Shooter's Bible GUIDE TO RIFLE BALLISTICS

Shooter's Bible
GUIDE TO RIFLE BALLISTICS

WAYNE VAN ZWOLL, Ph.D.

SKYHORSE PUBLISHING

To Alice, for her efforts on the computer, for her patient, forgiving spirit, and for those miserable hours when she'd rather have done just about anything than photograph a harried gun scribe with a rifle telling her exactly how to photograph a harried gun scribe with a rifle.

Skyhorse Publishing books may be purchased in bulk at special discounts for sales promotion, corporate gifts, fund-raising, or educational purposes. Special editions can also be created to specifications. For details, contact the Special Sales Department, Skyhorse Publishing, 307 West 36th Street, 11th Floor, New York, NY 10018 or info@skyhorsepublishing.com.

www.skyhorsepublishing.com

10 9 8 7 6 5 4 3 2 1

Library of Congress Cataloging-in-Publication Data on file.

ISBN: 978-1-61608-224-6

Printed in China

ACKNOWLEDGMENTS

Few worthwhile books come from one mind. This book builds on many. It also owes much to individuals not published. Some of the shooters and hunters who mentored me are no longer here. Some worked for companies like Speer and Sierra, Remington and Winchester, H-S Precision and McMillan—as have many friends and colleagues still able to critique this book. J.B. Hodgdon always answered my questions. So did Hornady's ballistics wizard Dave Emary, and Larry Werner, with his rich knowledge of DuPont and its products. Lee Reed, who started Swift Bullets, with Randy Brooks at Barnes and a host of knowledgeable riflemen at other bullet and ammunition firms contributed. Art Alphin, a standout in an industry of colorful men, added information on interior ballistics. Star competitive shooters Lones Wigger and Gary Anderson told me how to better direct bullets. Darrell Holland has reminded me. So, still, does friend Rich McClure, a soft–spoken rifle enthusiast whose long shooting career has garnered a wall of medals. Dr. Ken Oehler taught me a great deal about ballistics and tutored me on his superb chronographs. John Burns showed me how precise shooting with dead–center holds is possible to distances of over a mile. I've learned much from rifle- and barrel-makers too. Talented craftsmen like D'Arcy Echols and Gary Goudy have shown me how rifles are built from scratch. John Krieger has helped me understand how a bullet gets its best start. The list of contributors is really too long for this page. I'll truncate it here with a salute to Earl Wickman, who years ago in his basement range in central Michigan, coached an awkward young shooter with a DCM .22.

—Wayne van Zwoll

FOREWORD

This book is for hunters and shooters keen to know more about the behavior of bullets in flight. Until you know what affects a bullet, after all, you can't control its path. A bullet is moving so fast that air can't easily get out of its way. Air imposes tremendous pressure against the bullet's nose and shank, and a vacuum behind the heel. Pressure results in drag, which can amount to many times the force of gravity. As drag overcomes inertia, the bullet slows down. Meanwhile, gravity pushes it to earth. The slower the bullet goes, the more time gravity has to work on it, and the steeper its arc. That's why a bullet scribes a parabolic course, not one shaped like a rainbow. Wind bends that curve right or left.

Here you'll learn not only why bullets behave like they do but how to aim so they go where you want them to. You'll shoot better at long range, in wind, up and down hills and at moving targets. You'll find out what makes some rifles kick harder than others and some loads shoot more accurately than others. You'll get a short course on mirage—what causes it, how to read it, and why bullets riding three o'clock mirage may also rise, while mirage from the left commonly depresses the shot. You'll get straight talk on bullet deflection in brush, and the ballistic effects of temperature and elevation.

Terminal bullet performance matters to hunters, often even more so than accuracy and flat flight. This book sifts out the best loads for big game and examines the trend toward lead–free bullets. It tells how bullets are made and compares the most popular. There's also a concise treatise on powder manufacture. If you're a handloader, you'll appreciate knowing how the most popular propellants came to be, and how to choose among them. The chapter on handloading technique is your step-by-step guide to more effective ammunition.

After four decades studying ballistics then testing what I learned on the range and in the field, I'm still a student. Fortunately, you don't need a graduate degree in physics to understand exterior ballistics or to accurately direct a bullet. I'd like to say all you need is this book. In truth, you need trigger time, too.

—Wayne van Zwoll

CONTENTS

INTRODUCTION

Sure, there's math. But ballistics is also intuitive. It's how we describe things hurtling through air.

A basketball at rest in a corner of the gym is a lot like a bullet in the chamber of a rifle. Neither is very interesting, because neither is moving. Put the basketball in play or fire the rifle, and you set in motion a raft of variables that comprise the study of ballistics. Acceleration, deceleration, velocity, mass, energy, inertia, drag, profile, sectional density and the tug of gravity—to name just a few—affect the paths of all objects hurled through our atmosphere, from rocks to rockets. The name "ballistic missile" is oddly redundant, because every missile becomes "ballistic" at launch. Every projectile has ballistic properties.

In this book, ballistics has to do with bullet behavior. Once it leaves the muzzle, a bullet has only momentum to carry it (unlike a guided missile, which gets both power and direction during flight). A firm grasp of ballistics is a first step toward more effective shooting. Ballistics is really a three part discipline. *Interior* ballistics describes the turbulence inside a rifle: primer ignition, gas production and pressure, bullet release and acceleration. *Exterior* ballistics has to do with bullet flight—velocity, energy and trajectory as the bullet moves from muzzle to target. *Terminal* ballistics comes in after the strike; most commonly it's a measure of bullet penetration and upset in a game animal or an adversary.

Interior ballistics is mostly a laboratory science. Sophisticated instruments measure high pressures over tiny slices of time. Charting pressure curves, ballisticians assess performance and design propellants and bullets for commercial loads. Though it represents a small fraction of the eye–blink delay between striker fall and the bullet's impact 100 yards away, the launch has a profound effect on bullet trajectory and accuracy. Few shooters, though, are equipped to measure interior ballistics or manipulate them based on what happens before bullet exit. Riflemen have a much easier task with exterior ballistics. You can clock a bullet with a chronograph to determine its velocity. Plugging bullet speed and weight into a formula yields a measure of its energy. Drop and drift are a snap to determine—simply measure displacement at the target. By changing loads, you affect both interior and exterior ballistics, except for pressure signs on cartridge cases, meaningful measures of bullet performance all come forward of the muzzle.

Bullet velocity, energy, and trajectory have become standard items in ballistics charts provided by makers of ammunition and ammunition components. The properties of bullets in flight are relatively easy to quantify, very easy to compare in charts. With them, you can assess the practical reach of your rifle (as regards killing power, not accuracy) and its most efficient zero range.

Understanding ballistics, you can wring the most reach, accuracy, and power from your rifle.

Section I

BALLISTICS IN HISTORY

1. Hurling Things that Hurt

Long before they had bullets, people used other projectiles to kill game and adversaries. Rocks predated spears, boomerangs, arrows, darts, and bolts. All had limited range, because they depended directly on the power of the human arm.

By some accounts, the bow dates back 15,000 years, to early Oranian and Caspian cultures. It enabled the Persians to conquer the civilized world. Around 5,000 B.C., Egypt managed to free itself from Persian domination, at least in part because the Egyptians became skilled in the use of bows and arrows.

By 1,000 B.C. Persian archers had adapted the bow for use by horsemen. Short recurve bows, suitable for use while on horseback, arrived as early as 480 B.C. The Turks are credited with launching arrows half a mile in flight in contests with sinew–backed recurves.

Evidently it was the Greeks who first studied ballistics, around 300 B.C. Their inspiration was no doubt the development of better armament. At that time, little was known about gravity and air resistance, the two main forces impeding a projectile in flight. Later, such bright lights as Isaac Newton, Leonardo da Vinci, Galileo, Francis Bacon, and Leonard Euler would examine how these forces could be measured and countered.

▲ By becoming proficient in the use of bows and arrows, ancient Egyptians were able to free themselves from Persian domination.

▼ A hunter and his tracker scout for game atop a termite mound. Hunting is more than shooting.

Early on, arrows helped people understand the principles of ballistics. The arrow's arc was visible, and during the Middle Ages its role in battle can hardly be overstated. Years after gunpowder was invented, archers determined who would be the victor and the vanquished. At the Battle of Hastings in 1066,

▼ The crossbow could be shot as accurately as early firearms.

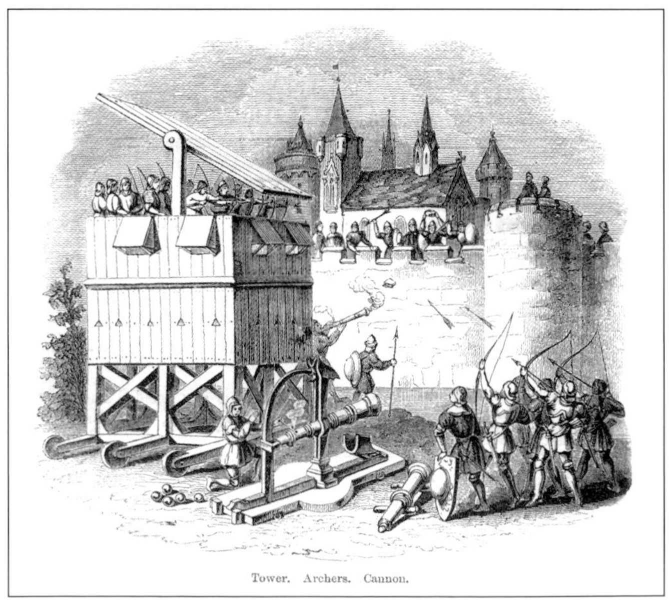

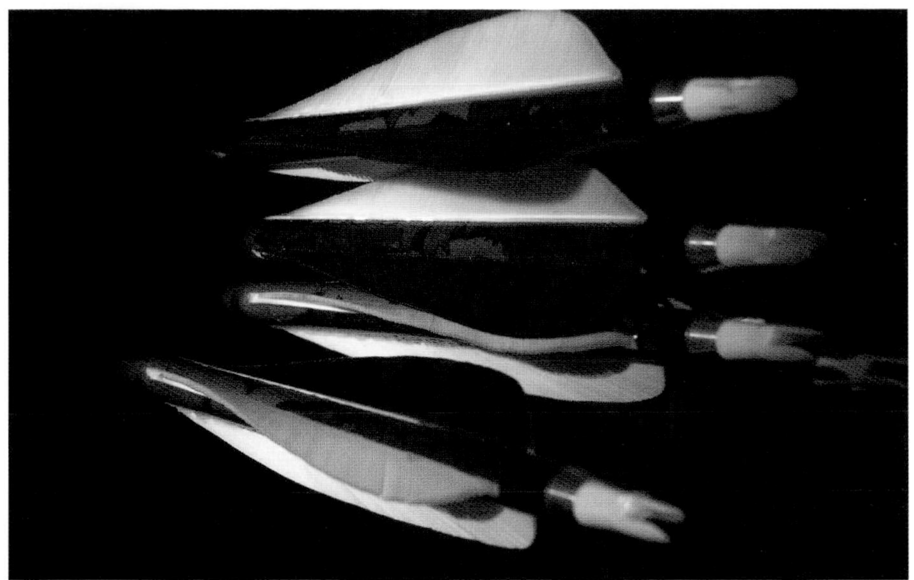

Modern arrows are colorful and accurate, uniform in weight and spine. But primitive shafts from longbows and recurves shaped history! ▶

Normans drew their English foes onto the field with a false retreat, then drove arrows *en masse* toward the oncoming troops, inflicting heavy casualties to win the day. Unlike the Turks, English archers preferred a one–piece bow. It was called a longbow not for its tip-to-tip measure, but for the manner of the archer's draw, with an anchor point at the ear or cheek. Short bows of the day were commonly drawn to the chest. The English adopted the Viking and Norman tactic of hailing arrows into distant troops. But they could be deadly up close, too. A charge toward well–positioned archers resulted in huge casualties, even when the attackers had armor. The armor wearied the advancing foot soldiers who wore it. English bowmen aimed for the joints in the armor and for the exposed head and neck of any man so foolish as to shed his helmet on a hot day. They shot deliberately at horses during a cavalry assault, not only to cripple and kill but to make the steeds unmanageable and spill their riders.

In those days, English conscripts were required to practice with their bows. Royal statutes dictated that anyone earning less than 100 pence a year had to own a bow and arrows—which could at any time be inspected! Poachers in Sherwood Forest (hung with their own bowstrings if caught in the act) were offered a pardon if they agreed to serve the king as archers. Many did, and a contingent of these outlaws won a spectacular victory at Halidon Hill in 1333. Their arrows killed 4,000 Scots in a conflict that left only 14 English dead. At Crecy (1346) and Agincourt (1415), England's archers vanquished the French army with volleys of arrows.

The English longbow became an everyday tool. Specimens were not embellished or displayed as were early firearms or swords. Bow wood deteriorated with age and weather. Only a few examples remain: unfinished staves in the Tower of London and a bow recovered in 1841 from the wreck of the *Mary Rose*, sunk in 1545. The "war" bow of English legend averaged six feet in length with a flat back and curved belly. Yew was the preferred wood, but English yew couldn't match that from Mediterranean countries for purity and straightness. Some of the best bows derived from Spanish wood. After the longbow gained its fearsome reputation, Spain forbade the growing of yew on the premise that it might find its way to England and thence to battlefields in which Spain might feel its sting. Desperate for staves, the English got around the

Longbows often spelled the difference between victory and defeat during the Middle Ages. ▶

▲ According to Samuel Colt, Indians could "shoot their bows faster than you can fire a revolver."

BALLISTICS IN HISTORY

ban by requiring that some staves be included with every shipment of Mediterranean wine!

In North America, bows varied regionally in shape and construction. Generally, those with wide, flat limbs were fashioned from soft woods like the yew preferred by Indians in the Pacific Northwest. Ash, hickory, and other hardwoods in the East, and Osage orange in the Midwest, provided the raw material for slender bows, rectangular in cross-section. Some tribes added sinew to protect the back of the bow at its extreme arch. Strips of horn occasionally found their way onto the bellies of bows. Unlike sinew, horn has no virtually no stretch; but it delivers resilience under compression.

Before horses became available on the plains, bows of Indians there averaged nearly five feet from tip to tip, almost as long as bows used by forest tribes east of the Mississippi. Mounted warriors soon switched to bows around 40 inches long, like those favored by Northwest tribes. Arrows favored by Eastern Indians were long and beautifully made, with short feathers to clear the bow handle while the hunter was stalking. Accuracy was of paramount importance because one shot was all that could be expected. On the plains, where hunters rode alongside bison and elk and shot several arrows quickly at short range, accuracy mattered less. And arrows driven through bison seldom survived for a second use. Fletching was long because the crude shafts needed strong steering and because the feathers spent little time against the bow handle before the shot. Raised nocks aided the "pinch" grip preferred by horsemen under pressure to shoot quickly. Most big game arrowheads were small, to penetrate, while arrows for smaller animals had bigger heads.

The plains Indian pushed the bow as much as he pulled the string. This technique enabled him to shoot quickly and get lots of thrust from a short but strong bow. He normally drew only to the chest, and well shy of the arrowhead—a 24 inch arrow might be pulled 20 inches. That draw stacked enough thrust to drive arrows through big animals. Indians did not soon abandon their bows for muskets. In fact, the speed with which repeat arrows could be launched kept the bow popular among mounted warriors until Samuel Colt's Walker revolver came along in 1839. "Bigfoot" Walker, the nineteenth century Texas Ranger who helped Colt develop that 4–pound handgun, respected the plains Indian and his bow. "I have seen a great many men in my time spitted with 'dogwood switches' . . . [Indians] can shoot their arrows faster than you can fire a revolver, and almost with the accuracy of a rifle at the distance of fifty or sixty yards."

Even in the East, the first flintlock muskets had little to offer red men skilled with the bow. These guns were not only slow to load; they were unwieldy and delivered poor accuracy—besides making a frightful noise and spewing thick smoke that obscured the animal or adversary. Powder and ball had to be bought or stolen, but arrows could be fashioned in the field.

2. Gunpowder!

The explosive "Chinese snow" appeared in fireworks a couple of centuries before Roger Bacon, an English friar and philosopher, described gunpowder in 1249. But those first compounds were hardly reliable propellants. Also, the idea of bottling gas pressure from burning powder and directing a projectile from a barrel had yet to be explored. Not until the early fourteenth century would crude guns appear in England, following experimental work on propulsion by Berthold Schwarz. In 1327 Edward II used guns as weapons during his invasion of Scotland.

Early gunpowder comprised roughly 40 percent saltpeter, with equal proportions of charcoal and sulfur. In 1338 French chemists changed the composition to 50-25-25. The English later settled on a mix of 75 percent saltpeter, 15 percent charcoal and 10 percent sulfur. That composition became established as black powder until the development of guncotton in 1846.

Powder manufacture in the US antedated gunbuilding. A powder mill in Milton, Mass., near Boston, was probably the first such facility. By the beginning of the Revolution, enterprising colonists had amassed, by manufacture or capture, 40 tons of black powder! Half went to Cambridge, where it was wasted before George Washington took charge of the Revolutionary Army. In short order, the Continental Army had no powder at all! New mills became a top priority, and by war's end American forces had stocks of powder totaling 1,000 tons. By 1800 the new nation's powder mills were producing 750 tons annually.

▼ Roger Bacon, friar and philosopher, wrote descriptions about gunpowder in the 13th century, more than 400 years after its invention in China.

▲ In the Revolutionary War, British troops were no match for the French-style flintlocks favored by the Americans.

Igniting black powder was easy in open air, not so easy in a chamber that bottled the expanding gas to launch a ball. The first guns, developed in Europe a century and a half before Columbus sailed for the New World, were heavy tubes that required two attendants. The Swiss called these firearms culverins. The culveriner held the tube, while his partner, the "gougat," lit a priming charge with a smoldering stick or rope. Culverins were clumsy and inaccurate and often misfired. Still, the noise and smoke they generated could unnerve an enemy armed with spears or pikes or even bows. Culverin muzzles were also fitted with ax heads, to make them useful when ignition failed. Eventually these firearms were modified so one soldier could load and fire unassisted. Mechanical rests helped shooters steady the heavy barrels. A forked brace adapted from fourteenth century artillery supported the petronel, a hand cannon held against the breast for firing. Forks could be made to support infantry guns or even used on the saddle of a mounted soldier.

Stationary guns aimed at a wall or a mass of men could be fired without regard to timing because gun and target had a fixed relationship. But soldiers on the move could ill afford to wait for a wick to burn through to the charge. They needed a mechanism to cause instant ignition. The first lock was a crude lever by which a long, smoldering wick was lowered to the touch-hole in the barrel. This wick was later replaced

▲ A Spanish arquebus, one of the first matchlocks.

by a shorter wick or match that got help from a cord kept smoldering atop the barrel. The shooter eased a serpentine device, holding the match, onto the cord until the match caught fire. Then he moved it to the side and lowered it to the touch-hole. A trigger adapted from crossbows afforded more control.

Guns with this crude mechanism became known as matchlocks. The Spanish arquebus was one. Arquebusiers carried extra wicks smoldering in perforated metal boxes on their belts. But no preparation could ensure steady or reliable discharges. In 1636, during eight hours of battle at Kuisyingen, one soldier managed only seven shots! At Wittenmergen two years later the rate of fire doubled to seven shots in four hours. Eliminating the wick became the priority of sixteenth century German gun designers, who developed the "monk's gun" with a spring–loaded jaw that held a piece of pyrite (flint) against a serrated bar. To fire, the shooter pulled a ring at the rear of the bar, scooting it across the pyrite to produce sparks. The sparks fell in a pan containing a trail of fine gunpowder that entered the barrel's touch-hole. This design led to another, in Nuremberg, around 1515. The wheellock had a spring–loaded sprocket wound with a spanner wrench and latched under tension. Pulling the trigger released the wheel to spin against a fixed shard of pyrite held

▼ White smoke from black powder: at ignition, a flintlock's discharge can obscure the target.

▲ After lifting thumbing frizzen (left) and hammer, a shooter charges a flintlock pan and touch-hole with powder. The frizzen is then lowered. The hammer's flint strikes it, sparks firing the powder.

by spring tension against the wheel's teeth. Sparks showered into the pan. Wheellocks were less affected by wet weather than were matchlocks. They also gave quicker ignition and were faster to set.

In the *Lock a la Miquelet*, the roles of pyrite and steel were reversed. Named after the Spanish *miquelitos* (marauders) operating in the Pyrenees, this design appears to have Dutch origins. It would later be modified to become what we Americans know as the flintlock. Guns of this type have a spring–loaded cock that holds a piece of flint and swings in an arc when released. At the end of its travel, the flint in the jaws of the cock hits a pan cover or hammer, knocking it back to expose the primed pan. Sparks shower into the pan, igniting a charge of priming powder, which conducts flame through the touch-hole. The cock eventually became known as a hammer, the hammer a frizzen. Flintlocks were less expensive to build than were wheellocks and in time proved more reliable.

The common weakness of matchlock, wheellock, and flintlock mechanisms was exposed priming. It was vulnerable to moisture which could quickly render the gun useless. A weak spark might fail to ignite even dry priming. If it did ignite, flame might not reach the main charge, yielding only a "flash in the pan." Generating spark inside the gun became possible early in the eighteenth century, with the discovery of fulminates. Chemists found that fulminic acid (an isomer of cyanic acid) produced shock sensitive salts. A sharp blow caused them to release their energy immediately and more reliably than flint generated sparks. In 1774 the chief physician to Louis XV wrote about the explosiveness of mercury fulminate. Adding saltpeter to fulminates of mercury produced a shock sensitive but stable explosive. Called "Howard's powder" after Englishman E. C. Howard who discovered it in 1799, this compound may have figured into experiments by Scotch clergyman Alexander John Forsythe. In 1806 Forsythe became the first on record to ignite a spark in the chamber of a gun. Two years later the Swiss gun maker Johannes Pauly designed a breech–loading percussion gun that employed a cartridge with a paper percussion cap on its base. A spring–loaded needle pierced the cap, detonating the fulminate. The Lefauchex needle gun came later.

Clearly a landmark development, the advent of internal combustion drew enormous interest from military and civilian circles. New ammunition and guns to fire it were developed simultaneously by legions of inventors. In 1818 Joseph Manton, an Englishman, built a gun with a spring–loaded catch that held a tiny tube of fulminate against the side of the barrel over the touch-hole. The hammer crushed the fulminate, and breech pressure blew the tube off to the side. The Merrill gun, 14,500 of which were bought by the British government, featured this mechanism. In 1821 the London firm of Westley Richards designed a percussion gun that used fulminate primers in a flintlock–style pan. The pan cover, forced open by the falling hammer, exposed a cup of fulminate. The hammer's sharp nose pierced it. Two years later American physician Dr. Samuel Guthrie found a way to make a much more convenient fulminate pellet.

Though many inventors have claimed credit for the percussion cap, its development is most commonly attributed to sea captain Joshua Shaw of Philadelphia. In 1814 Shaw was denied a patent for a steel cap because he was British–born and yet to become an American citizen. He persevered with a disposable pewter cap then one made of copper. The hollow nipple appeared soon. It provided a tunnel that caught sparks at their origin and funneled them to the chamber. In 1822 Shaw patented his own lock. Twenty-four years later, Congress awarded the 70-year-old inventor an honorarium for his work.

Between 1812 and 1825 the US patent office issued 72 patents for percussion caps. Only a few proved out. Some caps fragmented, splattering the shooter. Others had so little priming mixture they failed to ignite the main charge—or so much they started the ball before the burning powder could build pressure. To throttle primer blast, an Englishman named Nock designed an antechamber perpendicular to the bore and behind the chamber. Powder burning there ignited the main charge through a short tunnel.

Oddly enough, percussion rifles were slow to gain acceptance. In the early nineteenth century, chemistry was still viewed with suspicion by the masses, and fulminates were chemicals. Also, some early caps produced erratic results. Governments resisted replacing pyrite. Flintlocks, after all, had been refined mechanically and esthetically. Besides, percussion guns were rumored to kick harder while delivering a weaker blow downrange. Even Britain's Colonel Hawker, a firearms authority, throttled his praise of percussion ignition: "For killing single shots at wildfowl rapidly flying, and particularly by night, there is not a question in favor of the detonating system, as its trifling inferiority to the flint gun is tenfold repaid by the wonderful accuracy it gives in so readily obeying the eye. But in firing a heavy charge among a large flock of birds the flint has the decided advantage."

Eventually percussion caps would win over the doubters. Meanwhile, firearms were changing in other ways. The Pilgrims had landed with unwieldy smoothbores, typically 6-foot-long .75-caliber flintlocks. Though the superior accuracy of rifled bores was well known by that time (rifle matches had been held as early as 1498 in Leipzig, Germany, and 1504 in Zurich, Switzerland), rifled barrels were expensive and slow to load. But in the New World, battles between settlers and Indians did not follow the traditional European pattern. There was no wall of uniforms, squarely presented as a collective target. The enemy was commonly a single antagonist, partly hidden behind vegetation. Accuracy mattered to soldiers and hunters alike. Then too, the huge lead balls used in British muskets constituted a waste of valuable lead. For these reasons, Americans came to favor the French-style flintlock popular in Europe at the beginning of the eighteenth century. From it evolved the *jaeger* (hunter) rifle. The typical *jaeger* had a 24- to 30-inch barrel of .65 to .70-caliber, with seven to nine deep, slow–twist grooves. Most wore a rectangular patch box on a stock with a wide, flat butt. Double set triggers were common. To conserve lead, frontier gunsmiths started making *jaegers* with .50–, .45–, even .40–caliber bores. (A pound of lead will yield 70 .40–caliber balls, but only 15 of .70 inch diameter.) They lengthened the barrel, replaced the *jaeger's* sliding patch box cover with a hinged lid and trimmed the stock, giving it a "crescent" butt to fit comfortably against the shooter's upper arm. The result became known as the Kentucky rifle, though most of the changes were wrought in Pennsylvania by riflesmiths of German extraction.

The *jaeger's* rifled bore made it much more accurate than the Brown Bess musket British troops brought to the Revolutionary War. To speed loading, Americans learned early on to swath undersize balls in greased patches that took the rifling. Strangely, the crack *Jaeger* troops against whom they also fought, still loaded their rifles with tight–fitting balls. The colonists beat the *Jaegers* almost as handily as they defeated British regulars. The patched ball soon emerged as a standard for hunters, who appreciated the cleaning action of the patch and its protection of the bore against leading.

3. Rifles for a Frontier

In his father's forge on Staley Creek, four miles from the Mohawk River, Eliphalet ("Lite") Remington pumped the bellows. When the rod he had chosen for the barrel of his first rifle glowed red, he hammered it until it was half an inch square in cross-section. Then he wound it around an iron mandrel, heated it again until it was white-hot and sprinkled it with Borax and sand. He held one end with his tongs and pounded the other on the stone floor to seat the near–molten coils. After it cooled, Lite checked it for straightness and hammered out the curves. Then he ground and filed eight flats on the .45–caliber tube, because octagonal barrels were popular. Lite traveled to Utica to pay a gunsmith four double reales (about $1 in country currency, when $200 a year was a living wage) to rifle the .45–caliber bore. That took two days. Returning home, Remington bored a touch-hole and forged a breech plug and the lock parts. He shaped them with a file, then brazed the priming pan to the lock plate. He used uric acid and iron oxide, a preservative known as hazel brown, to finish the steel. Lite fashioned the walnut stock from scratch with draw-knife and chisel. He smoothed it with sandstone and sealed it with bees-wax. Hand–made screws and pins joined the parts.

The year was 1816. Lite Remington promptly took his new rifle to a local shooting match. He placed second. So impressed was the match winner that he asked if Lite would build a rifle for him. Lite agreed to deliver one in 10 days for $10.

As the US frontier edged south and west, hunters found their needs changing. Grizzly bears and bison didn't fall to the light charges fired from svelte Kentucky rifles. Neither were long barrels and fragile stocks ideal for hunting on horseback. While Daniel Boone was probing the Cumberlands in the late 1700s, gun makers began re-configuring the Kentucky rifle. They made it sturdier and gave it iron hardware and a bigger bore. The result: the "mountain" or "Tennessee" rifle. During this transition in rifle design, General W. H. Ashley, head of the Rocky Mountain Fur Company, promoted the rendezvous as a way to collect furs from trappers in the West. Tons of pelts funneled from frontier outposts to St. Louis. Among the many Easterners seeking fortunes in Missouri, then gateway to the West, was gunsmith Jacob Hawkins. In 1822 his brother Samuel closed a gun shop in Xenia, Ohio to join Jake. The two changed their name to the original Dutch "Hawken" and started building rifles.

▼ The elegant Kentucky rifle originated in Pennsylvania in the late 1700s.

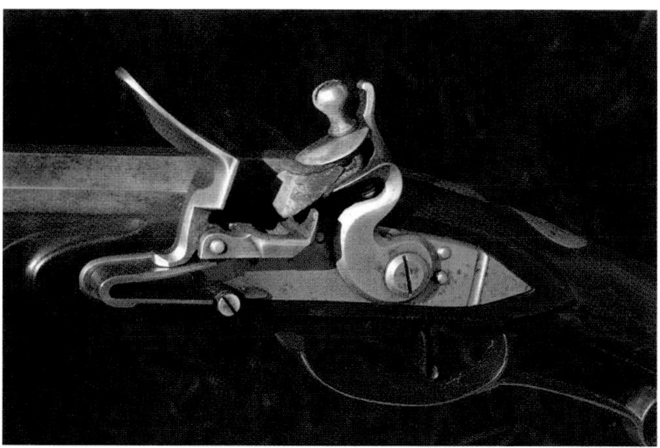

▲ The flint lock comprises a frizzen (here open), a pan, and a hammer holding flint. The percussion lock, more reliable, employs a primed copper cap on a short tube. A hammer blow ignites the cap.

As Youmans in North Carolina had become a pre-eminent maker of Tennessee rifles, the Hawken brothers would define the plains rifle. It borrowed from Youmans' design but had a shorter, heavier barrel for horseback carry and to accommodate bigger powder charges. The full length stock was replaced by a half-stock, typically maple with two. The traditional patch box was often omitted. Until 1840, the standard firing mechanism was a flintlock, sometimes purchased, more often fabricated in house. The Hawkens used Ashmore locks as well as their own, and typically installed double–set triggers. A typical Hawken weighed just under 10 lbs, with a 38 inch, .50–caliber octagonal barrel made of soft iron with a slow rifling twist. Hawken barrels were less susceptible to fouling problems than the hard, quick twist barrels common to "more advanced" English rifles of the day. They retained traces of bullet lube and delivered better accuracy with patched round balls. Other makers—notably Henry Lehman, James Henry, George Tryon—produced plains rifles that looked like (and in some cases were patterned after) Hawkens.

Hunters with Hawken rifles reported kills at 200 to 300 yards, long shooting in those days. Charge weights typically ran 150 to 215 grains. Bore size increased as

▲ Plains rifles by the Hawken brothers were favored by frontiersmen in the mid-1800s.

lead became easier to get and buffalo more valuable at market. In an article for the *Saturday Evening Post* (February 21, 1920 as cited by Hanson in "The Plains Rifle"), Horace Kephart wrote of finding a new Hawken rifle in St. Louis:

" . . . It would shoot straight with any powder charge up to a one-to-one load, equal weights of powder and ball. With a round ball of pure lead weighing 217 grains, patched with fine linen so that it fitted tight, and 205 grains of powder it gave very low trajectory and great smashing power, and yet the recoil was no more severe than that of a .45-caliber breech loader charged with 70 grains of powder and a 500–grain service bullet . . ."

In 1849, when the California Gold Rush began, you could buy a Hawken rifle for $22.50. That year Jake Hawken died of cholera. Sam continued building and repairing rifles alone. In 1859 he made his first trek to the Rocky Mountains, where many of his rifles had gone. Sam apparently worked in Colorado mines for a week, then started back to Missouri, where upon his return he was quoted as saying " . . . and here I am once more at more at my old trade, putting guns and pistols in order . . . ."

William Stewart Hawken, Sam's son, rode with Kit Carson's mounted rifles. He was wounded during the Battle of Monterey, September 23, 1847, when he and a small group of frontiersmen fought to hold a bridge over San Juan Creek. Vastly superior numbers gave Mexico the victory. The clash left only nine ambulatory men among 43 Texas Rangers. William Hawken, age 30, made his way back to Missouri.

When Sam went west he left William in charge of the Hawken facility. William got this letter:

Evans Landing Nov. 27th 1858
Mr. Wm. Hawkins

Sir, I have waited with patience for my gun, I am in almost in a hurry 2 weeks was out last Monday I will wait a short time for it and if it don't come I will either go or send. If you are still waiting to make me a good one it is all right. Please send as soon as possible.
Game is plenty and I have no gun. Yours a friend.
Daniel W. Boon.

After his return to St. Louis, Sam Hawken hired a shop hand. J. P. Gemmer had immigrated to the US from Germany in 1838. He proved capable and industrious and in 1862 bought the Hawken enterprise. He may have used the "S. Hawken" stamp on some rifles, but marked most "J. P. Gemmer, St. Louis." Sam Hawken continued to visit his shop in retirement and once built a complete rifle. He outlived Jim Bridger and Kit Carson and many other frontiersmen who had depended on Hawken rifles. When he died at age 92 the shop was still open for business! It closed in 1915; J. P. Gemmer died four years later.

▼ The Battle of Monterrey was a turning point in the Mexican-American War.

A patched ball can be loaded easier than bare lead. The patch takes the rifling, spinning the ball. ▶

4. Breech-Loaders at Last!

Development of the percussion cap energized inventors focused on a breech–loading rifle. While firearms with a hinged breech date to at least 1537, little practical advantage was possible without the percussion cap. Neither did early cartridges advance under flint ignition. The first, assembled in 1586, were of paper. They had no priming, and the guns were still loaded from the muzzle. Biting or ripping off the cartridge base was necessary before loading to expose the charge. The paper burned to ashes upon firing. Replacing pyrite with the percussion cap did away with the biting and tearing because the cap's more powerful spark could penetrate thin paper.

A major problem early on was building a breechloader stout enough to withstand the heavy powder charges used for hunting big game and reliable enough to keep functioning while hot and dirty. The first American breechloader that won popular acceptance was developed by John Harris Hall in 1811.

Six years later the US government issued a limited number of these rifles to soldiers. But the Hall was weak and crude, a flintlock firing paper cartridges. As war with Mexico threatened to drain US arsenals in 1845, factories fell back to producing the Harpers Ferry muzzle–loading rifle, a design dating to 1803!

Johann Nikolaus von Dreyse was among the first inventors to install a primer in a cartridge. The bullet, actually, held the pellet, inside a paper hull. A long striker penetrated the charge to pinch the pellet against the bullet. The von Dreyse "needle gun," developed in 1835, became very popular. About 300,000 were built for the Prussian army over the next 30 years. (Incidentally, the "needle gun" mentioned by post-Civil War writers was not the European Dreyse. It was the .50–70 Springfield that became in 1873 the .45–70 "trap–door" rifle used in the last of the Indian Wars. Its long breech block required a needle like striker.)

Meanwhile, Eliphalet Remington bought (for $2,581) the gun company and services of William Jenks, a bright Welsh engineer who had designed a breech loading service rifle but had wearied of awaiting a reply from the US government. Remington adapted the Jenks rifle to use Edward Maynard's percussion lock, which advanced caps on a strip of paper. Later J. H. Merrill improved the Jenks rifle. In government tests, its tallow coated cardboard cartridges fired reliably, even after a minute's submersion in water.

During the mid–nineteenth century, rail transport, meat markets, and immigrants establishing homesteads on the Great Plains exacted a heavy toll from wildlife. But development of self–contained rifle cartridges accelerated its decline as no single event had before.

In 1847 Stephen Taylor patented a hollow base bullet with an internal powder charge held in place by a perforated cap that admitted sparks from an external primer. The following year, New York inventor Walter Hunt devised a similar bullet with a paper–covered cork cap. Primer sparks shot through the paper to ignite the charge. What made Hunt's "rocket ball" exciting, however, was his repeating rifle to fire them. The Hunt "Volitional Repeater" had a brilliantly conceived tubular magazine, and a pillbox mechanism to advance the metallic primers. But the action, operated by a finger lever under the breech, was prone to malfunction. Lacking the money to promote or even improve his rifle, Hunt sold patent rights to fellow New Yorker and machinist George A. Arrowsmith. In Arrowsmith's shop a talented young engineer named Lewis Jennings began correcting design deficiencies in the Hunt repeater.

In 1849, after receiving patents for Jennings' work, Arrowsmith sold the Hunt rifle for $100,000 to railroad magnate and New York hardware merchant Courtland Palmer. With Palmer's financial backing, designers Horace Smith and Daniel Wesson began work in 1852

◀ The first popular American breechloader was developed by John Hall in 1811.

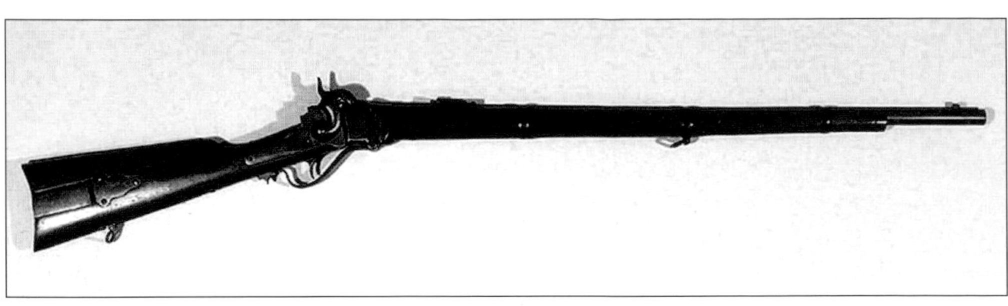

◀ The 1874 .50-caliber Sharps rifle was favored by many buffalo hunters.

on a metallic cartridge like that patented in 1846 and 1849 by the Frenchman Flobert. Rather than using a ball atop a primer as Flobert had, Smith and Wesson modified a rocket ball to include a copper base that held the fulminate priming. The pistols they fashioned for this ammunition failed to sell. In 1854 Courtland Palmer invested $10,000 in new tooling to bankroll a new partnership with his employees, and a firm that would become known as Smith and Wesson.

In 1855 a group of 40 New York and New Haven investors bought out Smith and Wesson and Palmer to form the Volcanic Repeating Arms Company. The investors chose one of their own as company director: a shirt salesman named Oliver F. Winchester. He moved the enterprise from Norwich to New Haven. When sluggish sales of Volcanic guns sent it into receivership in 1857, Winchester bought all assets for $40,000. He reorganized the company into the New Haven Arms Company, and hired Benjamin Tyler Henry as chief mechanic. In 1860 Henry received a patent for a 15–shot repeating rifle chambered for .44 rimfire cartridges. The brass–frame Henry would father Winchester's first lever rifles: the 1866, 1873, and 1876. Confederates called the Henry "that damned Yankee rifle you loaded on Sunday and fired all week." Underpowered, prone to leak gas, and marginally reliable, it was nonetheless coveted by hunters as well as soldiers because it could be recharged with a flick of the hand.

Oliver WInchester bought volcanic repeating arms for $40,000.

The middle of the nineteenth century was the most active period in the history of firearms design. Many inventors threw all their energy into repeating rifle designs, but young Christian Sharps decided to build a better breech–loading single–shot. Sharps, a New Jersey native, had worked under John Hall at the Harpers Ferry Arsenal. In 1848 he received his first patent for a mechanism with a sliding breechblock. Fitted to an altered 1841 Springfield, the prototype could handle powerful loads. Alas, Sharps failed to give it a proper launch at market. He was bailed out by businessman J. M. McCalla and gunsmith A. S. Nippes. A couple of decades later, five years before Christian Sharps succumbed to tuberculosis, the Sharps Rifle Manufacturing Company introduced the New Model 1869, its first rifle in metallic chamberings.

The New Model 1874 appeared the next year, a rifle targeted to market hunters. George Reighard was one. In a 1930 edition of the Kansas City Star, he explained how he shot bison:

> "In 1872 I organized my own outfit ... to shoot buffaloes for their hides. I furnished the team and wagon and did the killing. (My partners) furnished the supplies and did the skinning, stretching and cooking. They got half the hides and I got the other half. I had two big .50 Sharps rifle with telescopic sights....
>
> "The time I made my biggest kill I lay on a slight ridge, behind a tuft of weeds 100 yards from a bunch of a thousand buffaloes that had come a long distance to a creek, had drunk their fill and then strolled out upon the prairie to rest, some to lie down.... After I had killed about twenty-five my gun barrel became hot and began to expand. A bullet from an overheated gun does not go straight, it wobbles, so I put that gun aside and took the other. By the time that became hot the other had

cooled, but then the powder smoke in front of me was so thick I could not see through it; there was not a breath of wind to carry it away, and I had to crawl backward, dragging my two guns, and work around to another position on the ridge, from which I killed fifty-four more. In one and one-half hours I had fired ninety-one shots, as a count of the empty shells showed afterwards, and had killed seventy-nine buffaloes…."

The Sharps Rifle Company folded in 1880, having failed to market its hammerless Model 1878 rifle or design a practical repeater. A peacetime military budget and the decimation of game by commercial hunters contributed to the firm's collapse. By the early 1880s, so many bison had been killed that human scavengers would glean more than three million *tons* of bones from the plains.

Meanwhile, a young man began fashioning even more effective firearms. He was John Moses Browning, son of gunsmith Jonathan Browning, who arrived on Utah's Wasatch Front in 1852, five years after the first of his Mormon brethren completed the trip from Nauvoo, Illinois. John was born in 1855, one of Jonathan's 22 children. The lad showed an early knack for gun design and by the time he was 11 had built a working shotgun. Later he ran his father's shop. In 1878, shortly after turning 23, John designed a breech loading single–shot rifle. He built its prototype by hand, with files, chisels, and a foot-lathe his father had brought from Illinois. In May 1879, he received a patent for the dropping–block mechanism.

At this time, the Winchester Repeating Arms Company was a behemoth, with a net worth of $1.2 million. By 1875 it had reached an output of a million cartridges per day. Nonetheless, declining demand for military rifles and ammunition prompted the company to shift its focus in the late 1870s. For the next 36 years it would cater primarily to hunters. To that end it developed the Model 1876 lever rifle, a big, iron–frame version of the popular Model 1873, whose roots reached to Walter Hunt's Volitional repeater. But the 1876, while massive, lacked the strength to bottle pressures from the .45–70, a favorite not only of ex-soldiers but of elk and bison hunters. Then, in 1883, a Winchester salesman showed company president Thomas Bennett a single–shot rifle he had bought, used, during a trip west. The action was of clever design and evidenced great strength. The maker, whose name Bennett did not recognize, had a shop in Ogden. Bennett booked train passage there immediately.

America's premier gun designer John Browning brought stout, reliable repeating rifles to the western frontier. He later tapped the energy of fired cartridges to cycle autoloading mechanisms, as in the .22 rifle he's holding here. ▶

He arrived to find a group of brothers barely out of their teens, laboring in a small facility under a sign proclaiming it the "Largest Arms Factory Between Omaha and The Pacific." The boss, John, was 28. Bennett came straight to the point: He wanted to buy all rights to the single-shot. John said he could have them for $10,000. Bennett countered at $8,000; Browning accepted. It was the start of a relationship that would last 17 years and yield 40 gun designs for Winchester. Thomas Bennett was on the train back to New Haven six hours later.

Barely had Winchester dubbed Browning's rifle the Model 1885 than John and his brother Matt

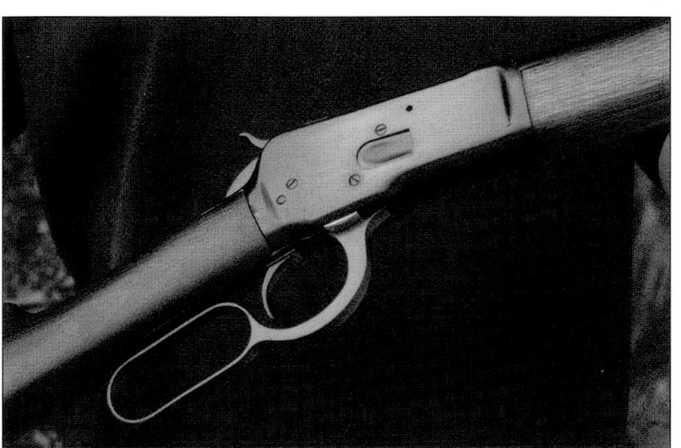

◀ Winchester's 92, a Browning design, was a huge hit. Phil Filing and Doug Mosier restored this one.

BALLISTICS IN HISTORY

◀ The Marlin Model 1894, not as celebrated as Winchester's M94, was sturdy, reliable, accurate. This modern version chambers the .357 Magnum.

arrived at company headquarters with a new idea: a repeating lever–action rifle that would handle the .45-70. Bennett bought the design, reportedly for $50,000—or, as John would say later, "more money than there was in Ogden." The rifle later became Winchester's Model 1886. John Browning returned from his two year Mormon mission in March, 1889, to design more firearms. During the next four years, he garnered 20 patents. His primary contribution to Winchester was the 1892, a petite lever–action with the Model 86's vertical locking lugs. The '92 would spawn the Model 1894, designed for black powder but chambered in 1895 for the .30-30, America's first centerfire smokeless round.

Development of the metallic cartridge accelerated the pace of rifle design in Europe too, thanks in large part to a talented young German.

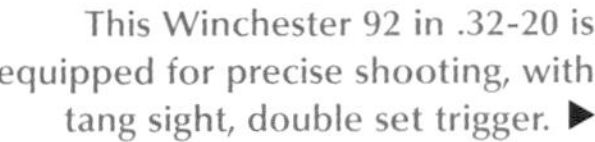

This Winchester 92 in .32-20 is equipped for precise shooting, with tang sight, double set trigger. ▶

5. Rifles from a Door Latch

Born in 1838 in the Swabian village of Oberndorf, Peter Paul Mauser did not succeed right away as a gun designer. His first project went nowhere. He and brother Wilhelm persevered to submit a viable infantry arm to the Prussian army. In 1872 the single–shot 11mm Mauser Model 1871 was accepted as the country's official infantry arm. Its rugged turn–bolt action derived, legend has it, from Paul's inspection of a door latch. Other governments took notice.

Mauser Bros. and Co. was founded in February, 1874. Following Wilhelm's premature death, it became a stock company. In 1889 Fabrique Nationale d'Armes de Guerre (FN) was established near Liege to build Mauser rifles for Belgium's military. The 1889 rifle, designed for smokeless–powder cartridges, confirmed Paul Mauser as the dominant rifle engineer in Europe. Over the next six years he improved the action. A staggered box magazine appeared in 1893. Two years later the Model 1895 incorporated most of the features that would make Mauser's 1898 the top choice of ordnance officers from eastern Europe to the tip of South America. By the late 1930s, Mauser was selling rifles to sportsmen in the US through A. F. Stoeger of New York. At one time Stoeger listed 20 types of Mauser actions, differing not only in length (four were available), but in magazine configuration. These rifles didn't come cheap. In 1939 retail prices ranged from $110 to $250. Since the second world war, modifications of Paul Mauser's Model 1898 action have appeared in all the world's game fields.

Peter Paul Mauser developed a single-shot 11mm Mauser Model 1871, soon accepted as Prussia's official infantry arm. It featured a turn-bolt action.

▲ Buzz Fletcher built this lovely custom rifle on a 98 Mauser action. It's chambered in .256 Newton.

The shift among American hunters to the centerfire bolt rifle began with their introduction to the Mauser–inspired 1903 Springfield. The Springfield's fine accuracy and the reach of its .30-06 cartridge quickly won converts. Smokeless powder and jacketed bullets offered new possibilities to experimenters seeking better ballistic performance.

One of the most active cartridge designers during the Springfield's heyday was Charles Newton. Educated as a lawyer, Newton designed the .250-3000 Savage, so named because its 87–grain bullet sped away at a reported 3,000 feet per second. He also fashioned, around 1912, the .25-06. With Fred Adolph, he designed other potent hunting cartridges. Newton started his own Newton Arms Company in August, 1914, intending to build his own rifles from DWM Mausers. Alas, his timing couldn't have been worse: Germany went to war a day before the first shipment of Mausers was due. Not easily deterred, Newton designed a new rifle from scratch and loaded his own rounds (he even designed and built softnose bullets that would penetrate tough game). But he depended on Remington for brass. The first production run of

▲ A 1903 Springfield.

Newton rifles was finished in January, 1917—just as America entered the war and the government seized control of all cartridge production.

Again making the best of bad luck, Newton tooled up to make cartridge cases. But in August 1918, the banks supporting his venture sent it into receivership. He persevered with the Chas. Newton Rifle Corporation in April 1919. A deal with Eddystone Arsenal to supply equipment fell through, however, and Newton sold only a few rifles on imported Mauser actions. Later he formed the Buffalo Newton Rifle Corporation, which manufactured rifles of his design. It failed in 1929, shortly before Newton's death.

More firmly grounded American gun companies began offering commercial bolt rifles soon after World War I. Remington's Model 30 was followed in 1922 by Winchester's Model 54. The versatile .30-06 proved the most popular chambering in both. In 1925 Winchester chambered its 54 for a new cartridge, the .270. Blessed with a receptive press, the .270 prospered. The .300 Holland & Holland Magnum, introduced at the same time, wooed some hunters, but its long case and belted head were not suited to standard–length military rifle actions. In 1937 Winchester replaced the Model 54 with the Model 70, destined to become the most popular centerfire rifle of the century. Chambered for every useful big game round, it had an action long enough to accommodate the .300 and

▼ Charles Newton was a brilliant inventor—of both cartridges and rifles like this late bolt gun.

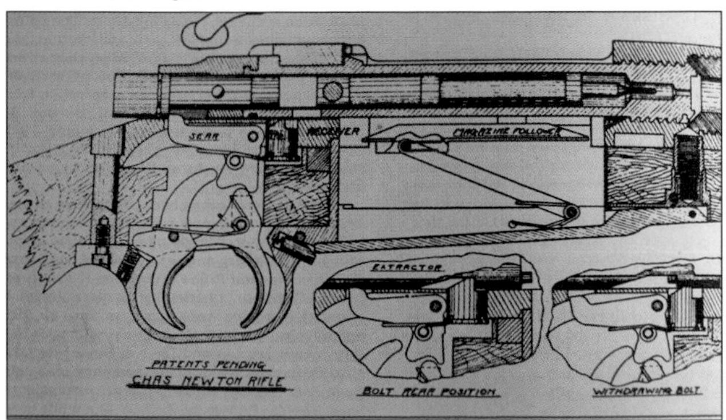

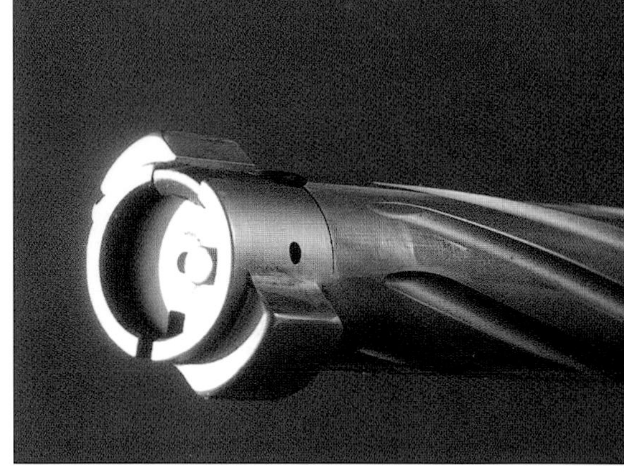

The two-lug Mauser bolt has evolved. McMillan rifles feature both fixed and plunger ejectors. ▶

.375 H&H Magnums. The strong Mauser–type extractor and a rugged but finely–adjustable trigger helped boost Model 70 sales.

About this time, Charles Newton's quest for more powerful hunting cartridges and innovative rifle designs was taken up by another experimenter. In 1937 insurance salesman Roy Weatherby moved from his native Kansas to California. To pursue his interest in firearms design, he bought a drill press and a lathe from Sears. He rebarreled or rechambered 1898 Mausers, 1903 Springfields, and 1917 Enfields to cartridges of his own design. His first publicized round, the .220 Weatherby Rocket, was a blown–out Swift. His next, the .270 Weatherby Magnum, became the first in a stable of fast stepping numbers on .300 Holland brass.

Weatherby soon made a business of his avocation, hawking high velocity as the path to lightning like kills at long range. His .270 Magnum drove a bullet 300 fps faster than a .270 Winchester. The .257 and 7mm Weatherby Magnums that followed were, like the .270 Magnum, based on a shortened Holland & Holland case to fit .30-06–length actions. The .300 Weatherby Magnum, a 1946 offering, had a full length

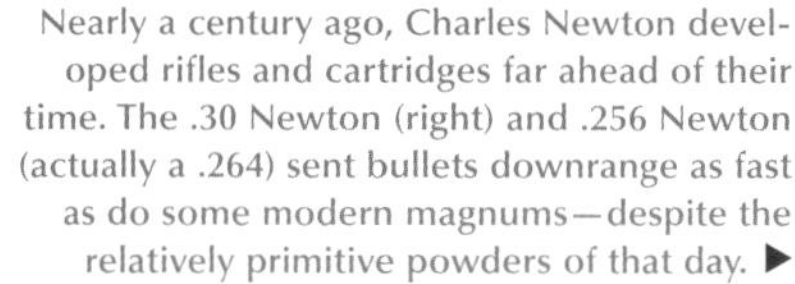

Nearly a century ago, Charles Newton developed rifles and cartridges far ahead of their time. The .30 Newton (right) and .256 Newton (actually a .264) sent bullets downrange as fast as do some modern magnums—despite the relatively primitive powders of that day. ▶

▲ Remington briefly produced this Mauser-action sporter in .375. Note crossbolts that reinforce the stock.

case. All Weatherby rounds were distinguished by minimal body taper and a double shoulder radius. Roy marketed these cartridges (and the rifles he built for them) expertly, making sure that prominent politicians and movie stars were photographed with Weatherby products. In 1948 he standardized the Weatherby rifle, using a commercial Fabrique Nationale (FN) action. Ten years later he and company engineer Fred Jennie completed work on a new action they called the Weatherby Mark V. Its full–diameter bolt had nine locking lugs in three rows of three. The stock gave the rifle a futuristic look.

During the last half-century, bolt–action rifles have changed little. The biggest shift, perhaps, has been in

Roy Weatherby pioneered high-velocity wildcats on the Holland case. His .300 appeared in 1945.

Paul Mauser's rifles saw dawn-to-dusk service in the African bush. Mauser-inspired rifles still do.

stock materials. Walnut has been replaced by hardwood like beech and birch in some instances but most commonly by synthetic materials. These range widely in quality, appearance, and fit. Detachable box magazines have become popular. So, too, stainless steel as an alternative to the traditional chrome–moly barrels and receivers. Iron sights have all but vanished as standard equipment, except on rifles intended for close shooting at dangerous game. Bolt–face extractors and plunger ejectors have largely replaced the stout Mauser claw and fixed ejector, but few shooters would say the 1898's action has been improved. Some new actions are smoother and safeties are more scope–friendly. Still, Paul Mauser's mechanism remains among the strongest and most reliable ever designed.

▼ A young Roy Weatherby poses with his wife Camille and first daughter Diane.

6. What the Numbers Mean

Since their inception around the time of our Civil War, metallic cartridges have been labeled for their dimensions. But the numbers don't all refer to the *same* dimensions. Also, units of measure can vary—inches and millimeters, for example. Other numbers can be thrown in: year of origin, bullet weight, even bullet speed. Sometimes numbers are rounded up or down so as not to duplicate numbers already in use.]

Best to start at the beginning. Labels on boxes of rifle cartridges usually specify bore diameter and parent firm (originator), plus the name of the manufacturer. So you'll find .243 Winchester ammunition loaded by Remington and .257 Roberts cartridges by Federal. Numbers designating caliber can confuse because in rifled barrels there are two diameters: one for the bore and one for the grooves cut to spin the bullet. The bore diameter (measured across the lands between grooves) is smaller than the groove diameter, and either number could be used as "caliber." The .250 Savage and .257 Roberts, for example, have bullets of the same diameter: .257 inch. That's groove diameter. Both .250 and .257 rifle bores have a .250 land diameter. The .270 Winchester is .277 across the grooves; all .300s mike .308 across the grooves, as do the .308 Winchester and .308 Norma Magnum. Centerfire .22's, from the .218 Bee to the .225 Winchester, use the same .224 bullets. Bullets for the .303 British measure .311. Those for modern .338's and Weatherby's .340 Magnums mike .338, for the .350 Remington and .358 Norma Magnums .358.

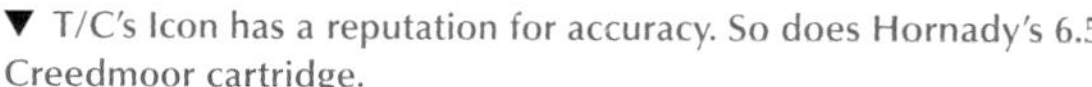
▼ T/C's Icon has a reputation for accuracy. So does Hornady's 6.5 Creedmoor cartridge.

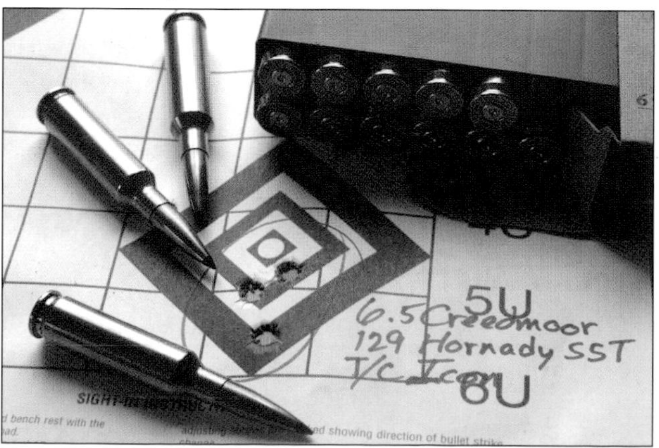

▲ The .416 Rigby is still popular after its first century. This hunter is loading a CZ rifle with solids.

What about two-digit designations like the .22 Hornet, .30 Carbine, and .45 Colt? These numbers simply indicate bore diameter in hundredths, not thousandths of an inch. Add a zero, and you'll often come up with the name of a similar cartridge and a good idea of the bullet diameter. Sometimes the rule doesn't hold, though. Handgunnners know the .38 Special uses the same .357 bullet as the .357 Magnum! Two two-digit numbers usually mean the cartridge dates to black powder days, the second pair indicating grains of black powder in an original load. The .45-70 was charged with 70 grains of black powder before it climbed aboard the smokeless wagon. Of course, "grains" here is a weight measure, not a physical description as in "grains of sand." There are 437.5 grains in one ounce. The best-known exception to the paired double-digit tradition is the .30-06. This is a .30 caliber cartridge adopted by the US Army for its new Springfield rifle in 1906. It replaced the .30-03. Another anomaly: the .250-3000 Savage. Developed by Charles Newton for Savage around 1913, it featured an 87-grain bullet at an advertised speed of 3,000 feet per second. The company wanted that velocity (high for that day) in the cartridge name. Some old cartridges wear a third set of numbers, designating bullet weight in grains, as in .45-70-405, a designation for the official US Army cartridge from 1873 to 1892. Three number sequences can also show caliber, bullet weight, and case length, as in .45-120-3 1/4 Sharps. The 3-1/4 inch case is exceptionally long.

In Europe, rifled bores are commonly measured in millimeters, not hundredths of an inch. Some American

At just 6 pounds, Kimber's 84M is still pleasant to shoot in 7mm-08, a fine plains game cartridge. ▶

rounds have been labeled this way. The 6mm Remington uses a .243 bullet, the 6.5 Remington Magnum a .264 bullet (like Winchester's .264 Magnum). The various 7mm's fire .284 bullets, the 8mm Remington Magnum a .323 bullet. European cartridge designations also include case length in millimeters: The 7x57 Mauser has a 7mm groove diameter and a case 57mm long. Our .308 Winchester cartridge is known in military circles as the 7.62x51 NATO (51mm is the case length).

"Wildcat" cartridges are those not commercially manufactured but fashioned by handloaders from existing cases. The .338-06 is the .30-06 with its case "necked up" to .33 caliber. Some wildcats, notably the .25-06 and .22-250 (on the .250 Savage case), have gone commercial. For years, hunters handloaded the .35 Whelen, a .30-06 derivative named after Colonel Townsend Whelen, a firearms authority in the decades between the world wars. Remington began producing .35 Whelen rifles and ammunition in 1988. Long-range enthusiasts necked the never-popular .284 Winchester hull to 6.5mm and liked it so well that Norma now loads it. Many commercial rounds have other cases in their ancestry. The 7x57 Mauser, circa 1892, was revamped to produce the .257 Roberts and, later, the 6mm Remington. The .308 Winchester case fathered the .243 and .358. Remington's 7mm-08 and .260, and the .338 Federal, later joined that group. The 7-30 Waters is a .30-30 case blown forward and necked to .284.

The selection of rimfire rounds has also grown of late. (The priming compound in rimfire lies in the rim itself instead of in a separate, central primer). The patriarch of this family could be the .22 BB Cap, designed in 1845 for what were then known as parlor or saloon (salon) rifles. The "BB" stands for "bulleted breech." This round initially held no powder; the priming alone delivered enough thrust for indoor target shooting. During the 1880s the CB (conical bullet) Cap appeared, loaded with 1-½ grains of black powder. The .22 Short and Long appeared early too. They differ in case length. Originally, the Long Rifle had the Long's case but a heavier bullet: 40 grains compared to 29. A 37-grain hollow point followed. Now some hyper-velocity .22 Long Rifle rounds feature bullets of 33 to 36 grains. The .22 Special is dead, but not the .22 WMR (Winchester Magnum Rimfire), available in a variety of loads and bullet weights. Hornady's wildly successful .17 HMR is based on that hull. The logical follow up, the .17 Mach 2 (also by Hornady, on the .22 Long Rifle case) has not achieved the HMR's success at market. Still, both give tiny (20-grain) bullets a very fast start.

Based on the .308 Winchester, the .338 Federal offers greater efficiency and more bullet weight.

The term "magnum" means a cartridge boasts extra-high energy or velocity. But some magnums are not as potent as others with the same bore diameter. Some rounds not called magnums (though they may come from magnum cases) outperform cartridges that carry the magnum label. Remington's 7mm STW (Shooting Times Westerner) derives from the 8mm Remington Magnum and has a bigger case than the 7mm Remington Magnum. "Belted magnum" refers to the belt in front of the extractor groove, present on cartridges based on the .300 H&H case and, later, the .378 Weatherby. Almost all belted magnum rifle cartridges were fashioned from the .300 H&H, itself an offshoot of the .375 H&H, circa 1912. The belt is a headspacing device; it has essentially nothing to do with structural reinforcement. The belt is a stop, to be arrested by the chamber to ensure proper fit between case, chamber and bolt head. The rim on a .30-30 hull, and the shoulder on a .270, perform the same function. All prevent the case from entering the chamber too far. End play in a chambered round can result in case separation on firing. Incidentally, magnum handgun rounds like the .357 and .44 magnums are much smaller than the .300 H&H and aren't belted.

"Nitro Express" is the British equivalent of "magnum." The name derives from nitroglycerine, the explosive used in some gunpowders and evokes images of a fast moving train. Mainly it applies to rifle cartridges designed for thick skinnned African game. "Black Powder Express" predated it, during the late 1800s. By the way, dual numbers on British cartridges signify parent cartridge and bore, in reverse order from American custom. A .450/.400 fires a .400 (actually .405) diameter bullet.

A word about shotshell nomenclature: Gauge is an early measure of bore diameter, indicating the number of lead balls the size of the bore that equal a pound. So the bigger the bore, the smaller the gauge. Balls that fit a 16 gauge shotgun bore weigh an ounce apiece; those that fit a 20 gauge weigh less because the bore is smaller in diameter and more small balls are required to equal one pound. An exception is the .410, actually a caliber designation: .410 inch bore diameter. The .410 is equivalent to 67-½ gauge. You can substitute

▲ This fine buck fell to a 412 yard shot with a GreyBull-stocked Remington 700, 7mm Magnum.

"bore" for "gauge" when referring to a shotgun, as in "a 12 bore double." Common shotgun gauges are 10, 12, 16, 20 and 28. During the late nineteenth century, "punt guns" of 4 gauge and even larger were mounted in small boats to kill waterfowl for market. Early African explorers used 1,250-grain bullets in 8 gauge muskets, delivering 3 tons of energy to big game, even at the sedate speed of 1,500 feet per second!

Labels on shotshell boxes show powder charges in "drams equivalent," the designation dating to black powder days. A dram is a unit of weight; 16 drams equal one ounce. When smokeless supplanted black powder at the turn of the century, it was of a type known as "bulk powder" and could be loaded in place of black "bulk for bulk" (not by weight). "Dense" smokeless powders came later. They took up less space in the shell, so neither bulk nor weight equivalents applied. A "3-¼ dram equivalent" charge is a smokeless charge that approximates the *performance* of a 3-¼ dram black powder charge. It has nothing to do with the amount of smokeless powder actually loaded. The other numbers on a shotshell box refer to shot charge weight and pellet size. A series that reads "3-¼—1-¼—6" tells you there's an ounce and a quarter of #6 shot in each shell.

Magnum shotshells may be longer than standard shells or may just have a heavier charge of shot. Standard length magnum shotshells commonly carry extra heavy payloads at modest velocities.

◀ Wayne fires a Ruger No.1, an elegant rifle that employs a dropping-block action much like the one John Browning used in many of his designs.

Section II

THE MUSCLE BEHIND THE SHOT

7. Primers: Sparkplugs with Bang!

Centerfire rifle primers hail from the percussion cap of the mid-nineteenth century. Drawn brass, solid head cartridge cases have no anvil, so beginning in 1880, primer cups have been manufactured with anvils. Installed in cases with a central flash hole, they're called Boxer style primers. They come in two sizes for rifle cartridges, two for handguns.

Large and small rifle primers are of the same diameter as large and small pistol primers respectively, but the pellets inside differ. You need more spark to ignite heavy charges of slow rifle powders. The spark of magnum primers lasts longer than that of standard primers. By the way, a large rifle primer weighs about 5.4 grains and carries .6-grain of priming compound.

Early on, European cartridge designers followed their own path, incorporating the anvil in the case and punching two flash holes in the primer pocket on either side of the anvil, which is part of the case. This Berdan design has a couple of advantages over the Boxer: there's more room in it for priming compound and the flame can go straight through the holes rather than having to scoot around the anvil and its braces. The Boxer primer owes its popularity largely to handloaders, who can pop the old primer out while sizing the case in a die with a decapping pin. Berdan primers must be pried out with a special hook or forced free with hydraulic pressure. Oddly, Edward Boxer, for whom American style primers are named, was British. Europeans named their primer after Hyram Berdan, an American. Both men were military officers.

Early Boxer primers ignited black powder easily but sometimes failed to fire smokeless. When more fulminate was added to the priming mix, cases began to

▲ A centerfire cartridge (left) holds a self-contained primer, with anvil and explosive. In a rimfire case, the priming mix is deposited inside the rim. The chamber lip serves as the anvil for the striker.

crack. Blame fell on the propellant, but the culprit was really mercury residue from the primer. Absorbed by black powder left in the cases, mercury accumulated to attack the zinc in case walls, causing them to split. A typical primer at this time contained 41 percent potassium chlorate, 33 percent antimony sulfide, 14 percent mercury fulminate, and 11 percent powdered glass.

The first successful non-mercuric primer for smokeless loads was the military H-48, developed in 1898 for the .30-40 Krag. Its primary detonating component was potassium chlorate, whose corrosive salts did not damage the case. It could wreak havoc with bores, however, by attracting water and causing rust. Cleaning with hot water and ammonia, followed by oiling, was required after shooting to keep rifling shiny.

In 1901 the German Company Rheinische-Westphalische Sprengstoff (RWS) introduced a primer with barium nitrate and picric acid instead of potassium chlorate. These compounds did not cause rust. Ten years later the Swiss had a non-corrosive primer and German rimfire ammunition featured *Rostfrei* (rust-free) priming. *Rostfrei* contained neither potassium chlorate nor ground glass, an element commonly used in other primers to generate friction when the striker hit. Unfortunately, this otherwise ideal sparkplug left a residue of barium oxide, which could scour a barrel as aggressively as did glass. American military primers were glass-free before World War I when the FH-42 supplanted the H-48.

Primer production during the Great War overloaded drying houses Stateside, causing sulfuric acid to build

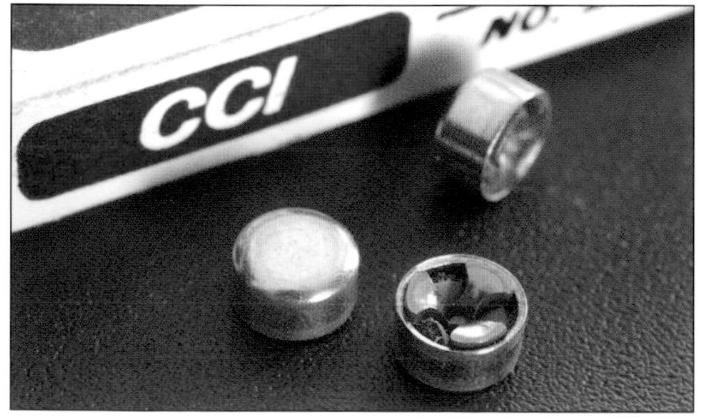

◀ Centerfire rifle primers feature an anvil, here a tripod-shaped fixture. The hardened mix of explosives beneath is ignited by the striker's blow, which crushes it against the anvil.

THE MUSCLE BEHIND THE SHOT

▲ The .22 rimfire cartridge dates to the 1850s and work by Horace Smith and Dan Wesson. Note the striker mark on the rim of this fired .22 cartridge.

up in priming mix. Misfires resulted. The FH-42 was replaced by the Winchester 35-NF primer, later known as the FA-70. This corrosive primer contained 53percent potassium chlorate, 25 percent lead thiocyanate, 17 percent antimony sulfide, and 5 percent TNT. It remained in military service through World War II.

Remington was the first US firm to announce non-corrosive priming in sporting ammo under the "Kleanbore" label in 1927. Winchester followed with "Staynless," Peters with "Rustless." All contained mercury fulminate. German chemists Rathburg and Von Hersz later managed to remove both potassium chlorate and mercury fulminate from primers. Again Remington took the lead with the first US version of a non-corrosive, non-mercuric primer. The main ingredient (then comprising up to 45 percent of the mix) was lead tri-nitro-resorcinate, or lead styphnate. It remains an important component in small arms primers. The US Army adopted non-corrosive, non-mercuric primers in 1948 and currently uses one designated FA-956. It comprises 37 percent lead styphnate, 32 percent barium nitrate, 15 percent antimony sulfide, 7 percent aluminum, 5 percent PETN, and 4 percent tetracene.

During the 1940s, development of big, broad-shouldered rounds and extra-slow-burning powders called for a stronger ignition flame. More priming compound was not the answer, because it might shatter powder directly in front of the flash hole, causing erratic pressures and performance. Dick Speer and Victor Jasaitis, a chemist from Speer Cartridge Works, came up with a better idea, adding boron and aluminum to the lead styphnate to make the primer burn longer. The result would be more heat and more complete ignition before primer fade. Other munitions companies latched onto this development. Speer primers, still made in Lewiston, Idaho, wear a different label these days: CCI (Cascade Cartridge Industries).

The same primer problems were visited on shotshell production—which found its salvation in the same quarters. But shotshell cup assemblies differ from rifle primers. A deep battery cup holds the anvil and a smaller cup containing the detonating material, protected by a foil cover. A shotshell's primer pocket has no bottom, hence, no flash hole. The flash hole is in the battery cup. Made of thin, folded brass like old balloon-head rifle cases, shotshell heads are reinforced with a dense paper base wad or a thick section of hull plastic. Battery cups seal the deep hole in the base wad.

While the machines that produce primers are more sophisticated now, primer manufacture is much the same as it was at the outbreak of the second world war. Huge batches of primer cups are still punched and drawn from sheet metal and indexed on large perforated metal tables. Perforated plates are smeared with wet priming compound the consistency of fresh dough and laid precisely on top of the tables so the dabs in the holes can be punched down into open faced cups.

▼ Winchester's Model 70, now in production again, has been chambered from .22 Hornet to .458.

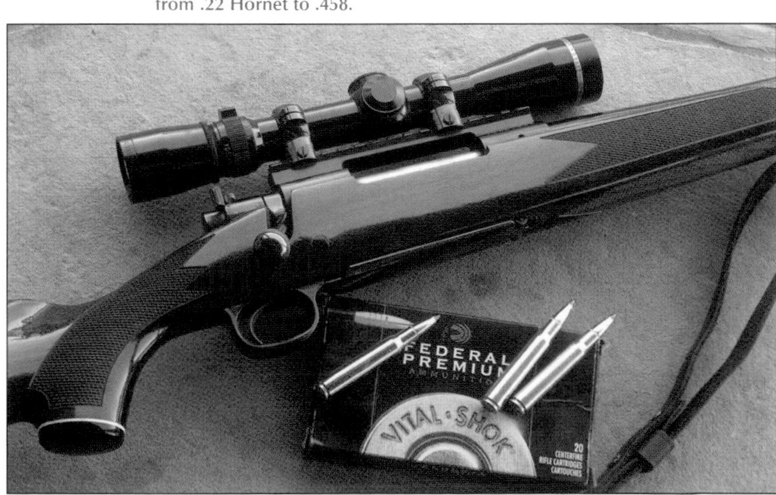

Or the cups are filled by workers brushing the compound across the face of the table. Next comes the thin foil disc (or a shellacked paper cover). Anvils, punched from another metal sheet, are inserted as the plates line up. Priming mix is stable when it is wet, but extremely hazardous to work with when dry. No mix is ever allowed to dry in the primer room.

Primer choice can influence pressures, velocity, and accuracy; however, most modern primers are both reliable and uniform in their ignition characteristics.

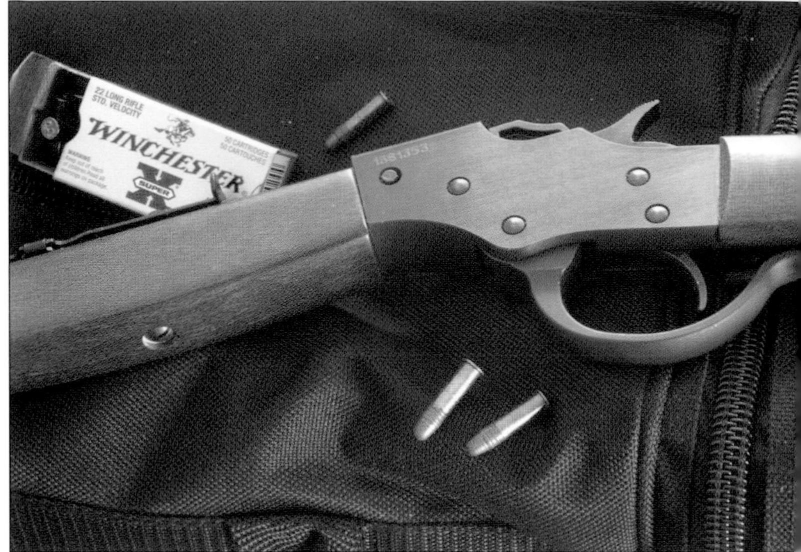

This modern rendition of the Stevens Favorite, a popular single-shot .22, has an exposed-hammer, dropping-block action with offset striker to hit the cartridge rim, where the priming mixture resides. ▶

8. Fuel for the Cartridge

From its inception in the fourteenth century until the middle of the nineteenth century, black powder generated the gas that pushed bullets out of gun barrels. Mild steels bottled its modest pressure. Nitroglycerine, discovered in 1846 by Ascanio Subrero in Italy, promised higher levels of performance at the expense of metal splitting pressure. "Nitro" is a colorless liquid comprising nitric and sulphuric acids plus glycerin. Unlike ordinary black powder, it's not a blend of fuels and oxidants; it is instead an unstable, oxygen rich compound that can almost instantly rearrange itself into more stable gases. All it needs is a jolt. With age, nitroglycerine can become more unstable, more dangerous.

In 1863 Swedish chemist Emmanuel Nobel and his son Alfred figured out how to put this touchy substance in cans. That made it easier to handle but no less hazardous. Several shipments blew up. So did the Nobel factory in Germany. Alfred later discovered that soaking the porous earth *Kieselguhr* with nitro rendered the chemical less sensitive to shock. This process paved the way for dynamite, patented in 1875.

During the 1840s Swiss chemist Christian Schoenbein had found that cotton treated with nitric and sulfuric acids formed a compound that burned so fast the fire would consume the cotton without setting fire to a heap of black powder on top of it! Schoenbein obtained an English patent for his work then sold the procedure to Austria. Shortly, John Hall and Sons built a guncotton plant in Faversham, England. It blew up.

▼ Early rifle powders were all packed in metal cans. The first powder enterprises endured some horrific accidents. But manufacture of propellants in modern factories is much safer.

▲ The mess attending black powder shooting led to the development of Pyrodex by Dan Pawlak. Hodgdon produces this black powder substitute, now available in convenient pellets as well as granules.

So did most of the other guncotton plants built at the time. Chemists concluded this substance had little use as a propellant because it burned too fast and was too unstable. History had witnessed such problems with chlorate powders, pioneered by Berthollet in the 1780s. When a French powder plant at Essons blew up in 1788, potassium chlorate was deemed too sensitive for use in firearms.

But eventually bright people figured out how to harness these frisky compounds. During the 1850s J. J. Pohl developed a fuel he called "white powder." It comprised 49 percent potassium chlorate, 28 percent yellow potash, and 23 percent sulfur. Though a second-rate propellant, it served the Confederacy when during the Civil War black powder became unavailable. Wartime backyard powder mills turned out propellants of widely varying compositions and behaviors. Some performed well enough. Others proved useless or dangerous. Formulas were marketed through the mail by con artists who baited customers with claims that coffee, sugar, and alum, plus potassium chlorate, gave lethal thrust to any lead ball!

Keen to improve upon black powder and heartened by Nobel's work with nitro, experimenters persevered. In 1869 German immigrant Carl Dittmar built a small plant to make "Dualin," sawdust treated with nitroglycerin. In his native Prussia, he had run out of money trying to make smokeless powder from nitrated wood. But his efforts in New England showed promise. A year after completing the Dualin plant, he introduced his "New Sporting Powder." By 1878 he was

◀ French engineer Paul Vielle is generally credited with the development of smokeless powder. In 1885 his "Poudre B" comprised ethyl alcohol and the ordinary proxylin known as celluloid. Poudre B is a single-base powder—no nitroglycerine.

building a mill in Binghampton, New York. It blew up, taking part wof Binghampton with it. When Dittmar's health failed, he sold what was left of his firm. One of his foreman, Milton Lindsey, landed at the King Powder Company, where he worked with president G. M. Peters to develop "King's Semi-Smokeless Powder." They patented their formula in 1899. Dupont's "Lesmoke," which appeared soon thereafter, had roughly the same composition: 60 percent saltpeter, 20 percent wood cellulose, 12 percent charcoal, and 8 percent sulfur. One of several semi-smokeless powders of that time, Lesmoke proved a fine propellant for .22 rimfires. Fouling remained a problem but the residue didn't harden as with black powder. Its soft residue gave semi-smokeless an advantage over the first smokeless powders, which left nothing to carry away residue from the corrosive primers of the day. Lesmoke was more hazardous to produce than smokeless, however. It was discontinued in 1947.

French engineer Paul Vielle is generally credited with developing the first successful smokeless powder. His "Poudre B" comprised ethyl alcohol and celluloid. But in the 1870s, a decade before Vielle's achievement, Austrian chemist Frederick Volkmann patented a cellulose-based powder. Unfortunately, Austrian patents were not acknowledged world wide and in 1875 Austria's government began enforcing its monopoly on the domestic powder supply. Volkmann closed his plant then disappeared. His claims of transparent smoke, less barrel residue, more power, and safer handling would be borne out.

By 1887 Alfred Nobel had increased the proportion of nitrocellulose in blasting gelatin and found he could use the new compound as a propellant. A year later he introduced "Ballistite." This double-base powder (it contained both nitrocellulose and nitroglycerin) was similar to a new powder developed at the same time by Hiram Maxim of machine gun fame. Concurrently, the British War Office started a search for a more effective

In 1863 Alfred Nobel, son of Swedish chemist Emmanuel Nobel, devised a way to put volatile nitroglycerine in cans. Later Alfred found that soaking porous earth with nitro stabilized the explosive. From this came dynamite, in 1875. ▶

rifle powder and came up with "Cordite." With elements of both Nobel's formula and Maxim's, Cordite was named for a stage in its manufacture, when the propellant paste could be squeezed through a die to form spaghetti-like cords. The early formula included 58 percent nitroglycerine and 37 percent guncotton. These proportions were later changed to 30 percent nitroglycerine and 65 percent guncotton, plus mineral jelly and acetone. Nobel and Maxim sued the British government for patent infringement but got nowhere.

Nitrated lignin gave early smokeless powders a lumpy or fuzzy appearance. Variations in density posed problems for handloaders. "Bulk" powders could be substituted, bulk for bulk, for black powder.

The .303 British, in the Short Magazine Lee Enfield, was one of the first military rounds fueled by smokeless powder, in the 1890s. ▶

▲ L-R: The 6.5x55 is much older than (but not as potent as) the .260 Remington, 6.5 Creedmoor.

"Dense" or gelatin powders could *not* be safely measured by bulk, because their energy/volume ratios were higher. The shooting industry responded by marking shotgun loads in "drams equivalent." In other words, the smokeless powder used gave the same performance as black-powder shotshells loaded with the marked number of drams. Handloaders charging rifle and pistol cases were advised to forget black-powder weights and treat smokeless as an entirely new fuel, with new rules.

The 8mm Lebel, adopted by the French army in 1886, became the first military cartridge designed for smokeless powder. Other countries soon followed: England with the .303 British in 1888, Switzerland with the 7.5x55 Schmidt-Rubin in 1889. By the mid-1890s nearly all nations that could muster an army were equipping soldiers with small-bore bolt rifles firing smokeless cartridges. The new propellant boosted bullet speed by a third and didn't give away a rifleman's position with lingering clouds of spent saltpeter.

Oddly enough, most powder firms established in the 1890s failed. Fierce competition and flawed product, combined with the hazards of powder manufacture, made this a tough business. Many ambitious entrepreneurs who saw huge profit potential in smokeless propellant failed to secure government contracts, believing mistakenly that private sales could sustain a young company. As with rifles, one military contract could mean salvation. Rejection by Ordnance boded ill—even if, as one industry scribe claimed, American sportsmen burned " . . . not less than three million pounds per annum."

Mergers among powder companies were common. In 1890, Samuel Rodgers, an English physician living in San Francisco, formed the United States Powder Company to produce ammonium nitrate. Then he partnered with the Giant Powder Company to make "Gold Dust Powder," comprising 55 percent ammonium picrate, 25 percent sodium or potassium nitrate, and 20 percent ammonium bichromate. The Giant Powder Company plant was destroyed by an explosion in 1898. At this time "Peyton Powder" by the California Powder Works was fueling .30-40 Krag ammunition for the US Army. Laflin & Rand manufactured its "W-A" double-base powder for the Krag (initials for developers Whistler and Aspinwall). "W-A" contained 30 percent nitroglycerin which contributed to its high burn temperatures and erosive tendencies.

Tennessee's Leonard Powder Company marketed "Ruby N" and "Ruby J" powders until it folded in 1894. The American Smokeless Powder Company, a New Jersey firm, succeeded it, producing powder under contract for the government. Creditor Laflin & Rand acquired ASPC in 1898. Earlier, Laflin & Rand had sought American rights to Ballistite but considered Nobel's price of $300,000 plus royalties too steep. Ballistite manufacture later came under the control of DuPont, which contracted that job to Laflin & Rand. "Lightning," "Unique," "Sharpshooter," and "L&R Smokeless" powders originated at Laflin & Rand.

The Robin Hood Powder Company of Vermont became the Robin Hood Ammunition Company before

▼ Alliant Powder (formerly Hercules Powder) offers eight ounce containers of its popular Reloder® series of smokeless powders for rifle reloaders. The product also is available in one pound and five pound offerings.

THE MUSCLE BEHIND THE SHOT

▲ Wayne killed this Idaho elk with a Ruger rifle in 7mm Winchester Short Magnum, a cartridge made possible by high-energy propellants whose roots go back to the development of guncotton and nitroglycerin in the 19th century.

it sold in 1915 to the Union Metallic Cartridge Company. The American E. C. & Schultz Powder Company was acquired by DuPont in 1903 then became part of Hercules when DuPont was split by court order in 1912. DuPont and the California Powder Works began filling military contracts in 1897 with nitrocellulose powders that resembled Cordite. Guncotton dissolved in ether and alcohol formed a colloid. Pressed into thin tubes, it was then chopped short. "Government Pyro" became one of the first of these powders to see military use, in the .30-06. DuPont later charged that cartridge with 1147 and 1185 powders. IMR (Improved Military Rifle) 4895 became the powder of choice for the .30-06 M2.

Even after Hercules started up its modern operation in Kenville, New Jersey, DuPont continued to dominate the market in small-arms powder. It manufactured up to a ton daily and produced large quantities of dynamite. By the onset of World War I, Hercules had established a factory in Parlin, New Jersey, there making nitrocellulose and popular rifle and pistol powders, including Bullseye, Infallible, and HiVel.

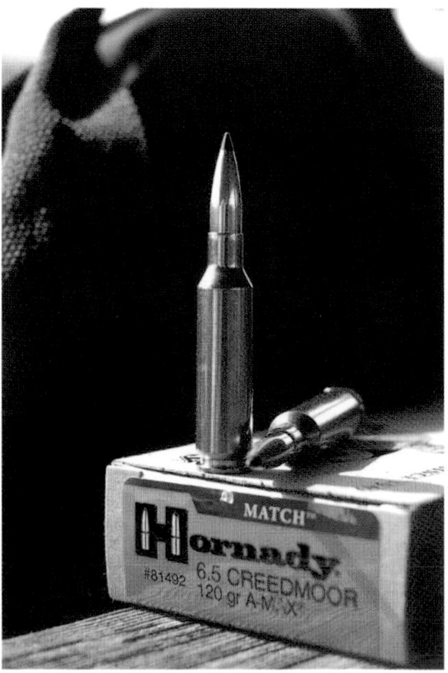

Hornady's 6.5mm Creedmoor and the firm's new Superperformance ammunition owe their success to powders that are far more efficient and temperature-stable than early propellants, the manufacture of which destroyed many factories. ▶

But DuPont got the big war contracts. It established plants in Old Hickory, Tennessee, and Nitro (really), West Virginia. Combined capacity was 1.5 million pounds per day! After the war DuPont bought the town of Old Hickory to build a rayon factory. The powder magazines remained, however. One day in August, 1924, they caught fire. More than 100 buildings and 50 million pounds of powder vanished in a fearsome blaze.

During the Great War, Hercules manufactured Cordite powder for the British government—up to 12,000 pounds a day. Wartime Cordite production totaled 46 million pounds. In addition, Hercules sold 3 million pounds of small arms propellants and 54 million pounds of cannon powder. The conflict spurred companies like Hercules to improve powders and production processes. Plagued by copper residue fouling cannon bores, US munitions experts took a tip from the French and added tin to their propellants. Soon rifle powders got the same treatment. With 4 percent tin DuPont's No. 17 became No. 17-½. No. 15 became No. 15-½. Tin levels were halved when dark rings appeared in the bores of National Match rifles, a result of tin cooling near the muzzle.

High-velocity magnums get their sauce from progressive-burning powders that yield a sustained burn to accelerate long, heavy bullets without generating ruinous pressures. Shooters in the 19th century didn't have them, didn't need them. ▼

9. Propellants from Cotton

Though most sportsmen know it as the traditional propellant for muzzle loading rifles and as the choice of purists in cartridge guns for Cowboy Action shooting, black powder still has military uses. It's in the detonating charges for high energy propellants in artillery shells and propels ejection seats clear of aircraft. As in the nineteenth century, it still comprises sulfur, charcoal and saltpeter. They're ground fine and mixed at 3 percent moisture. The powder "meal" is pressed into cakes, which are fed through a granulating machine where toothed cylinders chop them. After screening segregates particles by size, they're polished in revolving wooden barrels. Most black powder is labeled A-1, Fg, Ffg, FFFg, FFFFg and FFFFFg, in decreasing order of granule size. Bigger grains generally burn slowest and work best pushing heavy balls or bullets. Very fine black powder is suitable only for priming charges and pyrotechnics.

Smokeless powder derives from different materials and processes. It starts out as nitrocellulose—vegetable fiber soaked in nitric and sulfuric acids. Guncotton, a special kind of nitrocellulose, has slightly higher nitrogen content (13.2 percent compared to a standard 12.6) and lower solubility in ether-alcohol solution. Like other forms of nitrocellulose in powder production, it comes from short crude cotton fibers or linters which are boiled in caustic soda to remove oils. Water formed during nitrating is absorbed by the sulfuric acid, thus preventing decomposition by hydrolysis. A centrifuge next strips excess acid; then the linters are rinsed and boiled 48 hours to remove all traces of acid which can cause spontaneous combustion. The cotton is beaten and boiled several more times. Agitators fluff it. The nitrocellulose is washed in solvent, then heated to evaporate the solvent. Hard grains of powder (and water) remain. "Cooking" the solvent off with heat applied to a wet solution is less dangerous than the old air-dry method. Ether is used to dissolve the fibers in nitrocellulose marked for single-base powders, acetone is used for double-base. Nitroglycerin is then added to form the double-base powder.

The soup at this point in smokeless powder production is unstable. More mixing turns the soup to a jelly, which is squeezed through dies (extruded) to form slender tubes of precise dimensions. Rollers push these tubes through a plate, where a whirling knife shears them into measured increments. The resulting grains of single-base powders still contain ether, so they're sent to a warm solvent recovery room, where they soak in water for about two weeks. Wet single-base and freshly sheared double-base powders are then air-dried, sieved, and polished in drums that coat them with graphite. Tumbling smooths edges that might otherwise produce friction when the powder is jostled. Graphite further reduces friction while imparting the familiar slate color. Uncoated powder is yellow.

In 1933 Western Cartridge Company came up with the first successful ball powder. Ball powder manufacture differs from the production of extruded powders, though the raw materials are essentially the same. Nitrocellulose intended for ball powders goes

Accurate Arms powders serve a wide range of cartridges. The .308 Winchester likes several near mid-chart in burn rate. ▼

◀ Only about 30 percent of a cartridge's energy pushes the bullet. About 40 percent is lost as exhaust; less than 1 percent reaches you as recoil.

through a hammer mill that grinds it to a fine pumice. Blended with water and pumped in slurry form into a still, the nitrocellulose combines with chalk added to counteract the nitric acids. Ethyl acetate dissolves the nitrocellulose, producing a lacquer. Agitation and heat break the lacquer into small particles or it is pressed through plates much like extruded powders and chopped to bits by whirling knives. Tumbling and heating leave the grains round. When they're of proper size and roundness, the ethyl acetate is distilled off and salt is added to draw out moisture. In a slurry of fresh water, the powder rushes through sizing screens. A heated still adds nitroglycerin. Burn deterrents come next, to smooth the pressure curve by controlling burn rate. A centrifuge removes excess water. The grains are tumbled in graphite then sized again. Some ball powders are measured blends of sizes. Some are purposefully rolled or crushed to manipulate burning characteristics. Ball powders meter better than most extruded or stick powders, and their manufacture is quicker and simpler.

Extruded powders are shaped like little tubes. The central hole controls the burn rate and pressure curve. Powders whose grain surface area diminishes during the burn are classified as degressive. Ball and flake powders are like this. Powders whose grain surface stays about the same throughout most of the burn cycle

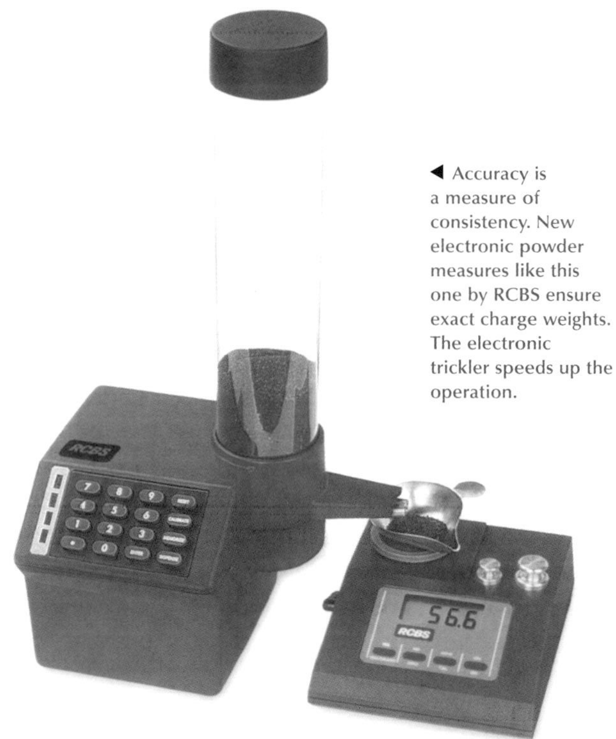

◀ Accuracy is a measure of consistency. New electronic powder measures like this one by RCBS ensure exact charge weights. The electronic trickler speeds up the operation.

RCBS PowderMaster™ Electronic Trickler & PowderPro™ Digital Scale

are said to be neutral. A one-hole extruded powder falls in this category because as flame eats away at the outer surface, it also consumes the grain from inside out. In the hole, burning increases surface area as the hole becomes bigger while flame on the outside reduces the grain's diameter. At that final point of gas release, of course, grain size shrinks rapidly. Large powder grains may have multiple holes—typically 7 or 19—that help them burn progressively.

Progressive or neutral powders are intuitively the ones you'd choose for a sustained thrust, the big push needed to launch heavy, small-diameter bullets fighting lots of bore friction. But ball powders work in this arena too. That's because additives throttle burn rate and gas release. Nearly all smokeless fuels have three additional components: a stabilizer to prevent decomposition of the nitrocellulose (commonly diphenylamine); graphite to make handling easier and increase electrical conductivity so static electricity doesn't pose a threat; and a flame retardant to reduce muzzle flash (potassium sulfate is one). Additives are present in such small quantities as to have negligible effect on bullet velocity.

▲ Vihtavouri makes high-energy double-base powders in a range of burn rates. Handloaders esteem these Finnish fuels.

Single-base powders use only nitrocellulose to generate pressure; double-base powders have the added kick of nitroglycerine. That extra oomph makes double base powders a logical choice in cartridges of modest case capacity. VihtaVuori 500-series powders, for example, have up to 25 percent nitroglycerin to give them more energy than 100-series single base rifle powders that burn at equivalent rates.

No matter what kind of powder you put in your handloads, or how much you pack into those hulls, expect only about a 30 percent return. That's right: Only a quarter to a third of the energy released by the propellant actually pushes your bullet up the bore. About the same amount of energy is lost as internal heat during firing. Nearly 40 percent jets out the muzzle as hot (and useless) exhaust! By the way, only about .1 percent of the powder's energy gets to you as felt recoil, which is good news. You wouldn't want much more, even from the slowest powders in the least efficient cases.

10. DuPont: Powder Pioneer

After its inception in 1802 on Delaware's Brandywine River, E. I. DuPont de Nemours had grown with the country. By the end of World War II, any list of major US corporations included the chemical giant. But the varied product line it fielded then could hardly have been imagined by its founder, French immigrant Eleuthere Irenee DuPont.

Not that DuPont lacked confidence in his products. "I can make better black powder than what your country has in its magazines," DuPont told Alexander Hamilton. Apparently the claim impressed our young government. Soon the enterprising DuPont built a plant in Wilmington. The new propellant satisfied US ordnance officers. Gunpowder remained the firm's primary product for most of the nineteenth century. In the 1880s DuPont added a plant at Carney's Point to boost capacity. During World War I, 25,000 people went to work at this Brandywine facility, providing more than 80 percent of the powders used by the Allies (the British and French, the Danes and Russians, as well as US troops)!

The 1930s humbled many mighty corporations. DuPont weathered not only the Depression, but scathing political attacks from some US senators who accused the company of war-mongering. As Hitler revved up his war machine and the US prepared to re-arm, DuPont boosted its production capacity. But the company was fed up with the treatment it had received from Congress. Larry Werner, who worked many years as a DuPont engineer, recalled that "Rather than build new plants, the company contracted to operate government facilities for $1 a year. That way, it could not be said to have had a stake in the hostilities. Of course, the US government had no powder works that could match DuPont's, so the firm supervised construction of seven factories modeled on its Carney's Point plant. Another went up in Canada. At the height of the second world war, these operations shipped *a million pounds of powder a day*. We fielded 16 million guys in uniform then, and they used a lot of ammo!"

After an armistice, the government took control of the propellant plants. Carney's Point stayed in production for DuPont. So did the Belin Works at Scranton, Penn. "Belin made black powder for the government," says Larry. It was used as an igniter in artillery shells. A plant explosion in 1971 sent debris over the nearby interstate and littered runways at the local airport. The plant closed right away but was reopened for military production to supply troops in Vietnam. "In 1973 Marv

DuPont's IMR (Improved Military Rifle) moniker dates way back. These early metal cans have been replaced by plastic. ▶

◀ For best accuracy with wildcats, the die set must match the chamber. Tight tolerances rule!

Gearhardt and Harold Owens bought the Belin Works for $400,000 and contracted to make powder," continued Larry. "Their company, GOEX, later moved to Louisiana, and the Scranton facility shut down."

Explosions at powder plants occur infrequently but can be serious. In June, 1969, an accident in the finishing area at Carney's Point leveled it. A new finishing area was built at DuPont's Potomac River Plant near Falling Waters, Va. In April, 1978, fire swept through the main mix house at Carney's Point, shutting it down. That summer, DuPont contracted with Valleyfield Chemical Products in Quebec to produce commercial smokeless propellants. The Valleyfield plant was a Canadian factory built during World War II and operated by CIL, or Canadian Industries, Limited, a branch of the government. In 1982 Valleyfield Chemical was bought by Welland Chemical, which became EXPRO.

In December, 1986 DuPont sold its smokeless powder business to EXPRO. The IMR Powder Company established itself as a testing and marketing firm for EXPRO. IMR's laboratory and offices in Plattsburg, New York, were kept to develop ballistics data for IMR powders and package and distribute them to dealers. EXPRO, with an annual manufacturing capacity of more than 10 million pounds, also produces powders for Alliant and other brands. Though DuPont owned 70 percent of Remington for decades, it also provided powder for competing ammunition firms.

After the transition from black to smokeless powders near the close of the nineteenth century, "MR" began appearing on cans of DuPont powders. It meant "military rifle." The IMR line of "improved military rifle" powders came along in the 1920s when four-digit numbers replaced two-digit numbers in DuPont designations. MR 10 and kin were supplanted by IMR fuels, beginning with 4198. The first had relatively fast burn rates because in those days rifle cartridges were small. In 1934 DuPont introduced IMR 4227. It announced IMR 4895 in the early 1940s, specifically for the .30-06 in the M1 Garand. About that time the first "magnum" IMR propellant made its debut. Developed for 20mm cannons, 4831 would become one of the signature fuels for the big bottleneck rounds designed by wildcatters Roy Weatherby and P. O. Ackley.

Incidentally, powder numbers have nothing to do with burning rate. According to long-timer Larry Werner, powder from DuPont is labeled chronologically. High numbers indicate recent propellants. Those under development have traditionally been tagged "EX" for "experimental." Larry, who started working with the company in 1954, recalls that "almost always, firearm design precedes cartridge design. Powder for a new round comes last. We'd start with a cookbook formula, then tweak the mix until we had it right." Once a customer was satisfied "and committed to a batch of 5,000 pounds or so," the "EX" was dropped from the designation and commercial labeling replaced it. Propellants made expressly for military use had no number prefix. "EX 7383 was developed for 50-caliber spotter rounds during the 1950s."

Powder charts by DuPont and other companies help handloaders compare burning rates so they can choose an efficient powder for a given cartridge. "Closed bomb" tests are used to measure burn rate. A charge of powder ignited in a chamber of known volume produces a pressure curve that's then compared to the curves from other propellants. But a powder's behavior relative to that of other propellants can change, not only with changes in case capacity and bore diameter, but also with bullet weight. IMR assigns all its powders a Relative Quickness value. IMR 4350 has an arbitrary value of 100. According to Larry, fast-burning IMR 4227 has an RQ of 180; IMR 4198 comes in at 165 and IMR 3031 at 135. IMR 4064, 4320 and 4895 are listed at 120, 115 and 110, respectively, though

◀ Rich McClure shot this half-minute group with 150-grain Hornadys, IMR 3031 in a Kimber '06.

some loading manuals suggest a different order. Savvy handloaders try a number of powders with similar burn rates to come up with a top load.

DuPont's old MR powders included single-base (nitrocellulose) and double-base (nitrocellulose with nitroglycerine) types. "All commercial ball powders are double-base," explains Larry Werner. "Nitro delivers more energy per grain. It also reduces the tendency for grains to pick up moisture. Its drawback is residue. Double-base powders don't burn as clean." Larry adds that to get the full effect of nitroglycerine, you need 8 to 12 percent in the mix, but that some powders advertised as double-base contain less.

▼ Heavy bullets in mid-capacity cases like the .30-06 call for powders like IMR or Hodgdon 4350.

11. The Hodgdon Story

After 1945, huge stocks of military powders remained in government arsenals. Bruce Hodgdon thought he could sell it to handloaders. He bought as much as he could store in underground rail cars and began parceling it out at a profit. His business grew and eventually his stocks of powder ran out. A lot of that powder was 4831. To get more powder for his customers, Bruce went to an Australian factory with a sample of the remnant. But the sample—and consequently the new 4831 that matched it—didn't quite equal the burn rate of the original. Time in storage can affect burning characteristics. That's why Hodgdon 4831 is a tad slower than IMR 4831. In magnum cases like the 7mm Remington and .300 Winchester, H4831 merits a charge weight increase of about 4 percent over IMR 4831 to get the same performance.

Years ago I was shown a keg of Hodgdon 4831 powder. "It's still gray," said its aged owner, as he unwrapped the tape holding the cardboard lid tight. He set the lid aside and plunged his hand into the silvery, slippery kernels. They dribbled through his fingers. "See. No red dust."

I didn't have enough .270 cases to use 50 pounds of powder, but the thought of owning that much appealed to me. I bought it. Thirty five years later, I fired a group with cartridges I'd loaded with that H4831 in the 1980s. The holes on the target touched.

Brewster E. Hodgdon was born in Joplin, Missouri, in 1910. His father and grandfather were civil engineers; he grew up as an apprentice. But one frigid day, riding in the back of an open 1917 Buick to survey a property, Bruce decided it was time to break the tradition. He studied business at Pittsburg State College, then at Washburn. He married high school sweetheart Amy Skipworth in 1934 and soon after he started work as a gas appliance salesman. Later, he and Amy bought two acres with a house and garage, a chicken coop, and a small orchard in Johnson County. That site would later serve as headquarters for Hodgdon Powder Company.

By all accounts, Bruce was a star gas company salesman, but he wasn't happy hewing to increasingly narrow mandates from the office. An avid shooter and reloader, he knew from his stint in the Navy during the 1940s that there was lots of powder left over from the war. Moreover, he figured there were plenty of riflemen who'd buy it from him. So he committed to 50,000 pounds, paid for with cash from a life insurance policy.

It was a gamble. Sure, this was 4895, a popular fuel for the popular .30-06. And it came really cheap. But Bruce had nowhere to store such a quantity and no market. He bought a derelict boxcar and moved it to a rented cow pasture. He placed a 1 inch ad in *The American Rifleman*. Mail-order price for that first Hodgdon powder was $30—for 150 pounds!

"Early on, the powder cans were metal," says son J. B. "My brother Bob and I glued on the labels and built shipping boxes from orange crates. On our way to school, we drove tons of 4895 to REA and Merriam Frisco terminals in the trunk of a 1940 Ford." Amy became bookkeeper. Orders soon included other reloading components and eventually rifles and ammunition. Copper-lined kegs were later replaced by cardboard. "We sold the salvaged copper for more than those first batches of powder," recalls J. B.

By 1952, brisk powder sales prompted Bruce to quit his appliance job in Kansas City to funnel all his energy into the powder business, B. E. Hodgdon, Incorporated. J. B. and Bob joined him after finishing school in 1959 and 1961. Ted Curtis, Homer Clark, and Dave Wolfe (founder, Wolfe Publishing) helped Bruce lobby the Interstate Commerce Commission to change the classification of some smokeless powders to "Flammable Solid." Containers under 8 pounds each, in shipments totaling less than 100 pounds, could then be delivered by common carrier. In 1966 the family separated the powder enterprise from its

▼ Slow powders like H4350 and H4831 excel in big cases with restrictive necks or heavy bullets.

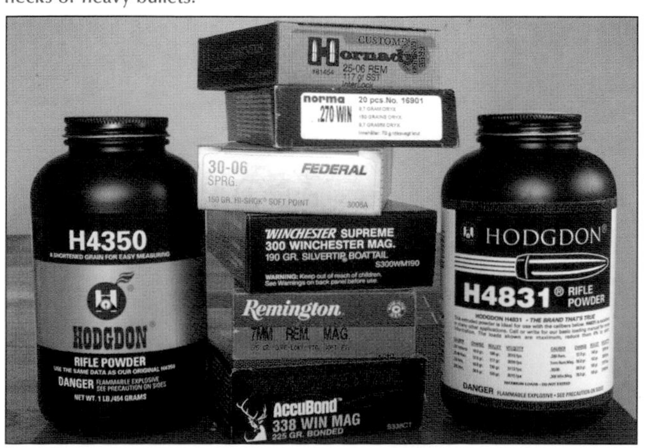

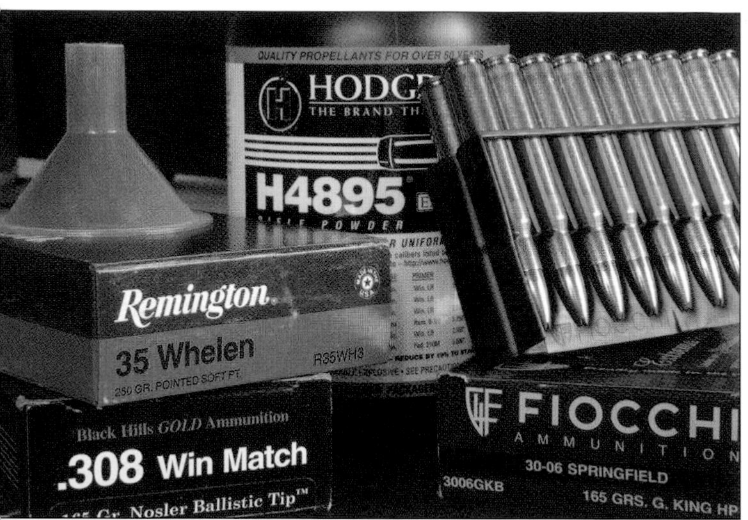

▲ H4895 is a versatile powder in popular cartridges, here the .35 Whelen, .308 and .30-06.

firearms business to form Hodgdon Powder Company. It would come to include powder magazines and packaging facilities on 160 acres six miles west of the office at 6231 Robinson in Overland Park, Kansas.

Bruce Hodgdon sold about four million pounds sterling of surplus powder, mostly H4831. Available in huge quantities, this slow cannon powder suited the belted magnum cartridges just beginning to snatch market share from the .30-06. "We got some surplus H4831 fresh," J. B. recalls. "Some came from disassembled ammo. To sell it fast, we offered primers with it, in a package deal. Primers weren't easy for handloaders to find then. One of Dad's packages included a 150-lb keg and 15,000 primers for $49.95." Or you could settle for a 50-lb keg with 10,000 primers, or a 20-lb keg with 5,000. "Bob and I screened that powder with a double-mesh drum cranked by hand. Big debris, such as wadding from 20mm shells, stayed in the middle. Fines sifted through to the floor. There were no SAAMI specs for performance, or practical ways to measure pressure. We tested powder uniformity with a crude electric chronograph and generated data by measuring heads of fired cases. Half a thousandth was too much expansion."

J. B. tells me H4831 was the most uniform of the early surplus powders.

Ron Reiber has worked at Hodgdon for nearly 20 years. He knows the origins of other popular surplus powders. "H870 was fuel for the .50 BMG. We no longer offer it. H335 was first designated WC 844, a powder for the 55-grain .223 load in the M16. It followed BL-C2, developed as WC 846 for 147-grain hardball in the .308." A powder that began as WC 852 took on a new moniker when Bruce found it gave excellent results in his .22-250. "He used 38 grains behind a 50-grain bullet for 3,800 fps," Ron tells me. "The powder became H380."

By 1959 surplus stocks had run dry. The Hodgdons looked for commercial sources. Before and during the war, the US government had subsidized Olin and DuPont, in the US and abroad. The French-owned Australian Thales plant that currently manufactures Hodgdon's extruded powders also got its start as a US-funded project. "After the war," says J.B., "countries transferred ownership to commercial interests. One of

▼ The .30-06 can use many powders to good effect. Two of the most useful are Hodgdon's H414 and BL-C(2). Also: H4895.

our first non-military sources was a plant in Scotland established to supply powder to the British."

The Hodgdons bought ball powder, pioneered by John Olin in 1933, from the Olin Corp. At first Bruce called ball powders ball powders. "But we soon learned Olin had registered that name," says J. B. "so we changed our designation to spherical." Olin's Winchester powder is currently made by St. Mark's, an industry supplier owned by General Dynamics and operated at a Florida location of that name. Since 2005 Hodgdon has marketed Winchester canister powders under a licensing agreement. IMR powders are made at a factory near Montreal. DuPont chose not to sell extruded powders to Hodgdon in the 1960s. Ironically, Hodgdon now owns DuPont's IMR business! "We also distribute Finland's Vihtavuori line," adds J. B. He stresses that Hodgdon is not a manufacturer. "But we do engineer powders. We developed Trail Boss with a high bulk density for Cowboy Action loads. It won't let you double-charge a case."

Brewster E. Hodgdon died in 1997. He lived modestly near the company he founded. A middle-class, three-bedroom home was enough. He didn't travel much or spend a lot on himself. He gave generously to the NRA Foundation and donated land to the local Millcreek Gun Club. His interests included goose hunting and smallbore rifle competition. He taught his sons from the Bible. When he turned the company over to them in 1976, it was with no strings. It's unlikely Bruce Hodgdon, borrowing on his life insurance for a mountain of surplus powder, could have imagined his firm marketing DuPont and Winchester lines, and cataloging 80 types of propellants. Then again, maybe that's *just* what he had in mind!

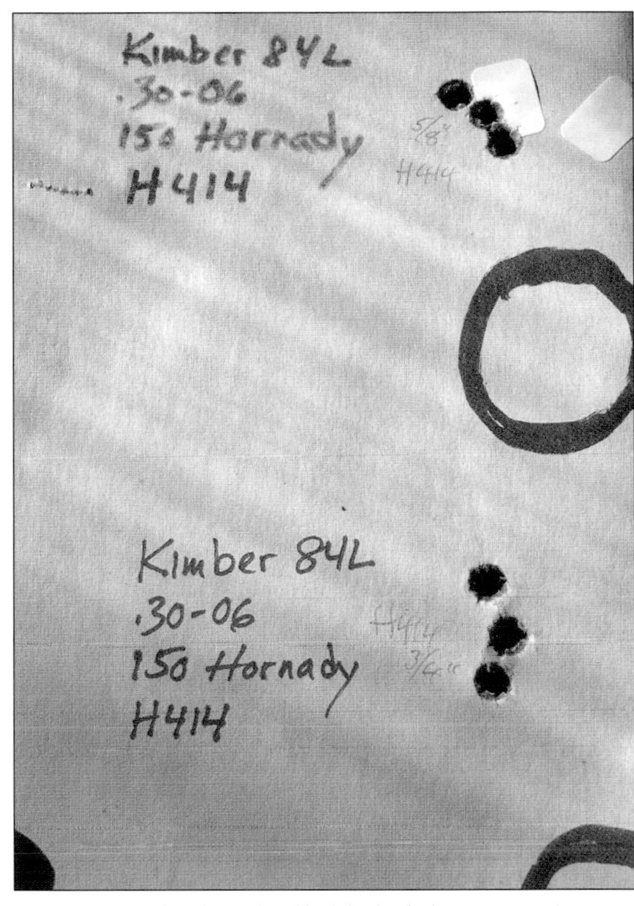

▲ As he predicted, Rich McClure liked this load of H414, 150-grain Hornadys in a .30-06 Kimber.

H380 excels in varmint cartridges like the .22-250. Hodgdon markets more than 80 propellants. ▶

THE MUSCLE BEHIND THE SHOT

12. Not Quite Black Powder

In 1976 Hodgdon agreed to distribute a new product called Pyrodex, a black-powder substitute that had its start far from Missouri, in the Seattle-area laboratory of a gifted young shooter named Dan Pawlak. Dan's goal during the early 1970s was to develop a fuel that would match black powder in appearance and density, generate similar smoke and smell, and yield comparable velocities at pressures any black powder gun could handle. The compound would be stable and safe and easy to ship, releasing shippers and shooters from the onerous regulations governing black powder. Pawlak aimed to provide a fuel that would stay outside the Class A, High Explosive category, where the Bureau of Explosives in the US Department of Transportation had placed black powder. Ideally his propellant would pass stringent Flammable Solids tests, so it could be handled like smokeless powder.

Pawlak teamed up with an experienced propellant engineer, Mike Levenson, and within two years the pair developed a steel-gray fuel that met some of Dan's criteria. The new substance was dubbed Pyrodex, an abbreviation for pyrotechnic deflagrating explosive.

Pawlak's work caught the eye of Warren Center at the gun firm of Thompson/Center. He phoned R. E. Hodgdon and urged him to consider a joint financial venture backing the young man. In January, 1975, Hodgdon traveled to Seattle and found the strapping 6'4" entrepreneur in his Issaquah mobile home, next to a private airstrip and a remarkably well-equipped ballistics laboratory. After examining the transducer pressure guns, oscilloscopes, and other sophisticated devices, R. E. knew Pawlak was both serious and talented. A quick study of pressure curves and some test firings convinced him that Pawlak was also onto something.

By this time Mike Levenson had left the project. With underwriting from Linn Emrich, Dan Pawlak continued to accumulate equipment, most of it used. He refined Pyrodex, increasing its potency, reducing its range of pressure variation, making it burn cleaner, adjusting components to make it smell like black powder. He

▼ Pyrodex, developed by Dan Pawlak then marketed by Hodgdon, was later offered in pellet form. Triple Seven pellets followed.

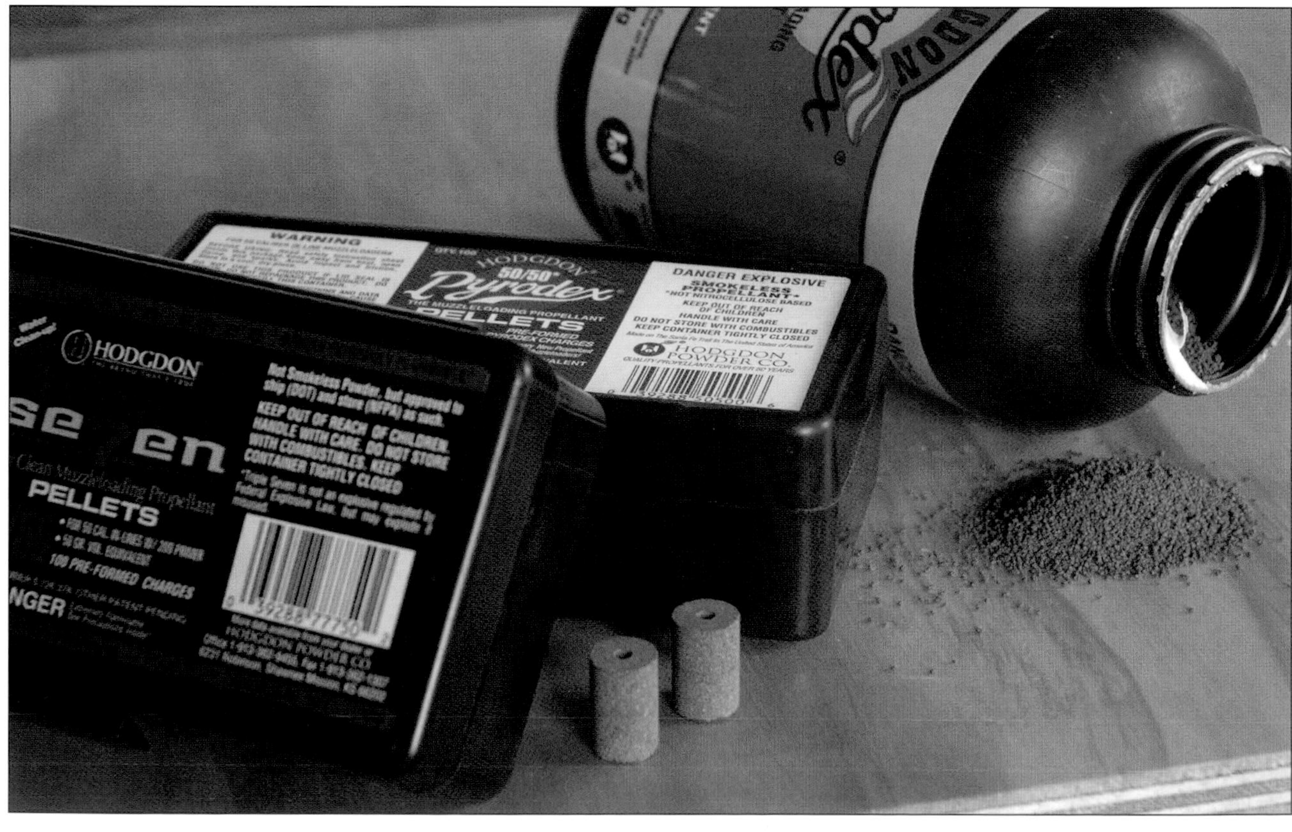

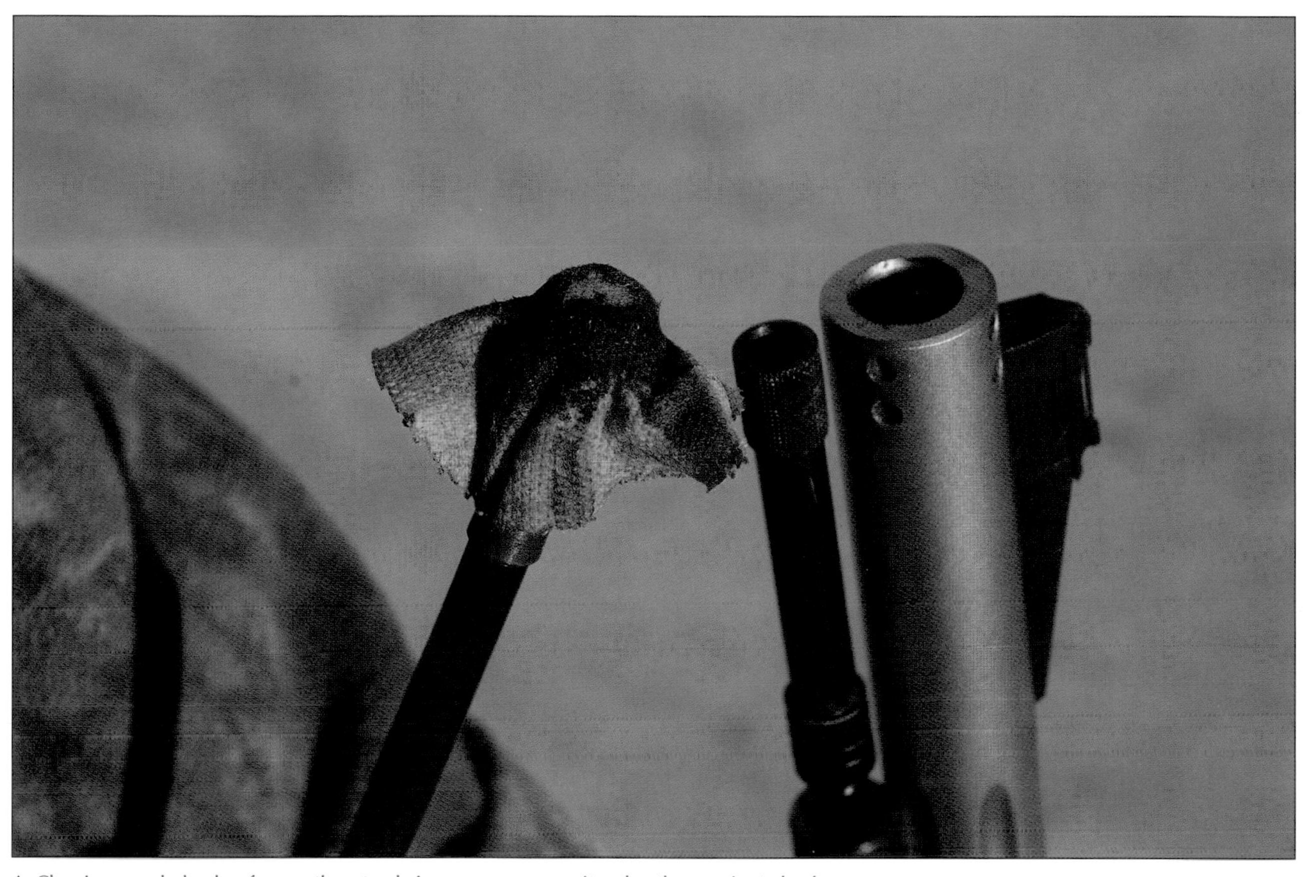

▲ Cleaning muzzle-loaders frequently not only improves accuracy; it makes them easier to load.

even changed the color to black. And he began to remodel a former explosives facility, Excoa, on Taylor Mountain north of Issaquah, for Pyrodex production.

Before submitting Pyrodex to government tests, Pawlak arranged his own. The detonator trials were most severe: An igniter was placed in one canister of 10 one-pound canisters in a case. The case was covered and surrounded with similar cases of the same size and weight but containing sand. To pass the test, the ignited can could not cause detonation in the others. Even smokeless powders occasionally fail this exercise. Pawlak, however, added rigor to the trial: He put a detonator *in each can* in the center case! Noise and flame ensued when the Pyrodex burned, but there was no detonation. In fact, the subsequent Department of Transportation laboratory report stated that "Pyrodex is probably a little safer than conventional smokeless powder because the ignition temperature is considerably higher."

Pawlak targeted the first shipment from Pyrodex Corporation for May, 1976. Hodgdon agreed to be the sole distributor for Pyrodex, and to market it as "the replica black powder." The launch gained momentum when Pyrodex was approved by the National Muzzleloading Rifle Association for use in NMLRA matches. Then, on January 27, 1977, tragedy struck the entrepreneur who had done what many thought impossible. At the Issaquah plant, three tons of Pyrodex flashed off, killing Dan Pawlak and three technicians..

In the aftermath, Pyrodex was again tested. Again, it was found to be less hazardous than smokeless propellants. The directors of Pyrodex Corporation met with Mrs. Pawlak and the board of Hodgdon Powder Company to discuss the product's future. Though initial demand had been strong, the Issaquah disaster would certainly affect shooters' perceptions. Still, the outcome of that somber January meeting in Issaquah may never have been in doubt. Dan Pawlak had been convinced his propellant would not only make money but encourage more people to take up black powder shooting. He also believed it would make the sport safer. Cathy Pawlak, Linn Emrich, Dave Wolfe, Neil Knox, and R. E. and J. B. Hodgdon agreed to build a new Pyrodex mill on an abandoned B-29 base eight miles from Herington, Kansas, 130 miles from Hodgdon's distribution center. In May, 1979, after three years and numerous delays, the $1.5 million plant began turning out canisters of Pyrodex. They reached retail stores in early 1980.

Pyrodex soon became available in three grades: RS, the equivalent to FFg black powder which works best as the main charge in most muzzle-loading rifles; P, which mimics FFFg in burning characteristics and is for small-bore rifles and pistols; and Pyrodex "Select" which appeared in 1991 as a specialty powder for sabot and heavy conical bullets. In 1997 Hodgdon announced Pyrodex pellets, 50-grain (equivalent) pills easy to pop into the muzzle. Use two or three for 100- and 150-grain charges. No measuring required.

The generation of black-powder enthusiasts now thumbing hammers in the field or at rendezvous shoots may not remember Dan Pawlak. They certainly know about Pyrodex. Legions would say it's the best fuel ever to feel the tamp of a ramrod. Dan would have liked to hear that.

Not many hunters see bucks this big, let alone shoot one with a muzzle-loader! Where? Illinois. ▶

Section III

BULLETS—THE INSIDE STORY

13. Bullets and Rifling

Bullets predated cartridges by centuries. But the first guns launched more primitive projectiles. During the 1300s, when firearms were new to warfare, hostilities turned lethal at very close range. Even after 17-horse teams drew big bronze culverins to the battlefront, hand-to-hand combat still accounted for most of the casualties. Arrows added reach to the sword and the pike. For the first soldiers bearing guns, accuracy mattered less than noise and smoke. In cannons, a load of rocks or metal scrap flew far enough to count. Iron balls wrought such devastation that they were outlawed in central Europe.

Lead became popular with shooters beginning in the fifteenth century. Lead's high density meant it had great inertia. Lead bullets held their speed against the push of the air, and they weren't easily stopped by obstacles like doors, saddles, and armor. Lead's low melting point made for easy molding to various bore sizes. It also made possible the use of rifling—spiral grooves cut into the bore to impart spin to a ball or a bullet. Lead 'took' the rifling as hard metal would not, the lands between the grooves engraving the surface of the bullet. For the Pilgrims, lead was a precious commodity. It remained so as frontiersmen pushed onto the plains. Rifles built in rural American shops were given small bores to conserve lead. No other material had lead's momentum. Lead balls were accurate and lethal. Under-sizing balls for use with a patch made them faster to load in dirty bores. A clean .50-caliber rifle may shoot accurately with a ball sized to .500, but after a few shots fouling can render it all but impossible to load with a bore-size ball. A .490 ball in a snug-fitting patch usually flies as accurately as a .500 ball in a clean bore and may outperform it after a few shots.

During the 1830s, when percussion ignition began to replace flint and the short, heavy, big-bore Plains rifle was edging out the elegant Kentucky in the West, conical bullets surged in popularity. At first, target shooters found the conical "picket" ball difficult to load and sensitive to loading technique. Alvin Clark invented the false muzzle in 1840, enabling riflemen to start a bullet square with the barrel proper. Paper-patched bullets and false muzzles soon became the choice in competition. But on the frontier patched balls remained popular. In fact, many frontiersmen chose smoothbore guns because they were faster than rifles to load and slower to foul!

A conical bullet in a smoothbore gun holds its velocity better than a ball because it has a higher sectional density (essentially, a ratio of weight to diameter). But its speed is wasted if it doesn't hit where it is aimed. A bullet shot from a smooth bore is likely to lose its point-forward orientation. It may even tumble. Once it starts to wobble, it loses the advantage of its sectional density because it is flying part of the time at an angle to the target, and is thus wasting some of its energy. Rifling prevents tumbling by stabilizing the bullet in flight, like a football thrown by a quarterback or a top spinning on a counter. The more perfect the rotation of the football, the farther and straighter it flies. The top remains upright until its speed of rotation drops below a certain threshold. Then it wobbles and falls down.

Loading a groove-diameter bullet from the muzzle of a rifled barrel is hard work because you're engraving the bullet with the lands all the way. And a bullet's shank puts up much more resistance than does the modest bearing surface of a ball. Patches don't wrap neatly on bullet shanks either. In 1826 Henri Gustave Delvigne of France attacked the problem of front-loading bullets with a new chamber design. His chamber had sharp corners that arrested and upset an

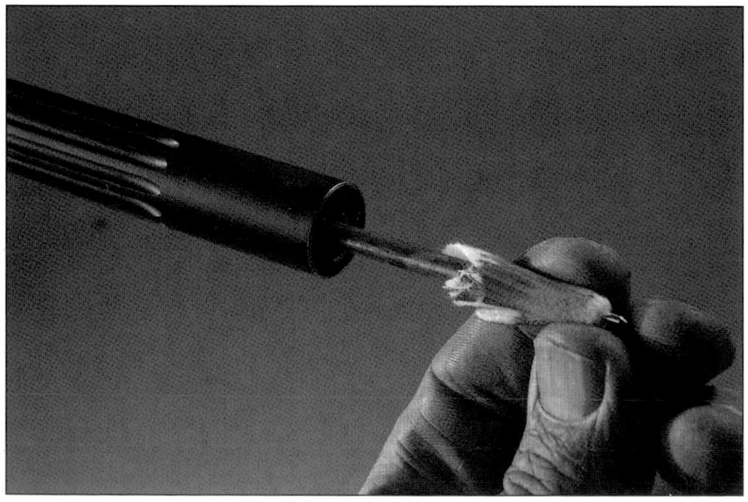

◀ Fouling impairs accuracy. Push patches only one way until the bore is clean enough to oil.

BULLETS—THE INSIDE STORY

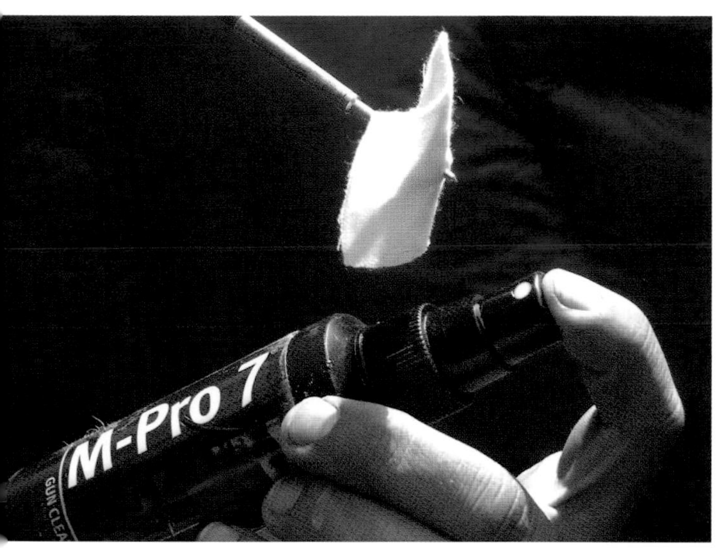

◀ Soaked patches loosen fouling; brushes remove it. Dry patches, then oiled, should follow.

undersize ball as it was rammed home. But the balls and bullets expanded to groove diameter in this process were also deformed. A chamber peg devised by another Frenchman, Thouvenin, gave similar results. In 1834 Captain Bernier of the British Brunswickers resurrected a century-old design to come up with a two-groove rifled bore and a ball with a belt that fit into the grooves. Originally proposed by a Spanish army officer, this arrangement required that the ball be oriented each time; still, pushing it home was easy. Shortly thereafter, English gun maker William Greener developed an oval ball with one flat end. A tapered hole from the flat end to the center of the ball held a metal peg whose round head conformed to the shape of the ball. Either end could be placed in the muzzle first. At launch, the peg drove into the undersize ball, expanding it to fit the grooves.

About this time, other British gun makers experimented with out-of-round bores that spun a bullet without engraving it. They didn't pass muster in military trials because the bullets had to be perfectly sized and oriented precisely. Producing out-of-round bullets also proved difficult. Delvigne took another route in 1841, with a hollow-base bullet sized to fit the grooves. Expanding gas would seal the bullet's skirt against the rifling. British Colonel Brunswick followed with a metal skirt soldered to the base of a ball. But these projectiles, like those upset by special chambers, often tipped in flight. British General John Jacobs came up with a four-finned bullet he mated to four-groove rifling. Failing to win a government contract, Jacobs invented a heavy conical bullet for long shooting and a 32-bore double rifle that fired an exploding bullet. African explorer and elephant hunter Sir Samuel Baker chose instead a 4-bore Gibbs with standard rifling. Its 36 inch barrel had two grooves, pitched one turn in 36 inches. As was customary then, the grooves were broad, the lands narrow to facilitate loading. (Barrels for patched balls had broad lands and narrow grooves to give more support to the undersize ball.) Baker's rifle used 16 drams of powder to hurl a 4-oz conical bullet. Recoil was at the nose-bleed level.

In 1847 French Captain Claude-Etienne Minie (pronounced me-nay) designed a bullet with an iron cup in its hollow base. Powder gas drove the cup forward, expanding the bullet into the rifling. Expansion was sometimes so violent, however, that it cut the bullet in two, leaving a ring of lead in the bore. Captain Minie modified his design and tested it against balls from smoothbore muskets. At 100 yards musketeers hit a 6x20-foot target 149 times out of 200 shots. Riflemen shooting the Minie bullet scored 189 hits. At 400 yards he recorded 9 hits for the muskets, 105 for the rifles. Minie would later sell his conical bullet to the British military establishment for 20,000 pounds. William Greener protested and was awarded 1,000 pounds for the base-expansion idea. Minie's bullet, lubricated with mutton fat or beeswax, became issue ammunition for the Union Army's Enfields during our Civil War. At first a wooden plug was placed in the bullet's hollow base to prompt expansion. This proved unnecessary.

Seeking more effective ammunition for its troops in 1854, the British government contracted with Joseph Whitworth. A brilliant technician, Whitworth was also persuasive; he requested and got an elaborate 500-yard range for his experiments. The range was destroyed by a storm soon after completion. Whitworth had another built and proceeded to try various rifling types and twist rates. Standard twist in military rifles then was 1-in-78 (one bullet rotation in 78 inches of travel). Whitworth found a better spin for short bullets was 1-in-20. Skeptics thought the sharp pitch would retard the bullet, but a hexagonal bullet of Whitworth's own design gave more than twice the penetration of a standard ball from a slow-twist barrel. His small-bore hexagonal bullets flew flat and at long range drilled groups a sixth the size of those shot with patched balls. Hexagonal bullets, however, were costly to make and slow to load.

Whitworth's efforts inspired more work on bullets and rifling. William Greener experimented with narrow-land rifling pitched 1-30, which stabilized small-bore (.40 to .52) bullets to 2,000 yards. Gun maker, James Purdey built two rifles featuring Greener-style barrels in 1856. He called them "Express Train" rifles because of their great power. "Express" became a common descriptor of potent British hunting cartridges.

Breech-loading mechanisms eliminated the need for an accurate bullet that could be loaded from the front. Bullets inserted from the rear could be made harder and longer and cast to full groove diameter. Hard bullets could be stabilized with shallower grooves and thus driven faster. Sharp rifling pitch could be used—even rifling that varied in pitch and depth, breech to muzzle. William Ellis Metford experimented with "gain twist" that allowed a bullet easy acceleration from the chamber but increased rate of spin during its barrel travel. His 34 inch barrel produced an exit spin of 1-in-17 but started bullets so gradually they turned over only once before reaching the muzzle! Metford favored the wide, shallow grooves that now work well with jacketed bullets. He also developed segmented rifling, with rounded lands and grooves. By the end of the century, gain twist and progressive grooving (deeper grooves at the breech than forward, as in England's Enfield and Martini-Henry rifles) were largely abandoned.

Charles Newton, American inventor, gun maker and wildcatter, reasoned that since a bullet bears on only one shoulder of a land, the other is unnecessary. His "ratchet rifling" tested this concept. Like the Lancaster oval bore derived from Bernier's elliptical design, Newton's idea had merit but did not succeed at market. To reduce bullet deformation that can lead to inaccuracy, Marlin introduced "Micro-Groove" rifling with 16 narrow, shallow grooves. They deliver excellent accuracy and have become a trademark of this venerable firm. But Marlin also uses Ballard-style six-groove rifling in its centerfire rifles.

Metford-style rifling features wide groove bottoms with the same radius as the bullet. They meet flat-topped, square-shouldered lands. Popular since its application in two-groove Springfields during World War I, Medford rifling has been adopted by many commercial makers, who commonly now use four and six grooves. Heckler and Koch rifles wear polygonal rifling.

A bullet's rotation is determined by rifling twist, expressed as distance traveled per revolution. A 1-in-14 twist means the bullet turns over one time for every 14 inches of forward travel. If all bullets were the same weight and shape and traveled at the same speed, one rate of twist would work for all. That's not the case, however. Proper twist rate varies. A patched round ball in a muzzleloader requires a slow twist, while a long bullet in small-bore rifle cartridge needs a quick twist to stabilize. Proper rate of spin for the muzzleloader might be 1-in-66 for a round ball, 1-in-32 for a conical bullet. Some muzzleloaders are rifled 1-in-48 as a compromise. Rifles designed for long .264 rifle bullets may have twist rates as short as 1-in-9.

A popular twist for 80-grain match bullets in the .223 is 1-in-7-½.

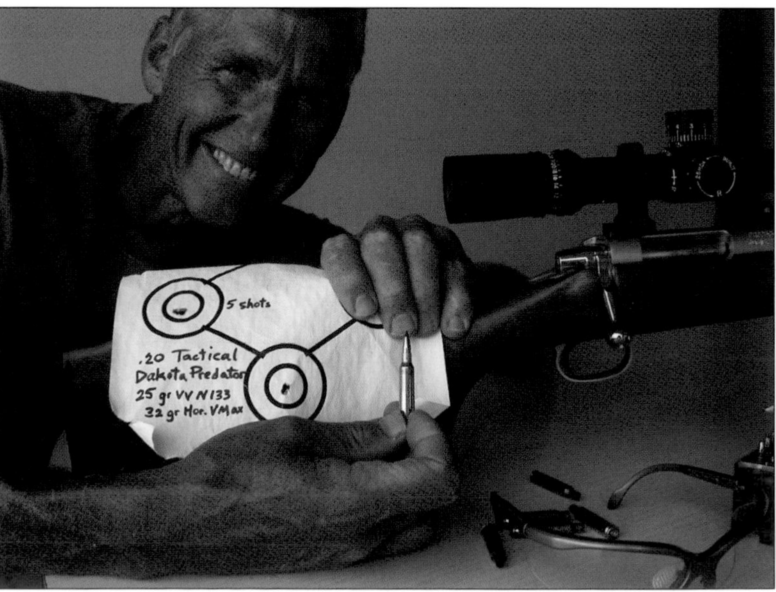

Wayne was pleased with this one-hole group, shot with a Nesika rifle in .20 Tactical. ▶

◀ Wayne drilled this 5/8 inch group with a .375 Blaser R93 and Norma ammo. Oryx bullets.

A .308 bullet spun one turn in 12 inches at a muzzle velocity of 3,000 fps reaches an animal 400 yards away in about half a second. (Average velocity: just under 2,500 fps.) In that half second, the bullet spins 1,500 times. Give it a 1-in-9 twist, and you boost rotational speed by 25 percent, to 3,750 rotations per second. Unlike a bullet's forward speed, which slows under the influence of drag, rotational velocity remains essentially constant. It affects the reaction of bullets to twigs and other obstructions in flight, and the expansion of softnose bullets in game. Jacket petals spread far to the side during upset add drag to both forward and rotational movement. So besides reducing penetration, they slow bullet rotation, reducing stability. Petals also act as lever arms to tip the bullet. They do inflict greater terminal damage because of their rotation—damage evident in high-speed film footage of bullets tearing ballistic gelatin. Contrary to what some shooters think, though, there's limited "buzz-saw" effect. A .308 bullet turning once in every 12 inches of travel barely gets through one revolution while penetrating the chest of a big deer.

In 1879 British ballistician Sir Alfred George Greenhill announced a formula to derive proper spin for all bullets with specific gravity 10.9. As the specific gravity of pure lead is 11.4, most jacketed bullets come close enough. Greenhill's formula was first published in the *British Textbook of Small Arms, 1929*: *Required twist in all calibers equals 150 divided by the length of the bullet in calibers.*

Thus, proper spin for a 180-grain .308 bullet 1-1/4 inch long is 150/4=37.5. Remember, 37.5 is caliber. To convert to inches, you multiply it by .308. Answer: just over 11 inches. Most .30-caliber barrels are rifled 1-in-10 or 1-in-12, so the formula confirms they have a useful pitch for that bullet at the speeds we launch such bullets from .308, .30-06, and most .300 Magnum rifles. Most modern barrels have proper twist for common bullet weights. Top accuracy *can* be hard to achieve with small-bore rounds loaded with a wide range of bullets. The .223, for example, is chambered in rifles with barrels rifled from 1-in-14 to 1-in-7-1/2. Varmint bullets of 50 to 53 grains work just fine with

Federal offers excellent heavy-game loads, with solid and softpoint bullets, for the .375 H&H. ▶

◀ The .22-250, a flat-shooting varmint cartridge, gave Wayne these groups, from a Remington 700.

a mild twist rate; but 75- and 80-grain match bullets require special fast-twist barrels.

Even gentle twist rates induce dizzying spins. A .308 bullet rotating one turn every 12 inches at a velocity of 3,000 fps rotates 1,500 times during a half second and 400 yards of forward travel. In contrast, an ordinary V-6 engine propelling an automobile at 65 mph turns perhaps 3,000 rpm. That's 50 crankshaft rotations per second, or just 25 per half-second!

Perfect, on-axis rotation is hard to achieve with bullets. The violent thrust accelerating them from a stand-still to 3,000 fps in an eye-blink puts great stress on core and jacket. Deformation from the rifling that imparts the spin can also make the bullet shudder. So can a damaged muzzle, a nicked bullet base or lack of concentricity in the jacket. The rotation of a bullet's nose into its own orbit around the bullet's axis is called precession. Of course, this is undesirable; but like a top that "goes to sleep" after you give it a hard spin, the bullet may rotate more smoothly, with less precession, after covering some distance. That's why sometimes you get smaller groups (in minutes of angle) at long range. A rifle that shoots into 1-½ inches at 100 yards may keep all bullets inside 3 inches at 300 yards.

Yaw is another aberration in bullet flight. It occurs when the bullet's axis does not line up with its direction of travel. Like precession, yaw is exacerbated by rifling with too sharp a pitch, or rate of twist.

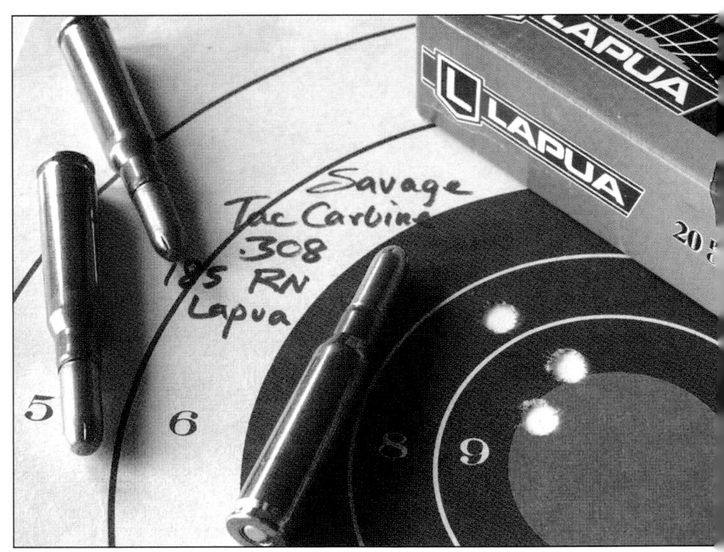

Lapua round-nose softpoints drilled this group for Wayne, from a Savage Model 10. ▶

14. Opening the Throttle

Jacketed bullets became necessary in the 1890s to withstand the higher velocities generated by smokeless powders. The jackets were of steel with a cupro-nickel coating. Satisfactory in the .30-40 Krag, they fouled badly at the higher velocities of the .30-06. Tiny lumps of jacket adhering to the relatively cool steel near a rifle's muzzle tore at the jackets of other bullets, accelerating the process. Shooters fought the fouling with "ammonia dope," a solution of .5 oz. ammonia bicarbonate, 1 oz. ammonia sulfate, 6 oz. ammonia water, and 4 oz. tap water. Poured into a plugged barrel and allowed to "work" for 20 minutes, this brew was then flushed out with hot water. Drying and oiling followed. Riflemen took care not to spill the ammonia, which could pit exposed metal.

To reduce metal fouling, the US Army issued "Mobilubricant" to soldiers on the eve of World War I. Unexpectedly, pressures in the .30-06 began bouncing from 51,000 to around 58,000 PSI. Coating *cartridges* with Mobilubricant sent pressures higher still. A lubricated case gave the neck no room to expand while it increased back-thrust on the bolt. This problem was exacerbated by tin-plated jackets. Tin sometimes "cold soldered" itself to the case neck. One bullet recovered at a shooting range still wore the case neck! The Army soon dropped Mobilubricant and tin-plated bullets, choosing instead to incorporate tin in the jacket alloy. Later cupro-nickel (60 percent copper, 40 percent nickel) became the jacket of choice. Gilding metal (90 percent copper, 10 percent zinc) was initially thought to be too soft for the high-speed 150-grain bullet in .30-06 service ammunition; but Western Cartridge Company's jacket of 90 percent copper, 8 percent zinc and 2 percent tin worked well. It was called Lubaloy. In 1922 Western provided Palma Match ammunition with 180-grain Lubaloy-coated bullets. That year, experiments at Frankfort Arsenal showed that gilding metal could stand up to high velocities. It remains a popular jacket material for hunting and target bullets. Most bullet-makers now favor jackets comprising 95 percent copper and 5 percent zinc (though Nosler stayed with a 90-10 alloy for its Partition bullets turned on screw machines before 1970). Softer, almost pure-copper jackets began showing up on bullets designed for deep penetration—like the Bitterroot Bonded Core, one of the first so-called "controlled expansion" bullets. Ductile jackets are less likely to break apart on contact with heavy muscle and bone. The liability of pure copper is its tendency to foul barrels.

The lead cores of big game bullets have a dash of antimony to make them harder. The usual ratio is 97.5 percent lead, 2.5 percent antimony. A little antimony makes a big difference; 6 percent is about the limit in hunting bullets. Sierra uses three alloys for rifle bullets, with antimony proportions of 1.5, 3, and 6 percent. A few game bullets have been described as having pure lead cores. Thick copper jackets on these bullets keep soft cores from disintegrating on impact. "Pure," incidentally, means unalloyed. But even pure bullet lead has traces of copper, zinc, nickel, arsenic, and aluminum. As little as .1 percent copper can cause hard spots. Cores are commonly cut from lead wire, extruded from bar stock in the appropriate diameter, then annealed to prevent expansion during forming.

Bullet jackets come about in one of two ways: "cup and draw" or impact extrusion. Drawn jackets begin as wafers punched from sheet metal. Formed over a series of dies, they become progressively deeper cups that are eventually trimmed to length and stuffed with lead. The bullet is then shaped and finished off at the nose. Jackets given the impact extrusion treatment begin as sections of metal rods that are annealed and fed into a punch press, which slams them into cups with 60 tons of force. Bullets like Nosler's Partition have cavities fore and aft so they must be punched twice. Nosler claims its current extruded jackets yield better accuracy than those on the original Partitions which were machine-turned and when completed had a hole in the dam of jacket material. The hole varied in location and hardly contributed to tight groups.

Cannelures help the jacket grip the core but serve mainly as crimping grooves. Cannelures have gradually disappeared on rifle bullets. They have been retained on bullets for heavy-recoiling rounds like the .458 Winchester (the crimp to prevent bullet creep in the magazine) and on pistol bullets (the crimp to keep short bullets with little case contact in place and smooth the cartridge profile for better feeding). Hornady, Winchester, and a few other makers routinely crimp bullets. Most cannelures are rolled on, but Nosler cuts the groove in its 210-grain .338 bullet.

▲ While it leaves no channel to measure, a cabbage can show the destructive power of a softpoint.

Claims that crimping impairs accuracy have not been substantiated.

Jacket and core dimensions must be held to tight tolerances for top accuracy. Sierra, renowned for match-winning target bullets, keeps jacket thickness within .0003 of a standard. The company limits bullet weight variation to .3-grain. Test lots of 168-grain 30-caliber match bullets that don't shoot into .250 inch at 100 yards can disqualify the entire batch.

Strict quality control has maintained Hornady's reputation for accuracy. "We shoot four five-shot groups to check lots," I was told on a factory visit. "The average must meet tough standards. For .30s it's .600 at 100 yards, for 6mms it's .450, for .17s it's .400." Match bullets face a high bar indeed. "We demand .350 from .22s. Our 30-caliber match bullets must stay inside .800 at 200 yards." Targets with their centers chewed out hang at each production station, proof of standards met.

Bullets from Walt Berger's shop, renowned among bench-rest shooters, have brought match-level accuracy into the hunting field. Nosler has grown its line the other way—from top-grade hunting bullets to boat-tail hollow points designed expressly to drill one-hole groups.

Demands on hunting bullets regarding dimensional uniformity are less stringent than on bullets for target shooting. Expansion, penetration, and weight retention usually matter more than gnat's-eye precision. An expanding bullet releases energy as it decelerates. Flattening, the nose does not *slide* through as would the sleek ogive of a jacketed bullet failing to open. It *pushes*, boosting deceleration rate and energy release. Its rotating nose petals tear tissue. Comparing channels made by a bullet that did not upset and one that opened to double diameter, you'll find the cross-sectional areas differ dramatically. The relationship is not 1:2—expanding bullets are much more destructive. Ragged petal edges, plus the hydraulic effect caused by displaced tissue, increase damage.

Securing jacket to core is crucial if a bullet is to maintain its integrity in heavy bone and muscle. Core-Lokt, Trophy Bonded, Bonded Core, Hot-Core, and AccuBond are trade names that play on this theme of bullet integrity. Remington's Core-Lokt has an inner belt (from the Peters Inner Belted bullet, progeny of the Peters Belted, with its exterior metal girdle). The Speer Hot-Core process ensures adhesion because the lead is warm enough to snuggle into every void in the jacket.

▼ A Winchester .223 takes a cabbage apart. The Ballistic Silvertip lead-free bullet pulps all!

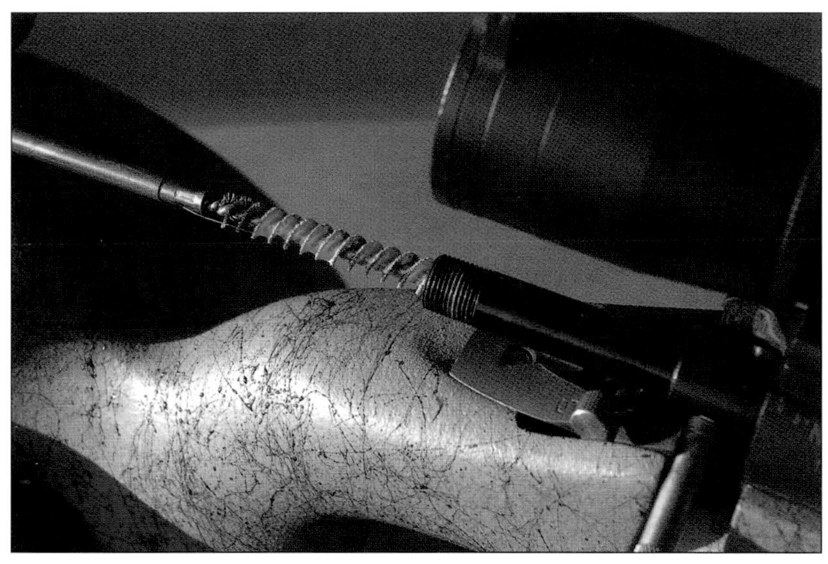

◀ A rifleman starts a brush in a bore guide. For large bores, attach the brush in front of the guide.

These days, chemical bonds have boosted retained weight above the 90-percent mark for many game bullets. Bonding is simply a way to keep jacket and core from separating under the tremendous stresses induced by high-speed bullet impact. John Nosler sought a mechanical solution in 1947, after bullets from his .300 Magnum disintegrated on a moose. His Partition bullet featured a wall of jacket material that divided the core. No matter how violent the forces tearing at the bullet nose, the heel core remained captive. It penetrated like a solid bullet, ensuring a long wound channel. The Partition remains hugely popular. Swift's A-Frame combines Nosler's Partition design with nose bonding that all but prevents core-jacket separation up front.

Incidentally, John Nosler wasn't the first engineer to employ a mechanical device to control upset. Before the Great Depression, American entrepreneur Charles Newton developed a wire-core bullet. During the 1940s the German H-Mantle bullet appeared, with a central dam much like Nosler's. A half-century later, Winchester took this idea to another level with its Fail Safe bullet. Now discontinued, it had a hollow nose of copper alloy, notched to deliver uniform four-petal upset. A steel heel cup was inserted after a few months' production to keep the lead core from ballooning the midsection and escaping jackets ruptured by the petal tips. Weight retention of Fail Safes typically approached 100 percent with pass-through penetration. A modified Partition, called the Partition Gold, was marketed by Winchester recently. Developed under the "Combined Technology" banner that marked collaboration between Winchester and Nosler, Partition Gold dams were moved forward to increase retained weight if the nose disintegrated. A steel heel cup prevented deformation of the rear jacket. Like the Fail Safe, the Partition Gold wore a black oxide finish.

One bore guide will serve for almost all the bolt rifles you'll likely encounter. ▶

Bullet nose design has a lot to do with how expansion proceeds. Hollow point bullets are typically used for target shooting and on thin-skinned animals. Small cavities and thicker jackets keep hollow points from breaking up on big game, but they also make expansion less dependable. Among early hollow points, the Western Tool and Copper Works bullet with a tiny nose cavity had perhaps the best reputation among hunters. Westley-Richards offered a bullet with a dimple covered by a metal cap that protected the nose and kept the jacket from rupturing prematurely. DWM's "strong-jacket" bullet had a long, narrow nose cavity lined with copper tubing and capped.

As new cartridges hiked muzzle velocities, the task confronting bullet designers got more difficult.

Game bullets had to withstand higher impact speeds; at the same time, hunters still expected them to open at modest velocities far from the muzzle. In the early days of smokeless cartridges, iron sights limited shot distances to a couple of hundred yards. So the velocity window in which game bullets had to perform well was relatively narrow. Most bullets left the muzzle clocking from 2,100 to 2,700 fps and reached 200 yards at 1,400 to 2,100 fps. A .300 magnum with a scope might now be used to clobber an elk at 50 steps, where the bullet is rocketing along at 3,200 fps, and then turned on a pronghorn at 500 yards, where velocity has dropped off to 2,000. The heavy shoulder of an elk exacerbates the tendency of a high-speed bullet to come apart, while the fragile pronghorn may not present enough resistance for a stout bullet, slowed by distance, to expand at all. Various solutions have been developed to ensure upset with penetration across a spectrum of impact speeds, on targets of varying resistance.

▼ Winchester's M 71 was dropped in 1957. Browning's recent, elegant copy is now discontinued.

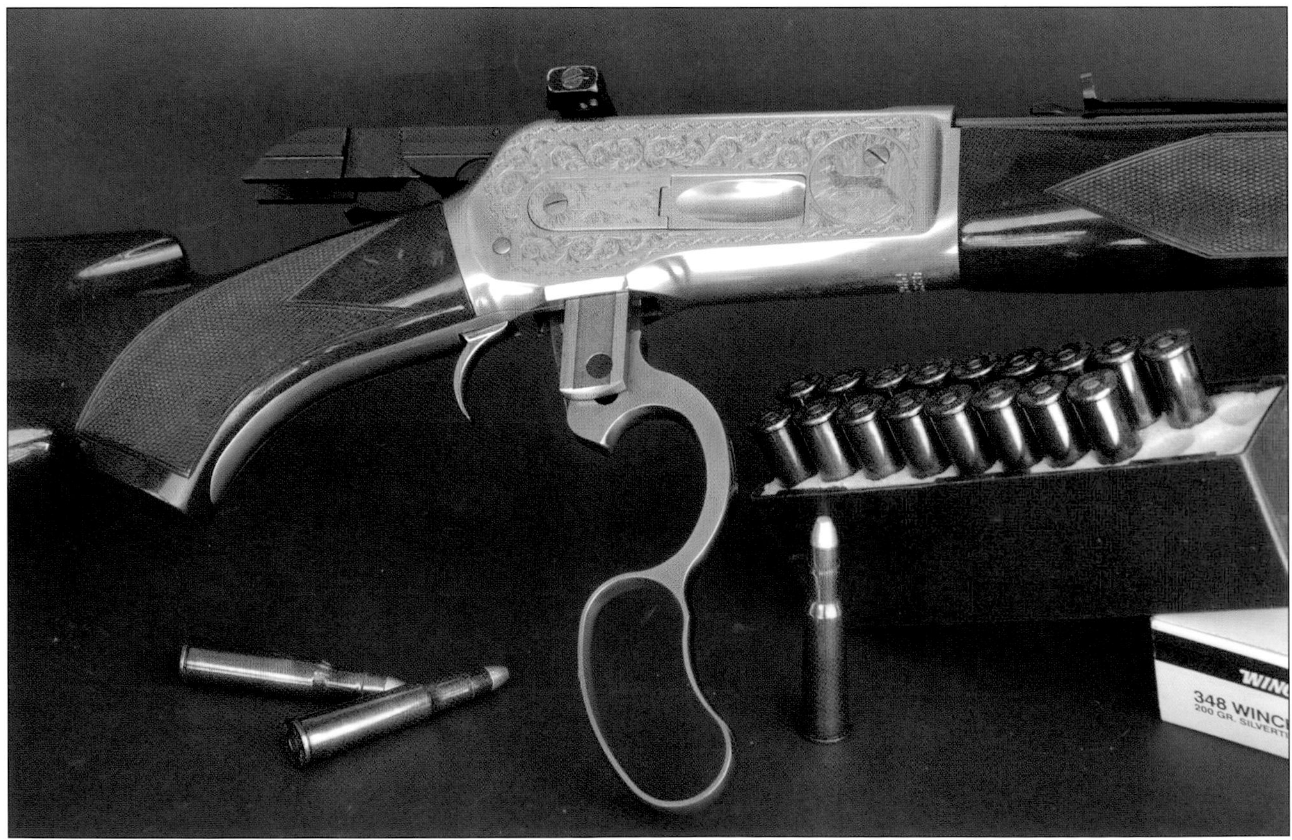

15. Controlled Upset, Then and Now

A sophisticate among early hollow point bullets was Peters' Protected Point. Its jacket enveloped a flat-topped core, the front third wrapped in a gilding metal band and crowned with a pointed metal cone. On impact the flattening nose drove the band down under the jacket, where it initiated and controlled the core's upset. The jacket split as expansion progressed. A Protected Point bullet required 51 operations and three hours to manufacture. Winchester's Silvertip, overhauled in 1960 and now discontinued, was a less costly rendition of this design. It lacked an inner band.

Remington put a hard peg in a hollow bullet nose to form its Bronze Point. Upon striking a target, this peg was driven back into the bullet to start expansion. Bronze Point bullets opened pretty violently at close range. RWS has counterparts to this design: the TIG (Torpedo Ideal) and TUG (Torpedo Universal) bullets.

Lead-free bullets, such as this Barnes X, can be designed to mushroom with deadly effect. Deep penetration and high weight retention are the hallmarks of the hollowpoint X and TSX, both engineered for big game hunting.

The TIG's tail section has a funnel-shaped mouth into which the nose core fits like a plug. Upset starts not only at the nose but at the core juncture. The rear core opens more reluctantly because it's harder. In TUG bullets the joint is reversed: A cavity in the nose accepts a conical protrusion from the rear section, which acts like a trailing bullet when the nose fragments. The pointed tail resists deformation, penetrating like the trunk of a Nosler Partition.

Bitterroot Bullet Company also used unalloyed copper for its jackets, which in .338 could be .060 inch thick. The nose of a Bitterroot bullet had a cavity to start expansion. These features made Bitterroots long for their weight, and the most renowned were heavy for their caliber. They required deep seating and an eye to pressures hiked by extended bearing surfaces.

Among the best known of bullet-makers specializing in tough bullets is Barnes. This firm started operations in 1939, predating John Nosler's by nine years. Barnes "Original" bullets, from .22 to .600, were available in a wide range of weights, many heavy for the caliber. The line has diminished of late, because Randy and Coni Brooks, who've owned Barnes for more than 35 years, designed and promote the sleeker, all-copper X and Triple Shock bullets. The Originals remain available for big-bore and obsolete cartridges like the .50-110 and .348 Winchester. Their jackets are of pure copper, .032 and .049 inch thick, depending on the application. The jackets have no taper, and the thick ones depend on a substantial jolt to open. One new bullet of similar design is the Barnes Buster, with a thick copper jacket and hard-cast lead core.

The dilemma confronting big game hunters these days is whether to choose the flattest-shooting bullet, the most accurate bullet or the bullet that penetrates best and retains the most weight after upset. It is unlikely one bullet will score at the top in all three categories. Despite what some shooters say, the sleek hollow point bullets that deliver flat flight and fine accuracy can also kill effectively at long range. I've even taken elk with lightweight bullets of this design. Distance is their friend, as it drains some of the velocity that can smash such bullets to pieces when they strike big muscles or bones at high speed close to the rifle. For heavy game at modest ranges, stout controlled-expansion bullets certainly make sense,

▲ Wayne shot this eland in Namibia with a Leupold-scoped Montana rifle in .375 H&H, Federal ammunition with 300-grain Barnes TSX bullet.

because reliable upset and penetration matters more than one-hole precision.

Here's a brief review of the best-known big game bullets:

Barnes X. This solid copper hollowpoint is sleek in form but lightweight for its length. So heavy X-Bullets must be seated deep to clear some magazine boxes and rifling (heed factory cautions here). On the other hand, the X is built to drive deep without losing significant weight. So you can use a lighter bullet and get fast flight, a taut trajectory and deep penetration at the same time. X-Bullets don't offer the frontal area of many lead-core bullets after expansion, and pass-throughs are common. Reports on accuracy vary from very good to sub-par.

Barnes Triple Shock. X-Bullets have now been replaced in the Barnes catalog by Triple Shock or TSX bullets, with shank grooves that reduce pressure while enhancing accuracy. The nose design is similar, and TSX bullets are of the same all-copper construction. New TSX Tipped bullets wear a polymer tip, more for cosmetic appeal than to boost ballistic coefficient. The MRX bullet has the TSX profile, but a denser-than-lead Silvex heel core. The shank can thus be shorter, an advantage when magazine length or throating limits over-all cartridge length.

Richard Mann and Charlie Sisk designed the "Test Tube" to assess bullet upset, wound channels. ▼

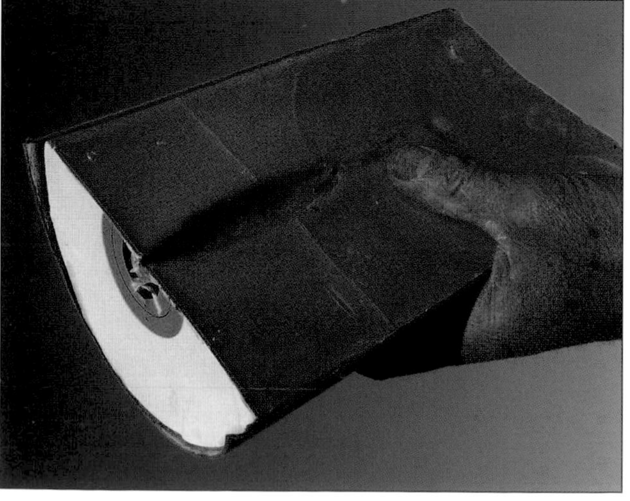

Nosler Partition. Developed in 1947 by John Nosler to penetrate better than bullets he could buy, the Partition was initially distributed only to his hunting buddies. The wall of jacket material between front and rear core sections stops expansion and ensures the shank will penetrate. Nosler Partitions commonly lose significant weight from the nose during penetration. But those fragments destroy a lot of tissue while the shank plows dependably forward. Hunters who have relied on Partitions know retained weight is hardly a measure of lethality! Partition jackets were once machined from solid stock; now they're impact-extruded, resulting in closer tolerances, better accuracy.

Remington Core-Lokt Ultra Bonded. Based on the tried-and-true Core-Lokt, the C-L Ultra has a jacket that is 20–50 percent heavier at mid-section, where the jacket is thickest, to arrest any tendency of the core to shift during penetration. As the name states, the core and jacket are bonded, further enhancing weight retention. Remington advertises the double-diameter upset typically seen with standard Core-Lokts. The Core-Lokt Ultra Bonded is available in many Remington Premier factory loads.

Speer Grand Slam. This dual-core bullet has a hard lead heel (5 percent antimony) held in place by an

▲ In Federal's ammunition plant, jackets are bonded to these cores to make Trophy Bonded bullets.

internal jacket lip. The nose core is softer, for quick upset and a broad mushroom. Grand Slam gilding metal jackets are 4 percent thicker than those on Speer Hot-Cor bullets. During manufacture, both types receive their cores in molten form, to eliminate voids that cause jacket-core separation. The Grand Slam has an aerodynamic ogive behind a protected (flat) nose.

Swift A-Frame. This bullet, developed by Lee Reed of Quinter, Kansas, features a bonded core *plus* a mid-section wall of jacket material. The result: very deep penetration with an intact but beautifully expanded nose. The A-Frame mushroom *looks* like a mushroom, and plows a broad wound channel. The A-Frame typically retains more than 90 percent of its weight, even in the toughest game. It ranks among the most dependable bullets for heavy animals, in rifles and in handguns.

Swift Scirocco. First available in 1999, the Scirocco combines the sleek form and polymer tip of Nosler's Ballistic Tip bullet with the ductile copper jacket and bonded core of the Swift A-Frame. It flies flatter than the A-Frame but still delivers controlled upset at high impact speeds. Weight retention averages a bit less than the A-Frame, but shooters can expect over 70 percent even at strike velocities of over 3,000 fps. The Scirocco opens at terminal speeds as low as 1,440 fps.

Trophy Bonded Bear Claw. Jack Carter designed this lead-core bullet for high weight retention in heavy muscle and bone. The thick, ductile copper jacket incorporates a heel section that extends to near the mid-point of the bullet. Mushrooming yields a broad nose that rarely loses more than 10 percent of its weight in the toughest going. Like the Swift A-Frame and Speer Grand Slam, the Trophy Bonded Bear Claw has a sleek ogive and a flat nose. Federal Cartridge Company acquired manufacturing rights from Jack Carter before his death and now manufactures the Trophy Bonded Bear Claw. A Trophy Bonded Tip bullet with a conical polymer nose insert has been added to the line. Both TB bullets are loaded by Federal.

Winchester Power Max Bonded. Otherwise of ordinary lead-core construction, the Super-X Power Max Bonded bullet features a core-jacket bond to improve weight retention. It takes the place of the Silver Tip in Winchester's Super-X line of loaded ammunition, complementing the Power-Point softpoint.

Winchester AccuBond. Developed with Nosler, Winchester's AccuBond has a sleek profile, with a polymer tip that caps a lead core bonded to a gilding metal jacket with reinforced shank and thick heel. It is loaded in Winchester's Supreme line of ammunition.

Winchester XP3. In some ways, the XP3 bullet resembles the discontinued Winchester Fail Safe. Its nose, of solid alloy, is an extension of the jacket, with a deep cavity under a polymer tip. The lead core fills the shank to mid-section and is bonded to the jacket.

A Swift bullet in a Norma load nips tight groups from Wayne's CZ 550 in 9.3x62. It's lethal too! ▶

Off-shore bullet companies offer competitive products. Australia's Woodleigh bullets, now loaded by Federal, have a fine reputation; core and jacket are as hard to separate as a pit bull and a burglar. Expansion tests in water (a severe medium) yield terminal weights that exceed 90 percent of initial weights. Petals open out wing-like, rather than collapsing to support a classic mushroom, as with Swift and Trophy Bonded bullets. But despite their action in braking the bullet and their exposure to rotational pressures, petals on Woodleighs seldom break or lose lead on their forward surfaces.

I have had excellent success with Norma's Oryx, increasingly popular among European hunters. It has a core-jacket bond that ensures deep penetration and high weight retention. Norma's Plastic Point, Soft Point, and Alaska bullets are designed to upset more easily and violently. So is the company's Vulkan, a hollowpoint with the jacket folded at the nose to minimize damage in the magazine.

Keen hunter interest in deep-driving bullets continues to drive a cottage industry. Blue Mountain Bullets and Elkhorn Bullets, both Oregon companies, have specialized in bullets for elk. Warren Jensen of Blackfoot, Idaho, improved on his sleek J-26 spitzer by replacing the polycarbonate tip with one of soft copper and making other, less visible changes. Mike Brady, of Glenrock, Wyoming, designed a controlled-expansion bullet with a ribbed heel to reduce bore friction. Northern Precision, initially focused on big-bore bullets, added smaller diameters and special-order weights. Hawk bullets, designed in Wyoming by Bob Fulton, have a rounded form but fly surprisingly flat (the bullet's ogive has a greater effect on trajectory than does tip profile). Like Kodiak bullets made in Alaska for tough game, they wear thick copper jackets.

▼ Bullet jackets come from great rolls of copper wire at Federal's Anoka, Minnesota plant.

▲ These Trophy Bonded bullets recovered from Australian buffalo show double-diameter upset, high weight retention.

If you hunt where oblique shots at elk or moose or big bear are common, you'll want a cohesive bullet that plows a long furrow. But most big game is taken with bullets through the ribs. Even animals that weigh more than half a ton usually succumb quickly to an ordinary softpoint driven through the front ribs. Here are some bullets that cost less (and may shoot more accurately) than bullets built to retain weight. On deer-size game, they can also kill quicker, because explosive energy release in the vitals kills right away.

Federal Hi-Shok Softpoint. The standard bullet for Federal's Classic line, Hi-Shok is available in roundnose, flat-nose, and spitzer form, in diameters .224 to .375. Like ordinary softpoint bullets loaded in PMC cartridges, the Hi-Shok is unremarkable in design. However, it is remarkably effective, a bargain in loaded ammunition.

Hornady Interlock. The reputation for fine accuracy that attended the company's flagship Spire Point for decades carried over to the Interlock. Inner jacket belting holds the lead core in place during upset. Roundnose versions are dependable killers and as accurate as their pointed brethren. Also, they pack more weight for any given length.

Hornady Super Shock Tip (SST). This bullet features the internal jacket belt of Hornady Interlock bullets. A sleek ogive that ends in a red polymer tip gives the SST an edge at extreme range. So does the tapered heel.

Initial tests showed the SST a bit fragile for tough game, so it was beefed up to better withstand high-speed impact. An accurate bullet, the SST routinely turns in half-minute groups at Hornady's range.

Nosler Ballistic Tip. The polycarbonate tip of this Nosler is color-coded by caliber and serves as a wedge to initiate expansion upon impact. Ballistic Tip bullets have an enviable reputation for accuracy and their sleek profile ensures flat flight. They're noted for quick upset and are not recommended for big-boned game. However, .338 Ballistic Tips have thick jackets for deeper penetration than expected from sub-.33s.

Remington Core-Lokt. In both roundnose and pointed form, Remington's veteran deer bullet may have killed more big game animals than any other softpoint. An internal lip behind the ogive holds the core in place during upset. Available in many diameters and weights, the Remington Core-Lokt delivers a lethal combination of double-diameter upset and deep penetration.

Sierra GameKing. Long renowned for superior accuracy and flat flight downrange, Sierra boat-tail bullets open violently. Expect lightning-like kills on deer from GameKing softpoints and hunting-style hollowpoints. The 250-grain .338 and 300-grain .375s have extra-heavy jackets to prevent break-up in big, tough animals.

Speer Hot-Cor. The huge selection of these solid performers adds to their popularity. You'll find bullets and weights not available elsewhere, even .366 spitzers for the 9.3x62 rifles popular in Europe and Africa. Traditional softnose construction and sleek profiles make Speer Hot-Cors ideal for long shooting at deer-size game.

▼ Bullet performance—upset, penetration, retained weight—is usually measured in ballistic gelatin.

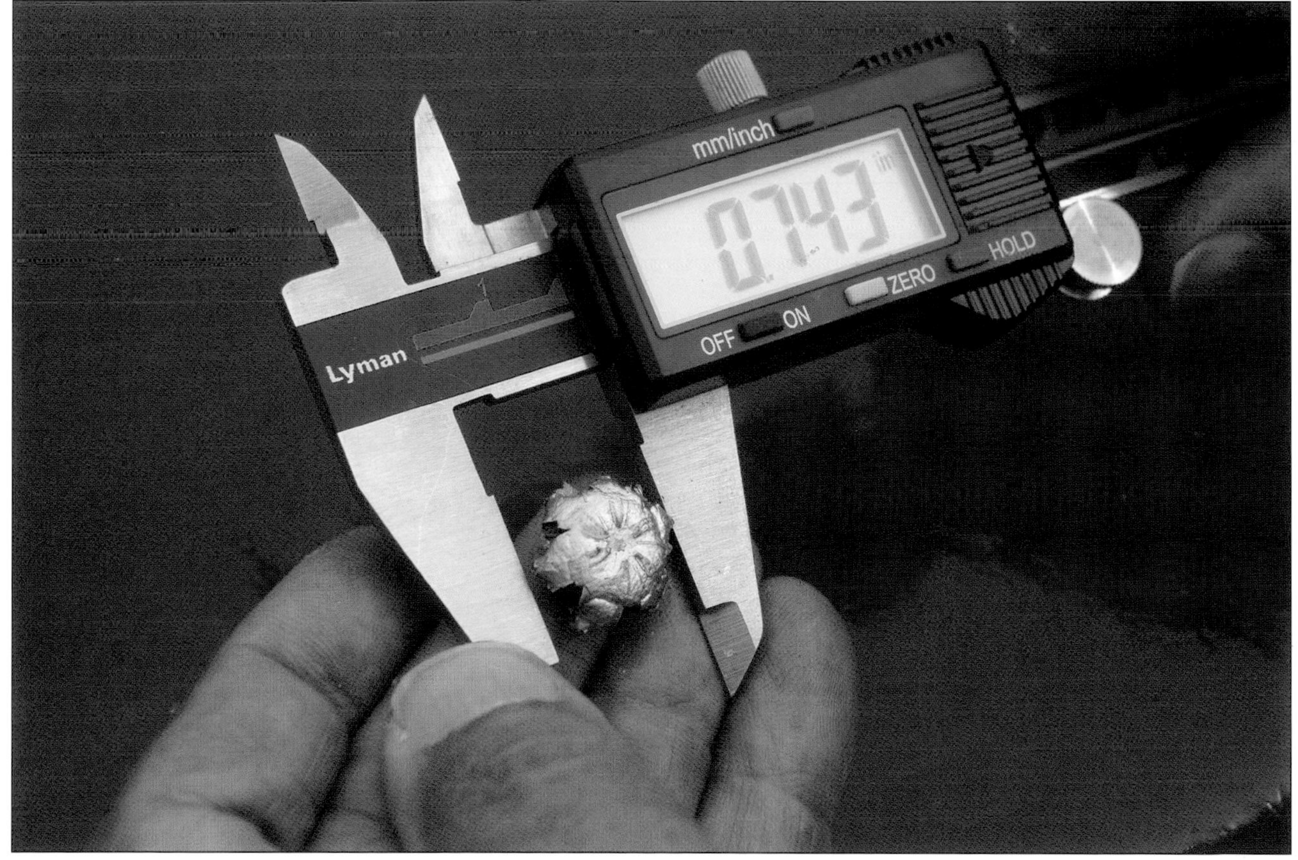

Winchester Power Point. This softpoint might well be considered an archetype. It has no special features, save the nose notches on its tapered jacket. They ensure ready upset. Still, penetration is often to the far side of moose-size game. Power Point bullets were recently moly-coated and loaded to stepped-up velocities in Winchester Power Point Plus ammunition.

Winchester Ballistic Silvertip. Developed at Nosler, this Combined Technology product is a cosmetic variant of the Nosler Ballistic Tip. Its gray polymer nose and black jacket coating distinguish it. Fine accuracy, violent upset, and flat flight are hallmarks. Available in a variety of weights and diameters, it is popular in Supreme factory loads.

The effect of velocity on bullet performance can hardly be overstated. If you choose a stout bullet and commonly shoot a deer with your .30-06 beyond 200 yards, terminal velocity (say 2,000 fps) may not give you the upset you want. I once asked a Nosler executive why there was a Partition-style 170-grain .30-30 bullet. He agreed with me that at .30-30 speeds a Partition didn't make sense, but added that retailers carrying the Nosler line wanted to stock bullets for hunters using .30-30s, and he wanted those bullets to be Noslers.

Actually, the drift toward stouter bullets is paradoxical. As hunters buy more powerful scopes and cartridges designed to give bullets flatter flight, they seem to be banking on long shots. The odds of having to shoot far and break both shoulders or thread an animal lengthwise are slim, as there is usually time to wait for a better angle. Also, by the time any high-velocity bullet has reached a distant target, it is moving considerably slower than when it started (figure about 25 percent loss in speed for a pointed bullet at 300 yards). Reduced impact velocity means less violent upset, less fragmentation.

Loads that shoot accurately and function faultlessly in your rifle inspire confidence and lead to more accurate shot placement afield. Confidence is a bigger asset than a bullet designed to thread six railroad ties, a stack of New York phone books and a 1950 John Deere engine block without losing more than 3 percent of its weight. What a bullet looks like when you dig it from a dead animal is not necessarily an indication of its lethality. After all, a set of worn tires may not look like much either. Before you settle on a bullet, buy several kinds, splitting boxes with friends to trim cost. You don't need 50 shots to tell you a given bullet is inaccurate or acts like a grenade in wet newspaper. Keep your mind open to different bullet weights. When thin-jacketed softpoints were the only option, heavy bullets made sense for tough game, because all bullets lost significant weight during expansion and hunters needed a substantial remnant to penetrate. But these days, bullets needn't be heavy to drive deep. Hiking bullet weight, you must reduce speed, trimming kinetic energy and making the bullet's arc steeper at distance.

Whether you handload or shoot factory rounds, there are more than enough bullet choices to keep you busy testing during the off season. More shooting means that whatever bullet you choose is more apt to land in the right place and kill right away.

16. The All-Copper Option

For centuries lead has remained unchallenged as bullet material, but lately the all-copper bullet has grabbed headlines. In 1981, after traditional soft-nose bullets failed to pass muster on a hunting trip, Randy Brooks hatched the idea of an expanding bullet with no lead core. Others had toyed with the idea; but no one had brought a viable product to market. Randy and wife Coni then owned Barnes Bullets. While he continued manufacturing Barnes Originals, Randy shifted the firm's focus to solid-copper hollowpoints. Soon the Barnes X became as well-known among hunters as Nosler's famous Partition, the dual-core big game bullet dating to 1947.

The X-Bullet drove deep, though its petals did not open as broadly as those on traditional lead-core bullets. Coated X-Bullets followed, the blue film reducing bore friction and copper fouling—both liabilities endemic to solid-copper bullets. Then came Barnes Triple Shock (TSX) bullets, with four circumferential grooves to reduce bearing surface and give shank material a place to move under land pressure. The Triple Shock soon became known for its deadly terminal performance, and for more consistent accuracy than the X-Bullet. The recent addition of a polymer tip gave the TSX a higher ballistic coefficient. Now this bullet has a rival: Barnes's own MRX. Its nose section is all copper, a hollowpoint with a polymer tip. It has the TSX profile with shank grooves. But inside the copper envelope of the shank, you'll find what Barnes calls a "tungsten-based Silvex" core. Extending from just behind the ogive to the heel, it adds heft without lead.

▼ A Browning X-Bolt in .308 drilled this half-minute group with 150-grain TSX bullets.

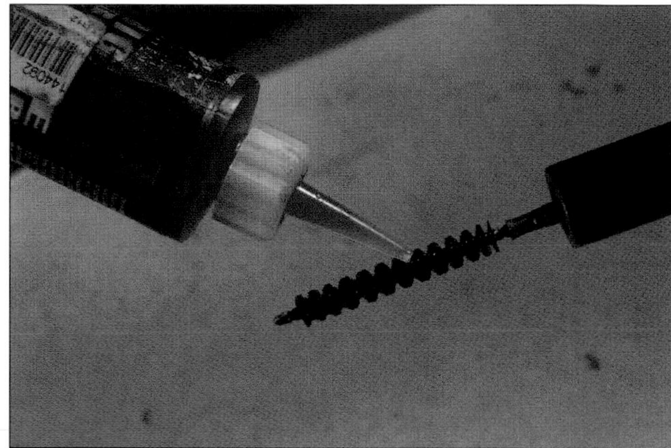

▲ Bore-cleaner on a brush removes metal fouling, a bigger problem with solid-copper bullets.

Now other bullet makers have introduced hunting bullets of copper or gilding metal construction, arguably in response to a lead-bullet ban in southern California condor range. Winchester and Remington, Nosler and Hornady plan to increase their lead-free bullet offerings. Ammunition firms will surely add to their lead-free loads. There is even a lead-free .22 WMR round from CCI (TNT Green). Are jacketed lead bullets on their way out? How do copper bullets compare ballistically with lead-core bullets?

First, a clarification: "Solid copper" is commonly used to describe these bullets. They are not solid in the sense that non-expanding bullets are solids. They're designed to mushroom. A hollow cavity ruptures the nose, enabling pre-scored petals to peel back, increasing diameter and destruction. Here "solid" refers to the bullet's composition: either solid ("pure") copper or gilding metal—copper/zinc alloy.

"Give up lead, and you give up speed in certain cartridges," says Hornady's chief engineer Dave Emary. "Cases designed for full-capacity charges behind heavy bullets don't do quite as well with copper or gilding metal bullets, because to make weight, so to speak, these bullets must be longer than lead-core bullets. You have to put that extra length *some*where. Seating a bullet deeper reduces case capacity. Seating it to greater overall length can cause interference in the magazine or throat. Any copper bullet with the dimensions of a lead-core bullet will be lighter. It will not retain its velocity as well or carry quite as much energy." Yes, you can start light bullets faster. "But a little more speed at the muzzle won't offset a higher ballistic coefficient

▲ A sabot sleeve falls away after exit endows shotgun slugs with the ballistic properties of rifle bullets. They have smaller diameters, sleeker profiles, higher sectional densities than traditional, bore-diameter Foster slugs. Note the huge nose cavity, to ensure upset at relatively low impact speeds.

downrange," says Dave. "And because copper is harder than lead, and gilding metal harder still, you can't accelerate a lightweight non-lead bullet quite as fast as a traditional softpoint without boosting pressure. There's too much bore friction from that hard shank."

Another concern that attends copper and gilding metal bullets is throat life. Most hunters needn't worry. While harder bullet material hikes friction and accelerates wear, few sportsmen shoot enough to ruin a throat with these bullets. And competitive shooters have so far stayed true to lead-core bullets.

Dave tells me that solid copper hunting bullets incorporate compromises in the nose. "You want an aerodynamic ogive, a pointed profile. But the small nose cavity in bullets of this shape doesn't initiate upset at low impact speeds. We can make the cavity bigger—but only at the expense of ballistic coefficient. An open nose also tends to shatter when driven fast into tough targets. Copper bullets expand satisfactorily in a relatively narrow velocity window. We can make lead-core bullets that penetrate well when striking an elk at 3,000 fps but still open reliably in deer at speeds as low as 1,600. It's difficult to make a copper bullet expand at less than 2,000 fps unless you make the cavity so big the front end disintegrates at 3,000." Small-diameter bullets—25-caliber and under—pose a challenge in nose design because there's so little material forward of the shank. A slender nose limits options for cavity diameter.

As for penetration, the copper bullet does just fine, typically retaining more of its original weight than lead bullets and delivering a more symmetrical blossom, which tends to drive straighter. On average, petals on copper rifle bullets don't gape quite as widely as jackets on lead bullets, assisted by the smashed core. But

▲ The TSX bullet from Wayne's iron-sighted Savage in .338 penetrated to the off-side shoulder knuckle of this Australian buffalo. The impact shattered the massive bone well below the joint.

while double-diameter upset of a fast lead bullet opens a huge cavity in the vitals, damage caused by a copper bullet 1 ½ times its original diameter can be stunning, and penetration deeper. Not long ago I shot a couple of Australian buffalo with Barnes .338 TSX bullets. Both drove to the off-side. One hit the massive knuckle of the off-shoulder so hard it shattered the wrist-thick bone at mid-section, inches from point of impact. I couldn't imagine any lead-core bullet dealing a more destructive blow.

Accuracy, too, can be on par with that of jacketed bullets. I've drilled tight groups with TSXs, and Dave Emary tells me the lead-free GMX bullet is as accurate as any of Hornady's lead-core hunting bullets. "GMX" stands for "gilding metal expanding." Designing it in 2009, Hornady chose gilding metal (5 percent zinc) over pure copper because it's less prone to fouling. It's also more brittle. Preventing breakage during upset proved a challenge. Hornady met it. Like the Barnes TSX, the GMX has circumferential grooves or driving bands. "We settled on two of standard .045 cannelure width," says Dave. "They proved significantly better than one; with three we gained no perceptible advantage. The grooves reduce full-diameter shank surface by about 20 percent and give the shank material room to move under land pressure."

"The gilding metal is the same material we've used for years in Hornady bullet jackets," explains Jeremy Millard, who headed the GMX project. He tells me the GMX bullet expands and penetrates reliably at impact velocities of just under 2,000 fps to 3,400 fps. "Typically, we get 99 percent weight retention in ballistic gelatin. All we lose is the tip." The GMX's scarlet plastic tip is just like that on the Hornady SST. In fact, the two bullets look the same when loaded. In flight, the GMX acts like the SST. "We designed the bullet to duplicate the SST's arc when driven at the same speed," Jeremy says. "The ballistic coefficient is almost identical. You can use SST load data."

But inside, these two bullets differ. Besides lacking the SST's lead core, the GMX has a unique cavity. "The front end is parallel-sided to accept the tip," says Jeremy. "As on the SST, that's roughly a 3/32 inch channel. But the GMX cavity tapers to a nearly a point even with the base of the ogive. That's where we want expansion to stop. And that's where it does."

Small but lethal at 3,800 fps: Winchester's .223 with 35-grain Ballistic Silvertip lead-free bullet. ▶

GMX bullets are cut from wire, swaged to shape. Jeremy emphasizes that dimensional tolerances are very tight. "We demand that these bullets not only deliver the upset hunters want, but that they shoot accurately." He concedes that they cost more than lead bullets. Though the price of lead has risen, it's still a fraction of the cost of copper, which has climbed to record levels over the last few years. "On average the GMX retails for about 40 percent more than our Interbond bullets," he says.

Shortly after a pre-production sample of 30-caliber GMX bullets became available, I hurried off to British Columbia to hunt moose with my friends and outfitters Lynn and Darrell Collins. We'd traveled southwest from their Quesnel base to the remote mountains below the Bella Coola Highway. Though local bulls had not yet felt the heat of rut, we eventually found one on a timbered hill. Shooting prone through a tight alley in the brush, I threaded a 150-grain GMX 105 yards to the shoulder. The moose fell backward and did not move. The bullet, from my Ruger Hawkeye in .300 RCM, had sailed through the near scapula into the spine. It had apparently stopped there; no exit wound was evident in the off-shoulder. Eviscerating the bull, I found considerable lung damage, from bone or bullet fragments or both. The massive chunk of bone comprising moose spine between its shoulders is, of course, a very tough assignment for any bullet.

Nosler knows about the challenges of making effective copper bullets. Its E-Tip bullet showed up first in Winchester ammunition. Now Nosler hawks 150- and 180-grain .30-caliber E-Tips as components. "This bullet is all gilding metal," explains Bob Nosler, "95 percent copper, 5 percent zinc. We call it 210 alloy. It has great tensile strength. E-Tips don't foul barrels as readily as copper bullets. A deep expansion cavity ensures upset in light game." That cavity is capped by a polymer tip for a high ballistic coefficient. It helps trigger expansion. The Nosler/Winchester E-Tip bullet features a tapered heel, or boat-tail. There are no circumferential grooves. E-Tips loaded by Winchester have the firm's familiar black Lubalox coating.

The E-Tip owes much to Glen Weeks, Winchester's centerfire ammo guru, who collaborated with the Nosler crew to deliver this bullet at record pace. Work began in October, 2006, and prototype bullets appeared at the April, 2007 NRA convention. "E-Tip's

◀ Neil Jacobson shot this outstanding gemsbok with a lead-free Winchester E-Tip bullet from his Remington .30-06.

metal is as hard as or slightly harder than copper," says Glen, "so it has less tendency to gall. That means easier bore cleaning and reduced metal fouling." I took E-Tip bullets to Africa recently and found that even on big, tough antelope they penetrated very deep.

A burly gemsbok bull dropped to one E-Tip from a .30-06. The spitzer passed through. An unnecessary follow-up shot gave me a recovered bullet, slightly deformed after shattering the shoulder, but very nearly as heavy as when it left the bore.

What about sealing in the bore? To cork powder gas and ensure an authoritative bite by the rifling, bullets must be malleable. Lead-core bullets "slug up" nicely to fill the grooves. Not so copper and gilding metal. I asked Glen about the bullet's accuracy and the pressure issue some companies have addressed with shank grooves.

"The secret to E-Tip's fine accuracy is its deep nose cavity," Glen says. "It extends well below the tip, down even below the ogive. So the leading portion of the shank can yield slightly as the rifling begins to engrave. Gas pressure on the bullet base clinches the deal, ensuring that E-Tip is securely gripped and seals the bore." The cavity also moves center of gravity back toward E-Tip's tapered heel. Better accuracy results. As for terminal performance, E-Tip delivers four-petal upset. But unlike solid-copper bullets, E-Tip winds up with a broad face, resembling that of a traditional softpoint. "It won't drive quite as deep as the AccuBond," adds Glen. "It behaves more like the XP3." That's Winchester's most recent lead-core bullet—one hailed for its versatility. The company loads 180-grain E-Tips to standard lead-bullet velocities.

Remington has a lead-free big game bullet, in a Premier Copper Solid line of hunting ammunition. The polymer-tipped spitzers have two shank grooves and tapered heels and are listed as solid copper. "They were designed to expand reliably over a wide range of velocities," explains Linda Powell, the company's press contact and a dedicated hunter who knows as much about Remington ammo as anyone. "Our goal was double-diameter upset with 98-percent weight retention in tough game. We're on target." Remington's lead-free ammo includes .223 and .22-250 Disintegrator loads with 45-grain bullets at 3,550 and 4,000 fps.

Frangible lead-free varmint bullets shatter the popular illusion that lead is necessary if you want explosive upset. Barnes serves prairie dog shooters with its Varmint Grenade, a flat-base hollowpoint bullet with a copper-tin core and gilding metal jacket. Like the Barnes MPG (multi-purpose green) bullet in 5.56 and 7.62mm, the Grenade ruptures immediately and violently. Randy Brooks is pleased with the reputation his X-Bullet and TSX have earned for deep penetration and high weight retention in tough game. But he's quick to praise his varmint bullets—and to point out that solid-copper bullets for deer-size animals deliver the accuracy and broad wound channels hunters have come to expect of lead-core softpoints. "Our hunting bullets aren't just for Volkswagen-size moose and bears. They're versatile. Match the bullet to the game, and you'll find them ideal for pronghorns and whitetails as well as for heavy animals with thick hides and big bones." He adds that solid-copper Expander MX hollowpoint muzzleloading bullets have performed superbly in deer-size game at modest impact speeds.

Winchester ballistician Glen Weeks covers gelatin with cloth in tests of bullet upset, penetration. ▶

What about other non-lead materials? Tungsten is denser than lead and performs successfully in shotshells. But it's frightfully expensive—several times the price of lead. "We considered tungsten for Dangerous Game solids," Dave Emary tells me. "But our jacketed lead-core bullets work as well and cost less." Those solids wear a laminated jacket, copper sandwiching steel.

"So we get the strength of steel with the surface properties of copper." A solid bullet for elephants could, of course, be constructed of copper or gilding metal. But sectional density matters a great deal when the bullet must drive through massive bones.

Of major US bullet companies, only Sierra and Swift have yet to list a lead-free centerfire bullet.

Carroll Pilant, shooter and long-time press liaison at Sierra, says tests of lead-free bullets have not shown them to be viable substitutes for lead. "Copper bullets won't deliver the accuracy we get with MatchKings. We'd be foolish to replace an iconic bullet like the MatchKing—the choice of an overwhelming majority of competitive shooters." Pilant hasn't heard of anyone at a high-power match choosing lead-free bullets. Nor does he think copper bullets equal Sierra's GameKing for either accuracy or devastation in deer-size game.

While Winchester and Remington have introduced their own lead-free bullets, Federal has not. Its preference: Offer bullets from the nation's top bulletsmiths. Jason Nash at Federal emphasizes that the firm has traditionally given hunters many options. "We'll continue that policy, with bullets from our house and specialty lines like Nosler, Barnes, Sierra and Woodleigh." Federal's Trophy Bonded Bear Claw has a big following among elk hunters. The company is currently pursuing a viable lead-free .22 Long Rifle round.

As lead-free bullets gain traction at market, they'll get more attention from engineers charged with improving them. During development of Hornady's GMX Dave Emary was keen to add Flex Tip polymer noses for use in rifles with tube magazines. It proved a tough assignment. "Lead-core bullets obligingly grip an FTX peg. A gilding metal nose isn't as malleable."

Does the addition of a soft or hard polymer nose affect the terminal performance of a gilding metal bullet? "A hard polymer tip makes upset more violent," Dave replies, "especially at high impact speeds. An FTX tip does not—but it helps trigger expansion at low velocities."

Pointed noses and long ogives help bullets cleave air. But the form factor is just one component of ballistic coefficient, which includes sectional density. Reducing weight reduces sectional density, so a lead bullet has a slightly higher ballistic coefficient than an all-copper bullet, given the same nose profiles. The shank of a lead bullet is shorter, so there's less skin friction. But the disparity is small. A 165-grain 30-bore jacketed bullet with a ballistic coefficient of .450 beats its copper or gilding metal rivals by only .015 or so. Currently, lead-free bullets cost more than traditional jacketed bullets. That could change as more makers develop more bullets of copper and gilding metal. The industry has made this commitment—though only Remington calls its bullets non-toxic. Other companies share my view that non-toxic is an unfortunate moniker. It implies that lead-core bullets *are* toxic.

Even outside the shooting industry, the toxicity of lead has become a headline topic of late. Most worrisome to shooters is the recent lead ban in California to prevent condors from eating bullet fragments while scavenging animals killed by hunters. The science behind this decision has been questioned. Despite warnings in the general press about lead fragments posing a threat to people who eat venison taken with softpoints, there's no substantiating evidence. After a politically motivated decision to pull tons of donated venison from food programs for the needy in North Dakota, the state has recanted. A report issued by the Epidemic Intelligence Service of the National Center of Environmental Health detailed a study of lead levels in 734 North Dakotans, 80 percent of whom claimed they ate venison year round. Blood tests showed mean lead levels of less than 1.5 ng/dl, with only 8 of participants (1.1 percent) testing over 5 ng/dl. The *highest* individual reading, an outlier, was still well below the 10 ng/dl considered by the Centers for Disease Control and Prevention (CDC) to warrant case management. A response by the National Shooting Sports Foundation noted that lead levels in workers exposed to lead would have to reach *60* ng/dl before OSHA would require employees to be furloughed. The difference in blood levels between people who ate venison and those who did not? Just .3 ng/dl. No wonder most companies making non-lead bullets hesitate to call them non-toxic!

Lead bullets remain the most popular bullets. The best of bullets made without lead simply give hunters more choice.

Choice is good. Which is why state efforts to limit bullet choice are not.

17. Speer, Nosler, Hornady

Vernon Speer was born in 1901 in Cedar Falls, Iowa. After a stint in the US Navy during World War I, he indulged an interest in aviation by building his own aircraft engine at age 21. He then installed it in a biplane and took to the sky in a test flight. Work as a tool foreman for John Deere grounded him for a while, but in 1941 he became chief ground instructor at a flying school in Lincoln, Nebraska. There he also started making bullets. Handloading was in its infancy; shooters still cast their own bullets. Jacketed bullets hadn't yet become widely available, and the war effort caused shortages in both brass and copper. Vernon Speer struck upon the idea of using .22 rimfire cases for bullet jackets. He built a machine to iron out the rims and draw the hulls to proper dimensions for .224 jackets. His partnership with Joyce Hornady proved as fragile as most, and in 1944 Speer left Hornady and Nebraska to establish his own business in Lewiston, Idaho. For two years he sold his jacketed .224 bullets in paper bags, while laying the groundwork for a new bullet manufacturing plant on the banks of the Snake River. That's still where Speer bullets come from.

War's end renewed the flow of gilding metal to the commercial ammunition industry. Speer took advantage by expanding his line of bullets to include all popular types and diameters. His son Ray joined the growing company in 1952. Two years later Ray produced the first Speer Reloading Manual. Ever the experimenter, Vernon Speer developed the Hot-Cor process to ensure better marriage of the bullet core and jacket. He realized early on the advantages of re-usable packaging and bought injection molding equipment to make sturdy plastic boxes for Speer products. In 1969 he began loading his bullets in handgun cartridges, introducing the Lawman line of ammo. Gold Dot bonded pistol bullets came along in 1994. They and the subsequent Gold Dot ammunition have earned enviable reputations among law enforcement officers. Speer remained a family-owned business until 1975, four years before Vernon Speer's death.

▲ Vernon Speer's firm became a leader in .22 rimfire ammo. It also makes the Gold Dot pistol line.

▼ Speer has made bullets and weights not available elsewhere—these .366 softpoints for the 9.3x26, for instance.

While Vernon's name is widely known among shooters, his brother Dick also contributed a great deal to the growth of handloading. Fourteen years younger than Vernon, he became a machinist at Boeing Aircraft in Seattle. After Speer's bullet factory began operation in Lewiston, Dick moved there to produce specialty cartridge cases. Shooters keen to brew handloads for discontinued, proprietary, or wildcat rounds took note. First selling the hulls under the label "Forged From Solid," Dick named his part of the business Speer Cartridge Works. While his extrusion processes were sound, the quality of raw stock

BULLETS—THE INSIDE STORY

varied widely in those days. Consequently, so did case quality. A high rejection rate, combined with the limited market in specialty brass, scuttled Dick's enterprise.

Not to be deterred, Dick looked to handloaders for another inspiration. He found that primers were a bottleneck on most loading benches. Major ammo firms couldn't (or wouldn't) ensure a steady supply of component primers. Dick Speer seized on this failing as an opportunity. In 1951 he hired explosives expert Dr. Victor Jasaitis from Lithuania to come up with percussive compounds to fuel a new business in primers for handloaders. His first products were FA-70 primers to fill government contracts. Later, Jasaitis came up with non-corrosive primers for sporting ammunition. To differentiate his business from Speer Bullets, Dick (with partner Arvid Nelson) changed his firm's name to Cascade Cartridge, Inc. Now known universally as CCI, it soon outgrew its corner in Vernon Speer's bullet plant. Dick bought a 17-acre chicken farm upriver, near the Lewiston Gun Club. In a converted coop under a tar-paper roof, he began producing rifle primers.

After the gun club moved, Dick bought that property, expanding his operation in 1957 to include manufacture of shotshell primers. Two years later he started making power loads—rimfire cartridges for nail guns and other industrial tools. Rimfire rifle cartridges were a natural sequel in 1963. CCI Mini-Mag ammunition soon became wildly popular. Four years after its debut, Dick Speer sold CCI to Omark.

The production of rimfire ammunition is highly specialized, and tooling up requires huge capital outlay. Consequently, there are few such factories in the US When Hornady decided to load its .17 HMR cartridge, it turned to CCI. Hornady's tiny polymer-tipped bullets, combined with CCI's manufacturing expertise and commitment to high quality, delivered to shooters accurate cartridges that became one of the greatest success stories of the industry in the last 40 years. By this time, CCI had improved its centerfire primers to give handloaders lower seating pressures and easier ignition. In 1991 it had opened a new primer plant in Lewiston and, subsequently, become a major supplier of cannon primers to the US armed forces.

Speer/CCI has become one of the most recognized brands in the shooting industry. Its bullets and primers and its handgun and rimfire ammunition are proven favorites. Now owned by ATK, which also counts Federal Cartridge, Weaver, and RCBS as assets, the enterprise Vernon Speer founded with Joyce Hornady continues to provide the best in ammo and loading components

Among the contemporaries of the Speer brothers was a hunting enthusiast who, in 1946 on a hunt in Canada, had to fire several shots to kill a moose. The bullets ruptured on the animal's mud-caked hide and didn't penetrate. "My .300 H&H was too powerful to kill a moose with the bullets of that day," he told me, years later. He decided to build a better softpoint.

John Amos Nosler, 33, ran a trucking business in western Oregon. His father Byrd had been born on the Oregon Trail and raised on a homestead in Coquille. John arrived after Byrd had moved to Brawley, in southern California. The boy grew up on a ranch near Bishop, where his family raised horses and mules. During the Great War, Byrd sold mules to the government.

Turning a dollar here and there in real estate and hardware sales and delivering fresh milk, Byrd Nosler moved his family to Pomona, then to a ranch near Huntington Beach. "I was seven," recalls John. "A year later, Dad took in an old Dort that needed service. I tinkered with it and got it started and sold it. What I wanted was a Model T. So I rode my bicycle around until I spotted one in permanent repose behind an old house. I went to the door and asked the lady there if she could use a bicycle. She eyed the derelict Model T and agreed to an even swap. I dragged that car home with Dad's mules, fixed it up, and sold it."

Automobiles became John's passion. From Western Auto Supply he got parts for overhead-valve engines, and built them. "I came to believe that problems were really opportunities to improve on current designs." John liked guns, too. He traded a set of Model T connecting rods for his first deer rifle, a .25-35 Winchester. But as the Depression tightened belts, the talented mechanic had to drop out of high school in his junior year. He went to work as clean-up boy at a Ford dealership in Chino for 15 cents an hour. That job led to more engine work, and racing. "A partner and I souped up a Model A with a B engine. I added counterweights to the B's crank. It ran smoothly at 100 mph. Ford liked that crank well enough to adopt it."

▲ Known for bullets, Nosler now sells ammunition and even rifles. This Model 48 is in .338 Federal.

John married Louise Booz in 1933. Shortly thereafter he sold his new 1935 Ford and bought a '29 coupe for $60. The young couple moved to Reedsport, Oregon, where John managed a Ford dealership. In response to worker demands for unions, local sawmills soon shut down. Jobless people didn't buy cars. To earn a living, John began trucking produce from California to southern Oregon. He bought one of the first Peterbilts ever made. It got only 6 miles to a gallon of diesel but could haul 20 tons—three times as much as a Ford. "Besides, diesel was 5 cents a gallon, gas 23." By this time, John was shooting competitively and experimenting with handloads. He killed his first elk near Burns, Oregon.

Bob Nosler was born in 1946, as his father shifted from trucking for the war effort back to civilian markets. After the moose hunt, he also committed time to a new bullet. He made a hand press and bought a screw machine. He drilled out both ends of 5/16 copper billets turned to size, and pressed them into shape around lead cores. Fred Huntington of RCBS gave him new presses from his Oroville, California shop. The first Partition bullets weren't accurate by current standards, but on their first hunt they put two moose down with two shoulder shots. John was on to something.

"That was more than sixty years ago," Bob grins. Now CEO of Nosler, Inc., he runs the company with wife Joan (vice-president of corporate services), son John (vice-president and general manager) and daughter Jill (manager of corporate services)—"plus our hard-working employees. We're very fortunate to have 125 dedicated people at Nosler." The plant now comprises two buildings totaling 60,000 square feet in Bend, Oregon. "Big John," 96, is still chairman of the board. "He drives a Lexus now," grins Bob. "but he'll talk to you about Model Ts and the Flying Mile at Long Beach."

The family-owned company has expanded its product line considerably with Ballistic Tip bullets in 1984, following the Nosler Solid Base. "We were the second North American firm to employ a polymer bullet tip," says Bob. "Canada's Dominion brand had the Saber Tip first. But that company is defunct." In contrast, many bullet and ammunition companies have adopted Nosler's polymer design, which has earned an enviable reputation for accuracy and flat flight. It was followed in 2002 by the AccuBond, Nosler's first bonded bullet. The lead-free E-Tip appeared in 2008. "Along the way we've also developed target bullets, handgun bullets, and brass solids for dangerous game. The Combined Technology bullets Winchester loads were designed mainly by Nosler."

There's also Custom brass with the Nosler headstamp. "We weigh-sort it, chamfer case mouths, de-burr primer pockets and true necks," says Bob. "It's top-end brass, ready for the powder charge right from the box." There's also a Custom ammunition line, with offerings from .204 Ruger to .416 Weatherby. Nosler

▼ Nosler's M48 in .338 Federal is a handsome rifle, potent enough for any North American game.

▲ John Nosler developed the Partition bullet in 1947. Here he cradles a favorite M70, in .280.

Trophy Grade ammo delivers all but the hand-finishing of Custom cases, at a lower price.

Bob points out that Nosler gave legitimacy to one of my pet cartridges: the .280 Ackley Improved.

"We developed factory loads and shepherded the round through SAAMI's approval process. It's a fine big game cartridge—especially in Nosler rifles!" The company builds two. The Custom wears a walnut stock and Timney trigger. Its hand-lapped, match-grade barrel has "half-minute accuracy potential." The 7-lb Nosler 48 features a Kevlar-laminated stock. CeraKote finish makes it just about impervious to rust. "We'll guarantee ¾ inch three-shot groups," says Bob.

Such high standards have distinguished Nosler products since John hand-turned the first Partitions.

One of America's premier bullet companies, Hornady, has been responsible for some of the most celebrated bullet designs of late. Sixty years ago, Joyce Hornady concluded that only uniform bullets would give him the "ten shots in one hole" he sought. In 1949 he decided he could make a bullet as any he could buy. Other riflemen apparently agreed; his first year's production brought $10,000 in sales.

The Grand Island, Nebraska company owes its beginnings to the partnership forged when Joyce Hornady and Vernon Speer fashioned bullet jackets from spent rimfire hulls. This idea not only helped them make varmint bullets cheaply; it kept them in business during metal shortages in the early 1940s. Joyce was quick to spot value in the specialized machinery and tooling dormant in government arsenals after the war.

◀ Wayne shot this pronghorn at 160 yards with a pointed FTX bullet from Hornady's LeverEvolution .30-30 load.

When he and Vernon Speer split up to seek their own fortunes, he bought as much as he could afford. The Hornady plant still employs Waterbury-Farrell transfer presses manufactured as early as the 1920s. Of course, they're updated with computerized controls.

War in Korea interrupted Joyce's budding bullet business. In 1958 he built an 8,000-square-foot factory that's still company headquarters. Shortly thereafter, Hornady Bullets announced a new bullet nose design for flatter flight and better accuracy. The Secant Ogive softpoint has since distinguished Hornady's hunting bullets. (Secant and tangent refer to the point from

▼ Hornady's FTX bullet has given new life to lever rifles, now lethal at distance as well as in timber.

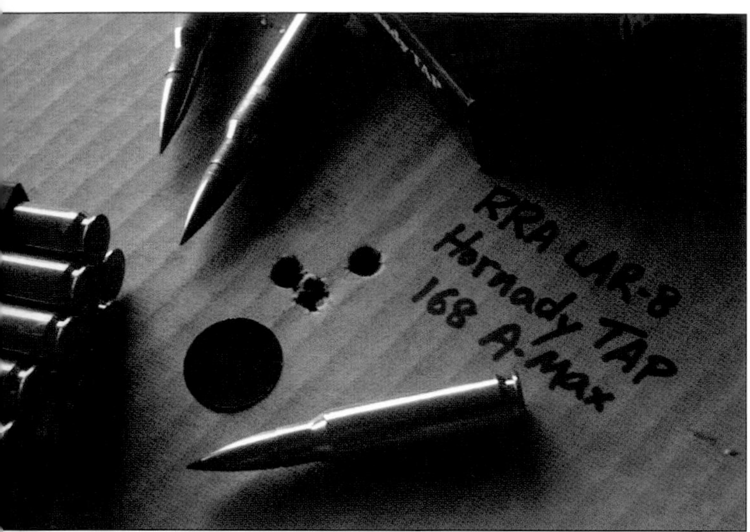

▲ Hornady's TAP ammunition delivers fine accuracy from Wayne's LAR-8 from Rock River Arms.

▲ Hornady began as a bullet company. Now it also produces loaded ammunition and loading tools.

which an arc, measured in calibers, scribes the outline of the bullet nose. The tangent measure is taken perpendicular to the bullet axis at the cylinder/cone juncture. Secant measurements occur behind that point.) Tangent ogives have a more rounded form. Secant ogives minimize nose weight and air friction. While they don't mandate a sharper junction between conical and cylindrical sections of a bullet, the secant ogive profile may appear more angular.

In 1964 Joyce Hornady entered the ammunition business with his Frontier line. He used canister powders in once-fired brass, and his own bullets. Initial offerings: .243, .270, .308 and .30-06. The Viet Nam War choked off brass supplies. Joyce began buying new cases in 1972. At the same time, son Steve moved back from Lincoln, where he'd been working for Pacific Tool. He brought the company with him.

Joyce Hornady lost his life in a plane crash in 1981, en route to the SHOT Show in New Orleans.

"No one was prepared," said Steve. "But our family was committed to growing the business. We were blessed with a talented crew."

In 1983 Hornady Bullets, Frontier Ammunition and Pacific Tool Company were absorbed into a new Hornady Manufacturing Company. They retained autonomy as Hornady Bullets, Hornady Custom Ammunition and Hornady Reloading Tools. A year later, the enterprise was making its own cartridge cases in-house, and loading them. The firm would soon launch itself as a major player in the ammunition field.

18. Inside an ammo factory

ave Emary, chief ballistics engineer, has been behind much of the innovation at Hornady. Like many of the company employees, he's an active shooter. In fact, he's an accomplished high-power rifle competitor and was even named to the President's Hundred at Camp Perry. Before coming to Hornady, he worked with artillery, "shooting 5-lb bullets at 7,000 fps and 12-lb bullets at 6,500" from 90mm and 120mm cannons. Expertise he acquired in the armed forces has helped him design 25-grain 17-caliber spitzers and 500-grain .458 solids for sportsmen.

Dave explains that Hornady gets its lead in ingots, which are melted and formed into cylindrical blocks about the size of a roll of freezer paper (but heavier!). A massive press squirts these cylinders, cold, through dies to form the lead wire that's cut into bullet lengths. Antimony content is specified at purchase, from 0 to 6 percent. More antimony means a harder bullet. Most bullet cores have 3 percent antimony.

Jacket cups are punched out of sheets. "Jacket uniformity and concentricity are vital to accuracy," Dave says. "We hold concentricity to .003."

Hornady's Spire Point softpoints have been a mainstay of big game hunters for decades. Now the firm also makes A-Max (Advanced Match Accuracy) spitzers for competitive shooting. V-Max bullets, introduced in 1995, share the A-Max's plastic nose insert. They're designed with thin jackets for explosive effect on small animals. The SST (Super Shock Tip) plastic-nose bullet for big game followed. "We got the SST designation from an old 1950s Hornady bullet board," explains Dave.

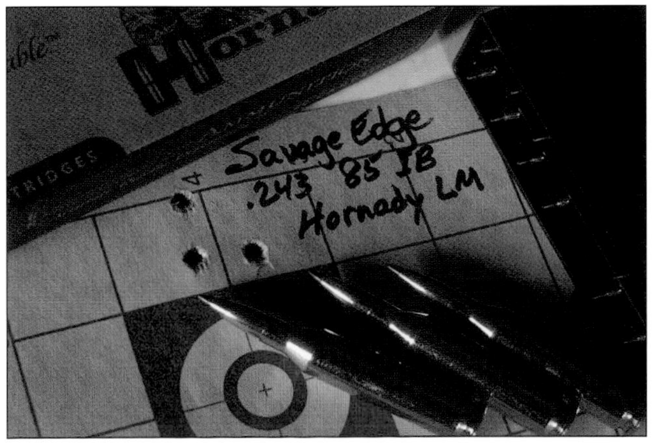

◀ Inexpensive rifles with good ammo can shoot well! Here: a Savage Edge rifle fired Hornady InterBonds.

Hornady has successfully mined niche markets too. After someone found the .50 BMG would detonate dynamite at 1,000 yards, this military round got lots of attention. When Hornady announced its A-Max bullet for the big .50 in 1994, it sold briskly. Its sleek profile and long aluminum tip kept weight to the rear for best accuracy. A ballistic coefficient of over .600 gave shooters the flat flight they wanted.

"We tried aluminum tips on 162-grain 7mm bullets as well," recalls Dave Emary. "They worked but proved too costly. We replaced them with a long plastic tip, but that gave erratic accuracy." The firm then switched to small plastic tips (all Hornady red) in both match and hunting bullets, refining the nose contours when necessary. These produced small groups consistently, partly because the tips were easier to manufacture to uniform dimensions, partly because the bullets come out a bit shorter and were thus less finicky about rifling twist. Aluminum is now used only in A-Max .50s.

Hornady bullets reflect Dave's experience at the 1,000-yard line. He points out that bullet design is an exercise in compromise. "Though it would reduce drag in the barrel, lengthening the nose to shorten the shank gives the nose greater leverage if it swings off the bullet's axis in flight," he says. A long nose also mandates a more gradual curvature forward of the shank, which increases odds for bullet misalignment in the throat, and for subsequent yaw. "A short transition is usually best, so the bullet is forced quickly into full contact with the rifling." Dave says he likes to keep the ratio of bullet bearing surface to diameter at 1.5 or higher, though nose type and other variables also affect that ratio.

Some shooters might question the need for new softpoint bullet designs, given the broad selection available from Hornady and other makers. Even at the sprawling Grand Island plant, there are too many to make at once. "Contrary to what many shooters think," says Steve Johnson, who represents Hornady to the press. "We can't forever dedicate one machine to, say, 200-grain .338 bullets. We run enough to build up our stock, then switch to another bullet on that machine." Batch size depends on market demand. Hornady production lines stay busy supplying handloaders and the company's own loading machines—but also other ammunition firms that feature Hornady bullets. "We just finished a run of two million FMJ bullets for Federal," Steve pointed out during one visit. "We make V-Max and boat-tail softpoints for Remington. In fact, we've manufactured bullets for every major ammo firm." Those lack the Hornady label.

Development of new bullets and ammunition requires extensive testing—and instruments like the sophisticated Heise Gauge. It's a hydraulic device for calibrating chamber pressure. A transducer with a quartz crystal registers pressure through electrical discharge, explains Dave Emary. He says peak pressure as commonly measured in copper units (CUP) tells little about the pressure *curve*. "Time matters. You can boost velocity by extending the peak of the curve forward without making the curve higher." He says that a strain gauge falls short because it can't be calibrated to a standard in the manner of the Heise. Dave allows that handloaders get adequate indication of high pressure by measuring web expansion. "But it's crucial that you mike all cases at the same spot, because a .001 bulge at the web can become .005 a touch farther forward. It's best to measure forward, because you get more reaction from the brass."

He adds that handloaders will notice pierced primers at 70,000 CUP, and blow cups at 80,000. Pressure that's high enough for most shooters to notice is already well above SAAMI spec. "We got higher speed from our Light and Heavy magnum ammo by pushing the pressure curve forward so the peak occurs when the bullet is 3 inches out. That powder has about 4 percent more nitroglycerin than ordinary double-base powders. Surface deterrents slowed the initial burn so the bullet didn't outrun the burn so soon."

Ammunition has become a bigger part of Hornady's business plan. "We launched Light Magnum ammo in 1995," recalls Dave, "after I saw at Olin-St. Marks how super-powerful loads could be concocted in ordinary cases, using new propellants that kept a lid on pressures." But those ball powders had to be compressed, hiking cost of manufacture. The stiffer charges also increased recoil. And some cartridges didn't lend themselves to turbo-charged loads. But many did, and the ballistic boost was often impressive: 150 fps at the muzzle. The Light Magnum line came to include several popular rimless rounds—and the .303 British. "The .303 has a great record on game," Dave says. "And we still get lots of orders for 174-grain FMJs from Australia." The Light Magnum load features a 150-grain Spire Point bullet at 2,830 fps. Hornady's .458 Heavy Magnum kicks a 500-grain bullet downrange at 2,300 fps. At this speed, the bullet hits harder than one from a .470 Nitro Express, yielding 15 percent more energy than ordinary .458 loads.

All told, Hornady's Light Magnum and Heavy Magnum (belted) rounds proved a good move, and Steve continued to look for other opportunities in the ammunition field.

"The .17 HMR wasn't on our radar," he concedes. "But Dave had worked out many of the early problems with sub-caliber rimfires. We had so much fun with that .17, I called Darrell Inman at CCI to see about loading it. Darrell told me I had to order five million cartridges *and* pay for the tooling! It was a dare. I took it." Weeks after its introduction, sales of the .17 Hornady Magnum Rimfire shot past the first year's projections. Hornady doubled its order for cartridges (still the only ones to bear the Hornady name). When in 1998 I reported on the first .17 HMR rifles, ammo back-orders totaled 12 million rounds!

The company went a step beyond load development when in 2001 it fashioned a new varmint round: the .204 Ruger. Sales of three million 33-grain bullets for the .20 Tactical had hinted of strong interest in

▼ This Ruger Hawkeye is carbine-quick, but the .300 RCM performs efficiently in its short barrel.

sub-.22s. With Ruger, Hornady assembled a lightning-fast load in a modified .222 magnum case, a 32-grain V-Max .204 bullet at 4,200 fps. Negligible recoil allowed riflemen a look at bullet impact. In conjunction with Ruger, Hornady also developed .375 and .416 Ruger cartridges, then .300 and .338 Ruger Compact Magnums—these two specifically for short-barreled rifles. The .450 Bushmaster for AR-type rifles came from Hornady's shop, and the .30 TC, for Thompson/Center. Hornady warmed to the task of loading such obscure numbers as the 9.3x74 R. It loads the 6.5 Grendel, the 6.8 SPC, the .376 Steyr, the 9.3x62, the .458 Lott. There's a .44-40 Cowboy load and both solid and softpoint ammunition for classic African rounds: the .404 Jeffery and .416 Rigby, the .450/400, .450, .470 and .500 Nitro Express. Hornady offers hunting loads for burly handgun rounds, from the .44 Magnum to the .476 Linebaugh and .500 S&W. Tactical and its own Critical Defense lines of rifle and pistol ammo complement what has become the company's most celebrated development to date: LeverEvolution ammunition.

It sprang in part from Dave Emary's growing interest in old lever rifles. Like other enthusiasts, he bemoaned the blunt bullet noses required in tube magazines to prevent accidental ignition when recoil jarred the stack. Blunt bullets traced steep arcs, limiting effective range. Dave tackled this problem with a resilient polymer bullet nose that would yield to sudden pressure, then spring back into aerodynamic shape when that pressure was released. Now streamlined bullets could be carried safely in lever-actions! Ballistic coefficients for the new .30-30 and .35 bullets were 20 percent higher than for blunt bullets. Hornady did not stop there. A "Light Magnum".30-30 load clocking 2,400 fps challenged the .300 Savage. At 250 yards, the 160-grain .30-30 spitzer hit half again as hard as flat-nose bullets from ordinary .30-30 loads.

Hornady quickly added the LeverEvolution Flex-Tip or FTX bullets to other traditional lever-rifle cartridges. The line came to include not only such rounds as the .32 Special and .45-70, but more modern numbers like the .444 and .450 Marlin and, eventually, handgun cartridges like the .357 and .44 Magnums. Next step: Marry the FTX bullet and new, efficient powders in a more potent cartridge for lever-actions.

▲ Dave Emary developed the .338 Marlin Express. Wayne has used this rifle on targets to 600 yards.

Dave Emary came up with the .308 Marlin Express, matching the ballistic muscle of the defunct but potent .307 Winchester. "It carries .300 Savage punch in a semi-rimmed case," he said. But pressures above 47,000 PSI didn't seem appropriate in traditional lever rifles. "So we throttled back to 46,500. No troubles." The 160-grain FTX developed for the .30-30 flew more accurately than the 165-grain spitzer intended for the new round. "The final rendition was a 160 with a

Hornady's LeverEvolution line now includes cartridges like the .357, used in Marlin's 1894 rifle. ▶

long ogive, the Interlock band pushed forward boost weight retention. A .395 ballistic coefficient gave it great reach. Exiting at 2,660 fps from the .308 Marlin Express, it clocks over 2,000 at 300 yards.

That fall, I shot the first elk to fall to the .308 ME, a New Mexico six-point.

Never one to sit still, Dave told me he planned to develop a lever-action round to trump all others, "one that equals the .30-06." With Mitch Mittelstaedt and other colleagues, he settled on a .33 bore. You could say Federal beat him to the punch. But the excellent .338 Federal—a .308 necked up—was designed for bolt actions, not rear-locking lever rifles. Dave and Mitch settled on the .376 Steyr hull as a model but changed the hull, beefing up the web. Loaded with a new 200-grain FTX bullet, the.338 Marlin Express is 2.60 inches long. At 2,565 fps, muzzle velocity matches that of the .348 Winchester's 200-grain flat-nose, then leaves it behind. The .338 ME bullet can't deliver the muzzle energy of the heavier (325-grain) .450 Marlin. But at 100 yards they're equals, and beyond that, the ballistically superior .338 takes over. It hews closely to the arc of a 210-grain Partition from the .338 Federal. At 400 yards, the payloads of 200-grain .338 ME and 180-grain .30-06 bullets are essentially the same: 1,760 ft-lbs.

While raising the bar on lever-rifle performance, Hornady was also developing new bolt-action rounds. Mitch Mittelstaedt worked with Dave in adapting new propellants to cartridges designed for short-action carbines. "Typically we sacrifice 160 fps when we chop a .30 magnum barrel from 24 to 20 inches," Mitch explained. "The .300 and .338 Ruger Compact Magnums leak only 100 fps in 4 inches." On a range with chronograph guru Ken Oehler, I set up one of his fine 35P instruments to check bullet speeds in Ruger rifles with 20 inch barrels. Three 180-grain .308 SST bullets averaged 2,840 fps. The Ruger in .338 RCM sent 225-grain softpoints out the muzzle at 2,675 fps. Groups measured just over an inch.

"The RCMs are really short versions of the .375 Ruger," Mitch told me. The .300 and .338 cases have .532 rims, mike 2.100 and 2.015, base to mouth, and are both loaded to 2.840-inches. "We designed the .338 hull to accept current .33 bullets," he said, "most of which were fashioned for the .338 Winchester. A 2.100 inch case would have put the mouth in front of cannelures and beyond the shanks of some bullets."

Amazingly, these powerful, efficient RCM loads didn't last long. Two years after their debut the company announced they'd be replaced. "We're dropping them in favor of Superformance loads that add nearly 100 fps," Steve Johnson confided to me. "We'll abandon the Light and Heavy Magnum lines too."

Sensing something important, I pressed him for details.

"Dave and his crew have found a way to apply what they've learned from LeverEvolution and the Marlin Express and RCM cartridges to ordinary ammunition. They're getting higher speeds under SAAMI pressure limits. We don't compress the powder. We're losing just 18 fps per inch of barrel when we whittle a .300

▲ More speed, more energy, standard pressures—new powders fuel Hornady Superperformance ammo.

BULLETS—THE INSIDE STORY

Winchester to carbine length. And it behaves the same at 15 below as at room temperature…."

Hornady's Superformance ammunition is truly a major industry development. Dave Emary calls it the most significant hike in centerfire performance since standards were set with IMR propellants in the 1930s. Steve Hornady looks me straight in the eye and declares: "No other sporting ammo can come close. Superformance delivers higher speeds, flatter flights, less recoil and lower pressures than its competition. It's as accurate as any ammo we've ever produced, less temperature-sensitive and more efficient in short barrels. It retails for less than cartridges souped up with compressed charges."

Still young at this writing, Superformance ammunition already comprises 28 loads, from 95-grain .243 to 225-grain .338 Winchester Magnum. All share feature ball powders chemically and physically treated to deliver that smooth, steep but flat-topped pressure curve that pushes bullets quickly from the case, accelerates them smoothly down the bore, then drops off decisively. Low muzzle pressure, even in short barrels, means you get less blast; and less energy is wasted at exit. "Superformance loads match the ballistic thrust of Light and Heavy Magnums, but with charges 10 to 15 percent lighter," says Dave Emary.

Steve Johnson adds: "Our tests show Superformance ammo delivers an increase of 100 to 300 fps over standard. In a Model 70 .270 with a 22 inch barrel, Superformance 130-grain loads gave us 3,100 fps, while same-weight bullets from two other ammunition makers clocked 2,920 and 2,780."

Tested in temperatures from -15 to 140 degrees F confirm that Superformance powders don't care a great deal about the weather. Some loads show *no* velocity change from room temperature to below zero, according to Dave. He says all demonstrate greater consistency than traditional loads. "We've even found them to show less sensitivity to variations in bore diameter."

The propellants in Superformance ammunition are not available to handloaders. Manufactured by St. Marks in Florida (home of Winchester ball powders, now sold in canisters by Hodgdon), they endure chemical tweaks and degrees of crushing to meet defined burning characteristics. "We do some blending of powders here at Hornady," smiles Steve Johnson. "Anyone trying to duplicate our efforts or back-engineer our propellants would take two years doing so. We're not worried."

In sum, Hornady Superformance ammunition is that rare product with no obvious flaws. It drives bullets significantly faster at pressures below SAAMI limits, while maintaining high levels of accuracy. It behaves consistently over a broad temperature range. It even costs less at the counter—just a dollar or two more than ordinary ammo, and $5 or so *less* than the current crop of hyper-velocity rounds.

◀ Alice van Zwoll loads up with Hornady Superperformance ammo, which delivers higher velocities.

Section IV

SPEED, ENERGY, AND ARC

19. Headspace first

When you release the hammer or striker in your rifle, a lot of important events follow right away. The blow to the primer crushes its face against the anvil inside, smashing the shock-sensitive priming mix between them. The compound ignites—actually, it detonates. The explosion shoots flame through the flash-hole in the primer pocket. When this flame reaches the gunpowder in the case, the powder starts to burn, producing gas that expands rapidly. Because the brass case is ductile, it expands under gas pressure, ironing itself to the chamber walls. Still expanding rapidly, the gas thrusts the bullet forward, out the neck of the case and into the bore. At the same time, it pushes the case head against the bolt face. During this mayhem, the chamber keeps the cartridge in place. Because cartridges vary slightly in dimensions, and each must chamber easily, the chamber must be a little bit bigger than the average case.

Then there's headspace, the distance from the face of the locked bolt to a datum line or shoulder in the chamber that arrests the forward movement of the cartridge.

"For every action there is an equal and opposite reaction." So you'd expect the gas to press the cartridge head against the bolt-face. What complicates things is the taper of the case wall, from thick at the web to very thin at the shoulder. The web itself is a solid partition of brass around the flash-hole. As the front of the case is ironed against the chamber wall, the rear section stays close to its original diameter, slightly smaller than the chamber and, thus, mobile.

Now, if the case is held tight to the bolt face, everything is OK. The shoulder blows forward, the case body and neck outward to contact the chamber. The case head simply absorbs the rearward thrust of gas without moving because it is supported by the bolt face. But it's unusual to have an unfired cartridge tight against the bolt face, because it would be very difficult to chamber—a press fit. A cartridge longer by a gnat's lash would not chamber without great effort. So chambers are cut, and cases formed, to allow a bit of play. Call it tolerance. A proper chamber is slightly large, so the case head does move very slightly to the rear upon firing. If there's too great a distance between the bolt face and the point in the chamber that stops the forward motion of a cartridge, however, you have a condition of excess headspace.

Understand that the striker's blow pushes the cartridge forward until it contacts the datum point in the chamber. Expansion sticks it there because the thin front part of the case yields readily to gas pressure. The case head isn't stuck because it is thick and doesn't expand as much, so it moves rearward to meet the bolt face. The bolt face isn't supporting the case head at this point, so the case stretches as gas pressure, leveraged against the bullet and the case shoulder, moves the head to the rear. The case wall just forward of the web can stretch a little without damage. But excess headspace may stretch it too far. Repeated firings "work harden" the case, reducing its ability to stretch. Given many repeated stretchings, a cartridge fired in a generous chamber can crack at the web, or even separate.

A cracked case is dangerous because it spills powder gas into the chamber. That gas seeks release, speeding down the tiniest corridors at velocities that can exceed bullet speed. It may jet along the bolt race, through the striker hole, into the magazine well. It can find your eye faster than you can blink....

Headspace is measured from the bolt-face to the mouth of a straight rimless case like the .45 ACP, whose mouth stops the case from going farther forward. In a belted magnum, the stop is the leading edge of the belt. On a .30-30 case it's the front of the rim. The datum line for rimless or rebated bottleneck rounds like the .270 and .284 lies on the shoulder. Semi-rimmed cartridges theoretically headspace on the rim, but sometimes (as with the .38 Super Automatic) the rim protrusion is insufficient given the action tolerances needed for sure function. The case mouth then serves as a secondary stop. The semi-rimmed .220 Swift has a more substantial lip; but most handloaders prefer to neck-size only, so after a first firing, the case actually headspaces on the shoulder. More on that later. The term "headspace" originated when all cartridges had rims, so the measurement was initially made only at the head. Now rimless and belted rounds are the rule. Headspace as a dimension includes all measures of bolt-face-to-cartridge stop.

Gunsmiths measure headspace with "go" and "no go" gauges. The "go" gauge is typically .004 to .006 shorter than the "no go" gauge for rimless and belted

▲ The wide variety of factory loads now available drains handloads of some of their exclusivity.

cartridges. The bolt should close on a "go" gauge but not on a "no go" gauge. Theoretically, if the bolt closes on a "no go" gauge, the barrel should be set back a thread and rechambered to achieve proper headspace. However, many chambers that accept "no go" gauges are still safe to shoot. The "field" gauge, seldom seen now, has been used to check these (mostly military) chambers. It's roughly .002 longer than a "no go" gauge.

Minimum and maximum headspace measurements are not the same as corresponding minimum and maximum case dimensions. For example, a .30-06 chamber should measure between 1.940 and 1.946, bolt face to shoulder datum line. A .30-06 cartridge usually falls between 1.934 and 1.940. Case gauges machined to close tolerances perform the same check on cartridges that headspace gauges do in chambers. An obvious difference: Case gauges are female and cannot accurately gauge headspace. They simply show whether a cartridge will work in a chamber that's correctly bored and fitted. Headspace is a steel-to-steel measure in the gun. Altering case dimensions *does* change the relationship of cartridge to chamber. And reducing the head-to-datum line length of a hull can result in a *condition* of excess headspace, even if the firearm checks out perfectly.

Once I was sizing cases for a wildcat 6mm cartridge, the .240 Hawk. The custom sizing die had been made to reduce the neck diameter of the .30-06 case without changing the shoulder or datum line. I set up the die initially to full-length resize, so I'd be starting with cartridges that would easily fit the chamber. After one firing, I would neck-size only to get a tighter fit and prolong case life.

My first shot blew gas from all the crevices of the stout Remington 700 action. The case showed a circumferential crack forward of the belt. Because the loads were not stiff, and because the bolt lift did not indicate high pressure, I fired another round. Same result. At the bench, I compared the sized cases with the fired cases. The sized .240 hulls were shorter by nearly .1 inch. I screwed the die into the press but left it 1/8 inch short of contacting the shell-holder. I ran a case into the die, then tried chambering it in the rifle. It wouldn't go. I ran the die down a thread and sized the case again. No go. Lowering the die incrementally and trying the case each time, I finally closed the bolt. It was a snug fit. I looked at the relationship of die and shell-holder. There was a gap of .1 inch—the measure of the difference between fired and unfired cases. Unlike most commercial dies, this one had not been machined to full-length size when flush with the shell-holder. Screwing it down that far, I had made the case .1 shorter than the rifle's chamber. When I fired, the striker drove the case forward .1 inch. The front of the case expanded into the chamber to grip it, and the rear of the case backed up .1 inch against the bolt, pulling the brass apart just ahead of the web.

Pressure spikes can result from an over-length case, when the case-mouth is pinched in the chamber. Case trimming to proper length ensures clean bullet release. This RCBS trimmer makes the job easy. ▶

If headspace can legitimately vary .006, and the corresponding case dimension another .006, it's possible to load a round .012 shorter than the chamber will allow, bolt face to stop. Full-length sizing dies, when set so the shell-holder presses tight at the end of the stroke, should not bring cases below minimum.

Even if rifles and cartridges could be manufactured to zero tolerances, you wouldn't want zero-tolerance chambering in a hunting rifle. The least bit of dust, water, snow or residual oil might prevent easy bolt closure and a missed opportunity. Changes in temperature can also affect cartridge fit. In a revolver, the breech face cannot have contact with the case head without risk of tying up the cylinder. Snug fit of straight cases in autoloading pistols means that any jump *at all* in case length keeps the slide out of battery.

Full-length resizing compresses a cartridge case; firing stretches it. Think for a second about what happens after the repeated bending of the tab on a can of soda pop. To prolong case life, you're better off to neck-size only, so the brass moves little upon firing. Because a cooling hull shrinks after firing (otherwise you couldn't easily extract it), there's no need to further reduce its dimensions *unless you plan to use the ammunition in another rifle that has a slightly smaller chamber*. The only other reason to full-length size (or to use small-base dies that squeeze cases down even further) is to accommodate autoloading or lever- or slide-action rifles that have little cramming power. Some hunters full-length size the cases they'll use on a hunt, to ensure easy chambering in the event they must fire quick follow-up shots.

◀ Weatherby's Mark V action, announced 1957, accommodates huge cartridges like the .378, .460.

Neck sizing is a particularly good practice with belted cases, because chambers for these hulls are often cut generously up front. The critical dimension, after all, is the distance from bolt face to belt face (.220 to .224, "go" to "no go"). If you full-length-size belted magnums, you may be shortening the *head-to-shoulder* span considerably each time—which means the case stretches a lot at each firing. Eventually (sometimes quite soon), you'll notice a white ring forming around the case just ahead of the belt. If you insert a straightened paper clip with a small "L" bend at the end and feel around the inside of the case, you may detect a slight indentation forward of the web. The white ring signals a thinning of the case and shows where the case will separate if you keep full-length sizing the case.

Rechambering rifles to Improved, or sharp-shouldered, cartridges should not change headspace measurement. The reduced body taper and steeper shoulder angle provide greater case capacity, but the datum point on an altered shoulder should remain the original distance from the bolt face. That's why you can fire factory ammunition in an Improved chamber safely. True wildcats that require case forming in dies must sometimes be given a false shoulder to serve as the chamber stop before firing full-power loads. For example, the Gibbs wildcats pioneered in Idaho by Rocky Gibbs in the 1950s, and the more recent Hawk cartridges, are based on the .30-06 with the shoulder moved forward. To fashion the .338 Hawk case, you might neck a .30-06 up to .375, then neck that hull down to .338 in a Hawk die. The result would be a case with two shoulders. The rear one would disappear upon firing. An alternative method would be to neck the .30-06 to .338, then seat a bullet to contact the lands as the bolt is closed. Hard against the lands, the bullet keeps the head of the case tight to the bolt face. Use a reduced powder charge. Handloaders who make false shoulders commonly employ small doses

▲ Few hunters think about headspace. But the shot that gave Dori Riggs this fine Namibian warthog depended on proper fit of the cartridge in the chamber.

of fast powder behind a case filler of corn meal, with a wax cap.

Often shooters who don't understand headspace blame it for all sorts of problems not related to headspace. The first centerfire rifle I owned was a surplus Short Magazine Lee Enfield. The rimmed .303 British cartridges fed like Vaselined sausages, but roughly one in four separated upon firing. Now, several things could have been wrong. Because headspacing on SMLE rifles can be changed merely by switching bolt heads, the bolt itself was even suspect. The cases in this instance were of new commercial brass, so my ammunition escaped scrutiny.

▲ Kimber's long-action 84L is one of the sleekest .30-06 sporters around, and, at 6 pounds, accurate.

I didn't know enough about rifles then to figure out what was wrong, but I did know that repeat shots at whitetails were improbable if I had to wait for the barrel to cool and use a rod with a tight brush to extract the fronts of broken cases. I was loath to part with the rifle, because I'd worked hard for the $15 it cost. My elders, mostly farmers with 97 Winchester pump guns and Krags as old as my .303, didn't know what to tell me. In desperation I took it to an ill-tempered gunsmith, who peered into the breech, examined one of my two-piece cases and declared that I had a "swelled chamber." I didn't know how chambers could swell, but he convinced me to sell him the rifle. My second SMLE cost twice as much, and I slapped down an additional $7.50 for a Herter's walnut stock blank that took weeks to fit. Somewhere I found $10 for a set of Williams sights. The cases all extracted, though, and some deer bit the dust.

Rimmed rifle cases (right) headspace on the rim. Rimless rounds headspace on the shoulder (straight rimless pistol cartridges on the case mouth). ▶

▲ L-R: .458, .338, .264 Winchester Magnums, 7mm Remington Magnum, introduced 1956-1962.

Some years later I spied queer marks on hulls kicked out of an M70 Winchester in .338 Magnum. They were white lines, but not in the usual place. Inspection of the chamber revealed an old gas cut. So I threaded the flash-hole of a fired .338 case and screwed in a ¼ inch rod. Then I chucked the rod in a variable-speed drill and secured the rifle in a vise. After smearing the case body (but not the belt!) with J-B's abrasive paste, I carefully fed the case into the chamber. The drill, turning slowly, polished the chamber without removing so much metal as to materially change its dimensions. It smoothed the edges of the gas cut and reduced its depth. The marks on fired cases all but vanished.

Headspace is a length measurement. It has nothing to do with diameter. Chambers that are egg-shaped or belled by unprincipled cleaning, or whose diameters are larger or smaller than normal may cause problems, but they're not headspace problems. Headspace hinges on reamer dimensions as well as on the machinist's eye and expertise. After long use, reamers cut slightly smaller chambers than when new. New reamers or those used aggressively can bore oversize chambers.

Headspace can change over time. With each firing of your centerfire rifle, some compression of the locking lugs and lug seats occurs. The elasticity of the steel keeps headspace essentially the same. But many firings with heavy loads can drain that elasticity and cause a permanent increase in headspace. A rifle with hard lugs and soft seats and generous headspace can eventually develop so much headspace that a field gauge can be chambered. At this point the rifle is unsafe.

Headspace is a chronic problem with early lever-action rifles built for rimmed rounds. Shooters seldom fret about it, partly because these cartridges, some originally loaded with black powder, develop relatively low pressures. Riflemen who handload for old lever guns wisely keep charges mild. Loose, rear-locking actions are intrinsically difficult to hold to the tolerances of front-locking bolt rifles. Handloaders with ailing saddle guns can keep them in service and prolong case life by peening the rims of cases before firing. Careful peening from the side, with frequent testing in the action, boosts rim thickness to match the chamber cut. Tedious but effective.

There's nothing mysterious about headspace. It's simply a measurement between the bolt-face and the place in the chamber that stops a cartridge from moving farther forward.

▲ With Federal-loaded 130-grain TSXs, the inexpensive T/C Venture shoots beyond its price.

20. Chaos in the rifle

When a primer spits fire into the powder charge and burning commences, gases form, increasing pressure inside the case and (because pressure produces heat), accelerating the burn. On a graph, you'll see a pressure peak that rises steeply after a short horizontal line reflecting the delay between primer detonation and powder ignition. Following the peak, which typically happens within a millisecond (1/1,000 second) after the powder starts to burn, the pressure curve arcs back down. This decline is relatively gradual as the bullet moves forward, increasing the volume behind it. The faster the powder, the steeper the curve on both sides. The area under this pressure/time curve translates to bullet velocity. Two to three milliseconds after the striker hits the primer, pressure has dropped to zero. The bullet is on its way.

A 180-grain bullet from a .300 Weatherby Magnum exits the muzzle of a 26 inch barrel about 1 ¼ milliseconds after it starts to move. This chart shows what happens (data adapted from a pressure/time curve in the excellent text "Any Shot You Want," a loading manual by Art Alphin's A-Square company):

Time (seconds)	Pressure (PSI)	Velocity (fps)	Distance (in)
0	0	0	0
0.0001	12,000	60	0.02
0.0003	36,000	500	0.60
0.0005	60,000 (near peak)	1,400	2.80
0.0007	42,000	2,350	7.40
0.0009	24,000	2,970	13.80
0.0011	6,000	3,250	21.30
0.0013	100	3,300	26.00

A few things to note: First, peak pressure comes when the bullet has moved only about 3 inches, even with the slow-burning fuels appropriate for a .300 magnum. The pressure drops off fast, too, losing 90 percent of its vigor in the next 18 inches of barrel. But the bullet continues to accelerate as pressure behind it diminishes. Between 14 and 21 inches, pressure loss totals 18,000 PSI. But bullet speed increases 300 fps! With very little pressure remaining behind it at the muzzle, the bullet is still accelerating! The value of a long barrel is clear, even if nearly all of it is used to control the tail of the pressure/time curve.

A pressure/distance curve differs from a pressure/time curve in slope, but it has the same general shape: steeper at the start than at the finish. The area under a pressure/distance curve represents the amount of energy available from the bullet. However, the energy generated is not all available downrange. A lot of it is lost in thermal (heat) transmission, expansion of the case into the chamber wall, bullet/rifling friction, even bullet rotation. Plotting a load's pressure/distance curve helps designers of gas-operated autoloading rifles because these rifles must tap the gas at some point in the bullet's travel. Too much pressure, and the slamming can damage rifle parts. Too little, and bolt travel is insufficient to clear the fired case.

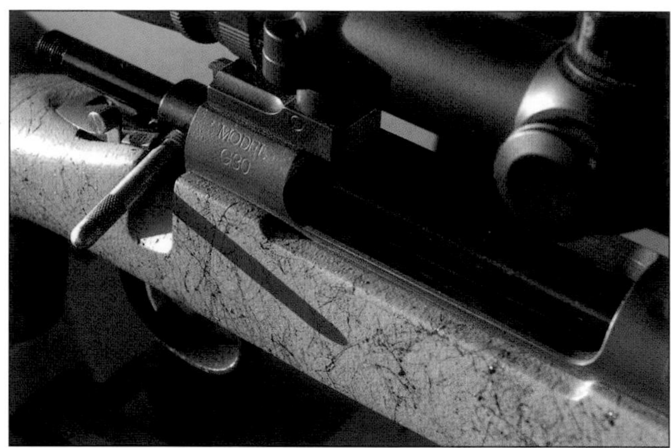

▲ Use a bore guide when cleaning to prevent wear in chamber or throat.

Measuring gas pressure proved as difficult at first as measuring bullet velocity. Then, in the mid-1800s, Alfred Nobel and an American named Rodman came up with solutions to that problem at the same time. Rodman's, the crusher system, is still in use. It's a factory procedure not easily or safely performed in a home shop. A small cylindrical piston is slid into a hole in the barrel of a test gun, and a copper or lead pellet is inserted snugly between the top of the piston and a stationary anvil. When the rifle is fired, the piston pushes against the pellet or crusher, shortening it. The difference in lengths of the crusher, before and after firing, is then converted mathematically to a pressure range, in units of CUP or LUP (copper units of pressure or lead units of pressure). Copper crushers are generally either .146 in diameter and .400 long to start with, or .225 in diameter and .500 long. The choice depends on application. Copper crushers work best for centerfire rifles and handguns that generate substantial pressures. Lead crushers (.325 x .500) typically register the low-pressure loads in rimfire guns and shotguns (though small-diameter copper crushers can be used

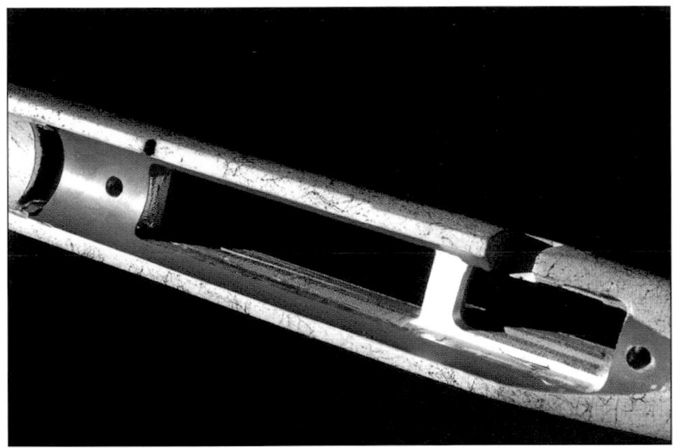

◀ Bedding can affect accuracy. Glass-bedding the action, floating a heavy barrel is popular practice.

too). Crushers are calibrated in a test press. Subsequent pressure measurements yield "Tarage Tables" that enable technicians to calculate the pressure in a rifle chamber tested with a similar crusher.

Pounded by high pressures, crushers don't register *peak* pressure accurately because the flow of the copper is slower than the change of pressure in the chamber. Also, the moving piston must be brought to a halt, which skews a reading in the opposite direction. There's no balancing out here, just conflicting forces. *Copper units of pressure and lead units of pressure are not the same; nor can they be interchanged with another common unit of pressure, pounds per square inch (PSI).* CUP value may coincide with PSI value; for example, SAAMI lists 28,000 as maximum average pressure for the .45-70. Both CUP and PSI units apply.

◀ Like its R93 predecessor, the Blaser R8 has a straight-feed magazine. But the R8's is removable.

But maximum average pressure for the .243 is 52,000 CUP and 60,000 PSI. Most cartridges show similar discrepancies. Sadly, there's no easy way to convert CUP to PSI or vice versa.

A more modern device for pressure measurement in firearms is the piezoelectric gauge. It registers an electric charge delivered through a transducer when a crystal is crushed. Pressure applied to the crystal yields a proportional transducer reading in pounds per square inch. Conformal transducers are installed in the barrel, just like crusher pistons, and become part of the barrel. External transducers can be mounted on the barrel, then removed for replacement or calibration checks.

▲ Phil Quick tries out a 50-caliber rifle. A brake tames recoil; the concussion is still formidable.

Another pressure tester that's become popular among shooters is the strain gauge. Developed for the consumer market by chronograph guru Ken Oehler, it's essentially a piece of wire that you glue to the outside of your chamber wall. When you fire the rifle, the chamber expands and the wire stretches. Wire length is then compared with a previous measure to get a stretch reading that translates into pressure. These readings do not equate with readings from a crusher or piezoelectric gauge. The way to use a strain gauge is to read pressures from factory loads and maximum recommended loads and determine relative pressures of hunting loads by comparing values.

21. Figuring bullet flight

Even a fast automobile moves at a glacial pace, compared to a bullet. A sedan traveling 60 miles per hour covers 88 feet per second. Relatively sedate rifle loads cough bullets out at 2,500 fps.

A bullet decelerates as soon as it escapes the thrust of powder gas—that is, as soon as it exits the barrel. Air resistance and friction, plus the turbulence set up in flight, act like brakes. All the while, gravity pulls the bullet toward earth at the accelerating rate of 32 fps. Energy measured in foot-pounds is a function of bullet weight and the square of bullet velocity, so as the bullet slows, it loses its authority.

Most bullets travel too fast for us to see. So measuring their speed and tracing their path proved difficult for the first shooters. Then in 1537 a brilliant Italian scientist named Trataglia wrote a ballistics book. He postulated that bullets traveled in arcs, a radical idea when many people assumed bullets flew straight until spent, then fell abruptly to earth. Trataglia also experimented to determine the launch angle that would give a bullet its greatest range, and found this angle to be near 45 degrees. This is much steeper than the angle you'd choose to give a .30-06 bullet its greatest reach. But Trataglia's conclusion was valid. At the very low velocities of his day, gravity has a far greater effect than air resistance on a bullet's flight. Modern high-speed bullets, in contrast, are influenced less by gravity than by drag.

A century later, in a trajectory study for the Venice arsenal, Galileo dropped cannon balls from the Leaning Tower of Pisa. He concluded that because the acceleration of gravity was constant, a bullet's path must be parabolic. Galileo affirmed Trataglia's finding of 45 degrees as the launch angle for maximum range. His experiments did not take drag into account because, again, in those days projectiles were very heavy, very slow. Compared to the acceleration of gravity, drag on a cannonball dropped from a window was inconsequential!

Another century passed before Englishman Benjamin Robins devised a ballistic pendulum. Firing a bullet of known weight into its heavy wooden bob, also precisely weighed, Robins calculated velocity by measuring the pendulum's swing. His colleagues in the 1740s could hardly believe that a 75-caliber musket ball traveled at the blinding speed of 1,500 fps! Low readings farther from the bob indicated that drag on the ball was 85 times as strong as the force of gravity! That too seemed incredible. Measurements of drag would eventually bear out the results of Robins' work, but they would have to wait many decades, for the development of the chronograph.

Robins was in good company. Sir Isaac Newton, who had died only 15 years before he began his pendulum experiments, had come up with important observations in the fields of physics and mathematics. One was the universal law of gravitation, which declares that the force of gravity varies with altitude. Sir Isaac's fundamental laws of mechanics, and his development of calculus (Leibnitz worked on calculus in Germany at the same time), were crucial pieces in the complex puzzle of ballistics. Newton showed that drag increases with the density of air and the cross-sectional area of the projectile. He also demon-

◀ Rich Folsland readies for a long shot, bipod supporting his rifle. He nailed a very fine pronghorn!

▼ Sam Shaw wrings out a CVA Apex rifle at the bench, testing several types of .308 ammunition.

strated a relationship between drag and the *square* of the projectile's speed. Because he had no way to measure the speed of musket balls, he could not know that drag increases dramatically when projectiles approach the speed of sound (1,120 fps).

Late in the nineteenth century, scientists hit upon the idea of a "standard" bullet, of certain dimensions and weight and with specific flight characteristics. Deriving ballistic coefficient, or C, was a logical next step. Ballisticians the world over were soon making drag calculations. The best-known were by Krupp in Germany and the Gavre Commission in France. The Krupp standard bullet was a flat-based conical, 3-calibers long, with a 2-caliber ogive. Shortly after the Krupp data was published, a Russian colonel named Mayevski developed a mathematical model that showed the drag deceleration of this bullet. A formula by Russian Colonel Mayevski became the basis for tables by US Army Colonel James Ingalls. Published in 1893 and revised in 1917, the Ingalls tables feature a standard Krupp bullet, similar in form to modern hunting bullets. While matching bullets by shape and weight provides serviceable C values, velocity affects ballistic coefficient too. Because drag increases with speed, you can't expect shooting tests of the same bullet at different speeds to yield the same C. For the same reason, tests of different bullets at different speeds are invalid for determining C.

"It's common to see differences of 10 percent between calculated Cs and those determined by our firing tests," say technical experts at Sierra Bullets. Lacking facilities to test C by shooting, you can get a usable value with this formula: C = w/id2, where w is bullet weight in pounds, d is bullet diameter in inches and i is the form factor. C includes sectional density and the bullet's weight divided by the square of its diameter (w/d2). Form factor, i, has to do with the bullet's profile. Long, pointed bullets with tapered heels have high sectional densities and high Cs. Blunt bullets of the same weight have high sectional densities, but less aerodynamic form, which means lower Cs and steeper deceleration rates.

The most streamlined match and VLD (very low drag) bullets have C values approaching .600. Magazine length and seating depth can make use of VLD bullets impractical in hunting rifles that accept bullets with C values of .400. Changes in drag, which most directly affects bullet drop, do not correspond linearly to changes in C. A bullet with a C of .600 and a starting velocity of 3,000 fps falls about 58 inches at 500 yards. A bullet with a C of .400 sags 65 inches—not much more, given the 33-percent change in C. Remaining energy more closely reflects changes in point of impact than differences in C: here, 2,256 ft-lbs for the first

Factory charts are sometimes inaccurate. A chronograph (here Pact screens) reveal true speed. ▶

▲ Don Ward fires a custom 10/22 Ruger. A .22 Long Rifle bullet hits top speed in a 16 inch barrel.

bullet, 1,929 for the second. At distance, high C helps you more than does a fast launch. A faster bullet has a higher deceleration rate and has shed its advantage at long range, where the high C exerts proportionately more influence.

If you reduce velocity by 500 fps, to 2,500 fps, both bullets drop much farther over 500 yards. The bullet with a C of .600 drops 85 inches—27 inches more than it did at a starting velocity of 3,000 fps. The bullet with a C of .400 drops 96 inches—31 inches more than it did with the faster start. Remaining energy: 1,835 and 1,551 ft-lbs. It seems that *a reduction in velocity only half as great (by percentage) as a reduction in ballistic coefficient* can have a *greater* effect on bullet drop and remaining energy at distance.

A couple of other things to remember: A change in C has a larger effect on remaining velocities at high muzzle velocities than at low ones, because as bullets speed up, drag increases as a percentage of the forces impeding bullet flight. Secondly, a change in C has a greater effect on drop at lower velocities than at high ones, because at low speeds, gravity takes a more active hand than drag in depressing a bullet's arc.

Ballistic coefficients change markedly near the speed of sound.

The retarding effect of air friction is enormous. In a vacuum, a 150-grain .30-06 bullet fired at 2,700 fps at a 45-degree upward angle can fly 43 miles! The same bullet fired at the same speed and angle through our atmosphere falls to earth just two miles out, victim of air resistance 56 times as strong as gravity! The higher the velocity, the stronger the drag. Drag comprises several factors. Their sum depends on bullet speed, weight and profile, as well as axial spin and atmospheric conditions. Jacket texture affects drag via "skin friction." A sharp nose reduces "pressure drag," but so does supersonic speed. "Wave drag" results from the shock of a bullet traveling above the speed of sound. "Base drag" comes in the bullet's wake; a tapered heel or boat-tail bullet minimizes base drag at distance.

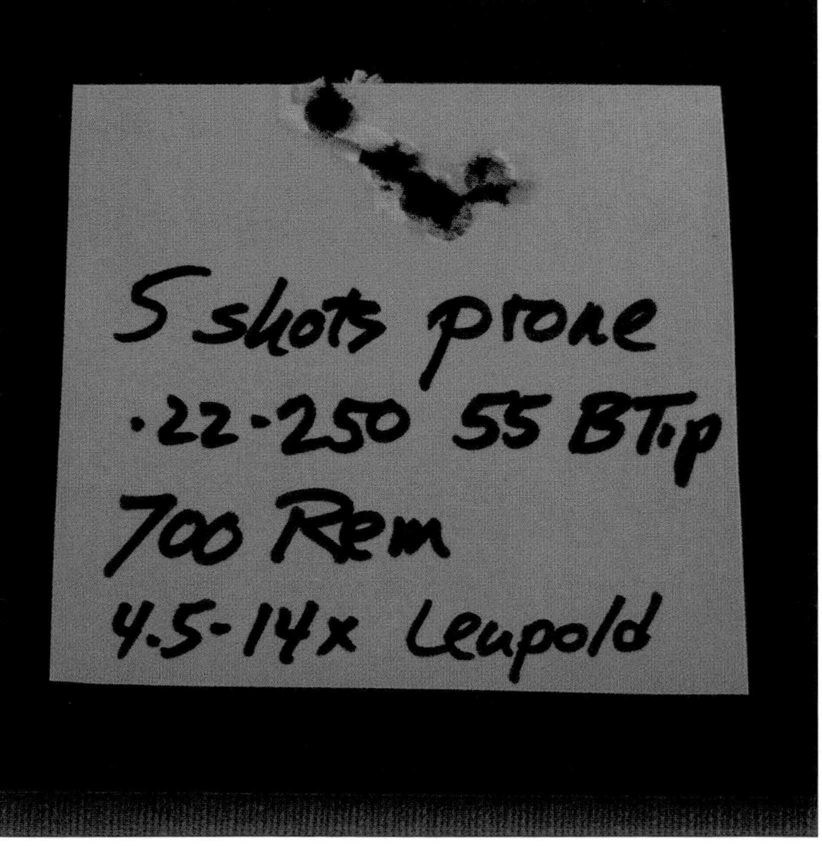

Wayne fired this 1 inch five-shot group prone, the sling taut on a Remington 700 in .22-250. ▶

22. More on speed

The first instruments to gauge bullet speed were mechanical—notably Robins' pendulum in the eighteenth century. Movement of the pendulum when it was struck gave Mr. Robins the information he needed to calculate the bullet's speed, because speed is a component of momentum. We no longer measure velocity with pendulums, but with electric eyes that register the passage of a bullet's shadow as the bullet travels a known distance. The device is a chronograph.

Chronographs are a century old, but it wasn't that long ago that Texan Dr. Ken Oehler designed and built the first chronographs meant for consumer use. Before Oehler's instruments, chronographs were found only in the laboratories and shooting tunnels of ammunition companies. They were fixed in place. They were very costly. Consequently, shooters could only take the catalog ballistics charts at face value, and hope their handloads were producing the pressures and bullet speeds listed in the loading manuals. Now every serious shooter I know has a chronograph. Portable and easy to use, some are less expensive than an ordinary rifle-scope!

Dick Williams set up a Chrony chronograph. Reading velocities is essential in tuning handloads. ▼

▲ One of the first riflemen to test the .300 RCM, Wayne used an Oehler 35 chronograph.

Portable chronographs have "screens"—electric eyes—set up a short distance apart on a bar or even directly on the electronic box that gives you a velocity reading. The chronograph measures the time (hence, "chrono") between the bullet's passage over the first screen and its passage over the second. Just as you could drive a car a quarter mile and compute the number of miles per hour your car would travel at that speed, so you can time bullet flight for a short distance and extrapolate. Some chronographs allow you to

SPEED, ENERGY, AND ARC

adjust the distance between screens. The greater the distance, the more accurate the read. The chronograph must be precisely calibrated for the span between screens, or it won't read velocities correctly. Also, you must shoot squarely through the opening above the screens, as an angled shot, horizontally or vertically, effectively increases the distance the bullet travels during its timed flight.

You get lots of information from a chronograph: bullet speed for each shot, of course, but also average bullet speed for a string of several shots. The average, or mean velocity, is the sum of all recorded velocities divided by the number of shots you fired. The instrument will also tell you the extreme spread (ES)—that is, the range of velocities, slowest to fastest. ES is useful because you want a load that delivers uniform velocity. While it's unrealistic to expect all shots to stay within 5 fps of each other, I've often seen more than 100 fps variation between slowest and fastest readings. If a hunting load delivers good accuracy and adequate speed, and ES stays within 25 fps, that ammunition shouldn't disappoint you on a hunt. Some loads do better; some work hard to meet that standard.

Another number you'll get from modern chronographs is standard deviation. Credited to American statistician Karl Pearson, this statistical term appeared in the late 1890s. Without wading into mathematics, which had me in a headlock from grammar school through my PhD program, I can summarize standard deviation as the positive square root of the variance. What's variance? It's simply the sum of the squares of the deviations from the mean of your chronograph readings, divided by a number that's one less than the number of times you shot. A high standard deviation indicates a lot of spread in your data—that is, a great deal of variability among your readings. A low SD means that most of your readings were clustered close to your mean.

Texas rifle-maker Charlie Sisk deftly uses a computer to asses wildcat cartridge performance. ▼

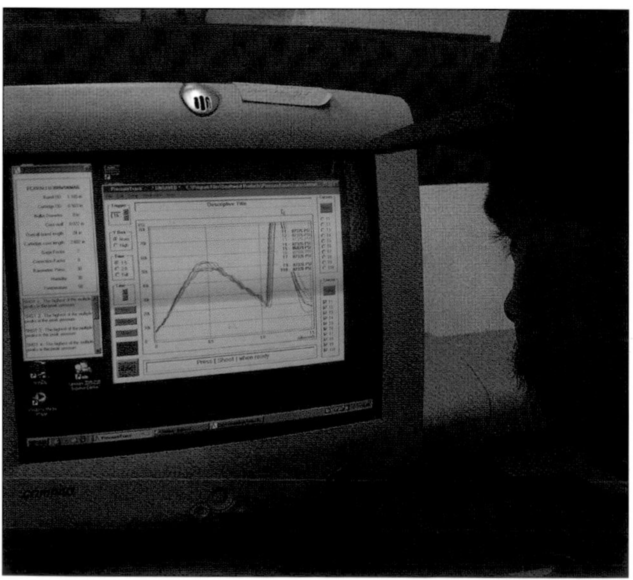

There's more to milk from standard deviation. With it, you can construct a bell curve that shows how your velocities grouped around the mean, and, for any given speed range, the percentage of shots likely to fall within that range. Occasionally you'll get a velocity reading you don't believe. It may be the chronograph didn't register the bullet's passage properly. Or the load was somehow defective. One rule of thumb to keep SD useful: Throw out any reading more than 2 ½ times the SD from the mean.

Bullet velocity varies not only with the powder type and charge and bullet weight; it's influenced by chamber and barrel dimensions, throat shape and length and bore finish. A tight chamber reduces the amount of energy lost in case expansion. So does a tight throat. But a long throat that allows the bullet to move before engaging the rifling and permits long seating of the bullet to increase powder space enables a handloader to add fuel, boosting velocity. That long throat is generally thought to be less than desirable for accuracy; but on hunting rifles it's not a liability. Roy Weatherby used long throats and ambitious Norma loadings to give his magnums lots of pep. My pal John Burns, one of the principals in GreyBull Precision, insists that long throats *cut to a minimum diameter* sacrifice no accuracy but give you more throttle than the short throats commonly associated with target rifles.

Bore dimensions and rifling type affect pressures and bullet speed. Some barrels seem to "shoot faster" than others that by all appearances should give the same performance. Bore finish is pretty much invisible, but you can feel it. The consensus of many barrel-makers is that smooth lands and grooves boost accuracy. "But you can get a bore *too* smooth," one pointed out. "If you make it glass-smooth, you increase friction. It's sticky, like the surface of a glass table." Increased friction means higher pressures, which can increase speed; however, if your ammunition already tops the velocity charts, cork-popping pressure is not what you want. More velocity *without* higher pressure is the goal.

Barrel length also makes a difference in bullet speed. How much difference per inch depends on the original and finished lengths, the original velocity, the cartridge and powder and bullet. The only way to tell for sure how much velocity you gain with a long barrel or lose with a short barrel is to chop a very long barrel shorter an inch at a time. Such tests show great variation. One, conducted by A-Square with a .300 Winchester pressure barrel, measured velocities at 1 inch increments from 28 down to 16 inches. Loads of 70.5 grains IMR 4350 with a 150-grain Nosler Ballistic Tip, and 78.0 grains RL-22 with a 180-grain Sierra Spitzer gave these results:

BARREL LENGTH	VELOCITY, FPS, 150-GR	VELOCITY, FPS, 180-GR	VELOCITY LOSS, FPS, 150/180
28 inches	3346	3134	
26 inches	3268	3089	78/45
24 inches	3211	3016	57/73
22 inches	3167	2966	44/50
20 inches	3108	2930	59/36
18 inches	3014	2874	94/56
16 inches	2903	2748	111/126

Velocity loss per inch of barrel length varies from a low of 22 fps to a high of 56 fps for the 150-grain bullet, and 18 fps to 63 fps for the 180-grain bullet. That range could be expected to vary with other .300 Winchester Magnum loads. Certainly it would differ for other cartridges with faster-burning powders. Note that rate of velocity loss increases substantially as the barrel is lopped to less than 20 inches in length.

Logic tells us that we're cutting into the descending sector of the pressure curve, before it flattens out. A lot of pressure is being released to the atmosphere instead of staying in harness behind the bullet. Based on the figures presented here, you lose relatively little speed and energy chopping a barrel from 24 to 22 inches.

Hornady's .300 and .338 RCM cartridges were designed to deliver high speeds in carbine-length barrels. The cutting-edge propellants in these rounds are also used in the company's Superformance ammo. No doubt that powder technology will find its way into other loads, industry-wide. Expect a shift in the conventional ballistic wisdom that has favored long barrels over short.

Changing components affects pressures and velocities. Substituting magnum primers for standard primers, for example, can hike pressure by several percentage points. At full throttle, increasing pressure (by whatever means) kicks velocity up a little—but not proportionately. Similar changes occur when you substitute cases with smaller powder chambers (thicker walls or webs). Pressure goes up; velocity follows but not at the same rate. Switching bullets, you may see no significant change in velocity. However, if the new bullet has a longer shank and generates more friction in the bore, or is seated closer to the lands on take-off, or is very slightly larger in diameter, or has a "sticky" jacket, pressures can rise. Remington's use of Nosler Partition bullets for the first .300 Ultra Mag loads no doubt disappointed the folks at Swift, who were already supplying Partition-style A-Frame bullets to Remington. The rationale: A-Frame jackets were softer, resulting in more bore friction and higher pressures. To get 180-grain bullets going as fast as they wanted them too in the new Ultra Mag, Remington engineers chose the Noslers.

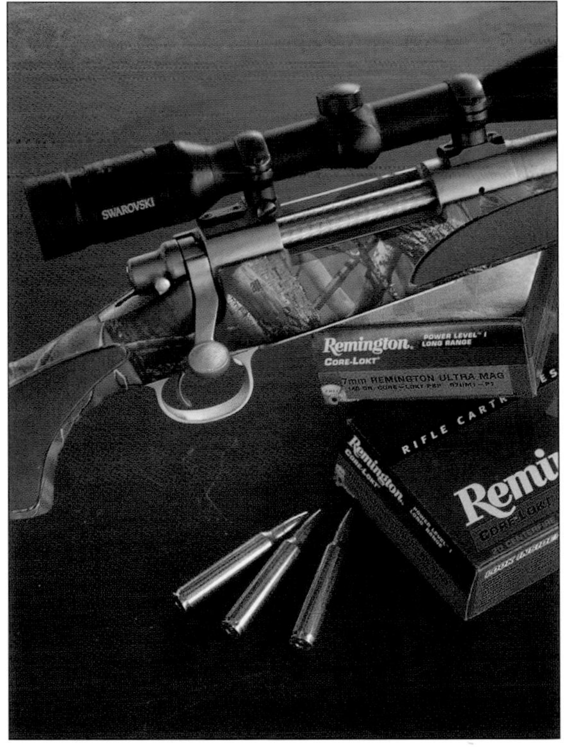

This Swarvoski-scoped Remington 700 is chambered to the fast-stepping 7mm Ultra Mag. ▶

23. Knockdown is a myth

Not long ago I met on safari a fellow toting a rifle in .416 Weatherby Magnum. It is a truly potent cartridge, its 400-grain bullets pummeling targets with 6,400 ft-lbs of energy. The ferocious recoil can be throttled back to merely unpleasant by a muzzle brake, if you can brook the land-mine concussion. "Nice rifle," I said, admiring the Mark V's lovely walnut. A couple of days later, this fellow had to follow blue wildebeest he had crippled with that .416. Raw power, it seems, is no substitute for precise shooting.

In Sweden, where thousands of moose are shot each year, sportsmen favor the old 6.5x55 cartridge over more potent rounds. The .30-06 is next in popularity, then the .308 Winchester. As a hunting guide, I've watched hunters tip over elk with lightweight bullets from .270-class rifles. I've also seen elk run after being hammered repeatedly with bullets that dumped frightful doses of energy. The key to sure kills: bullet placement. Only when you've learned to shoot accurately can you get tangible benefits from turbo-charged bullets that fly flatter than the curve of the earth and deliver a ton of smash in the next time zone.

The notion that your bullet must carry a certain level of kinetic energy to kill big game is widely accepted because it makes sense. In truth, it is flawed. I have it on good report that a couple of fellows, on a dare, once killed an elephant with a .22 rimfire. They downed this huge beast by swatting it with less than 140 ft-lbs of energy. Most assuredly a stunt, it points up the absurdity of measuring lethality in foot-pounds.

Norma's Africa PH series features tough bullets for tough game, like the .300-grain Woodleigh softpoints in .375. ▼

Dale Gardner made an excellent shot with his Kimber in 7mm-08 to down this magnificent kudu. ▶

The counter argument is that most sportsmen want to take advantage of the first reasonable shot opportunity. They might concede that a pellet from a frisky air gun would kill a deer shot through the ear at spitwad range. But who courts that limitation? If we see a buck climbing the next ridge, we expect the rifle in our hands to down it quickly with a shot to the front ribs.

When you can't insert a bullet like a needle in a vein, you need extra energy to knock an animal down. At least, that's the common conclusion. It's only partly valid. More energy does result in more tissue damage, which can hasten or ensure death. On the other hand, a more powerful blow does not necessarily mean the animal will fall down right away. That's because animals are rarely knocked down by bullets. A bullet, after all, is not an automobile or a locomotive, both of which knock animals down regularly. Even a big bullet is tiny, compared to the animal. Its lethality depends in large measure on its speed. For example, a centerfire rifle bullet moving 2,000 fps is now considered sluggish. A bullet striking a deer at less than 1,400 fps may not even upset properly. In comparison, a sedan traveling at 88 fps (60 mph) not only kills a deer instantly upon collision, but throws it, inflicting terrific internal damage and perhaps dismembering it.

Dangerous animals must not only be killed but stopped. Hunters in Africa rely on cartridges like the .458 Winchester Magnum to drop game as big as elephants right away. I've seen elephants struck by .458 bullets collapse as if struck by lightning. The .458 sends about 5,000 ft-lbs of energy out the muzzle—2 ½ tons of knock-down punch, say some. But the bullet energy-to-animal weight ratio of a .458 to an elephant is about the same as that of a .22 Long Rifle to a big whitetail deer. If a .458 can be counted on to stop an elephant, why doesn't the .22 deck big deer?

I'll recount here a clever experiment one fellow devised to test knock-down power. He fashioned handles for a thick steel plate so he could support it in front of him on the edge of a table. Then, from close range, a friend fired into the plate with a 500-grain softnose from a .458. The bullet spent its 2-½ tons of kinetic energy on the plate without knocking the man down! **Caution!** *Despite previous firings to ensure that the bullet would not penetrate the steel, this exercise entailed some risk; firing a bullet toward another person is never a safe practice and cannot be recommended!* Firearms etiquette aside, the results of this exercise are insightful. They suggest there's no such thing as knock-down power in bullets. Animals fall down when they are fatally stricken—either weakened by blood loss or denied the function of a vital organ. A bullet can appear to slap the animal to earth when it hits a supporting bone or destroys nerves that control the legs. A bullet doesn't kill deer in the woods the way a dump truck kills deer on the highway.

▲ The powerful .450 Alaskan, a wildcat on the .348 Winchester, was once popular in the Model 71.

The reaction of game to a bullet, like the lethality of a hit, depends on bullet placement as well as on the energy package. It also depends on what the bullet does. Hiking energy increases the likelihood of a quick kill only if the bullet can translate that energy into the destruction of vital organs. More power can mean deeper penetration (a longer wound channel) or more violent expansion (a wider wound channel) or both. You may get more value from one than from the other.

The notion that very fast bullets kill quicker has some merit. High velocity means more violent bullet expansion, all else equal. Quick energy release can be instantly lethal. The results of explosive bullet action on small animals are often used to argue the case for high-speed. But there is no shoulder-fired rifle that can kill deer in the manner that a .22-250 unhinges prairie dogs.

◀ In Africa, reliability counts as much as accuracy, power. This PH favors a CZ rifle in .416 Rigby.

◀ L-R: .338 Winchester, .338 Ultra Mag, .340 Weatherby. All deliver over 4,000 ft-lbs of energy.

Deer and other big game animals commonly survive some seconds or minutes after a well-placed and lethal shot from a powerful cartridge. Once, I fired at a whitetail that slipped into view 80 yards away. I called a good hit in the forward ribs. But the buck ran off as if not hurt at all. I eased over to where the deer had stood and found nothing but a faint scuff-mark in the forest floor. No blood. No hair. Carefully I circled the mark. Eventually I found a bit of lung tissue the size of a BB. Tracks put me on an exit trail. On the third try I caught the buck's right-angle turn and found blood. Shortly, I came upon my prize, dead. The 150-grain .300 Savage bullet had penetrated both lungs. The buck had died in mid-stride only seconds after the hit. Would it have been a quicker kill with a faster bullet? That's hard to say. Explosive bullet action can drop an animal that might stagger off or run when hit in the same place by a slower or less frangible bullet. But the outcome is the same: an animal soon dead. Explosive rupture works against you when the animal is big and quartering and you must have a deep-penetrating bullet to reach the vitals.

I borrowed a .30-30 rifle once to hunt blacktail deer. As luck would have it, I spied a dandy four-point as it bounced from a blackberry thicket only 30 yards off. I led him too much at first, then corrected and hit his shoulder. The last of my four shots caught him in the rear ribs as he cleared a deadfall going away. He lay dead perhaps 40 yards beyond. A more powerful round, especially one firing a fast-opening bullet, might have put the skids under that buck with the first hit. The second might have sent him into a somersault. But those pokey .30-30 bullets were still lethal.

I think the allure of super-potent cartridges has to do, at least in part, with the perverse notion that recoil tests manliness. That is, if you shoot a big cartridge, you're more of a male than someone who shoots a small cartridge. As Jack O'Connor might have said, this is the purest of applesauce. You can set a very powerful rifle against a sack of rolled oats and shoot it comfortably all day long. What does this say about rolled oats? Shooting is not about absorbing recoil; it's

L-R: .338-06 A-Square, .338 Federal, .338 RCM. Great alternatives to heavy-bullet .30-06 loads. ▶

▲ Phil Quick approaches a deer after it fell to a long shot from a GreyBull rifle in 7mm Rem. Mag.

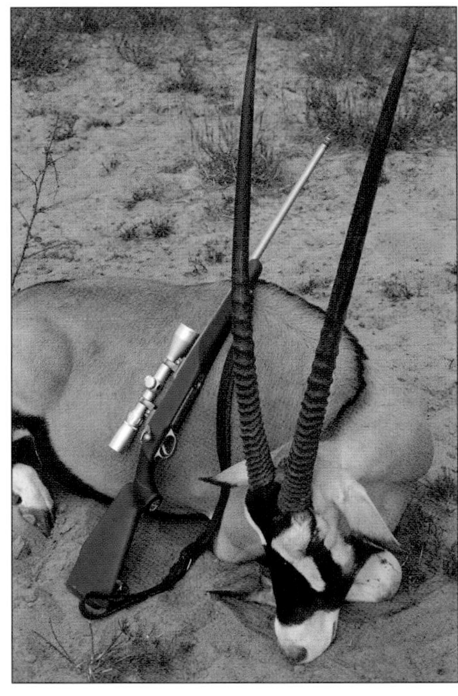

◀ Wayne killed this Namibian gemsbok with a Sako rifle in .30-06. Using Federal ammunition.

▼ Gemsbok are notoriously tough, but Shannon Jackson got her bull with one well-placed shot.

Wayne heart-shot this buffalo with an iron-sighted Savage rifle. His TSX bullet drove through. ▶

▲ Professional hunter Jamy Traut tries out a .470 Heym double, plain but trim and finely balanced.

about hitting a target. There *are* legitimate reasons for buying rifles in magnum chamberings. But you might do some math before selling that '06.

Without accuracy, bullet speed and energy accomplish as much as a locomotive jumping the rails.

Over the years, various measures of killing power have been proposed. Naturally, bullet speed, weight, diameter and upset all contribute to the terminal effects of a shot. Some hunters (famously, Elmer Keith) have argued that in the calculation of energy commonly used in ballistics tables, velocity plays too big a part. Alternative formulae put more emphasis on bullet weight. To get more speed is to accept lighter bullets; to get heavier bullets, we concede velocity. Wherever in the weight-velocity spectrum a bullet falls, its construction must match. That is, it must deliver a wide wound channel deep enough to penetrate the vitals. But some shots are taken obliquely, and the vitals may lie behind a shoulder the size of a truck axle. A bullet that delivers explosive upset and adequate penetration through deer ribs at 200 yards will likely fail on a quartering elk at 20.

Given the variable endemic to any field shooting, the all-around hunting bullet is at best a bullet that performs adequately most of the time and perfectly once in a while. Still, shooters have pursued for decades a scale to rank the relative effectiveness of big game loads. Many break down at the extremes of bullet weight and velocity. Among the few with real merit is the H.I.T.S scale. Developed by my colleague Steve Johnson, who works at Hornady, it incorporates all the important factors that make hunting bullets lethal. Here's how it works:

▼ Wayne killed this caribou with a .300 Ultra Mag. A .243 would have worked every bit as well.

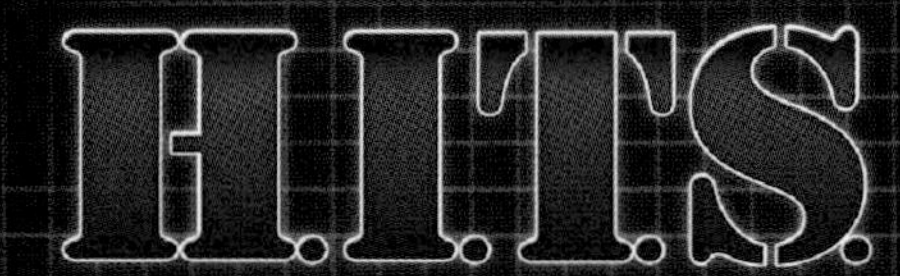

Hornady Index of Terminal Standards

Provided courtesy of Hornady

The Hornady Index of Terminal Standards (H.I.T.S.) is intended as a **guideline** to help hunters compare cartridge and bullet combinations. Beginners and seasoned hunters alike will find these standards useful when sorting through online chat room discussions and gun shop "hype" to make sense of an onslaught of varying information.

The index considers variables such as impact velocity, ballistic coefficient, sectional density and bullet weight. Bullet construction is another important factor in determining the best combination. H.I.T.S. is intended for use with hunting bullets, as match bullets may perform unpredictably on game animals.

Remember, H.I.T.S. is merely a **guideline** to help you choose the proper bullet/cartridge combination. Be sure to consider impact velocity and bullet construction and select a bullet that is appropriate for your situation. A quick reference guide of Hornady bullets is listed on the right.

The H.I.T.S. rating on Hornady ammunition is based on: 100 yard impact velocities for rifles,muzzleloaders, and shotguns and 50 yard impact velocities for handguns. **See how your favorite handload stacks up: Visit www.hornady.com/ballistics to use the online H.I.T.S. calculator.**

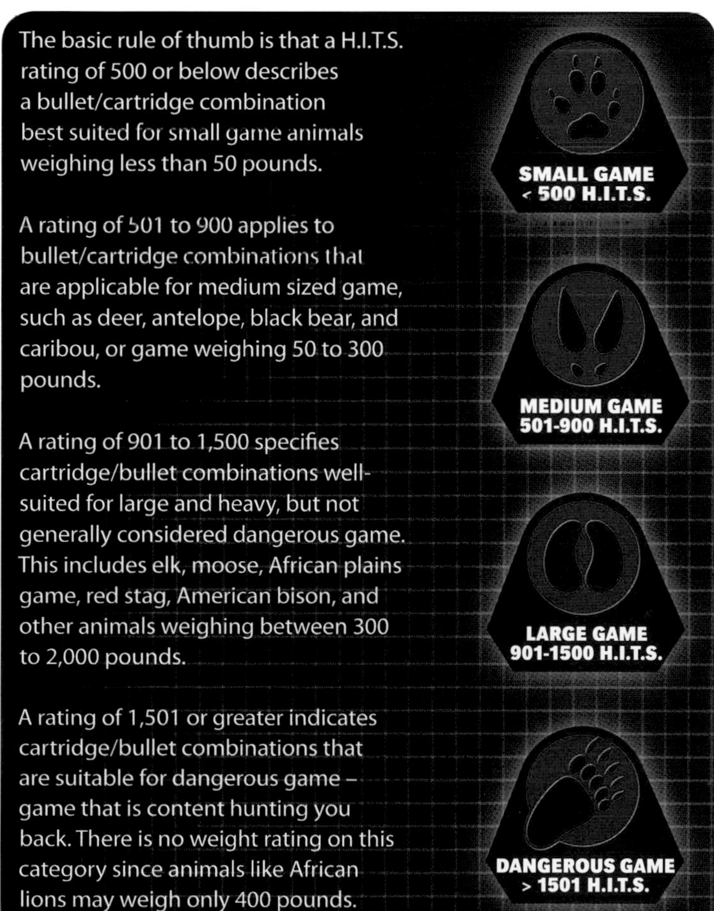

The basic rule of thumb is that a H.I.T.S. rating of 500 or below describes a bullet/cartridge combination best suited for small game animals weighing less than 50 pounds.

A rating of 501 to 900 applies to bullet/cartridge combinations that are applicable for medium sized game, such as deer, antelope, black bear, and caribou, or game weighing 50 to 300 pounds.

A rating of 901 to 1,500 specifies cartridge/bullet combinations well-suited for large and heavy, but not generally considered dangerous game. This includes elk, moose, African plains game, red stag, American bison, and other animals weighing between 300 to 2,000 pounds.

A rating of 1,501 or greater indicates cartridge/bullet combinations that are suitable for dangerous game – game that is content hunting you back. There is no weight rating on this category since animals like African lions may weigh only 400 pounds.

Hornady Bullet Guide

V-MAX™ and Traditional Varmint - Rapid, explosive expansion. Recommended muzzle velocity range: 2000 to 4000+ fps

InterBond™ - Rapid, controlled expansion with deep penetration. Recommended muzzle velocity range: 2000 to 3600 fps

SST® (Super Shock Tip) - Rapid, controlled expansion with deep penetration. Recommended muzzle velocity range: 2000 to 3300 fps

Traditional Hunting InterLock™ (RN, SP, SP-RP, FP, HP) - Controlled expansion with deep penetration. Recommended muzzle velocity range: 2000 to 3300 fps

FTX™ (available only in factory loaded ammunition) - Rapid, controlled expansion with deep penetration. Recommended muzzle velocity range: Handgun 800 to 2100 fps and Rifle 1800 to 3000 fps.

DGX™ Dangerous Game eXpanding - Deep penetration with highly controlled expansion. Recommended muzzle velocity range: 1700 to 3000+ fps

DGS™ Dangerous Game Solid - Deepest penetration with NO expansion. Recommended muzzle velocity range: 1700 to 3000+fps

FMJ (rifle and handgun) -No expansion, deep penetration. Recommended muzzle velocity range: N/A

XTP™ -Controlled expansion with deep penetration. Recommended muzzle velocity range: 700 to 1500 fps

XTP MAG™ -Controlled expansion with deep penetration at higher velocities than the original XTP. Recommended muzzle velocity range: 1200 to 2300 fps

FPB™ and SST-ML w/ Flex-Tip® technology -Rapid, controlled expansion with deep penetration. Recommended muzzle velocity range: 800 to 2300 fps

A-MAX™ and BTHP Match -Rapid, explosive expansion with limited penetration. Recommended muzzle velocity range: 2000+ fps. These bullets are not recommended for hunting medium and large game.

HORNADY PRODUCT LINES

V Varmint Express™ **LE** LEVERevolution® **C** Custom™ **LM** Light Mag™ **HM** Heavy Mag™ **T** TAP FPD™ **M** Match **DG** Dangerous Game Series

	Ammo Description				Velocity (fps) / Energy (ft/lb)						Trajectory Tables					
	CARTRIDGE	BULLET	ITEM #	HITS #	MUZZLE	100 yds	200 yds	300 yds	400 yds	500 yds	MUZZLE	100 yds	200 yds	300 yds	400 yds	500 yds
V	17 Mach 2	17 gr. V-MAX	83177	21	2100/166	1530/88	1134/49	–	–	–	-1.5	0	-14.0	–	–	–
V	17 HMR	17 gr. V-MAX	83170	26	2550/245	1901/136	1378/72	–	–	–	-1.5	0	-8.5	–	–	–
V	17 HMR	20 gr. XTP	83172	34	2375/250	1776/140	1304/75	–	–	–	-1.5	0	-9.9	–	–	–
V	204 Ruger	32 gr. V-MAX	83204	129	4225/1268	3645/944	3137/699	2683/512	2272/367	1899/256	-1.5	0.6	0	-4.1	-13.1	-29.0
V	204 Ruger	40 gr. V-MAX	83206	191	3900/1351	3482/1077	3103/855	2755/674	2433/526	2133/404	-1.5	0.7	0	-4.3	-13.2	-28.1
V	204 Ruger	45 gr. SP	83208	222	3625/1313	3188/1015	2792/778	2428/589	2093/438	1787/319	-1.5	1.0	0	-5.5	-16.9	-36.3
V	22 WMR	30 gr. V-MAX	83202	36	2200/322	1421/134	1002/67	–	–	–	-1.5	0	-16.5	–	–	–
V	22 Hornet	35 gr. V-MAX	8302	79	3100/747	2271/401	1590/197	1126/99	923/66	806/50	-1.5	2.8	0	-17.1	-61.6	-146.7
V	222 Rem	40 gr. V-MAX	8310	140	3600/1151	3074/839	2606/603	2184/424	1803/289	1474/193	-1.5	1.1	0	-6.2	-19.9	-44.4
V	222 Rem	50 gr. V-MAX w/Moly	83153	195	3140/1094	2743/835	2380/629	2045/464	1740/336	1471/240	-1.5	1.6	0	-7.8	-23.9	-51.7
V	223 Rem	40 gr. V-MAX	8325	148	3800/1282	3249/937	2762/677	2324/479	1928/330	1578/221	-1.5	0.9	0	-5.5	-17.6	-39.1
V	223 Rem	40 gr. V-MAX w/Moly	83253	148	3800/1282	3249/937	2762/677	2324/479	1928/330	1578/221	-1.5	0.9	0	-5.5	-17.6	-39.1
V	223 Rem	55 gr. V-MAX	8327	246	3240/1282	2854/995	2500/763	2172/576	1871/427	1598/312	-1.5	1.4	0	-7.0	-21.4	-45.9
M	223 Rem	53 gr. HP W/C	8023	230	3330/1305	2873/971	2460/712	2083/510	1742/357	1446/246	-1.5	1.4	0	-7.2	-22.5	-49.4
V	223 Rem	55 gr. V-MAX w/Moly	83273	246	3240/1282	2854/995	2500/763	2172/576	1871/427	1598/312	-1.5	1.4	0	-7.0	-21.4	-45.9
T	223 Rem	55 gr. TAP-FPD	83278	246	3240/1282	2854/995	2500/763	2172/576	1871/427	1598/312	-1.5	1.4	0	-7.0	-21.4	-45.9
T	223 Rem	60 gr. TAP-FPD	83288	283	3115/1293	2754/1010	2420/780	2110/593	1824/443	1567/327	-1.5	1.6	0	-7.5	-22.9	-48.9
M	223 Rem	75 gr. BTHP Match	8026	411	2790/1296	2561/1092	2344/915	2137/760	1941/627	1757/514	-1.5	1.9	0	-8.3	-24.1	-49.3
T	223 Rem	75 gr. TAP-FPD	80268	411	2790/1296	2561/1092	2344/915	2137/760	1941/627	1757/514	-1.5	1.9	0	-8.3	-24.1	-49.3
V	22-250 Rem	40 gr. V-MAX	8335	162	4150/1529	3553/1121	3032/816	2568/585	2148/410	1771/278	-1.5	0.6	0	-4.5	-14.2	-31.7
V	22-250 Rem	40 gr. V-MAX w/Moly	83353	162	4150/1529	3553/1121	3032/816	2568/585	2148/410	1771/278	-1.5	0.6	0	-4.5	-14.2	-31.7
V	22-250 Rem	50 gr. V-MAX	8336	237	3800/1603	3339/1238	2925/949	2546/720	2198/536	1878/392	-1.5	0.8	0	-4.9	-15.2	-32.8
V	22-250 Rem	50 gr. V-MAX w/Moly	83363	237	3800/1603	3339/1238	2925/949	2546/720	2198/536	1878/392	-1.5	0.8	0	-4.9	-15.2	-32.8
V	22-250 Rem	55 gr. V-MAX	8337	281	3680/1654	3253/1292	2867/1003	2511/770	2183/582	1880/432	-1.5	0.9	0	-5.2	-15.9	-33.9
V	22-250 Rem	55 gr. V-MAX w/Moly	83373	281	3680/1654	3253/1292	2867/1003	2511/770	2183/582	1880/432	-1.5	0.9	0	-5.2	-15.9	-33.9
C	22-250 Rem	60 gr. SP	8039	328	3600/1726	3195/1360	2826/1063	2485/823	2169/627	1877/470	-1.5	1.0	0	-5.3	-16.3	-34.8
V	220 Swift	40 gr. V-MAX w/Moly	83203	164	4200/1566	3597/1149	3070/837	2602/601	2179/422	1798/287	-1.5	0.6	0	-4.3	-13.8	-30.8
V	220 Swift	50 gr. V-MAX w/Moly	83213	240	3850/1645	3384/1271	2965/976	2583/741	2232/553	1910/405	-1.5	0.8	0	-4.8	-14.8	-31.8
V	220 Swift	55 gr. V-MAX	8324	281	3680/1654	3253/1292	2867/1003	2511/770	2183/582	1880/432	-1.5	0.9	0	-5.2	-15.9	-33.9
V	220 Swift	55 gr. V-MAX w/Moly	83243	281	3680/1654	3253/1292	2867/1003	2511/770	2183/582	1880/432	-1.5	0.9	0	-5.2	-15.9	-33.9
C	220 Swift	60 gr. HP	8122	328	3600/1726	3195/1360	2826/1063	2485/823	2169/627	1877/470	-1.5	1.0	0	-5.3	-16.3	-34.8
V	243 Win	58 gr. V-MAX w/Moly	83423	269	3750/1811	3308/1409	2909/1090	2544/833	2206/627	1896/463	-1.5	0.8	0	-5.0	-15.4	-33.0
C	243 Win	75 gr. HP	8040	414	3400/1925	3051/1550	2729/1240	2428/982	2147/768	1886/592	-1.5	1.1	0	-5.8	-17.6	-36.9
LM	243 Win	85 gr. InterBond LM	85469	519	3175/1902	2926/1615	2690/1366	2467/1148	2254/958	2051/794	-1.5	1.3	0.0	-6.1	-17.9	-36.6
LM	243 Win	95 gr. SST LM Interlock	85464	618	3100/2027	2828/1687	2572/1396	2331/1146	2102/932	1887/751	-1.5	1.4	0	-6.7	-19.8	-40.8
C	243 Win	95 gr. SST InterLock	80464	587	2950/1835	2687/1523	2439/1255	2205/1025	1983/829	1776/665	-1.5	1.7	0	-7.5	-22.2	-45.8
LM	243 Win	100 gr. BTSP LM InterLock	8546	692	3100/2133	2861/1817	2634/1541	2419/1299	2213/1087	2018/904	-1.5	1.4	0	-6.4	-18.8	-38.2
C	243 Win	100 gr. BTSP InterLock	8046	660	2960/1945	2728/1653	2508/1397	2299/1173	2099/978	1910/810	-1.5	1.6	0	-7.1	-20.9	-42.5
C	6MM Rem	95 gr. SST InterLock	81664	618	3100/2027	2828/1687	2572/1396	2331/1146	2102/932	1887/751	-1.5	1.4	0	-6.7	-19.8	-40.8
LM	6MM Rem	100 gr. BTSP LM InterLock	8566	727	3250/2345	3003/2001	2769/1702	2547/1440	2335/1211	2134/1011	-1.5	1.2	0	-5.7	-16.8	-34.3
C	6MM Rem	100 gr. BTSP Interlock	8166	692	3100/2133	2861/1817	2634/1541	2419/1299	2213/1087	2018/904	-1.5	1.4	0	-6.4	-18.8	-38.2
LM	257 Roberts	117 gr. SST LM InterLock	85354	800	2940/2245	2701/1895	2474/1589	2258/1324	2053/1095	1859/898	-1.5	1.6	0	-7.3	-21.5	-39.9
C	257 Roberts	117 Gr. BTSP InterLock	8135	755	2780/2007	2550/1688	2331/1411	2122/1170	1925/963	1740/787	-1.5	1.9	0	-8.4	-24.4	-49.9
C	25-06 Rem	117 gr. SST InterLock	81454	813	2990/2322	2748/1962	2519/1648	2301/1375	2093/1138	1897/935	-1.5	1.6	0	-7.1	-20.7	-42.3
C	25-06 Rem	117 gr. BTSP InterLock	8145	814	2990/2322	2749/1962	2520/1649	2302/1377	2095/1141	1900/938	-1.5	1.6	0	-7.0	-20.7	-42.2
LM	25-06 Rem	117 gr. BTSP LM InterLock	8545	847	3110/2512	2862/2128	2627/1793	2405/1502	2193/1249	1992/1030	-1.5	1.4	0	-6.4	-18.9	-38.6
C	6.5 x 55 Swed Maus	140 gr. SP InterLock	8147	941	2525/1982	2341/1704	2165/1457	1996/1239	1836/1048	1685/882	-1.5	2.4	0	-9.9	-28.5	-57.4
M	6.5 Creedmoor	120 gr. A-MAX (28"Bbl)	81492	831	3020/2430	2815/2111	2619/1827	2431/1574	2251/1350	2079/1151	-1.5	1.4	0	-6.5	-18.9	-38.2
M	6.5 Creedmoor	140 gr. A-MAX (28"Bbl)	81494	1066	2820/2472	2654/2179	2494/1915	2339/1679	2190/1467	2046/1279	-1.5	1.7	0	-7.2	-20.6	-41.1
V	6.8 SPC	110 gr. V-MAX	8346	523	2550/1588	2319/1313	2100/1077	1893/875	1700/706	1524/567	-1.5	2.5	0	-10.4	-30.6	-62.8
C	6.8 SPC	110 gr. BTHP	8146	522	2550/1588	2313/1306	2088/1065	1877/860	1680/689	1500/550	-2.4	2.1	0	-10.1	-30.0	-62.4
C	270 Win	130 gr. InterBond	80549	897	3060/2702	2851/2345	2651/2028	2460/1746	2277/1496	2101/1275	-1.5	1.4	0	-6.3	-18.5	-37.3
LM	270 Win	130 gr. InterBond LM	85549	943	3215/2983	2998/2594	2792/2249	2595/1943	2406/1671	2225/1429	-1.5	1.2	0	-5.7	-16.5	-33.3
C	270 Win	130 gr. SST InterLock	8054	897	3060/2702	2851/2345	2651/2028	2460/1746	2277/1496	2101/1275	-1.5	1.4	0	-6.3	-18.5	-37.3
C	270 Win	130 gr. SP InterLock	8055	889	3060/2702	2825/2304	2603/1955	2391/1649	2188/1382	1996/1150	-1.5	1.4	0	-6.6	-19.3	-39.2
C	270 Win	140 gr. BTSP InterLock	8056	1004	2940/2687	2747/2345	2562/2040	2384/1767	2214/1523	2050/1307	-1.5	1.6	0	-6.9	-19.8	-39.9
LM	270 Win	140 gr. BTSP LM InterLock	8556	1060	3100/2987	2900/2614	2709/2280	2525/1982	2349/1715	2180/1477	-1.5	1.3	0	-6.1	-17.6	-35.4
C	270 Win	140 gr. SST InterLock	80564	1005	2940/2687	2750/2351	2569/2051	2394/1781	2226/1540	2065/1325	-1.5	1.6	0	-6.8	-19.7	-39.7
C	270 Win	150 gr. SP InterLock	8058	1106	2840/2686	2642/2324	2452/2002	2270/1716	2095/1462	1929/1239	-1.5	1.7	0	-7.5	-21.8	-44.1

	Ammo Description				Velocity (fps) / Energy (ft/lb)						Trajectory Tables					
	CARTRIDGE	BULLET	ITEM #	HITS #	MUZZLE	100 yds	200 yds	300 yds	400 yds	500 yds	MUZZLE	100 yds	200 yds	300 yds	400 yds	500 yds
LM	7 x 57 Mauser	139 gr. SST LM InterLock	85554	903	2830/2471	2642/2153	2461/1869	2287/1615	2121/1388	1961/1187	-1.5	1.7	0	-7.5	-21.6	-43.5
C	7 x 57 Mauser	139 gr. BTSP InterLock	8155	839	2680/2216	2455/1860	2241/1550	2038/1282	1846/1052	1667/858	-1.5	2.1	0	-9.1	-26.6	-54.3
C	7MM-08 Rem	139 gr. SST InterLock	80574	906	2840/2489	2651/2169	2470/1883	2296/1627	2129/1399	1969/1197	-1.5	1.7	0.0	-7.4	-21.5	-43.2
LM	7MM-08 Rem	139 gr. SST LM InterLock	85574	959	3000/2777	2804/2427	2617/2113	2437/1833	2265/1583	2099/1360	-1.5	1.5	0	-6.5	-19.0	-38.2
LM	7MM-08 Rem	139 gr. SP LM InterLock	8557	943	3000/2777	2759/2348	2530/1975	2312/1650	2106/1368	1910/1126	-1.5	1.5	0	-7.0	-20.5	-41.9
LM	280 Rem	139 gr. SST w/Moly LM InterLock	85584	995	3110/2985	2909/2612	2718/2279	2534/1981	2357/1715	2188/1477	-1.5	1.3	0	-6.0	-17.5	-35.2
C	280 Rem	139 gr. SST	81584	959	3000/2777	2804/2427	2617/2113	2437/1833	2265/1583	2099/1360	-1.5	1.5	0	-6.5	-19.0	-38.2
C	7MM Rem Mag	139 gr. BTSP InterLock	8059	1003	3150/3062	2933/2655	2727/2294	2529/1974	2341/1691	2160/1440	-1.5	1.3	0	-6.0	-17.4	-35.1
C	7MM Rem Mag	139 gr. InterBond	80599	1008	3150/3062	2948/2681	2754/2341	2569/2037	2391/1764	2220/1521	-1.5	1.3	0	-5.8	-17.0	-34.2
HM	7MM Rem Mag	139 gr. InterBond HM w/Moly	85599	1041	3250/3259	3043/2857	2845/2498	2656/2177	2475/1890	2301/1634	-1.5	1.1	0	-5.4	-15.8	-31.8
HM	7MM Rem Mag	139 gr. SST w/Moly HM InterLock	85594	1041	3250/3259	3043/2857	2845/2498	2656/2177	2475/1890	2301/1634	-1.5	1.1	0	-5.4	-15.8	-31.8
C	7MM Rem Mag	154 gr. InterBond	80629	1200	3035/3149	2854/2784	2680/2455	2512/2158	2351/1890	2196/1648	-1.5	1.4	0	-6.2	-18.0	-36.0
C	7MM Rem Mag	154 gr. SP InterLock	8060	1183	3035/3149	2814/2708	2604/2318	2403/1975	2212/1672	2029/1407	-1.5	1.4	0	-6.6	-19.2	-38.9
C	7MM Rem Mag	154 gr. SST InterLock	8062	1199	3035/3149	2852/2781	2677/2449	2508/2150	2345/1880	2189/1638	-1.5	1.4	0	-6.2	-18.0	-36.1
C	7MM Rem Mag	162 gr. BTSP InterLock	8063	1282	2940/3109	2757/2734	2582/2397	2413/2094	2251/1822	2094/1577	-1.5	1.5	0	-6.8	-19.5	-39.1
C	7MM Wby Mag	154 gr. InterBond	80689	1266	3200/3501	3012/3101	2832/2741	2659/2416	2492/2123	2331/1858	-1.5	1.2	0	-5.5	-15.9	-32.0
C	30-30 Win	150 gr. RN InterLock	8080	664	2390/1902	1959/1278	1581/832	1276/542	–	–	-1.5	0	-7.7	-29.6	–	–
LE	30-30 Win	160 gr. FTX	82730	826	2400/2046	2150/1643	1916/1304	1699/1025	–	–	-1.5	3.0	0.2	-12.1	–	–
C	30-30 Win	170 gr. FP InterLock	8085	782	2200/1827	1796/1218	1450/793	1186/530	–	–	-1.5	0	-9.4	-35.7	–	–
LE	308 Marlin Express	160 gr. FTX	82733	933	2660/2513	2430/2111	2226/1761	2026/1457	1836/1197	1659/978	-1.5	3.0	1.7	-6.7	-23.5	-50.7
T	308 Win	110 gr. TAP-FPD	80898	517	3165/2446	2830/1956	2519/1549	2228/1212	1957/935	1708/712	-1.5	1.4	0	-6.9	-20.9	-44.1
C	308 Win	150 gr. InterBond	80939	882	2820/2648	2601/2252	2392/1905	2192/1601	2003/1336	1823/1107	-1.5	1.8	0	-7.9	-23.1	-47.0
LM	308 Win	150 gr. SST LM InterLock	8593	940	3000/2997	2772/2558	2555/2173	2348/1836	2151/1540	1963/1283	-1.5	1.5	0	-6.9	-20.0	-40.7
LM	308 Win	150 gr. SP LM InterLock	8590	922	3000/2997	2721/2466	2459/2014	2212/1629	1979/1305	1762/1034	-1.5	1.6	0	-7.4	-21.9	-45.3
C	308 Win	150 gr. BTSP InterLock	8091	868	2820/2648	2560/2183	2315/1785	2084/1446	1866/1159	1664/922	-1.5	1.9	0	-8.4	-24.9	-51.4
C	308 Win	150 gr. SST InterLock	8093	882	2820/2648	2601/2252	2392/1905	2192/1601	2003/1336	1823/1107	-1.5	1.8	0	-7.9	-23.1	-47.0
T	308 Win	155 gr. TAP-FPD	80928	931	2785/2669	2577/2285	2379/1947	2189/1649	2008/1387	1836/1160	-1.5	1.9	0	-8.0	-23.3	-47.3
LM	308 Win	165 gr. BTSP LM InterLock	8598	1092	2880/3038	2668/2607	2465/2226	2272/1890	2087/1595	1911/1337	-1.5	1.7	0	-7.4	-21.6	-43.8
C	308 Win	165 gr. BTSP InterLock	8098	1021	2700/2670	2496/2282	2301/1939	2115/1638	1937/1375	1770/1147	-1.5	2.0	0	-8.6	-25.1	-50.8
M	308 Win	168 gr. BTHP Match	8097	1064	2700/2719	2503/2336	2314/1997	2133/1697	1960/1433	1797/1204	-1.5	2.0	0	-8.5	-24.7	-50.0
M	308 Win	168 gr. BTHP Match w/Moly	80973	1064	2700/2719	2503/2336	2314/1997	2133/1697	1960/1433	1797/1204	-1.5	2.0	0	-8.5	-24.7	-50.0
M	308 Win	168 gr. A-MAX Match	8096	1068	2700/2719	2513/2355	2333/2030	2161/1742	1996/1486	1839/1261	-1.5	2.0	0	-8.4	-24.3	-48.9
T	308 Win	168 gr. TAP-FPD	80968	1068	2700/2719	2513/2355	2333/2030	2161/1742	1996/1486	1839/1261	-1.5	2.0	0	-8.4	-24.3	-48.9
LM	30-06 Sprg	150 gr. SST LM InterLock	8519	972	3100/3200	2867/2736	2645/2330	2434/1973	2233/1660	2041/1387	-1.5	1.4	0	-6.4	-18.6	-37.8
LM	30-06 Sprg	150 gr. SP LM InterLock	8510	954	3100/3200	2815/2639	2548/2161	2295/1754	2057/1410	1835/1121	-1.5	1.5	0	-6.8	-20.3	-42.0
LM	30-06 Sprg	150 gr. InterBond LM	85199	972	3100/3200	2867/2736	2645/2330	2434/1973	2233/1660	2041/1387	-1.5	1.4	0	-6.4	-18.6	-37.8
C	30-06 Sprg	150 gr. SP InterLock	8110	894	2910/2820	2637/2315	2380/1886	2137/1521	1909/1213	1697/959	-1.5	1.8	0	-7.9	-23.5	-48.7
C	30-06 Sprg	150 gr. BTSP InterLock	8111	897	2910/2820	2645/2330	2395/1911	2159/1553	1937/1249	1729/996	-1.5	1.7	0	-7.8	-23.1	-47.8
C	30-06 Sprg	150 gr. SST InterLock	8109	911	2910/2820	2686/2403	2473/2037	2270/1716	2077/1436	1893/1193	-1.5	1.7	0	-7.4	-21.5	-43.7
C	30-06 Sprg	150 gr. InterBond	81099	911	2910/2820	2686/2403	2473/2037	2270/1716	2077/1436	1893/1193	-1.5	1.7	0	-7.4	-21.5	-43.7
C	30-06 Sprg	165 gr. BTSP InterLock	8115	1060	2800/2872	2591/2460	2392/2096	2202/1776	2020/1495	1848/1251	-1.5	1.8	0	-7.9	-23.0	-46.7
LM	30-06 Sprg	165 gr. BTSP LM InterLock	8515	1144	3015/3330	2796/2864	2588/2453	2389/2090	2199/1771	2017/1490	-1.5	1.5	0	-6.7	-19.5	-39.5
LM	30-06 Sprg	165 gr. SST LM InterLock	85154	1147	3015/3330	2802/2876	2599/2474	2405/2118	2219/1803	2041/1526	-1.5	1.5	0	-6.6	-19.3	-39.0
LM	30-06 Sprg	165 gr. InterBond LM	85159	1147	3015/3330	2802/2876	2599/2474	2405/2118	2219/1803	2041/1526	-1.5	1.5	0	-6.6	-19.3	-39.0
C	30-06 Sprg	165 gr. SST InterLock	81154	1063	2800/2872	2597/2470	2403/2115	2217/1800	2039/1523	1870/1281	-1.5	1.8	0	-7.9	-22.8	-46.2
C	30-06 Sprg	165 gr. InterBond	81159	1063	2800/2872	2597/2470	2403/2115	2217/1800	2039/1523	1870/1281	-1.5	1.8	0	-7.9	-22.8	-46.2
LM	30-06 Sprg	180 gr. BTSP LM InterLock	8518	1315	2900/3361	2695/2902	2498/2494	2310/2133	2131/1814	1959/1533	-1.5	1.6	0	-7.2	-21.0	-42.4
C	30-06 Sprg	180 gr. SP InterLock	8118	1215	2700/2913	2491/2480	2292/2099	2102/1765	1921/1475	1751/1225	-1.5	2.1	0	-8.7	-25.3	-51.3
C	30-06 Sprg	180 gr. SST InterLock	81184	1227	2700/2913	2515/2527	2337/2182	2166/1875	2003/1603	1847/1363	-1.5	2.0	0	-8.4	-24.2	-48.7
C	30TC	150 gr. SST InterLock	81004	940	3000/2997	2772/2558	2555/2173	2348/1836	2151/1540	1963/1283	-1.5	1.5	0	-6.9	-20.0	-40.7
C	30TC	165 gr. SST InterLock	81014	1082	2850/2975	2644/2560	2447/2193	2258/1868	2078/1582	1906/1331	-1.5	1.7	0	-7.6	-22.0	-44.4
C	300 RCM	150 gr. SST	82231	1036	3300/3627	3056/3110	2825/2658	2606/2262	2397/1914	2198/1609	-1.5	1.1	0	-5.4	-16.0	-32.6
C	300 RCM	165 gr. SST	82232	1195	3140/3612	2921/3126	2713/2697	2514/2316	2324/1979	2142/1681	-1.5	1.3	0	-6.0	-17.5	-35.4
C	300 RCM	180 gr. SST	82235	1367	3000/3597	2802/3139	2613/2729	2432/2363	2258/2037	2091/1747	-1.5	1.5	0	-6.5	-18.9	-38.2
C	300 Win Mag	150 gr SST InterLock.	82014	1028	3275/3572	3032/3061	2802/2615	2584/2223	2375/1879	2177/1578	-1.5	1.1	0	-5.6	-16.4	-33.4
C	300 Win Mag	150 gr. BTSP InterLock	8201	1013	3275/3572	2988/2972	2718/2460	2464/2022	2224/1648	1998/1329	-1.5	1.2	0	-5.9	-17.6	-36.3
C	300 Win Mag	150 gr. InterBond	82019	1028	3275/3572	3032/3061	2802/2615	2584/2223	2375/1879	2177/1578	-1.5	1.1	0	-5.6	-16.4	-33.4
C	300 Win Mag	165 gr. BTSP Interlock	8202	1177	3100/3520	2877/3032	2665/2601	2462/2221	2269/1886	2084/1591	-1.5	1.4	0	-6.3	-18.3	-37.0
C	300 Win Mag	165 gr. SST InterLock	82024	1180	3100/3520	2883/3044	2676/2623	2478/2250	2289/1920	2108/1628	-1.5	1.3	0	-6.2	-18.1	-36.6
C	300 Win Mag	165 gr. InterBond	82029	1180	3100/3520	2883/3044	2676/2623	2478/2250	2289/1920	2108/1628	-1.5	1.3	0	-6.2	-18.1	-36.6
C	300 Win Mag	180 gr. SP InterLock	8200	1336	2960/3501	2739/2998	2528/2555	2328/2165	2136/1823	1953/1525	-1.5	1.6	0	-7.0	-20.5	-41.6
HM	300 Win Mag	180 gr. SP HM InterLock	8500	1401	3100/3840	2872/3296	2655/2817	2448/2396	2251/2025	2063/1701	-1.5	1.4	0	-6.3	-18.4	-37.4
C	300 Win Mag	180 gr. SST InterLock	82194	1348	2960/3501	2764/3052	2576/2651	2396/2293	2223/1974	2057/1690	-1.5	1.5	0	-6.8	-19.6	-39.5

Ammo Description					Velocity (fps) / Energy (ft/lb)						Trajectory Tables					
	CARTRIDGE	BULLET	ITEM #	HITS #	MUZZLE	100 yds	200 yds	300 yds	400 yds	500 yds	MUZZLE	100 yds	200 yds	300 yds	400 yds	500 yds
C	300 Wby Mag	150 gr. InterBond	82219	1060	3375/3793	3126/3255	2891/2784	2669/2371	2456/2009	2254/1692	-1.5	1.0	0	-5.2	-15.3	-31.2
C	300 Wby Mag	180 gr. SP InterLock	8222	1410	3120/3890	2891/3840	2673/2856	2466/2429	2268/2055	2079/1727	-1.5	1.3	0	-6.2	-18.1	-36.9
LE	32 Special	165 gr. FTX	82732	810	2410/2128	2145/1685	1897/1318	1669/1020	–	–	-1.5	2.0	0	-13.0	–	–
C	303 British	150 gr. SP InterLock	8225	806	2685/2401	2441/1984	2210/1627	1992/1321	1787/1064	1598/851	-1.5	2.2	0	-9.3	-27.4	-56.5
C	8 x 57 JS Mauser	195 gr. SP	8229	1194	2500/2706	2293/2277	2096/1902	1909/1578	1734/1301	1571/1608	-1.5	2.6	0	-10.5	-30.6	-62.2
C	338 RCM	200 gr. SST	82236	1372	2950/3865	2744/3344	2547/2881	2359/2471	2179/2108	2006/1787	-1.5	1.6	0	-6.9	-20.0	-40.5
C	338 RCM	225 gr. SST	82237	1643	2775/3847	2598/3372	2427/2944	2264/2560	2106/2216	1955/1909	-1.5	1.8	0	-7.7	-22.2	-44.6
C	338 Win Mag	225 gr. SST	82234	1628	2785/3875	2575/3313	2375/2818	2184/2382	2001/2000	1828/1670	-1.5	1.9	0	-8.0	-23.4	-47.4
HM	338 Win Mag	225 gr. SP-RP HM InterLock	8505	1716	2950/4347	2714/3680	2491/3098	2278/2591	2075/2151	1884/1772	-1.5	1.6	0	-7.2	-21.2	-43.2
LE	35 Rem	200 gr. FTX	82735	875	2225/2198	1963/1711	1721/1315	1503/1003	–	–	-1.5	3.0	-1.3	-17.5	–	–
DG	9.3 x 74R	286 gr. SP-RP	82304	1863	2360/3536	2136/2896	1924/2351	1727/1893	1545/1516	1383/1214	-1.5	0	-6.1	-21.7	-49.0	-90.9
DG	376 Steyr	225 gr. SP-RP InterLock	8234	1201	2600/3377	2331/2714	2078/2157	1842/1694	1625/1319	1431/1023	-1.5	2.5	0	-10.6	-31.4	-65.5
DG	376 Steyr	270 gr. SP-RP InterLock	8237	1755	2600/4052	2372/3373	2156/2787	1951/2283	1759/1855	1582/1500	-1.5	2.3	0	-9.9	-28.9	-59.2
DG	375 H&H	270 gr. SP-RP HM InterLock	8508	1944	2870/4937	2628/4141	2399/3450	2182/2853	1976/2339	1782/1903	-1.5	1.8	0	-7.8	-23.0	-47.1
DG	375 H&H	270 gr. SP-RP	82312	1818	2700/4370	2458/3621	2229/2977	2012/2425	1811/1967	1619/1571	-1.5	2.1	0	-9.2	-26.0	-55.4
DG	375 H&H	300 gr. DGS	8509	2183	2705/4873	2386/3792	2089/2908	1817/2198	1568/1637	1354/1221	-1.5	2.3	0	-10.1	-31.3	-66.5
DG	375 H&H	300 gr. DGS	82322	2034	2530/4263	2223/3292	1938/2503	1678/1875	1448/1396	1256/1050	-1.5	2.8	0	-12.1	-36.7	-77.9
DG	375 H&H	300 gr. DGX	82332	2034	2530/4263	2223/3292	1938/2503	1678/1875	1448/1396	1256/1050	-1.5	2.8	0	-12.1	-36.7	-77.9
DG	375 Ruger	270 gr. SP-RP	8231	1923	2840/4835	2600/4052	2372/3373	2156/2786	1951/2283	1759/1855	-1.5	1.8	0	-8.0	-23.6	-48.2
DG	375 Ruger	300 gr. DGS	8232	2145	2660/4713	2344/3660	2050/2800	1780/2110	1536/1572	1328/1174	-1.5	2.4	0	-10.8	-32.6	-69.2
DG	375 Ruger	300 gr. DGX	82333	2145	2660/4713	2344/3660	2050/2800	1780/2110	1536/1572	1328/1174	-1.5	2.4	0	-10.8	-32.6	-69.2
C	405 Win	300 gr. SP InterLock	8241	1423	2200/3224	1890/2379	1610/1727	1370/1250	–	–	-1.5	0	-8.3	-30.2	–	–
C	405 Win	300 gr. FP InterLock	8240	1398	2200/3224	1857/2297	1553/1607	1300/1126	–	–	-1.5	0	-8.7	-31.9	–	–
DG	416 Rigby	400 gr. DGX	82663	2793	2415/5179	2116/3977	1840/3006	1590/2244	–	–	-0.9	3.5	0	-13.8	–	–
DG	416 Rigby	400 gr. DGS	8265	2793	2415/5179	2116/3977	1840/3006	1590/2244	–	–	-0.9	3.5	0	-13.8	–	–
LM	444 Marlin	265 gr. FP LM InterLock	85444	1036	2325/3180	1907/2140	1542/1400	1251/921	–	–	-1.5	0	-8.2	-31.3	–	–
LE	444 Marlin	265 gr. FTX	82744	1071	2325/3180	1971/2285	1652/1606	1380/1120	–	–	-1.5	3.0	-1.4	-18.6	–	–
LE	45-70 Govt	325 gr. FTX	82747	1242	2050/3032	1729/2158	1450/1516	1225/1083	–	–	-1.5	3.0	-4.1	-27.8	–	–
LE	450 Marlin	325 gr. FTX	82750	1355	2225/3572	1887/2569	1585/1813	1331/1278	–	–	-1.5	3.0	-2.2	-21.3	–	–
C	450 Marlin	350 gr. FP InterLock	8250	1433	2100/3427	1720/2298	1397/1516	1156/1039	–	–	-1.5	0	-10.4	-38.9	–	–
DG	450/400 Nit Exp	400 gr. DGS	8242	2468	2050/3732	1815/2924	1595/2259	1402/1746	–	–	-1.5	0.0	-10.0	-33.4	–	–
DG	450/400 Nit Exp	400 gr. DGX	82433	2468	2050/3732	1815/2924	1595/2259	1402/1746	–	–	-1.5	0.0	-10.0	-33.4	–	–
DG	450 Nitro Express	480 gr. DGX	8255	2938	2150/4927	1872/3733	1618/2792	1397/2080	–	–	-1.5	0	-8.5	-30.4	–	–
DG	450 Nitro Express	480 gr. DGS	8256	2938	2150/4927	1872/3733	1618/2792	1397/2080	–	–	-1.5	0	-8.5	-30.4	–	–
DG	450 Bushmaster	250 gr. FTX	82244	805	2200/2686	1840/1879	1524/1289	1268/893	–	–	-2.0	2.5	-3.4	-24.5	–	–
DG	458 Win	500 gr. DGX HM	85833	3395	2260/5670	1991/4401	1743/3372	1519/2562	–	–	-1.5	0	-7.4	-26.5	–	–
DG	458 Win	500 gr. DGS HM	8585	3395	2260/5670	1991/4401	1743/3372	1519/2562	–	–	-1.5	0	-7.3	-26.2	–	–
DG	458 Lott	500 gr. DGX	82613	3446	2300/5872	2021/4535	1764/3453	1532/2604	–	–	-1.5	0	-7.1	-25.4	–	–
DG	458 Lott	500 gr. DGS	8262	3458	2300/5872	2028/4567	1777/3506	1549/2665	–	–	-1.5	0	-7.0	-25.1	–	–

All rifle ballistics are established with a 24" SAAMI standard test barrel.

Shotgun Ammunition

Ammo Description				Velocity (fps) / Energy (ft/lb)					Trajectory Tables				
AMMO DESCRIPTION	WEIGHT	ITEM #	HITS #	MUZZLE	50 yds	100 yds	150yds	200 yds	MUZZLE	50 yds	100 yds	150 yds	200 yds
20 ga. SST Shotgun Slug	250 gr.	86232	643	1800/1798	1628/1471	1470/1200	1331/983	1212/815	-1.5	2.5	3.3	0	-8.2
12 ga. SST Shotgun Slug	300 gr.	8623	842	2000/2664	1816/2196	1641/1793	1482/1463	1341/1198	-1.5	2.4	2.7	0	-6.7
GAUGE	SHELL LENGTH	ITEM #	MUZZLE	10 yds	20 yds	30 yds	40 yds	MUZZLE	10 yds	20 yds	30 yds	40 yds	
12 Gauge 00 Buck (8 Pellets)	12/2¾"	8624	1600	1510	1425	1346	1274	2415	2150	1915	1709	1531	
12 Gauge TAP-FPD	12/2¾"	86278	1600	1510	1425	1346	1274	2415	2150	1915	1709	1531	

All shotgun ballistics are established with a 30" SAAMI standard test barrel.

Muzzleloader Projectiles

Description				Velocity (fps) / Energy (ft/lb)						Trajectory Tables					
DESCRIPTION	WEIGHT	ITEM #	HITS #	MUZZLE	50 yds	100 yds	150yds	200 yds	250 yds	MUZZLE	50 yds	100 yds	150 yds	200 yds	250 yds
45 Cal. SST-ML	200 gr.	67132	724	2325/2400	2171/2092	2022/1815	1880/1569	1744/1351	1616/1160	-1.5	1.7	3.0	2.2	-1.0	-7.1
50 Cal. SST-ML Low Drag	250 gr.	67270	810	2250/2735	2031/2290	1852/1904	1684/1574	1529/1297	1389/1070	-1.5	1.8	3.0	1.7	-2.7	-11.0
50 Cal. SST-ML Low Drag	300 gr.	67271	1150	2130/3022	1974/2597	1826/2221	1686/1893	1554/1609	1433/1368	-1.5	1.9	3.0	1.6	-2.9	-11.1
50 Cal. SST-ML	250 gr.	67275	810	2250/2735	2031/2290	1852/1904	1684/1574	1529/1297	1389/1070	-1.5	1.8	3.0	1.7	-2.7	-11.0
50 Cal. SST-ML	300 gr.	67265	1150	2130/3022	1974/2597	1826/2221	1686/1893	1554/1609	1433/1368	-1.5	1.9	3.0	1.6	-2.9	-11.1
50 Cal. FPB	350 gr.	6600	1188	1950/2955	1821/2577	1697/2238	1581/1942	1473/1685	1372/1463	-1.5	2	3.0	0.9	-4.7	-14.2
50 Cal. FPB (100 gr. charge)	350 gr.	6600	984	1620/2039	1509/1769	1406/1536	1312/1338	1230/1176	1159/1043	-1.5	2.7	3.0	-1.1	-10.2	-25.0

All data developed in a stock T/C Omega inline muzzleloader with 150 gr. charges except when noted. Zero your rifle 3" high at 100 yards for a 6" shooting window to 200 yards with 3 pellets or 150 gr. charges.

Handgun Ammunition

Handgun Ammunition

Ammo Description					Velocity (fps)			Energy (ft/lb)		
CARTRIDGE	BULLET	ITEM #	HITS #	BARREL LENGTH	MUZZLE	50 yds	100 yds	MUZZLE	50 yds	100 yds
25 Auto	35 gr. JHP/XTP	90012	22	2"	900	813	742	63	51	43
32 Auto	60 gr. JHP/XTP	90062	48	4"	1000	906	834	133	112	96
380 Auto	90 gr. JHP/XTP	90102	84	4"	1000	913	846	200	167	143
9MM Luger	115 gr. JHP/XTP	90252	157	4"	1155	1047	971	341	280	241
9MM Luger	124 gr. JHP/XTP	90242	180	4"	1110	1030	971	339	292	259
9MM Luger	124 gr. TAP-FPD	90248	180	4"	1110	1030	971	339	292	259
9MM Luger	147 gr. JHP/XTP	90282	230	4"	975	935	899	310	285	264
9MM Luger	147 gr. TAP-FPD	90288	230	4"	975	935	899	310	285	264
9 x 18MM Makarov	95 gr. JHP/XTP	91002	90	4"	1000	930	874	211	182	161
38 Special	125 gr. JHP/XTP	90322	151	4"	900	856	817	225	203	185
38 Special	158 gr. JHP/XTP	90362	214	4"	800	765	735	199	183	168
357 Magnum	125 gr. JHP/XTP	90502	230	8"	1500	1314	1166	624	479	377
357 Magnum	140 gr. JHP/XTP	90552	266	8"	1350	1208	1100	566	454	376
357 Magnum	140 gr. FTX	92755	280	8"	1440	1274	1143	644	504	406
357 Magnum	158 gr. JHP/XTP	90562	322	8"	1250	1150	1073	548	464	404
357 SIG	124 gr. JHP/XTP	9130	211	4"	1350	1208	1108	502	405	338
357 SIG	147 gr. JHP/XTP	9131	279	4"	1225	1138	1072	490	422	375
40 S&W	155 gr. JHP/XTP	9132	227	4"	1180	1061	980	479	388	331
40 S&W	155 gr. TAP-FPD	91328	227	4"	1180	1061	980	479	387	331
40 S&W	180 gr. JHP/XTP	9136	262	4"	950	903	862	361	326	297
40 S&W	180 gr. TAP-FPD	91368	262	4"	950	903	862	361	326	297
10MM Auto	155 gr. HP/XTP	9122	239	5"	1265	1119	1020	551	431	358
10MM Auto	180 gr. JHP/XTP	9126	312	5"	1180	1077	1004	556	464	403
10MM Auto	200 gr. JHP/XTP	9129	376	5"	1050	994	948	490	439	399
44-40 Cowboy	205 gr. Cowboy	9075	227	7½"	725	689	655	239	216	195
44 Special	180 gr. JHP/XTP	9070	234	7½"	1000	935	882	400	349	311
44 Rem Mag	180 gr. JHP/XTP	9081	335	7½"	1550	1340	1173	960	717	550
44 Rem Mag	200 gr. JHP/XTP	9080	413	7½"	1500	1333	1196	999	789	635
44 Rem Mag	225 gr. FTX	92782	485	7½"	1410	1240	1111	993	768	617
44 Rem Mag	240 gr. JHP/XTP	9085	547	7½"	1350	1231	1134	971	807	685
44 Rem Mag	300 gr. JHP/XTP	9088	754	7½"	1150	1084	1031	881	782	708
45 Auto	185 gr. JHP/XTP	9090	219	5"	970	910	860	386	340	304
45 Auto	200 gr. JHP/XTP	9112	240	5"	900	856	817	360	325	296
45 Auto+P	200 gr. TAP-FPD	91128	275	5"	1055	982	926	949	428	380
45 Auto+P	200 gr. JHP/XTP	9113	275	5"	1055	982	926	494	428	380
45 Auto+P	230 gr. JHP/XTP	9096	338	5"	950	908	872	461	421	385
45 Auto	230 gr. FMJ RN ENC	9097	305	5"	850	818	788	369	342	317
45 Auto+P	230 gr. TAP-FPD	90958	338	5"	950	908	872	461	421	388
45 Colt	255 gr. Cowboy	9115	310	4¾"	725	687	651	298	267	240
454 Casull	240 gr. XTP MAG	9148	680	7½"	1900	1678	1478	1923	1500	1163
454 Casull	300 gr. XTP MAG	9150	939	7½"	1650	1490	1348	1813	1480	1210
460 S&W	200 gr. FTX	9152	545	8⅜"	2200	1948	1715	2149	1685	1305
475 Linebaugh	400 gr. XTP MAG	9140	1191	7½"	1300	1177	1084	1501	1231	1043
480 Ruger	325 gr. XTP MAG	9138	799	7½"	1350	1193	1078	1315	1026	839
480 Ruger	400 gr. XTP MAG	9144	1039	7½"	1100	1027	971	1075	937	838
50 AE	300 gr. XTP/HP	9245	643	6"	1475	1253	1095	1449	1046	799
500 S&W	300 gr. FTX	9249	967	10"	2075	1885	1706	2868	2366	1939
500 S&W	350 gr. XTP MAG	9250	1113	10"	1900	1656	1439	2805	2131	1610
500 S&W	500 gr. FP-XTP	9252	1793	10"	1425	1281	1164	2254	1823	1505

BT .... Boat-tail
DGS .... Dangerous Game Solid
DGX .... Dangerous Game Expanding
ENC .... Encapsulated
FMJ .... Full Metal Jacket
FP .... Flat Point
FPB .... Flex Tip® Projectile Blackpowder
FTT .... Flex Tip® Technology
FTX .... Flex Tip® eXpanding
HP .... Hollow Point
HM .... Heavy Magnum™
I .... InterLock™ Bullet
IB .... InterBond™ Bullet
L .... Swaged Lead Bullet
LM .... Light Magnum™
LRN .... Lead Round Nose
ML .... Muzzleloading
w/Moly .... Moly-Coated
RN .... Round Nose
SIL .... Silhouette
SJ .... Short Jacket
SP .... Spire Point
SP-RP ..... Spire Point Recoil Proof
SST .... Super Shock Tipped™
SSP .... Single Shot Pistol
XTP .... Extreme Terminal Performance™

CUSTOM HANDGUN

AMMUNITION

Hornady's Custom Handgun ammunition starts by meeting the demands of the hunters and shooters who design the cartridges.

Carefully chosen components matching brass, powder, primer and our XTP™, fully encapsulated FMJ or new FTX (Flex Tip eXpanding) bullets all come together to achieve peak accuracy and performance.

Hornady's Custom™ handgun ammunition is all that you'd expect from Hornady: Hard hitting, deadly, accurate and proven. Try some in your favorite handgun today.

1) HIGH PERFORMANCE HORNADY BULLETS

All Hornady Custom™ pistol ammo is loaded with either the famous Hornady XTP™ (Extreme Terminal Performance) bullet, our fully-encapsulated FMJ or our new FTX bullet. All are supremely accurate, and deliver dependable knockdown power.

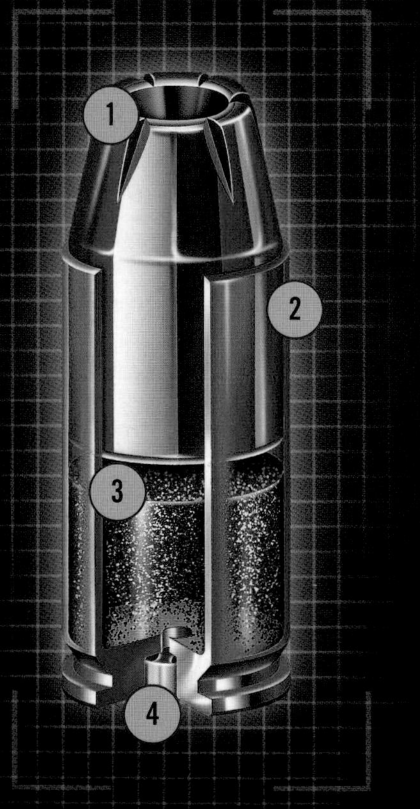

2) SELECT CASES

Hornady produces much of the brass for Hornady Custom™ pistol ammo. All other brass is chosen to ensure it meets our unusually high standards for reliable feeding, corrosion resistance, proper hardness and the ability to withstand maximum chamber pressures.

3) POWDER

Each powder is matched with each load to ensure optimal pressure, velocity, volume, consistency from lot to lot, and accuracy. We use only the highest quality powder, and each new lot is double-checked for consistency.

4) PRIMERS

Like the powder, each primer is carefully matched to its load. All are chosen for their ability to quickly, completely, and reliably ignite the powder charge.

Hornady rides tall in the saddle for Cowboy Action Shooting.

44-40 Cowboy

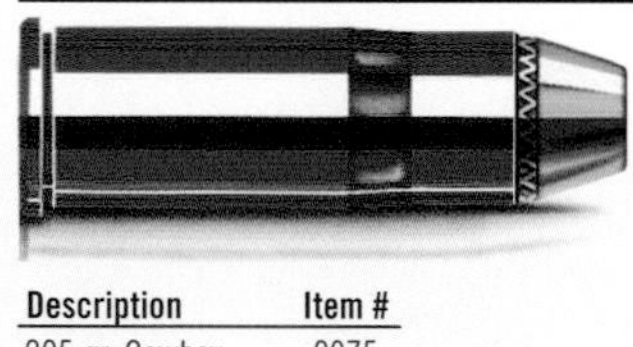

Description	Item #
205 gr. Cowboy	9075

45 Colt

Description	Item #
255 gr. Cowboy	9115

Cowboy Action Shooters demand total reliability from their ammo – and Hornady delivers! Like all Hornady ammo, our Cowboy Action rounds are engineered to perform flawlessly. Thanks to our swaged bullets, the projectile flattens at the target instead of fragmenting. Our propellants are the cleanest burning, and the diamond knurling means the bullet is lubed the entire length of the bearing surface. It all adds up to the highest quality cowboy ammo on the market.

Richard Voss took this deer at 186 yards with Hornday's 460 S&W 200 gr. SST. This was his fourth deer in two days. "All the deer I shot went down like a ton of bricks!" said Richard.

MATCH

Hornady's match ammunition is so incredibly accurate, you might think it's a handload.

We achieve that level of success by hand-picking every component to ensure uniformity. Then the cases, powder, primer and match-grade bullets are loaded to stringent specifications to provide pinpoint accuracy — shot after shot.

Each cartridge is loaded with either Hornady A-MAX™ bullets or our high-performance boat-tail hollow points. Both represent the cutting edge of match bullet technology and accuracy. Stringent quality control ensures that we achieve proper bullet seating, consistent charges and pressures, optimal velocity, and repeatable accuracy.

Loads that are designed, tested and shot in competition by the engineers who design them add up to a cartridge worthy of the world's best shooters.

223 Remington

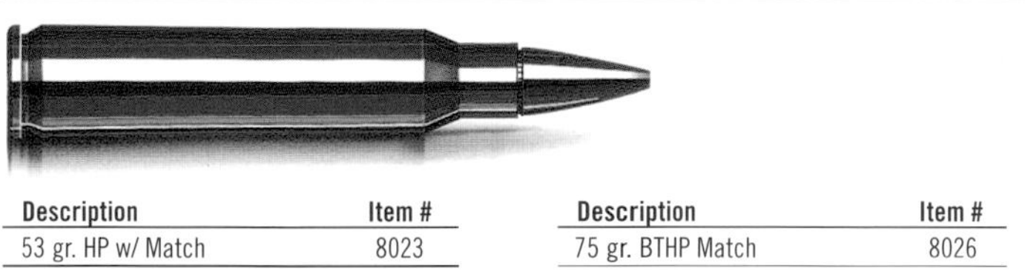

Description	Item #	Description	Item #
53 gr. HP w/ Match	8023	75 gr. BTHP Match	8026

6.5 Creedmoor

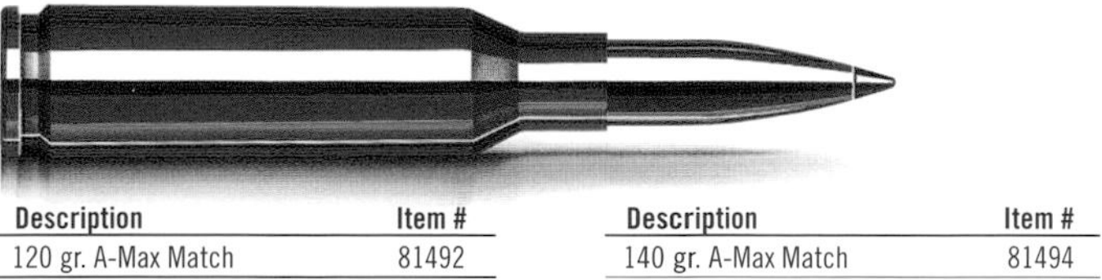

Description	Item #	Description	Item #
120 gr. A-Max Match	81492	140 gr. A-Max Match	81494

308 Winchester

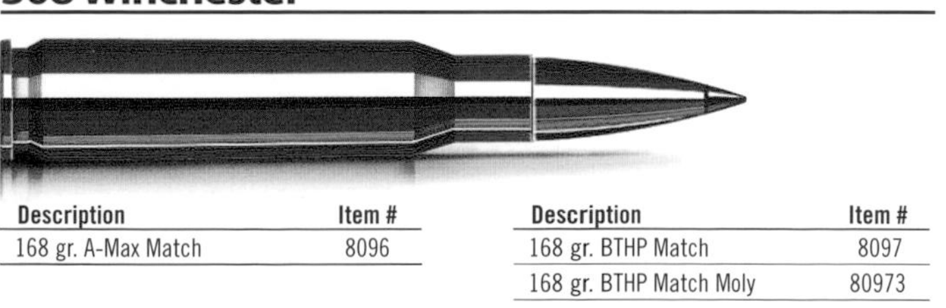

Description	Item #	Description	Item #
168 gr. A-Max Match	8096	168 gr. BTHP Match	8097
		168 gr. BTHP Match Moly	80973

1) TOP PERFORMING HORNADY MATCH BULLETS

Hornady match rifle ammunition is loaded with the most accurate, consistent match bullets in the world: our sophisticated boat-tail hollow point match bullets and our technologically advanced A-MAX™ match bullets.

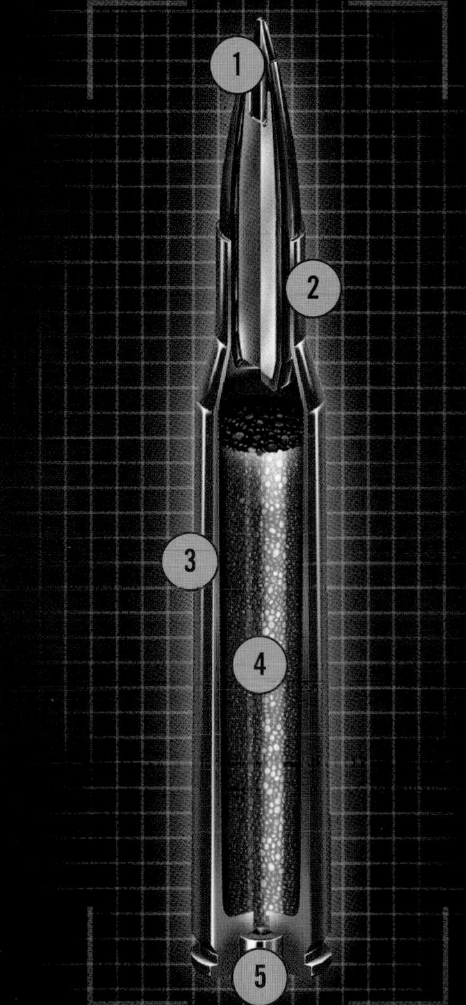

2) SPECIALLY SELECTED CASES

Cases are hand selected based on strict criteria: wall thickness uniformity, internal capacity, case weight and consistent wall concentricity.

3) HAND INSPECTED

The loading process for our match rifle ammo begins with hand selected components and a final hand inspection.

4) POWDER

Powder is matched carefully to each specific load for optimal pressure, velocity and consistent accuracy.

5) PRIMERS

Like the powder, the primers we select are the highest quality available, perfectly matched to the load.

Hornady has a product line to meet every shooting need in any environment. From small game to dangerous game– match competitions to muzzleloading, Hornady loads it all!

Varmint Express™

Varmint Express™ ammunition is loaded with our venerable V-MAX™ bullet, which is specially designed for long-range shooting. From our popular 17-caliber rimfire loads to the 243 Winchester 58 gr. Varmint Express,™ this line will handle anything from plinking to hunting small game.

Custom™ Rifle

With over 70 custom loads to choose from, you'll find something that meets your needs in Hornady's Custom™ Rifle Line. With InterBond™, SST®, Interlock, Spire Point or FMJ bullets, you'll be shooting the finest factory-loaded ammunition on the market today.

LEVERevolution®

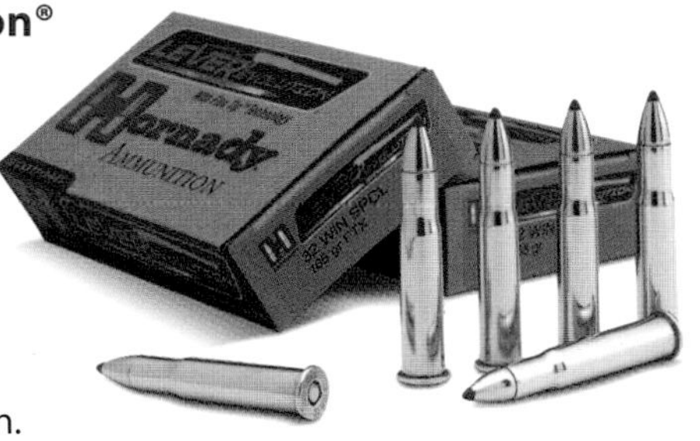

LEVERevolution® ammo with Flex Tip™ technology represents the piercing tip of ammunition design. Loaded with Flex Tip™ eXpanding (FTX) bullets, this ammo delivers 40% more energy than traditional loads while remaining safe to use in tubular magazines. And with the introduction of the 357 Mag and 44 Mag, we're expanding the line to the handgun arena, too.

Custom™ Handgun

Hard hitting and deadly accurate, Hornady's Custom Handgun ammo is loaded with both our newly introduced FTX™ (Flex Tip™ eXpanding) or time tested XTP™ (Extreme Terminal Performance), or FMJ bullets. Each one delivers superior accuracy and dependable knockdown power.

Light/Heavy Mag™

Hornady's full line of Light Mag™ and Heavy Mag™ ammunition utilizes cooler-burning powder, revolutionary loading techniques and the most accurate bullets on the market to deliver the highest velocity, hardest hitting factory ammo possible!

Dangerous Game Series

The new DGS™ (Dangerous Game Solid) and DGX™ (Dangerous Game eXpanding) bullets are composed of an extremely hard lead alloy core and a copper clad steel jacket that allow Hornady's new Dangerous Game Series™ ammo to cover every need a dangerous game hunt offers. Extra attention is given to the internal and external ballistics to ensure regulation in doubles and consistent performance no matter how harsh the conditions.

Match

Hornady's hand-picked cases, powder, primer, and superior match grade bullets are loaded to strict specifications to provide surgical accuracy with every shot. Case in point: the new 6.5 Creedmoor delivers world-class performance in a factory-loaded cartridge that the handloader will have no trouble duplicating. Having the best R&D team in the ammunition industry allows us to deliver the most accurate and consistent match ammo in the world.

TAP FPD™

Specifically designed for personal defense, Hornady's TAP-FPD takes the superior design of our TAP ammo used by elite military groups and law enforcement agencies throughout the world and adds a revolutionary nickel-coated case that extends the reliability, functionality and corrosion resistance o these superbly engineered cartridges.

24. Of drop and drift

You're smart to think beyond the muzzle and consider the bullet not as a rocket but as a fragment driven yonder by an explosion. This mindless sliver of lead, spinning madly, must rip through powerful forces we know collectively as air. Air is not a void. It is like water. It offers resistance to penetration. If you dip your hand in water, you feel a little resistance but not much. When you swim, you feel much more resistance. A belly-flop from the 7-meter board shows you more resistance still. Bullets trace paths unique to themselves and subject to conditions. Looking through a high-power target scope as you launch a .22 match bullet downrange, you'll see the trajectory as a hook, fore-shortened in the lens. Thinking of bullets as curve balls thrown by a pitcher can help you put them in the vitals of big game. It's important that you know the range and shoot to that yardage. This may seem elementary. Still, many hunters make poor shots because they think in straight lines.

▲ Wayne fires a Magnum Research rifle in 6.5 Creedmoor, designed for long reach with light recoil.

▼ Bill Dermody shoots a Zeiss-scoped Savage tactical rifle in .338 Lapua, a favored sniper round.

A BB is hardly more accurate than a stone from a slingshot. But long ago my Daisy lever-action hit small targets at ranges to 50 yards. The reason I shot it well was that I shot it so much. I learned how the steel pellets reacted to air and gravity. Their lazy arcs came to me in my sleep. Intuitively, it seemed, the coarse steel blade would find some corner of space above and to the side of what I wanted to hit, and in due time the BB would land there. BBs behaved much like the 25-cent arrows I launched from the fiberglass bow I bought with Green Stamps to harass local starlings. From these crude tools I learned that aiming is simply an attempt to arrange a collision at some point in space.

Seeing a bullet's arc is a distinct advantage in learning about trajectory. That's why machine guns and anti-aircraft cannons are fed tracer bullets at regular intervals. Drag, drift and deceleration all show up with great clarity in tracer paths. Gunners trained to shoot at Axis airplanes during World War II were often started with BB guns that made trajectory and flight time easy to comprehend.

As soon as a bullet leaves the muzzle of your rifle, it starts to drop at an accelerating rate of 32.16 feet per second. But bullets seldom stay aloft for an entire second. A 160-grain 7mm magnum bullet started at

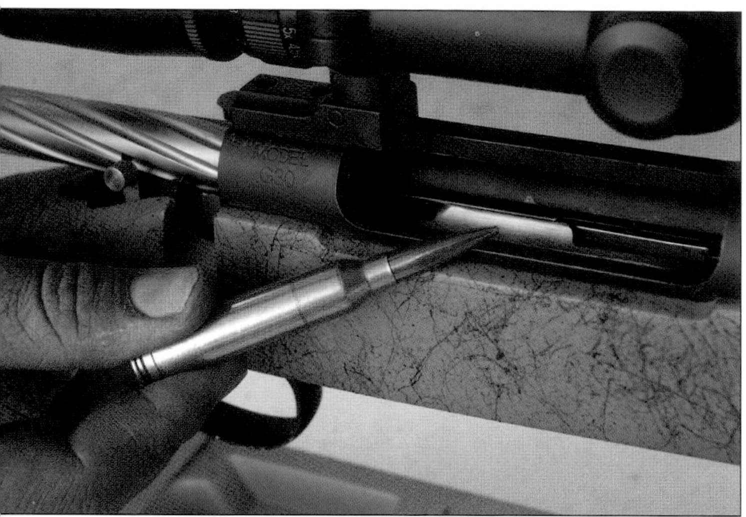

▲ VLD bullets, as in this 7mm Remington Magnum round, reduce drop and drift distance.

3,150 fps will hit a deer 250 yards away in about a quarter of a second, given deceleration that brings average velocity to 3,000 fps. During that quarter-second the bullet drops 3 feet (not 8 feet, as gravity pulls it faster and farther the last quarter second than the first). If your line of sight were parallel and tangent to line of bore, the bullet would strike 3 feet low. A slower bullet drops the same distance during the same time. It just doesn't cover as much ground in flight. Say your 165-grain .300 Savage bullet clocks an average 2,400 fps (800 yards per second) over its first 200 yards. After a quarter second it will pass that 200 yard mark. So instead of landing 3 feet low at 250 yards, as with the 7mm magnum, it prints 3 feet low at 200. Bullet speed doesn't affect gravity; it simply determines the reach of the bullet's parabolic arc.

Crude illustrations of trajectories show them as rainbows. As Galileo found, they are not. Because air is pushing against the bullet's nose, sucking on its tail and clawing at its shank, the bullet slows down as soon as there's no more thrust on its base. The slower it goes, the less ground it covers per unit of time. The arc gets steeper downrange. If you dropped a bullet from your fingers at the same time a bullet was fired horizontally from a rifle the same distance above the ground, *the two bullets would come to earth at very nearly the same time*. It's true!

Cartridges like the .30-378 Weatherby excel at long range because the velocity that gives them the impact of a wrecking ball also flattens trajectory. A moose 450 yards away will escape your bullet if you're shooting a .30-06 and underestimate the range as 350. A .30-378 bullet flies flatter and will still strike the vitals, albeit several inches low. Many shooters have been bamboozled into thinking a bullet rises above line of bore during its flight. It does not. The misunderstanding results from illustrations of trajectory that aren't carefully drawn. *Sight-line is not parallel to bore-line*, but at a slight converging angle. Sight-line dips below bore-line and the bullet's arc. Sight-line never meets bore-line again, because both are straight. They cross and forever get farther apart. A bullet will hit above sight-line at midrange, but only because sight-line angles down through its trajectory. Sighting in or zeroing a rifle is simply adjusting the sights so you are looking where the bullet hits. Zero range is not point-blank range. Shooting point-blank is shooting with no compensation for a bullet's trajectory. Hunting big game, you can ignore small differences between point of aim and point of impact. If you can abide a 2-½ inch deviation, a 200-yard zero will give your .30-06 a point-blank range of 230 yards or so, depending on the load. Maximum point-blank range is the distance

▼ This Leupold scope has a parallax dial, plus a GreyBull elevation knob for a 7mm magnum load.

▲ The straight-pull Blaser R93, here in .375 H&H, is beautifully engineered, lightning-fast to cycle.

at which a bullet falls so far below line of sight that you must compensate for gravity's pull by raising your point of aim.

Another force that moves your bullet from sight-line is wind. Wind is like gravity on a horizontal plane. As the bullet slows, a constant wind has greater effect. But, unlike gravity, wind force and direction are *not* constant. In competition, I've often fired through wind that straightened the target flags one way while swinging mechanical wind vanes the opposite direction on the line. While wind at the muzzle has more effect on impact point than does an equivalent shift downrange, the bullet is more easily moved the farther it gets from the muzzle because downrange there's more time per unit of distance traveled for the wind to work its mayhem. A slight pick-up or let-off or fish-tail can flip your bullet wild after you press the last ounce from that trigger. A "full value" or 3 to 9 o'clock wind has the greatest effect on strike point.

You'll get a good start as a wind-doper with a ballistics program from Ken Oehler or the people at Sierra Bullets, or Nikon computer program that shows wind deflection for popular loads. Punch in the velocity and ballistic coefficient of your bullet, and Oehler's Ballistic Explorer will plot a bullet track, telling you about energy, point-blank range and wind drift beside showing bullet drop. The Sierra program is fully as useful. There's even a way to calculate ballistic coefficient from simple flight data you collect at the range.

Air temperature also affects bullet behavior. Warm air is thinner than cold air, so your bullet meets less resistance on a warm day, just as an airplane gets less lift on a warm day. Honestly, you won't see much difference in bullet impact due to the effect of air temperature *on bullet flight.* Figure no more than half a minute of elevation *for every 100 degrees* change in temperature. But trajectory is also affected by breech pressure: the higher the pressure, the faster the bullet. A hot day can raise the temperature of the powder, generating higher pressure. A cold day can make the cartridge perform sluggishly. Tests run by Art Alphin (A-Square) with a .30-06 showed that at 40 degrees a charge of 51 grains RL-15 generated 54,600 PSI to push a 180-grain Nosler Ballistic Tip at 2,675 fps. The same rifle and load registered 59,900 PSI and 2,739 fps when the temperature was 120 degrees. The temperature of the ammunition is what's important. A cartridge kept in a warm pocket and fired soon after loading in a rifle on a cold morning will perform as if the chamber temperature were warmer than the ambient temperature. Cartridges left on a hot dashboard in a safari vehicle can get much warmer than the rifle and cause higher pressures than ambient temperature would indicate. The effect of changes in temperature on ammunition varies with the load. Some powders are more sensitive than others, and if you're approaching the safe pressure limit, you may get a dangerous spike in pressure with a relatively modest increase in temperature. Rule of thumb: Figure a velocity change of 3 fps for every degree of temperature change.

▼ This bear roamed open tundra, where bullet drop matters. A flat-flying Swift Scirocco from Wayne's .300 Remington Ultra Mag landed on target.

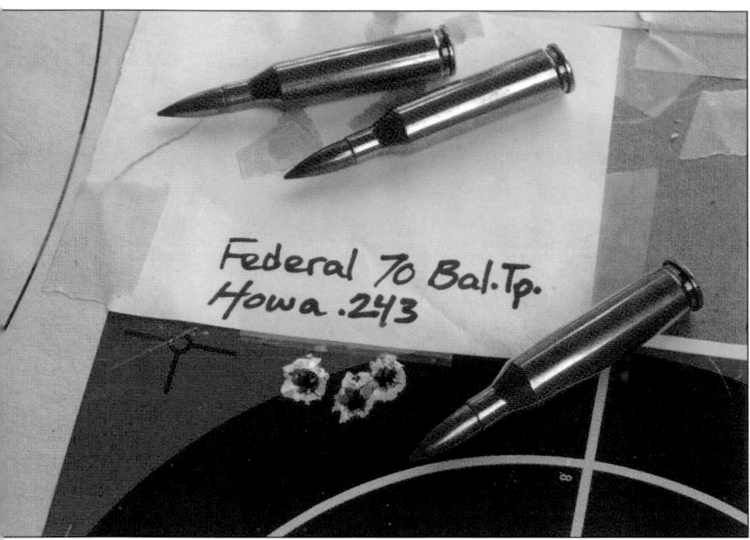

▲ This .243 load shoots flat and accurately from Wayne's Howa rifle—a good choice for pronghorns. But a heavier bullet would reduce drift in windy conditions, and suit the round for bigger game.

As you'd expect, altitude also influences bullet flight. The higher you go, the thinner the air and the less resistance it offers. The effect is greatest with flat-nose bullets. According to T.D. Smith, a former fighter pilot who has used his military experience to develop long-range shooting aids for small arms, a .30-30 bullet hits about 9 inches higher at 300 yards when fired at 10,000 feet than when fired at sea level. In contrast, a ballistically more efficient 175-grain bullet from a 7mm Remington Magnum strikes less than 3 inches higher in the thinner air. The longer the range, the greater the difference in point of impact due to changes in air resistance. Hunters, however, know that as you climb into thinner air, temperatures typically drop. So elevation and air temperature changes can cancel each other out. In the mountains, air resistance can be greater (because of the cold) and less (because of the elevation) than its resistance at sea level. On a hunt, I ignore these variables.

SPEED, ENERGY, AND ARC

Another thing to ignore is the Coriolis effect. The earth's rotation causes a bullet to drift slightly right in the northern hemisphere, slightly left in the southern hemisphere. Get on a merry-go-round moving clockwise and toss a ball to someone else on the merry-go-round. The ball seems to curve left. It doesn't; only your frame of reference imposes that illusion. Coriolis acceleration for any bullet can be described by this mathematical equation: Y=2wVsin(latitude), where w is the earth's rate of rotation (.0000729 degrees per second) and V is average bullet speed in feet per second. For a bullet traveling 2,800 fps at a latitude of 45 degrees north, Coriolis acceleration comes out to .30 fps/second, or roughly 1 percent of the acceleration of gravity. At 350 yards, you'll get half an inch of displacement. That's not enough to notice, because your hunting rifle probably won't shoot 1 inch groups at 350 yards. At long range, the Coriolis effect can be significant. Air Force F-16 fighter cannons are not wired for Coriolis correction, says T.D. Smith. "But the on-board computer *is* programmed for a 6 inch correction at 5,000 yards with the Mark 82 or Mark 84 dive bomb." Longer bombing ranges require a higher correction value. Here's a rule of thumb for hitting distant targets with a sporting rifle: Figure a 1 inch Coriolis correction for each second of bullet flight time.

A rotating bullet generates other forces that cause drift. One of these is gyroscopic effect, which amounts to twice the Coriolis drift—and is thus negligible in most hunting situations. Spun by a right-twist bore, a bullet moves slightly right. Left-twist rifling pushes bullets left. The reason: Torque within the bullet throws its nose slightly in the direction of spin. There's a vertical component to gyroscopic effect too, albeit you'll need a very accurate rifle to see it. The right-hand twist in my Remington 37 smallbore match rifle sends bullets to 4 o'clock in wind from the left, to 10 o'clock in wind from the right.

Nosler and most other bullet-makers publish comprehensive manuals. Their load data makes them a must for handloaders—and anyone interested in ballistics. ▶

Section V

PUTTING BALLISTICS TO WORK

25. How to zero

"Gun must be off." You've heard it too—this shopworn excuse for poor shooting.

Truth is, a gun is not a flashlight with an on-and-off switch. Nor do bullets land on or off the target by themselves. What the fellow meant was that his scope reticle was not adjusted to bring his line of aim into the bullet's arc at a certain range. That adjustment is called zeroing. Zero range is the distance at which line of sight and bullet trajectory coincide for the second time.

A rifle cannot be manipulated to change the bullet's path; the scope alone can be adjusted. So in fact zeroing is a sight function. Windage and elevation adjustments move the scope's reticle so it directs your eye to where the bullet is at a given distance. You pick the range.

Because a bullet follows the bore axis out the muzzle, it will fly nearly parallel to the line of sight until gravity pulls it noticeably off course. Bear in mind that a bullet's path is never straight. The projectile yields to gravity as soon as it leaves the rifle. Zeroing, you adjust the sight so your straight line of vision intersects the bullet's parabolic path not far from the muzzle, then travels below it until the two merge at the zero distance. Beyond that, the bullet drops ever more steeply away from line of sight.

To make efficient use of time and ammunition, you're smart to separate zeroing into two stages: bore-sighting and shooting. Bore-sighting isn't necessary; it's merely a short-cut to the end of the shooting stage. Shooting *is* necessary. A rifle that is bore-sighted *only* is not zeroed!

▼ Before zeroing, adjust the focus of the scope's reticle by rotating the eyepiece. Then leave it alone.

▲ In the field, protect your rifle's zero by keeping the firearm cased until you're ready to carry it.

By the way, factory technicians can roughly align iron sights, but they can't know which load you want to use, or at what range you want to zero; and they may not see the sights the way you do. You can't farm out the job of zeroing a scope either, because you're unlikely to find someone who holds a rifle quite like you do, or sees the scope field quite the same.

An intelligent first step is to find your load in ballistics tables. Knowing the bullet's arc, you can determine the most useful zero range and correct holdover for longer shots.

It's possible to adjust the scope so your line of sight comes tangent to the bullet's arc, but a better practice is to thread the line of sight *through* the arc. Two intersections give you a zero range at the second crossing. If you're a target shooter, you may well want to re-zero each time the target distance changes on the course. As a hunter, that's impractical because shots can come quickly, and you'll seldom know the exact yardage. So before zeroing, specify a maximum gap that you'll tolerate between line of sight and the bullet's arc at mid-range (between crossing points). In other words, adjust the sight so the sight-line stays close enough to the arc that you can ignore the gap between first and second bullet crossings. For big game hunting, many riflemen tolerate a mid-range gap of 3 inches. If a bullet hits 3 inches above point of aim on a deer's chest, you'll still kill the deer. By the same logic, you should be able to hold center on big animals to the range at which your bullet drops 3 inches *below* sightline. This is maximum point-blank range. Fast, flat-shooting bul-

◀ Donna Gulden uses a rest to check her rifle's zero on safari. The exercise also boosts confidence.

lets have a longer point-blank range than do slow bullets that drop quickly.

The first intersection of sight-line and bullet arc is pretty close to the muzzle. The exact distance depends on the ballistic performance of your bullet, your chosen zero range and the height of the sight over the bore. The best zero for a .30-30 carbine may have less to do with the limited range of the cartridge than the more limited range at which you can shoot accurately with its iron sights—or the even *more* limited distance you can see in the cover you generally hunt! Remington tables show 170-grain .30-30 Core-Lokt bullets 2 inches high at midrange for a 150-yard zero. A 200-yard zero pulls those bullets nearly 5 inches above sight-line at midrange. While the 150-yard zero seems the best choice, a 100-yard zero may be even more practical, especially if you hunt in dense timber and most of your shots come very close.

Faster bullets give you longer zeros. At 100 yards, a sleek 180-grain .30-06 bullet hits roughly 2 inches above line of sight with a 200-yard zero. At 300 yards it's 8 inches low. The top of the arc comes a little

▲ Attaching a scope, be sure you get enough eye relief in prone, which pushes your face forward.

▼ Bench technique must be consistent. This rifleman holds the forend firmly on a lightweight AR.

beyond the 100-yard point (remember, the arc is parabolic). With this load, you could zero your rifle a bit beyond 200 yards, increasing maximum point-blank range. If you'd accept a 3-½ inch mid-range gap, you could zero at 225 yards and stretch point-blank range to nearly 300. A .300 Weatherby, whose 180s leave at a scorching 3,250 fps, is easily zeroed at 250 yards. Maximum point-blank range exceeds 300.

Sight height affects zero because it determines the angle of the sight-line to bullet path. Ballistics tables typically specify a 1-½ inch gap between bore and sight-line at the muzzle. A flat line of sight will cross the arc a second time closer than will a sight-line raised by high scope mounts or an AR-style rifle.

I zero almost all my big game rifles at 200 yards. When the animal is farther than my maximum point-blank range of 250 yards or so, I shade a bit high. A top-of-the-back hold with my .270 brings down the curtain on deer to 350 yards. Firearms and ammo designed for close shooting—Marlin lever guns in .45-70, for example—are best zeroed inside 150 yards.

Before you start a zeroing routine, make sure the scope is mounted firmly, the base screws tight and the rings secured to the base. Dovetail rings are best turned into alignment with a 1 inch dowel; don't use the scope for this or to check ring alignment. When the scope drops easily into the belly of horizontally split rings, slip the tops of rings over the tube, but don't snug

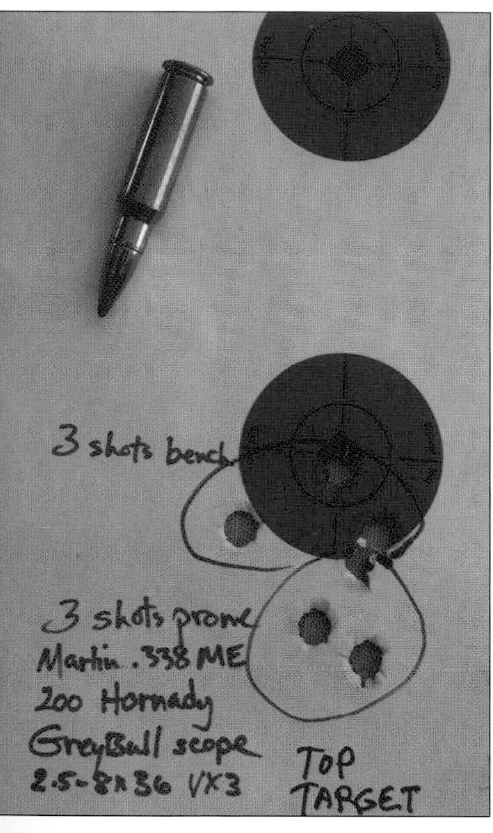

◀ The low group here was fired at the top target prone, after zeroing from the bench at the bottom target. Note the 6 inch difference in impact caused by pressure from a tight sling on the barrel!

them. Shoulder the rifle to see that the reticle is square with the world and you have the proper eye relief. You should see a full field of view when your face rests naturally on the comb. I like the scope a little farther forward than most shooters, for two reasons: First, when I cheek the rifle quickly, I want the field to open up as I thrust my head forward. I don't want to waste any time pulling it back to see more through the scope. Secondly, I want room between the ocular bell and my eye should I have to shoot uphill or from the sit hunkered over the rifle. My rule of thumb is to start with the ocular lens directly over the rear guard screw on a bolt rifle, then refine.

After you lock the scope in place by cinching ring screws (alternately, as you'd tighten lug nuts on an automobile hub), secure the rifle in a cleaning cradle or sandbags or a shooting rest like Midway's Lead Sled. You're ready to bore-sight. No need to be at the range, only someplace that affords you a clear view of a small, distant object. First, remove the bolt. Then, looking through the bore, align the barrel with your object of choice. It can be anything, from a rock to a paper target—something one you can easily center in the bore. Without disturbing the rifle, adjust the scope until the object also falls on the aiming axis. I often bore-sight on a transformer box atop an electrical pole. It's about a mile away, but the box is clearly visible. There's nothing unsafe about this, because the bolt is necessarily out of the rifle!

The other way of aligning sight with bore is with a collimator, an optical device you attach to the rifle's muzzle by means of a close-fitting stud that slides into the bore. The collimator's screen appears in your sightline. On common versions, you adjust windage and elevation dials on the scope so the reticle centers the screen's grid. The collimator's main advantage: You can use it on rifles with bolts that aren't easily removable. Special collimators are necessary for rifles with muzzle brakes that are best left in place.

While bore-sighting saves time and ammo, it's no substitute for shooting. A rifle bore-sighted is like a new automobile before its wheels are aligned. It is fully assembled, with the parts roughly oriented.

You don't need first-cabin range facilities to zero. Or commercial target faces. For targets, I prefer cardboard slabs with white paper squares. For most iron sights at 100 yards, a sheet of typing paper works fine. For a 4x scope, I use 6 inch squares, for a 6-x scope, 4 inch squares. The white paper shows up plainly against brown cardboard, and holes are easy to see wherever the bullets land. Black lines and bullseyes hide holes. Not to disparage commercial targets. Fluorescent stick-on dots excel for high-power scopes. Targets designed to show a rim of fluorescent color around each bullet hole—Birchwood-Casey's Shoot-N-C and Caldwell's Orange Peel—make hits easy to spot at distance.

An adjustable rest helps you shoot well because with it you can position the rifle exactly, bringing its natural point of aim to the bullseye. You can then relax behind it. If you must *hold* the rifle on target, you introduce muscle tension, pulse and nerve tremors that can kick your bullet off course. Sandbags are OK, but positioning the rifle the same, shot to shot, is more difficult with sandbags. Consistency matters!

In most cases, your rifle is best supported on a firm but forgiving rest just behind the forend swivel and at the stock's toe. Protect sandbags from swivel studs during recoil by wadding a washcloth in front of the bag. Never zero a rifle with the barrel touching a rest! The barrel will vibrate away from the rest and throw the shot wide. I use my left hand to pull the forend of a lightweight rifle into the rest from behind. You can also tug the sling, which pulls the rifle into the rest from the front. With heavy-barreled rifles, it's usually better to put your left hand instead on the rear bag. A little hand pressure here can shift the rifle just enough to bring the sight to the exact center of the target. The rifle's mass will deal with the recoil.

I've heard snickers when swathing my shoulder in extra padding. "Can't take it?" Well, yes, I *can* take it. But my purpose behind the rifle is not to see how much recoil I can absorb. It's to shoot accurately. Zeroing, you'll want to minimize the human element. To flinch is human. For the same reason, you'll want still air. Wind adds a variable that is best dealt with *after* you've established a zero.

First shots to zero should be at 35 yards, whether or not you've bore-sighted. You can't make any changes until you see exactly where bullets hit. After each shot at 35 yards, move the rear sight or scope dial in the direction you want the bullet to go until you hit point of aim. (Mind the dial arrows! European scope knobs typically turn clockwise to move impact up and right, while clockwise rotation on scopes built for the American market moves impact down and left.) Now switch to a 100-yard target. For a 200-yard zero, your bullets should print just above point of aim at 100 (I prefer 2 inches to 3). In the last stages of zeroing, make sight changes after three-shot groups. A single shot can be misleading.

Dial "clicks" or graduations are specified in inches of movement at 100 yards. Call them minutes of angle. A minute of angle is actually 1.047 inches at 100 yards, but it's commonly rounded to an inch. At 200 yards, a minute is 2 inches, at 300 it's 3 inches. Scope adjustments with quarter-minute clicks move point of impact an inch with every four clicks at 100 yards. A target scope may have graduations as fine as 1/8 minute; scopes intended for long shooting incorporate coarser elevation detents—half-minute or even 1-minute clicks—to lift point of impact with less dial movement. Advantages: faster adjustment and greater range of adjustment. When you can't turn the dial past zero, you also avoid the possibility of "full rotation" error, which can cause spectacular misses.

As fast as counting clicks is to secure your rifle so the sight centers the target as it did when you last fired. Then, *without moving the rifle*, turn the dials until your reticle kisses the previous bullet hole.

Group size is partly a function of rifle and load. But mainly it's a function of how still you hold the rifle and how well you execute the shot. Even with a benchrest, it's easy to make a bad shot. In fact, a bench can give you a false sense of stability, prompting fast, sloppy shooting. No matter how steady you think you are, check your position before each shot and fire carefully. Call your shots. To check your zero and refine, fire at 200 yards, then 300. For hunting, that's as far as you'll likely have occasion to shoot. If longer pokes are on the agenda, find a place to test your rifle (and your hold!) at extended range.

Tactical rifles chambered for the .338 Lapua and .50 BMG and built for use with match bullets at extreme range have been joined by sporting rifles with exceptional reach. Zeroing at long range introduces a couple of special considerations the average deer hunter needn't consider. One of them is the range of dial movement on the scope's elevation adjustment. Consider installing a slanted Picatinny rail—one whose front end is lower than the rear. Such a rail is said to have "gain" and puts the scope at an angle to the bore, so when you center the elevation adjustment dial in its range, the scope's axis (your line of sight) crosses the bullet's arc farther downrange. You get a longer zero without using all the adjustment. The closer to center you keep the erector assembly (the tube

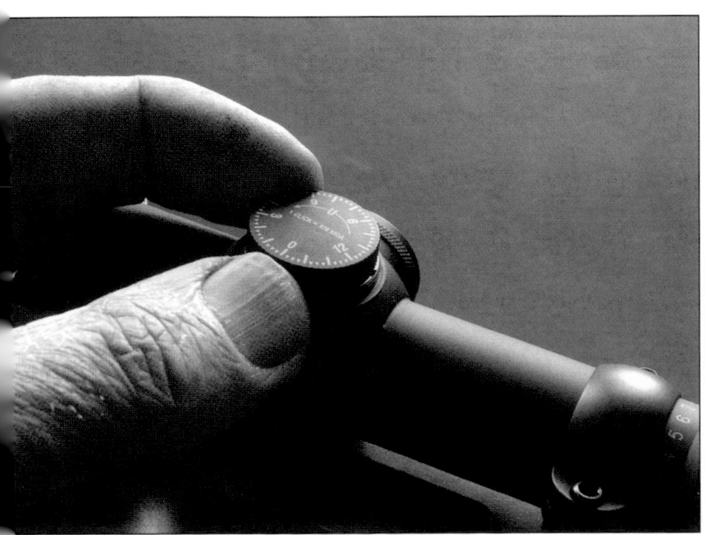

◀ Finger-friendly dials, here on a new Redfield, make zeroing easier. Assume quarter-minute clicks.

◀ Before hunting season, take a target frame to the hills and check your zero. Confidence matters!

that holds your reticle inside the scope), the better. A lens gives you the best picture through its middle. Barrett supplies rails with gain for its 50-caliber rifles.

Tactical rifles with bipods are best zeroed from them, rather than from sandbags or a commercial rest. Sporting rifles can also be zeroed from a bipod, or from a sling. You don't need a one-hole group. The purpose of zeroing is to align the sight with a repeatable bullet track. If you use a bench to zero a hunting rifle, follow up by getting off the bench to check zero from hunting positions. I shoot a lot with a taut sling. Typically, the sling pulls the rifle down and left. One .30 magnum put a sitting group 9 inches below the group I'd fired from the bench! A barrel-mounted sling swivel exacerbates this problem. So does a swivel on the forend cap of a lever rifle with its magazine tube dovetailed to the barrel up front. Not long ago, after confirming a 100-yard zero at the bench, I slinged up my Marlin 1895 in .338 Marlin Express and fired three shots prone. They formed a 1 inch group 6 inches below point of aim! When my bench zero differs a great deal from where my bullets hit from prone with a tight sling, I adjust the sight to accommodate the prone group.

Keep the barrel cool. I fire no more than 10 shots before setting the rifle aside, bolt open, to bring bore temperature down. If I must take more than 30 shots, or if groups open up, I clean the bore. Bringing two or three rifles to the line makes sense. A second and third keep you occupied while the first cools.

After zeroing, thoroughly scrub your rifle's bore and follow with a lightly oiled patch. If you have time to let the barrel get stone-cold, shoot then at 200 yards to check point of impact. Pay attention to the first and second shots. Those are the shots that count on a hunt. Save that target. Next time at the range, fire another cold-barrel shot at that target. Composite first-shot groups from different days on the same target should form a tight knot.

If you don't zero carefully, or check zero often, you may be hunting for a shot you can't make.

▼ Adjusting a high-power Nightforce scope, Wayne refines zero. Target knobs make it easy.

26. Never a miss

Ask any rifleman why he shot a 9 instead of a 10, or missed an elk. He'll expound on tricky winds or deceptive terrain or a hidden limb that caught his bullet—or a bad barrel or squirrely scope, an unproven load.

In truth, we miss because the bullet is pointed in the wrong direction when we launch it. There is no other way to miss. We can't help but hit when the bullet heads in the right direction.

Long ago I was shooting a regional smallbore match in the Midwest. The competitor to my right was Johnny Moschkau, an unflappable old man who consistently shot tiny groups. The morning sun soon flooded the targets with heavy mirage. With a bit of luck I managed a ragged but still perfect 200 with my first 20 shots. Moschkau, I noticed, dropped a point. This made me feel very good indeed.

During the next stage of the 1600-point match, I kept one eye on Johnny's target, the other on mirage. I shaded a few into the X-ring, listening for pauses in rifle fire on the windward end of the line to warn me of impending let-ups or reversals. Moschkau apparently wasn't aware of all that. Still as a corpse on the mat, his left eye pressed to the spotting scope and his right in the sight-cup, he didn't move except to finger the bolt up-back-down, up-back-down, with a mechanical drop of his hand to the loading block somewhere in the middle. Shooting fast. Then Johnny stopped.

I looked at his target. Just 12 record shots. I kept firing. Johnny would run out of clock….

Suddenly the wind died, and my next bullet looped for a 9. My second. Heart thumping, I put three

◀ Position, breathing, trigger control. Make sure the rifle's natural point of aim is on target!

▼ Among the most popular .22s ever, Ruger's 10/22 is easily customized. It can be very accurate.

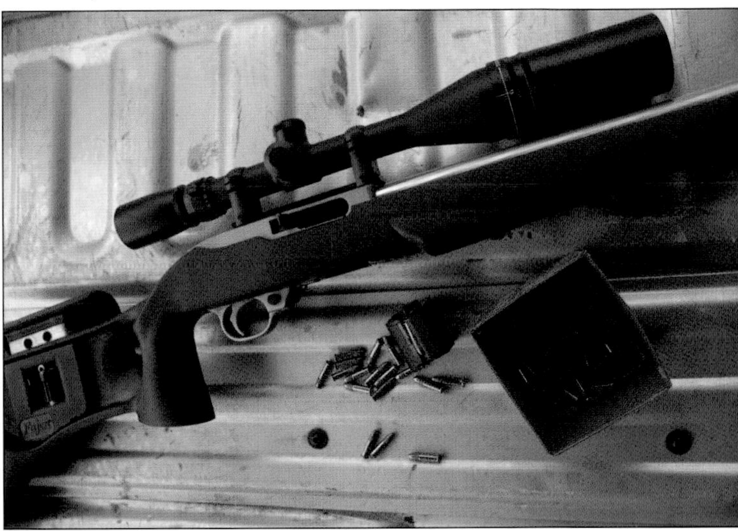

X's in the sighter bull and lost two more points for score before finishing with a minute left. I swung my scope to Moschkau's target: 16 holes. He lay like a beached crocodile, waiting for the condition he demanded. Then, with fewer than 25 seconds remaining, Moschkau's rifle spat a bullet. X. The efficient bolt manipulation and loading resumed. The .22 cracked rhythmically. X. X. Ten seconds. Bang. Now five. Bang. Bang. X. X.

"Cease fire!" The range officer called it before Moschkau had ejected his last case. Johnny unlatched his sling, rolled over and asked how I'd weathered the bumps. Not too well, I said. He told me there were still lots of X's left out there for people who aimed carefully and didn't let a shot go until everything looked good.

I must report that Johnny Moschkau whipped me soundly at this event. His cool, focused attention to the target and to shooting fundamentals won out. My sidelong glances at other targets broke my concentration. I knew how to shoot an X, but dividing my attention netted me sloppy 10s. And 9s. "Hitting is easier when you keep bullets on a tight rein," Johnny grinned.

He was right, of course. Executing shots carefully helps you hit. But that's not all there is to know.

After you've established your zero, you must trust it, putting the intersection of the crosswire right where you want to hit. One of the most common failings of hunters is thinking when they should be shooting. The reticle should stick where you want the bullet to strike.

▲ Tom Gallagher bolts in another round during practice. Follow-up shots should be automatic.

Compensation for range and wind is not necessary as often as most hunters think it is. They typically overestimate range. Wind has little appreciable effect on hunting bullets at the ranges most game is killed.

Another hunter and I once trailed a herd of elk along the side of a deep coulee. Just at dusk, we peeked over a rise and spied them 150 yards off. The hunter fired, dropping a bull. But the animal got up and staggered away. The man shot his rifle dry, then reloaded. None of the bullets hit. Meanwhile, the elk went down again. We ran forward and finished it up close. The bull's front legs had been shattered by the first shot; this fellow later admitted he had aimed low every time. Why? He couldn't say.

I've had a great deal of experience aiming where I shouldn't. Once I drew a bead on an elk that gave me one shot at about 280 yards. My 160-grain handloaded bullet would land about 4 inches low, I figured—no need for holdover. Perversely, I aimed at the spine. The elk died quickly, but the hit was most certainly high. Another time, I surprised a group of elk on their way to bed. The animals were walking fast, but at 60 yards a dead-on hold made sense. Maybe I confused the speed of my pulse with that of the elk—anyway, my bullet whizzed in front of the bull's chest. I got a second chance after tracking this animal, and made the most of it.

▼ Weather shouldn't affect your focus. This hunter cycles her Blaser smoothly, from long practice.

In pronghorn country, shots can be long. Ballistic superiority won't trump a steady position. ▶

Another bull was not so generous. When my Nosler clipped a wad of hair from his brisket, he throttled up. Dutifully I took the trail. It was easy to follow, but as bloodless as cabbage.

My willingness to aim anywhere but where I want to hit may derive from my youth, when BBs cost a nickel a pack and I amused myself attempting impossibly long shots with an air gun. The lazy coppery arc of a BB is more like that of an arrow than a bullet. Beyond 20 feet, I had to elevate. The fickle ball sidestepped at the mere suggestion of a breeze. Aiming at the mark was the surest way to miss it.

Later, shooting rimfire rifles in competition at 50 feet, I had no worries about gravity or wind. But my pulse and quivering muscles wouldn't allow the sights to settle. A slow trigger squeeze was OK for shooting from a bench or solid position, but offhand the only way I could nip an occasional 10 was to

Aperture sights can deliver fine accuracy—as far as you can clearly see the target. ▶

◀ Shooting sticks get you above tall grass and make offhand shooting almost as steady as sitting.

grab the last ounce as the muzzle strafed center. This technique was known by those of us who adopted it as a controlled jerk. Like any other jerk, it moved the rifle; so we had to correct not only for rifle movement before the jerk, but for the barrel's leap or dip when our adolescent fingers bumped the striker into free-fall.

While I still shoot poorly offhand, my bullets don't stray quite as far as they used to. That's because I learned, after many misses, to trust my rifle and hold it still.

Trust is more than using a center hold within point-blank range. It means you jettison every excuse having to do with rifle, sight and ammunition. If your equipment isn't good enough, buy better. In competitive circles, amateurs remain so until they get rifles that shoot tight enough to win every match. They can then forget about equipment and build their skills to that standard. On the other hand, hunting rifles needn't shoot as well or cost nearly as much as target rifles. A big game rifle that shoots into an inch and a half at 100 yards should earn your confidence. A rifle that manages no better than 2 minutes of angle won't cause you to miss. At some point, you'll have to accept your gear as adequate and hold yourself accountable for each shot. Practice, not excuses, makes you confident and competent. How would you like to board a 747 behind a pilot who, as he settled into the cockpit, told passengers the flight would be smoother, safer and faster if he had a *good* airplane?

Left-handed, this moose guide favors a Browning autoloader. He makes good use of field rests. ▼

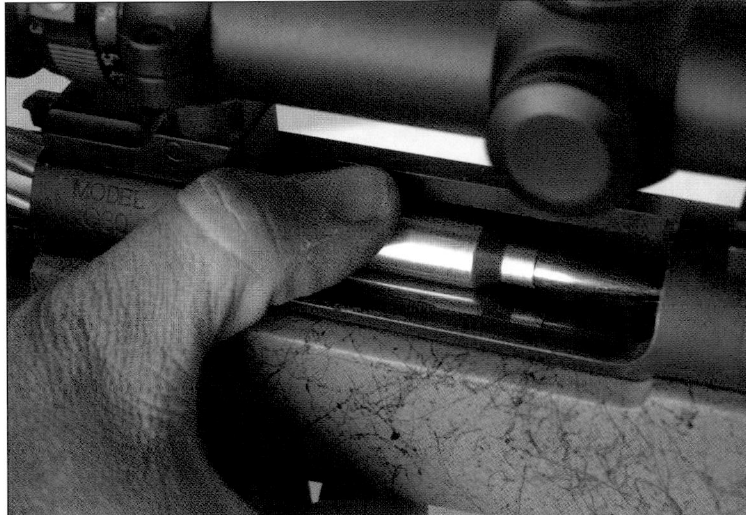

▲ Before hunting make sure all handloads feed smoothly—down and up. Practice with a full box.

Some rifles are choosy about ammunition. If you have a rifle that doesn't like *any* brand you feed it, sell it. You didn't marry it. The same goes for scopes. While you can wager your mother-in-law's good graces on the reliability of modern scopes, the one you bought must satisfy you. If it doesn't, get rid of it. You must have confidence in your hardware. If top-flight marksmanship is your goal, you'll do well

Savage engineers developed AccuStock, with a molded-in alloy rib and action frame, and a wedge that pulls the recoil lug tight in its seal. More consistent bedding means more accurate shooting. ▶

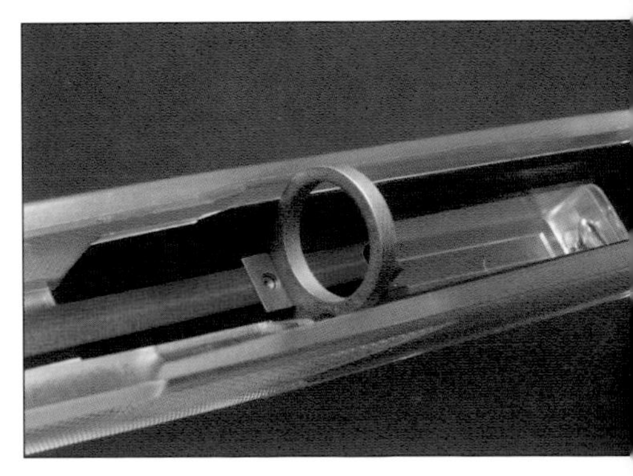

Practice! Wayne peppered this steel rodent prone from 500 yards, with a Remington 700, .22-250. ▶

to get beyond the equipment hurdle right away, so you can invest your time learning to steady a rifle and control its trigger.

Holding a rifle still without a rest is so hard that hunters commonly refuse to try it in public, shooting only from the bench. But your body won't train itself as a shooting platform until you deprive it of that bench.

You can save money by dry-firing in your living room at a thumbtack on the wall. Dry-firing won't hurt most centerfire rifles. It enables you to practice much more often. An understudy rifle can help with live fire. The J. Stevens Arms & Tool Company developed, in 1887, the .22 long rifle cartridge, and it's been the best training aid for shooters ever since! Match-quality .22 rifles and ammunition are expensive, but they're not necessary for practice. Taping tire weights to a cheap .22 can give it the balance of your hunting rifle.

I once watched a hunter miss an elk about 160 yards distant. His rifle was resting across a spotting scope on a tripod. The bull stood obligingly, waiting. When dirt flew from the hillside, both elk and hunter showed some surprise. In the firestorm that ensued the elk expired and the hunter said he couldn't fathom how he missed a target the size of a California beach towel. I fathomed it because I'd been a dispassionate observer. The fellow had laid his rifle across the scope without padding it with his hand. He shook. He fired too quickly. He yanked the trigger. "Some shots just can't be figured out," I said generously.

▼ Tight groups from a rest may not be as valuable as a target reflecting practice from field positions.

▲ A logical sequence to the Icon sporting rifle, the heavier T/C Tactical rifle has an adjustable stock.

27. Wind wisdom

If Wyoming weren't anchored to Utah, Idaho and Montana, it might blow away. I've shot in wind from many quarters, but a Wyoming wind always gets my attention. It has a breadth and depth that makes the earth itself hunker down. A Wyoming wind bends thick trees and dulls the edges of big rocks. It has its way with little things like bullets.

I thought about that as I bellied into the short sage on the ridge and peeked through my 4x Lyman Challenger. Wind-tears blurring my aim, I snugged the sling and set the horizontal wire on the antelope's back. Then I nudged the rifle against the wind—which seemed strong enough to push a 6mm spitzer into South Dakota. I let my lungs collapse and crushed the trigger. The buck ran off, then slowed as I cranked in another round. I doubled my wind allowance, holding the vertical wire well into the sage in front of the chest. The Remington 722 bounced again. My 90-grain Remington softpoint found the buck's heart. He dashed away, stumbled and fell. Gravity had pulled my bullet nearly 18 inches low, and wind had moved it as far. No matter how accurate your rifle or how solid your position, you won't hit if you ignore wind.

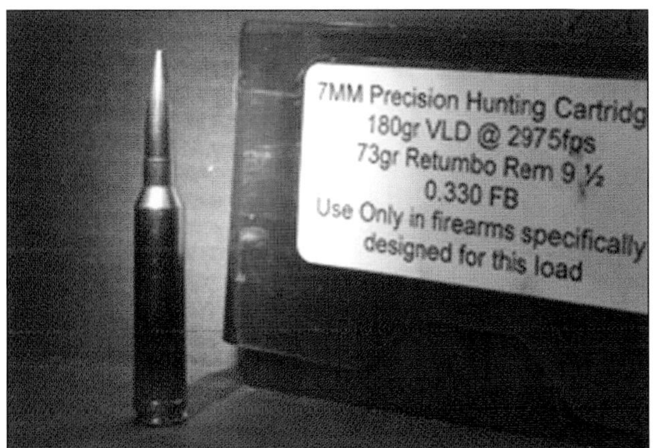

▲Long and lean, VLD (very low drag) bullets add effective reach, especially in wind.

Adding a minute for wind drift, Wayne kept these five .243 bullets on the gong at 540 yards. ▼

Wind speed and angle both affect bullet flight. A "full-value" wind from 3 or 9 o'clock gives you the most trouble because, like gravity acting on a bullet fired horizontally, it is pushing at right angles to the bullet's path. Vulnerability to wind also depends on bullet velocity and ballistic coefficient, or C. Bullets of similar C show about the same wind drift. Consider a quartet of Nosler Partitions: a 130-grain .270 bullet, a 140-grain 7mm, a 165-grain .308 and a 210-grain .338. All have essentially the same nose shape, and they have similar C values—from about .390 to .440. Launched at 3,000 fps, all these bullets drift about 6 inches at 200 yards in a 20-mph crosswind. Drop C to .289, with a 150-grain .308 protected-point bullet, and drift goes up 50 percent, to 9 inches.

A wind from 12 o'clock or 6 o'clock has essentially no effect unless it is very strong, and then the result may not be what you think. A bullet fired at a distant target across level ground is actually launched slightly nose-up *and remains nose-up*. Surface exposure due to the bullet's in-flight attitude affects shot displacement. Unlike an arrow, a bullet is not heavy at the front and

Excepting bullseye shooting in a prevailing wind, it's usually best to shade, not click, for wind. ▲

does not "porpoise." You can ignore most head-winds and tail-winds. Remember that a bullet moving 3,000 fps bucks tremendous air resistance even in still conditions. It is, in fact, generating its own headwind—a *2,000-mph* gale! What difference do you think a 20-mph head-wind or tail-wind will have on this bullet's flight?

My introduction to wind came in smallbore prone matches. When I moved outside from indoor three-position, shooting, I felt as though I'd been plucked from a hotel pool and dropped into the North Atlantic. Outdoors, you had to hold, execute *and dope the wind*. To ignore the wind was to lose.

Wind flags and "windicators"—small, delicately mounted fans with tails that swung atop stems on ball bearings—kept me apprized of wind speed and direction. I soon learned to pay them close attention. Even a light breeze could shove a .22 bullet across a couple of scoring rings.

Sometimes windicators at the line wouldn't catch a let-off or pick-up, or even a reversal. They'd hum lazily with nary a flip of their tails, while my bullets jumped in and out of the 10-ring. The flags at 50 and 100 yards, however, affirmed that downrange conditions were unstable. Wind at the target could even run opposite that at the line! I'd see flags in full flap at 100 yards, other flags limp at 50. Occasionally the windicators would spin furiously to the left, while the mid-range flag lifted to the right, and the 100-yard flag kicked out left again. A bullet sent through that gauntlet would, quite literally, chart a zig-zag course. Shooting during mixed signals was pretty risky. When the wind was visibly undecided, the spatter of shots at the line would die out as shooters waited for more favorable conditions.

Favorable didn't necessarily mean still. It's possible to shoot well in stiff breeze, as long as you're zeroed for that condition or "shade" for it. Zeroed for predominate drift, you get more shooting time during a match. You can afford to hold your fire during let-offs and pickups, or at least reduce the number of shots you must fire under those conditions. Savvy shooters make notes about the wind on a range so they learn its idiosyncrasies. The Spokane rifle range, where I often competed, is on a river-bank. Wind typically angles across the firing line from 7 or 8 o'clock, then bounces off the bank and hits the targets from 4 o'clock. If you minded only wind at the line, you'd make a mistake. Wind may also vary from one end to the other on a firing line, depending on obstructions like trees and club houses, and the local terrain.

Hunting big game, you're not using a .22 rimfire or shooting at X-rings the size of a dime. Bullets from most centerfire rifles can drive through pretty strong winds without significant deflection. Even a 170-grain flat-nose .30-30 bullet drifts less than 2 inches in a 10-mph full-value wind at 100 yards. A 25-mph wind, strong enough to sway trees, pushes that .30-30 bullet only 4 inches off course. Pointed bullets from .30-06-class cartridges buck the wind better. So at woods ranges, you really needn't fret about the wind. Remember too that deflection is generally figured for wind at right angles to the bullet's path. Even wind that howls through the trees and picks up small dogs and trash can lids has little effect at modest ranges if the angle is acute. But just as the trajectory of a bullet becomes steeper the farther it gets from the muzzle, so wind deflection becomes greater at long range. A constant wind is, in effect, much like gravity. Bullets scribe a parabolic arc under the press of wind for the same reasons their trajectory is parabolic.

Double the wind speed, and you double the drift. Halve the wind speed, and you halve the drift.

Reduce the wind's angle from 90 degrees, and you reduce drift proportionately. Change the shot distance, however, and the drift may surprise you. For example, a 130-grain .270 bullet launched at 3,000 fps drifts less than an inch at 100 yards in a 10-mph wind. At 200 yards, it is 3 inches off course—four times as far as it was at 100! At 300 yards it drifts 7 inches, at 400, 13. There's negligible drift at 100 yards because the bullet arrives in just 1/10 second. There's not much drop at 100 yards either. While wind speed and angle determine actual deflection, adding distance dramatically increases drift for every bullet. In fact, wind drift for the .270 bullet at 500 yards is about 60 percent greater than at 400. For most popular big game loads, a handy rule of thumb is to assume an inch of drift at 100 yards, then double that at 200. Triple the 200 drift at 300 and double the 300 drift at 400. Here's how that works for a 180-grain .30-06 bullet at 2,700 fps:

Drift for .30-06 bullet (180 grains) in 10-mph right-angle wind

	Actual drift (inches):	*Rule of thumb drift (inches):*
100 yards	0.7	1
200 yards	2.9	2
300 yards	7.0	6
400 yards	12.9	12

In this case, the estimate is within an inch of actual drift. Nobody I know can hold within an inch at 400 yards under field conditions, and darn few rifles will shoot even half that tight. If you're shooting a .30-30 with a flat-nose bullet, the rule of thumb fails beyond 100 yards because the bullet is wind-sensitive and decelerating quickly. The rule works well enough for very fast bullets like a 140-grain spitzer at 3,300 fps from the 7 STW. Out to 300 yards, actual and estimated drift are close; but at 400 yards the STW bullet stays about 2 inches closer to line of sight than does the .30-06 bullet.

You might think the formula fails the .30-30 bullet because of its blunt nose. That's true, in part. A bullet the shape of a soup can is not very well adapted for flight. There's a lot of air pressure on the nose, a high rate of deceleration. But lightweight spitzers, like 70-grain .243s, also have low ballistic coefficients. Their low sectional density (ratio of a bullet's weight to the square of its diameter) acts like a blunt nose to reduce C. A sleek bullet short for its diameter can

▼ A Rock River LAR-8—with AR-10-size action—likes this Federal load of wind-bucking 175s.

have as much trouble cleaving air as a longer bullet with a blunt nose. The 70-grain .243 Nosler has a ballistic coefficient of .252; the .30-30's is higher, at .268. Its pointed nose gives the .243 an advantage in wind. Drift at 100, 200, 300 and 400 yards is 1.0, 4.3, 10.3 and 19.7 inches respectively, while drift for the 170-grain .30-30 is 1.7, 7.6, 18,1 and 34.4. But both bullets give up more to the wind than do .30-06-class big game bullets. Velocity, by the way, is not a main factor until it drops well below "normal" for the distance. While the .30-30 starts sluggishly at 2,200 fps, 70-grain .243s give their dismal performance in wind after leaving the muzzle at 3,400 fps! Deceleration rates for both are substantial, contributing to their lackluster performance in wind downrange.

All else equal, fast bullets buck wind better than slow ones. For instance:

Deflection in a 10-mph, right-angle wind

	RANGE, YARDS:	0	100	200	300	400	500
30-30 150-grain	velocity (fps)	2390				1040	
	drift (inches)		2	8	21	39	65
.30-06 150-grain	velocity (fps)	2910				1620	
drift (inches)		1	4	10	19	31	
.300 Win	velocity (fps)	3290					1810
150-grain	drift (inches)		1	4	9	17	28

A couple things are operating here. First, at 500 yards the .300 Winchester bullet drops 3 inches less than the same bullet from a .30-06. Not much difference, considering the 380 fps disparity in starting velocities. Note, though, that the 500-yard velocity spread is less than 200 fps. In other words, the .300 bullet slowed at a greater rate. Moving faster, it met stiffer air resistance, just as you feel the wind on your face grow stronger as you pedal faster on a bicycle.

Launched from a .30-30, a bullet of the same weight but with a blunt nose lags well behind the others and yields more readily to the wind. Though its muzzle speed comes within 80 percent of the .30-06's, it drifts *more than twice as far* at 500 yards. Why? The .30-30 bullet has a low ballistic coefficient and decelerates much more rapidly. Its 500-yard velocity is only 40 percent of its launch speed. The '06 and .300 retain about 60 percent of initial velocity at that range. Rate of deceleration heavily influences long-range drop and drift. Muzzle speed, in fact, becomes all but irrelevant. Consider this comparison:

Deflection in a 10-mph, right-angle wind

	RANGE (YARDS)	0	100	200	300	400	500
.30-06	velocity (fps)	3330					1240
110-grain	drift (inches)		1	6	15	30	52
.308 Win	velocity (fps)	2620					1210
180-grain	drift (inches)		1	6	15	29	49

These bullets leave the gate 700 fps apart but at 500 yards register nearly identical speeds. Drift is the same out to 300 yards, as the greater weight of the .308 bullet offsets the velocity edge of the .30-06. But at long range the heavier .308 bullet better resists wind. It is catching up to the 110-grain spitzer, whose rapid deceleration erases the speed advantage that held wind deflection even at the start.

Do heavier bullets always perform better in wind? Not always. A .223 bullet half the weight of the 110-grain .30-06 and started at about the same speed shows almost identical vulnerability to wind:

Deflection in a 10-mph, right-angle wind

	RANGE (YARDS)	0	100	200	300	400	500
.223 Rem.,	velocity (fps)	3240					1270
55-grain	drift (inches)		1	6	15	29	50

Bullet weight, ballistic coefficient and velocity all affect drift because they all affect deceleration.

These three bullets show why you can't ignore any of these factors:

Deflection in a 10-mph, right-angle wind

	RANGE (YARDS)	0	100	200	300	400	500
.300 Wby	velocity (fps)	3250					1990
180-grain	drift (inches)		1	3	8	14	23
.375 H&H	velocity (fps)	2530					1130
300-grain	drift (inches)		2	7	17	33	56
.458 Win	velocity (fps)	2040					1160
500-grain	drift (inches)		2	6	15	28	45

The 180-grain bullet from a .300 Weatherby, driven as fast as a 150-grain spitzer from the .300 Winchester (first block of figures) drifts 5 inches less at 500 yards, a function of the additional weight and 176 fps less lag at that range. Given the same bullet shape and diameter, you reduce deceleration as you add weight. Despite their greater surface area, heavier bullets resist crosswind better than do light ones,

The effect of deceleration is confirmed by the greater drift of the .375 bullet compared to the .458. Terminal velocities at 500 yards are nearly identical, but the .458 loses only about 800 fps en route, while the .375 drops 1,400 fps. (This .375 solid, incidentally, is one of the least aerodynamic of many .375 bullets available). So here the faster bullet drifts nearly a foot farther than the slower bullet—albeit the .375's C value is only slightly lower than that of the .458's. The great weight of the .458 bullet hikes inertia, which extends maximum range and reduces wind drift.

Sharp bullet tips have become popular of late, lending an aerodynamic shape to the missile. But it's easy to assign too much importance to the bullet nose. Winchester ballistician Alan Corzine told me long ago that the first 1/10th inch of the nose can be flat, round or pointed without affecting trajectory or drift. The ogive—the leading curve of the bullet between tip and shank—matters more.

Boat-tail bullets become an asset only at very long ranges or in gale-force winds. A 30-mph wind that shoves a flat-base 7mm bullet 17 inches at 350

▲ GreyBull Precision manufactures load-specific dials retrofitted to Leupold scopes for dead-on aim at long range.

◀ Before you shoot long at game, shoot long at paper. It's instructive—and humbling in wind.

yards moves a boat-tail bullet 15-½ inches. The lesser drift afforded by a tapered heel at higher wind speeds is academic, given how hard it is to estimate drift in a wind that strong, or to hold a crosswire within a couple of inches at 350 yards. Also, *percentage* difference in wind deflection between the two bullets is about the same for a 10-mph wind and a 30-mph wind.

No matter how well your bullet resists wind, hitting consistently at distance can depend on your ability to predict drift. To do that you must accurately read the wind.

Wind doping is an acquired skill. Early in my competitive shooting career, fellow rifleman Dick Nelson (who also helped Boeing engineer the first moon vehicle) took me aside. "Mind the mirage. Learn to read that, and your bullets will hop through the 10-ring like trained pigs."

Mirage is a visual distortion caused by heat waves rising from the earth's surface. If you don't see it, it isn't there. Mirage does not move bullets; its dance shows you wind that does. Mirage can also show you a target that isn't there, by "floating" the target image in the direction the air currents are moving. You can't see mirage at all distances at once. You'll either see the strongest mirage or the mirage at the range for which your scope is focused. To get the most information about the wind that most affects their bullets, match shooters typically focus their spotting scopes to read mirage just short of the targets.

Mirage that's really bumpy and moving slowly indicates a light breeze. Mirage that's flat and fast indicates stronger breeze. When mirage disappears suddenly with no change in light conditions, it's often because the wind has picked up. Mirage that boils vertically shows you a still condition—but beware, as a boil commonly precedes a reversal in wind direction. Many competitive shooters zero for light prevailing breeze, then hold their fire during boils and reversals, shading and shooting during pick-ups and let-offs.

In the field, you may seldom see mirage. Fall hunting seasons bring cold weather, which all but cancels mirage. To read wind then, you must rely on coarser signs: nodding trees and grass, the leaves and snow and mist that yield to wind. Remember that wind at the target can be as important as wind up close, because downrange the bullet is moving slower, and wind has more time for any given distance to work its mischief. Wind at muzzle has great leverage, and you're better able to read it—but it's not the only wind that can make you miss!

◀ A young shooter puts her training to the test on the prairie. A steady rifle makes long shots possible.

28. When the target moves

Obligingly, the moose comes clear. Bang! Flicking the Blaser rifle's bolt, I'm back on target right away, the dot of the Aimpoint sweeping ahead of the shoulder, even with the ear. Bang! The moose is gone.

After a few more runs, right and left, the score comes up electronically. The Swede in the control house smiles sympathetically.

There's no reason I shouldn't garner a perfect score on this target. It is only 100 yards away, and though the bullseye is invisible from the line, it is in the logical place on the moose, and big enough to hit offhand. When the carriage moves, it is at a predictable speed, and smoothly. There's no change of speed or direction, no brush in the way. Still, few shooters keep their bullets inside that five-spot. In fact, I lost one shot outside all the scoring circles and put several bullets in the three ring. Hardly a stellar performance for someone who's been shooting rifles regularly for 35 years.

▲ After a long trail, Wayne killed this leopard in tall grass with a quick 12-yard shot from his .375.

▲ For shooting moving game at modest ranges, red dot sights excel. So do short, lightweight rifles.

Hitting a moving target with a rifle is not so easy as some shooters would have you believe. One fellow told me he routinely killed running pronghorns at a quarter mile. But the next day he crippled a fine buck that was standing still as a post at 200 yards. Another fellow boasted of tumbling an elk on a dead run 300 yards off. A little probing revealed that his bullet clipped the skull, nearly 3 feet from where he had intended to hit. A couple of years ago, I watched a guide miss a wounded grizzly three times at less than 80 yards as it scampered across an open hillside.

The Swedes know that most riflemen think too highly of their own marksmanship, and that lucky hits simply encourage irresponsible shooting. That's why a passable score on the moving moose target is a prerequisite for big game hunters in Sweden. It may not teach you how to hit running animals, but it *will* give you a healthy dose of humility.

I'm poorly qualified to write about shooting game on the run, because I avoid it. Actually, I started strong, with a one-shot kill on a whitetail streaking through aspens. Flushed with my achievement, I figured my keen eye and iron-sighted .303 were a match for anything on hooves. Then I repeatedly missed a buck waltzing across an alfalfa field, and a wounded deer

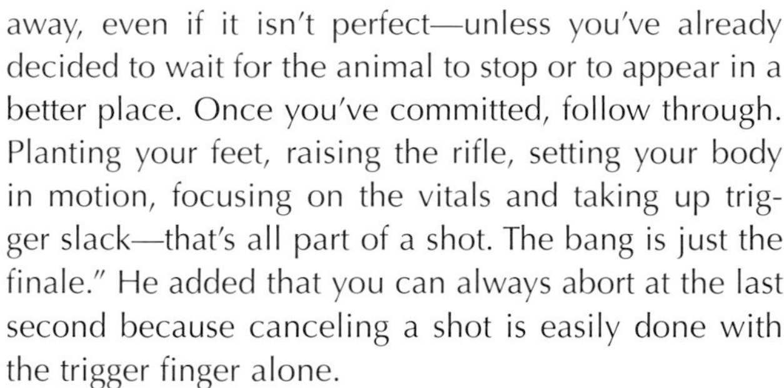

scrambling for cover. I shot behind a pronghorn and well ahead of a blacktail buck close enough to nail with a beanbag.

Hitting with a rifle is harder than hitting with a shotgun because not only does your bullet lack the pancake-skillet breadth of a shot charge; it also lacks depth. A cloud of shot may be several feet long by the time it gets near the target. A lot of birds are killed by trailing pellets, so you can afford to be generous with lead. A bullet gives you no such latitude. You're spot-on, or you miss.

With this mandate for precision, it's easy to be stiff and tardy. Shooting moving game with a rifle calls for the same instant response and fluid body movement as using a shotgun. If you dawdle or interrupt your swing trying to refine that sight picture, you'll miss, or lose your chance to shoot at all.

One deer hunter who taught me a lot about shooting in the woods said that it is like boxing: "Get your feet right first. The rest is easy." He pointed out that many hunters fire at running deer before they get their balance, before they position their feet so the rifle comes *naturally* on-target. Easing through cover, he was careful to keep his weight over his feet and never get "twisted up." With each step, he made sure he could shoot accurately in any direction a deer might appear, just by moving one foot. When he paused, it was always where he had good opportunities to shoot, but more importantly, where his feet could rest and pivot easily for a quick offhand shot. "Deer most often break cover when you stop moving," he observed. "If you stop where your feet can't help you shoot... well, that's just dumb."

◀ Jason Nash and his Australian guide approach a buffalo Jason downed with a Federal .375 load.

My mentor swung as gracefully with his little 6.5x55 carbine as with his favorite 20-bore double. His knees were bent slightly, most of his weight on the balls of his feet as he leaned into the rifle. "Prepare for the shot right away, even if it isn't perfect—unless you've already decided to wait for the animal to stop or to appear in a better place. Once you've committed, follow through. Planting your feet, raising the rifle, setting your body in motion, focusing on the vitals and taking up trigger slack—that's all part of a shot. The bang is just the finale." He added that you can always abort at the last second because canceling a shot is easily done with the trigger finger alone.

Surely, it's irresponsible to fling bullets at every running deer in range. But to swing tentatively is to miss. Forget about light brush. In timber, you should have a shot alley picked out before the butt strikes your shoulder. As soon as the sight sweeps in front of the target, the rifle ought to fire itself.

Try to apply the same discipline as when shooting at stationary game. I don't shoot unless I think there's a 90 percent chance my bullet will hit vitals. Making that decision instantly is part of shooting well at running game. There's no disgrace in passing up a shot. But if you miss often, you're probably shooting too often. When trees catch my bullets, I'm more generous with my scorecard than I am in open country, because in timber even dead-center shots will occasionally be short-stopped.

How much you lead an animal depends on its apparent speed (actual speed mitigated by the angle) and bullet flight time (distance x average velocity). A deer running straight away absolves you of lead, no matter the distance, because its path is in line with the bullet's. A buck racing across your front at slingshot range requires *almost* no lead, if your swing is fast enough to keep the sight in the vitals, because bullet flight time is so short. To ranges of, say, 50 yards, your bullet should hit close enough to point of aim for a sure kill. Computing lead takes time; better to shoot fast squarely at the target.

As soon as that deer bursts into view, determine the lead *based on what you know*. Temper your instinctive urge to fire blindly. Think. Running deer up close seem jet-propelled, and your tendency is to snap-shoot. You generally have time for an aimed shot, and if you don't, you have no shot at all. The same animal farther out requires more lead than you think. Like a goose in the distance, it *appears* to be cruising slowly. Steep shot angles at long range can require *less* lead than seems

▲ Linda Powell took this southeastern whitetail with her lightweight Remington bolt rifle.

right, because you're smitten by the animal's actual speed and may not recognize its displacement relative to the bullet's path.

To kill moving game regularly, you must move that rifle too! Your reaction time and the rifle's lock time add to the bullet's flight time to extend the lead you think is right. Also, the interval between your brain's signal to fire and the striker's release can vary. With a moving rifle, you have only flight time to fret about. If you prefer to "swing through" with a rifle moving fast enough to pass the target, you'll have extra lead built in, so you won't need as much air between sight and target as with a sustained lead.

Keep both eyes open. In concert, they'll help you track the animal and maintain a sight picture. A squint handicaps you even when you're shooting at still targets. More so when the game is moving.

I was once asked how much lead was required to tumble an elk running, at right angles, 20 mph at 200 yards, with a 180-grain bullet from a .30-06.

For a sustained lead, you calculate first the speed of the animal in feet per second. As anyone who took Driver Education when automobiles had bias-ply tires knows, a car traveling 60 mph moves 88 fps. So an elk at 20 mph covers about a third that distance—say, 30 feet—in one second. Chart velocity for a 180-grain .30-06 bullet is 2,700 fps. Now, because the bullet slows down as soon as it leaves the rifle, we must find its average speed over 200 yards to calculate its flight time. With a 200-yard speed of just over 2,300 fps, the bullet averages about 2,500 fps. But that's a little skewed, because deceleration rate changes. Let's put the *real* average at 2,450. A couple of hundred yards is 600 feet, so the bullet takes only a quarter-second to reach the bull. During that time, the elk travels a quarter of 30 feet, or about 7 ½ feet. So you'd aim 6 ½ feet ahead of the shoulder.

If the animal were running at a 45-degree angle, you'd halve the lead.

Here's another example: Say you're shooting a rifle chambered for the hot .338 Remington Ultra Mag, and on a moose hunt a bull with huge antlers trots across your front at 300 yards. It's an open shot, and you're sitting, with the rifle over a stump and steady enough for a smooth lead. But the bull is moving into a stiff 20-mph headwind. Your handloaded 210-grain Nosler exits the muzzle at 3,100 fps. Remember, though, that fast bullets decelerate faster than slow ones because they meet heavier air resistance. And that moose is covering ground at about 10 mph, or 15 fps. The math: Your bullet, averaging 2,700 fps, covers 300 yards (900 feet) in 1/3 second, during which time the target moves

▲ The centenarian .30-06 now boasts many loads adequate for the biggest North American game. Here: a Nosler Ballistic Tip in Federal ammo.

▲ Getting to game is always more fun than shooting long. And the kills are more certain.

5 feet. Your hold, then, should be four feet in front of the shoulder—if you were zeroed for 300 yards and there were no wind. But you rifle is zeroed, most properly, at 200 yards, so you'll have to hold about 6 inches above where you want the bullet to hit. And since the 20-mph wind will drift your bullet back toward the animal, you must add the drift into your lead. That's another foot. Swinging five feet ahead with the vertical wire, and keeping the horizontal just above center, you squeeze off.

Then again, you may choose not to shoot at all. Long pokes, especially those that beg elevation or wind correction, are chancy when the target isn't still. Truly, a 300-yard *standing* shot can be a challenge under most field conditions. If you aren't sure, you're smart to decline.

A running shot properly executed is a delightful thing, an accomplishment not soon forgotten. The fast, fluid moments up close—shots begun and finished in a heartbeat—are best of all. I've not made many. One I recall happened long ago, when a whitetail buck exploded from cover a few feet away. I fired as if at a partridge, decking the deer instantly. The entire episode lasted less than three seconds.

Another time, on the last day of a demanding quest for a big eland in Zimbabwe, my tracker and I happened upon a fresh track in dense thorn. We followed. As luck would have it, we had moved a scant hundred yards when an eland cow erupted from the cover. She vanished instantly. Then a huge eland bull burst into view at spitwad range. Phillip shouted something in Endebele that I took to mean *"Shoot!"* A patch of shoulder came clear for a millisecond as the scope field swept up from behind, a blur of eland and thorn. I fired with the memory of that shoulder in my mind's eye; and a ton of hard-won trophy crashed to earth. The Core-Lokt bullet from my .300 Holland had broken the bull's neck.

Such is the stuff a hunter's dreams are made of. To make them come true, you must instantly pick your lead and shot alley. Point your feet. Stay balanced and fluid. Use both eyes. Swing smoothly. When your brain tells you the sight picture looks right, the only thing between you and success is delay.

▲ Donna Gulden's kudu fell to a shoulder shot, recovered, and required a finisher. Always be ready to follow up!

29. Minding the angles

Most of the time, we shoot with the rifle held sights up, trigger down, at targets that allow the barrel to remain more or less horizontal. If we tip or cant the rifle so the trigger is no longer vertical, point of impact will change. It will also change if we fire at steep uphill or downhill angles.

"Canting isn't bad," a shooting coach told me long ago, "so long as you do it the same each time." Doing it the same each time presupposes that you know you're doing it in the first place. It's quite easy to spot a cant if you're coaching, just as it's easy to see the tilt of a truck loaded heavily on one side if you're driving behind it. In the truck's cab, you might not be able to sense the lean of its bed; and when you're looking through the sights you may be unaware of cant.

You may have thrown a pal's rifle to your shoulder and found the reticle's vertical wire is not even close to vertical.

"Good grief," you say. "How can you shoot with the reticle tilted like that?"

"It's not tilted."

"Is too."

"Is not."

Such arguments can deteriorate quickly. One way to settle them is to lay the rifle in a rest or across sandbags, using one of the compact levels designed to help ensure squared-up rifles and reticles.

A canted reticle will not necessarily cause a miss. In fact, you can rotate the scope so the crosswire looks like an "X" and use it with deadly effect. The disadvantage is that you won't have a vertical wire to help you correct for wind or show you the line of bullet drop at distance. You won't have a horizontal wire to help you lead running animals.

A canted *rifle*, however, is another story. No matter how the reticle appears, if the rifle is tipped, you'll have problems hitting beyond zero range because the bullet path is not going to fall along the vertical wire

◀ Sitting is a fine hunting position. Wayne shot this group at 200 yards with a GreyBull rifle.

▼ How you support a rifle affects point of impact. Here an adjustable Caldwell rest cradles a Nesika.

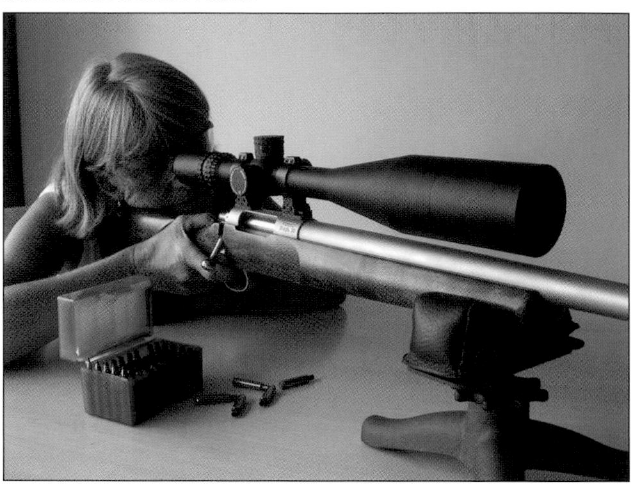

or directly below the intersection. If your sight-line is directly over the bore, a long shot requires you only to hold high. If the sight-line is forced by a canted rifle to the *side* of a vertical plane through the bore, you'll not only have to hold high, but to one side. Here's why:

Given that your scope is mounted directly above the bore, your line of sight crosses the bullet path twice. The first crossing happens at about 35 yards; the second is at zero range—say 200 yards. If the rifle is rotated so the scope falls to the side of the barrel, the sight-line crosses only once, because gravity sucks the bullet straight down, while the line of sight has a horizontal component. Put another way, whether the scope is on top of the rifle or a bit to the side, the line of sight will converge with the bullet path and slice

▲ Prone is the steadiest position because it lowers center of gravity while increasing ground contact.

through it, then angle away. If the scope is on top of the rifle, gravity pulls the bullet in an arc back into and through the straight line of sight. If the scope is *not* on top, the bullet's path still dips below the horizontal plane; but the sight-line doesn't follow it down. The rifle shoots to the side of where you look.

A cant that escapes your notice won't cause a noticeable shift in bullet impact at normal hunting ranges. As the targets get smaller and the range longer, cant starts to matter.

When I shot on the Michigan State University rifle team, I marveled at a colleague who posted top scores but used a pronounced cant. In the offhand position, not only the line of sight but the rifle's center of gravity fell near the centerline of his torso. Because he had time to position himself the same for each shot, and because the targets were all at a set distance, it proved no handicap at all.

Hunters don't shoot at just one distance, however, or with adjustable stocks. So although a few degrees of cant seldom affect field accuracy, it's a good idea to shoot with the sights squarely on top of the rifle. Cant is just one more thing to worry about, one more distraction, a small but thorny threat to the self-confidence that can help you shoot well.

Sometimes shooters slip a cant into their shooting routine without knowing it. They affix the scope carelessly, then subconsciously adjust the way they hold the rifle to correct for a tilted reticle. One culprit here is the ubiquitous Weaver Tip-Off scope ring. This inexpensive ring has been around a long time, and for good reason. It's strong and lightweight. But because the top half hooks the base on one side and its two screws take up all the slack on the opposite side, tightening a Tip-Off ring can rotate the scope tube down toward the screws. If they're installed on the right-hand side, you put a clockwise tilt into your reticle as you cinch them up. You may have aligned the reticle perfectly with the butt-plate before installing the ring tops, but now the crosswire is tipped! Solution: Back off the screws and twist the scope counterclockwise about as far as you think it moved. Tighten again, and check the reticle.

▼ Offhand is an unsteady position—so merits practice! Chris shows how, with a Browning A-Bolt.

Canting isn't the only way you can compromise your aim at long range. When I was growing up, side-mounted scopes were common. With them, you could attach a scope to a top-ejecting Model 94 or 71 Winchester, so you could use your iron sights *and* a scope without removing the scope. But a sight-line to the side of the receiver introduces the same error you get with a cant.

Top mounts centered above the bore can give you problems with sight angles too, if the bases are extra high. It's easy to see this in exaggeration. Picture a scope with ring bases three feet high. If you adjust that scope to put its bullets on point of aim at 35 yards, you can't expect a 200-yard zero. Sight-line now diverges quickly from the bullet's trajectory, diving under it in a straight but steeply descending path. The bullet will eventually meet it, courtesy gravity, provided it doesn't strike the ground first. The angle issue here isn't a sideways tilt, it's a steep forward tipping of the scope.

I once watched an elk hunter miss a huge bull from prone, with a rest. The range was perhaps 300 yards. He asked me where to hold, and I suggested high behind the shoulder, assuming his rifle was zeroed at 200. I checked it later, shooting to ranges of 400 yards. It was actually zeroed at 330. My client had fired it previously only at 100 yards, and someone had told him that bullets striking 3 inches high at 100 would be dead on at 200. Alas, the extra-high rings that put his Hubbel-size scope clear of the barrel set the line of sight at a steep angle to the trajectory, moving the second intersection of bullet arc and sight-line far away.

By far the most common questions about angles have to do with uphill and downhill shooting. The

◀ For steep uphill or downhill shots, hold for the horizon component of the actual distance.

net effect on point of impact is essentially the same. As your shot deviates from the horizontal, the effect of gravity on the bullet over any given shot distance diminishes. That's because gravity acts perpendicular to the earth; it's always pulling things toward the earth's center. Just as wind at right angles to a bullet has a greater effect on the bullet's flight than wind coming from 7 o'clock, so gravity applied at right angles has its strongest influence.

Imagine a bullet fired straight up, or one fired straight down through a hole deep enough to reach China. In both cases, gravity's pull would act parallel to the bullet's flight. Both bullets would fly straight until gravity and drag stopped them (Coriolis effect aside). You could argue that the bullet fired into the sky fights gravity immediately, while the bullet sent to China gets an initial *boost* from gravity. Truly, the effect of gravity on the nose and heel of bullets shot parallel with gravity's pull is negligible at normal distances. The drag exerted on a speeding bullet is many times more powerful than the force of gravity.

When you shoot at any angle to horizontal, gravity's effect is the same as you might expect if you considered only the horizontal component of the bullet's flight. Say that you're firing at a 45-degree angle at a deer 280 yards away. From geometry, you remember that a right triangle with one 45-degree angle has another also, and that the hypotenuse is roughly 1.4 times as long as either leg. In this case, the hypotenuse represents your bullet's flight path in a triangle whose horizontal leg is the distance your bullet would cover if the target was moved vertically until it gave you a flat shot. That leg is the horizontal component of your bullet's flight, whether you're shooting uphill or down. If actual distance to the target at 45 degrees is 280 yards, the horizontal leg is roughly 200 yards. If you're zeroed at 200, hold center. Shading high, as you would for a 280-yard shot on the horizontal, you'll miss high.

You can determine effective range from the actual range if you know shot angle. The actual range is the hypotenuse of a right triangle whose horizontal leg is your effective range. If your math is a bit rusty, divide the actual range by these numbers:

degrees angle	*divisor*
10	1.02
15	1.04
20	1.06
25	1.10
30	1.15
35	1.22
40	1.31
45	1.41

The short magnums now include Winchester's .325 WSM. It helped Wayne take this fine goat. ▶

▲ While Africa's plains game doesn't often impose steep angles, Lauri Homer shot this springbok uphill, and Wayne once killed a kudu by shooting almost straight down.

A lot of hunters overestimate the effect of shot angle. A useful rule of thumb: With most popular big game loads, don't adjust aim for shot angle if the animal is closer than 200 yards, unless the angle Is very steep—more than 45 degrees. When the shot is 300 yards, and the angle around 45 degrees, hold 6 inches lower than you normally would for a 300-yard shot. At 400 yards, hold a foot lower than you would for a horizontal 400-yard shot. Steeper angles require a little more adjustment, of course—I once bungled three shots at kudu that stood at 100 yards almost directly below me as I hung out over a bluff. Still, it's not often that you'll have to shoot long at angles of greater than 45 degrees. For gentle angles, keep your reticle on the animal and shade slightly for the reduced bullet drop.

Flat-shooting cartridges offer a bonus if you're not shooting horizontally:

Adjustments in aim for targets at 45 degrees to horizontal

	RANGE, YARDS	0	100	200	300	400	500
.300 Sav	velocity (fps)	2350					1410
180-grain	hold (inches under)		1	4	10	20	33
.308 Win	velocity (fps)	2620					1600
180-grain	hold (inches under)		1	3	8	15	26
.30-06	velocity (fps)	2700					1660
180-grain	hold (inches under)		1	3	8	15	25
.300 Win	velocity (fps)		2960				1980
180-grain	hold (inches under)		1	3	6	12	19
.300 Wby	velocity (fps)	3250					1990
180-grain	hold (inches under)		1	2	5	10	17

Truly, errors caused by cant and steep shot angles pale beside those resulting from rifles that move as the bullet leaves. Holding a rifle steady and executing a shot smoothly still matter most.

◀ Coaching from her tracker, and well-placed shooting sticks, help this huntress make a tough shot.

30. Recoil!

Accelerating a bullet from a stand-still to warp speed in a blink is not without cost. We feel it as recoil. Sir Isaac Newton described recoil when he figured out that for every action there must be an equal and opposite reaction. You can calculate recoil's kinetic energy easily enough with this formula: KE = MV2 / GC, where M is the rifle's mass and V its velocity. GC is a gravitational constant for earth: 64.32.

Now, mass and weight aren't the same. Mass is the measure of an object's inertia. The theory of relativity tells us that two objects have equal mass if the same force gives them equal acceleration. Using gravity as the force, we can equate mass with weight. That is, weight is a measure of the force by which gravity draws an object to earth. Because rifles respond pretty much the same to gravity, rifles of the same weight have essentially the same mass.

To get rifle velocity we must crunch some numbers. We already know most of them. The formula:

V = bullet weight (grs.) / 7000 x bullet velocity (fps) + powder weight (grs.) / 7000 x powder gas velocity (fps).

Powder and its gas figure in because like the bullet they are "ejecta" and contribute to recoil. You can get powder weight from factory rounds by pulling bullets and weighing charges. Gas velocity varies, but Art Alphin, in his A-Square handloading manual, claims that 5,200 fps is a useful average. The "7000" denominators simply convert grains to pounds so units make sense in the end.

Steve Kerby fires his Winchester 71 in .450 Alaskan, a cartridge with the muscle of the .450/400. ▶

For a 180-grain bullet fired at 3,000 fps from my 8-½-lb .30-338, .300 Winchester or .308 Norma rifles, I'd calculate recoil this way: 180 / 7000 x 3000 + 70 / 7000 x 5200 = 8.5 x V. That simplifies to (77.143 + 52) 8.5 = V = 15.19 fps. Then I can calculate recoil using the first formula: KE = MV2 / GC. The result looks like this: 8.5 (15.19)2 / 64.32 = 30.49 ft-lbs of recoil.

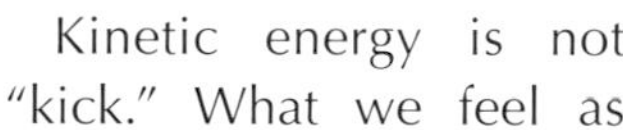

Kinetic energy is not "kick." What we feel as kick can vary significantly among rifles delivering the same amount of recoil in foot-pounds. There are a couple of reasons for this. One is that while bullet speed figures into the energy calculation, its contribution to rifle "slap," or the blow of quick recoil, does not. A bullet that exits fast dumps all its energy fast too. The rifle seems to slap you instead of shoving you.

For example, a Ruger Number One launching a 405-grain .45-70 bullet at 1,800 fps (don't try that load in

▼ L-R: .30-06, .300 Winchester, .30-378 Weatherby. More powder extends reach – and hikes recoil!

▼ Similar to the .340 Weatherby, Remington's .338 Ultra Mag kicks hard, requires long action.

your 1873 Springfield!) delivers about the same recoil force as a .338 Winchester Magnum thrusting a 225-grain spitzer at 2,800 fps. While you absorb about the same bundle of energy, the .338 may feel more brutal because the bullet and its reactive force leave the rifle more quickly.

Some shooters say rifles chambered for big-bore British cartridges merely push you, while sharp-shouldered magnums belt you, as if initiation by cordite somehow makes bullet launch more civil. I'm not convinced. There's more than a push to a .600 Nitro in recoil! Even .470s light enough for safaris without gunbearers can get vicious. To add insult, the short breech section of a double puts the muzzles closer to your face, and those off-center bores cause the rifle to pivot. True, doubles have twice the barrel steel up front, and velocities and breech pressures are low. But bullets that weigh more than an ounce, in front of powder columns as long as a shotshell, ensure that you'll get quite a jab. Inexperienced shooters or faulty locks that fire both barrels in quick succession make recoil more memorable. Also, there's less fore-hand control with a double. While you can *point* surely and quickly, the double's slender forend and slick barrels won't match the checkered fore-stock of a bolt rifle for grip in absorbing recoil.

It does seem that sharp-shouldered magnum cartridges sometimes kick harder than they should. Combining heavy bullets with high pressures and big charges of powder behind abrupt shoulders makes rifles bounce violently. The .378 Weatherby Magnum and its progeny can bring on a flinch fast.

▼ A long barrel and big brake distinguish this custom rifle by David Smith, here fired by Ken Nagel.

▼ The .308 is versatile, in bolt guns or ARs. Here Wayne fires a Rock River LAR-8. Trijicon scope.

A muzzle brake reduces recoil by reducing jet effect at the muzzle. It bleeds gas pressure through vents instead of letting it erupt suddenly with explosive force. In siphoning the gas, a brake also provides opposing surfaces fore and aft of each vent for the gas to push against. So not all the thrust of escaping gas is rearward. Brakes boost muzzle blast. Noisy rifles are easy to shoot at the bench, where you can wear ear protection. But you won't don muffs when you hunt. Shooting through a brake without them can ruin your hearing. Hunting guides, who often find themselves beside a hunter at the shot, by and large hate brakes.

A brake can also affect your shooting from low positions. Lying prone in dry dirt or snow, you'll trigger a tornado that leaves residue on your scope lens and in your barrel, maybe in your eyes. At best, it will hang aloft long enough to obscure your view of the animal's reaction. Without wind it can hang there after the animal and your chance for a second shot are gone.

Brakes needn't be unsightly. Many are barrel-diameter, with unobtrusive vents. Lex Webernick, the Texas gun maker who oper-

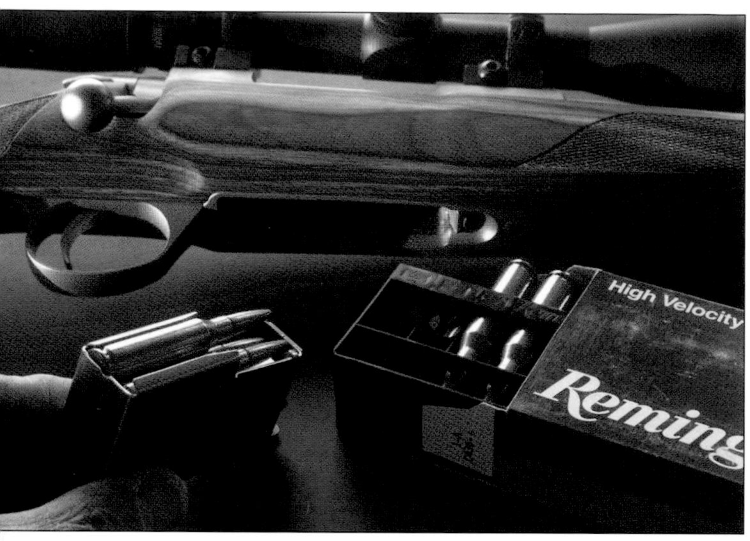

◀ Chambered in .260 Remington, Sako's handsome Grey Wolf is a versatile sporter with light recoil.

ates under the Rifles, Inc. shingle, has studied brake design, even measured noise output with vents of various sizes and locations. His brakes are very trim, and so closely fitted as to be all but indistinguishable from the barrel. Winchester and Browning incorporated a brake into their BOSS (Ballistic Optimizing Shooting System) device. Apparently a lot of hunters are willing to take recoil over noise, because now the BOSS comes without vents. Anyone ordering a brake is wise to ask for a cap to protect barrel threads with the brake off. A Mark X Mauser in my rack, barreled by Intermountain Arms, has a brake installed only finger-tight. At the bench, this .338 is docile but noisy. I replace the brake with a cap for hunting. Not all barrels shoot to the same point of impact with and without a brake. This one does.

A long barrel reduces felt recoil, partly because it delays the jet effect of powder gas at the muzzle, partly because it thrusts the blast farther from you. It also adds weight to the rifle's front end, counteracting muzzle jump—which means there's less lift to slam the rifle into your chops.

Another thing that keeps recoil from hurting you is a well-designed stock. The comb should have just enough drop to put your eye behind the sight. It should be straight from front to rear (no more drop at the rearmost area of cheek contact). A well-rounded top mitigates the bite. Cast-off (the comb offset to the right) is typically an option only on custom rifles.

Early cartridge rifles from central Europe have "Tyrolean" cheekpieces with pronounced dishing. They're comfortable if you're shooting deliberately but awkward on the trail and ill-suited for quick shots from unorthodox positions. Combs that slope up at the rear (as on Weatherby Mark Vs) reduce the damage to my cheek. Proper stock pitch (angle of butt to bore) matters too. Not only does it help you aim quickly; it affects the muzzle's arc at bullet exit. A soft butt-pad of generous dimensions slows and spreads recoil.

Shooting position and form affect felt recoil. When I was young I wondered why anyone would build a rifle with a crescent butt-plate. The butts of old lever rifles dug into my shoulder like bar-b-q forks when I aimed them at imaginary bears above the wood stove in the hardware store. I had fired a handful of carbines so equipped, and they all hurt me. What I learned later was that people who shot them in the days when crescent butts were in vogue placed the butts on their upper arms, not tight against their tender necks. They bent their heads over the stocks instead of relying on the comb for cheek support.

The .450 Bushmaster packs about as much punch into an AR-15 action as possible. It kicks hard. ▶

▲ When you rest a rifle against a tree, pad it with your hand, or it will bounce from the hard surface.

▲ This Montana/Serengeti rifle in .257 Roberts is handsome, accurate, and a pleasure to shoot!

Some rifles have a reputation for wicked kick. The Winchester 95 in .405 was one. Lots of power coupled with a low, sharp comb made this a molar-masher. Perhaps the most fearsome rifle in my rack is a Mauser in .458. Its stock is proportioned just right for the iron sights, and the rifle has the lively field of an upland bird gun. It doesn't weigh much more. This .458 kicks as fast as lightning on skids. After three shots my head throbs. My jaw comes out of numb after the fourth. When the sights again settle on the target, I'd almost trade places with it. If this four-five-eight with the hooves of a mule didn't point like a Rizzini and stick 500-grain solids into walnut-size groups, I'd trade it off.

◀ You don't need a hard-kicking cartridge to kill big animals. This Utah elk fell to Wayne's .308.

Brutal rifles give you little mercy at a bench. Leaning over a rifle on a table, you put your shoulder hard into the butt. The weight of your torso keeps you hard against it, so you absorb all the violence of a hard-kicking rifle. One way to make bench shooting more pleasant and keep flinching at bay is to use extra padding on your shoulder. In T-shirt weather folded bath towels work well because you can just drape them over your shoulder and shed them between strings. You'll need a soft pad for your right elbow, too, or the bench top will skin it. An old sweatshirt works well here—better than small pads because you won't tweak your position or put tension in your arm to keep it on the pad.

Recoil feels most severe when you're prone, partly because your body has lots of ground contact and can't move easily. That means you don't act as a shock absorber to help the rifle decelerate; you stop it suddenly. Shooting uphill from prone can exacerbate the effects of recoil because it puts the scope closer to your noggin. A short stock and a scope set well to the rear give you an even chance of drawing more blood from your skull than from the animal.

You'll absorb recoil most comfortably from offhand. Your body can flex and rock, damping the jolt. It's good form to aim with your head erect and your eyes straight forward. You'll get the clearest sight picture. But for shooters like me, with lots of neck between

▲ Properly a bit front-heavy, and an armload even with open sights, this CZ in .505 Gibbs still kicks!

chin and shoulder, there's a problem. We can't get full shoulder contact with the butt while holding our head up and keeping our cheek in contact with the stock. So we move the butt up so only the toe bears on our shoulder. All the recoil lands on a tiny section of clavicle, bringing to mind that 5th-grade bully who used to zap us there with an electrical device that was once marketed as a toy but would now be classified as an assault weapon. Toe-only contact is still better than bending over the stock and squinting up to seek a patch of target and a hyphen of reticle.

▲ Ruger's Alaskan in .375 Ruger is nicely balanced, quick to point, and handles recoil well.

Flinching is a real problem offhand because there's no brace for your torso to counteract the tug of suddenly-tensed muscles. The crosswire gyrates wildly as you run short of breath trying to settle it. Your trigger finger tries in vain to time the shot. The sear is about to drop. Then you remember the jab you felt at this stage last time. Oh my, did that hurt! Yikes! It's gonna git me again! Now! NOW!

On a recoil tolerance scale of gun-shy to Godzilla, I'm a notch above wimpish. My muscles are scattered in places that don't arrest butt-pads. I'm painfully aware when I pull triggers that save for a slice of rubber, all that lies between my clavicle and an aspirin-bottle load of IMR 4350 are brass, steel, and hardwood. People make hammers and mallets out of that stuff. Pounding such objects into my body with charges of gunpowder makes as much sense to me as sitting on stumps over dynamite. On the other hand, I like to put holes in things far away, and shooting is the best way to do that. So I work at controlling those muscles that bunch when they sense I'm taking up the last ounce on a trigger.

Repeated flinching is flinching well-practiced—a routine you don't want to learn.

Section VI

FOR LONGER REACH

31. Faster and shorter

In the 1890s, long, blunt military bullets in cases of modest capacity gave riflemen their first shooting with smokeless powder. The 7x57 launched a 173-grain bullet, the .30-40 Krag a 220-grain, the .303 British a 215-grain, the 8x57 (then the 7.9x57) a 226-grain. All traveled at roughly 2,200 fps from long barrels. When streets were still mostly dirt and our Civil War still sharp in collective memory, 2,200 fps was pretty fast.

But fast didn't stay fast. When Germany announced a new 154-grain bullet for its 8x57 cartridge in 1905, it raised the standard. This missile had a pointed nose and left the muzzle at a scorching 2,880 fps. Not to be outdone, the US scrapped the 220-grain .30-03 bullet (adopted from the Krag) and replaced it with a 150-grain spitzer. Velocity: 2,700 fps. Both countries made other changes in their service cartridges at that time. Germany increased bullet diameter from .318 to .323, the present diameter of 8mm bullets. A "J" was used to designate the original round (J meaning I for infantry), and an "S" (for Spitzgeschoss; also JS or JRS) given to the new one. American ordnance people shortened the .30-03's case .07, then renamed it the "Ball Cartridge, Caliber .30, Model 1906."

Other nations also recognized the advantages of pointed bullets moving fast. Flat trajectory made precise range estimation less critical and hitting easier. By the time the Archduke Ferdinand was felled by an assassin, most countries had rifles that far outstripped their sights. The .30-06 was claimed to be lethal at 4,700 yards, farther than most doughboys could keep

▼ This pronghorn fell at 300 yards to a shot from Dave Anderson's .257 Weatherby Magnum.

▲ Wayne got this moose with a single Hornady GMX bullet from his Ruger Hawkeye in .300 RCM.

'06 bullets on the side of a commercial granary. Still, like arrows loosed en masse at Agincourt, a volley of bullets raining on distant enemy positions was bound to be felt. *Effective* range and the range at which a soldier could hit a single combatant were quite different!

Small-arms reach became important to generals trying to conserve their troops under the withering artillery fire cratering battle-fields farther and farther from the cannon's mouth. So it was with consternation that in battle they found the 150-grain .30 Springfield bullet mostly useless beyond 3,400 yards. So the US changed its service bullet again, this time to a 173-grain spitzer with 9-degree boat-tail and long, 7-caliber ogive (radial curvature between shank and tip). Muzzle velocity dropped—but not much. This new "M1" bullet, issued in 1925, left the barrel at 2,647 fps. Its higher ballistic coefficient carried it 5,500 yards!

In 1939 the Army went back to a lighter bullet, a 152-grain spitzer designated the M2. The reason for this switch was the brutal recoil delivered by the M1 load. Even at 2,805 fps, the 152-grain bullet was easier to shoot. Like the M1, it had a gilding metal (zinc and copper) jacket to prevent metal fouling. With the M2 we fought the second world war. . . . .

Modern hunting bullets resemble the pointed German infantry bullets of 1905. About the only blunt bullets still popular are for heavy African games shot up close, where sectional density matters most. Oddly, hunters often talk about weight as if it were the crucial variable. To show how *small* a difference bullet weight can make in killing game, here's a look at two Nosler Partition bullets in the .300 Ultra Mag (zero: 250 yards).

	VELOCITY, FPS			*ENERGY, FT-LB*			*DROP, INCHES*	
	muz.	*200*	*400*	*muz.*	*200*	*400*	*300*	*400*
180-grain	3250	2834	2454	4221	3201	2407	-3.0	-12.7
200-grain	3025	2636	2279	4063	3086	2308	-3.4	-14.6

Either would work fine on the big game for which this cartridge was designed. The relatively even rate of velocity loss shows these bullets have nearly identical ballistic coefficients (.474 to .481). There's negligible difference in bullet drop to 300 yards, and the 2 inch disparity at 400 is just half as great as the bullet dispersion from a minute-of-angle rifle. It surely doesn't matter when you're shooting at a moose. The edge in velocity enjoyed by the 180 is offset by the greater mass and sectional density of the 200.

Another comparison worth a look is between bullets of the same weight but different nose shape. These two Wincheseter 150-grain .308 loads both clock 2,900 fps at the muzzle:

	VELOCITY, FPS			*ENERGY, FT-LB*			*DROP, INCHES*	
	muz.	*200*	*400*	*muz.*	*200*	*400*	*300*	*400*
Power-Pt. Plus	2900	2241	1678	2802	1672	938	-8.9	-27.0
Partition Gold	2900	2405	1962	2802	1972	1282	-7.8	-22.9

You might choose a Partition Gold bullet over a Power Point on the basis of this chart—and forget that most big game is shot closer than 200 yards, where either bullet would kill quickly. Accuracy counts for something, and maybe the Power Point Plus load shoots better in your rifle. I once chose a Power Point bullet over a Nosler Partition for an elk hunt simply because the Power Point gave me exceptionally tight groups. I killed a bull with one shot. If you expect close shots at tough game you'll want the Partition for its penetrating qualities, not for its flatter flight.

▲ L-R: the .308, .243, and .358 all appeared in the mid-fifties. The .260, 7mm-08 and .338 Federal followed, on the same case. Short-action rifles were proportioned for this family of cartridges.

Case size used to indicate relative performance. Not anymore, Remington's .300 Ultra Mag merely matches Weatherby's load for its .300 Magnum, though the Ultra Mag has 13 percent more case capacity. As capacity increases, efficiency drops. The .30-378 Weatherby Magnum and 7.82 Lazzeroni Warbird hit just a little harder than the .300 Weatherby, which gets almost equal velocity from 20 percent less powder.

Hiking bullet velocity once required adding powder and enduring more recoil. But some shooters have worked hard to wring high speed from compact cartridges that don't kick hard. In 1974 benchrest competitor Dr. Lou Palmisano reshaped the .220 Russian round to form what he and cohort Ferris Pindell would call the .22 PPC. A 6mm PPC came later. These cartridges were short and squat. From the base to the 30-degree shoulder measured barely over an inch, though basal diameter approached that of the .30-06. Palmisano thought a shorter powder column would yield better accuracy. In benchrest matches, where quarter-minute groups are commonplace, the PPC would have a tough test. The .222 Remington and 6x47 (a necked-up .222 Magnum) had been the darlings of serious competitors long enough that they held most of the records. Their popularity also meant that the "triple deuce" and 6x47 were chambered in the best rifles and used by the most competent riflemen. The PPC not only had to be superior; it needed time in the hands of shooters who didn't like to lose points experimenting, who might replace a barrel to try a new round but would be a lot more reluctant to change the bolt face on their pet bench rifle.

Palmisano and Pindell were convinced that the PPC case had promise. Soon their champion-level shooting and careful handloading produced winning groups. Other shooters followed. In the 1975 NBRSA championships, two of the top 20 shooters in the sporter class used PPCs. By 1980, 15 of the top 20 were so equipped. In 1989 *all* of them used the short, fat rounds. Even more impressive: The top 20 entrants in the demanding Unlimited class shot PPCs. And 18 of the 20 best in Light Varmint and Heavy Varmint categories favored them. Sako eventually chambered rifles for the PPCs, but despite vigorous campaigning by Palmisano, American gun companies demurred. The East Coast physician then took it upon himself to supply the benchrest community with PPC brass, importing more than a million .220 Russian cases! At this writing, 35 years later, the short, squat profile of the PPC has become commonplace in hunting camps.

Rick Jamison and John Lazzeroni pioneered the short powder column in big game rounds, albeit John is perhaps best known for his long magnums. Ballistically, his rimless 7.82 Warbird rivals the .30-378 Weatherby. His 8.59 Titan matches the .338-378. Lazzeroni's long cartridges range in caliber from 257 to 416. The cases are of his own design and manufacture. "If I'd done my homework," admits John, "I might have based them

▲ L-R: The 6.5 Creedmoor's hull is a tad shorter than the .260 Remington's, to accept longer bullets.

on the .404 Jeffery. Head dimensions of my rounds are ridiculously close to the .404's."

The Lazzeroni short magnums have the same heads, just .750 less case up front. The heads for his .243 and .264 short cartridges mike .532, same as for an ordinary belted magnum like the 7mm Remington or .300 Winchester, and identical to the head on Lazzeroni's long .257 Scramjet. The short 7mm, .300, .338 and .416 Lazzeronis feature .580 heads, like their longer counterparts. There used to be a .264 and a 7mm on a .546 case, but John discontinued them. He dropped the long .264 altogether and revived the 7mm on a bigger case. John lists these velocities for his compact versions:

6.17 (.243) Spitfire: 85-grain bullet at 3618 fps
6.71 (.264) Phantom: 120-grain bullet at 3312 fps

FOR LONGER REACH

◀ How to get rifle performance from a handgun? Use a strong rifle action, as Remington did by adaptingthe M600 bolt mechanism to its XP-100 pistol. Note the cantilever design, action to the rear, that allows a long but balanced barrel.

▲ The 8.59 Galaxy (a .33) is Wayne's favorite among a handful of short, potent Lazzeroni magnums.

7.21 (.284) Tomahawk: 140-grain bullet at 3379 fps
7.82 (.308) Patriot: 180-grain bullet at 3184 fps
8.59 (.338) Galaxy: 225-grain bullet at 2968 fps
10.57 (.416) Maverick: 400-grain bullet at 2454 fps.

These cartridges are short enough to fit .308-length rifle actions. Of course, the magazine and bolt face must be altered for the fatter case. Or you can buy John's rifle, the L2000SA. Appropriately dubbed the Mountain Rifle, it weighs only 6 ½ lbs. The McMillan action gets the same treatment as on long-action models: oversize Sako-style extractor, custom bottom metal, three-position safety, fluted Schneider cut-rifled barrel and Jewell trigger. John bores out the standard 6-48 scope mount holes, then drills and taps them to 8-40 for dead-center spacing and a more secure hold. Except for the magazine spring, all steel in this Lazzeroni rifle is stainless, jacketed with a satin-silver NP3 electroless nickel finish. It wears a classic-style synthetic stock, with a long, slender grip, straight comb, sharp checkering and a soft buttpad.

This Lazzeroni rifle is comfortable to shoot, partly because of the case shape. According to John, a squat hull "concentrates powder around the primer, so ignition at the front of the column occurs faster. Less powder starts moving with the bullet. Since powder following a bullet out the case mouth is ejecta, the less you send down the bore, the better. Recoil reflects both the burned and unburned weight of heavy charges."

Short cases give you the option of using faster fuel. John loads RL-15 behind 225-grain bullets in the Galaxy to get 2,760 fps—velocity you'd expect from the longer .338 Winchester and H4350.

Short Lazzeroni cartridges preceded Winchester's 2001 announcement of stubby rimless .30 with a .532 base. Slightly longer than the Lazzeroni Patriot, the .300 Winchester Short Magnum duplicates its performance. That is, it shoots as flat and hits as hard as a belted .300 Winchester Magnum. But with an overall length of 2.76 inches, it's half an inch shorter than the .300 Winchester. In fact, a .300 WSM *cartridge* is shorter than the *hull* of a .300 H&H, granddaddy of all belted magnums. And out-performs it.

Actually, Browning approached Winchester with the idea for a short .300 magnum early in 1999. Winchester ammunition engineers finalized the dimensions. Browning and US Repeating Arms Company (USRAC, manufacturer of Winchester firearms) redesigned their flagship bolt rifles—the A-Bolt and the Model 70—for the .300 WSM. Winchester followed with short .270 and 7mm rounds on the same case.

▲ L-R: .340 Weatherby, .338 Winchester, 8.59 Lazzeroni Galaxy. The Galaxy out-performs the .338.

Increasing bullet diameter proved problematic, given the ogive of .338 bullets and limited seating options in short actions. Eventually the .325 (8mm) WSM appeared. It offered a fine alternative to hunters wanting more bullet weight for elk, moose and big bears. Meanwhile, Winchester took short cartridges another step, with Super Short Magnums: .223, .243 and .25. The ballistic equal of much longer rounds, they did not feed smoothly. Hunters decided that there was nothing wrong with the .22-250, .243 Winchester or .25-06.

Remington was late to the party with short magnums, though it could have announced the first of them soon after the WSM debut. It chose instead to promote its just-introduced line of Ultra Mags, the full-length 7mm, .300, .338 and .375. When the .300 and 7mm Short Action Ultra Mags arrived, Winchester had established its WSMs as *the* short magnums of record. In truth, Remington's SAUM cartridges differ so little from their rivals that some chatter ensued on the possible hazards of switching ammunition. The Remington's .300 is the better round, in my view. It's very slightly shorter and, as slightly, more efficient. Also, it fits the compact Model Seven action, which does not as readily accept WSM rounds. I downed the first elk taken with the Remington .300 SAUM, using a Custom Shop Model Seven that's still a favorite.

Other short cartridges have followed the Winchester and Remington offerings, notably the .300 and .338 Ruger Compact Magnums, engineered by Hornady not only to deliver belted-magnum speed from short actions, but to outperform high-octane competition in short *barrels*. Mitch Mittelstaedt, who headed the project, explained to me that with new proprietary powders, his team was able to "tighten" pressure curves so the .300 RCM behaves like ordinary .30 magnums in 24 inch barrels but doesn't lose as much enthusiasm

▼ Prototype rifles in .300 RCM were synthetic-stocked Ruger 77 Mark IIs like this. They shot well!

▼ Remington's R-15 rifle gave Wayne this group. The short .30 Remington AR cartridge is mild in recoil, deadly on deer.

▲ L-R: .300 SAUM, .300 RCM, .300 WSM. They all outperform the longer and venerable .30-06.

▲ L-R: .300 WSM, .300 RCM, .300 SAUM. All wring .30-magnum speed from short actions.

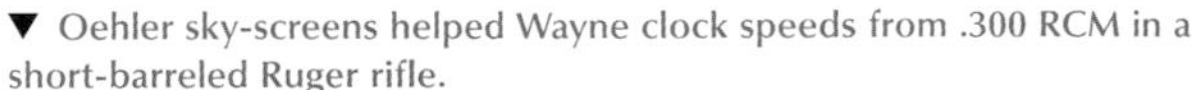
▼ Oehler sky-screens helped Wayne clock speeds from .300 RCM in a short-barreled Ruger rifle.

in carbines. "Velocity of .300 WSM bullets drops 160 to 180 fps when barrels are chopped from 24 to 20 inches; RCMs lose 100." With chronograph legend Ken Oehler, I chronographed .300 RCM loads from the 20 inch barrel of a Ruger carbine. The Oehler 35 gave me readings of around 2,840 fps with 180-grain bullets. Groups stayed around an inch. The accuracy was gratifying; short barrels are stiff.

Inspired by the 2.58 inch .375 Ruger, the .300 and .338 RCM share its .532 head and base. WSM rounds are bigger, with rebated .535 heads. RCM shoulder angles are 30 degrees. Case capacities average 68 and 72 grains of water to the mouth. For comparison, Remington .30-06 hulls hold 67 grains of water, Winchester .300 WSM cases 79 grains. Ruger Compact Magnums cycle through WSM magazines, but you can sneak four RCMs into most three-round WSM boxes. They're loaded to the same overall length (2.84).

Long cartridges may be going the way of long automobiles. For riflemen keen to boost velocity without getting a haymaker punch to the chops, modern short magnums make sense!

32. Notes on handloading

Last month I visited Cooper's Landing, Alaska half a century ago. Well, not really. I was at the loading bench concocting loads for the .450 Alaskan. This wildcat cartridge, attributed to Harold Johnson, who plied his trade as a gunsmith in the post-war Far North, is a powerful round that hurls 400-grain bullets at 2,150 fps. It beats the British .450/400 that in another day seemed a match for Bengal tigers and even big African game. Handloading the .450 Alaskan took me to Alaska's frontier when the state was still new. Hardy men in woolens and shin-high leather boots probed alder jungles for brown bears and threaded willow thickets for moose.

Among the most revered rifles for such duty was Winchester's Model 71, descendant of John Browning's powerful, elegant Model 1886, the first successful vertical-lug lever rifle. The 71 chambered a new cartridge, the rimmed .348 Winchester. The 250-grain bullet at 2,350 fps churned up 3,000 ft-lbs—as much as a .30-06. But the blunt noses required of bullets in the 71's tube magazine limited reach. By the rifle's 1935 debut, hunters were lusting after scoped bolt rifles launching rocket-shaped bullets. The 71 didn't last long; production ended in 1957.

"See what you can do with it." Steve Kerby had loaned me his converted 71, with a batch of expanded .348 cases, months earlier. Other projects got in the way. At last I shut the door to the twenty-first century and pawed through my stash of powders. I picked Scot 3032, H322, H4895 and Winchester 748, with bullets from Northern Precision and Hornady and Speer, 325 to 400 grains.

▼ Wayne used handloads in this high-performance 6.5 by Greybull to shoot a gong at a range of one mile.

▲ Wayne's handloads for the .250 Savage produced this group. Handloading can make old rounds shine.

Expanding a .348 case to 45-caliber is best done in two steps. RCBS forming dies with .30-to-.40 then .40-to-.45 expander balls yield a straight, tapered case. Firing a loaded round in a .450 Alaskan chamber puts a shoulder into the hull and reduces body taper. I hand-weighed charges of powder and seated bullets without crimping. Had these been hunting loads, I would have crimped the bullets in place, because the stiff recoil of the .450 Alaskan can overcome neck tension and jam bullets back in their cases in the magazine. To form cases, I'd load singly.

Boom! Even without game in the sights, shooting the 71 and home-brewed loads was great fun. The cases emerged beautifully formed, with no pressure signs—though one charge drove 400-grain Speers at nearly 2,100 fps.

You don't have to fashion wildcat cartridges to get something out of handloading. Stoking your own

▼ For years, the .22-250 was a wildcat. Shooters had to load their own ammunition. Then Remington adopted the popular varminter.

▼ Redding dies and Norma brass and Accurate 3100 powder: recipe for a potent load. Bullet? Your choice!

▼ At the moment of truth, we depend on one cartridge. Handloads can be as reliable as factory ammo.

.270 with cartridges you assembled yourself is like tying your own flies or making your own arrows. Handloading gives you a bigger role in the shot, more investment in a trophy. If you shoot as much as necessary to shoot confidently, rolling your own will save you money.

When I first considered handloading, I wondered if the investment in tools would ever be erased by savings in ammunition. After all, a Herter's press cost $15, and I'd pay that much more for a powder scale. I'd need dies too, at $10 per set. Components—bullets, cases, powder and primers—hiked the tab. With factory-loaded .303 softpoints at $5 a box, I almost demurred.

Having since saved enough money handloading to buy a well-equipped sedan, I find that earlier reasoning absurd. But many hunters still hesitate. If you shoot only a box of ammo each year, any savings will take a long time to appear. On the other hand, if you're not shooting more than that, you're not getting much practice as a marksman.

Another traditional reason to handload was to improve rifle performance. Handloaders enjoyed more bullet options and could tweak components and velocities to improve ballistic performance and accuracy. These days, that rationale carries less weight. The best of current factory loads are good indeed. Bullet choices rival those available to handloaders, because ammo firms are partnering with bullet makers to load bullets once sold only as components. Still, you have many more options as a handloader. Powders have proliferated too. "We carry 120 kinds, including Winchester and IMR powders," says J.B. Hodgdon. "That's 70 percent of the market." Incidentally, Bruce Hodgdon started his business 60 years ago with just one powder: war-surplus H4895. Next came H4831, a 20mm cannon powder available in huge quantities after the war. During my college days, I bought a 50-lb keg for $150. With barely enough cash left for primers, bullets, tomato soup and the month's rent, I plunged into handloading. In my .270, a 130-grain Sierra and 59 grains H4831 sent mule deer head over heels. I killed my first elk with a 180-grain Speer atop 69 grains H4831 in a .300 H&H. Today H4831 remains a top choice for magnum hulls. The Short Cut version sifts easier. (Note: Slow powders like H4831 should not be used in reduced charges. Detonation can occur, perhaps due to colliding pressure waves when primer flame spans the half-charge to start a secondary burn.)

Another fine traditional powder is H4350. Slightly faster than H4831, it's perfect for heavy-bullet loads in the .30-06, and for middle-weight bullets in medium-bore magnums. There's no better powder in the .257 Roberts or .280 Remington. My .25 Souper (a necked-up .243) uses 46 grains H4350 to launch 100-grain Speers at 3,240 fps. With 55 grains I get 3,010 from 140 Nosler Ballistic Tips in my .270s.

Versatility is the hallmark of H4895. Mid-range on burning-rate charts, it excels in the .308 and .30-06, and accommodates a wide range of bullets in most mid-capacity cases. It excels in big-bore rounds like the .375 H&H, yet remains a favorite in the .223. In a .338-06, 57 grains milks 2,850 fps from 200-grain Hornadys; 49 grains drives 180-grain Nosler Ballistic Tips at 2,800 from the .338 Federal.

▲ Some new factory ammo—here Hornady's for the .300 RCM—is hard to match at the loading bench.

▲ Accuracy like this, plus sizzling velocity, now comes in factory ammo. Hard to beat with handloads!

Practical pressure ceilings limit how far you can hike performance. When handloading cartridges like the 6.5x55 and .45-70, developed in rifles more than a century old, you can easily beat chart velocities. Modern actions and barrels permit friskier loads than would be safe in original rifles, whose presence dictates that ammunition firms observe conservative pressure lids. But high-octane cartridges, like Norma-loaded Weatherby Magnums and short magnums introduced during the last decade, may be up against the throttle peg from the start. Matching velocities of Hornady Superformance or Federal High Energy ammo can push pressures to case-sticking levels. That's because we handloaders lack access to some powders and loading techniques that make such hot-rod factory loads possible.

You'll still benefit from handloads with components matched and assembled to deliver the best accuracy in your rifle. You can tune loads to make certain bullets shoot faster or more accurately. To learn techniques that yield the best results quickly, consult manuals from Barnes, Hornady, Norma, Nosler, Sierra, Speer, Swift and Vihtavuori. Handloading is mostly science, and technique matters. Here are a few tips for better handloads—and caveats that might prevent wasted hulls, malfunctions, a wrecked rifle or a face-lift.

Try as many combinations of bullets and powders as you can, after comparing at least three manual listings for the cartridge. Why three? Test procedures and rifles vary; so may barrel lengths used to develop velocity tables. Reconcile differences between manuals; pick powders that generate the highest velocities in all three. Pay attention to case volume; slow powders that deliver acceptable speed may require such high charges weights that you run out of powder space. Getting all the powder you can into a case is best done with a drop tube, and by tapping the base of the case as you rotate it on its rim. Crushing powder by seating the bullet should have no effect on accuracy, velocity or safety. But compressed charges are slow to load. Ball powders don't compress as well as stick powders, and you may find bullets creeping out of severely compressed loads. My rule of thumb: Keep powder levels at mid-neck—the base of the neck for ball powders. If you need more fuel than that to reach target velocities, try a faster powder.

To make your dollar go farther when trying new powders, split canisters with friends. Ditto for boxes of bullets. Load three, four or five cartridges at a time.

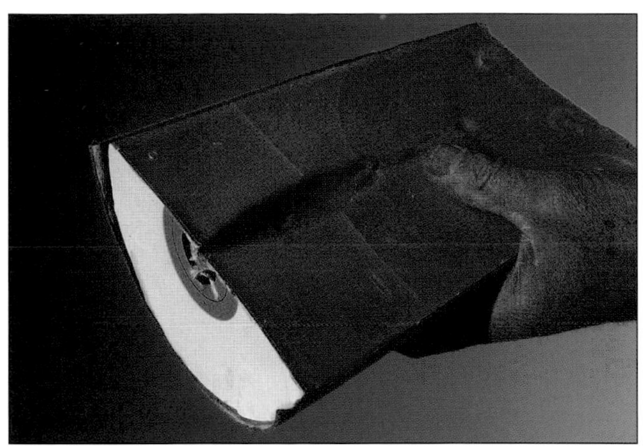

▲ "The Tube" was developed by Richard Mann, who wanted a convenient way to assess a bullet's terminal performance. A softpoint from a small-caliber rifle plowed this channel.

Chronograph them. After you whittle your options, assemble 10 or 12 cartridges at a time and shoot enough groups to find the most accurate. Then buy components in quantity.

You'll lubricate cases before sizing. A light coating is enough—too much lube will dent the case shoulder. Don't forget the inside of the neck. Use dry lube on a brush, or press the case mouth into a pad soaked in liquid lube to put a bead on the rim. The expander ball will have an easier job, and it won't tug the neck on exit.

Neck-size if loading for one rifle. Full-length sizing unnecessarily works brass, reducing case life. Belted cases, full-length-sized and fired in generous chambers, can fail quickly just ahead of the belt. You'll see damage there as a light-colored ring that portends case separation. A thin dark line in this pale belt is a crack waiting to spill gas. Discard that case, and examine carefully other cases from that lot. Gas loosed in the chamber can find its way back through the bolt. If the case head separates, you may need a tool to remove the front—which you won't have when an elk is staring you down in the lodgepoles. Gas also cuts chambers like a blow-torch. Once you've fired a belted case, baby it by setting your die a dime's thickness above the shell-holder. The sized case should fit nicely in the chamber it came from, and will grip a bullet securely. When loading a round for different rifles or to ensure easy chambering, size the shoulder only as much as necessary. (Shabbily-cut chambers that are out of round may resist neck-sized rounds oriented differently than when they were first fired; but this is a rifle problem, and one to correct.)

Don't test pressure limits. Sticky extraction, flattened primers and shiny ejector marks on case heads warn of pressures that impair accuracy and rifle function and reduce case life. By the time extraction becomes difficult, pressures are already beyond reasonable. Back off! Measuring case head expansion helps you keep tabs on pressure.

Keep cases trimmed to recommended length. A long case may not chamber. If the case mouth contacts the end of the chamber and you manage to close the bolt, the mouth will collapse into the bullet, effectively crimping it. But unlike a deliberate crimp, which releases after ignition as the neck expands to release the bullet, a case mouth up against the chamber end has no place to go. Its compression of the bullet greatly increases drag. Pressures can spike.

There's nothing wrong with trimming rifle cases a tad short. That way you can get several firings before having to trim again. (Avoid this practice when trimming cases that headspace on the mouth—like the .45 ACP.) Be sure to de-burr case mouths inside and out after trimming, for easy bullet seating and sure function in the rifle. If you crimp, set the die to deliver no more mouth compression than you need. Crimp only on a crimping groove or a cannelure.

When not crimping, you're free to seat bullets farther out than the cannelure indicates—within the limits imposed by your magazine and throat. Cartridges must fit comfortably in your magazine, and when you chamber one, the bullet's shank must lie shy of the rifling. Seating a bullet so far out that the rifling grips the bullet can be bad news. Not only does the contact deprive the bullet of an easy release; if the rifling engraves far enough onto the shank, it can win in a tug of war when you try to extract the loaded round. That is, you'll pull the case off the bullet, spilling powder into your magazine and leaving the bullet stuck in the bore. I like to seat bullets to within about .1 inch of the rifling. Accuracy can suffer if the bullet must make a long leap. To check throat length, seat a series of bullets progressively farther out until you feel one contact the rifling. Check for rifling marks (smoking a bullet with a match before chambering, you'll see them more clearly). Then set your seating die at least .1 deeper.

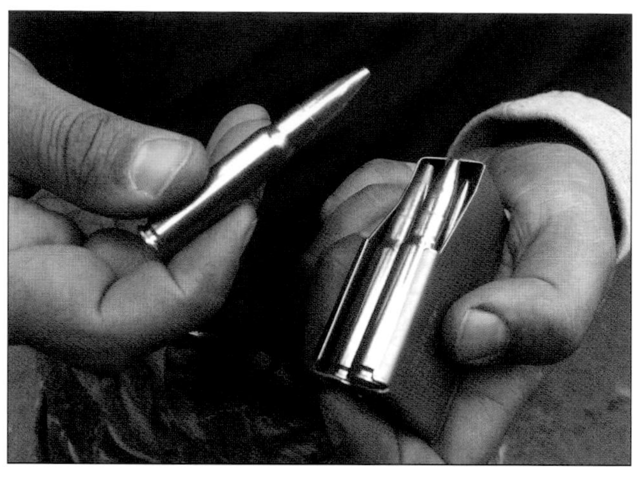

▲ Load all handloads into your rifle's magazine and cycle them before you hunt or enter a match!

When finished, label all handloads immediately. You will not remember powder charges tomorrow!

Run all handloads through your rifle, from the bottom of the magazine up, to ensure function. You want to know they'll feed now, before you cycle the bolt on an irate leopard or a spruce-bound Boone and Crockett moose.

▲ Faultless feeding is a requisite in hunting rifles. This Blaser R93 slicks up well-assembled .375 handloads.

At the range, as at the bench, mind what you're doing. Handloading requires only ordinary intelligence but extraordinary vigilance.

Once, on the range with a fellow who'd bought a lovely .270 from me, I heard a loud report. A quavering call for help brought me running. My amigo was bleeding around his shooting glasses, but didn't seem badly hurt. His rifle, though, was in shambles, its

▲ A

▼ B

◄ C

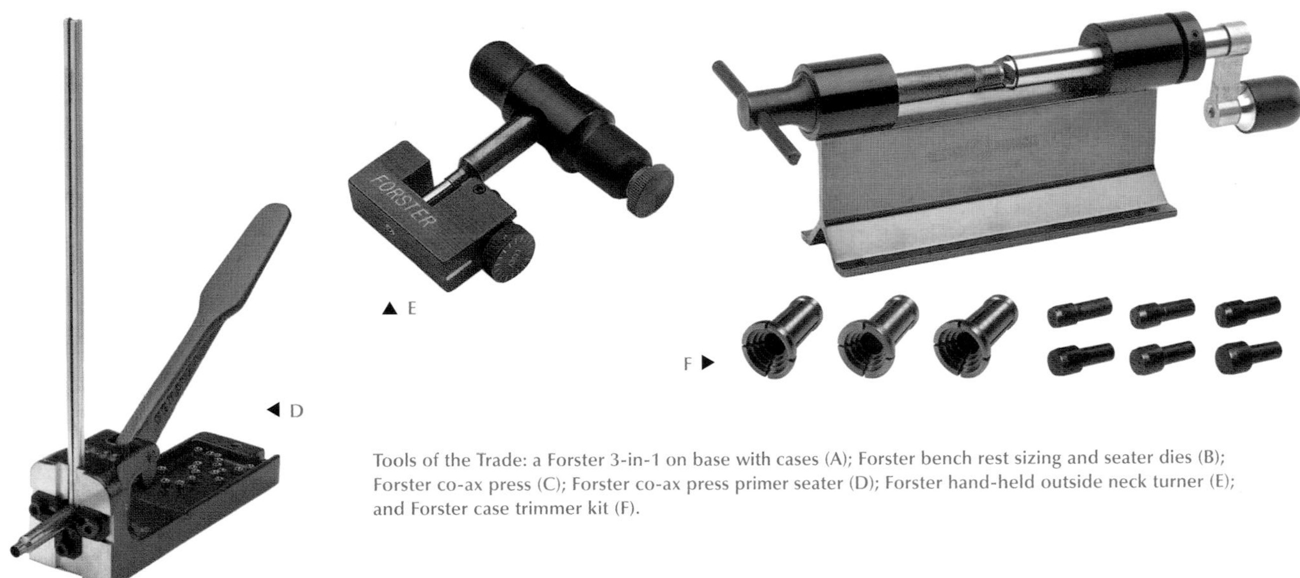

Tools of the Trade: a Forster 3-in-1 on base with cases (A); Forster bench rest sizing and seater dies (B); Forster co-ax press (C); Forster co-ax press primer seater (D); Forster hand-held outside neck turner (E); and Forster case trimmer kit (F).

French walnut stock split in three pieces, the extractor gone, the bolt frozen. "Those handloads of yours..." He winced as he wiped his brow. I examined the box of .270s. I'd loaded them with H4831. It's nigh impossible to get enough H4831 in a .270 case to blow up a 98 Mauser. In fact, I was sure I could card off a charge and seat a 130-grain bullet without exceeding safe pressures. The box in my hand wore my label, in my writing. H4831. The only thing wrong, I noticed suddenly, was that the box was full. I pointed this out, asking where the delinquent round had come from. Dave picked up another box. I saw instantly that it held .308 cartridges—suitable for the other rifle he owned. In haste he'd grabbed that ammo by mistake. Chambered in a .270, a .308 is poison. The shorter case slides right in. But squeezing a .308 bullet through that .277 bore, the rifle became a bomb.

More recently, on the bench with a borrowed lever rifle, I thumbed back the hammer and squeezed. Clack. I held the rifle securely for several seconds, in case of a hang-fire. When I opened the action, an empty case tumbled out. First thing to mind: "I forgot to cycle." But it's always wise to consider every possibility. Action open, I looked into the muzzle. Dark. The wildcat cartridge I'd chambered had been taken apart by the rifle's owner, formed, then reloaded with the original powder charge and bullet. Except he had forgotten to include the powder. When I pulled the trigger, the primer blast pushed the bullet into the throat. The primer's report couldn't escape from case or bore; it was further muffled by the hammer fall. Had I levered in a live round and fired it, the results would have been jarring. Expanding gas would have had to shove two 200-grain bullets down the bore. To make matters infinitely worse, the front bullet would have interrupted the forward travel of the one behind just as gas pressure was peaking!

Handloading is great fun. It can bring you to a different place and time, wring more accuracy and possibly even more power from your rifle. It becomes a personal investment in your hunt, your own signature at its climax.

Handloading treats most kindly riflemen who mind what they're doing.

33. Long shots at school

I shifted the phone to my other hand and wrote as Darrell Holland dictated the address. "Get there the night before. Bring your rifle and 300 rounds of ammo."

Highway 42 snaked through the southern Coast Range over a low pass and onto the South Fork of the Coquille. Powers, Oregon was a dot on the map upstream; I stayed with the river into Myrtle Point and checked into the only motel. The proprietor's small-town hospitality was genuine. He told me there were lots of elk in the hills and that logging strictures had squeezed local businesses. From the office we watched the sun's last light on Coquille backwaters—a glistening apron below the forest. "It's still a pretty place."

Next morning, after threading timber on a twisty macadam road, I came to Powers and a clapboard building—a Rotarian lodge that could have been a church, or a church that had once been a schoolhouse.

▼ Tactical rifles chambered for long-range rounds are typically heavy and have many adjustments.

▲ Notebooks and the Mil Dot Master are required on the line at Darrell Holland's shooting school.

"Safety first," barked Darrell, after introductions. This long-range shooting class numbered 20 or so, including those who'd been through the course and returned to help. David Brauneis was one. Pairing up recruits in shooter-spotter teams left David with me so I could run my camera when not on the line.

◀ Good notes help all students—especially shooters learning the vagaries of wind at distance!

Rules and procedures out of the way, Darrell launched into the contents of a three-ring notebook. I had thumbed the prodigious text, provided, with fruit bars and coffee, by Darrell's wife Rosita, She and son Jonathan also distributed shooting gear Holland sells from his shop where Powers meets the forest.

That morning I struggled a bit. Not because the information was foreign; rather, I'd not before had to recite it. Quickly now, what's a minute of angle? It's not an inch at 100 yards; it's 1.047 inch. A mil? It's a mil-radian, but also 3.6 inches per 100 yards and 3.438 minutes of angle. What's the formula for finding distance with a mil measurement? Uh.... "Math a little rusty, van Zwoll? Multiply target height in inches by 29. Divide the product by the number of mils." Darrell grinned wickedly. He had this memorized. "For example: A buck measures 18 inches through the chest; 18 times 29 comes to 522. The reticle brackets that deer with 1.5 mils; 522 divided by 1.5 is 348 yards." Simple enough.

But not everyone shoots at long range or has a scope reticle that shows mil measurements. Darrell read my mind. "You can get pretty skilled at estimating ranges out to 300, even 400 yards," he said. "But steep country can fool your eye. So can partially hidden targets, and changing light. So even at point-blank range, you can misjudge distance." Practice with a laser rangefinder can improve estimates. Darrell leans heavily on a rangefinding reticle because "it gives you an instant read when you're behind the trigger. It will help you hit game farther than you ever thought possible." He adds, however, that your first job on a hunt is to get as close as you can. "Don't shoot long when you can shoot short."

The best all-around reticle? Darrell had shipped me a Schmidt & Bender 3-12x50 fitted with his ART, or Advanced Reticle Technology crosswire. Tics indicate mils and minutes. But it's straightforward and easy to use. There's minimal clutter, so it also works for instinctive shooting. Darrell pointed out that most rangefinding reticles "don't offer enough precision for distant targets, where bullet trajectory is very steep. Their elevation ladders won't handle the arcs of many popular cartridges at ranges beyond 500 yards. And unlike the ART, they don't have numerical *values* you can plug into mil and m.o.a. formulas."

We finished the day on a windy saddle in the Siskiyous, one of the loveliest settings I've ever seen from a firing line. Then the rain came, as I should have expected even in May. We zeroed at 100 yards. I'd brought .308 ammunition from Black Hills, Federal, Hornady, Remington. Most loads featured 168-grain Sierra MatchKings or similar bullets. I included some 175-grain boat-tails, which hew closely to the same path to 400 yards but retain velocity and battle wind better at long range. My Kimber LPT shot both well.

I observed that most hunters wouldn't carry a .308 zeroed at just 100 yards, or use match bullets.

"Actually, I've shot more than 100 animals with a 168-grain MatchKings," Darrell said, hunching against the wind as I opened another box of 175-grain Black Hills Match. "They drive deeper than you'd think. And they're accurate. The 100-yard zero is fine for most shots. I crank in elevation for long pokes."

We shot until light ran out. By the time I'd micro-waved a cup of soup back in Myrtle Point, it was 9:30. Then on to homework: Clean the rifle, read in the workbook, and practice bolt cycling 150 times.

Next morning I drove fast with the window down, listening on the blind corners for that rattle of jake brakes. Log trucks had the right of way. I arrived before 8 to Rosita's fresh fruit bars. "Position and natural sight alignment first," harped Holland. "Controlled breathing next, then trigger squeeze and follow-through." He recommended the Harris bipod most of us had installed, and a toe pad he designed to support the rifle's butt. "Squeeze it with your off-side hand to nudge the muzzle."

Still, Holland cautioned against relying on gadgets. "A couple of data cards in one pocket and the toe pad in another is really all you need besides a good rifle and scope, and the bipod." He had printed and laminated cards for all of us, with info specific to loads we'd brought and chronographed. My card showed a 168-grain BTHP at 2,700 fps falling nearly 20 m.o.a. at 700 yards. That's 144 inches! Over the next 50 yards,

▲ A shooter adjusts a scope dial calibrated for long shooting with a 105-grain VLD bullet in a .243.

it would drop another 20 inches! Drift from a mild 12-mph full-value breeze would amount to more than 4 feet! Obviously, a hit at extreme range *without* data would be the purest of luck.

At the saddle again, we shot steel silhouettes from 200 yards out, finding yardages with the ART reticle. A Kestrel anemometer helped us gauge wind speed. "Zeroes are best established in still air," said Darrell. "After that, you can chase drift with the windage knob, or shade. If the wind is steady and you're firing repeatedly in a match, a dial change makes sense." He urged me to click up to add elevation, rather than hold over, to zero the resettable knob on my Schmidt & Bender at 100 yards.

Next afternoon, we spilled more brass on the saddle, then moved to a nearby hill to test our skills at ranges exceeding 800 yards. Humbling. I found that to 400 yards my sling scores matched those from the bipod. But at extreme distances, pulse bounce gave the gongs a rest.

Each morning we gathered to plow through a new chapter in the workbook, waiting for the fog to lift and hoping like 5th-graders that we'd not bungle a response when called upon. "What's the yardage if 7 ½ minutes of reticle brackets an elk's chest?" "How many mils in a circle?" "When is a corrected cosine helpful?" Hoo boy. "Wayne, how many mils high would you hold to kill a deer at 400 yards if bullet drop is 30 inches?" After a long, awkward moment with my

▲ At Holland's Shooting School, discussions turn to shots lost in frisky winds about Myrtle Point.

calculator, I managed a tentative: "2.18 mils high—30 inches divided by 3.438 equals 8.72, divided by 4 equals 2.18 mils."

Each afternoon the hills tested our wind savvy. They throttled the air but also put more spin on it, vertical as well as horizontal. The breeze bent around the hills, and anemometer readings at the line differed from what distant grass told us. Cool, gray skies denied us the mirage that would have warned of pick-ups, let-offs and changes in wind direction.

"Think of wind passing over a clock," said Darrell. "You're at the center. A full-value wind is one that comes from right or left, 3 o'clock or 9. A half-value wind comes from 4 or 10 o'clock, quarter-value wind from 5 or 11. Give 80 percent allowance for half-value wind, 50 percent for quarter-value wind." No matter how strong a head-wind or tail-wind, he said, it will not displace a shot laterally. The threat as wind hits you from in front or behind is a let-up. Sudden stillness often signals a change. When a 6 o'clock wind subsides, you'll be tempted to shoot. But when that indolent breeze flips its tail, you'll hit right or left—and wonder how a wiggle of air could have its way with a bullet unaffected by the gale that blew your hat off.

Besides our pocket calculators, we brought Mil Dot Master to the line. It's a slide rule developed as a math shortcut, with formulas and conversions and corrections. Plug in the numbers you know—drop or drift, minutes or mils, even shot angles. Mil Dot Master delivers the information you need.

The last day was a test: Twenty shots at unspecified ranges, from a new place so you couldn't use wind dope accumulated after four days on the saddle. No sight-in shots. You had to know the rifle and how the scope responded to adjustment. You had to use mil and/or m.o.a. scales on the reticle. You hit the steel or missed. If you dinged the heart-shaped paint in the middle you got an extra point—though recoil and/or distance hid the bullet strike so you couldn't adjust to better your odds for a center hit with the next shot. When the last target, an extra-credit javelina hung between 500 and 600 yards, swung slowly, and the echo of a hit floated back, I slid the Kimber's bolt open knowing I should have shot better.

▼ The Mil Dot Master is a bit like a slide rule for shooters – helpful even on the line.

▲ A chronograph session helps Darrell Holland correctly chart bullet paths for long-range shooters.

▲ To ensure quick follow-up shots afield, practice cycling the rifle's action every time you fire.

One of the class tallied a higher score, with a .280 Improved built by Holland. My Kimber would have cleaned the course, had I done my part.

Darrell Holland's Shooting School is one of several courses available for would-be sharpshooters. Gunsite Academy in Arizona is another. These classes *will* make you a better shot. The reason: For a week, you'll focus only on *shooting*. You'll fire more cartridges than many hunters fire in a decade. You'll iron out problems with gear and shooting positions. You'll pick up tips from instructors and other shooters.

For example, Darrell recommended that we fire with empty lungs, that we use our trigger finger to raise the bolt handle and our thumb to return it, that for long-range practice we hang butcher paper behind the target to catch all shots. Did you know that when part of a scope field "blacks out," your bullet will hit to the opposite side? That front and rear action screws are best torqued to 55 inch-pounds but center screws should be only snug? Darrell free-floats his barrels, with .080 forend clearance. He pillar-beds with alloy columns and gives his triggers generous over-travel. "You don't want your finger coming up against a stop and disturbing the rifle just as it fires."

Common-sense tips can save you from common errors: Cycle the action quickly after each shot so you're never caught with an empty chamber. Shoot from the lowest position possible. Let the rifle find its natural point of aim; shift your position, not your arms, to get on target. Treat each shot as the only one you'll get. Never rest your barrel, and always pad the forend.

Holland included some insight you won't find elsewhere unless you're deep into Sierra's Infinity ballistics program. For instance, you know thin air at high elevation can affect bullet flight—though lower temperatures at altitude increase density and thus offset the influence of elevation. But how *much* lift does thin air give a bullet? Well, a 150-grain bullet shot from a .300 Weatherby at 3,400 fps drops 34 inches at 500 yards. That's if you're at 1,000 feet elevation. Climb to 3,000, and you hit an inch higher. Add another inch as you approach timberline at 7,000 feet. Near Colorado's roof, at 12,000, your bullet sinks just over 30 inches. Such differences in bullet strike (for this load ½ m.o.a. for 7,000 feet of elevation gain at 500

FOR LONGER REACH

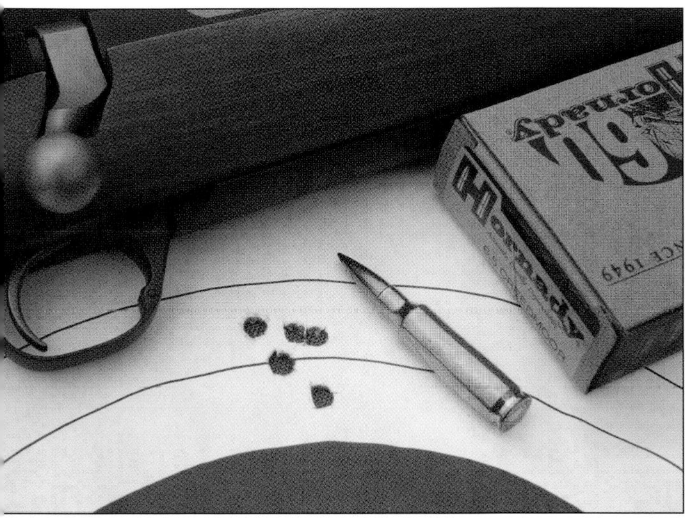

▲ Ruger's Hawkeye in 6.5 Creedmoor is a lithe, light-recoiling hunting rifle with great reach.

yards!) are tiny compared to bullet displacement from a horsed trigger.

An overlooked bonus from long-range shooting schools is their contribution to better accuracy up close, where you're most likely to kill game. It's easy to get sloppy from a bench at 100 yards. Snuggle into the rifle prone and try to hit a gong at unmarked range beyond a quarter mile, and you must focus. Small errors obscured by up-close shooting bring ragged groups at 500 yards—and silence from the gongs. You must shoot more carefully at long range to gain proficiency, and more often. Time behind the rifle makes you more familiar with it. Hunters who handle their rifles once a year stand out like. Saddle-bronc riders who warm a saddle that often. Neither a rifle nor a horse becomes familiar at a distance.

To say that a hunting rifle is ill-suited to long shots is to say a gelding trained to cut cattle won't pack elk. A rifle designed for 1,000-yard competition will perform better there than in the lodgepoles. But you can apply your hunting hardware at ranges that are long *for that rifle, scope and load.* Variable scopes with 3x or 4x magnification at the low end give you plenty of power for long pokes without compromising fast aim in thickets. Scopes like Leupold's Mark 4 and Zeiss and Schmidt &Bender variables, when paired with reticles like the Holland ART, can deliver fast offhand shots or

▼ Norma loads the 6.5/284. As a wildcat, the round became the darling of 1,000-yard shooters.

▲ Riflemen bear down on distant targets at Darrell Holland's shooting school in southwest Oregon.

help you find and compensate for wind and gravity at distance. Barrels and bullets that excel in the thickets can also deliver fine accuracy far away.

Another benefit from Holland's school is ranking. Few shooters can (or choose to) honestly assess their own prowess. Competition, even informal, is instructive and humbling. One unusually good shot takes you nowhere on a scoreboard; you're compelled to fire a *series* of bullets, and claim the misses. You must improve aggregate scores. Long courses of fire reward consistency, which is another way to say accuracy. Checking your ego at the door is a requisite in Powers, Oregon. Because eventually you'll bungle a shot or get the question you dread:

"OK, van Zwoll, calculate the difference in 600-yard drop caused by a 45-degree shot angle. Your .308 is zeroed at 100 yards with 168-grain MatchKings."

"Why of course, Mr. Holland. The cosine for 45 degrees is .707, corrected cosine .300. Multiply the drop from bore by .3. Subtract the result from drop from line of sight at that distance, and divide that result by 1.047 minutes of angle. Finally, divide this number by 6, the range in hundreds of yards.... Oh, you mean the *easy* way. Well, you just take the straight-line distance and multiply it by .7, a handy cosine multiplier: 600 times .7 equals 420. Hold for 420 yards. For a 30-degree shot angle, the cosine multiplier is .9; for 60 degrees, it's .5."

Invariably I wake up at this point, as was the case decades ago the night before an algebra exam.

If math has *you* in a hammerlock, know that Holland's Long Range Shooting School gives partial credit for showing up and won't report your tenuous grasp of ballistics to anyone who thinks you never miss. Just be sure, each night, to scrub your bore until patches come out white. And when you'd rather go to bed, cycle that bolt 150 times. Follow with 150 trigger squeezes. Next day, after the fog lifts through the oaks over the Coquille, shooting mechanics must come naturally. You must be free to engineer the landing of a steeply-descending bullet on a slab of steel so far off you can eat a fruit bar before you hear it ring.

34. A day in the desert

He produced a photograph, poorly composed, taken in difficult light. The men inside, dark and out of focus, stared beyond, over the rifle to a spot of orange. It had been a vehicle of some sort. The incendiary bullet had unhinged it. A bright spot in the desert, a memorable moment in a long tour.

The Army is supposed to break things. When things blow up, it's a good day.

"We were there together," says Jon Weiler. "Ryan nailed that one." Jon—lean, bright-eyed and intense—hails from Tennessee. He logged six years in the 10th Mountain Division and 82nd Airborne before coming to work for Barrett as a shooting instructor. Ryan Cannon—stocky, with a gunnery sergeant's jaw and a ready smile—served in the 82nd Airborne. He's from Omaha.

▼ Note-taking on the line distinguishes savvy shooters. As in academic classes, it's a habit of top students.

"Here's your rifle." Ryan lifts an M82 Barrett from its coffin-like case, upper in one hand, lower in the other. He presents them with practiced ease, and as if they weighed much less than their combined 18 lbs. "You assemble it like this," he continues, rescuing me from embarrassment. "Pull this collar… The springs are stout … Takes some practice." The rifle comes together on its own. He hands it to me. "Both these pins must be in place or the gun comes apart." He smiles and ponderous lengths of steel capitulate. I repeat the exercise. Ryan smiles again. "You'll get faster."

Enrollees in Barrett's Tactical Long Range Class have all now arrived. Jon wastes no time. "We'll use M33 ball ammo. Its 660-grain copper-jacketed bullet has a soft steel core. It starts at 2,700 fps from a 29 inch barrel. Chamber pressure averages 55,000 PSI. Expect 2-minute accuracy—that is, 12 inches at 600 yards." We sit like high school students in trig class as Jon scrolls quickly through a Power Point summary of external ballistics. "Some of the 50-caliber ammo you'll see is de-linked machine gun fodder. A lot of BMG is manufactured off-shore." He says these cartridges vary, one to the next, "in case dimensions and hardness. Soft brass can cause extraction problems." He passes around a fired hull with the rim badly bent.

The group, a dozen of us, breaks for lunch, motoring a mile to the Whittington Center's cafeteria.

"You could have joined us for PT," grins John when he learns I'd run a marathon a week earlier. But I had traveled late, in a rental car from Denver, passing through Raton after midnight.

"Slept like a log. Maybe tomorrow."

The Whittington Center could pass for a piece of Afghanistan. It sprawls across the eastern hem of rugged hills shadowing a great, dry basin. Rock and sand and grizzled desert plants—"a touch of home," grins Ryan, recalling his recent deployment as a sniper in Iraq. Like Jon, he's employed now by Barrett. Like Jon, he gets on well with these men in fatigues and black T-shirts—men young enough to squander hours on bordello humor, old enough to have survived battle and get serious about shooting. A generation removed, I am qualified to observe them and share the line with them

▲ Dust from the .50's blast through a brake engulfs shooters on the line at Barrett's shooting school.

but not to count myself one of them. I'm here to report on the training of 50-caliber riflemen, to get a story and perhaps glimpse desert warfare through the dust.

The Center is no longer an NRA facility. It retains a strong affiliation but has its own board. Its vast complex of shooting ranges, plus on-site housing, makes the Center a destination resort for firearms enthusiasts. It hosts 170,000 visitors annually. Under Mike Ballew and now Wayne Armacost, the facility also offers two Adventure Camps for youth during the summer "to ensure that youngsters learn not only about firearms, but about the land and wildlife and their conservation." They learn resourcefulness too in the Center's rugged back-country. It's home to a variety of game animals: mule deer, elk, pronghorn, cougar and black bear. Hunts in Whittington's hills go to sportsmen lucky in the tag draws.

But we aren't here for big game. Our shooting will be limited to the 1,000-yard range.

We reconvene in the classroom. Jon talks about the Barrett M82. "The Army calls it the M107." He adds that for my benefit. All the other students seem to know; they're soldiers and law officers. "It's a short-recoil autoloader with a 10-round detachable box magazine. The barrel is button-rifled, lands pitched one-in-15." He tells us the Leupold Mark IV scope sits 2-½ inches above bore-line, that one revolution of its elevation dial moves impact 15 minutes, that to find the paper quickly at 300 yards we should bottom the dial, then turn it up 22 clicks. He advises us to keep a light coating of high-pressure grease on the barrel extension and bolt head. "The trigger pulls 8 lbs and is not adjustable. You'll get used to it. When you fire, keep pulling the trigger and hold it back for a count of two—to ensure that you follow through."

Jon continues with a monologue on distance. "Shooting far, you must contend with variables most riflemen never have to think about. Like air density. Cold air is denser than warm. Air at sea level is denser than air in the mountains. As humidity goes up, air density goes down—strange but true." He tells us that "dope"—as a shooter dopes

▼ At 1,000 yards even this target looks small. The pit crew is protected by a berm and concrete.

▲ This Kestrel gauge delivers a digital read on wind. Long-range shooters heed those numbers!

▲ The .50 BMG gives you an edge in wind at distance. But it's a violent, hard-kicking cartridge.

the wind—is an acronym for "data of previous engagement" and that keeping accurate records of range conditions is the first step to learning how they affect bullet flight. "Most data is standardized for shooting at sea level at 59 degrees Fahrenheit. Hot and frigid weather, and high altitudes, can affect your bullet noticeably at extended range."

He talks about ballistic coefficient—how it changes with speed and why the most accurate bullets don't always have highest C values. "A football is aerodynamic," he points out. "But it's very unstable."

Suddenly, the afternoon is over. Jon briefs us on the next day's schedule. "We'll fire 15 rounds to zero at 200 yards, 20 each at 600, 800 and 1,000."

Next morning, I join the pit crew first. We plug and paste to the rhythmic thump of rifles hundreds of yards away, the crack of their bullets close overhead.

Relay number one takes all day to finish. In fact, it doesn't. Each shooter has a spotter, as in the field. So essentially two relays must fire through before switching with the pit crew. I abandon the pits early to photograph the line against New Mexico's red evening sun. The gaping brakes hurl amber dust high over the prone marksmen and the spotters on their flanks. Brass cases the size of whisky flasks wink as they spin forward through the haze. The rifles, hard against the sand-filled feed sacks in the shooters' armpits, shuffle reluctantly to the cycling of the bolts. Powder residue and dirt ring the eyes of the young men as they peer intently through spotting scopes and the Leupold Mark IVs.

"Call 'em!" snaps Jon. "Keep your body behind the rifle! Good shot! Watch the wind, spotter!

What's the temperature? Talk to him...!"

At 600 yards lots of shots find the 10-ring; at 800, fewer. At 1,000 mirage and wind flags often tell different stories. The men must balance midrange drift against that at the target. As with .22 bullets in 100-yard matches, the spotting scopes show rippling wakes of bullets hooking through the mirage.

"Mirage doesn't affect bullet flight," I remind my team-mate the next morning as he bellies onto the mat. "But it shows you wind that does." I've little experience shooting .50s; on the other hand, wind is wind, and its harsh treatment of my bullets in smallbore matches remains clear in memory. I hunch over the spotting scope, marking hits in the log book, coaching as best I can. "Hold 10-ring at 9 o'clock."

"You mean 3 o'clock, don't you?" Jon crowds my shoulder. "It's a 4 o'clock wind."

I concede that is so. "But he's set up for that. The mirage at 1,000 has big waves. Wind is putting on the brakes. He'll leak right if he holds center." Age gives you some prerogatives, such as telling young, bright people with better eyes that your call is correct, if counterintuitive. "Conditions same. Hold at 9," I repeat. "Four minutes out."

Boommm! Frank triggers it well. The target sinks slowly behind the orange dust. When it comes up it

▲ A shooter lines up his 50-caliber Barrett on a 600-yard target. The heavy bullet still yields to wind.

wears a plug close to center at 6 o'clock. "Good call," Jon smiles, rising.

Then it is my turn to shoot. I've fired plenty of rounds prone, but almost all with sling support and rifles of modest weight. The Barrett's stout bipod is more than an accessory. Without it, the rifle would be as useful as a chair without legs. And without the bag I would never endure a 20-round string. Recoil and the great weight of the rifle's butt quickly make themselves felt.

"Lie on *top* of the bag," urges Jon. "Take some sand out if it won't conform to your body. Bring the toe well into it. Do it exactly the same for each shot."

That much I know. Accuracy is a measure of consistency. But getting that simple bag to behave under my bicep proves a challenge. So does the long, hard trigger pull.

"You're doing well," says Jon, putting a rosy spin on mediocre shooting. At 1,000 I leak a couple to the edge of the last scoring ring, 30 inches from center. "Two-minute ammunition," Jon consoles. Still, making a silk purse from this performance will be tough. I've noted during the last relay that other riflemen have missed the target altogether.

Launching bullets of 660 to 750 grains at .30-06 velocities, the .50 BMG is a formidable round! ▶

▲ Shooters and spotters take their turn in the pits, pulling and marking targets, then pasting them.

The .50 is not brutal. Blast from the brake rocks me, but recoil is tolerable. While some shooters have padded the steel combs of their stocks (tampons seem the cheek-rest of choice), I find no such need.

The last day of my visit, we arrange a war zone in the pits, with cardboard silhouettes mounted on long poles. Some silhouettes are roughly the shape of human torsos. Others, smaller, offer a chest-up target only. Painted various colors, the cut-outs are designated friendly and hostile by hue. Shooters must tell at a glance, and hold fire until a legitimate target is in the clear. With the first relay on the 300-yard line, those of us manning the silhouettes raise them briefly at random places. Then we march with them, sometimes crossing friendly and hostile.

"It's like that over there," says Ryan. "Not much time to shoot. A high risk of collateral damage." The exercise reminded me that these riflemen are not primarily sport hunters or target shooters. For some, Barrett's school is grounding for additional combat. A couple are explosives experts on domestic police teams. One is returning to Iraq as a civilian contractor.

A tight schedule denies me the last day of tactical shooting with the Barrett M82. Pity. "We'll be firing at distances of up to 1,700 yards," Jon says. "That's about as far as we can correct for elevation on a Mark IV when the scope base has 27 minutes of gain. The targets will be randomly placed in hilly terrain; some will be hard to see. Shooters will have to range them, determine atmospheric conditions with Kestrel instruments and make appropriate adjustments in their hold or scope settings."

Packing up as the other shooters dismantle their 82s for cleaning, I feel a bit out of place. These are warriors, with experience in hostile environments and the prospect of using their big rifles against men who want them dead. Barrett's Tactical Long Range Class is tailored to them. Perhaps someday I'll attend its civilian counterpart. Right now I'll drive north while the soldiers prepare for the final day's event. The practice, and the Barrett .50s, might one day save them.

35. Dial up at distance

Extending reach is a fundamental purpose for firearms. One shooter who has made long reach a mission is John Burns, a Wyoming gun-builder who, with Coloradans Scott Downs and Don Ward, operate GreyBull Precision. They fashion hunting rifles for hunters who expect to shoot far. Chamberings: .243 and 7mm Remington Magnum.

Just two? "They're all you need for western big game," shrugs John. "We load 105- and 180-grain VLD bullets. We program our scopes so you can click to any yardage, even beyond 1,000 yards." John and Scott have taken game at extreme range. "But that doesn't mean we shoot irresponsibly," John insists. "A hunter must know his limits and hew to them." Maximum effective range depends on conditions that affect your precision. A close offhand shot can be tougher than a long poke with bipod or sling. Wind complicates a shot. So does your physical state; hitting gets hard when you're catching your breath after a climb.

Targets also play a role, and not just as regards size. Shooting steel gongs and paper bulls-eyes at half a mile is great fun—and worthwhile practice! But even with a steady position and the best equipment, the risk of a crippling hit at such distances keeps me from shooting game that far. In fact, reaching a quarter mile with accuracy demands excellent marksmanship and favorable conditions.

Optics are a key component of GreyBull rifles. The firm contracts with Leupold to install its own reticle in Leupold's 4.5-14x VX III sight. It's essentially a Duplex with a few fine horizontal lines for range estimation, and one-minute tics to help you shade for wind. The elevation dial is meant to move; each is cut for a specific load and marked so you can quickly dial to the distance and hold center. Adjusting windage dials, most hunters agree, is bad business. Wind is always changing, and you can easily get lost dialing off zero. Numbers scribed atop distance marks on the elevation knob show minutes of lateral correction needed in a 10-mph crosswind. Testing these scopes, I've found yardage and windage marks accurate. Of course, a laser rangefinder is all but necessary to get the most from the elevation dial.

▲ Offhand, John Burns draws a bead with a Leupold scope featuring his load-specific elevation dial.

"Calibrating a dial to match the arc of a bullet is a demanding job," John concedes. "We have to know starting velocity and 700-yard drop to calculate the ballistic coefficient and accurately mark the dial." GreyBull can supply scopes with dials for nearly any cartridge, provided that data is available. "Ballistic coefficients listed in catalogs aren't always right," John

▼ Wayne fired this group with a GreyBull rifle, prone, at 780 yards. Chambering: 7mm Rem. Mag.

FOR LONGER REACH

adds. "If that C number is off a little, you won't notice it at under 400 yards. But the farther the bullet travels, the steeper its arc, and the more important the accuracy of the data." John builds in third-minute clicks to replace standard quarter-minute detents. That's so he can milk more distance from one dial revolution. "Then you won't get a full-rotation error."

Before you can benefit from a sight that tracks trajectory, you need ammo that delivers precision where arcs get steep. High-performance handloads help. John's aren't much if any faster than ambitious factory loads. However, VLD (very low drag) bullets *retain* velocity better than ordinary spitzers. That's crucial at long range. You need the highest ballistic coefficient practical. In other words, the bullet must be heavy for its diameter (high sectional density) and sleek in form. Reducing rate of deceleration at distance matters a lot more than increasing muzzle velocity. A 180-grain 7mm bullet lies at the heavy end of the weight range; so too 105-grain .243s. These bullets, driven by Hodgdon's Retumbo powder, shoot flat "and with enough precision for 1,000-yard hits," says John. Because distance saps velocity, terminal behavior (upset and penetration) from hollow-point bullets can improve at long range—even as energy diminishes.

Long bullet ogives make seating a problem in short actions, so John prefers the roomy Remington 700 long actions, even for the .243. "Seating those 105-grain missiles out increases case capacity." John cuts relatively long throats in his barrels, because "short bullet jump hasn't produced the best accuracy for us. Besides, bullets seated into the rifling can become a problem in the field. One cartridge a tad long may stick the bullet when you close the bolt." Instead, John guides bullets with a lengthy throat "the thickness of a fly's wing" over bullet diameter. "Bullet alignment is crucial. Many factory chambers are too generous."

GreyBull rifles wear 26 inch medium-heavy barrels from custom makers like Kreiger, Schneider and Lilja. John floats the barrel and glass-beds actions in a synthetic (hand laid) stock he and his partners designed. It has a steep, full grip and ample forend. A special stud accepts a Stoney Point flexible bipod.

Like me, John and his crew think stiff recoil and harsh muzzle blast can offset benefits afforded by accurate loads, costly barrels and sophisticated optics.

▲ Prone, firing one shot each at 100, 200, 300, 400, 500, and 600 yards with his Marlin 1895, .338 Marlin Express, Wayne used only the GreyBull dial on his Leupold to add elevation. All shots hit!

"If you're afraid of the rifle, you can't shoot well," he declares. A range session near our camp last fall confirmed that observation. I watched several hunters fire powerful rifles. Softball-size groups predominated—at 100 yards! One fellow had trouble hitting with his .338 Magnum. No wonder! At each pull of the trigger he shut his eyes and ducked away from the comb!

The GreyBull crew says mild recoil is one reason they like the .243 and 7mm Magnum. Both have accounted for deer and elk at extreme range.

"Nail that gong." John handed me a GreyBull rifle in .243. Good grief! The 16 inch steel plate was so far it appeared a mere dot in the Wyoming sage. "It's as big as a deer's chest," he said matter-of-factly. "Dial up to 800 yards. It's actually 780, so take a click off." I indexed the knob and settled onto the bipod. A sharp wind quartered toward us at roughly 15 mph. "Give it 4 minutes left windage." At 780 steps, that's 30 inches. Lots of air gaped between crosswire and plate!

Bang! The 2-lb Jewell trigger broke cleanly. "Add a minute left," John advised. I did. Seconds after my next shot, we heard the distant pop of a solid hit. "We don't advocate shooting at game half a mile off," John emphasized. "But minute-of-angle precision at long range gives you great confidence at normal distances. It's an ace in the hole if you must anchor an elk far away."

Trusting the dial can be hard. "We loaned a rifle to a neighbor," recalls John. "At 780 yards he hit high. I was perplexed until he admitted he *held* high. Of course, adding a few inches of elevation that way is absurd.

Were it not for the *dialed* adjustment, he would still have planted his bullets several *feet* shy!"

More shooting at gongs, and a one-shot kill on a distant deer, convinced me the GreyBull system works. Hit on the shoulder, that buck and others killed by my camp-mates demonstrated the lethal effect of the VLDs. "Of course," John reminded me, "aiming for the right spot is a requisite. You must also steady the rifle and break the shot without disturbing your sight picture."

To see if the GreyBull scope would add reach to my lever-action Marlin in .338 Marlin Express, I had Don Ward cut an elevation dial for Hornady's 200-grain FTX load. Installed on a 2 ½-8x36 Leupold, it didn't look *too* much like a target knob. Mounted low, the scope complemented the 1895 Marlin nicely. But would it really benefit a lever gun? We tested it on the Wyoming prairie. After establishing a zero with a sling from prone, I bellied into the sage and fired one shot at a 10 inch steel gong from 100 yards. Then I moved back to 200, dialed up to "2" on the GreyBull knob and fired another shot. I repeated at 300, 400, 500 and 600 yards, one bullet at each range, trusting the dial and holding center. Every shot hit the 10 inch gong. Now, on a hunt, I limit my shooting to modest ranges. In fact, with that rifle I passed up my only shot of the season at a six-point elk. It was standing just 300 yards off, and I had a steady position. But the angle and the thick surrounding cover signaled caution. Almost surely I could have clobbered that bull; declining a shot, however, is never a bad choice.

Recently, I put GreyBull hardware to the test on a hunt. The scope wore a dial carefully scribed to

▼ This Marlin 1895 in .338 Marlin Express wears a Leupold scope with GreyBull dial for distance.

▲ John Burns hoists a coyote that came to his call and fell to Wayne's 6.5 Creedmoor at 250 yards.

match the arc of a 129-grain SST bullet in Hornady's then-new 6.5 Creedmoor. The cartridge derived from Dave Emary's discussions with 1,000-yard shooters, who favored a mild 6.5. An accomplished marksman himself, Emary distilled the requisites: high ballistic coefficient, low recoil and easy adaption to short-action bolt rifles. Dave revamped the compact .30 T/C hull (also from Hornady), whose neck would keep long, pointed bullets within the limits imposed by short magazines. He used powder technology from the firm's Superformance Ammunition to get eye-popping speed from 129-grain SSTs. The Creedmoor starts on the heels of 130-grain .270 loads. Beyond 400 yards, its superior ballistic coefficient narrows the gap, then erases it. "It's a great round," Dave enthused, after he'd shot a couple of bucks far away. "It's easy to shoot but deadly on deer. And we've punched half-minute groups with a T/C Icon!"

I ordered a Ruger Hawkeye in 6.5 Creedmoor. But hunting season arrived before I had a chance to scope it. Then Todd Seyfert at Magnum Research delivered a test rifle barreled to the Creedmoor on a long 700 action. Magnum Research rifles have impressed me in the past—a trim .280 killed a pronghorn at 393 steps—so this 6.5 got my quick attention. Its long carbon-fiber barrel had a stainless core rifled by Kreiger. GreyBull Precision provided the stock and the 4.5-14x Leupold. Prone, with a sling, I was soon zeroed at 200 yards. After a spin of the dial and a shading for wind, every bullet rang iron at 500 yards.

A few days later, on a frosty morning with no wind, I managed to miss a New Mexico coyote from the sit at 200 yards. "Yanked the trigger," I admitted. Fate was kind, however. John and Phil called expertly at a second spot to coax another hungry coyote across a sunny mesa. As the dog skidded to a halt 250 yards off, I began a measured crush, again from the sit. The coyote slumped without a twitch.

▼ This elk fell to a single 129-grain Hornady bullet from a 6.5 Creedmoor at very long range.

Alas, the elk that year were proving more elusive. After John and Phil and I joined Ray Milligan near Chama, we saw plenty of animals; but the season was already weeks along, and branch-antlered bulls had felt the pressure.

Then, one evening on the hem of a huge sage basin, we got a break. Scant minutes of legal light remained. The elk sifted through the purple shadows half a mile distant. They were moving away.

"We can get closer." Ray Milligan tried to inject optimism. He'd had plenty of practice. Milligan Brand Outfitting hosts many elk hunters in northern New Mexico each year. Dozens go home with bulls.

"Let's do it fast," I hissed, picking up the pace.

Phil, John and Ray stayed close on my heels through the pinions. We scooted up the spine until it fell off abruptly, the sage a sea below us, the elk edging toward a ridge on its far shore.

"Six hundred." Ray's Leica Geovid binocular confirmed John's read.

"Too far." I shook my head, gulping wind.

"Get ready." Ray urged. Roger that. This five-point might be our only chance. Whatever the range, you make final decisions *after* you're ready to fire, not before.

Sliding the sling up my arm, I flopped prone and chambered a round, then spun the elevation dial to 6. Dead-still air promised zero drift. Confident in the Magnum Research rifle after its stellar performance on distant steel, I was equally sure GreyBull's dial had accurately corrected for the bullet's steepening arc. Still, I hesitated. This elk was twice as far as any elk I had shot at in 35 years of hunting. I had passed shots at many closer bulls, one just this morning. The smallest errors in hold and execution become problems at extended range. What if the bullet strayed? A follow-up shot would be almost impossible if the elk moved. Certainly they would. And trailing a hit animal would be difficult at best. I didn't *have* to shoot this elk....

Still, my position was solid, the air dead-calm. I felt my excuses slipping away.

"Trust the dial," John whispered. "Remember, you kept *all* the bullets in a 12 inch gong at 500."

▲ Wayne tests a Burris Eliminator range-compensation scope on a SIG-Sauer SSG 3000 in .308.

▲ Laser-ranging scopes, like this one from Zeiss, make hitting at long range easier: If you're steady.

The raghorn bull was quartering to, almost entirely exposed. Not yet. My finger came taut against the trigger. The crosswire quivered in the shoulder crease. The bull turned slightly.

Still uncommitted, I saw him stop, tawny ribs golden in the orange, slanting light of dusk. Of such moments are memories made.

FOR LONGER REACH

36. The wrong shot

▲ Big country suggests long shooting. But short shots are usually possible, almost always easier.

Had my chance come a few minutes sooner, I might have killed the buck. It was a gorgeous high-country deer, heavily muscled, with a gray coat, grizzled face and thick, broad mahogany antlers. I'd been on its trail all day, tracking through patchy snow and soggy meadows, cutting fast across basins, glimpsing movement twice—too far and too quickly gone. The buck had stayed along the rims, just above timber.

Now dusk had come, and with it a brute of a storm, borne by a cold, keening wind. Deep-violet clouds turned black as they enveloped the mountains to the west. Sheets of snow tumbled like a curtain to hide the Wallowa Valley. I'd have to descend soon.

The deer appeared below me, silently. It wasn't moving now, just standing, regarding me as if to say, politely, "This is where we part." I eased the rifle up as the storm hurled itself onto the slope, popcorn snow pelting me and the wind wresting the rifle off target. I wanted badly to fire. But I didn't.

Neither did I shoot at the biggest elk I've seen in 35 years afield. The bull faced me 300 yards off, at the far end of a meadow. Ivory tines reach high and wide, Prone, it was a makeable shot—heck, it was a cinch. But I wasn't prone, couldn't get prone or even sitting without losing the elk below the hump of the ridge. Offhand, the crosswire bounced crazily, on and off the chest. As it had with the deer many seasons before. Again, I considered the odds and declined. A lethal hit shouldn't depend on good luck.

Long shots require precise shooting more than they beg powerful loads and optics. If you can't steady the reticle, shooting is simply an exercise in hope. Declining a shot, you reveal standards. Without them, the decision to fire depends only on how badly you want to kill.

▼ Before hunting with his Magnum Research rifle, the author shot it extensively at distance, prone.

Risky shots aren't all long. Once, still-hunting through thick lodgepoles, I caught a wink of russet color. In the Leupold it became an elk ear, 18 steps away. I was not gulping air; the reticle quivered, but in a tight, controlled way like an eager shorthair anticipating the shot. Problem was, brush blocked the bullet's path to brain and spine. I could only guess where the shoulder lay. Seconds later, breeze kissed the back of my neck. The ear vanished.

No one can specify a sure-kill distance for shots at big game, as no one can declare a maximum speed safe on a highway. Conditions matter. Hunters who

▲ Long shots aren't reprehensible if they're lethal 90 percent of the time. Short shots aren't all easy.

boast of long shots may in fact be conscientious—a long lethal hit is no less legitimate than one taken up close. Arguably, sniping from afar diminishes the thrill of the chase; and the cynical might say a habit of reaching beyond point-blank range indicates you're lazy or inept. But neither long shooting nor fast driving is irresponsible of itself. Years before distant shots at game became fashionable, I rolled a deer at roughly 480 yards, judging by bullet drop. The hit—through the heart—followed two misses with my .30-06. The buck looked very small in my 4x scope, and I had to double my initial allowance for drift. The killing shot was a good one, intelligently engineered and well executed. It was also as reprehensible as the first two. These days, I fire only when 90 percent sure of a kill—that is, when under prevailing conditions I can expect to land a bullet in the vitals nine times in 10 tries.

▲ Bonnie Shirk rests her rifle on a log for a long shot. Accuracy at distance requires a steady rifle!

▼ Her first African trophy! Donna Gulden waited for a good shot at this gemsbok, fired carefully.

▲ After a long crawl to within 90 yards, Wayne killed this gemsbok with a Montana rifle in .375 and Federal ammunition.

Distance is only one of several factors that influence a shot. Of course your hardware has limits. But rifle, cartridge and optics seldom count for as much as shooting position and shot execution. Wind matters most at long range. Steep angles, quartering presentations and intervening brush can scuttle shots up close. So can other animals in the background.

"Anyone who says he wouldn't take a risky shot at a big bull on the last day is a liar!" A reader once posted me that note, after I had suggested that neither an animal's trophy value nor the likelihood of another shot qualify as conditions. If your aim is to kill, only variables that affect the probability of a lethal hit matter. Wishing that you'll kill doesn't justify a shot any more than wishing earns you a gold medal, a winning lottery number or a PhD.

Shooting when you're not sure of the shot is like poaching in this way: Both events show you can't abide discipline. Hewing to standards in shot selection is like obeying game laws. You restrict yourself so that, whatever the outcome of a hunt, you will have acquitted yourself well.

Such high ground can be costly to hold. Pass a shot at a records-class animal, and you may have passed the only one you'll ever have. No shoulder mount. No accolades from pals. No listing in the book. "Your one chance to be a celebrity, and you turn it down—why? Because there's only a 50-50 chance of killing? Good grief! At least put a bullet in the air! If the shot's off the mark, no one needs to know…."

If you're with a guide or a partner, someone *will* know when you botch a shot—and remember. You might also confront the rule, increasingly common, that blood drawn is a tag filled. Guiding an elk hunter years ago, I spied a fine bull on a distant spine. Quickly we scooted closer. Setting up my spotting scope in a copse of aspens, I was startled by the blast of my client's .300. He had wanted that elk badly and opened up—offhand—at ridiculously long range. My objection was drowned by his second shot. Grimly, I trudged to where the bull had stood and found blood. We trailed the animal until the blood petered out. Then, because I could not dismiss the wound as superficial, we spent the rest of that week passing up other bulls to find the injured elk. We failed.

If you're alone, a "first blood" rule still makes sense. You're not afield to spray the scenery with softpoints and hope something falls over. In its pure sense, sport hunting is testing yourself. It is not simply carcass collection.

Sometimes others in your party may test you too. A guide who really wants rid of your company or to visit his girl or attend Saturday night festivities at Billy Bob's will want you to shoot early. Ditto an outfitter looking to bump his success rate or spare the groceries or beat a storm. Resisting that pressure can make for a tense camp. But taking risky shots to please your companions won't sit well in memory.

Once, in Africa, my PH and his tracker led me on the trail of an eland bull. We were all physically fit, but by mid-afternoon, sun, sand and thorn had exacted a toll. Then Komati snapped his fingers. I heard it: the faint

▲ Wayne used Norma's .270 Weatherby ammo in a Weatherby rifle to take this bull at 300 yards.

▲ A 300-yard shot anchored this fine Alberta mule deer. Longer pokes are usually ill-advised.

click of eland hooves. We crept forward. The tufted face of a huge bull appeared 60 yards away. Slowly the crossed sticks rose, and I slid my rifle into place. But a screen of acacia loomed in the sight.

"Shoot," hissed the PH. "Your bullet will get through."

I shook my head. A second later the eland vanished. We began a long hike back in uncomfortable silence. As luck would have it, I killed an eland later, a fine bull that dropped to one shot. All was forgiven.

But you're foolish to count on second chances. Not long ago, on assignment for a television show, I turned my ankle on a rocky hillside and fell so quickly I couldn't save my rifle from a bruising—a freak event. Of course, our party spotted an elk barely an hour later, quartering away in a small window in dense alder. Ordinarily I'd have bellied down and fired. But there was no divining how my tumble had affected my scope. "Sorry," I mumbled to guide, cameraman and company. The rest of that week was an exercise in public relations, as no other elk appeared. The scope, by the way, had not lost zero. But conduct matters. A lucky hit on the heels of a risky shot simply means an animal died *in spite of* your judgment.

Shots at crippled game needn't meet a 90-percent standard. I recall a partner hitting a grizzly not quite well enough. The bear roared, spun in a tight circle, then dashed for cover. We both let fly, though neither of us would have fired at a running grizzly that was unhurt.

Another time, I took an ill-advised poke at a Cape buffalo. Tense moments, a dash through thorn and several Winchester solids later, the animal died. It was not a neat kill, but once you commit, your task is clear. The time for deliberation is *before* losing that first bullet.

No matter how confident you are of a lethal hit, be ready to follow one shot with another. Animal reaction to a hit in the paunch often mimics response to a heart or lung shot. Game escapes when hunters reload slowly or don't reload at all. Fast bolt work can give you a second hit.

Animals that drop instantly worry me; the bullet may have clipped a spinal process, delivering shock that floors the beast but causes no lethal damage. A bullet severing the forward spine or breaking both shoulders yields the same result. You can't know exactly where the bullet landed, so be ready! Make fast bolt throw

▲ Even the .243 can take big game at distance with 105-grain VLD bullets – and accurate shooting.

the bullet landed, so be ready! Make fast bolt throw part of your practice routine. A handloader, I fight my habit of opening the action slowly to pluck and pocket the empty. Such a delay could one day cost me the chance to finish an injured animal.

The best place from which to fire a second shot is usually where you fired the first. You're in shooting position, you know the range, you may still have a clear shot alley. If you move forward to close the distance, odds are that a second chance will come quickly, when you're least able to capitalize on it. You'll lose time getting ready to shoot and taming your pulse. Terrain or brush may prevent a shot from a low position. Finally, you risk alerting the animal to your location. A rifle's report and a bullet's strike give the game little information about you. Instinct tells it to identify a threat before committing to an escape tactic or direction. Stay still until there's reason to move! A pal once set up to shoot far at a big mule deer, then waited patiently for an hour for the bedded buck to get up and expose a shoulder. Eventually that happened.

▲ Using coulees and low sage as cover, the author crept up on this buck on its bed. Note iron sights.

▼ Blake Anderson carries camp on his back in caribou country. Broken terrain affords close shots.

▲ Nimble, lightweight rifles often trump those designed for long shots, especially on long treks!

The bullet struck; the deer rolled out of sight. Wisely my amigo stayed put a few seconds. But that wasn't long enough. As he climbed through brush toward the bed, he heard the buck scramble off. He never recovered it.

Once the animal is gone—down or out of sight—your best strategy is to stay still for *two minutes*. Watch and listen, rifle ready. A delay costs you nothing. Why rush to a carcass? If the beast is ambulatory, silence works in your favor. You can hear movement without revealing your position. Wounded game that thinks it is hidden will likely stay where it fell or bed nearby.

Long shooting is controversial partly because recovering distant game can be problematic. No matter how well you mark the spot, you can lose it after crossing a deep, brushy defile. Off course by a few yards, you may not see that buck. Besides, not all game dies close to the impact site. If you're nearby, you can hear hooves, twigs, a cough, a stumble. Far away, game that reaches cover in a jump gives you no clue as to its mobility, speed or direction. By the time you arrive, it may have altered its route, found a hidden bed or simply put so much distance behind it that you'll run out of daylight catching up.

Then there are dolts who don't check after a shot. They might stroll across a meadow. But lose a quarter-mile elevation and labor up the far side of an abyss and return? "Nah. Probably missed. Won't find blood anyway. Knees can't take that. Not enough time." I've found animals shot dead where recovery was probably not attempted. Once, guiding a deer hunter, I spied a buck loafing just 200 yards away, but across a steep coulee. The fellow fired. The deer ran off. I suspected a hit. The hunter insisted he'd missed. I told him we were going to check anyway, and since I had no rifle, he'd have to follow me. Grumbling, he relented. We descended, then climbed to where the deer had stood.

▲ Wayne killed this Nebraska buck with a CZ Model 550 rifle in .30–06. He fired from prone at 100 yards, after a long stalk through tall grass.

into cover, where I found a tiny drop of blood. The buck lay dead a few yards farther on.

Now, it matters not to an animal whether a lethal bullet comes from 50 yards or 500. Nor does shot distance figure into wildlife policy. Harvest is harvest.

It seems to me foolish to measure hunting ethics in yards. I once killed an elk at just over 600—twice as far as any other I've shot. My rifle was chambered to a mild round most hunters would think more suitable for deer, even at modest ranges. But it was an accurate rifle, with a scope designed for shooting at extended range. More importantly, I had time to sling up, settle into prone and confirm dead-still air. *Most* importantly, I had practiced with this rifle on distant targets. My bullet lanced both lungs. Had the elk been a coyote, I'd have hit it.

I'm not especially proud of that kill. I took the shot not because light was fading and an approach nearly impossible, but because it was a 90-percent shot. A 30-yard hit after a long sneak would have been more satisfying; but conditions this time narrowed my options. I could fire or decline.

Those options are yours always, regardless of other opportunity. One evening, hunting kudu, I came upon an old bull browsing in thick thorn. Wind and luck were with me as I edged close for a shot with an open-sighted .470 double. At 23 steps I fired. The animal reeled at the impact, then vanished. I could have emptied my second barrel as the bull suddenly re-appeared, jetting through a gap; but I thought better of it. What if this were another kudu and the first lay dead in the thicket? To my chagrin, the track showed only a trace of blood; In the failing light, I'd nudged the front sight too high in the notch, merely clipping the neck. Apparently 23 steps had been too far.

Another time, in Alaska, I stalked a black bear in tall coastal grass. When the wind spun abruptly, the bear loped toward cover. I rose to my knees, swung and fired. Forest enveloped the bear. My guide was not impressed. My .30-30 he considered marginal at best; now dusk was closing after a hasty shot. We hurried forward. Under a dense canopy, the blood trail—indeed everything—got dark fast. We pushed through giant fern and found the bear dying. My bullet had struck its heart. I breathed a prayer of thanks, and an apology. Success aside, 90 yards had really been too far.

Launching a bullet is properly a weighty decision. Riflemen who shoot cavalierly or beyond sure-kill range boost crippling loss. They also color the public's perception of sport hunting. Sadly, declining a wrong shot is not as easy as it is noble, because it means foregoing shots that *would* have killed.

BALLISTICS

FEDERAL
PREMIUM
AMMUNITION
LOW RECOIL
20
CENTERFIRE PISTOL
CARTRIDGES/CARTOUCHES

Ballistics Tables for Modern Sporting Rifles

Introduction: Ballistics tables for modern sporting rifle cartridges

Most ammunition manufacturers publish exterior ballistics data to help shooters compare loads. The data also shows what can be reasonably expected of both the factory ammo and handloads. Tables here combine information from a variety of manufacturers, so you don't have to scrounge catalogs or flip pages in one to find a corresponding load in another. Of course, new loads are appearing all the time, so these tables are in truth "almost complete." Some offerings here have been discontinued or replaced but are still in common use (Hornady's Light and Heavy Magnum ammunition, for example, has been supplanted by its more inclusive Superformance line).

Most bullet-type abbreviations are self-explanatory: FMJ=full metal jacket; HP=hollow-point; SP=softpoint —except in the case of Hornady ammunition, where SP=Spire Point, the trade name for the firm's signature pointed softpoint. HE=Federal High Energy; LM and HM=Hornady Light and Heavy Magnum.

Zero range is 200 yards for most flat-shooting cartridges; however, some data was compiled with a zero at middle yardage—150 or 250 yards. These zeros are obvious. When, say, a bullet strikes high at 100 yards and low at 200, assume the zero is 150.

Barrel length influences velocity. Chronograph readings from high-velocity rifle rounds are typically taken from 24 and 26 inch barrels. Figure roughly 50 fps loss per inch in shorter barrels, though actual differences vary by load.

.17 REMINGTON TO .221 REMINGTON FIREBALL

CARTRIDGE BULLET	RANGE, YARDS:	0	100	200	300	400
.17 Remington						
Rem. 20 AccuTip BT	velocity, fps:	4250	3594	3028	2529	2081
	energy, ft-lb:	802	574	407	284	192
	arc, inches:		+1.3	+1.3	-2.5	-11.8
Rem. 20 Fireball	velocity, fps	4000	3380	2840	2360	1930
	energy, ft-lb	710	507	358	247	165
	arc, inches		+1.6	+1.5	-2.8	-13.5
Rem. 25 HP Power-Lokt	velocity, fps:	4040	3284	2644	2086	1606
	energy, ft-lb:	906	599	388	242	143
	arc, inches:		+1.8	0	-3.3	-16.6
.204 Ruger						
Federal 32 Nosler Ballistic Tip	velocity, fps	4030	3465	2968	2523	2119
	arc, inches		+0.7	0	-4.7	-14.9
Hornady 32 V-Max	velocity, fps:	4225	3632	3114	2652	2234
	energy, ft-lb:	1268	937	689	500	355
	arc, inches:		+0.6	0	-4.2	-13.4
Hornady 40 V-Max	velocity, fps:	3900	3451	3046	2677	2335
	energy, ft-lb:	1351	1058	824	636	485
	arc, inches:		+0.7	0	-4.5	-13.9
Rem. 32 AccuTip	velocity, fps:	4225	3632	3114	2652	2234
	Energy, ft-lb:	1268	937	689	500	355
	Arc, inches:		+0.6	0	-4.1	-13.1
Rem. 40 AccuTip	velocity, fps:	3900	3451	3046	2677	2336
	energy, ft-lb:	1351	1058	824	636	485
	arc, inches:		+0.7	0	-4.3	-13.2
Win. 32 Ballistic Silver Tip	velocity, fps	4050	3482	2984	2537	2132
	energy, ft-lb	1165	862	632	457	323
	arc, inches		+0.7	0	-4.6	-14.7
Win. 34 HP	velocity, fps:	4025	3339	2751	2232	1775
	energy, ft-lb:	1223	842	571	376	238
	arc, inches:		+0.8	0	-5.5	-18.1
.218 Bee						
Win. 46 Hollow Point	velocity, fps:	2760	2102	1550	1155	961
	energy, ft-lb:	778	451	245	136	94
	arc, inches:		0	-7.2	-29.4	
.22 Hornet						
Hornady 35 V-Max	velocity, fps:	3100	2278	1601	1135	929
	energy, ft-lb:	747	403	199	100	67
	arc, inches:		+2.8	0	-16.9	-60.4
Rem. 35 AccuTip	velocity, fps:	3100	2271	1591	1127	924
	energy, ft-lb:	747	401	197	99	66
	arc, inches:		+1.5	-3.5	-22.3	-68.4
Rem. 45 Pointed Soft Point	velocity, fps:	2690	2042	1502	1128	948
	energy, ft-lb:	723	417	225	127	90
	arc, inches:		0	-7.1	-30.0	
Rem. 45 Hollow Point	velocity, fps:	2690	2042	1502	1128	948
	energy, ft-lb:	723	417	225	127	90
	arc, inches:		0	-7.1	-30.0	
Win. 34 Jacketed HP	velocity, fps:	3050	2132	1415	1017	852
	energy, ft-lb:	700	343	151	78	55
	arc, inches:		0	-6.6	-29.9	
Win. 45 Soft Point	velocity, fps:	2690	2042	1502	1128	948
	energy, ft-lb:	723	417	225	127	90
	arc, inches:		0	-7.7	-31.3	
Win. 46 Hollow Point	velocity, fps:	2690	2042	1502	1128	948
	energy, ft-lb:	739	426	230	130	92
	arc, inches:		0	-7.7	-31.3	
.221 Remington Fireball						
Rem. 50 AccuTip BT	velocity, fps:	2995	2605	2247	1918	1622
	energy, ft-lb:	996	753	560	408	292
	arc, inches:		+1.8	0	-8.8	-27.1

BALLISTICS

Ballistics Tables for Modern Sporting Rifles

.222 Remington to .223 Remington

CARTRIDGE BULLET	RANGE, YARDS:	0	100	200	300	400
.222 Remington						
Federal 50 Hi-Shok	velocity, fps:	3140	2600	2120	1700	1350
	energy, ft-lb:	1095	750	500	320	200
	arc, inches:		+1.9	0	-9.7	-31.6
Federal 55 FMJ boat-tail	velocity, fps:	3020	2740	2480	2230	1990
	energy, ft-lb:	1115	915	750	610	484.
	arc, inches:		+1.6	0	-7.3	-21.5
Hornady 40 V-Max	velocity, fps:	3600	3117	2673	2269	1911
	energy, ft-lb:	1151	863	634	457	324
	arc, inches:		+1.1	0	-6.1	-18.9
Hornady 50 V-Max	velocity, fps:	3140	2729	2352	2008	1710.
	energy, ft-lb:	1094	827	614	448	325
	arc, inches:		+1.7	0	-7.9	-24.4
Norma 50 Soft Point	velocity, fps:	3199	2667	2193	1771	
	energy, ft-lb:	1136	790	534	348	
	arc, inches:		+1.7	0	-9.1	
Norma 50 FMJ	velocity, fps:	2789	2326	1910	1547	
	energy, ft-lb:	864	601	405	266	
	arc, inches:		+2.5	0	-12.2	
Norma 62 Soft Point	velocity, fps:	2887	2457	2067	1716	
	energy, ft-lb:	1148	831	588	405	
	arc, inches:		+2.1	0	-10.4	
PMC 50 Pointed Soft Point	velocity, fps:	3044	2727	2354	2012	1651
	energy, ft-lb:	1131	908	677	494	333
	arc, inches:		+1.6	0	-7.9	-24.5
PMC 55 Pointed Soft Point	velocity, fps:	2950	2594	2266	1966	1693
	energy, ft-lb:	1063	822	627	472	350
	arc, inches:		+1.9	0	-8.7	-26.3
Rem. 50 Pointed Soft Point	velocity, fps:	3140	2602	2123	1700	1350.
	energy, ft-lb:	1094	752	500	321	202
	arc, inches:		+1.9	0	-9.7	-31.7
Rem. 50 HP Power-Lokt	velocity, fps:	3140	2635	2182	1777	1432.
	energy, ft-lb:	1094	771	529	351	228
	arc, inches:		+1.8	0	-9.2	-29.6
Rem. 50 AccuTip BT	velocity, fps:	3140	2744	2380	2045	1740
	energy, ft-lb:	1094	836	629	464	336.
	arc, inches:		+1.6	0	-7.8	-23.9
Win. 40 Ballistic Silvertip	velocity, fps:	3370	2915	2503	2127	1786
	energy, ft-lb:	1009	755	556	402	283
	arc, inches:		+1.3	0	-6.9	-21.5
Win. 50 Pointed Soft Point	velocity, fps:	3140	2602	2123	1700	1350
	energy, ft-lb:	1094	752	500	321	202
	arc, inches:		+2.2	0	-10.0	-32.3
.223 Remington						
Black Hills 40 Nosler B. Tip	velocity, fps:	3600				
	energy, ft-lb:	1150				
	arc, inches:					
Black Hills 50 V-Max	velocity, fps:	3300				
	energy, ft-lb:	1209				
	arc, inches:					
Black Hills 52 Match HP	velocity, fps:	3300				
	energy, ft-lb:	1237				
	arc, inches:					
Black Hills 55 Softpoint	velocity, fps:	3250				
	energy, ft-lb:	1270				
	arc, inches:					
Black Hills 60 SP or V-Max	velocity, fps:	3150				
	energy, ft-lb:	1322				
	arc, inches:					
Black Hills 60 Partition	velocity, fps:	3150				
	energy, ft-lb:	1322				
	arc, inches:					
Black Hills 68 Heavy Match	velocity, fps:	2850				
	energy, ft-lb:	1227				
	arc, inches:					
Black Hills 69 Sierra MK	velocity, fps:	2850				
	energy, ft-lb:	1245				
	arc, inches:					
Black Hills 73 Berger BTHP	velocity, fps:	2750				
	energy, ft-lb:	1226				
	arc, inches:					
Black Hills 75 Heavy Match	velocity, fps:	2750				
	energy, ft-lb:	1259				
	arc, inches:					
Black Hills 77 Sierra MKing	velocity, fps:	2750				
	energy, ft-lb:	1293				
	arc, inches:					
Federal 50 Jacketed HP	velocity, fps:	3400	2910	2460	2060	1700
	energy, ft-lb:	1285	940	675	470	320
	arc, inches:		+1.3	0	-7.1	-22.7
Federal 50 Speer TNT HP	velocity, fps:	3300	2860	2450	2080	1750
	energy, ft-lb:	1210	905	670	480	340
	arc, inches:		+1.4	0	-7.3	-22.6
Federal 52 Sierra MatchKing BTHP	velocity, fps:	3300	2860	2460	2090	1760
	energy, ft-lb:	1255	945	700	505	360
	arc, inches:		+1.4	0	-7.2	-22.4
Federal 55 Hi-Shok	velocity, fps:	3240	2750	2300	1910	1550
	energy, ft-lb:	1280	920	650	445	295
	arc, inches:		+1.6	0	-8.2	-26.1
Federal 55 FMJ boat-tail	velocity, fps:	3240	2950	2670	2410	2170
	energy, ft-lb:	1280	1060	875	710	575
	arc, inches:		+1.3	0	-6.1	-18.3
Federal 55 Sierra GameKing BTHP	velocity, fps:	3240	2770	2340	1950	1610
	energy, ft-lb:	1280	935	670	465	315
	arc, inches:		+1.5	0	-8.0	-25.3
Federal 55 Trophy Bonded	velocity, fps:	3100	2630	2210	1830	1500.
	energy, ft-lb:	1175	845	595	410	275
	arc, inches:		+1.8	0	-8.9	-28.7
Federal 55 Nosler Bal. Tip	velocity, fps:	3240	2870	2530	2220	1920
	energy, ft-lb:	1280	1005	780	600	450
	arc, inches:		+1.4	0	-6.8	-20.8
Federal 55 Sierra BlitzKing	velocity, fps:	3240	2870	2520	2200	1910
	energy, ft-lb:	1280	1005	775	590	445
	arc, inches:		+-1.4	0	-6.9	-20.9
Federal 62 FMJ	velocity, fps:	3020	2650	2310	2000	1710
	energy, ft-lb:	1225	970	735	550	405
	arc, inches:		+1.7	0	-8.4	-25.5
Federal 64 Hi-Shok SP	velocity, fps:	3090	2690	2325	1990	1680
	energy, ft-lb:	1360	1030	770	560	400
	arc, inches:		+1.7	0	-8.2	-25.2
Federal 69 Sierra MatchKing BTHP	velocity, fps:	3000	2720	2460	2210	1980
	energy, ft-lb:	1380	1135	925	750	600
	arc, inches:		+1.6	0	-7.4	-21.9
Hornady 40 V-Max	velocity, fps:	3800	3305	2845	2424	2044
	energy, ft-lb:	1282	970	719	522	371
	arc, inches:		+0.8	0	-5.3	-16.6
Hornady 53 Hollow Point	velocity, fps:	3330	2882	2477	2106	1710
	energy, ft-lb:	1305	978	722	522	369
	arc, inches:		+1.7	0	-7.4	-22.7
Hornady 55 V-Max	velocity, fps:	3240	2859	2507	2181	1891.
	energy, ft-lb:	1282	998	767	581	437
	arc, inches:		+1.4	0	-7.1	-21.4
Hornady 55 TAP-FPD	velocity, fps:	3240	2854	2500	2172	1871
	energy, ft-lb:	1282	995	763	576	427

BALLISTICS

Ballistics Tables for Modern Sporting Rifles

.223 Remington to .22-250 Remington

CARTRIDGE BULLET	RANGE, YARDS:	0	100	200	300	400
	arc, inches:		+1.4	0	-7.0	-21.4
Hornady 55 Urban Tactical	velocity, fps:	2970	2626	2307	2011	1739
	energy, ft-lb:	1077	842	650	494	369
	arc, inches:		+1.5	0	-8.1	-24.9
Hornady 60 Soft Point	velocity, fps:	3150	2782	2442	2127	1837
	energy, ft-lb:	1322	1031	795	603	450
	arc, inches:		+1.6	0	-7.5	-22.5
Hornady 60 TAP-FPD	velocity, fps:	3115	2754	2420	2110	1824
	energy, ft-lb:	1293	1010	780	593	443
	arc, inches:		+1.6	0	-7.5	-22.9
Hornady 60 Urban Tactical	velocity, fps:	2950	2619	2312	2025	1762
	energy, ft-lb:	1160	914	712	546	413
	arc, inches:		+1.6	0	-8.1	-24.7
Hornady 75 BTHP Match	velocity, fps:	2790	2554	2330	2119	1926
	energy, ft-lb:	1296	1086	904	747	617
	arc, inches:		+2.4	0	-8.8	-25.1
Hornacy 75 TAP-FPD	velocity, fps:	2790	2582	2383	2193	2012
	energy, ft-lb:	1296	1110	946	801	674
	arc, inches:		+1.9	0	-8.0	-23.2
Hornady 75 BTHP Tactical	velocity, fps:	2630	2409	2199	2000	1814
	energy, ft-lb:	1152	966	805	666	548
	arc, inches:		+2.0	0	-9.2	-25.9
PMC 40 non-toxic	velocity, fps:	3500	2606	1871	1315	
	energy, ft-lb:	1088	603	311	154	
	arc, inches:		+2.6	0	-12.8	
PMC 50 Sierra BlitzKing	velocity, fps:	3300	2874	2484	2130	1809
	energy, ft-lb:	1209	917	685	504	363
	arc, inches:		+1.4	0	-7.1	-21.8
PMC 52 Sierra HPBT Match	velocity, fps:	3200	2808	2447	2117	1817
	energy, ft-lb:	1182	910	691	517	381
	arc, inches:		+1.5	0	-7.3	-22.5
PMC 53 Barnes XLC	velocity, fps:	3200	2815	2461	2136	1840
	energy, ft-lb:	1205	933	713	537	398
	arc, inches:		+1.5	0	-7.2	-22.2
PMC 55 HP boat-tail	velocity, fps:	3240	2717	2250	1832	1473
	energy, ft-lb:	1282	901	618	410	265
	arc, inches:		+1.6	0	-8.6	-27.7
PMC 55 FMJ boat-tail	velocity, fps:	3195	2882	2525	2169	1843
	energy, ft-lb:	1246	1014	779	574	415
	arc, inches:		+1.4	0	-6.8	-21.1
PMC 55 Pointed Soft Point	velocity, fps:	3112	2767	2421	2100	1806
	energy, ft-lb:	1182	935	715	539	398
	arc, inches:		+1.5	0	-7.5	-22.9
PMC 64 Pointed Soft Point	velocity, fps:	2775	2511	2261	2026	1806
	energy, ft-lb:	1094	896	726	583	464
	arc, inches:		+2.0	0	-8.8	-26.1
PMC 69 Sierra BTHP Match	velocity, fps:	2900	2591	2304	2038	1791
	energy, ft-lb:	1288	1029	813	636	492
	arc, inches:		+1.9	0	-8.4	-25.3
Rem. 50 AccuTip BT	velocity, fps:	3300	2889	2514	2168	1851
	energy, ft-lb:	1209	927	701	522	380
	arc, inches:		+1.4	0	-6.9	-21.2
Rem. 55 Pointed Soft Point	velocity, fps:	3240	2747	2304	1905	1554
	energy, ft-lb:	1282	921	648	443	295
	arc, inches:		+1.6	0	-8.2	-26.2
Rem. 55 HP Power-Lokt	velocity, fps:	3240	2773	2352	1969	1627
	energy, ft-lb:	1282	939	675	473	323
	arc, inches:		+1.5	0	-7.9	-24.8
Rem. 55 AccuTip BT	velocity, fps:	3240	2854	2500	2172	1871
	energy, ft-lb:	1282	995	763	576	427
	arc, inches:		+1.5	0	-7.1	-21.7
Rem. 55 Metal Case	velocity, fps:	3240	2759	2326	1933	1587
	energy, ft-lb:	1282	929	660	456	307

CARTRIDGE BULLET	RANGE, YARDS:	0	100	200	300	400
	arc, inches:		+1.6	0	-8.1	-25.5
Rem. 62 HP Match	velocity, fps:	3025	2572	2162	1792	1471
	energy, ft-lb:	1260	911	643	442	298
	arc, inches:		+1.9	0	-9.4	-29.9
Rem. 69 BTHP Match	velocity, fps:	3000	2720	2457	2209	1975
	energy, ft-lb:	1379	1133	925	747	598
	arc, inches:		+1.6	0	-7.4	-21.9
Win. 40 Ballistic Silvertip	velocity, fps:	3700	3166	2693	2265	1879
	energy, ft-lb:	1216	891	644	456	314
	arc, inches:		+1.0	0	-5.8	-18.4
Win. 45 JHP	velocity, fps:	3600				
	energy, ft-lb:	1295				
	arc, inches:					
Win. 50 Ballistic Silvertip	velocity, fps:	3410	2982	2593	2235	1907
	energy, ft-lb:	1291	987	746	555	404
	arc, inches:		+1.2	0	-6.4	-19.8
Win. 53 Hollow Point	velocity, fps:	3330	2882	2477	2106	1770
	energy, ft-lb:	1305	978	722	522	369
	arc, inches:		+1.7	0	-7.4	-22.7
Win. 55 Pointed Soft Point	velocity, fps:	3240	2747	2304	1905	1554
	energy, ft-lb:	1282	921	648	443	295
	arc, inches:		+1.9	0	-8.5	-26.7
Win. 55 Super Clean NT	velocity, fps:	3150	2520	1970	1505	1165
	energy, ft-lb:	1212	776	474	277	166
	arc, inches:		+2.8	0	-11.9	-38.9
Win. 55 FMJ	velocity, fps:	3240	2854			
	energy, ft-lb:	1282	995			
	arc, inches:					
Win. 55 Ballistic Silvertip	velocity, fps:	3240	2871	2531	2215	1923
	energy, ft-lb:	1282	1006	782	599	451
	arc, inches:		+1.4	0	-6.8	-20.8
Win. 64 Power-Point	velocity, fps:	3020	2656	2320	2009	1724
	energy, ft-lb:	1296	1003	765	574	423
	arc, inches:		+1.7	0	-8.2	-25.1
Win. 64 Power-Point Plus	velocity, fps:	3090	2684	2312	1971	1664
	energy, ft-lb:	1357	1024	760	552	393
	arc, inches:		+1.7	0	-8.2	-25.4

.5.6 x 52 R

CARTRIDGE BULLET	RANGE, YARDS:	0	100	200	300	400
Norma 71 Soft Point	velocity, fps:	2789	2446	2128	1835	
	energy, ft-lb:	1227	944	714	531	
	arc, inches:		+2.1	0	-9.9	

.22 PPC

CARTRIDGE BULLET	RANGE, YARDS:	0	100	200	300	400
A-Square 52 Berger	velocity, fps:	3300	2952	2629	2329	2049
	energy, ft-lb:	1257	1006	798	626	485
	arc, inches:		+1.3	0	-6.3	-19.1

.225 Winchester

CARTRIDGE BULLET	RANGE, YARDS:	0	100	200	300	400
Win. 55 Pointed Soft Point	velocity, fps:	3570	3066	2616	2208	1838
	energy, ft-lb:	1556	1148	836	595	412
	arc, inches:		+2.4	+2.0	-3.5	-16.3

.224 Weatherby Magnum

CARTRIDGE BULLET	RANGE, YARDS:	0	100	200	300	400
Wby. 55 Pointed Expanding	velocity, fps:	3650	3192	2780	2403	2056
	energy, ft-lb:	1627	1244	944	705	516
	arc, inches:		+2.8	+3.7	0	-9.8

.22-250 Remington

CARTRIDGE BULLET	RANGE, YARDS:	0	100	200	300	400
Black Hills 50 Nos. Bal. Tip	velocity, fps:	3700				
	energy, ft-lb:	1520				
	arc, inches:					
Black Hills 60 Nos. Partition	velocity, fps:	3550				
	energy, ft-lb:	1679				
	arc, inches:					

Ballistics Tables for Modern Sporting Rifles

.22-250 REMINGTON TO .223 WSSM

CARTRIDGE BULLET	RANGE, YARDS:	0	100	200	300	400
Federal 40 Nos. Bal. Tip	velocity, fps:	4150	3610	3130	2700	2300
	energy, ft-lb:	1530	1155	870	645	470
	arc, inches:		+0.6	0	-4.2	-13.2
Federal 40 Sierra Varminter	velocity, fps:	4000	3320	2720	2200	1740
	energy, ft-lb:	1420	980	660	430	265
	arc, inches:		+0.8	0	-5.6	-18.4
Federal 55 Hi-Shok	velocity, fps:	3680	3140	2660	2220	1830
	energy, ft-lb:	1655	1200	860	605	410
	arc, inches:		+1.0	0	-6.0	-19.1
Federal 55 Sierra BlitzKing	velocity, fps:	3680	3270	2890	2540	2220
	energy, ft-lb:	1655	1300	1020	790	605
	arc, inches:		+0.9	0	-5.1	-15.6
Federal 55 Sierra GameKing BTHP	velocity, fps:	3680	3280	2920	2590	2280
	energy, ft-lb:	1655	1315	1040	815	630
	arc, inches:		+0.9	0	-5.0	-15.1
Federal 55 Trophy Bonded	velocity, fps:	3600	3080	2610	2190	1810.
	energy, ft-lb:	1585	1155	835	590	400.
	arc, inches:		+1.1	0	-6.2	-19.8
Hornady 40 V-Max	velocity, fps:	4150	3631	3147	2699	2293
	energy, ft-lb:	1529	1171	879	647	467
	arc, inches:		+0.5	0	-4.2	-13.3
Hornady 50 V-Max	velocity, fps:	3800	3349	2925	2535	2178
	energy, ft-lb:	1603	1245	950	713	527
	arc, inches:		+0.8	0	-5.0	-15.6
Hornady 53 Hollow Point	velocity, fps:	3680	3185	2743	2341	1974.
	energy, ft-lb:	1594	1194	886	645	459
	arc, inches:		+1.0	0	-5.7	-17.8
Hornady 55 V-Max	velocity, fps:	3680	3265	2876	2517	2183
	energy, ft-lb:	1654	1302	1010	772	582
	arc, inches:		+0.9	0	-5.3	-16.1
Hornady 60 Soft Point	velocity, fps:	3600	3195	2826	2485	2169
	energy, ft-lb:	1727	1360	1064	823	627
	arc, inches:		+1.0	0	-5.4	-16.3
Norma 53 Soft Point	velocity, fps:	3707	3234	2809	1716	
	energy, ft-lb:	1618	1231	928	690	
	arc, inches:		+0.9	0	-5.3	
PMC 50 Sierra BlitzKing	velocity, fps:	3725	3264	2641	2455	2103
	energy, ft-lb:	1540	1183	896	669	491
	arc, inches:		+0.9	0	-5.2	-16.2
PMC 50 Barnes XLC	velocity, fps:	3725	3280	2871	2495	2152
	energy, ft-lb:	1540	1195	915	691	514.
	arc, inches:		+0.9	0	-5.1	-15.9.
PMC 55 HP boat-tail	velocity, fps:	3680	3104	2596	2141	1737
	energy, ft-lb:	1654	1176	823	560	368
	arc, inches:		+1.1	0	-6.3	-20.2
PMC 55 Pointed Soft Point	velocity, fps:	3586	3203	2852	2505	2178
	energy, ft-lb:	1570	1253	993	766	579
	arc, inches:		+1.0	0	-5.2	-16.0
Rem. 50 AccuTip BT (also in EtronX)	velocity, fps:	3725	3272	2864	2491	2147
	energy, ft-lb:	1540	1188	910	689	512
	arc, inches:		+1.7	+1.6	-2.8	-12.8
Rem. 55 Pointed Soft Point	velocity, fps:	3680	3137	2656	2222	1832
	energy, ft-lb:	1654	1201	861	603	410
	arc, inches:		+1.9	+1.8	-3.3	-15.5
Rem. 55 HP Power-Lokt	velocity, fps:	3680	3209	2785	2400	2046.
	energy, ft-lb:	1654	1257	947	703	511
	arc, inches:		+1.8	+1.7	-3.0	-13.7
Rem. 60 Nosler Partition (also in EtronX)	velocity, fps:	3500	3045	2634	2258	1914
	energy, ft-lb:	1632	1235	924	679	488
	arc, inches:		+2.1	+1.9	-3.4	-15.5
Win. 40 Ballistic Silvertip	velocity, fps:	4150	3591	3099	2658	2257
	energy, ft-lb:	1530	1146	853	628	453
	arc, inches:		+0.6	0	-4.2	-13.4
Win. 50 Ballistic Silvertip	velocity, fps:	3810	3341	2919	2536	2182
	energy, ft-lb:	1611	1239	946	714	529.
	arc, inches:		+0.8	0	-4.9	-15.2
Win. 55 Pointed Soft Point	velocity, fps:	3680	3137	2656	2222	1832
	energy, ft-lb:	1654	1201	861	603	410
	arc, inches:		+2.3	+1.9	-3.4	-15.9
Win. 55 Ballistic Silvertip	velocity, fps:	3680	3272	2900	2558	2240
	energy, ft-lb:	1654	1307	1027	799	613
	arc, inches:		+0.9	0	-5.0	-15.4
Win. 64 Power-Point	velocity, fps:	3500	3086	2708	2360	2038
	energy, ft-lb:	1741	1353	1042	791	590
	arc, inches:		+1.1	0	-5.9	-18.0

.220 Swift

CARTRIDGE BULLET	RANGE, YARDS:	0	100	200	300	400
Federal 52 Sierra MatchKing BTHP	velocity, fps:	3830	3370	2960	2600	2230
	energy, ft-lb:	1690	1310	1010	770	575
	arc, inches:		+0.8	0	-4.8	-14.9
Federal 55 Sierra BlitzKing	velocity, fps:	3800	3370	2990	2630	2310.
	energy, ft-lb:	1765	1390	1090	850	650
	arc, inches:		+0.8	0	-4.7	-14.4
Federal 55 Trophy Bonded	velocity, fps:	3700	3170	2690	2270	1880
	energy, ft-lb:	1670	1225	885	625	430
	arc, inches:		+1.0	0	-5.8	-18.5
Hornady 40 V-Max	velocity, fps:	4200	3678	3190	2739	2329
	energy, ft-lb:	1566	1201	904	666	482
	arc, inches:		+0.5	0	-4.0	-12.9
Hornady 50 V-Max	velocity, fps:	3850	3396	2970	2576	2215.
	energy, ft-lb:	1645	1280	979	736	545
	arc, inches:		+0.7	0	-4.8	-15.1
Hornady 50 SP	velocity, fps:	3850	3327	2862	2442	2060.
	energy, ft-lb:	1645	1228	909	662	471
	arc, inches:		+0.8	0	-5.1	-16.1
Hornady 55 V-Max	velocity, fps:	3680	3265	2876	2517	2183
	energy, ft-lb:	1654	1302	1010	772	582
	arc, inches:		+0.9	0	-5.3	-16.1
Hornady 60 Hollow Point	velocity, fps:	3600	3199	2824	2475	2156
	energy, ft-lb:	1727	1364	1063	816	619
	arc, inches:		+1.0	0	-5.4	-16.3
Norma 50 Soft Point	velocity, fps:	4019	3380	2826	2335	
	energy, ft-lb:	1794	1268	887	605	
	arc, inches:		+0.7	0	-5.1	
Rem. 50 Pointed Soft Point	velocity, fps:	3780	3158	2617	2135	1710
	energy, ft-lb:	1586	1107	760	506	325
	arc, inches:		+0.3	-1.4	-8.2	
Rem. 50 V-Max boat-tail (also in EtronX)	velocity, fps:	3780	3321	2908	2532	2185
	energy, ft-lb:	1586	1224	939	711	530
	arc, inches:		+0.8	0	-5.0	-15.4
Win. 40 Ballistic Silvertip	velocity, fps:	4050	3518	3048	2624	2238.
	energy, ft-lb:	1457	1099	825	611	445
	arc, inches:		+0.7	0	-4.4	-13.9
Win. 50 Pointed Soft Point	velocity, fps:	3870	3310	2816	2373	1972
	energy, ft-lb:	1663	1226	881	625	432
	arc, inches:		+0.8	0	-5.2	-16.7

.223 WSSM

CARTRIDGE BULLET	RANGE, YARDS:	0	100	200	300	400
Win. 55 Ballistic Silvertip	velocity, fps:	3850	3438	3064	2721	2402
	energy, ft-lb:	1810	1444	1147	904	704
	arc, inches:		+0.7	0	-4.4	-13.6
Win. 55 Pointed Softpoint	velocity, fps:	3850	3367	2934	2541	2181
	energy, ft-lb:	1810	1384	1051	789	581
	arc, inches:		+0.8	0	-4.9	-15.1
Win. 64 Power-Point	velocity, fps:	3600	3144	2732	2356	2011
	energy, ft-lb:	1841	1404	1061	789	574
	arc, inches:		+1.0	0	-5.7	-17.7

Ballistics Tables for Modern Sporting Rifles

6MM PPC TO .243 WINCHESTER

6mm PPC

CARTRIDGE BULLET	RANGE, YARDS:	0	100	200	300	400
A-Square 68 Berger	velocity, fps:	3100	2751	2428	2128	1850
	energy, ft-lb:	1451	1143	890	684	516
	arc, inches:		+1.5	0	-7.5	-22.6

6x70 R

CARTRIDGE BULLET	RANGE, YARDS:	0	100	200	300	400
Norma 95 Nosler Bal. Tip	velocity, fps:	2461	2231	2013	1809	
	energy, ft-lb:	1211	995	810	654	
	arc, inches:		+2.7	0	-11.3	

6.8mm SPC

CARTRIDGE BULLET	RANGE, YARDS:	0	100	200	300	400
Hornady 110 V-Max	velocity, fps:	2550	2319	2100	1893	1700
	energy, ft-lb:	1588	1313	1077	875	706
	arc, inches:		+2.5	0	-10.4	-30.6

.243 Winchester

CARTRIDGE BULLET	RANGE, YARDS:	0	100	200	300	400
Black Hills 55 Nosler B. Tip	velocity, fps:	3800				
	energy, ft-lb:	1763				
	arc, inches:					
Black Hills 95 Nosler B. Tip	velocity, fps:	2950				
	energy, ft-lb:	1836				
	arc, inches:					
Federal 70 Nosler Bal. Tip	velocity, fps:	3400	3070	2760	2470	2200
	energy, ft-lb:	1795	1465	1185	950	755.
	arc, inches:		+1.1	0	-5.7	-17.1
Federal 70 Speer TNT HP	velocity, fps:	3400	3040	2700	2390	2100
	energy, ft-lb:	1795	1435	1135	890	685
	arc, inches:		+1.1	0	-5.9	-18.0
Federal 80 Sierra Pro-Hunter	velocity, fps:	3350	2960	2590	2260	1950
	energy, ft-lb:	1995	1550	1195	905	675
	arc, inches:		+1.3	0	-6.4	-19.7
Federal 85 Sierra GameKing BTHP	velocity, fps:	3320	3070	2830	2600	2380
	energy, ft-lb:	2080	1770	1510	1280	1070
	arc, inches:		+1.1	0	-5.5	-16.1
Federal 90 Trophy Bonded	velocity, fps:	3100	2850	2610	2380	2160.
	energy, ft-lb:	1920	1620	1360	1130	935
	arc, inches:		+1.4	0	-6.1	-19.2
Federal 100 Hi-Shok	velocity, fps:	2960	2700	2450	2220	1990
	energy, ft-lb:	1945	1615	1330	1090	880
	arc, inches:		+1.6	0	-7.5	-22.0
Federal 100 Sierra GameKing BTSP	velocity, fps:	2960	2760	2570	2380	2210
	energy, ft-lb:	1950	1690	1460	1260	1080
	arc, inches:		+1.5	0	-6.8	-19.8
Federal 100 Nosler Partition	velocity, fps:	2960	2730	2510	2300	2100
	energy, ft-lb:	1945	1650	1395	1170	975.
	arc, inches:		+1.6	0	-7.1	-20.9
Hornady 58 V-Max	velocity, fps:	3750	3319	2913	2539	2195
	energy, ft-lb:	1811	1418	1093	830	620
	arc, inches:		+1.2	0	-5.5	-16.4
Hornady 75 Hollow Point	velocity, fps:	3400	2970	2578	2219	1890
	energy, ft-lb:	1926	1469	1107	820	595
	arc, inches:		+1.2	0	-6.5	-20.3
Hornady 100 BTSP	velocity, fps:	2960	2728	2508	2299	2099
	energy, ft-lb:	1945	1653	1397	1174	979
	arc, inches:		+1.6	0	-7.2	-21.0
Hornady 100 BTSP LM	velocity, fps:	3100	2839	2592	2358	2138
	energy, ft-lb:	2133	1790	1491	1235	1014
	arc, inches:		+1.5	0	-6.8	-19.8
Norma 80 FMJ	velocity, fps:	3117	2750	2412	2098	
	energy, ft-lb:	1726	1344	1034	782	
	arc, inches:		+1.5	0	-7.5	
Norma 100 FMJ	velocity, fps:	3018	2747	2493	2252	
	energy, ft-lb:	2023	1677	1380	1126	
	arc, inches:		+1.5	0	-7.1	
Norma 100 Soft Point	velocity, fps:	3018	2748	2493	2252	
	energy, ft-lb:	2023	1677	1380	1126	
	arc, inches:		+1.5	0	-7.1	
Norma 100 Oryx	velocity, fps:	3018	2653	2316	2004	
	energy, ft-lb:	2023	1563	1191	892	
	arc, inches:		+1.7	0	-8.3	
PMC 80 Pointed Soft Point	velocity, fps:	2940	2684	2444	2215	1999
	energy, ft-lb:	1535	1280	1060	871	709
	arc, inches:		+1.7	0	-7.5	-22.1
PMC 85 Barnes XLC	velocity, fps:	3250	3022	2805	2598	2401
	energy, ft-lb:	1993	1724	1485	1274	1088
	arc, inches:		+1.6	0	-5.6	16.3
PMC 85 HP boat-tail	velocity, fps:	3275	2922	2596	2292	2009
	energy, ft-lb:	2024	1611	1272	991	761
	arc, inches:		+1.3	0	-6.5	-19.7
PMC 100 Pointed Soft Point	velocity, fps:	2743	2507	2283	2070	1869
	energy, ft-lb:	1670	1395	1157	951	776
	arc, inches:		+2.0	0	-8.7	-25.5
PMC 100 SP boat-tail	velocity, fps:	2960	2742	2534	2335	2144
	energy, ft-lb:	1945	1669	1425	1210	1021
	arc, inches:		+1.6	0	-7.0	-20.5
Rem. 75 AccuTip BT	velocity, fps:	3375	3065	2775	2504	2248
	energy, ft-lb:	1897	1564	1282	1044	842
	arc, inches:		+2.0	+1.8	-3.0	-13.3
Rem. 80 Pointed Soft Point	velocity, fps:	3350	2955	2593	2259	1951
	energy, ft-lb:	1993	1551	1194	906	676
	arc, inches:		+2.2	+2.0	-3.5	-15.8
Rem. 80 HP Power-Lokt	velocity, fps:	3350	2955	2593	2259	1951
	energy, ft-lb:	1993	1551	1194	906	676
	arc, inches:		+2.2	+2.0	-3.5	-15.8
Rem. 90 Nosler Bal. Tip (also in EtronX) or Scirocco	velocity, fps:	3120	2871	2635	2411	2199
	energy, ft-lb:	1946	1647	1388	1162	966
	arc, inches:		+1.4	0	-6.4	-18.8
Rem. 95 AccuTip	velocity, fps:	3120	2847	2590	2347	2118
	energy, ft-lb:	2053	1710	1415	1162	946
	arc, inches:		+1.5	0	-6.6	-19.5
Rem. 100 PSP Core-Lokt (also in EtronX)	velocity, fps:	2960	2697	2449	2215	1993
	energy, ft-lb:	1945	1615	1332	1089	882
	arc, inches:		+1.6	0	-7.5	-22.1
Rem. 100 PSP boat-tail	velocity, fps:	2960	2720	2492	2275	2069
	energy, ft-lb:	1945	1642	1378	1149	950
	arc, inches:		+2.8	+2.3	-3.8	-16.6
Speer 100 Grand Slam	velocity, fps:	2950	2684	2434	2197	
	energy, ft-lb:	1932	1600	1315	1072	
	arc, inches:		+1.7	0	-7.6	-22.4
Win. 55 Ballistic Silvertip	velocity, fps:	4025	3597	3209	2853	2525
	energy, ft-lb:	1978	1579	1257	994	779
	arc, inches:		+0.6	0	-4.0	-12.2
Win. 80 Pointed Soft Point	velocity, fps:	3350	2955	2593	2259	1951.
	energy, ft-lb:	1993	1551	1194	906	676
	arc, inches:		+2.6	+2.1	-3.6	-16.2
Win. 95 Ballistic Silvertip	velocity, fps:	3100	2854	2626	2410	2203
	energy, ft-lb:	2021	1719	1455	1225	1024
	arc, inches:		+1.4	0	-6.4	-18.9
Win. 95 Supreme Elite XP3	velocity, fps	3100	2864	2641	2428	2225
	energy, ft-lb	2027	1730	1471	1243	1044
	a rc, inches		+1.4	0	-6.4	-18.7
Win. 100 Power-Point	velocity, fps:	2960	2697	2449	2215	1993
	energy, ft-lb:	1945	1615	1332	1089	882
	arc, inches:		+1.9	0	-7.8	-22.6.
Win. 100 Power-Point Plus	velocity, fps:	3090	2818	2562	2321	2092
	energy, ft-lb:	2121	1764	1458	1196	972
	arc, inches:		+1.4	0	-6.7	-20.0

Ballistics Tables for Modern Sporting Rifles

6MM REMINGTON TO .25-06 REMINGTON

6mm Remington

CARTRIDGE BULLET	RANGE, YARDS:	0	100	200	300	400
Federal 80 Sierra Pro-Hunter	velocity, fps:	3470	3060	2690	2350	2040
	energy, ft-lb:	2140	1665	1290	980	735
	arc, inches:		+1.1	0	-5.9	-18.2
Federal 100 Hi-Shok	velocity, fps:	3100	2830	2570	2330	2100
	energy, ft-lb:	2135	1775	1470	1205	985
	arc, inches:		+1.4	0	-6.7	-19.8
Federal 100 Nos. Partition	velocity, fps:	3100	2860	2640	2420	2220
	energy, ft-lb:	2135	1820	1545	1300	1090
	arc, inches:		+1.4	0	-6.3	-18.7
Hornady 100 SP boat-tail	velocity, fps:	3100	2861	2634	2419	2231
	energy, ft-lb:	2134	1818	1541	1300	1088
	arc, inches:		+1.3	0	-6.5	-18.9
Hornady 100 SPBT LM	velocity, fps:	3250	2997	2756	2528	2311
	energy, ft-lb:	2345	1995	1687	1418	1186
	arc, inches:		+1.6	0	-6.3	-18.2
Rem. 75 V-Max boat-tail	velocity, fps:	3400	3088	2797	2524	2267
	energy, ft-lb:	1925	1587	1303	1061	856
	arc, inches:		+1.9	+1.7	-3.0	-13.1
Rem. 100 PSP Core-Lokt	velocity, fps:	3100	2829	2573	2332	2104.
	energy, ft-lb:	2133	1777	1470	1207	983
	arc, inches:		+1.4	0	-6.7	-19.8
Rem. 100 PSP boat-tail	velocity, fps:	3100	2852	2617	2394	2183.
	energy, ft-lb:	2134	1806	1521	1273	1058
	arc, inches:		+1.4	0	-6.5	-19.1
Win. 100 Power-Point	velocity, fps:	3100	2829	2573	2332	2104
	energy, ft-lb:	2133	1777	1470	1207	983
	arc, inches:		+1.7	0	-7.0	-20.4

.243 WSSM

CARTRIDGE BULLET	RANGE, YARDS:	0	100	200	300	400
Win. 55 Ballistic Silvertip	velocity, fps:	4060	3628	3237	2880	2550
	energy, ft-lb:	2013	1607	1280	1013	794
	arc, inches:		+0.6	0	-3.9	-12.0
Win. 95 Ballistic Silvertip	velocity, fps:	3250	3000	2763	2538	2325
	energy, ft-lb:	2258	1898	1610	1359	1140
	arc, inches:		+1.2	0	5.7	16.9
Win. 95 Supreme Elite XP3	velocity, fps	3150	2912	2686	2471	2266
	energy, ft-lb	2093	1788	1521	1287	1083
	arc, inches		+1.3	0	-6.1	-18.0
Win. 100 Power Point	velocity, fps:	3110	2838	2583	2341	2112
	energy, ft-lb:	2147	1789	1481	1217	991
	arc, inches:		+1.4	0	-6.6	-19.7

.240 Weatherby Magnum

CARTRIDGE BULLET	RANGE, YARDS:	0	100	200	300	400
Wby. 87 Pointed Expanding	velocity, fps:	3523	3199	2898	2617	2352
	energy, ft-lb:	2397	1977	1622	1323	1069
	arc, inches:		+2.7	+3.4	0	-8.4
Wby. 90 Barnes-X	velocity, fps:	3500	3222	2962	2717	2484
	energy, ft-lb:	2448	2075	1753	1475	1233
	arc, inches:		+2.6	+3.3	0	-8.0
Wby. 95 Nosler Bal. Tip	velocity, fps:	3420	3146	2888	2645	2414
	energy, ft-lb:	2467	2087	1759	1475	1229
	arc, inches:		+2.7	+3.5	0	-8.4
Wby. 100 Pointed Expanding	velocity, fps:	3406	3134	2878	2637	2408
	energy, ft-lb:	2576	2180	1839	1544	1287
	arc, inches:		+2.8	+3.5	0	-8.4
Wby. 100 Partition	velocity, fps:	3406	3136	2882	2642	2415
	energy, ft-lb:	2576	2183	1844	1550	1294
	arc, inches:		+2.8	+3.5	0	-8.4

.25-20 Winchester

CARTRIDGE BULLET	RANGE, YARDS:	0	100	200	300	400
Rem. 86 Soft Point	velocity, fps:	1460	1194	1030	931	858
	energy, ft-lb:	407	272	203	165	141
	arc, inches:		0	-22.9	-78.9	-173.0
Win. 86 Soft Point	velocity, fps:	1460	1194	1030	931	858.
	energy, ft-lb:	407	272	203	165	141
	arc, inches:		0	-23.5	-79.6	-175.9

.25-35 Winchester

CARTRIDGE BULLET	RANGE, YARDS:	0	100	200	300	400
Win. 117 Soft Point	velocity, fps:	2230	1866	1545	1282	1097
	energy, ft-lb:	1292	904	620	427	313
	arc, inches:		+2.1	-5.1	-27.0	-70.1

.250 Savage

CARTRIDGE BULLET	RANGE, YARDS:	0	100	200	300	400
Rem. 100 Pointed SP	velocity, fps:	2820	2504	2210	1936	1684.
	energy, ft-lb:	1765	1392	1084	832	630
	arc, inches:		+2.0	0	-9.2	-27.7
Win. 100 Silvertip	velocity, fps:	2820	2467	2140	1839	1569
	energy, ft-lb:	1765	1351	1017	751	547
	arc, inches:		+2.4	0	-10.1	-30.5

.257 Roberts

CARTRIDGE BULLET	RANGE, YARDS:	0	100	200	300	400
Federal 120 Nosler Partition	velocity, fps:	2780	2560	2360	2160	1970
	energy, ft-lb:	2060	1750	1480	1240	1030
	arc, inches:		+1.9	0	-8.2	-24.0
Hornady 117 SP boat-tail	velocity, fps:	2780	2550	2331	2122	1925
	energy, ft-lb:	2007	1689	1411	1170	963
	arc, inches:		+1.9	0	-8.3	-24.4
Hornady 117 SP boat-tail LM	velocity, fps:	2940	2694	2460	2240	2031
	energy, ft-lb:	2245	1885	1572	1303	1071
	arc, inches:		+1.7	0	-7.6	-21.8
Rem. 117 SP Core-Lokt	velocity, fps:	2650	2291	1961	1663	1404
	energy, ft-lb:	1824	1363	999	718	512
	arc, inches:		+2.6	0	-11.7	-36.1
Win. 117 Power-Point	velocity, fps:	2780	2411	2071	1761	1488
	energy, ft-lb:	2009	1511	1115	806	576.
	arc, inches:		+2.6	0	-10.8	-33.0

.25-06 Remington

CARTRIDGE BULLET	RANGE, YARDS:	0	100	200	300	400
Black Hills 100 Nos. Bal. Tip	velocity, fps:	3200				
	energy, ft-lb:	2273				
	arc, inches:					
Black Hills 100 Barnes XLC	velocity, fps:	3200				
	energy, ft-lb:	2273				
	arc, inches:					
Black Hills 115 Barnes X	velocity, fps:	2975				
	energy, ft-lb:	2259				
	arc, inches:					
Federal 90 Sierra Varminter	velocity, fps:	3440	3040	2680	2340	2030
	energy, ft-lb:	2365	1850	1435	1100	825
	arc, inches:		+1.1	0	-6.0	-18.3
Federal 100 Barnes XLC	velocity, fps:	3210	2970	2750	2540	2330
	energy, ft-lb:	2290	1965	1680	1430	1205
	arc, inches:		+1.2	0	-5.8	-17.0
Federal 100 Nosler Bal. Tip	velocity, fps:	3210	2960	2720	2490	2280
	energy, ft-lb:	2290	1940	1640	1380	1150.
	arc, inches:		+1.2	0	-6.0	-17.5
Federal 115 Nosler Partition	velocity, fps:	2990	2750	2520	2300	2100
	energy, ft-lb:	2285	1930	1620	1350	1120
	arc, inches:		+1.6	0	-7.0	-20.8
Federal 115 Trophy Bonded	velocity, fps:	2990	2740	2500	2270	2050
	energy, ft-lb:	2285	1910	1590	1310	1075
	arc, inches:		+1.6	0	-7.2	-21.1
Federal 117 Sierra Pro Hunt.	velocity, fps:	2990	2730	2480	2250	2030
	energy, ft-lb:	2320	1985	1645	1350	1100
	arc, inches:		+1.6	0	-7.2	-21.4
Federal 117 Sierra GameKing BTSP	velocity, fps:	2990	2770	2570	2370	2190
	energy, ft-lb:	2320	2000	1715	1465	1240
	arc, inches:		+1.5	0	-6.8	-19.9

BALLISTICS

Ballistics Tables for Modern Sporting Rifles

.25-06 REMINGTON TO 6.5X55 SWEDISH

CARTRIDGE BULLET	RANGE, YARDS:	0	100	200	300	400
Hornady 117 SP boat-tail	velocity, fps:	2990	2749	2520	2302	2096
	energy, ft-lb:	2322	1962	1649	1377	1141
	arc, inches:		+1.6	0	-7.0	-20.7
Hornady 117 SP boat-tail LM	velocity, fps:	3110	2855	2613	2384	2168
	energy, ft-lb:	2512	2117	1774	1476	1220
	arc, inches:		+1.8	0	-7.1	-20.3
PMC 100 SPBT	velocity, fps:	3200	2925	2650	2395	2145
	energy, ft-lb:	2273	1895	1561	1268	1019
	arc, inches:		+1.3	0	-6.3	-18.6
PMC 117 PSP	velocity, fps:	2950	2706	2472	2253	2047
	energy, ft-lb:	2261	1900	1588	1319	1088
	arc, inches:		+1.6	0	-7.3	-21.5
Rem. 100 PSP Core Lokt	velocity, fps:	3230	2893	2580	2287	2014
	energy, ft-lb:	2316	1858	1478	1161	901
	arc, inches:		+1.3	0	-6.6	-19.8
Rem. 115 Core-Lokt Ultra	velocity, fps:	3000	2751	2516	2293	2081
	energy, ft-lb:	2298	1933	1616	1342	1106
	arc, inches:		+1.6	0	-7.1	-20.7
Rem. 120 PSP Core-Lokt	velocity, fps:	2990	2730	2484	2252	2032
	energy, ft-lb:	2382	1985	1644	1351	1100
	arc, inches:		+1.6	0	-7.2	-21.4
Speer 120 Grand Slam	velocity, fps:	3130	2835	2558	2298	
	energy, ft-lb:	2610	2141	1743	1407	
	arc, inches:		+1.4	0	-6.8	-20.1
Win. 85 Ballistic Silvertip	velocity, fps	3470	3156	2863	2589	2331
	energy, ft-lb:	2273	1880	1548	1266	1026
	arc, inches:		+1.0	0	-5.2	-15.7
Win. 90 Pos. Exp. Point	velocity, fps:	3440	3043	2680	2344	2034
	energy, ft-lb:	2364	1850	1435	1098	827
	arc, inches:		+2.4	+2.0	-3.4	-15.0
Win. 110 AccuBond CT	velocity, fps:	3100	2870	2651	2442	2243
	energy, ft-lb:	2347	2011	1716	1456	1228
	arc, inches:		+1.4	0	-6.3	-18.5
Win. 115 Ballistic Silvertip	velocity, fps:	3060	2825	2603	2390	2188
	energy, ft-lb:	2391	2038	1729	1459	1223
	arc, inches:		+1.4	0	-6.6	-19.2
Win. 120 Pos. Pt. Exp.	velocity, fps:	2990	2717	2459	2216	1987
	energy, ft-lb:	2382	1967	1612	1309	1053
	arc, inches:		+1.6	0	-7.4	-21.8

.25 WINCHESTER SUPER SHORT MAGNUM

CARTRIDGE BULLET	RANGE, YARDS:	0	100	200	300	400
Win. 85 Ballistic Silvertip	velocity, fps:	3470	3156	2863	2589	2331
	energy, ft-lb:	2273	1880	1548	1266	1026
	arc, inches:		+1.0	0	-5.2	-15.7
Win. 110 AccuBond CT	velocity, fps:	3100	2870	2651	2442	2243.
	energy, ft-lb:	2347	2011	1716	1456	1228
	arc, inches:		+1.4	0	-6.3	-18.5
Win. 115 Ballistic Silvertip	velocity, fps:	3060	2844	2639	2442	2254
	energy, ft-lb:	2392	2066	1778	1523	1298
	arc, inches:		+1.4	0	-6.4	-18.6
Win. 120 Pos. Pt. Exp.	velocity, fps:	2990	2717	2459	2216	1987
	energy, ft-lb:	2383	1967	1612	1309	1053
	arc, inches:		+1.6	0	-7.4	-21.8

.257 WEATHERBY MAGNUM

CARTRIDGE BULLET	RANGE, YARDS:	0	100	200	300	400
Federal 115 Nosler Partition	velocity, fps:	3150	2900	2660	2440	2220.
	energy, ft-lb:	2535	2145	1810	1515	1260
	arc, inches:		+1.3	0	-6.2	-18.4
Federal 115 Trophy Bonded	velocity, fps:	3150	2890	2640	2400	2180
	energy, ft-lb:	2535	2125	1775	1470	1210
	arc, inches:		+1.4	0	-6.3	-18.8
Wby. 87 Pointed Expanding	velocity, fps:	3825	3472	3147	2845	2563
	energy, ft-lb:	2826	2328	1913	1563	1269
	arc, inches:		+2.1	+2.8	0	-7.1
Wby. 100 Pointed Expanding	velocity, fps:	3602	3298	3016	2750	2500
	energy, ft-lb:	2881	2416	2019	1680	1388
	arc, inches:		+2.4	+3.1	0	-7.7
Wby. 115 Nosler Bal. Tip	velocity, fps:	3400	3170	2952	2745	2547
	energy, ft-lb:	2952	2566	2226	1924	1656.
	arc, inches:		+3.0	+3.5	0	-7.9
Wby. 115 Barnes X	velocity, fps:	3400	3158	2929	2711	2504
	energy, ft-lb:	2952	2546	2190	1877	1601
	arc, inches:		+2.7	+3.4	0	-8.1
Wby. 117 RN Expanding	velocity, fps:	3402	2984	2595	2240	1921
	energy, ft-lb:	3007	2320	1742	1302	956
	arc, inches:		+3.4	+4.31	0	-11.1
Wby. 120 Nosler Partition	velocity, fps:	3305	3046	2801	2570	2350
	energy, ft-lb:	2910	2472	2091	1760	1471
	arc, inches:		+3.0	+3.7	0	-8.9

6.53 (.257) SCRAMJET

CARTRIDGE BULLET	RANGE, YARDS:	0	100	200	300	400
Lazzeroni 85 Nosler Bal. Tip	velocity, fps:	3960	3652	3365	3096	2844
	energy, ft-lb:	2961	2517	2137	1810	1526
	arc, inches:		+1.7	+2.4	0	-6.0
Lazzeroni 100 Nosler Part.	velocity, fps:	3740	3465	3208	2965	2735
	energy, ft-lb:	3106	2667	2285	1953	1661.
	arc, inches:		+2.1	+2.7	0	-6.7

6.5X50 JAPANESE

CARTRIDGE BULLET	RANGE, YARDS:	0	100	200	300	400
Norma 156 Alaska	velocity, fps:	2067	1832	1615	1423	
	energy, ft-lb:	1480	1162	904	701	
	arc, inches:		+4.4	0	-17.8	

6.5X52 CARCANO

CARTRIDGE BULLET	RANGE, YARDS:	0	100	200	300	400
Norma 156 Alaska	velocity, fps:	2428	2169	1926	1702	
	energy, ft-lb:	2043	1630	1286	1004	
	arc, inches:		+2.9	0	-12.3	

6.5X55 SWEDISH

CARTRIDGE BULLET	RANGE, YARDS:	0	100	200	300	400
Federal 140 Hi-Shok	velocity, fps:	2600	2400	2220	2040	1860
	energy, ft-lb:	2100	1795	1525	1285	1080
	arc, inches:		+2.3	0	-9.4	-27.2
Federal 140 Trophy Bonded	velocity, fps:	2550	2350	2160	1980	1810
	energy, ft-lb:	2020	1720	1450	1220	1015
	arc, inches:		+2.4	0	-9.8	-28.4
Federal 140 Sierra MatchKg.	velocity, fps:	2630	2460	2300	2140	2000
BTHP	energy, ft-lb:	2140	1880	1640	1430	1235
	arc, inches:		+16.4	+28.8	+33.9	+31.8
Hornady 129 SP LM	velocity, fps:	2770	2561	2361	2171	1994
	energy, ft-lb:	2197	1878	1597	1350	1138
	arc, inches:		+2.0	0	-8.2	-23.2
Hornady 140 SP Interlock	velocity, fps	2525	2341	2165	1996	1836
	energy, ft-lb:	1982	1704	1457	1239	1048
	arc, inches:		+2.4	0	-9.9	-28.5
Hornady140 SP LM	velocity, fps:	2740	2541	2351	2169	1999
	energy, ft-lb:	2333	2006	1717	1463	1242
	arc, inches:		+2.4	0	-8.7	-24.0
Norma 120 Nosler Bal. Tip	velocity, fps:	2822	2609	2407	2213	
	energy, ft-lb:	2123	1815	1544	1305	
	arc, inches:		+1.8	0	-7.8	
Norma 139 Vulkan	velocity, fps:	2854	2569	2302	2051	
	energy, ft-lb:	2515	2038	1636	1298	
	arc, inches:		+1.8	0	-8.4	
Norma 140 Nosler Partition	velocity, fps:	2789	2592	2403	2223	
	energy, ft-lb:	2419	2089	1796	1536	
	arc, inches:		+1.8	0	-7.8	
Norma 156 TXP Swift A-Fr.	velocity, fps:	2526	2276	2040	1818	
	energy, ft-lb:	2196	1782	1432	1138	

BALLISTICS

Ballistics Tables for Modern Sporting Rifles

6.5X55 SWEDISH TO .270 WINCHESTER

CARTRIDGE BULLET	RANGE, YARDS:	0	100	200	300	400
	arc, inches:		+2.6	0	-10.9	
Norma 156 Alaska	velocity, fps:	2559	2245	1953	1687	
	energy, ft-lb:	2269	1746	1322	986	
	arc, inches:		+2.7	0	-11.9	
Norma 156 Vulkan	velocity, fps:	2644	2395	2159	1937	
	energy, ft-lb:	2422	1987	1616	1301	
	arc, inches:		+2.2	0	-9.7	
Norma 156 Oryx	velocity, fps:	2559	2308	2070	1848	
	energy, ft-lb:	2269	1845	1485	1183	
	arc, inches:		+2.5	0	-10.6	
PMC 139 Pointed Soft Point	velocity, fps:	2850	2560	2290	2030	1790
	energy, ft-lb:	2515	2025	1615	1270	985
	arc, inches:		+2.2	0	-8.9	-26.3
PMC 140 HP boat-tail	velocity, fps:	2560	2398	2243	2093	1949
	energy, ft-lb:	2037	1788	1563	1361	1181
	arc, inches:		+2.3	0	-9.2	-26.4
PMC 140 SP boat-tail	velocity, fps:	2560	2386	2218	2057	1903
	energy, ft-lb:	2037	1769	1529	1315	1126
	arc, inches:		+2.3	0	-9.4	-27.1
PMC 144 FMJ	velocity, fps:	2650	2370	2110	1870	1650
	energy, ft-lb:	2425	1950	1550	1215	945
	arc, inches:		+2.7	0	-10.5	-30.9
Rem. 140 PSP Core-Lokt	velocity, fps:	2550	2353	2164	1984	1814
	energy, ft-lb:	2021	1720	1456	1224	1023
	arc, inches:		+2.4	0	-9.8	-27.0
Speer 140 Grand Slam	velocity, fps:	2550	2318	2099	1892	
	energy, ft-lb:	2021	1670	1369	1112	
	arc, inches:		+2.5	0	-10.4	-30.6
Win. 140 Soft Point	velocity, fps:	2550	2359	2176	2002	1836
	energy, ft-lb:	2022	1731	1473	1246	1048.
	arc, inches:		+2.4	0	-9.7	-28.1

6.5 Creedmoor

CARTRIDGE BULLET	RANGE, YARDS:	0	100	200	300	400
120 A-Max (Hornady)	velocity, fps	2910	2712	2522	2340	2166
	energy, ft-lbs	2256	1959	1695	1459	1250
	arc, inches	-1.5	1.6	0	-7.1	-20.5
129 SST (Hornady)	velocity, fps	2950	2756	2570	2392	2221
	energy, ft-lbs	2492	2175	1892	1639	1417
	arc, inches	-1.5	1.5	0	-6.8	-19.7
140 A-Max (Hornady)	velocity, fps	2710	2557	2409	2266	2128
	energy, ft-lbs	2238	2032	1804	1596	1408
	arc, inches	-1.5	1.9	0	-7.9	-22.6

.260 Remington

CARTRIDGE BULLET	RANGE, YARDS:	0	100	200	300	400
Federal 140 Sierra GameKing	velocity, fps:	2750	2570	2390	2220	2060
BTSP	energy, ft-lb:	2350	2045	1775	1535	1315
	arc, inches:		+1.9	0	-8.0	-23.1
Federal 140 Trophy Bonded	velocity, fps:	2750	2540	2340	2150	1970
	energy, ft-lb:	2350	2010	1705	1440	1210
	arc, inches:	+1.9	0	-8.4	-24.1	
Rem. 120 Nosler Bal. Tip	velocity, fps:	2890	2688	2494	2309	2131
	energy, ft-lb:	2226	1924	1657	1420	1210
	arc, inches:		+1.7	0	-7.3	-21.1
Rem. 120 AccuTip	velocity, fps:	2890	2697	2512	2334	2163
	energy, ft-lb:	2392	2083	1807	1560	1340
	arc, inches:		+1.6	0	-7.2	-20.7
Rem. 125 Nosler Partition	velocity, fps:	2875	2669	2473	2285	2105.
	energy, ft-lb:	2294	1977	1697	1449	1230
	arc, inches:	+1.71	0	-7.4	-21.4	
Rem. 140 PSP Core-Lokt	velocity, fps:	2750	2544	2347	2158	1979
(and C-L Ultra)	energy, ft-lb:	2351	2011	1712	1448	1217
	arc, inches:		+1.9	0	-8.3	-24.0

CARTRIDGE BULLET	RANGE, YARDS:	0	100	200	300	400
Speer 140 Grand Slam	velocity, fps:	2750	2518	2297	2087	
	energy, ft-lb:	2351	1970	1640	1354	
	arc, inches:		+2.3	0	-8.9	-25.8

6.5/284 Norma

CARTRIDGE BULLET	RANGE, YARDS:	0	100	200	300	400
Norma 120 Nosler Bal. Tip	velocity, fps:	3117	2890	2674	2469	
	energy, ft-lb:	2589	2226	1906	1624	
	arc, inches:		+1.3	0	-6.2	
Nosler 120 Ballistic Tip	velocity, fps:	3000	2792	2594	2404	2223
	energy, ft-lbs	2398	2077	1793	1540	1316
	arc, inches	-1.5	+1.4	0	-6.6	-17.1
Nosler 130 AccuBond	velocity, fps	2900	2709	2526	2351	2182
	energy, ft-lbs	2427	2118	1842	1595	1374
	arc, inches	-1.5	+1.5	0	-6.9	-18.4
Norma 140 Nosler Part.	velocity, fps:	2953	2750	2557	2371	
	energy, ft-lb:	2712	2352	2032	1748	
	arc, inches:		+1.5	0	-6.8	

6.5 Remington Magnum

CARTRIDGE BULLET	RANGE, YARDS:	0	100	200	300	400
Rem. 120 Core-Lokt PSP	velocity, fps:	3210	2905	2621	2353	2102
	energy, ft-lb:	2745	2248	1830	1475	1177
	arc, inches:		+2.7	+2.1	-3.5	-15.5

.264 Winchester Magnum

CARTRIDGE BULLET	RANGE, YARDS:	0	100	200	300	400
Nosler 100 Ballistic Tip	velocity, fps	3400	3105	2829	2569	2324
	energy, ft-lbs	2567	2141	1777	1465	1199
	arc, inches	-1.5	+1.0	0	-5.5	-16.1
Nosler 130 AccuBond	velocity, fps	3100	2900	2709	2527	2351
	energy, ft-lbs	2774	2428	2119	1843	1595
	arc, inches	-1.5	+1.2	0	-6.0	-17.5
Rem. 140 PSP Core-Lokt	velocity, fps:	3030	2782	2548	2326	2114
	energy, ft-lb:	2854	2406	2018	1682	1389
	arc, inches:		+1.5	0	-6.9	-20.2
Win. 140 Power-Point	velocity, fps:	3030	2782	2548	2326	2114.
	energy, ft-lb:	2854	2406	2018	1682	1389
	arc, inches:		+1.8	0	-7.2	-20.8

6.8mm Remington SPC

CARTRIDGE BULLET	RANGE, YARDS:	0	100	200	300	400
Rem. 115 Open Tip Match	velocity, fps:	2800	2535	2285	2049	1828
(and HPBT Match)	energy, ft-lb:	2002	1641	1333	1072	853
	arc, inches:		+2.0	0	-8.8	-26.2
Rem. 115 Metal Case	velocity, fps:	2800	2523	2262	2017	1789
	energy, ft-lb:	2002	1625	1307	1039	817
	arc, inches:		+2.0	0	-8.8	-26.2
Rem. 115 Sierra HPBT	velocity, fps:	2775	2511	2263	2028	1809
(2005; all vel. @ 2775)	energy, ft-lb:	1966	1610	1307	1050	835
	arc, inches:		+2.0	0	-8.8	-26.2.
Rem. 115 CL Ultra	velocity, fps:	2775	2472	2190	1926	1683
	energy, ft-lb:	1966	1561	1224	947	723
	arc, inches:		+2.1	0	-9.4	-28.2

.270 Winchester

CARTRIDGE BULLET	RANGE, YARDS:	0	100	200	300	400
Black Hills 130 Nos. Bal. T.	velocity, fps:	2950				
	energy, ft-lb:	2512				
	arc, inches:					
Black Hills 130 Barnes XLC	velocity, ft-lb:	2950				
	energy, ft-lb:	2512				
	arc, inches:					
Federal 130 Hi-Shok	velocity, fps:	3060	2800	2560	2330	2110
	energy, ft-lb:	2700	2265	1890	1565	1285
	arc, inches:		+1.5	0	-6.8	-20.0
Federal 130 Sierra Pro-Hunt.	velocity, fps:	3060	2830	2600	2390	2190

BALLISTICS

Ballistics Tables for Modern Sporting Rifles

.270 WINCHESTER TO .270 WINCHESTER

CARTRIDGE BULLET	RANGE, YARDS:	0	100	200	300	400
	energy, ft-lb:	2705	2305	1960	1655	1390
	arc, inches:		+1.4	0	-6.4	-19.0
Federal 130 Sierra GameKing	velocity, fps:	3060	2830	2620	2410	2220.
	energy, ft-lb:	2700	2320	1980	1680	1420
	arc, inches:		+1.4	0	-6.5	-19.0
Federal 130 Nosler Bal. Tip	velocity, fps:	3060	2840	2630	2430	2230
	energy, ft-lb:	2700	2325	1990	1700	1440
	arc, inches:		+1.4	0	-6.5	-18.8
Federal 130 Nos. Partition	velocity, fps:	3060	2830	2610	2400	2200
And Solid Base	energy, ft-lb:	2705	2310	1965	1665	1400
	arc, inches:		+1.4	0	-6.5	-19.1.
Federal 130 Barnes XLC	velocity, fps:	3060	2840	2620	2420	2220
And Triple Shock	energy, ft-lb:	2705	2320	1985	1690	1425
	arc, inches:		+1.4	0	-6.4	-18.9
Federal 130 Trophy Bonded	velocity, fps:	3060	2810	2570	2340	2130
	energy, ft-lb:	2705	2275	1905	1585	1310
	arc, inches:		+1.5	0	-6.7	-19.8
Federal 140 Trophy Bonded	velocity, fps:	2940	2700	2480	2260	2060
	energy, ft-lb:	2685	2270	1905	1590	1315
	arc, inches:		+1.6	0	-7.3	-21.5
Federal 140 Tr. Bonded HE	velocity, fps:	3100	2860	2620	2400	2200.
	energy, ft-lb:	2990	2535	2140	1795	1500
	arc, inches:		+1.4	0	-6.4	-18.9
Federal 140 Nos. AccuBond	velocity, fps:	2950	2760	2580	2400	2230.
	energy, ft-lb:	2705	2365	2060	1790	1545
	arc, inches:		+1.5	0	-6.7	-19.6
Federal 150 Hi-Shok RN	velocity, fps:	2850	2500	2180	1890	1620
	energy, ft-lb:	2705	2085	1585	1185	870
	arc, inches:		+2.0	0	-9.4	-28.6
Federal 150 Sierra GameKing	velocity, fps:	2850	2660	2480	2300	2130
	energy, ft-lb:	2705	2355	2040	1760	1510
	arc, inches:		+1.7	0	-7.4	-21.4
Federal 150 Sierra GameKing	velocity, fps:	3000	2800	2620	2430	2260
HE	energy, ft-lb:	2995	2615	2275	1975	1700
	arc, inches:		+1.5	0	-6.5	-18.9
Federal 150 Nosler Partition	velocity, fps:	2850	2590	2340	2100	1880.
	energy, ft-lb:	2705	2225	1815	1470	1175
	arc, inches:		+1.9	0	-8.3	-24.4
Hornady 130 SST	velocity, fps:	3060	2845	2639	2442	2254
(or Interbond)	energy, ft-lb:	2700	2335	2009	1721	1467
	arc, inches:		+1.4	0	-6.6	-19.1
Hornady 130 SST LM	velocity, fps:	3215	2998	2790	2590	2400
(or Interbond)	energy, ft-lb:	2983	2594	2246	1936	1662
	arc, inches:		+1.2	0	-5.8	-17.0
Hornady 140 SP boat-tail	velocity, fps:	2940	2747	2562	2385	2214
	energy, ft-lb:	2688	2346	2041	1769	1524
	arc, inches:		+1.6	0	-7.0	-20.2
Hornady 140 SP boat-tail LM	velocity, fps:	3100	2894	2697	2508	2327.
	energy, ft-lb:	2987	2604	2261	1955	1684
	arc, inches:		+1.4	0	6.3	-18.3
Hornady 150 SP	velocity, fps:	2800	2684	2478	2284	2100
	energy, ft-lb:	2802	2400	2046	1737	1469
	arc, inches:		+1.7	0	-7.4	-21.6
Norma 130 SP	velocity, fps:	3140	2862	2601	2354	
	energy, ft-lb:	2847	2365	1953	1600	
	arc, inches:		+1.3	0	-6.5	
Norma 130 FMJ	velocity, fps:	2887	2634	2395	2169	
	energy, ft-lb:					
	arc, inches:		+1.8	0	-7.8	
Norma 150 SP	velocity, fps:	2799	2555	2323	2104	
	energy, ft-lb:	2610	2175	1798	1475	
	arc, inches:		+1.9	0	-8.3	
Norma 150 Oryx	velocity, fps:	2854	2608	2376	2155	
	energy, ft-lb:	2714	2267	1880	1547	
	arc, inches:		+1.8	0	-8.0	
PMC 130 Barnes X	velocity, fps:	2910	2717	2533	2356	2186
	energy, ft-lb:	2444	2131	1852	1602	1379
	arc, inches:		+1.6	0	-7.1	-20.4
PMC 130 SP boat-tail	velocity, fps:	3050	2830	2620	2421	2229
	energy, ft-lb:	2685	2312	1982	1691	1435
	arc, inches:		+1.5	0	-6.5	-19.0
PMC 130 Pointed Soft Point	velocity, fps:	2950	2691	2447	2217	2001
	energy, ft-lb:	2512	2090	1728	1419	1156
	arc, inches:		+1.6	0	-7.5	-22.1
PMC 150 Barnes X	velocity, fps:	2700	2541	2387	2238	2095
	energy, ft-lb:	2428	2150	1897	1668	1461
	arc, Inches:		+2.0	0	-8.1	-23.1
PMC 150 SP boat-tail	velocity, fps:	2850	2660	2477	2302	2134
	energy, ft-lb:	2705	2355	2043	1765	1516.
	arc, Inches:		+1.7	0	-7.4	-21.4
PMC 150 Pointed Soft Point	velocity, fps:	2750	2530	2321	2123	1936
	energy, ft-lb:	2519	2131	1794	1501	1248
	arc, inches:		+2.0	0	-8.4	-24.6
Rem. 100 Pointed Soft Point	velocity, fps:	3320	2924	2561	2225	1916
	energy, ft-lb:	2448	1898	1456	1099	815
	arc, inches:		+2.3	+2.0	-3.6	-16.2
Rem. 115 PSP Core-Lokt mr	velocity, fps:	2710	2412	2133	1873	1636
	energy, ft-lb:	1875	1485	1161	896	683
	arc, inches:		+1.0	-2.7	-14.2	-35.6
Rem. 130 PSP Core-Lokt	velocity, fps:	3060	2776	2510	2259	2022
	energy, ft-lb:	2702	2225	1818	1472	1180
	arc, inches:		+1.5	0	-7.0	-20.9
Rem. 130 Bronze Point	velocity, fps:	3060	2802	2559	2329	2110
	energy, ft-lb:	2702	2267	1890	1565	1285
	arc, inches:		+1.5	0	-6.8	-20.0
Rem. 130 Swift Scirocco	velocity, fps:	3060	2838	2677	2425	2232
	energy, ft-lb:	2702	2325	1991	1697	1438
	arc, inches:		+1.4	0	-6.5	-18.8
Rem. 130 AccuTip BT	velocity, fps:	3060	2845	2639	2442	2254
	energy, ft-lb:	2702	2336	2009	1721	1467
	arc, inches:		+1.4	0	-6.4	-18.6
Rem. 140 Swift A-Frame	velocity, fps:	2925	2652	2394	2152	1923
	energy, ft-lb:	2659	2186	1782	1439	1150
	arc, inches:		+1.7	0	-7.8	-23.2
Rem. 140 PSP boat-tail	velocity, fps:	2960	2749	2548	2355	2171
	energy, ft-lb:	2723	2349	2018	1724	1465
	arc, inches:		+1.6	0	-6.9	-20.1
Rem. 140 Nosler Bal. Tip	velocity, fps:	2960	2754	2557	2366	2187
	energy, ft-lb:	2724	2358	2032	1743	1487
	arc, inches:		+1.6	0	-6.9	-20.0
Rem. 140 PSP C-L Ultra	velocity, fps:	2925	2667	2424	2193	1975
	energy, ft-lb:	2659	2211	1826	1495	1212
	arc, inches:		+1.7	0	-7.6	-22.5
Rem. 150 SP Core-Lokt	velocity, fps:	2850	2504	2183	1886	1618
	energy, ft-lb:	2705	2087	1587	1185	872
	arc, inches:		+2.0	0	-9.4	-28.6
Rem. 150 Nosler Partition	velocity, fps:	2850	2652	2463	2282	2108
	energy, ft-lb:	2705	2343	2021	1734	1480
	arc, inches:		+1.7	0	-7.5	-21.6
Speer 130 Grand Slam	velocity, fps:	3050	2774	2514	2269	
	energy, ft-lb:	2685	2221	1824	1485	
	arc, inches:		+1.5	0	-7.0	-20.9
Speer 150 Grand Slam	velocity, fps:	2830	2594	2369	2156	
	energy, ft-lb:	2667	2240	1869	1548	
	arc, inches:		+1.8	0	-8.1	-23.6
Win. 130 Power-Point	velocity, fps:	3060	2802	2559	2329	2110
	energy, ft-lb:	2702	2267	1890	1565	1285.
	arc, inches:		+1.8	0	-7.1	-20.6

CARTRIDGE BULLET	RANGE, YARDS:	0	100	200	300	400
Win. 130 Power-Point Plus	velocity, fps:	3150	2881	2628	2388	2161
	energy, ft-lb:	2865	2396	1993	1646	1348
	arc, inches:		+1.3	0	-6.4	-18.9
Win. 130 Silvertip	velocity, fps:	3060	2776	2510	2259	2022.
	energy, ft-lb:	2702	2225	1818	1472	1180
	arc, inches:		+1.8	0	-7.4	-21.6
Win. 130 Ballistic Silvertip	velocity, fps:	3050	2828	2618	2416	2224
	energy, ft-lb:	2685	2309	1978	1685	1428
	arc, inches:		+1.4	0	-6.5	-18.9
Win. 140 AccuBond	velocity, fps:	2950	2751	2560	2378	2203
	energy, ft-lb:	2705	2352	2038	1757	1508
	arc, inches:		+1.6	0	-6.9	-19.9
Win. 140 Fail Safe	velocity, fps:	2920	2671	2435	2211	1999
	energy, ft-lb:	2651	2218	1843	1519	1242
	arc, inches:		+1.7	0	-7.6	-22.3
Win. 150 Power-Point	velocity, fps:	2850	2585	2336	2100	1879
	energy, ft-lb:	2705	2226	1817	1468	1175
	arc, inches:		+2.2	0	-8.6	-25.0
Win. 150 Power-Point Plus	velocity, fps:	2950	2679	2425	2184	1957
	energy, ft-lb:	2900	2391	1959	1589	1276
	arc, inches:		+1.7	0	-7.6	-22.6
Win. 150 Partition Gold	velocity, fps:	2930	2693	2468	2254	2051
	energy, ft-lb:	2860	2416	2030	1693	1402
	arc, inches:		+1.7	0	-7.4	-21.6
Win. 150 Supreme Elite XP3	velocity, fps:	2950	2763	2583	2411	2245
	energy, ft-lb:	2898	2542	2223	1936	1679
	arc, inches:		+1.5	0	-6.9	-15.5

.270 Winchester Short Magnum

CARTRIDGE BULLET	RANGE, YARDS:	0	100	200	300	400
Black Hills 140 AccuBond	velocity, fps:	3100				
	energy, ft-lb:	2987				
	arc, inches:					
Federal 130 Nos. Bal. Tip	velocity, fps:	3300	3070	2840	2630	2430
	energy, ft-lb:	3145	2710	2335	2000	1705
	arc, inches:		+1.1	0	-5.4	-15.8
Federal 130 Nos. Partition And Nos. Solid Base And Barnes TS	velocity, fps:	3280	3040	2810	2590	2380
	energy, ft-lb:	3105	2665	2275	1935	1635
	arc, inches:		+1.1	0	-5.6	-16.3
Federal 140 Nos. AccuBond	velocity, fps	3200	3000	2810	2630	2450
	energy, ft-lb:	3185	2795	2455	2145	1865
	arc, inches:		+1.2	0	-5.6	-16.2
Federal 140 Trophy Bonded	velocity, fps:	3130	2870	2640	2410	2200
	energy, ft-lb:	3035	2570	2160	1810	1500
	arc, inches:		+1.4	0	-6.3	18.7
Federal 150 Nos. Partition	velocity, fps:	3160	2950	2750	2550	2370
	energy, ft-lb:	3325	2895	2515	2175	1870
	arc, inches:		+1.3	0	-5.9	-17.0
Norma 130 FMJ	velocity, fps:	3150	2882	2630	2391	
	energy, ft-lb:					
	arc, inches:		+1.5	0	-6.4	
Norma 130 Ballistic ST	velocity, fps:	3281	3047	2825	2614	
	energy, ft-lb:	3108	2681	2305	1973	
	arc, inches:		+1.1	0	-5.5	
Norma 140 Barnes X TS	velocity, fps:	3150	2952	2762	2580	
	energy, ft-lb:	3085	2709	2372	2070	
	arc, inches:		+1.3	0	-5.8	
Norma 150 Nosler Bal. Tip	velocity, fps:	3280	3046	2824	2613	
	energy, ft-lb:	3106	2679	2303	1972	
	arc, inches:		+1.1	0	-5.4	
Norma 150 Oryx	velocity, fps:	3117	2856	2611	2378	
	energy, ft-lb:	3237	2718	2271	1884	
	arc, inches:		+1.4	0	-6.5	
Win. 130 Bal. Silvertip	velocity, fps:	3275	3041	2820	2609	2408
	energy, ft-lb:	3096	2669	2295	1964	1673
	arc, inches:		+1.1	0	-5.5	-16.1
Win. 140 AccuBond	velocity, fps:	3200	2989	2789	2597	2413
	energy, ft-lb:	3184	2779	2418	2097	1810
	arc, inches:		+1.2	0	-5.7	-16.5
Win. 140 Fail Safe	velocity, fps:	3125	2865	2619	2386	2165
	energy, ft-lb:	3035	2550	2132	1769	1457
	arc, inches:		+1.4	0	-6.5	-19.0
Win. 150 Ballistic Silvertip	velocity, fps:	3120	2923	2734	2554	2380.
	energy, ft-lb:	3242	2845	2490	2172	1886.
	arc, inches:		+1.3	0	-5.9	-17.2
Win. 150 Power Point	velocity, fps:	3150	2867	2601	2350	2113
	energy, ft-lb:	3304	2737	2252	1839	1487
	arc, inches:		+1.4	0	-6.5	-19.4
Win. 150 Supreme Elite XP3	velocity, fps:	3120	2926	2740	2561	2389
	energy, ft-lb:	3242	2850	2499	2184	1901
	arc, inches:		+1.3	0	-5.9	-17.1

.270 Weatherby Magnum

CARTRIDGE BULLET	RANGE, YARDS:	0	100	200	300	400
Federal 130 Nosler Partition	velocity, fps:	3200	2960	2740	2520	2320
	energy, ft-lb:	2955	2530	2160	1835	1550
	arc, inches:		+1.2	0	-5.9	-17.3
Federal 130 Sierra GameKing BTSP	velocity, fps:	3200	2980	2780	2580	2400
	energy, ft-lb:	2955	2570	2230	1925	1655
	arc, inches:		+1.2	0	-5.7	-16.6
Federal 140 Trophy Bonded	velocity, fps:	3100	2840	2600	2370	2150.
	energy, ft-lb:	2990	2510	2100	1745	1440
	arc, inches:		+1.4	0	-6.6	-19.3
Wby. 100 Pointed Expanding	velocity, fps:	3760	3396	3061	2751	2462
	energy, ft-lb:	3139	2560	2081	1681	1346
	arc, inches:		+2.3	+3.0	0	-7.6
Wby. 130 Pointed Expanding	velocity, fps:	3375	3123	2885	2659	2444
	energy, ft-lb:	3288	2815	2402	2041	1724
	arc, inches:		+2.8	+3.5	0	-8.4
Wby. 130 Nosler Partition	velocity, fps:	3375	3127	2892	2670	2458.
	energy, ft-lb:	3288	2822	2415	2058	1744
	arc, inches:		+2.8	+3.5	0	-8.3
Wby. 140 Nosler Bal. Tip	velocity, fps:	3300	3077	2865	2663	2470.
	energy, ft-lb:	3385	2943	2551	2204	1896
	arc, inches:		+2.9	+3.6	0	-8.4
Wby. 140 Barnes X	velocity, fps:	3250	3032	2825	2628	2438
	energy, ft-lb:	3283	2858	2481	2146	1848
	arc, inches:		+3.0	+3.7	0	-8.7
Wby. 150 Pointed Expanding	velocity, fps:	3245	3028	2821	2623	2434
	energy, ft-lb:	3507	3053	2650	2292	1973
	arc, inches:		+3.0	+3.7	0	-8.7
Wby. 150 Nosler Partition	velocity, fps:	3245	3029	2823	2627	2439.
	energy, ft-lb:	3507	3055	2655	2298	1981
	arc, inches:		+3.0	+3.7	0	-8.

7-30 Waters

CARTRIDGE BULLET	RANGE, YARDS:	0	100	200	300	400
Federal 120 Sierra GameKing BTSP	velocity, fps:	2700	2300	1930	1600	1330.
	energy, ft-lb:	1940	1405	990	685	470
	arc, inches:		+2.6	0	-12.0	-37.6

7mm Mauser (7x57)

CARTRIDGE BULLET	RANGE, YARDS:	0	100	200	300	400
Federal 140 Sierra Pro-Hunt.	velocity, fps:	2660	2450	2260	2070	1890.
	energy, ft-lb:	2200	1865	1585	1330	1110
	arc, inches:		+2.1	0	-9.0	-26.1
Federal 140 Nosler Partition	velocity, fps:	2660	2450	2260	2070	1890.
	energy, ft-lb:	2200	1865	1585	1330	1110
	arc, inches:		+2.1	0	-9.0	-26.1
Federal 175 Hi-Shok RN	velocity, fps:	2440	2140	1860	1600	1380
	energy, ft-lb:	2315	1775	1340	1000	740
	arc, inches:		+3.1	0	-13.3	-40.1

Ballistics Tables for Modern Sporting Rifles

7MM MAUSER TO 7X64 BRENNEKE

CARTRIDGE BULLET	RANGE, YARDS:	0	100	200	300	400
Hornady 139 SP boat-tail	velocity, fps:	2700	2504	2316	2137	1965
	energy, ft-lb:	2251	1936	1656	1410	1192
	arc, inches:		+2.0	0	-8.5	-24.9
Hornady 139 SP Interlock	velocity, fps:	2680	2455	2241	2038	1846
	energy, ft-lb:	2216	1860	1550	1282	1052
	arc, inches:		+2.1	0	-9.1	-26.6
Hornady 139 SP boat-tail LM	velocity, fps:	2830	2620	2450	2250	2070
	energy, ft-lb:	2475	2135	1835	1565	1330
	arc, inches:		+1.8	0	-7.6	-22.1
Hornady 139 SP LM	velocity, fps:	2950	2736	2532	2337	2152.
	energy, ft-lb:	2686	2310	1978	1686	1429
	arc, inches:		+2.0	0	-7.6	-21.5
Norma 150 Soft Point	velocity, fps:	2690	2479	2278	2087	
	energy, ft-lb:	2411	2048	1729	1450	
	arc, inches:		+2.0	0	-8.8	
PMC 140 Pointed Soft Point	velocity, fps:	2660	2450	2260	2070	1890
	energy, ft-lb:	2200	1865	1585	1330	1110.
	arc, inches:		+2.4	0	-9.6	-27.3
PMC 175 Soft Point	velocity, fps:	2440	2140	1860	1600	1380
	energy, ft-lb:	2315	1775	1340	1000	740
	arc, inches:		+1.5	-3.6	-18.6	-46.8
Rem. 140 PSP Core-Lokt	velocity, fps:	2660	2435	2221	2018	1827
	energy, ft-lb:	2199	1843	1533	1266	1037
	arc, inches:		+2.2	0	-9.2	-27.4
Win. 145 Power-Point	velocity, fps:	2660	2413	2180	1959	1754
	energy, ft-lb:	2279	1875	1530	1236	990
	arc, inches:		+1.1	-2.8	-14.1	-34.4

7x57 R

CARTRIDGE BULLET	RANGE, YARDS:	0	100	200	300	400
Norma 150 FMJ	velocity, fps:	2690	2489	2296	2112	
	energy, ft-lb:	2411	2063	1756	1486	
	arc, inches:		+2.0	0	-8.6	
Norma 154 Soft Point	velocity, fps:	2625	2417	2219	2030	
	energy, ft-lb:	2357	1999	1684	1410	
	arc, inches:		+2.2	0	-9.3	
Norma 156 Oryx	velocity, fps:	2608	2346	2099	1867	
	energy, ft-lb:	2357	1906	1526	1208	
	arc, inches:		+2.4	0	-10.3	

7mm-08 Remington

CARTRIDGE BULLET	RANGE, YARDS:	0	100	200	300	400
Black Hills 140 AccuBond	velocity, fps:	2700				
	energy, ft-lb:					
	arc, inches:					
Federal 140 Nosler Partition	velocity, fps:	2800	2590	2390	2200	2020
	energy, ft-lb:	2435	2085	1775	1500	1265
	arc, inches:		+1.8	0	-8.0	-23.1
Federal 140 Nosler Bal. Tip And AccuBond	velocity, fps:	2800	2610	2430	2260	2100
	energy, ft-lb:	2440	2135	1840	1590	1360.
	arc, inches:		+1.8	0	-7.7	-22.3
Federal 140 Tr. Bonded HE	velocity, fps:	2950	2660	2390	2140	1900
	energy, ft-lb:	2705	2205	1780	1420	1120
	arc, inches:		+1.7	0	-7.9	-23.2
Federal 150 Sierra Pro-Hunt.	velocity, fps:	2650	2440	2230	2040	1860
	energy, ft-lb:	2340	1980	1660	1390	1150
	arc, inches:		+2.2	0	-9.2	-26.7
Hornady 139 SP boat-tail LM	velocity, fps:	3000	2790	2590	2399	2216
	energy, ft-lb:	2777	2403	2071	1776	1515
	arc, inches:		+1.5	0	-6.7	-19.4
Norma 140 Ballistic ST	velocity, fps:	2822	2633	2452	2278	
	energy, ft-lb:	2476	2156	1870	1614	
	arc, inches:		+1.8	0	-7.6	
PMC 139 PSP	velocity, fps:	2850	2610	2384	2170	1969
	energy, ft-lb:	2507	2103	1754	1454	1197
	arc, inches:		+1.8	0	-7.9	-23.3
Rem. 120 Hollow Point	velocity, fps:	3000	2725	2467	2223	1992
	energy, ft-lb:	2398	1979	1621	1316	1058
	arc, inches:		+1.6	0	-7.3	-21.7
Rem. 140 PSP Core-Lokt	velocity, fps:	2860	2625	2402	2189	1988
	energy, ft-lb:	2542	2142	1793	1490	1228
	arc, inches:		+1.8	0	-7.8	-22.9
Rem. 140 PSP boat-tail	velocity, fps:	2860	2656	2460	2273	2094
	energy, ft-lb:	2542	2192	1881	1606	1363
	arc, inches:		+1.7	0	-7.5	-21.7
Rem. 140 AccuTip BT	velocity, fps:	2860	2670	2488	2313	2145
	energy, ft-lb:	2543	2217	1925	1663	1431
	arc, inches:		+1.7	0	-7.3	-21.2
Rem. 140 Nosler Partition	velocity, fps:	2860	2648	2446	2253	2068
	energy, ft-lb:	2542	2180	1860	1577	1330
	arc, inches:		+1.7	0	-7.6	-22.0
Speer 145 Grand Slam	velocity, fps:	2845	2567	2305	2059	
	energy, ft-lb:	2606	2121	1711	1365	
	arc, inches:		+1.9	0	-8.4	-25.5
Win. 140 Power-Point	velocity, fps:	2800	2523	2268	2027	1802.
	energy, ft-lb:	2429	1980	1599	1277	1010
	arc, inches:		+2.0	0	-8.8	-26.0
Win. 140 Power-Point Plus	velocity, fps:	2875	2597	2336	2090	1859
	energy, ft-lb:	2570	1997	1697	1358	1075
	arc, inches:		+2.0	0	-8.8	26.0
Win. 140 Fail Safe	velocity, fps:	2760	2506	2271	2048	1839
	energy, ft-lb:	2360	1953	1603	1304	1051
	arc, inches:		+2.0	0	-8.8	-25.9
Win. 140 Ballistic Silvertip	velocity, fps:	2770	2572	2382	2200	2026
	energy, ft-lb:	2386	2056	1764	1504	1276
	arc, inches:		+1.9	0	-8.0	-23.8

7x64 Brenneke

CARTRIDGE BULLET	RANGE, YARDS:	0	100	200	300	400
Federal 160 Nosler Partition	velocity, fps:	2650	2480	2310	2150	2000
	energy, ft-lb:	2495	2180	1895	1640	1415
	arc, inches:		+2.1	0	-8.7	-24.9
Norma 140 AccuBond	velocity, fps:	2953	2759	2572	2394	
	energy, ft-lb:	2712	2366	2058	1782	
	arc, inches:		+1.5	0	-6.8	
Norma 154 Soft Point	velocity, fps:	2821	2605	2399	2203	
	energy, ft-lb:	2722	2321	1969	1660	
	arc, inches:		+1.8	0	-7.8	
Norma 156 Oryx	velocity, fps:	2789	2516	2259	2017	
	energy, ft-lb:	2695	2193	1768	1410	
	arc, inches:		+2.0	0	-8.8	
Norma 170 Vulkan	velocity, fps:	2756	2501	2259	2031	
	energy, ft-lb:	2868	2361	1927	1558	
	arc, inches:		+2.0	0	-8.8	
Norma 170 Oryx	velocity, fps:	2756	2481	2222	1979	
	energy, ft-lb:	2868	2324	1864	1478	
	arc, inches:		+2.1	0	-9.2	
Norma 170 Plastic Point	velocity, fps:	2756	2519	2294	2081	
	energy, ft-lb:	2868	2396	1987	1635	
	arc, inches:		+2.0	0	-8.6	
PMC 170 Pointed Soft Point	velocity, fps:	2625	2401	2189	1989	1801
	energy, ft lb:	2601	2175	1808	1493	1224
	arc, inches:		+2.3	0	-9.6	-27.9
Rem. 175 PSP Core-Lokt	velocity, fps:	2650	2445	2248	2061	1883
	energy, ft-lb:	2728	2322	1964	1650	1378
	arc, inches:		+2.2	0	-9.1	-26.4
Speer 160 Grand Slam	velocity, fps:	2600	2376	2164	1962	
	energy, ft-lb:	2401	2006	1663	1368	
	arc, inches:		+2.3	0	-9.8	-28.6
Speer 175 Grand Slam	velocity, fps:	2650	2461	2280	2106	

Ballistics Tables for Modern Sporting Rifles

7X65 R TO 7MM REMINGTON MAGNUM

CARTRIDGE BULLET	RANGE, YARDS:	0	100	200	300	400
	energy, ft-lb:	2728	2353	2019	1723	
	arc, inches:		+2.4	0	-9.2	-26.2

7x65 R

CARTRIDGE BULLET	RANGE, YARDS:	0	100	200	300	400
Norma 150 FMJ	velocity, fps:	2756	2552	2357	2170	
	energy, ft-lb:	2530	2169	1850	1569	
	arc, inches:		+1.9	0	-8.2	
Norma 156 Oryx	velocity, fps:	2723	2454	2200	1962	
	energy, ft-lb:	2569	2086	1678	1334	
	arc, inches:		+2.1	0	-9.3	
Norma 170 Plastic Point	velocity, fps:	2625	2390	2167	1956	
	energy, ft-lb:	2602	2157	1773	1445	
	arc, inches:		+2.3	0	-9.7	
Norma 170 Vulkan	velocity, fps:	2657	2392	2143	1909	
	energy, ft-lb:	2666	2161	1734	1377	
	arc, inches:		+2.3	0	-9.9	
Norma 170 Oryx	velocity, fps:	2657	2378	2115	1871	
	energy, ft-lb:	2666	2135	1690	1321	
	arc, inches:		+2.3	0	-10.1	

.284 Winchester

CARTRIDGE BULLET	RANGE, YARDS:	0	100	200	300	400
Win. 150 Power-Point	velocity, fps:	2860	2595	2344	2108	1886
	energy, ft-lb:	2724	2243	1830	1480	1185
	arc, inches:		+2.1	0	-8.5	-24.8

.280 Remington

CARTRIDGE BULLET	RANGE, YARDS:	0	100	200	300	400
Federal 140 Sierra Pro-Hunt.	velocity, fps:	2990	2740	2500	2270	2060
	energy, ft-lb:	2770	2325	1940	1605	1320
	arc, inches:		+1.6	0	-7.0	-20.8
Federal 140 Trophy Bonded	velocity, fps:	2990	2630	2310	2040	1730
	energy, ft-lb:	2770	2155	1655	1250	925
	arc, inches:		+1.6	0	-8.4	-25.4
Federal 140 Tr. Bonded HE	velocity, fps:	3150	2850	2570	2300	2050
	energy, ft-lb:	3085	2520	2050	1650	1310
	arc, inches:		+1.4	0	-6.7	-20.0
Federal 140 Nos. AccuBond	velocity, fps:	3000	2800	2620	2440	2260
And Bal. Tip	energy, ft-lb:	2800	2445	2130	1845	1590
And Solid Base	arc, inches:		+1.5	0	-6.5	-18.9
Federal 150 Hi-Shok	velocity, fps:	2890	2670	2460	2260	2060
	energy, ft-lb:	2780	2370	2015	1695	1420
	arc, inches:		+1.7	0	-7.5	-21.8
Federal 150 Nosler Partition	velocity, fps:	2890	2690	2490	2310	2130
	energy, ft-lb:	2780	2405	2070	1770	1510.
	arc, inches:		+1.7	0	-7.2	-21.1
Federal 150 Nos. AccuBond	velocity, fps	2800	2630	2460	2300	2150
	energy, ft-lb:	2785	2455	2155	1885	1645
	arc, inches:		+1.8	0	-7.5	-21.5
Federal 160 Trophy Bonded	velocity, fps:	2800	2570	2350	2140	1940
	energy, ft-lb:	2785	2345	1960	1625	1340
	arc, inches:		+1.9	0	-8.3	-24.0
Hornady 139 SPBT LMmoly	velocity, fps:	3110	2888	2675	2473	2280.
	energy, ft-lb:	2985	2573	2209	1887	1604
	arc, inches:		+1.4	0	-6.5	-18.6
Norma 156 Oryx	velocity, fps:	2789	2516	2259	2017	
	energy, ft-lb:	2695	2193	1768	1410	
	arc, inches:		+2.0	0	-8.8	
Norma 170 Plastic Point	velocity, fps:	2707	2468	2241	2026	
	energy, ft-lb:	2767	2299	1896	1550	
	arc, inches:		+2.1	0	-9.1	
Norma 170 Vulkan	velocity, fps:	2592	2346	2113	1894	
	energy, ft-lb:	2537	2078	1686	1354	
	arc, inches:		+2.4	0	-10.2	
Norma 170 Oryx	velocity, fps:	2690	2416	2159	1918	
	energy, ft-lb:	2732	2204	1760	1389	
	arc, inches:		+2.2	0	-9.7	
Rem. 140 PSP Core-Lokt	velocity, fps:	3000	2758	2528	2309	2102
	energy, ft-lb:	2797	2363	1986	1657	1373
	arc, inches:		+1.5	0	-7.0	-20.5
Rem. 140 PSP boat-tail	velocity, fps:	2860	2656	2460	2273	2094
	energy, ft-lb:	2542	2192	1881	1606	1363
	arc, inches:		+1.7	0	-7.5	-21.7
Rem. 140 Nosler Bal. Tip	velocity, fps:	3000	2804	2616	2436	2263
	energy, ft-lb:	2799	2445	2128	1848	1593
	arc, inches:		+1.5	0	-6.8	-19.0
Rem. 140 AccuTip	velocity, fps:	3000	2804	2617	2437	2265
	energy, ft-lb:	2797	2444	2129	1846	1594
	arc, inches:		+1.5	0	-6.8	-19.0
Rem. 150 PSP Core-Lokt	velocity, fps:	2890	2624	2373	2135	1912
	energy, ft-lb:	2781	2293	1875	1518	1217
	arc, inches:		+1.8	0	-8.0	-23.6
Rem. 165 SP Core-Lokt	velocity, fps:	2820	2510	2220	1950	1701
	energy, ft-lb:	2913	2308	1805	1393	1060.
	arc, inches:		+2.0	0	-9.1	-27.4
Speer 145 Grand Slam	velocity, fps:	2900	2619	2354	2105	
	energy, ft-lb:	2707	2207	1784	1426	
	arc, inches:		+2.1	0	-8.4	-24.7
Speer 160 Grand Slam	velocity, fps:	2890	2652	2425	2210	
	energy, ft-lb:	2967	2497	2089	1735	
	arc, inches:		+1.7	0	-7.7	-22.4
Win. 140 Fail Safe	velocity, fps:	3050	2756	2480	2221	1977
	energy, ft-lb:	2893	2362	1913	1533	1216
	arc, inches:		+1.5	0	-7.2	-21.5
Win. 140 Ballistic Silvertip	velocity, fps:	3040	2842	2653	2471	2297
	energy, ft-lb:	2872	2511	2187	1898	1640
	arc, inches:		+1.4	0	-6.3	-18.4

.280 Ackley Improved

CARTRIDGE BULLET	RANGE, YARDS:	0	100	200	300	400
Nosler 140 AccuBond	velocity, fps	3150	2947	2753	2567	2389
	energy, ft-lbs	3084	2700	2355	2048	1774
	arc, inches	-1.5	+1.1	0	-5.0	-16.8
Nosler 160 Partition	velocity, fps	2950	2752	2562	2380	2206
	energy, ft-lbs	3091	2690	2332	2013	1729
	arc, inches	-1.5	+1.5	0	-6.7	-19.4

7mm Remington Magnum

CARTRIDGE BULLET	RANGE, YARDS:	0	100	200	300	400
A-Square 175 Monolithic	velocity, fps:	2860	2557	2273	2008	1771
Solid	energy, ft-lb:	3178	2540	2008	1567	1219
	arc, inches:		+1.92	0	-8.7	-25.9
Black Hills 140 Nos. Bal. Tip	velocity, fps:	3150				
	energy, ft-lb:	3084				
	arc, inches:					
Black Hills 140 Barnes XLC	velocity, fps:	3150				
	energy, ft-lb:	3084				
	arc, inches:					
Black Hills 140 Nos. Partition	velocity, fps:	3150				
	energy, ft-lb:	3084				
	arc, inches:					
Federal 140 Nosler Bal. Tip	velocity, fps:	3110	2910	2720	2530	2360.
And AccuBond	energy, ft-lb:	3005	2630	2295	1995	1725
	arc, inches:		+1.3	0	-6.0	-17.4
Federal 140 Nosler Partition	velocity, fps:	3150	2930	2710	2510	2320
	energy, ft-lb:	3085	2660	2290	1960	1670
	arc, inches:		+1.3	0	-6.0	-17.5
Federal 140 Trophy Bonded	velocity, fps:	3150	2910	2680	2460	2250.

BALLISTICS

Ballistics Tables for Modern Sporting Rifles

7MM REMINGTON MAGNUM TO 7MM REMINGTON MAGNUM

CARTRIDGE BULLET	RANGE, YARDS:	0	100	200	300	400
	energy, ft-lb:	3085	2630	2230	1880	1575
	arc, inches:		+1.3	0	-6.1	-18.1
Federal 150 Hi-Shok	velocity, fps:	3110	2830	2570	2320	2090
	energy, ft-lb:	3220	2670	2200	1790	1450
	arc, inches:		+1.4	0	-6.7	-19.9
Federal 150 Sierra GameKing	velocity, fps:	3110	2920	2750	2580	2410
BTSP	energy, ft-lb:	3220	2850	2510	2210	1930
	arc, inches:		+1.3	0	-5.9	-17.0
Federal 150 Nosler Bal. Tip	velocity, fps:	3110	2910	2720	2540	2370
	energy, ft-lb:	3220	2825	2470	2150	1865
	arc, inches:		+1.3	0	-6.0	-17.4
Federal 150 Nos. Solid Base	velocity, fps:	3100	2890	2690	2500	2310
	energy, ft-lb:	3200	2780	2405	2075	1775
	arc, inches:		+1.3	0	-6.2	-17.8
Federal 160 Barnes XLC	velocity, fps:	2940	2760	2580	2410	2240
	energy, ft-lb:	3070	2695	2360	2060	1785
	arc, inches:		+1.5	0	-6.8	-19.6
Federal 160 Sierra Pro-Hunt.	velocity, fps:	2940	2730	2520	2320	2140
	energy, ft-lb:	3070	2640	2260	1920	1620
	arc, inches:		+1.6	0	-7.1	-20.6
Federal 160 Nosler Partition	velocity, fps:	2950	2770	2590	2420	2250.
	energy, ft-lb:	3090	2715	2375	2075	1800
	arc, inches:		+1.5	0	-6.7	-19.4
Federal 160 Nos. AccuBond	velocity, fps:	2950	2770	2600	2440	2280.
	energy, ft-lb:	3090	2730	2405	2110	1845
	arc, inches:		+1.5	0	-6.6	-19.1
Federal 160 Trophy Bonded	velocity, fps:	2940	2660	2390	2140	1900
	energy, ft-lb:	3070	2505	2025	1620	1280.
	arc, inches:		+1.7	0	-7.9	-23.3
Federal 165 Sierra GameKing	velocity, fps:	2950	2800	2650	2510	2370.
BTSP	energy, ft-lb:	3190	2865	2570	2300	2050
	arc, inches:		+1.5	0	-6.4	-18.4
Federal 175 Hi-Shok	velocity, fps:	2860	2650	2440	2240	2060
	energy, ft-lb:	3180	2720	2310	1960	1640
	arc, inches:		+1.7	0	-7.6	-22.1
Federal 175 Trophy Bonded	velocity, fps:	2860	2600	2350	2120	1900
	energy, ft-lb:	3180	2625	2150	1745	1400
	arc, inches:		+1.8	0	-8.2	-24.0
Hornady 139 SPBT	velocity, fps:	3150	2933	2727	2530	2341
	energy, ft-lb:	3063	2656	2296	1976	1692
	arc, inches:		+1.2	0	-6.1	-17.7
Hornady 139 SST	velocity, fps:	3150	2948	2754	2569	2391
(or Interbond)	energy, ft-lb:	3062	2681	2341	2037	1764
	arc, inches:		+1.1	0	-5.7	-16.7
Hornady 139 SST LM	velocity, fps:	3250	3044	2847	2657	2475
(or Interbond)	energy, ft-lb:	3259	2860	2501	2178	1890
	arc, inches:		+1.1	0	-5.5	-16.2
Hornady 139 SPBT HMmoly	velocity, fps:	3250	3041	2822	2613	2413
	energy, ft-lb:	3300	2854	2458	2106	1797.
	arc, inches:		+1.1	0	-5.7	-16.6
Hornady 154 Soft Point	velocity, fps:	3035	2814	2604	2404	2212
	energy, ft-lb:	3151	2708	2319	1977	1674
	arc, inches:		+1.3	0	-6.7	-19.3
Hornady 154 SST	velocity, fps:	3035	2850	2672	2501	2337
(or Interbond)	energy, ft-lb:	3149	2777	2441	2139	1867
	arc, inches:		+1.4	0	-6.5	-18.7
Hornady 162 SP boat-tail	velocity, fps:	2940	2757	2582	2413	2251
	energy, ft-lb:	3110	2735	2399	2095	1823
	arc, inches:		+1.6	0	-6.7	-19.7
Hornady 175 SP	velocity, fps:	2860	2650	2440	2240	2060.
	energy, ft-lb:	3180	2720	2310	1960	1640
	arc, inches:		+2.0	0	-7.9	-22.7
Norma 140 Nosler Bal. Tip	velocity, fps:	3150	2936	2732	2537	

CARTRIDGE BULLET	RANGE, YARDS:	0	100	200	300	400
	energy, ft-lb:	3085	2680	2320	2001	
	arc, inches:		+1.2	0	-5.9	
Norma 140 Barnes X TS	velocity, fps:	3117	2912	2716	2529	
	energy, ft-lb:	3021	2637	2294	1988	
	arch, inches:		+1.3	0	-6.0	
Norma 150 Scirocco	velocity, fps:	3117	2934	2758	2589	
	energy, ft-lb:	3237	2869	2535	2234	
	arc, inches:		+1.2	0	-5.8	
Norma 156 Oryx	velocity, fps:	2953	2670	2404	2153	
	energy, ft-lb:	3021	2470	2002	1607	
	arc, inches:		+1.7	0	-7.7	
Norma 170 Vulkan	velocity, fps:	3018	2747	2493	2252	
	energy, ft-lb:	3439	2850	2346	1914	
	arc, inches:		+1.5	0	-2.8	
Norma 170 Oryx	velocity, fps:	2887	2601	2333	2080	
	energy, ft-lb:	3147	2555	2055	1634	
	arc, inches:		+1.8	0	-8.2	
Norma 170 Plastic Point	velocity, fps:	3018	2762	2519	2290	
	energy, ft-lb:	3439	2880	2394	1980	
	arc, inches:		+1.5	0	-7.0	
PMC 140 Barnes X	velocity, fps:	3000	2808	2624	2448	2279
	energy, ft-lb:	2797	2451	2141	1863	1614
	arc, inches:		+1.5	0	-6.6	18.9
PMC 140 Pointed Soft Point	velocity, fps:	3099	2878	2668	2469	2279
	energy, ft-lb:	2984	2574	2212	1895	1614
	arc, inches:		+1.4	0	-6.2	-18.1
PMC 140 SP boat-tail	velocity, fps:	3125	2891	2669	2457	2255
	energy, ft-lb:	3035	2597	2213	1877	1580
	arc, inches:		+1.4	0	-6.3	-18.4
PMC 160 Barnes X	velocity, fps:	2800	2639	2484	2334	2189
	energy, ft-lb:	2785	2474	2192	1935	1703
	arc, inches:		+1.8	0	-7.4	-21.2
PMC 160 Pointed Soft Point	velocity, fps:	2914	2748	2586	2428	2276
	energy, ft-lb:	3016	2682	2375	2095	1840
	arc, inches:		+1.6	0	-6.7	-19.4
PMC 160 SP boat-tail	velocity, fps:	2900	2696	2501	2314	2135
	energy, ft-lb:	2987	2582	2222	1903	1620
	arc, inches:		+1.7	0	-7.2	-21.0
PMC 175 Pointed Soft Point	velocity, fps:	2860	2645	2442	2244	2957
	energy, ft-lb:	3178	2718	2313	1956	1644
	arc, inches:		+2.0	0	-7.9	-22.7
Rem. 140 PSP Core-Lokt mr	velocity, fps:	2710	2482	2265	2059	1865
	energy, ft-lb:	2283	1915	1595	1318	1081
	arc, inches:		+1.0	-2.5	-12.8	-31.3
Rem. 140 PSP Core-Lokt	velocity, fps:	3175	2923	2684	2458	2243
	energy, ft-lb:	3133	2655	2240	1878	1564
	arc, inches:		+2.2	+1.9	-3.2	-14.2
Rem. 140 PSP boat-tail	velocity, fps:	3175	2956	2747	2547	2356
	energy, ft-lb:	3133	2715	2345	2017	1726
	arc, inches:		+2.2	+1.6	-3.1	-13.4
Rem. 150 AccuTip	velocity, fps:	3110	2926	2749	2579	2415
	energy, ft-lb:	3221	2850	2516	2215	1943
	arc, inches:		+1.3	0	-5.9	-17.0
Rem. 150 PSP Core-Lokt	velocity, fps:	3110	2830	2568	2320	2085
	energy, ft-lb:	3221	2667	2196	1792	1448
	arc, inches:		+1.3	0	-6.6	-20.2
Rem. 150 Nosler Bal. Tip	velocity, fps:	3110	2912	2723	2542	2367
	energy, ft-lb:	3222	2825	2470	2152	1867
	arc, inches:		+1.2	0	-5.9	-17.3
Rem. 150 Swift Scirocco	velocity, fps:	3110	2927	2751	2582	2419
	energy, ft-lb:	3221	2852	2520	2220	1948
	arc, inches:		+1.3	0	-5.9	-17.0
Rem. 160 Swift A-Frame	velocity, fps:	2900	2659	2430	2212	2006

Ballistics Tables for Modern Sporting Rifles

7MM REMINGTON MAGNUM TO 7MM WEATHERBY MAGNUM

CARTRIDGE BULLET	RANGE, YARDS:	0	100	200	300	400
	energy, ft-lb:	2987	2511	2097	1739	1430
	arc, inches:		+1.7	0	-7.6	-22.4
Rem. 160 Nosler Partition	velocity, fps:	2950	2752	2563	2381	2207
	energy, ft-lb:	3091	2690	2333	2014	1730
	arc, inches:		+0.6	-1.9	-9.6	-23.6
Rem. 175 PSP Core-Lokt	velocity, fps:	2860	2645	2440	2244	2057
	energy, ft-lb:	3178	2718	2313	1956	1644
	arc, inches:		+1.7	0	-7.6	-22.1
Speer 145 Grand Slam	velocity, fps:	3140	2843	2565	2304	
	energy, ft-lb:	3174	2602	2118	1708	
	arc, inches:		+1.4	0	-6.7	
Speer 175 Grand Slam	velocity, fps:	2850	2653	2463	2282	
	energy, ft-lb:	3156	2734	2358	2023	
	arc, inches:		+1.7	0	-7.5	-21.7
Win. 140 Fail Safe	velocity, fps:	3150	2861	2589	2333	2092
	energy, ft-lb:	3085	2544	2085	1693	1361
	arc, inches:		+1.4	0	-6.6	-19.5
Win. 140 Ballistic Silvertip	velocity, fps:	3100	2889	2687	2494	2310
	energy, ft-lb:	2988	2595	2245	1934	1659.
	arc, inches:		+1.3	0	-6.2	-17.9
Win. 140 AccuBond CT	velocity, fps:	3180	2965	2760	2565	2377
	energy, ft-lb:	3143	2733	2368	2044	1756
	arc, inches:		+1.2	0	-5.8	-16.9
Win. 150 Power-Point	velocity, fps:	3090	2812	2551	2304	2071
	energy, ft-lb:	3181	2634	2167	1768	1429
	arc, inches:		+1.5	0	-6.8	-20.2
Win. 150 Power-Point Plus	velocity, fps:	3130	2849	2586	2337	2102
	energy, ft-lb:	3264	2705	2227	1819	1472
	arc, inches:		+1.4	0	-6.6	-19.6
Win. 150 Ballistic Silvertip	velocity, fps:	3100	2903	2714	2533	2359
	energy, ft-lb:	3200	2806	2453	2136	1853
	arc, inches:		+1.3	0	-6.0	-17.5
Win. 160 AccuBond	velocity, fps:	2950	2766	2590	2420	2257
	energy, ft-lb:	3091	2718	2382	2080	1809
	arc, inches:		+1.5	0	-6.7	-19.4
Win. 160 Partition Gold	velocity, fps:	2950	2743	2546	2357	2176
	energy, ft-lb:	3093	2674	2303	1974	1682
	arc, inches:		+1.6	0	-6.9	-20.1
Win. 160 Fail Safe	velocity, fps:	2920	2678	2449	2331	2025
	energy, ft-lb:	3030	2549	2131	1769	1457
	arc, inches:		+1.7	0	-7.5	-22.0
Win. 175 Power-Point	velocity, fps:	2860	2645	2440	2244	2057
	energy, ft-lb:	3178	2718	2313	1956	1644
	arc, inches:		+2.0	0	-7.9	-22.7

7MM REMINGTON SHORT ULTRA MAGNUM

CARTRIDGE BULLET	RANGE, YARDS:	0	100	200	300	400
Rem. 140 PSP C-L Ultra	velocity, fps:	3175	2934	2707	2490	2283
	energy, ft-lb:	3133	2676	2277	1927	1620.
	arc, inches:		+1.3	0	-6.0	-17.7
Rem. 150 PSP Core-Lokt	velocity, fps:	3110	2828	2563	2313	2077
	energy, ft-lb:	3221	2663	2188	1782	1437
	arc, inches:		+2.5	+2.1	-3.6	-15.8
Rem. 160 Partition	velocity, fps:	2960	2762	2572	2390	2215
	energy, ft-lb:	3112	2709	2350	2029	1744
	arc, inches:		+2.6	+2.2	-3.6	-15.4
Rem. 160 PSP C-L Ultra	velocity, fps:	2960	2733	2518	2313	2117
	energy, ft-lb:	3112	2654	2252	1900	1592
	arc, inches:		+2.7	+2.2	-3.7	-16.2

7MM WINCHESTER SHORT MAGNUM

CARTRIDGE BULLET	RANGE, YARDS:	0	100	200	300	400
Federal 140 Nos. AccuBond	velocity, fps:	3250	3040	2840	2660	2470
	energy, ft-lb:	3285	2875	2515	2190	1900
	arc, inches:		+1.1	0	-5.5	-15.8
Federal 140 Nos. Bal. Tip	velocity, fps:	3310	3100	2900	2700	2520
	energy, ft-lb:	3405	2985	2610	2270	1975
	arc, inches:		+1.1	0	-5.2	15.2
Federal 150 Nos. Solid Base	velocity, fps:	3230	3010	2800	2600	2410
	energy, ft-lb:	3475	3015	2615	2255	1935
	arc, inches:		+1.3	0	-5.6	-16.3
Federal 160 Nos. AccuBond	velocity, fps:	3120	2940	2760	2590	2430
	energy, ft-lb:	3460	3065	2710	2390	2095
	arc, inches:		+1.3	0	-5.9	-16.8
Federal 160 Nos. Partition	velocity, fps:	3160	2950	2750	2560	2380.
	energy, ft-lb:	3545	3095	2690	2335	2015.
	arc, inches:		+1.2	0	-5.9	-16.9
Federal 160 Barnes TS	velocity, fps:	2990	2780	2590	2400	2220
	energy, ft-lb:	3175	2755	2380	2045	1750
	arc, inches:		+1.5	0	-6.6	-19.4
Federal 160 Trophy Bonded	velocity, fps:	3120	2880	2650	2440	2230
	energy, ft-lb:	3460	2945	2500	2105	1765
	arc, inches:		+1.4	0	-6.3	-18.5
Win. 140 Bal. Silvertip	velocity, fps:	3225	3008	2801	2603	2414
	energy, ft-lb:	3233	2812	2438	2106	1812
	arc, inches:		+1.2	0	-5.6	-16.4
Win. 140 AccuBond CT	velocity, fps:	3225	3008	2801	2604	2415
	energy, ft-lb:	3233	2812	2439	2107	1812
	arc, inches:		+1.2	0	-5.6	-16.4
Win. 150 Power Point	velocity, fps:	3200	2915	2648	2396	2157
	energy, ft-lb:	3410	2830	2335	1911	1550
	arc, inches:		+1.3	0	-6.3	-18.6
Win. 160 AccuBond	velocity, fps:	3050	2862	2682	2509	2342
	energy, ft-lb:	3306	2911	2556	2237	1950
	arc, inches:		1.4	0	-6.2	-17.9
Win. 160 Fail Safe	velocity, fps:	2990	2744	2512	2291	2081
	energy, ft-lb:	3176	2675	2241	1864	1538
	arc, inches:		+1.6	0	-7.1	-20.8

7MM WEATHERBY MAGNUM

CARTRIDGE BULLET	RANGE, YARDS:	0	100	200	300	400
Federal 160 Nosler Partition	velocity, fps:	3050	2850	2650	2470	2290
	energy, ft-lb:	3305	2880	2505	2165	1865
	arc, inches:		+1.4	0	-6.3	-18.4
Federal 160 Sierra GameKing BTSP	velocity, fps:	3050	2880	2710	2560	2400
	energy, ft-lb:	3305	2945	2615	2320	2050
	arc, inches:		+1.4	0	-6.1	-17.4
Federal 160 Trophy Bonded	velocity, fps:	3050	2730	2420	2140	1880.
	energy, ft-lb:	3305	2640	2085	1630	1255
	arc, inches:		+1.6	0	-7.6	-22.7
Hornady 154 Soft Point	velocity, fps:	3200	2971	2753	2546	2348.
	energy, ft-lb:	3501	3017	2592	2216	1885
	arc, inches:		+1.2	0	-5.8	-17.0
Hornady 154 SST (or Interbond)	velocity, fps:	3200	3009	2825	2648	2478
	energy, ft-lb:	3501	3096	2729	2398	2100
	arc, inches:		+1.2	0	-5.7	-16.5
Hornady 175 Soft Point	velocity, fps:	2910	2709	2516	2331	2154
	energy, ft-lb:	3290	2850	2459	2111	1803
	arc, inches:		+1.6	0	-7.1	-20.6
Wby. 139 Pointed Expanding	velocity, fps:	3340	3079	2834	2601	2380.
	energy, ft-lb:	3443	2926	2478	2088	1748
	arc, inches:		+2.9	+3.6	0	-8.7
Wby. 140 Nosler Partition	velocity, fps:	3303	3069	2847	2636	2434
	energy, ft-lb:	3391	2927	2519	2159	1841
	arc, inches:		+2.9	+3.6	0	-8.5
Wby. 150 Nosler Bal. Tip	velocity, fps:	3300	3093	2896	2708	2527
	energy, ft-lb:	3627	3187	2793	2442	2127
	arc, inches:		+2.8	+3.5	0	-8.2
Wby. 150 Barnes X	veloctiy, fps:	3100	2901	2710	2527	2352
	energy, ft-lb:	3200	2802	2446	2127	1842
	arc, inches:		+3.3	+4.0	0	-9.4

Ballistics Tables for Modern Sporting Rifles

7mm Weatherby Magnum to .30 T/C Hornaday

Cartridge Bullet	Range, yards:	0	100	200	300	400
Wby. 154 Pointed Expanding	velocity, fps:	3260	3028	2807	2597	2397
	energy, ft-lb:	3634	3134	2694	2307	1964
	arc, inches:		+3.0	+3.7	0	-8.8
Wby. 160 Nosler Partition	velocity, fps:	3200	2991	2791	2600	2417
	energy, ft-lb:	3638	3177	2767	2401	2075.
	arc, inches:		+3.1	+3.8	0	-8.9
Wby. 175 Pointed Expanding	velocity, fps:	3070	2861	2662	2471	2288
	energy, ft-lb:	3662	3181	2753	2373	2034
	arc, inches:		+3.5	+4.2	0	-9.9

7mm Dakota

Cartridge Bullet	Range, yards:	0	100	200	300	400
Dakota 140 Barnes X	velocity, fps:	3500	3253	3019	2798	2587
	energy, ft-lb:	3807	3288	2833	2433	2081
	arc, inches:		+2.0	+2.1	-1.5	-9.6
Dakota 160 Barnes X	velocity, fps:	3200	3001	2811	2630	2455
	energy, ft-lb:	3637	3200	2808	2456	2140
	arc, inches:		+2.1	+1.9	-2.8	-12.5

7mm STW

Cartridge Bullet	Range, yards:	0	100	200	300	400
A-Square 140 Nos. Bal. Tip	velocity, fps:	3450	3254	3067	2888	2715
	energy, ft-lb:	3700	3291	2924	2592	2292
	arc, inches:		+2.2	+3.0	0	-7.3
A-Square 160 Nosler Part.	velocity, fps:	3250	3071	2900	2735	2576.
	energy, ft-lb:	3752	3351	2987	2657	2357
	arc, inches:		+2.8	+3.5	0	-8.2
A-Square 160 SP boat-tail	velocity, fps:	3250	3087	2930	2778	2631
	energy, ft-lb:	3752	3385	3049	2741	2460
	arc, inches:		+2.8	+3.4	0	-8.0
Federal 140 Trophy Bonded	velocity, fps:	3330	3080	2850	2630	2420
	energy, ft-lb:	3435	2950	2520	2145	1815
	arc, inches:		+1.1	0	-5.4	-15.8
Federal 150 Trophy Bonded	velocity, fps:	3250	3010	2770	2560	2350.
	energy, ft-lb:	3520	3010	2565	2175	1830
	arc, inches:		+1.2	0	-5.7	-16.7
Federal 160 Sierra GameKing	velocity, fps:	3200	3020	2850	2670	2530.
BTSP	energy, ft-lb:	3640	3245	2890	2570	2275
	arc, inches:		+1.1	0	-5.5	-15.7
Rem. 140 PSP Core-Lokt	velocity, fps:	3325	3064	2818	2585	2364
	energy, ft-lb:	3436	2918	2468	2077	1737
	arc, inches:		+2.0	+1.7	-2.9	-12.8
Rem. 140 Swift A-Frame	velocity, fps:	3325	3020	2735	2467	2215
	energy, ft-lb:	3436	2834	2324	1892	1525
	arc, inches:		+2.1	+1.8	-3.1	-13.8
Speer 145 Grand Slam	velocity, fps:	3300	2992	2075	2435	
	energy, ft-lb:	3506	2882	2355	1909	
	arc, inches:		+1.2	0	-6.0	-17.8
Win. 140 Ballistic Silvertip	velocity, fps:	3320	3100	2890	2690	2499
	energy, ft-lb:	3427	2982	2597	2250	1941
	arc, inches:		+1.1	0	-5.2	-15.2
Win. 150 Power-Point	velocity, fps:	3250	2957	2683	2424	2181
	energy, ft-lb:	3519	2913	2398	1958	1584
	arc, inches:		+1.2	0	-6.1	-18.1
Win. 160 Fail Safe	velocity, fps:	3150	2894	2652	2422	2204
	energy, ft-lb:	3526	2976	2499	2085	1727
	arc, inches:		+1.3	0	-6.3	-18.5

7mm Remington Ultra Magnum

Cartridge Bullet	Range, yards:	0	100	200	300	400
Rem. 140 PSP Core-Lokt	velocity, fps:	3425	3158	2907	2669	2444
	energy, ft-lb:	3646	3099	2626	2214	1856
	arc, inches:		+1.8	+1.6	-2.7	-11.9
Rem. 140 Nosler Partition	velocity, fps:	3425	3184	2956	2740	2534
	energy, ft-lb:	3646	3151	2715	2333	1995
	arc, inches:		+1.7	+1.6	-2.6	-11.4
Rem. 160 Nosler Partition	velocity, fps:	3200	2991	2791	2600	2417
	energy, ft-lb:	3637	3177	2767	2401	2075
	arc, inches:		+2.1	+1.8	-3.0	-12.9

7.21 (.284) Firehawk

Cartridge Bullet	Range, yards:	0	100	200	300	400
Lazzeroni 140 Nosler Part.	velocity, fps:	3580	3349	3130	2923	2724
	energy, ft-lb:	3985	3488	3048	2656	2308
	arc, inches:		+2.2	+2.9	0	-7.0
Lazzeroni 160 Swift A-Fr.	velocity, fps:	3385	3167	2961	2763	2574
	energy, ft-lb:	4072	3565	3115	2713	2354
	arc, inches:		+2.6	+3.3	0	-7.8

7.5x55 Swiss

Cartridge Bullet	Range, yards:	0	100	200	300	400
Norma 180 Soft Point	velocity, fps:	2651	2432	2223	2025	
	energy, ft-lb:	2810	2364	1976	1639	
	arc, inches:		+2.2	0	-9.3	
Norma 180 Oryx	velocity, fps:	2493	2222	1968	1734	
	energy, ft-lb:	2485	1974	1549	1201	
	arc, inches:		+2.7	0	-11.8	

7.62x39 Russian

Cartridge Bullet	Range, yards:	0	100	200	300	400
Federal 123 Hi-Shok	velocity, fps:	2300	2030	1780	1550	1350
	energy, ft-lb:	1445	1125	860	655	500.
	arc, inches:		0	-7.0	-25.1	
Federal 124 FMJ	velocity, fps:	2300	2030	1780	1560	1360
	energy, ft-lb:	1455	1135	875	670	510
	arc, inches:		+3.5	0	-14.6	-43.5
PMC 123 FMJ	velocity, fps:	2350	2072	1817	1583	1368
	energy, ft-lb:	1495	1162	894	678	507
	arc, inches:		0	-5.0	-26.4	-67.8
PMC 125 Pointed Soft Point	velocity, fps:	2320	2046	1794	1563	1350
	energy, ft-lb:	1493	1161	893	678	505.
	arc, inches:		0	-5.2	-27.5	-70.6
Rem. 125 Pointed Soft Point	velocity, fps:	2365	2062	1783	1533	1320
	energy, ft-lb:	1552	1180	882	652	483
	arc, inches:		0	-6.7	-24.5	
Win. 123 Soft Point	velocity, fps:	2365	2033	1731	1465	1248
	energy, ft-lb:	1527	1129	818	586	425
	arc, inches:		+3.8	0	-15.4	-46.3

.30 Carbine

Cartridge Bullet	Range, yards:	0	100	200	300	400
Federal 110 Hi-Shok RN	velocity, fps:	1990	1570	1240	1040	920
	energy, ft-lb:	965	600	375	260	210
	arc, inches:		0	-12.8	-46.9	
Federal 110 FMJ	velocity, fps:	1990	1570	1240	1040	920
	energy, ft-lb:	965	600	375	260	210
	arc, inches:		0	-12.8	-46.9	
Magtech 110 FMC	velocity, fps:	1990	1654			
	energy, ft-lb:	965	668			
	arc, inches:		0			
PMC 110 FMJ	(and RNSP)velocity, fps:	1927	1548	1248		
	energy, ft-lb:	906	585	380		
	arc, inches:		0	-14.2		
Rem. 110 Soft Point	velocity, fps:	1990	1567	1236	1035	923
	energy, ft-lb:	967	600	373	262	208
	arc, inches:		0	-12.9	-48.6	
Win. 110 Hollow Soft Point	velocity, fps:	1990	1567	1236	1035	923
	energy, ft-lb:	967	600	373	262	208
	arc, inches:		0	-13.5	-49.9	

.30 T/C Hornaday

Cartridge Bullet	Range, yards:	0	100	200	300	400
Hornady 150	velocity, fps	3000	2772	2555	2348	
	energy, ft-lb	2997	2558	2176	1836	
	arc, inches	-1.5	+1.5	0	-6.9	
Hornady 165	velocity, fps	2850	2644	2447	2258	
	energy, ft-lb	2975	2560	2193	1868	

Ballistics Tables for Modern Sporting Rifles

CARTRIDGE BULLET	RANGE, YARDS:	0	100	200	300	400
	arc, inches	-1.5	+1.7	0	-7.6	

.30-30 Winchester

CARTRIDGE BULLET	RANGE, YARDS:	0	100	200	300	400
Federal 125 Hi-Shok HP	velocity, fps:	2570	2090	1660	1320	1080
	energy, ft-lb:	1830	1210	770	480	320
	arc, inches:		+3.3	0	-16.0	-50.9
Federal 150 Hi-Shok FN	velocity, fps:	2390	2020	1680	1400	1180
	energy, ft-lb:	1900	1355	945	650	460
	arc, inches:		+3.6	0	-15.9	-49.1
Federal 170 Hi-Shok RN	velocity, fps:	2200	1900	1620	1380	1190
	energy, ft-lb:	1830	1355	990	720	535
	arc, inches:		+4.1	0	-17.4	-52.4
Federal 170 Sierra Pro-Hunt.	velocity, fps:	2200	1820	1500	1240	1060
	energy, ft-lb:	1830	1255	845	575	425
	arc, inches:		+4.5	0	-20.0	-63.5
Federal 170 Nosler Partition	velocity, fps:	2200	1900	1620	1380	1190
	energy, ft-lb:	1830	1355	990	720	535
	arc, inches:		+4.1	0	-17.4	-52.4
Hornady 150 Round Nose	velocity, fps:	2390	1973	1605	1303	1095
	energy, ft-lb:	1902	1296	858	565	399
	arc, inches:		0	-8.2	-30.0	
Hornady 160 Evolution	velocity, fps:	2400	2150	1916	1699	
	energy, ft-lb:	2046	1643	1304	1025	
	arc, inches:		+3.0	0.2	-12.1	
Hornady 170 Flat Point	velocity, fps:	2200	1895	1619	1381	1191
	energy, ft-lb:	1827	1355	989	720	535
	arc, inches:		0	-8.9	-31.1	
Norma 150 Soft Point	velocity, fps:	2329	2008	1716	1459	
	energy, ft-lb:	1807	1344	981	709	
	arc, inches:		+3.6	0	-15.5	
PMC 150 Starfire HP	velocity, fps:	2100	1769	1478		
	energy, ft-lb:	1469	1042	728		
	arc, inches:		0	-10.8		
PMC 150 Flat Nose	velocity, fps:	2300	1943	1627		
	energy, ft-lb:	1762	1257	881		
	arc, inches:		0	-7.8		
PMC 170 Flat Nose	velocity, fps:	2150	1840	1566		
	energy, ft-lb:	1745	1277	926		
	arc, inches:		0	-8.9		
Rem. 55 PSP (sabot)	velocity, fps:	3400	2693	2085	1570	1187
"Accelerator"	energy, ft-lb:	1412	886	521	301	172
	arc, inches:		+1.7	0	-9.9	-34.3
Rem. 150 SP Core-Lokt	velocity, fps:	2390	1973	1605	1303	1095
	energy, ft-lb:	1902	1296	858	565	399
	arc, inches:		0	-7.6	-28.8	
Rem. 170 SP Core-Lokt	velocity, fps:	2200	1895	1619	1381	1191
	energy, ft-lb:	1827	1355	989	720	535
	arc, inches:		0	-8.3	-29.9	
Rem. 170 HP Core-Lokt	velocity, fps:	2200	1895	1619	1381	1191
	energy, ft-lb:	1827	1355	989	720	535
	arc, inches:		0	-8.3	-29.9	
Speer 150 Flat Nose	velocity, fps:	2370	2067	1788	1538	
	energy, ft-lb:	1870	1423	1065	788	
	arc, inches:		+3.3	0	-14.4	-43.7
Win. 150 Hollow Point	velocity, fps:	2390	2018	1684	1398	1177
	energy, ft-lb:	1902	1356	944	651	461
	arc, inches:		0	-7.7	-27.9	
Win. 150 Power-Point	velocity, fps:	2390	2018	1684	1398	1177
	energy, ft-lb:	1902	1356	944	651	461
	arc, inches:		0	-7.7	-27.9	
Win. 150 Silvertip	velocity,fps:	2390	2018	1684	1398	1177
	energy, ft-lb:	1902	1356	944	651	461
	arc, inches:		0	-7.7	-27.9	
Win. 150 Power-Point Plus	velocity, fps:	2480	2095	1747	1446	1209
	energy, ft-lb:	2049	1462	1017	697	487
	arc, inches:		0	-6.5	-24.5	
Win. 170 Power-Point	velocity, fps:	2200	1895	1619	1381	1191
	energy, ft-lb:	1827	1355	989	720	535
	arc, inches:		0	-8.9	-31.1	
Win. 170 Silvertip	velocity, fps:	2200	1895	1619	1381	1191
	energy, ft-lb:	1827	1355	989	720	535
	arc, inches:		0	-8.9	-31.1	

.300 Savage

CARTRIDGE BULLET	RANGE, YARDS:	0	100	200	300	400
Federal 150 Hi-Shok	velocity, fps:	2630	2350	2100	1850	1630
	energy, ft-lb:	2305	1845	1460	1145	885
	arc, inches:		+2.4	0	-10.4	-30.9
Federal 180 Hi-Shok	velocity, fps:	2350	2140	1940	1750	1570
	energy, ft-lb:	2205	1825	1495	1215	985
	arc, inches:		+3.1	0	-12.4	-36.1
Rem. 150 PSP Core-Lokt	velocity, fps:	2630	2354	2095	1853	1631
	energy, ft-lb:	2303	1845	1462	1143	806
	arc, inches:		+2.4	0	-10.4	-30.9
Rem. 180 SP Core-Lokt	velocity, fps:	2350	2025	1728	1467	1252
	energy, ft-lb:	2207	1639	1193	860	626
	arc, inches:		0	-7.1	-25.9	
Win. 150 Power-Point	velocity, fps:	2630	2311	2015	1743	1500
	energy, ft-lb:	2303	1779	1352	1012	749
	arc, inches:		+2.8	0	-11.5	-34.4

.307 Winchester

CARTRIDGE BULLET	RANGE, YARDS:	0	100	200	300	400
Win. 180 Power-Point	velocity, fps:	2510	2179	1874	1599	1362
	energy, ft-lb:	2519	1898	1404	1022	742
	arc, inches:		+1.5	-3.6	-18.6	-47.1

.30-40 Krag

CARTRIDGE BULLET	RANGE, YARDS:	0	100	200	300	400
Rem. 180 PSP Core-Lokt	velocity, fps:	2430	2213	2007	1813	1632
	energy, ft-lb:	2360	1957	1610	1314	1064
	arc, inches, s:		0	-5.6	-18.6	
Win. 180 Power-Point	velocity, fps:	2430	2099	1795	1525	1298
	energy, ft-lb:	2360	1761	1288	929	673
	arc, inches, s:		0	-7.1	-25.0	

7.62x54R Russian

CARTRIDGE BULLET	RANGE, YARDS:	0	100	200	300	400
Norma 150 Soft Point	velocity, fps:	2953	2622	2314	2028	
	energy, ft-lb:	2905	2291	1784	1370	
	arc, inches:		+1.8	0	-8.3	
Norma 180 Alaska	velocity, fps:	2575	2362	2159	1967	
	energy, ft-lb:	2651	2231	1864	1546	
	arc, inches:		+2.9	0	-12.9	

.308 Marlin Express

CARTRIDGE BULLET	RANGE, YARDS:	0	100	200	300	400
Hornady 160	velocity, fps	2660	2438	2226	2026	1836
	energy, ft-lb	2513	2111	1761	1457	1197
	arc, inches	-1.5	+3.0	+1.7	-6.7	-23.5

.308 Winchester

CARTRIDGE BULLET	RANGE, YARDS:	0	100	200	300	400
Black Hills 150 Nosler B. Tip	velocity, fps:	2800				
	energy, ft-lb:	2611				
	arc, inches:					
Black Hills 165 Nosler B. Tip	velocity, fps:	2650				
(and SP)	energy, ft-lb:	2573				
	arc, inches:					
Black Hills 168 Barnes X	velocity, fps:	2650				
(and Match)	energy, ft-lb:	2620				
	arc, inches:					
Black Hills 175 Match	velocity, fps:	2600				
	energy, ft-lb:	2657				
	arc, inches:					

Ballistics Tables for Modern Sporting Rifles

.308 WINCHESTER TO .308 WINCHESTER

CARTRIDGE BULLET	RANGE, YARDS:	0	100	200	300	400
Black Hills 180 AccuBond	velocity, fps:	2600				
	energy, ft-lb:	2701				
	arc, inches:					
Federal 150 Hi-Shok	velocity, fps:	2820	2530	2260	2010	1770
	energy, ft-lb:	2650	2140	1705	1345	1050
	arc, inches:		+2.0	0	-8.8	-26.3
Federal 150 Nosler Bal. Tip.	velocity, fps:	2820	2610	2410	2220	2040
	energy, ft-lb:	2650	2270	1935	1640	1380
	arc, inches:		+1.8	0	-7.8	-22.7
Federal 150 FMJ boat-tail	velocity, fps:	2820	2620	2430	2250	2070
	energy, ft-lb:	2650	2285	1965	1680	1430
	arc, inches:		+1.8	0	-7.7	-22.4
Federal 150 Barnes XLC	velocity, fps:	2820	2610	2400	2210	2030
	energy, ft-lb:	2650	2265	1925	1630	1370
	arc, inches:		+1.8	0	-7.8	-22.9
Federal 155 Sierra MatchKg. BTHP	velocity, fps:	2950	2740	2540	2350	2170
	energy, ft-lb:	2995	2585	2225	1905	1620
	arc, inches:		+1.9	0	-8.9	-22.6
Federal 165 Sierra GameKing BTSP	velocity, fps:	2700	2520	2330	2160	1990
	energy, ft-lb:	2670	2310	1990	1700	1450
	arc, inches:		+2.0	0	-8.4	-24.3
Federal 165 Trophy Bonded	velocity, fps:	2700	2440	2200	1970	1760
	energy, ft-lb:	2670	2185	1775	1425	1135
	arc, inches:		+2.2	0	-9.4	-27.7
Federal 165 Tr. Bonded HE	velocity, fps:	2870	2600	2350	2120	1890
	energy, ft-lb:	3020	2485	2030	1640	1310
	arc, inches:		+1.8	0	-8.2	-24.0
Federal 168 Sierra MatchKg. BTHP	velocity, fps:	2600	2410	2230	2060	1890
	energy, ft-lb:	2520	2170	1855	1580	1340.
	arc, inches:		+2.1	0	+8.9	+25.9
Federal 180 Hi-Shok	velocity, fps:	2620	2390	2180	1970	1780
	energy, ft-lb:	2745	2290	1895	1555	1270
	arc, inches:		+2.3	0	-9.7	-28.3
Federal 180 Sierra Pro-Hunt.	velocity, fps:	2620	2410	2200	2010	1820
	energy, ft-lb:	2745	2315	1940	1610	1330
	arc, inches:		+2.3	0	-9.3	-27.1
Federal 180 Nosler Partition	velocity, fps:	2620	2430	2240	2060	1890
	energy, ft-lb:	2745	2355	2005	1700	1430.
	arc, inches:		+2.2	0	-9.2	-26.5
Federal 180 Nosler Part. HE	velocity, fps:	2740	2550	2370	2200	2030
	energy, ft-lb:	3000	2600	2245	1925	1645
	arc, inches:		+1.9	0	-8.2	-23.5
Hornady 110 TAP-FPD	velocity, fps:	3165	2830	2519	2228	1957
	energy, ft-lb:	2446	1956	1649	1212	935
	arc, inches:		+1.4	0	-6.9	-20.9
Hornady 110 Urban Tactical	velocity, fps:	3170	2825	2504	2206	1937
	energy, ft-lb:	2454	1950	1532	1189	916
	arc, inches:		+1.5	0	-7.2	-21.2
Hornady 150 SP boat-tail	velocity, fps:	2820	2560	2315	2084	1866
	energy, ft-lb:	2648	2183	1785	1447	1160
	arc, inches:		+2.0	0	-8.5	-25.2
Hornady 150 SST (or Interbond)	velocity, fps:	2820	2593	2378	2174	1984
	energy, ft-lb:	2648	2240	1884	1574	1311
	arc, inches:		+1.9	0	-8.1	-22.9
Hornady 150 SST LM (or Interbond)	velocity, fps:	3000	2765	2541	2328	2127
	energy, ft-lb:	2997	2545	2150	1805	1506.
	arc, inches:		+1.5	0	-7.1	-20.6
Hornady 150 SP LM	velocity, fps:	2980	2703	2442	2195	1964
	energy, ft-lb:	2959	2433	1986	1606	1285
	arc, inches:		+1.6	0	-7.5	-22.2
Hornady 155 A-Max	velocity, fps:	2815	2610	2415	2229	2051
	energy, ft-lb:	2727	2345	2007	1709	1448
	arc, inches:		+1.9	0	-7.9	-22.6
Hornady 155 TAP-FPD	velocity, fps:	2785	2577	2379	2189	2008
	energy, ft-lb:	2669	2285	1947	1649	1387
	arc, inches:		+1.9	0	-8.0	-23.3
Hornady 165 SP boat-tail	velocity, fps:	2700	2496	2301	2115	1937
	energy, ft-lb:	2670	2283	1940	1639	1375
	arc, inches:		+2.0	0	-8.7	-25.2
Hornady 165 SPBT LM	velocity, fps:	2870	2658	2456	2283	2078
	energy, ft-lb:	3019	2589	2211	1877	1583
	arc, inches:		+1.7	0	-7.5	-21.8
Hornady 165 SST LM (or Interbond)	velocity, fps:	2880	2672	2474	2284	2103
	energy, ft-lb:	3038	2616	2242	1911	1620
	arc, inches:		+1.6	0	-7.3	-21.2
Hornady 168 BTHP Match	velocity, fps:	2700	2524	2354	2191	2035.
	energy, ft-lb:	2720	2377	2068	1791	1545
	arc, inches:		+2.0	0	-8.4	-23.9
Hornady 168 BTHP Match LM	velocity, fps:	2640	2630	2429	2238	2056
	energy, ft-lb:	3008	2579	2201	1868	1577
	arc, inches:		+1.8	0	-7.8	-22.4
Hornady 168 A-Max Match	velocity fps:	2620	2446	2280	2120	1972
	energy, ft-lb:	2560	2232	1939	1677	1450
	arc, inches:		+2.6	0	-9.2	-25.6
Hornady 168 A-Max	velocity, fps:	2700	2491	2292	2102	1921
	energy, ft-lb:	2719	2315	1959	1648	1377
	arc, inches:		+2.4	0	-9.0	-25.9
Hornady 168 TAP-FPD	velocity, fps:	2700	2513	2333	2161	1996
	energy, ft-lb:	2719	2355	2030	1742	1486
	arc, inches:		+2.0	0	-8.4	-24.3
Hornady 178 A-Max	velocity, fps:	2965	2778	2598	2425	2259
	energy, ft-lb:	3474	3049	2666	2323	2017
	arc, inches:		+1.6	0	-6.9	-19.8
Hornady 180 A-Max Match	velocity, fps:	2550	2397	2249	2106	1974
	energy, ft-lb:	2598	2295	2021	1773	1557
	arc, inches:		+2.7	0	-9.5	-26.2
Norma 150 Nosler Bal. Tip	velocity, fps:	2822	2588	2365	2154	
	energy, ft-lb:	2653	2231	1864	1545	
	arc, inches:		+1.6	0	-7.1	
Norma 150 Soft Point	velocity, fps:	2861	2537	2235	1954	
	energy, ft-lb:	2727	2144	1664	1272	
	arc, inches:		+2.0	0	-9.0	
Norma 165 TXP Swift A-Fr.	velocity, fps:	2700	2459	2231	2015	
	energy, ft-lb:	2672	2216	1824	1488	
	arc, inches:		+2.1	0	-9.1	
Norma 180 Plastic Point	velocity, fps:	2612	2365	2131	1911	
	energy, ft-lb:	2728	2235	1815	1460	
	arc, inches:		+2.4	0	-10.1	
Norma 180 Nosler Partition	velocity, fps:	2612	2414	2225	2044	
	energy, ft-lb:	2728	2330	1979	1670	
	arc, inches:		+2.2	0	-9.3	
Norma 180 Alaska	velocity, fps:	2612	2269	1953	1667	
	energy, ft-lb:	2728	2059	1526	1111	
	arc, inches:		+2.7	0	-11.9	
Norma 180 Vulkan	velocity, fps:	2612	2325	2056	1806	
	energy, ft-lb:	2728	2161	1690	1304	
	arc, inches:		+2.5	0	-10.8	
Norma 180 Oryx	velocity, fps:	2612	2305	2019	1755	
	energy, ft-lb:	2728	2124	1629	1232	
	arc, inches:		+2.5	0	-11.1	
Norma 200 Vulkan	velocity, fps:	2461	2215	1983	1767	
	energy, ft-lb:	2690	2179	1747	1387	
	arc, inches:		+2.8	0	-11.7	
PMC 147 FMJ boat-tail	velocity, fps:	2751	2473	2257	2052	1859

Ballistics Tables for Modern Sporting Rifles

.308 WINCHESTER TO .30-06 SPRINGFIELD

CARTRIDGE BULLET	RANGE, YARDS:	0	100	200	300	400
	energy, ft-lb:	2428	2037	1697	1403	1150
	arc, inches:		+2.3	0	-9.3	-27.3
PMC 150 Barnes X	velocity, fps:	2700	2504	2316	2135	1964
	energy, ft-lb:	2428	2087	1786	1518	1284
	arc, inches:		+2.0	0	-8.6	-24.7
PMC 150 Pointed Soft Point	velocity, fps:	2750	2478	2224	1987	1766
	energy, ft-lb:	2519	2045	1647	1315	1039
	arc, inches:		+2.1	0	-9.2	-27.1
PMC 150 SP boat-tail	velocity, fps:	2820	2581	2354	2139	1935
	energy, ft-lb:	2648	2218	1846	1523	1247.
	arc, inches:		+1.9	0	-8.2	-24.0
PMC 168 Barnes X	velocity, fps:	2600	2425	2256	2095	1940
	energy, ft-lb:	2476	2154	1865	1608	1379
	arc, inches:		+2.2	0	-9.0	-26.0
PMC 168 HP boat-tail	velocity, fps:	2650	2460	2278	2103	1936
	energy, ft-lb:	2619	2257	1935	1649	1399
	arc, inches:		+2.1	0	-8.8	-25.6
PMC 168 Pointed Soft Point	velocity, fps:	2559	2354	2160	1976	1803
	energy, ft-lb:	2443	2067	1740	1457	1212
	arc, inches:		+2.4	0	-9.9	-28.7
PMC 168 Pointed Soft Point	velocity, fps:	2600	2404	2216	2037	1866
	energy, ft-lb:	2476	2064	1709	1403	1142
	arc, inches:		+2.3	0	-9.8	-28.7
PMC 180 Pointed Soft Point	velocity, fps:	2550	2335	2132	1940	1760
	energy, ft-lb:	2599	2179	1816	1504	1238.
	arc, inches:		+2.5	0	-10.1	-29.5
PMC 180 SP boat-tail	velocity, fps:	2620	2446	2278	2117	1962
	energy, ft-lb:	2743	2391	2074	1790	1538
	arc, inches:		+2.2	0	-8.9	-25.4
Rem. 125 PSP C-L MR	velocity, fps:	2660	2348	2057	1788	1546
	energy, ft-lb:	1964	1529	1174	887	663
	arc, inches:		+1.1	-2.7	-14.3	-35.8
Rem. 150 PSP Core-Lokt	velocity, fps:	2820	2533	2263	2009	1774
	energy, ft-lb:	2648	2137	1705	1344	1048
	arc, inches:		+2.0	0	-8.8	-26.2
Rem. 150 PSP C-L Ultra	velocity, fps:	2620	2404	2198	2002	1818
	energy, ft-lb:	2743	2309	1930	1601	1320
	arc, inches:		+2.3	0	-9.5	-26.4
Rem. 150 Swift Scirocco	velocity, fps:	2820	2611	2410	2219	2037
	energy, ft-lb:	2648	2269	1935	1640	1381
	arc, inches:		+1.8	0	-7.8	-22.7
Rem. 165 AccuTip	velocity, fps:	2700	2501	2311	2129	1958.
	energy, ft-lb:	2670	2292	1957	1861	1401.
	arc, inches:		+2.0	0	-8.6	-24.8
Rem. 165 PSP boat-tail	velocity, fps:	2700	2497	2303	2117	1941.
	energy, ft-lb:	2670	2284	1942	1642	1379
	arc, inches:		+2.0	0	-8.6	-25.0
Rem. 165 Nosler Bal. Tip	velocity, fps:	2700	2613	2333	2161	1996
	energy, ft-lb:	2672	2314	1995	1711	1460
	arc, inches:		+2.0	0	-8.4	-24.3
Rem. 165 Swift Scirocco	velocity, fps:	2700	2513	2233	2161	1996
	energy, fps:	2670	2313	1994	1711	1459
	arc, inches:		+2.0	0	-8.4	-24.3
Rem. 168 HPBT Match	velocity, fps:	2680	2493	2314	2143	1979
	energy, ft-lb:	2678	2318	1998	1713	1460
	arc, inches:		+2.1	0	-8.6	-24.7
Rem. 180 SP Core-Lokt	velocity, fps:	2620	2274	1955	1666	1414
	energy, ft-lb:	2743	2066	1527	1109	799
	arc, inches:		+2.6	0	-11.8	-36.3
Rem. 180 PSP Core-Lokt	velocity, fps:	2620	2393	2178	1974	1782
	energy, ft-lb:	2743	2288	1896	1557	1269
	arc, inches:		+2.3	0	-9.7	-28.3

CARTRIDGE BULLET	RANGE, YARDS:	0	100	200	300	400
Rem. 180 Nosler Partition	velocity, fps:	2620	2436	2259	2089	1927.
	energy, ft-lb:	2743	2371	2039	1774	1485
	arc, inches:		+2.2	0	-9.0	-26.0
Speer 150 Grand Slam	velocity, fps:	2900	2599	2317	2053	
	energy, ft-lb:	2800	2249	1788	1404	
	arc, inches:		+2.1	0	-8.6	-24.8
Speer 165 Grand Slam	velocity, fps:	2700	2475	2261	2057	
	energy, ft-lb:	2670	2243	1872	1550	
	arc, inches:		+2.1	0	-8.9	-25.9
Speer 180 Grand Slam	velocity, fps:	2620	2420	2229	2046	
	energy, ft-lb:	2743	2340	1985	1674	
	arc, inches:		+2.2	0	-9.2	-26.6
Win. 150 Power-Point	velocity, fps:	2820	2488	2179	1893	1633
	energy, ft-lb:	2648	2061	1581	1193	888
	arc, inches:		+2.4	0	-9.8	-29.3
Win. 150 Power-Point Plus	velocity, fps:	2900	2558	2241	1946	1678
	energy, ft-lb:	2802	2180	1672	1262	938
	arc, inches:		+1.9	0	-8.9	-27.0
Win. 150 Partition Gold	velocity, fps:	2900	2645	2405	2177	1962
	energy, ft-lb:	2802	2332	1927	1579	1282.
	arc, inches:		+1.7	0	-7.8	-22.9
Win. 150 Ballistic Silvertip	velocity, fps:	2810	2601	2401	2211	2028
	energy, ft-lb:	2629	2253	1920	1627	1370.
	arc, inches:		+1.8	0	-7.8	-22.8
Win. 150 Fail Safe	velocity, fps:	2820	2533	2263	2010	1775
	energy, ft-lb:	2649	2137	1706	1346	1049
	arc, inches:		+2.0	0	-8.8	-26.2
Win. 150 Supreme Elite XP3	velocity, fps:	2825	2616	2417	2226	2044
	energy, ft-lb:	2658	2279	1945	1650	1392
	arc, inches:		+1.8	0	-7.8	-22.6
Win. 168 Ballistic Silvertip	velocity, fps:	2670	2484	2306	2134	1971
	energy, ft-lb:	2659	2301	1983	1699	1449
	arc, inches:		+2.1	0	-8.6	-24.8
Win. 168 HP boat-tail Match	velocity, fps:	2680	2485	2297	2118	1948
	energy, ft-lb:	2680	2303	1970	1674	1415
	arc, inches:		+2.1	0	-8.7	-25.1
Win. 180 Power-Point	velocity, fps:	2620	2274	1955	1666	1414
	energy, ft-lb:	2743	2066	1527	1109	799
	arc, inches:		+2.9	0	-12.1	-36.9
Win. 180 Silvertip	velocity, fps:	2620	2393	2178	1974	1782
	energy, ft-lb:	2743	2288	1896	1557	1269
	arc, inches:		+2.6	0	-9.9	-28.9

.30-06 SPRINGFIELD

CARTRIDGE BULLET	RANGE, YARDS:	0	100	200	300	400
A-Square 180 M & D-T	velocity, fps:	2700	2365	2054	1769	1524
	energy, ft-lb:	2913	2235	1687	1251	928
	arc, inches:		+2.4	0	-10.6	-32.4
A-Square 220 Monolythic Solid	velocity, fps:	2380	2108	1854	1623	1424
	energy, ft-lb:	2767	2171	1679	1287	990
	arc, inches:		+3.1	0	-13.6	-39.9
Black Hills 150 Nosler B. Tip	velocity, fps:	2900				
	energy, ft-lb:	2770				
	arc, inches:					
Black Hills 165 Nosler B. Tip	velocity, fps:	2750				
	energy, ft-lb:	2770				
	arc, inches:					
Black Hills 168 Hor. Match	velocity, fps:	2700				
	energy, ft-lb:	2718				
	arc, inches:					
Black Hills 180 Barnes X	velocity, fps:	2650				
	energy, ft-lb:	2806				
	arc, inches:					

BALLISTICS

Ballistics Tables for Modern Sporting Rifles

.30-06 SPRINGFIELD TO .30-06 SPRINGFIELD

CARTRIDGE BULLET	RANGE, YARDS:	0	100	200	300	400
Black Hills 180 AccuBond	velocity, ft-lb:	2700				
	energy, ft-lb:					
	arc, inches:					
Federal 125 Sierra Pro-Hunt.	velocity, fps:	3140	2780	2450	2140	1850
	energy, ft-lb:	2735	2145	1660	1270	955
	arc, inches:		+1.5	0	-7.3	-22.3
Federal 150 Hi-Shok	velocity, fps:	2910	2620	2340	2080	1840
	energy, ft-lb:	2820	2280	1825	1445	1130
	arc, inches:		+1.8	0	-8.2	-24.4
Federal 150 Sierra Pro-Hunt.	velocity, fps:	2910	2640	2380	2130	1900
	energy, ft-lb:	2820	2315	1880	1515	1205
	arc, inches:		+1.7	0	-7.9	-23.3
Federal 150 Sierra GameKing	velocity, fps:	2910	2690	2480	2270	2070
BTSP	energy, ft-lb:	2820	2420	2040	1710	1430
	arc, inches:		+1.7	0	-7.4	-21.5
Federal 150 Nosler Bal. Tip	velocity, fps:	2910	2700	2490	2300	2110
	energy, ft-lb:	2820	2420	2070	1760	1485
	arc, inches:		+1.6	0	-7.3	-21.1
Federal 150 FMJ boat-tail	velocity, fps:	2910	2710	2510	2320	2150
	energy, ft-lb:	2820	2440	2100	1800	1535
	arc, inches:		+1.6	0	-7.1	-20.8
Federal 165 Sierra Pro-Hunt.	velocity, fps:	2800	2560	2340	2130	1920
	energy, ft-lb:	2875	2410	2005	1655	1360
	arc, inches:		+1.9	0	-8.3	-24.3
Federal 165 Sierra GameKing	velocity, fps:	2800	2610	2420	2240	2070.
BTSP	energy, ft-lb:	2870	2490	2150	1840	1580
	arc, inches:		+1.8	0	-7.8	-22.4
Federal 165 Sierra GameKing	velocity, fps:	3140	2900	2670	2450	2240.
HE	energy, ft-lb:	3610	3075	2610	2200	1845
	arc, inches:		+1.5	0	-6.9	-20.4
Federal 165 Nosler Bal. Tip	velocity, fps:	2800	2610	2430	2250	2080
	energy, ft-lb:	2870	2495	2155	1855	1585
	arc, inches:		+1.8	0	-7.7	-22.3
Federal 165 Trophy Bonded	velocity, fps:	2800	2540	2290	2050	1830.
	energy, ft-lb:	2870	2360	1915	1545	1230
	arc, inches:		+2.0	0	-8.7	-25.4
Federal 165 Tr. Bonded HE	velocity, fps:	3140	2860	2590	2340	2100
	energy, ft-lb:	3610	2990	2460	2010	1625.
	arc, inches:		+1.6	0	-7.4	-21.9
Federal 168 Sierra MatchKg.	velocity, fps:	2700	2510	2320	2150	1980
BTHP	energy, ft-lb:	2720	2350	2010	1720	1460
	arc, inches:		+16.2	+28.4	+34.1	+32.3
Federal 180 Hi-Shok	velocity, fps:	2700	2470	2250	2040	1850
	energy, ft-lb:	2915	2435	2025	1665	1360
	arc, inches:		+2.1	0	-9.0	-26.4
Federal 180 Sierra Pro-Hunt.	velocity, fps:	2700	2350	2020	1730	1470
RN	energy, ft-lb:	2915	2200	1630	1190	860
	arc, inches:		+2.4	0	-11.0	-33.6
Federal 180 Nosler Partition	velocity, fps:	2700	2500	2320	2140	1970
	energy, ft-lb:	2915	2510	2150	1830	1550
	arc, inches:		+2.0	0	-8.6	-24.6
Federal 180 Nosler Part. HE	velocity, fps:	2880	2690	2500	2320	2150
	energy, ft-lb:	3315	2880	2495	2150	1845
	arc, inches:		+1.7	0	-7.2	-21.0
Federal 180 Sierra GameKing	velocity, fps:	2700	2540	2380	2220	2080
BTSP	energy, ft-lb:	2915	2570	2260	1975	1720
	arc, inches:		+1.9	0	-8.1	-23.1
Federal 180 Barnes XLC	velocity, fps:	2700	2530	2360	2200	2040.
	energy, ft-lb:	2915	2550	2220	1930	1670
	arc, inches:		+2.0	0	-8.3	-23.8
Federal 180 Trophy Bonded	velocity, fps:	2700	2460	2220	2000	1800
	energy, ft-lb:	2915	2410	1975	1605	1290
	arc, inches:		+2.2	0	-9.2	-27.0

CARTRIDGE BULLET	RANGE, YARDS:	0	100	200	300	400
Federal 180 Tr. Bonded HE	velocity, fps:	2880	2630	2380	2160	1940
	energy, ft-lb:	3315	2755	2270	1855	1505
	arc, inches:		+1.8	0	-8.0	-23.3
Federal 220 Sierra Pro-Hunt.	velocity, fps:	2410	2130	1870	1630	1420
RN	energy, ft-lb:	2835	2215	1705	1300	985
	arc, inches:		+3.1	0	-13.1	-39.3
Hornady 150 SP	velocity, fps:	2910	2617	2342	2083	1843
	energy, ft-lb:	2820	2281	1827	1445	1131
	arc, inches:		+2.1	0	-8.5	-25.0
Hornady 150 SP LM	velocity, fps:	3100	2815	2548	2295	2058
	energy, ft-lb:	3200	2639	2161	1755	1410
	arc, inches:		+1.4	0	-6.8	-20.3
Hornady 150 SP boat-tail	velocity, fps:	2910	2683	2467	2262	2066.
	energy, ft-lb:	2820	2397	2027	1706	1421
	arc, inches:		+2.0	0	-7.7	-22.2
Hornady 150 SST	velocity, fps:	2910	2802	2599	2405	2219
(or Interbond)	energy, ft-lb:	3330	2876	2474	2118	1803
	arc, inches:		+1.5	0	-6.6	-19.3
Hornady 150 SST LM	velocity, fps:	3100	2860	2631	2414	2208
	energy, ft-lb:	3200	2724	2306	1941	1624
	arc, inches:		+1.4	0	-6.6	-19.2
Hornady 165 SP boat-tail	velocity, fps:	2800	2591	2392	2202	2020
	energy, ft-lb:	2873	2460	2097	1777	1495
	arc, inches:		+1.8	0	-8.0	-23.3
Hornady 165 SPBT LM	velocity, fps:	3015	2790	2575	2370	2176
	energy, ft-lb:	3330	2850	2428	2058	1734
	arc, inches:		+1.6	0	-7.0	-20.1
Hornady 165 SST	velocity, fps:	2800	2598	2405	2221	2046
(or Interbond)	energy, ft-lb:	2872	2473	2119	1808	1534
	arc, inches:		+1.9	0	-8.0	-22.8
Hornady 165 SST LM	velocity, fps:	3015	2802	2599	2405	2219
	energy, ft-lb:	3330	2878	2474	2118	1803.
	arc, inches:		+1.5	0	-6.5	-19.3
Hornady 168 HPBT Match	velocity, fps:	2790	2620	2447	2280	2120.
	energy, ft-lb:	2925	2561	2234	1940	1677.
	arc, inches:		+1.7	0	-7.7	-22.2
Hornady 180 SP	velocity, fps:	2700	2469	2258	2042	1846
	energy, ft-lb:	2913	2436	2023	1666	1362
	arc, inches:		+2.4	0	-9.3	-27.0
Hornady 180 SPBT LM	velocity, fps:	2880	2676	2480	2293	2114
	energy, ft-lb:	3316	2862	2459	2102	1786
	arc, inches:		+1.7	0	-7.3	-21.3
Norma 150 Nosler Bal. Tip	velocity, fps:	2936	2713	2502	2300	
	energy, ft-lb:	2872	2453	2085	1762	
	arc, inches:		+1.6	0	-7.1	
Norma 150 Soft Point	velocity, fps:	2972	2640	2331	2043	
	energy, ft-lb:	2943	2321	1810	1390	
	arc, inches:		+1.8	0	-8.2	
Norma 180 Alaska	velocity, fps:	2700	2351	2028	1734	
	energy, ft-lb:	2914	2209	1645	1202	
	arc, inches:		+2.4	0	-11.0	
Norma 180 Nosler Partition	velocity, fps:	2700	2494	2297	2108	
	energy, ft-lb:	2914	2486	2108	1777	
	arc, inches:		+2.1	0	-8.7	
Norma 180 Plastic Point	velocity, fps:	2700	2455	2222	2003	
	energy, ft-lb:	2914	2409	1974	1603	
	arc, inches:		+2.1	0	-9.2	
Norma 180 Vulkan	velocity, fps:	2700	2416	2150	1901	
	energy, ft-lb:	2914	2334	1848	1445	
	arc, inches:		+2.2	0	-9.8	
Norma 180 Oryx	velocity, fps:	2700	2387	2095	1825	
	energy, ft-lb:	2914	2278	1755	1332	
	arc, inches:		+2.3	0	-10.2	

Ballistics Tables for Modern Sporting Rifles

.30-06 SPRINGFIELD TO .30-06 SPRINGFIELD

CARTRIDGE BULLET	RANGE, YARDS:	0	100	200	300	400
Norma 180 TXP Swift A-Fr.	velocity, fps:	2700	2479	2268	2067	
	energy, ft-lb:	2914	2456	2056	1708	
	arc, inches:		+2.0	0	-8.8	
Norma 180 AccuBond	velocity, fps:	2674	2499	2331	2169	
	energy, ft-lb:	2859	2497	2172	1881	
	arc, inches:		+2.0	0	-8.5	
Norma 200 Vulkan	velocity, fps:	2641	2385	2143	1916	
	energy, ft-lb:	3098	2527	2040	1631	
	arc, inches:		+2.3	0	-9.9	
Norma 200 Oryx	velocity, fps:	2625	2362	2115	1883	
	energy, ft-lb:	3061	2479	1987	1575	
	arc, inches:		+2.3	0	-10.1	
PMC 150 X-Bullet	velocity, fps:	2750	2552	2361	2179	2005
	energy, ft-lb:	2518	2168	1857	1582	1339
	arc, inches:		+2.0	0	-8.2	-23.7
PMC 150 Pointed Soft Point	velocity, fps:	2773	2542	2322	2113	1916
	energy, ft-lb:	2560	2152	1796	1487	1222.
	arc, inches:		+1.9	0	-8.4	-24.6
PMC 150 SP boat-tail	velocity, fps:	2900	2657	2427	2208	2000
	energy, ft-lb:	2801	2351	1961	1623	1332
	arc, inches:		+1.7	0	-7.7	-22.5
PMC 150 FMJ	velocity, fps:	2773	2542	2322	2113	1916
	energy, ft-lb:	2560	2152	1796	1487	1222
	arc, inches:		+1.9	0	-8.4	-24.6
PMC 168 Barnes X	velocity, fps:	2750	2569	2395	2228	2067
	energy, ft-lb:	2770	2418	2101	1818	1565
	arc, inches:		+1.9	0	-8.0	-23.0
PMC 180 Barnes X	velocity, fps:	2650	2487	2331	2179	2034
	energy, ft-lb:	2806	2472	2171	1898	1652
	arc, inches:		+2.1	0	-8.5	-24.3
PMC 180 Pointed Soft Point	velocity, fps:	2650	2430	2221	2024	1839
	energy, ft-lb:	2807	2359	1972	1638	1351
	arc, inches:		+2.2	0	-9.3	-27.0
PMC 180 SP boat-tail	velocity, fps:	2700	2523	2352	2188	2030
	energy, ft-lb:	2913	2543	2210	1913	1646
	arc, inches:		+2.0	0	-8.3	-23.9
PMC 180 HPBT Match	velocity, fps:	2800	2622	2456	2302	2158
	energy, ft-lb:	3133	2747	2411	2118	1861
	arc, inches:		+1.8	0	-7.6	-21.7
Rem. 55 PSP (sabot)	velocity, fps:	4080	3484	2964	2499	2080
"Accelerator"	energy, ft-lb:	2033	1482	1073	763	528.
	arc, inches:		+1.4	+1.4	-2.6	-12.2
Rem. 125 PSP C-L MR	velocity, fps:	2660	2335	2034	1757	1509
	energy, ft-lb:	1964	1513	1148	856	632
	arc, inches:		+1.1	-3.0	-15.5	-37.4
Rem. 125 Pointed Soft Point	velocity, fps:	3140	2780	2447	2138	1853
	energy, ft-lb:	2736	2145	1662	1269	953.
	arc, inches:		+1.5	0	-7.4	-22.4
Rem. 150 AccuTip	velocity, fps:	2910	2686	2473	2270	2077
	energy, ft-lb:	2820	2403	2037	1716	1436
	arc, inches:		+1.8	0	-7.4	-21.5
Rem. 150 PSP Core-Lokt	velocity, fps:	2910	2617	2342	2083	1843
	energy, ft-lb:	2820	2281	1827	1445	1131
	arc, inches:		+1.8	0	-8.2	-24.4
Rem. 150 Bronze Point	velocity, fps:	2910	2656	2416	2189	1974
	energy, ft-lb:	2820	2349	1944	1596	1298
	arc, inches:		+1.7	0	-7.7	-22.7
Rem. 150 Nosler Bal. Tip	velocity, fps:	2910	2696	2492	2298	2112.
	energy, ft-lb:	2821	2422	2070	1769	1485
	arc, inches:		+1.6	0	-7.3	-21.1
Rem. 150 Swift Scirocco	velocity, fps:	2910	2696	2492	2298	2111
	energy, ft-lb:	2820	2421	2069	1758	1485
	arc, inches:		+1.6	0	-7.3	-21.1

CARTRIDGE BULLET	RANGE, YARDS:	0	100	200	300	400
Rem. 165 AccuTip	velocity, fps:	2800	2597	2403	2217	2039
	energy, ft-lb:	2872	2470	2115	1800	1523
	arc, inches:		+1.8	0	-7.9	-22.8
Rem. 165 PSP Core-Lokt	velocity, fps:	2800	2534	2283	2047	1825.
	energy, ft-lb:	2872	2352	1909	1534	1220
	arc, inches:		+2.0	0	-8.7	-25.9
Rem. 165 PSP boat-tail	velocity, fps:	2800	2592	2394	2204	2023
	energy, ft-lb:	2872	2462	2100	1780	1500
	arc, inches:		+1.8	0	-7.9	-23.0
Rem. 165 Nosler Bal. Tip	velocity, fps:	2800	2609	2426	2249	2080.
	energy, ft-lb:	2873	2494	2155	1854	1588
	arc, inches:		+1.8	0	-7.7	-22.3
Rem. 168 PSP C-L Ultra	velocity, fps:	2800	2546	2306	2079	1866
	energy, ft-lb:	2924	2418	1984	1613	1299
	arc, inches:		+1.9	0	-8.5	-25.1
Rem. 180 SP Core-Lokt	velocity, fps:	2700	2348	2023	1727	1466
	energy, ft-lb:	2913	2203	1635	1192	859
	arc, inches:		+2.4	0	-11.0	-33.8
Rem. 180 PSP Core-Lokt	velocity, fps:	2700	2469	2250	2042	1846
	energy, ft-lb:	2913	2436	2023	1666	1362
	arc, inches:		+2.1	0	-9.0	-26.3
Rem. 180 PSP C-L Ultra	velocity, fps:	2700	2480	2270	2070	1882
	energy, ft-lb:	2913	2457	2059	1713	1415
	arc, inches:		+2.1	0	-8.9	-25.8
Rem. 180 Bronze Point	velocity, fps:	2700	2485	2280	2084	1899.
	energy, ft-lb:	2913	2468	2077	1736	1441
	arc, inches:		+2.1	0	-8.8	-25.5
Rem. 180 Swift A-Frame	velocity, fps:	2700	2465	2243	2032	1833
	energy, ft-lb:	2913	2429	2010	1650	1343
	arc, inches:		+2.1	0	-9.1	-26.6
Rem. 180 Nosler Partition	velocity, fps:	2700	2512	2332	2160	1995
	energy, ft-lb:	2913	2522	2174	1864	1590
	arc, inches:		+2.0	0	-8.4	-24.3
Rem. 220 SP Core-Lokt	velocity, fps:	2410	2130	1870	1632	1422
	energy, ft-lb:	2837	2216	1708	1301	988
	arc, inches, s:		0	-6.2	-22.4	
Speer 150 Grand Slam	velocity, fps:	2975	2669	2383	2114	
	energy, ft-lb:	2947	2372	1891	1489	
	arc, inches:		+2.0	0	-8.1	-24.1
Speer 165 Grand Slam	velocity, fps:	2790	2560	2342	2134	
	energy, ft-lb:	2851	2401	2009	1669	
	arc, inches:		+1.9	0	-8.3	-24.1
Speer 180 Grand Slam	velocity, fps:	2690	2487	2293	2108	
	energy, ft-lb:	2892	2472	2101	1775	
	arc, inches:		+2.1	0	-8.8	-25.1
Win. 125 Pointed Soft Point	velocity, fps:	3140	2780	2447	2138	1853
	energy, ft-lb:	2736	2145	1662	1269	953
	arc, inches:		+1.8	0	-7.7	-23.0
Win. 150 Power-Point	velocity, fps:	2920	2580	2265	1972	1704
	energy, ft-lb:	2839	2217	1708	1295	967
	arc, inches:		+2.2	0	-9.0	-27.0
Win. 150 Power-Point Plus	velocity, fps:	3050	2685	2352	2043	1760
	energy, ft-lb:	3089	2402	1843	1391	1032
	arc, inches:		+1.7	0	-8.0	-24.3
Win. 150 Silvertip	velocity, fps:	2910	2617	2342	2083	1843
	energy, ft-lb:	2820	2281	1827	1445	1131
	arc, inches:		+2.1	0	-8.5	-25.0
Win. 150 Partition Gold	velocity, fps:	2960	2705	2464	2235	2019
	energy, ft-lb:	2919	2437	2022	1664	1358.
	arc, inches:		+1.6	0	-7.4	-21.7
Win. 150 Ballistic Silvertip	velocity, fps:	2900	2687	2483	2289	2103
	energy, ft-lb:	2801	2404	2054	1745	1473
	arc, inches:		+1.7	0	-7.3	-21.2

Ballistics Tables for Modern Sporting Rifles

.30-06 Springfield to .300 Winchester Magnum

CARTRIDGE BULLET	RANGE, YARDS:	0	100	200	300	400
Win. 150 Fail Safe	velocity, fps:	2920	2625	2349	2089	1848
	energy, ft-lb:	2841	2296	1838	1455	1137
	arc, inches:		+1.8	0	-8.1	-24.3
Win. 165 Pointed Soft Point	velocity, fps:	2800	2573	2357	2151	1956
	energy, ft-lb:	2873	2426	2036	1696	1402
	arc, inches:		+2.2	0	-8.4	-24.4
Win. 165 Fail Safe	velocity, fps:	2800	2540	2295	2063	1846
	energy, ft-lb:	2873	2365	1930	1560	1249
	arc, inches:		+2.0	0	-8.6	-25.3
Win. 168 Ballistic Silvertip	velocity, fps:	2790	2599	2416	2240	2072
	energy, ft-lb:	2903	2520	2177	1872	1601
	arc, inches:		+1.8	0	-7.8	-22.5
Win. 180 Ballistic Silvertip	velocity, fps:	2750	2572	2402	2237	2080
	energy, ft-lb:	3022	2644	2305	2001	1728
	arc, inches:		+1.9	0	-7.9	-22.8
Win. 180 Power-Point	velocity, fps:	2700	2348	2023	1727	1466
	energy, ft-lb:	2913	2203	1635	1192	859
	arc, inches:		+2.7	0	-11.3	-34.4
Win. 180 Power-Point Plus	velocity, fps:	2770	2563	2366	2177	1997
	energy, ft-lb:	3068	2627	2237	1894	1594
	arc, inches:		+1.9	0	-8.1	-23.6
Win. 180 Silvertip	velocity, fps:	2700	2469	2250	2042	1846
	energy, ft-lb:	2913	2436	2023	1666	1362
	arc, inches:		+2.4	0	-9.3	-27.0
Win. 180 AccuBond	velocity, fps:	2750	2573	2403	2239	2082
	energy, ft-lb:	3022	2646	2308	2004	1732
	arc, inches:		+1.9	0	-7.9	-22.8
Win. 180 Partition Gold	velocity, fps:	2790	2581	2382	2192	2010
	energy, ft-lb:	3112	2664	2269	1920	1615
	arc, inches:		+1.9	0	-8.0	-23.2
Win. 180 Fail Safe	velocity, fps:	2700	2486	2283	2089	1904
	energy, ft-lb:	2914	2472	2083	1744	1450
	arc, inches:		+2.1	0	-8.7	-25.5
Win. 150 Supreme Elite XP3	velocity, fps:	2925	2712	2508	2313	2127
	energy, ft-lb:	2849	2448	2095	1782	1507
	arc, inches:		+1.6	0	-7.2	-20.8
Win. 180 Supreme Elite XP3	velocity, fps:	2750	2579	2414	2256	2103
	energy, ft-lb:	3022	2658	2330	2034	1768
	arc, inches:		+1.9	0	-7.8	-22.5

.300 H&H Magnum

CARTRIDGE BULLET	RANGE, YARDS:	0	100	200	300	400
Handload, 165 Sierra HP	velocity, fps	3000	2784	2579	2382	2195
	energy, ft-lbs	3297	2840	2436	2079	1764
	arc, inches	-1.5	+1.5	0	-6.7	-19.5
Federal 180 Barnes TSX	velocity, fps	2880	2680	2480	2290	2120
	energy, ft-lbs	3315	2860	2460	2105	1790
	arc, inches	-1.5	+1.7	0	-7.3	-21.3
Hornady 180 InterBond	velocity, fps	2870	2678	2493	2316	2146
	energy, ft-lbs	3292	2865	2484	2144	1841
	arc, inches	-1.5	+1.7	0	-7.3	-21.0
Federal 180 Nosler Partition	velocity, fps:	2880	2620	2380	2150	1930
	energy, ft-lb:	3315	2750	2260	1840	1480
	arc, inches:		+1.8	0	-8.0	-23.4
Win. 180 Fail Safe	velocity, fps:	2880	2628	2390	2165	1952
	energy, ft-lb:	3316	2762	2284	1873	1523
	arc, inches:		+1.8	0	-7.9	-23.2
Handload, 190 Hornady	velocity, fps	2800	2615	2437	2266	2102
	energy, ft-lbs	3307	2884	2505	2166	1864
	arc, inches	-1.5	+1.8	0	-7.7	-22.1

.308 Norma Magnum

CARTRIDGE BULLET	RANGE, YARDS:	0	100	200	300	400
Norma 180 TXP Swift A-Fr.	velocity, fps:	2953	2704	2469	2245	
	energy, ft-lb:	3486	2924	2437	2016	
	arc, inches:		+1.6	0	-7.3	
Norma 180 Oryx	velocity, fps:	2953	2630	2330	2049	
	energy, ft-lb:	3486	2766	2170	1679	
	arc, inches:		+1.8	0	-8.2	
Norma 200 Vulkan	velocity, fps:	2903	2624	2361	2114	
	energy, ft-lb:	3744	3058	2476	1985	
	arc, inches:	0	+1.8	0	-8.0	

.300 Winchester Magnum

CARTRIDGE BULLET	RANGE, YARDS:	0	100	200	300	400
A-Square 180 Dead Tough	velocity, fps:	3120	2756	2420	2108	1820
	energy, ft-lb:	3890	3035	2340	1776	1324
	arc, inches:		+1.6	0	-7.6	-22.9
Black Hills 180 Nos. Bal. Tip	velocity, fps:	3100				
	energy, ft-lb:	3498				
	arc, inches:					
Black Hills 180 Barnes X	velocity, fps:	2950				
	energy, ft-lb:	3498				
	arc, inches:					
Black Hills 180 AccuBond	velocity, fps:	3000				
	energy, ft-lb:	3597				
	arc, inches:					
Black Hills 190 Match	velocity, fps:	2950				
	energy, ft-lb:	3672				
	arc, inches:					
Federal 150 Sierra Pro Hunt.	velocity, fps:	3280	3030	2800	2570	2360.
	energy, ft-lb:	3570	3055	2600	2205	1860
	arc, inches:		+1.1	0	-5.6	-16.4
Federal 150 Trophy Bonded	velocity, fps:	3280	2980	2700	2430	2190
	energy, ft-lb:	3570	2450	2420	1970	1590
	arc, inches:		+1.2	0	-6.0	-17.9
Federal 180 Sierra Pro Hunt.	velocity, fps:	2960	2750	2540	2340	2160
	energy, ft-lb:	3500	3010	2580	2195	1860
	arc, inches:		+1.6	0	-7.0	-20.3
Federal 180 Barnes XLC	velocity, fps:	2960	2780	2600	2430	2260
	energy, ft-lb:	3500	3080	2700	2355	2050
	arc, inches:		+1.5	0	-6.6	-19.2
Federal 180 Trophy Bonded	velocity, fps:	2960	2700	2460	2220	2000
	energy, ft-lb:	3500	2915	2410	1975	1605
	arc, inches:		+1.6	0	-7.4	-21.9
Federal 180 Tr. Bonded HE	velocity, fps:	3100	2830	2580	2340	2110
	energy, ft-lb:	3840	3205	2660	2190	1790
	arc, inches:		+1.4	0	-6.6	-19.7
Federal 180 Nosler Partition	velocity, fps:	2960	2700	2450	2210	1990
	energy, ft-lb:	3500	2905	2395	1955	1585
	arc, inches:		+1.6	0	-7.5	-22.1
Federal 190 Sierra MatchKg. BTHP	velocity, fps:	2900	2730	2560	2400	2240
	energy, ft-lb:	3550	3135	2760	2420	2115
	arc, inches:		+12.9	+22.5	+26.9	+25.1
Federal 200 Sierra GameKing BTSP	velocity, fps:	2830	2680	2530	2380	2240
	energy, ft-lb:	3560	3180	2830	2520	2230
	arc, inches:		+1.7	0	-7.1	-20.4
Federal 200 Nosler Part. HE	velocity, fps:	2930	2740	2550	2370	2200
	energy, ft-lb:	3810	3325	2885	2495	2145
	arc, inches:		+1.6	0	-6.9	-20.1
Federal 200 Trophy Bonded	velocity, fps:	2800	2570	2350	2150	1950
	energy, ft-lb:	3480	2935	2460	2050	1690
	arc, inches:		+1.9	0	-8.2	-23.9
Hornady 150 SP boat-tail	velocity, fps:	3275	2988	2718	2464	2224
	energy, ft-lb:	3573	2974	2461	2023	1648
	arc, inches:		+1.2	0	-6.0	-17.8
Hornady 150 SST (and Interbond)	velocity, fps:	3275	3027	2791	2565	2352
	energy, ft-lb:	3572	3052	2593	2192	1842
	arc, inches:		+1.2	0	-5.8	-17.0
Hornady 165 SP boat-tail	velocity, fps:	3100	2877	2665	2462	2269.
	energy, ft-lb:	3522	3033	2603	2221	1887

Ballistics Tables for Modern Sporting Rifles

.300 WINCHESTER MAGNUM TO .300 WINCHESTER MAGNUM

CARTRIDGE BULLET	RANGE, YARDS:	0	100	200	300	400
	arc, inches:		+1.3	0	-6.5	-18.5
Hornady 165 SST	velocity, fps:	3100	2885	2680	2483	2296
	energy, ft-lb:	3520	3049	2630	2259	1930
	arc, inches:		+1.4	0	-6.4	-18.6
Hornady 180 SP boat-tail	velocity, fps:	2960	2745	2540	2344	2157
	energy, ft-lb:	3501	3011	2578	2196	1859
	arc, inches:		+1.9	0	-7.3	-20.9
Hornady 180 SST	velocity, fps:	2960	2764	2575	2395	2222
	energy, ft-lb:	3501	3052	2650	2292	1974
	arc, inches:		+1.6	0	-7.0	-20.1
Hornady 180 SPBT HM	velocity, fps:	3100	2879	2668	2467	2275
	energy, ft-lb:	3840	3313	2845	2431	2068
	arc, inches:		+1.4	0	-6.4	-18.7
Hornady 190 SP boat-tail	velocity, fps:	2900	2711	2529	2355	2187
	energy, ft-lb:	3549	3101	2699	2340	2018
	arc, inches:		+1.6	0	-7.1	-20.4
Norma 150 Nosler Bal. Tip	velocity, fps:	3250	3014	2791	2578	
	energy, ft-lb:	3519	3027	2595	2215	
	arc, inches:		+1.1	0	-5.6	
Norma 150 Barnes TS	velocity, fps:	3215	2982	2761	2550	
	energy, ft-lb:	3444	2962	2539	2167	
	arc, inches:		+1.2	0	-5.8	
Norma 165 Scirocco	velocity, fps:	3117	2921	2734	2554	
	energy, ft-lb:	3561	3127	2738	2390	
	arc, inches:		+1.2	0	-5.9	
Norma 180 Soft Point	velocity, fps:	3018	2780	2555	2341	
	energy, ft-lb:	3641	3091	2610	2190	
	arc, inches:		+1.5	0	-7.0	
Norma 180 Plastic Point	velocity, fps:	3018	2755	2506	2271	
	energy, ft-lb:	3641	3034	2512	2062	
	arc, inches:		+1.6	0	-7.1	
Norma 180 TXP Swift A-Fr.	velocity, fps:	2920	2688	2467	2256	
	energy, ft-lb:	3409	2888	2432	2035	
	arc, inches:		+1.7	0	-7.4	
Norma 180 AccuBond	velocity, fps:	2953	2767	2588	2417	
	energy, ft-lb:	3486	3061	2678	2335	
	arc, inches:		+1.5	0	-6.7	
Norma 180 Oryx	velocity, fps:	2920	2600	2301	2023	
	energy, ft-lb:	3409	2702	2117	1636	
	arc, inches:		+1.8	0	-8.4	
Norma 200 Vulkan	velocity, fps:	2887	2609	2347	2100	
	energy, ft-lb:	3702	3023	2447	1960	
	arc, inches:		+1.8	0	-8.2	
Norma 200 Oryx	velocity, fps:	2789	2510	2248	2002	
	energy, ft-lb:	3455	2799	2245	1780	
	arc, inches:		+2.0	0	-8.9	
PMC 150 Barnes X	velocity, fps:	3135	2918	2712	2515	2327
	energy, ft-lb:	3273	2836	2449	2107	1803
	arc, inches:		+1.3	0	-6.1	-17.7
PMC 150 Pointed Soft Point	velocity, fps:	3150	2902	2665	2438	2222
	energy, ft-lb:	3304	2804	2364	1979	1644
	arc, inches:		+1.3	0	-6.2	-18.3
PMC 150 SP boat-tail	velocity, fps:	3250	2987	2739	2504	2281
	energy, ft-lb:	3517	2970	2498	2088	1733
	arc, inches:		+1.2	0	-6.0	-17.4
PMC 180 Barnes X	velocity, fps:	2910	2738	2572	2412	2258
	energy, ft-lb:	3384	2995	2644	2325	2037
	arc, inches:		+1.6	0	-6.9	-19.8
PMC 180 Pointed Soft Point	velocity, fps:	2853	2643	2446	2258	2077
	energy, ft-lb:	3252	2792	2391	2037	1724
	arc, inches:		+1.7	0	-7.5	-21.9
PMC 180 SP boat-tail	velocity, fps:	2900	2714	2536	2365	2200
	energy, ft-lb:	3361	2944	2571	2235	1935
	arc, inches:		+1.6	0	-7.1	-20.3
PMC 180 HPBT Match	velocity, fps:	2950	2755	2568	2390	2219
	energy, ft-lb:	3478	3033	2636	2283	1968
	arc, inches:		+1.5	0	-6.8	-19.7
Rem. 150 PSP Core-Lokt	velocity, fps:	3290	2951	2636	2342	2068
	energy, ft-lb:	3605	2900	2314	1827	1859
	arc, inches:		+1.6	0	-7.0	-20.2
Rem. 150 PSP C-L MR	velocity, fps:	2650	2373	2113	1870	1646
	energy, ft-lb:	2339	1875	1486	1164	902
	arc, inches:		+1.0	-2.7	-14.3	-35.8
Rem. 150 PSP C-L Ultra	velocity, fps:	3290	2967	2666	2384	2120
	energy, ft-lb:	3065	2931	2366	1893	1496
	arc, inches:		+1.2	0	-6.1	-18.4
Rem. 180 AccuTip	velocity, fps:	2960	2764	2577	2397	2224
	energy, ft-lb:	3501	3053	2653	2295	1976
	arc, inches:		+1.5	0	-6.8	-19.6
Rem. 180 PSP Core-Lokt	velocity, fps:	2960	2745	2540	2344	2157
	energy, ft-lb:	3501	3011	2578	2196	1424
	arc, inches:		+2.2	+1.9	-3.4	-15.0
Rem. 180 PSP C-L Ultra	velocity, fps:	2960	2727	2505	2294	2093
	energy, ft-lb:	3501	2971	2508	2103	1751
	arc, inches:		+2.7	+2.2	-3.8	-16.4
Rem. 180 Nosler Partition	velocity, fps:	2960	2725	2503	2291	2089
	energy, ft-lb:	3501	2968	2503	2087	1744
	arc, inches:		+1.6	0	-7.2	-20.9
Rem. 180 Nosler Bal. Tip	velocity, fps:	2960	2774	2595	2424	2259
	energy, ft-lb:	3501	3075	2692	2348	2039
	arc, inches:		+1.5	0	-6.7	-19.3
Rem. 180 Swift Scirocco	velocity, fps:	2960	2774	2595	2424	2259
	energy, ft-lb:	3501	3075	2692	2348	2039
	arc, inches:		+1.5	0	-6.7	-19.3
Rem. 190 PSP boat-tail	velocity, fps:	2885	2691	2506	2327	2156
	energy, ft-lb:	3511	3055	2648	2285	1961
	arc, inches:		+1.6	0	-7.2	-20.8
Rem. 190 HPBT Match	velocity, fps:	2900	2725	2557	2395	2239
	energy, ft-lb:	3547	3133	2758	2420	2115
	arc, inches:		+1.6	0	-6.9	-19.9
Rem. 200 Swift A-Frame	velocity, fps:	2825	2595	2376	2167	1970
	energy, ft-lb:	3544	2989	2506	2086	1722
	arc, inches:		+1.8	0	-8.0	-23.5
Speer 180 Grand Slam	velocity, fps:	2950	2735	2530	2334	
	energy, ft-lb:	3478	2989	2558	2176	
	arc, inches:		+1.6	0	-7.0	-20.5
Speer 200 Grand Slam	velocity, fps:	2800	2597	2404	2218	
	energy, ft-lb:	3481	2996	2565	2185	
	arc, inches:		+1.8	0	-7.9	-22.9
Win. 150 Power-Point	velocity, fps:	3290	2951	2636	2342	2068
	energy, ft-lb:	3605	2900	2314	1827	1424
	arc, inches:		+2.6	+2.1	-3.5	-15.4
Win. 150 Fail Safe	velocity, fps:	3260	2943	2647	2370	2110
	energy, ft-lb:	3539	2884	2334	1871	1483
	arc, inches:		+1.3	0	-6.2	-18.7
Win. 165 Fail Safe	velocity, fps:	3120	2807	2515	2242	1985
	energy, ft-lb:	3567	2888	2319	1842	1445
	arc, inches:		+1.5	0	-7.0	-20.0
Win. 180 Power-Point	velocity, fps:	2960	2745	2540	2344	2157
	energy, ft-lb:	3501	3011	2578	2196	1859
	arc, inches:		+1.9	0	-7.3	-20.9
Win. 180 Power-Point Plus	velocity, fps:	3070	2846	2633	2430	2236
	energy, ft-lb:	3768	3239	2772	2361	1999
	arc, inches:		+1.4	0	-6.4	-18.7
Win. 180 Ballistic Silvertip	velocity, fps:	2950	2764	2586	2415	2250
	energy, ft-lb:	3478	3054	2673	2331	2023

Ballistics Tables for Modern Sporting Rifles

.300 WINCHESTER MAGNUM TO .300 WEATHERBY MAGNUM

CARTRIDGE BULLET	RANGE, YARDS:	0	100	200	300	400
	arc, inches:		+1.5	0	-6.7	-19.4
Win. 180 AccuBond	velocity, fps:	2950	2765	2588	2417	2253
	energy, ft-lb:	3478	3055	2676	2334	2028
	arc, inches:		+1.5	0	-6.7	-19.4
Win. 180 Fail Safe	velocity, fps:	2960	2732	2514	2307	2110
	energy, ft-lb:	3503	2983	2528	2129	1780
	arc, inches:		+1.6	0	-7.1	-20.7
Win. 180 Partition Gold	velocity, fps:	3070	2859	2657	2464	2280
	energy, ft-lb:	3768	3267	2823	2428	2078
	arc, inches:		+1.4	0	-6.3	-18.3
Win. 150 Supreme Elite XP3	velocity, fps:	3260	3030	2811	2603	2404
	energy, ft-lb:	3539	3057	2632	2256	1925
	arc, inches:		+1.1	0	-5.6	-16.2
Win. 180 Supreme Elite XP3	velocity, fps:	3000	2819	2646	2479	2318
	energy, ft-lb:	3597	3176	2797	2455	2147
	arc, inches:		+1.4	0	-6.4	-18.5

.300 Remington Short Ultra Magnum

CARTRIDGE BULLET	RANGE, YARDS:	0	100	200	300	400
Rem. 150 PSP C-L Ultra	velocity, fps:	3200	2901	2672	2359	2112
	energy, ft-lb:	3410	2803	2290	1854	1485
	arc, inches:		+1.3	0	-6.4	-19.1
Rem. 165 PSP Core-Lokt	velocity, fps:	3075	2792	2527	2276	2040
	energy, ft-lb:	3464	2856	2339	1828	1525
	arc, inches:		+1.5	0	-7.0	-20.7
Rem. 180 Partition	velocity, fps:	2960	2761	2571	2389	2214
	energy, ft-lb:	3501	3047	2642	2280	1959
	arc, inches:		+1.5	0	-6.8	-19.7
Rem. 180 PSP C-L Ultra	velocity, fps:	2960	2727	2506	2295	2094
	energy, ft-lb:	3501	2972	2509	2105	1753
	arc, inches:		+1.6	0	-7.1	-20.9
Rem. 190 HPBT Match	velocity, fps:	2900	2725	2557	2395	2239
	energy, ft-lb:	3547	3133	2758	2420	2115
	arc, inches:		+1.6	0	-6.9	-19.9

.300 Winchester Short Magnum

CARTRIDGE BULLET	RANGE, YARDS:	0	100	200	300	400
Black Hills 175 Sierra MKing	velocity, fps:	2950				
	energy, ft-lb:	3381				
	arc, inches:					
Black Hills 180 AccuBond	velocity, fps:	2950				
	energy, ft-lb:	3478				
	arc, inches:					
Federal 150 Nosler Bal. Tip	velocity, fps:	3200	2970	2755	2545	2345
	energy, ft-lb:	3410	2940	2520	2155	1830
	arc, inches:		+1.2	0	-5.8	-17.0
Federal 165 Nos. Partition	velocity, fps:	3130	2890	2670	2450	2250
	energy, ft-lb:	3590	3065	2605	2205	1855
	arc, inches:		+1.3	0	-6.2	-18.2
Federal 165 Nos. Solid Base	velocity, fps:	3130	2900	2690	2490	2290
	energy, ft-lb:	3590	3090	2650	2265	1920
	arc, inches:		+1.3	0	-6.1	-17.8
Federal 180 Barnes TS	velocity, fps:	2980	2780	2580	2400	2220
And Nos. Solid Base	energy, ft-lbs:	3550	3085	2670	2300	1970
	arc, inches:		+1.5	0	-6.7	-19.5
Federal 180 Grand Slam	velocity, fps:	2970	2740	2530	2320	2130
	energy, ft-lb:	3525	3010	2555	2155	1810
	arc, inches:		+1.5	0	-7.0	-20.5
Federal 180 Trophy Bonded	velocity, fps:	2970	2730	2500	2280	2080
	energy, ft-lb:	3525	2975	2500	2085	1725
	arc, inches:		+1.5	0	-7.2	-21.0
Federal 180 Nosler Partition	velocity, fps:	2975	2750	2535	2290	2126
	energy, ft-lb:	3540	3025	2570	2175	1825
	arc, inches:		+1.5	0	-7.0	-20.3
Federal 180 Nos. AccuBond	velocity, fps:	2960	2780	2610	2440	2280
	energy, ft-lb:	3500	3090	2715	2380	2075
	arc, inches:		+1.5	0	-6.6	-19.0
Federal 180 Hi-Shok SP	velocity, fps:	2970	2520	2115	1750	1430
	energy, ft-lb:	3525	2540	1785	1220	820
	arc, inches:		+2.2	0	-9.9	-31.4
Norma 150 FMJ	velocity, fps:	2953	2731	2519	2318	
	energy, ft-lb:					
	arc, inches:		+1.6	0	-7.1	
Norma 150 Barnes X TS	velocity, fps:	3215	2982	2761	2550	
	energy, ft-lb:	3444	2962	2539	2167	
	arc, inches:		+1.2	0	-5.7	
Norma 180 Nosler Bal. Tip	velocity, fps:	3215	2985	2767	2560	
	energy, ft-lb:	3437	2963	2547	2179	
	arc, inches:		+1.2	0	-5.7	
Norma 180 Oryx	velocity, fps:	2936	2542	2180	1849	
	energy, ft-lb:	3446	2583	1900	1368	
	arc, inches:		+1.9	0	-8.9	
Win. 150 Power-Point	velocity, fps:	3270	2903	2565	2250	1958
	energy, ft-lb:	3561	2807	2190	1686	1277
	arc, inches:		+1.3	0	-6.6	-20.2
Win. 150 Ballistic Silvertip	velocity, fps:	3300	3061	2834	2619	2414
	energy, ft-lb:	3628	3121	2676	2285	1941
	arc, inches:		+1.1	0	-5.4	-15.9
Win. 165 Fail Safe	velocity, fps:	3125	2846	2584	2336	2102
	energy, ft-lb:	3577	2967	2446	1999	1619
	arc, inches:		+1.4	0	-6.6	-19.6
Win. 180 Ballistic Silvertip	velocity, fps:	3010	2822	2641	2468	2301
	energy, ft-lb:	3621	3182	2788	2434	2116
	arc, inches:		+1.4	0	-6.4	-18.6
Win. 180 AccuBond	velocity, fps:	3010	2822	2643	2470	2304
	energy, ft-lb:	3622	3185	2792	2439	2121
	arc, inches:		+1.4	0	-6.4	-18.5
Win. 180 Fail Safe	velocity, fps:	2970	2741	2524	2317	2120
	energy, ft-lb:	3526	3005	2547	2147	1797
	arc, inches:		+1.6	0	-7.0	-20.5
Win. 180 Power Point	velocity, fps:	2970	2755	2549	2353	2166
	energy, ft-lb:	3526	3034	2598	2214	1875
	arc, inches:		+1.5	0	-6.9	-20.1
Win. 150 Supreme Elite XP3	velocity, fps:	3300	3068	2847	2637	2437
	energy, ft-lb:	3626	3134	2699	2316	1978
	arc, inches:		+1.1	0	-5.4	-15.8
Win. 180 Supreme Elite XP3	velocity, fps:	3010	2829	2655	2488	2326
	energy, ft-lb:	3621	3198	2817	2473	2162
	arc, inches:		+1.4	0	-6.4	-18.3

.300 Ruger Compact Magnum

CARTRIDGE BULLET	RANGE, YARDS:	0	100	200	300	400
Hornady 150 SST	velocity, fps	3310	3065	2833	2613	2404
	energy, ft-lbs	3648	3128	2673	2274	1924
	arc, inches	-1.5	+1.1	0	-5.4	-16.0
Hornady 165 GMX	velocity, fps	3130	2911	2703	2504	2314
	energy, ft-lbs	3589	3105	2677	2297	1963
	arc, inches	-1.5	+1.3	0	-6.1	-17.7
Hornady 180 SST	velocity, fps	3040	2840	2649	2466	2290
	energy, ft-lbs	3693	3223	2804	2430	2096
	arc, inches	-1.5	+1.4	0	-6.4	-18.5

.300 Weatherby Magnum

CARTRIDGE BULLET	RANGE, YARDS:	0	100	200	300	400
A-Square 180 Dead Tough	velocity, fps:	3180	2811	2471	2155	1863
	energy, ft-lb:	4041	3158	2440	1856	1387
	arc, inches:		+1.5	0	-7.2	-21.8
A-Square 220 Monolythic	velocity, fps:	2700	2407	2133	1877	1653
Solid	energy, ft-lb:	3561	2830	2223	1721	1334
	arc, inches:		+2.3	0	-9.8	-29.7
Federal 180 Sierra GameKing	velocity, fps:	3190	3010	2830	2660	2490
BTSP	energy, ft-lb:	4065	3610	3195	2820	2480

BALLISTICS

Ballistics Tables for Modern Sporting Rifles

.300 WEATHERBY MAGNUM TO .30-378 WEATHERBY MAGNUM

CARTRIDGE BULLET	RANGE, YARDS:	0	100	200	300	400
	arc, inches:		+1.2	0	-5.6	-16.0
Federal 180 Trophy Bonded	velocity, fps:	3190	2950	2720	2500	2290
	energy, ft-lb:	4065	3475	2955	2500	2105
	arc, inches:		+1.3	0	-5.9	-17.5
Federal 180 Tr. Bonded HE	velocity, fps:	3330	3080	2850	2750	2410
	energy, ft-lb:	4430	3795	3235	2750	2320
	arc, inches:		+1.1	0	-5.4	-15.8
Federal 180 Nosler Partition	velocity, fps:	3190	2980	2780	2590	2400
	energy, ft-lb:	4055	3540	3080	2670	2305
	arc, inches:		+1.2	0	-5.7	-16.7
Federal 180 Nosler Part. HE	velocity, fps:	3330	3110	2810	2710	2520
	energy, ft-lb:	4430	3875	3375	2935	2540
	arc, inches:		+1.0	0	-5.2	-15.1
Federal 200 Trophy Bonded	velocity, fps:	2900	2670	2440	2230	2030
	energy, ft-lb:	3735	3150	2645	2200	1820
	arc, inches:		+1.7	0	-7.6	-22.2
Hornady 150 SST	velocity, fps:	3375	3123	2882	2652	2434
(or Interbond)	energy, ft-lb:	3793	3248	2766	2343	1973
	arc, inches:		+1.0	0	-5.4	-15.8
Hornady 180 SP	velocity, fps:	3120	2891	2673	2466	2268.
	energy, ft-lb:	3890	3340	2856	2430	2055
	arc, inches:		+1.3	0	-6.2	-18.1
Hornady 180 SST	velocity, fps:	3120	2911	2711	2519	2335
	energy, ft-lb:	3890	3386	2936	2535	2180
	arc, inches:		+1.3	0	-6.2	-18.1
Rem. 180 PSP Core-Lokt	velocity, fps:	3120	2866	2627	2400	2184
	energy, ft-lb:	3890	3284	2758	2301	1905
	arc, inches:		+2.4	+2.0	-3.4	-14.9
Rem. 190 PSP boat-tail	velocity, fps:	3030	2830	2638	2455	2279
	energy, ft-lb:	3873	3378	2936	2542	2190.
	arc, inches:		+1.4	0	-6.4	-18.6
Rem. 200 Swift A-Frame	velocity, fps:	2925	2690	2467	2254	2052
	energy, ft-lb:	3799	3213	2701	2256	1870
	arc, inches:		+2.8	+2.3	-3.9	-17.0
Speer 180 Grand Slam	velocity, fps:	3185	2948	2722	2508	
	energy, ft-lb:	4054	3472	2962	2514	
	arc, inches:		+1.3	0	-5.9	-17.4
Wby. 150 Pointed Expanding	velocity, fps:	3540	3225	2932	2657	2399
	energy, ft-lb:	4173	3462	2862	2351	1916
	arc, inches:		+2.6	+3.3	0	-8.2
Wby. 150 Nosler Partition	velocity, fps:	3540	3263	3004	2759	2528
	energy, ft-lb:	4173	3547	3005	2536	2128
	arc, inches:		+2.5	+3.2	0	-7.7
Wby. 165 Pointed Expanding	velocity, fps:	3390	3123	2872	2634	2409
	energy, ft-lb:	4210	3573	3021	2542	2126
	arc, inches:		+2.8	+3.5	0	-8.5
Wby. 165 Nosler Bal. Tip	velocity, fps:	3350	3133	2927	2730	2542
	energy, ft-lb:	4111	3596	3138	2730	2367
	arc, inches:		+2.7	+3.4	0	-8.1
Wby. 180 Pointed Expanding	velocity, fps:	3240	3004	2781	2569	2366
	energy, ft-lb:	4195	3607	3091	2637	2237
	arc, inches:		+3.1	+3.8	0	-9.0
Wby. 180 Barnes X	velocity, fps:	3190	2995	2809	2631	2459
	energy, ft-lb:	4067	3586	3154	2766	2417
	arc, inches:		+3.1	+3.8	0	-8.7
Wby. 180 Bal. Tip	velocity, fps:	3250	3051	2806	2676	2503
	energy, ft-lb:	4223	3721	3271	2867	2504
	arc, inches:		+2.8	+3.6	0	-8.4
Wby. 180 Nosler Partition	velocity, fps:	3240	3028	2826	2634	2449
	energy, ft-lb:	4195	3665	3193	2772	2396
	arc, inches:		+3.0	+3.7	0	-8.6
Wby. 200 Nosler Partition	velocity, fps:	3060	2860	2668	2485	2308
	energy, ft-lb:	4158	3631	3161	2741	2366
	arc, inches:		+3.5	+4.2	0	-9.8
Wby. 220 RN Expanding	velocity, fps:	2845	2543	2260	1996	1751.
	energy, ft-lb:	3954	3158	2495	1946	1497
	arc, inches:		+4.9	+5.9	0	-14.6

.300 Dakota

CARTRIDGE BULLET	RANGE, YARDS:	0	100	200	300	400
150 Barnes TTSX	velocity, fps	3300	3064	2840	2627	2424
	energy, ft-lbs	3628	3127	2687	2300	1958
	arc, inches	-1.5	2.0	1.7	-2.9	-12.5
165 Swift Scirocco	velocity, fps	3200	2988	2787	2594	2409
	energy, ft-lbs	3753	3273	2846	2466	2127
	arc, inches	-1.5	2.1	1.8	-3.0	-13.0
180 Swift Scirocco	velocity, fps	3100	2913	2733	2561	2395
	energy, ft-lbs	3842	3392	2986	2621	2292
	arc, inches	-1.5	2.2	1.9	-3.1	-13.2
Dakota 200 Barnes X	velocity, fps:	3000	2824	2656	2493	2336
	energy, ft-lb:	3996	3542	3131	2760	2423
	arc, inches:		+2.2	+1.5	-4.0	-15.2

.300 Pegasus

CARTRIDGE BULLET	RANGE, YARDS:	0	100	200	300	400
A-Square 180 SP boat-tail	velocity, fps:	3500	3319	3145	2978	2817
	energy, ft-lb:	4896	4401	3953	3544	3172
	arc, inches:		+2.3	+2.9	0	-6.8
A-Square 180 Nosler Part.	velocity, fps:	3500	3295	3100	2913	2734
	energy, ft-lb:	4896	4339	3840	3392	2988
	arc, inches:		+2.3	+3.0	0	-7.1
A-Square 180 Dead Tough	velocity, fps:	3500	3103	2740	2405	2095
	energy, ft-lb:	4896	3848	3001	2312	1753
	arc, inches:		+1.1	0	-5.7	-17.5

.300 Remington Ultra Magnum

CARTRIDGE BULLET	RANGE, YARDS:	0	100	200	300	400
Federal 180 Trophy Bonded	velocity, fps:	3250	3000	2770	2550	2340
	energy, ft-lb:	4220	3605	3065	2590	2180
	arc, inches:		+1.2	0	-5.7	-16.8
Rem. 150 Swift Scirocco	velocity, fps:	3450	3208	2980	2762	2556
	energy, ft-lb:	3964	3427	2956	2541	2175
	arc, inches:		+1.7	+1.5	-2.6	-11.2
Rem. 180 Nosler Partition	velocity, fps:	3250	3037	2834	2640	2454
	energy, ft-lb:	4221	3686	3201	2786	2407
	arc, inches:		+2.4	+1.8	-3.0	-12.7
Rem. 180 Swift Scirocco	velocity, fps:	3250	3048	2856	2672	2495
	energy, ft-lb:	4221	3714	3260	2853	2487
	arc, inches:		+2.0	+1.7	-2.8	-12.3
Rem. 180 PSP Core-Lokt	velocity, fps:	3250	2988	2742	2508	2287
	energy, ft-lb:	3517	2974	2503	2095	1741
	arc, inches:		+2.1	+1.8	-3.1	-13.6
Rem. 200 Nosler Partition	velocity, fps:	3025	2826	2636	2454	2279
	energy, ft-lb:	4063	3547	3086	2673	2308
	arc, inches:		+2.4	+2.0	-3.4	-14.6

.30-378 Weatherby Magnum

CARTRIDGE BULLET	RANGE, YARDS:	0	100	200	300	400
Wby. 165 Nosler Bal. Tip	velocity, fps:	3500	3275	3062	2859	2665
	energy, ft-lb:	4488	3930	3435	2995	2603
	arc, inches:		+2.4	+3.0	0	-7.4
Wby. 180 Nosler Bal. Tip	velocity, fps:	3420	3213	3015	2826	2645
	energy, ft-lb:	4676	4126	3634	3193	2797
	arc, inches:		+2.5	+3.1	0	-7.5
Wby. 180 Barnes X	velocity, fps:	3450	3243	3046	2858	2678.
	energy, ft-lb:	4757	4204	3709	3264	2865
	arc, inches:		+2.4	+3.1	0	-7.4
Wby. 200 Nosler Partition	velocity, fps:	3160	2955	2759	2572	2392.
	energy, ft-lb:	4434	3877	3381	2938	2541
	arc, inches:		+3.2	+3.9	0	-9.1

BALLISTICS

Ballistics Tables for Modern Sporting Rifles

7.82 (.308) WARBIRD TO .325 WSM

CARTRIDGE BULLET	RANGE, YARDS:	0	100	200	300	400
7.82 (.308) Warbird						
Lazzeroni 150 Nosler Part.	velocity, fps:	3680	3432	3197	2975	2764
	energy, ft-lb:	4512	3923	3406	2949	2546
	arc, inches:		+2.1	+2.7	0	-6.6
Lazzeroni 180 Nosler Part.	velocity, fps:	3425	3220	3026	2839	2661
	energy, ft-lb:	4689	4147	3661	3224	2831
	arc, inches:		+2.5	+3.2	0	-7.5
Lazzeroni 200 Swift A-Fr.	velocity, fps:	3290	3105	2928	2758	2594
	energy, ft-lb:	4808	4283	3808	3378	2988
	arc, inches:		+2.7	+3.4	0	-7.9
7.65x53 Argentine						
Norma 174 Soft Point	velocity, fps:	2493	2173	1878	1611	
	energy, ft-lb:	2402	1825	1363	1003	
	arc, inches:		+2.0	0	-9.5	
Norma 180 Soft Point	velocity, fps:	2592	2386	2189	2002	
	energy, ft-lb:	2686	2276	1916	1602	
	arc, inches:		+2.3	0	-9.6	
.303 British						
Federal 150 Hi-Shok	velocity, fps:	2690	2440	2210	1980	1780
	energy, ft-lb:	2400	1980	1620	1310	1055
	arc, inches:		+2.2	0	-9.4	-27.6
Federal 180 Sierra Pro-Hunt.	velocity, fps:	2460	2230	2020	1820	1630
	energy, ft-lb:	2420	1995	1625	1315	1060
	arc, inches:		+2.8	0	-11.3	-33.2
Federal 180 Tr. Bonded HE	velocity, fps:	2590	2350	2120	1900	1700
	energy, ft-lb:	2680	2205	1795	1445	1160
	arc, inches:		+2.4	0	-10.0	-30.0
Hornady 150 Soft Point	velocity, fps:	2685	2441	2210	1992	1787
	energy, ft-lb:	2401	1984	1627	1321	1064
	arc, inches:		+2.2	0	-9.3	-27.4
Hornady 150 SP LM	velocity, fps:	2830	2570	2325	2094	1884
	energy, ft-lb:	2667	2199	1800	1461	1185
	arc, inches:		+2.0	0	-8.4	-24.6
Norma 150 Soft Point	velocity, fps:	2723	2438	2170	1920	
	energy, ft-lb:	2470	1980	1569	1228	
	arc, inches:		+2.2	0	-9.6	
PMC 174 FMJ (and HPBT)	velocity, fps:	2400	2216	2042	1876	1720
	energy, ft-lb:	2225	1898	1611	1360	1143
	arc, inches:		+2.8	0	-11.2	-32.2
PMC 180 SP boat-tail	velocity, fps:	2450	2276	2110	1951	1799
	energy, ft-lb:	2399	2071	1779	1521	1294
	arc, inches:		+2.6	0	-10.4	-30.1
Rem. 180 SP Core-Lokt	velocity, fps:	2460	2124	1817	1542	1311
	energy, ft-lb:	2418	1803	1319	950	687
	arc, inches, s:		0	-5.8	-23.3	
Win. 180 Power-Point	velocity, fps:	2460	2233	2018	1816	1629
	energy, ft-lb:	2418	1993	1627	1318	1060
	arc, inches, s:		0	-6.1	-20.8	
7.7x58 Japanese Arisaka						
Norma 174 Soft Point	velocity, fps:	2493	2173	1878	1611	
	energy, ft-lb:	2402	1825	1363	1003	
	arc, inches:		+2.0	0	-9.5	
Norma 180 Soft Point	velocity, fps:	2493	2291	2099	1916	
	energy, ft-lb:	2485	2099	1761	1468	
	arc, inches:		+2.6	0	-10.5	
.32-20 Winchester						
Rem. 100 Lead	velocity, fps:	1210	1021	913	834	769
	energy, ft-lb:	325	231	185	154	131
	arc, inches:		0	-31.6	-104.7	
Win. 100 Lead	velocity, fps:	1210	1021	913	834	769
	energy, ft-lb:	325	231	185	154	131
	arc, inches:		0	-32.3	-106.3	
.32 Winchester Special						
Hornady 165 FTX	velocity, fps	2410	2145	1897	1669	
	energy, ft-lbs	2128	1685	1318	1020	
	arc, inches	-1.5	+3.0	0	-12.8	
Federal 170 Hi-Shok	velocity, fps:	2250	1920	1630	1370	1180
	energy, ft-lb:	1910	1395	1000	710	520
	arc, inches:		0	-8.0	-29.2	
Rem. 170 SP Core-Lokt	velocity, fps:	2250	1921	1626	1372	1175
	energy, ft-lb:	1911	1393	998	710	521
	arc, inches:		0	-8.0	-29.3	
Win. 170 Power-Point	velocity, fps:	2250	1870	1537	1267	1082
	energy, ft-lb:	1911	1320	892	606	442
	arc, inches:		0	-9.2	-33.2	
8mm Mauser (8x57)						
Federal 170 Hi-Shok	velocity, fps:	2360	1970	1620	1330	1120
	energy, ft-lb:	2100	1465	995	670	475
	arc, inches:		0	-7.6	-28.5	
Hornady 195 SP	velocity, fps:	2550	2343	2146	1959	1782
	energy, ft-lb:	2815	2377	1994	1861	1375
	arc, inches:		+2.3	0	-9.9	-28.8
Hornady 195 SP (2005)	velocity, fps:	2475	2269	2074	1888	1714
	energy, ft-lb:	2652	2230	1861	1543	1271
	arc, inches:		+2.6	0	-10.7	-31.3
Norma 123 FMJ	velocity, fps:	2559	2121	1729	1398	
	energy, ft-lb:	1789	1228	817	534	
	arc, inches:		+3.2	0	-15.0	
Norma 196 Oryx	velocity, fps:	2395	2146	1912	1695	
	energy, ft-lb:	2497	2004	1591	1251	
	arc, inches:		+3	0	-12.6	
Norma 196 Vulkan	velocity, fps:	2395	2156	1930	1720	
	energy, ft-lb:	2497	2023	1622	1289	
	arc, inches:		3.0	0	-12.3	
Norma 196 Alaska	velocity, fps:	2395	2112	1850	1611	
	energy, ft-lb:	2714	2190	1754	1399	
	arc, inches:		0	-6.3	-22.9	
Norma 196 Soft Point (JS)	velocity, fps:	2526	2244	1981	1737	
	energy, ft-lb:	2778	2192	1708	1314	
	arc, inches:		+2.7	0	-11.6	
Norma 196 Alaska (JS)	velocity, fps:	2526	2248	1988	1747	
	energy, ft-lb:	2778	2200	1720	1328	
	arc, inches:		+2.7	0	-11.5	
Norma 196 Vulkan (JS)	velocity, fps:	2526	2276	2041	1821	
	energy, ft-lb:	2778	2256	1813	1443	
	arc, inches:		+2.6	0	-11.0	
Norma 196 Oryx (JS)	velocity, fps:	2526	2269	2027	1802	
	energy, ft-lb:	2778	2241	1789	1413	
	arc, inches:		+2.6	0	-11.1	
PMC 170 Pointed Soft Point	velocity, fps:	2360	1969	1622	1333	1123
	energy, ft-lb:	2102	1463	993	671	476
	arc, inches:		+1.8	-4.5	-24.3	-63.8
Rem. 170 SP Core-Lokt	velocity, fps:	2360	1969	1622	1333	1123
	energy, ft-lb:	2102	1463	993	671	476
	arc, inches:		+1.8	-4.5	-24.3	-63.8
Win. 170 Power-Point	velocity, fps:	2360	1969	1622	1333	1123
	energy, ft-lb:	2102	1463	993	671	476
	arc, inches:		+1.8	-4.5	-24.3	-63.8
.325 WSM						
Win. 180 Ballistic ST	velocity, fps:	3060	2841	2632	2432	2242
	energy, ft-lb:	3743	3226	2769	2365	2009

Ballistics Tables for Modern Sporting Rifles

.325 WSM to .338 Winchester Magnum

Cartridge Bullet	Range, yards:	0	100	200	300	400
	arc, inches:		+1.4	0	-6.4	-18.7
Win. 200 AccuBond CT	velocity, fps:	2950	2753	2565	2384	2210
	energy, ft-lb:	3866	3367	2922	2524	2170
	arc, inches:		+1.5	0	-6.8	-19.8
Win. 220 Power-Point	velocity, fps:	2840	2605	2382	2169	1968
	energy, ft-lb:	3941	3316	2772	2300	1893
	arc, inches:		+1.8	0	-8.0	-23.3

8mm Remington Magnum

Cartridge Bullet	Range, yards:	0	100	200	300	400
A-Square 220 Monolythic Solid	velocity, fps:	2800	2501	2221	1959	1718
	energy, ft-lb:	3829	3055	2409	1875	1442
	arc, inches:		+2.1	0	-9.1	-27.6
Rem. 200 Swift A-Frame	velocity, fps:	2900	2623	2361	2115	1885
	energy, ft-lb:	3734	3054	2476	1987	1577
	arc, inches:		+1.8	0	-8.0	-23.9

.338 Federal

Cartridge Bullet	Range, yards:	0	100	200	300	400
Federal 180 AccuBond	velocity, fps	2830	2590	2350	2130	1930
	energy, ft-lbs	3200	2670	2215	1820	1480
	arc, inches	-1.5	+1.8	0	-8.2	-23.9
Federal 185 Barnes TSX	velocity, fps	2750	2500	2260	2030	1820
	energy, ft-lbs	3105	2560	2090	1695	1355
	arc, inches	-1.5	+2.0	0	-8.9	-26.2
Federal 200 Tr. Bonded T	velocity, fps	2630	2430	2240	2060	1890
	energy, ft-lbs	3070	2625	2230	1885	1580
	arc, inches	-1.5	+2.2	0	-9.2	-26.3
Federal 210 Partition	velocity, fps	2630	2410	2200	2010	1820
	energy, ft-lbs	3225	2710	2265	1880	1545
	arc, inches	-1.5	+2.3	0	-9.4	-27.3

.338 Marlin Express

Cartridge Bullet	Range, yards:	0	100	200	300	400
Hornady 200 FTX	velocity, fps	2565	2365	2174	1992	1820
	energy, ft-lbs	2922	2484	2099	1762	1471
	arc, inches	-1.5	+3.0	+1.2	-7.9	-25.9

.338-06

Cartridge Bullet	Range, yards:	0	100	200	300	400
A-Square 200 Nos. Bal. Tip	velocity, fps:	2750	2553	2364	2184	2011
	energy, ft-lb:	3358	2894	2482	2118	1796
	arc, inches:		+1.9	0	-8.2	-23.6
A-Square 250 SP boat-tail	velocity, fps:	2500	2374	2252	2134	2019
	energy, ft-lb:	3496	3129	2816	2528	2263
	arc, inches:		+2.4	0	-9.3	-26.0
A-Square 250 Dead Tough	velocity, fps:	2500	2222	1963	1724	1507
	energy, ft-lb:	3496	2742	2139	1649	1261
	arc, inches:		+2.8	0	-11.9	-35.5
Wby. 210 Nosler Part.	velocity, fps:	2750	2526	2312	2109	1916
	energy, ft-lb:	3527	2975	2403	2074	1712
	arc, inches:		+4.8	+5.7	0	-13.5

.338 Ruger Compact Magnum

Cartridge Bullet	Range, yards:	0	100	200	300	400
Hornady 185 GMX	velocity, fps	2980	2755	2542	2338	2143
	energy, ft-lbs	3647	3118	2653	2242	1887
	arc, inches	-1.5	+1.5	0	-6.9	-20.3
Hornady 200 SST	velocity, fps	2950	2744	2547	2358	2177
	energy, ft-lbs	3846	3342	2879	2468	2104
	arc, inches	-1.5	+1.6	0	-6.9	-20.1
Hornady 225 SST	velocity, fps	2750	2575	2407	2245	2089
	energy, ft-lbs	3778	3313	2894	2518	2180
	arc, inches	-1.5	+1.9	0	-7.9	-22.7

.338 Winchester Magnum

Cartridge Bullet	Range, yards:	0	100	200	300	400
A-Square 250 SP boat-tail	velocity, fps:	2700	2568	2439	2314	2193
	energy, ft-lb:	4046	3659	3302	2972	2669
	arc, inches:		+4.4	+5.2	0	-11.7
A-Square 250 Triad	velocity, fps:	2700	2407	2133	1877	1653
	energy, ft-lb:	4046	3216	2526	1956	1516
	arc, inches:		+2.3	0	-9.8	-29.8
Federal 210 Nosler Partition	velocity, fps:	2830	2600	2390	2180	1980
	energy, ft-lb:	3735	3160	2655	2215	1835
	arc, inches:		+1.8	0	-8.0	-23.3
Federal 225 Sierra Pro-Hunt.	velocity, fps:	2780	2570	2360	2170	1980
	energy, ft-lb:	3860	3290	2780	2340	1960
	arc, inches:		+1.9	0	-8.2	-23.7
Federal 225 Trophy Bonded	velocity, fps:	2800	2560	2330	2110	1900
	energy, ft-lb:	3915	3265	2700	2220	1800
	arc, inches:		+1.9	0	-8.4	-24.5
Federal 225 Tr. Bonded HE	velocity, fps:	2940	2690	2450	2230	2010
	energy, ft-lb:	4320	3610	3000	2475	2025
	arc, inches:		+1.7	0	-7.5	-22.0
Federal 225 Barnes XLC	velocity, fps:	2800	2610	2430	2260	2090
	energy, ft-lb:	3915	3405	2950	2545	2190
	arc, inches:		+1.8	0	-7.7	-22.2
Federal 250 Nosler Partition	velocity, fps:	2660	2470	2300	2120	1960
	energy, ft-lb:	3925	3395	2925	2505	2130.
	arc, inches:		+2.1	0	-8.8	-25.1
Federal 250 Nosler Part HE	velocity, fps:	2800	2610	2420	2250	2080
	energy, ft-lb:	4350	3775	3260	2805	2395
	arc, inches:		+1.8	0	-7.8	-22.5
Hornady 225 Soft Point HM	velocity, fps:	2920	2678	2449	2232	2027
	energy, ft-lb:	4259	3583	2996	2489	2053
	arc, inches:		+1.8	0	-7.6	-22.0
Norma 225 TXP Swift A-Fr.	velocity, fps:	2740	2507	2286	2075	
	energy, ft-lb:	3752	3141	2611	2153	
	arc, inches:		+2.0	0	-8.7	
Norma 230 Oryx	velocity, fps:	2756	2514	2284	2066	
	energy, ft-lb:	3880	3228	2665	2181	
	arc, inches:		+2.0	0	-8.7	
Norma 250 Nosler Partition	velocity, fps:	2657	2470	2290	2118	
	energy, ft-lb:	3920	3387	2912	2490	
	arc, inches:		+2.1	0	-8.7	
PMC 225 Barnes X	velocity, fps:	2780	2619	2464	2313	2168
	energy, ft-lb:	3860	3426	3032	2673	2348.
	arc, inches:		+1.8	0	-7.6	-21.6
Rem. 200 Nosler Bal. Tip	velocity, fps:	2950	2724	2509	2303	2108
	energy, ft-lb:	3866	3295	2795	2357	1973
	arc, inches:		+1.6	0	-7.1	-20.8
Rem. 210 Nosler Partition	velocity, fps:	2830	2602	2385	2179	1983
	energy, ft-lb:	3734	3157	2653	2214	1834
	arc, inches:		+1.8	0	-7.9	-23.2
Rem. 225 PSP Core-Lokt	velocity, fps:	2780	2572	2374	2184	2003
	energy, ft-lb:	3860	3305	2815	2383	2004
	arc, inches:		+1.9	0	-8.1	-23.4
Rem. 225 PSP C-L Ultra	velocity, fps:	2780	2582	2392	2210	2036
	energy, ft-lb:	3860	3329	2858	2440	2071
	arc, inches:		+1.9	0	-7.9	-23.0
Rem. 225 Swift A-Frame	velocity, fps:	2785	2517	2266	2029	1808
	energy, ft-lb:	3871	3165	2565	2057	1633
	arc, inches:		+2.0	0	-8.8	-25.2
Rem. 250 PSP Core-Lokt	velocity, fps:	2660	2456	2261	2075	1898
	energy, ft-lb:	3927	3348	2837	2389	1999
	arc, inches:		+2.1	0	-8.9	-26.0
Speer 250 Grand Slam	velocity, fps:	2645	2442	2247	2062	
	energy, ft-lb:	3883	3309	2803	2360	
	arc, inches:		+2.2	0	-9.1	-26.2
Win. 200 Power-Point	velocity, fps:	2960	2658	2375	2110	1862
	energy, ft-lb:	3890	3137	2505	1977	1539

BALLISTICS

Ballistics Tables for Modern Sporting Rifles

.338 WINCHESTER MAGNUM TO .338 EXCALIBER

CARTRIDGE BULLET	RANGE, YARDS:	0	100	200	300	400
	arc, inches:		+2.0	0	-8.2	-24.3
Win. 200 Ballistic Silvertip	velocity, fps:	2950	2724	2509	2303	2108
	energy, ft-lb:	3864	3294	2794	2355	1972
	arc, inches:		+1.6	0	-7.1	-20.8
Win. 225 AccuBond	velocity, fps:	2800	2634	2474	2319	2170
	energy, ft-lb:	3918	3467	3058	2688	2353
	arc, inches:		+1.8	0	-7.4	-21.3
Win. 230 Fail Safe	velocity, fps:	2780	2573	2375	2186	2005
	energy, ft-lb:	3948	3382	2881	2441	2054
	arc, inches:		+1.9	0	-8.1	-23.4
Win. 250 Partition Gold	velocity, fps:	2650	2467	2291	2122	1960
	energy, ft-lb:	3899	3378	2914	2520	2134
	arc, inches:		+2.1	0	-8.7	-25.2

.340 Weatherby Magnum

CARTRIDGE BULLET	RANGE, YARDS:	0	100	200	300	400
A-Square 250 SP boat-tail	velocity, fps:	2820	2684	2552	2424	2299
	energy, ft-lb:	4414	3999	3615	3261	2935
	arc, inches:		+4.0	+4.6	0	-10.6
A-Square 250 Triad	velocity, fps:	2820	2520	2238	1976	1741
	energy, ft-lb:	4414	3524	2781	2166	1683
	arc, inches:		+2.0	0	-9.0	-26.8
Federal 225 Trophy Bonded	velocity, fps:	3100	2840	2600	2370	2150
	energy, ft-lb:	4800	4035	3375	2800	2310
	arc, inches:		+1.4	0	-6.5	-19.4
Wby. 200 Pointed Expanding	velocity, fps:	3221	2946	2688	2444	2213
	energy, ft-lb:	4607	3854	3208	2652	2174
	arc, inches:		+3.3	+4.0	0	-9.9
Wby. 200 Nosler Bal. Tip	velocity, fps:	3221	2980	2753	2536	2329
	energy, ft-lb:	4607	3944	3364	2856	2409
	arc, inches:		+3.1	+3.9	0	-9.2
Wby. 210 Nosler Partition	velocity, fps:	3211	2963	2728	2505	2293
	energy, ft-lb:	4807	4093	3470	2927	2452
	arc, inches:		+3.2	+3.9	0	-9.5
Wby. 225 Pointed Expanding	velocity, fps:	3066	2824	2595	2377	2170
	energy, ft-lb:	4696	3984	3364	2822	2352
	arc, inches:		+3.6	+4.4	0	-10.7
Wby. 225 Barnes X	velocity, fps:	3001	2804	2615	2434	2260
	energy, ft-lb:	4499	3927	3416	2959	2551
	arc, inches:		+3.6	+4.3	0	-10.3
Wby. 250 Pointed Expanding	velocity, fps:	2963	2745	2537	2338	2149
	energy, ft-lb:	4873	4182	3572	3035	2563
	arc, inches:		+3.9	+4.6	0	-11.1
Wby. 250 Nosler Partition	velocity, fps:	2941	2743	2553	2371	2197
	energy, ft-lb:	4801	4176	3618	3120	2678
	arc, inches:		+3.9	+4.6	0	-10.9

.330 Dakota

CARTRIDGE BULLET	RANGE, YARDS:	0	100	200	300	400
Dakota 200 Barnes X	velocity, fps:	3200	2971	2754	2548	2350
	energy, ft-lb:	4547	3920	3369	2882	2452
	arc, inches:		+2.1	+1.8	-3.1	-13.4
Dakota 250 Barnes X	velocity, fps:	2900	2719	2545	2378	2217
	energy, ft-lb:	4668	4103	3595	3138	2727
	arc, inches:		+2.3	+1.3	-5.0	-17.5

Lazzeroni 8.59 Galaxy

CARTRIDGE BULLET	RANGE, YARDS:	0	100	200	300	400
185 Barnes TTSX	velocity, fps	3201	3002	2811	2629	2454
	energy, ft-lbs	4210	3703	3248	2840	2474
	arc, inches	-1.5	1.2	0	-5.9	-16.8
225 Nosler BallisticTip	velocity, fps	2968	2786	2611	2443	2281
	energy, ft-lbs	4402	3879	3407	2983	2600
	arc, inches	-1.5	1.4	0	-6.7	-19.6
250 Nosler AccuBond	velocity, fps	2761	2594	2433	2277	2128
	energy, ft-lbs	4232	3736	3287	2881	2515
	arc, inches	-1.5	1.6	0	-7.4	-21.8

.338 Remington Ultra Magnum

CARTRIDGE BULLET	RANGE, YARDS:	0	100	200	300	400
Federal 210 Nosler Partition	velocity, fps:	3025	2800	2585	2385	2190
	energy, ft-lb:	4270	3655	3120	2645	2230
	arc, inches:		+1.5	0	-6.7	-19.5
Federal 250 Trophy Bonded	velocity, fps:	2860	2630	2420	2210	2020
	energy, ft-lb:	4540	3850	3245	2715	2260.
	arc, inches:		+0.8	0	-7.7	-22.6
Rem. 250 Swift A-Frame	velocity, fps:	2860	2645	2440	2244	2057
	energy, ft-lb:	4540	3882	3303	2794	2347
	arc, inches:		+1.7	0	-7.6	-22.1
Rem. 250 PSP Core-Lokt	velocity, fps:	2860	2647	2443	2249	2064
	energy, ft-lb:	4540	3888	3314	2807	2363
	arc, inches:		+1.7	0	-7.6	-22.0

.338 Lapua

CARTRIDGE BULLET	RANGE, YARDS:	0	100	200	300	400
Black Hills, 250-grain BTHP	velocity, fps	2950	2800	2660	2530	2410
	energy, ft-lbs	4840	4352	3958	3564	3290
	arc, inches	-1.5	+3	+4	0	-9
Black Hills, 300-grain BTHP	velocity, fps	2800	2670	2542	2418	2310
	energy, ft-lbs	5010	4765	4300	3890	3556
	arc, inches	-1.5	+4	+5	0	10
Black Hills 250 Sierra MKing	velocity, fps:	2950				
	energy, ft-lb:	4831				
	arc, inches:					
Lapua 250 Scenar	velocity, fps	2970	2823	2680	2539	2141
	energy, ft-lbs	4896	4424	3985	3579	2545
	arc, inches	-1.5	+3.0	+4.0	0	-47.0
Black Hills 300 Sierra MKing	velocity, fps:	2800				
	energy, ft-lb:	5223				
	arc, inches:					
Lapua 300 Scenar	velocity, fps	2723	2600	2482	2367	2042
	energy, ft-lbs	4938	4504	4102	3731	2778
	arc, inches	-1.5	+4.0	+5.0	0	-54.0

.338-378 Weatherby Magnum

CARTRIDGE BULLET	RANGE, YARDS:	0	100	200	300	400
Wby. 200 Nosler Bal. Tip	velocity, fps:	3350	3102	2868	2646	2434
	energy, ft-lb:	4983	4273	3652	3109	2631
	arc, inches:	0	+2.8	+3.5	0	-8.4
Wby. 225 Barnes X	velocity, fps:	3180	2974	2778	2591	2410.
	energy, ft-lb:	5052	4420	3856	3353	2902
	arc, inches:	0	+3.1	+3.8	0	-8.9
Wby. 250 Nosler Partition	velocity, fps:	3060	2856	2662	2475	2297
	energy, ft-lb:	5197	4528	3933	3401	2927
	arc, inches:	0	+3.5	+4.2	0	-9.8

8.59 (.338) Titan

CARTRIDGE BULLET	RANGE, YARDS:	0	100	200	300	400
Lazzeroni 200 Nos. Bal. Tip	velocity, fps:	3430	3211	3002	2803	2613
	energy, ft-lb:	5226	4579	4004	3491	3033
	arc, inches:		+2.5	+3.2	0	-7.6
Lazzeroni 225 Nos. Partition	velocity, fps:	3235	3031	2836	2650	2471
	energy, ft-lb:	5229	4591	4021	3510	3052
	arc, inches:		+3.0	+3.6	0	-8.6
Lazzeroni 250 Swift A-Fr.	velocity, fps:	3100	2908	2725	2549	2379
	energy, ft-lb:	5336	4697	4123	3607	3143
	arc, inches:		+3.3	+4.0	0	-9.3

.338 A-Square

CARTRIDGE BULLET	RANGE, YARDS:	0	100	200	300	400
A-Square 200 Nos. Bal. Tip	velocity, fps:	3500	3266	3045	2835	2634
	energy, ft-lb:	5440	4737	4117	3568	3081
	arc, inches:		+2.4	+3.1	0	-7.5
A-Square 250 SP boat-tail	velocity, fps:	3120	2974	2834	2697	2565.
	energy, ft-lb:	5403	4911	4457	4038	3652
	arc, inches:		+3.1	+3.7	0	-8.5
A-Square 250 Triad	velocity, fps:	3120	2799	2500	2220	1958
	energy, ft-lb:	5403	4348	3469	2736	2128
	arc, inches:		+1.5	0	-7.1	-20.4.

Ballistics Tables for Modern Sporting Rifles

.338 EXCALIBER TO 9.3X74 R

.338 Excaliber

CARTRIDGE BULLET	RANGE, YARDS:	0	100	200	300	400
A-Square 200 Nos. Bal. Tip	velocity, fps:	3600	3361	3134	2920	2715
	energy, ft-lb:	5755	5015	4363	3785	3274
	arc, inches:		+2.2	+2.9	0	-6.7
A-Square 250 SP boat-tail	velocity, fps:	3250	3101	2958	2684	2553
	energy, ft-lb:	5863	5339	4855	4410	3998
	arc, inches:		+2.7	+3.4	0	-7.8
A-Square 250 Triad	velocity, fps:	3250	2922	2618	2333	2066
	energy, ft-lb:	5863	4740	3804	3021	2370
	arc, inches:		+1.3	0	-6.4	-19.2

.348 Winchester

CARTRIDGE BULLET	RANGE, YARDS:	0	100	200	300	400
Win. 200 Silvertip	velocity, fps:	2520	2215	1931	1672	1443.
	energy, ft-lb:	2820	2178	1656	1241	925
	arc, inches:		0	-6.2	-21.9	

.357 Magnum

CARTRIDGE BULLET	RANGE, YARDS:	0	100	200	300	400
Federal 180 Hi-Shok HP Hollow Point	velocity, fps:	1550	1160	980	860	770
	energy, ft-lb:	960	535	385	295	235
	arc, inches:		0	-22.8	-77.9	-173.8
Win. 158 Jacketed SP	velocity, fps:	1830	1427	1138	980	883
	energy, ft-lb:	1175	715	454	337	274
	arc, inches:		0	-16.2	-57.0	-128.3

.35 Remington

CARTRIDGE BULLET	RANGE, YARDS:	0	100	200	300	400
Federal 200 Hi-Shok	velocity, fps:	2080	1700	1380	1140	1000
	energy, ft-lb:	1920	1280	840	575	445
	arc, inches:		0	-10.7	-39.3	
Hornady 200 Evolution	velocity, fps:	2225	1963	1721	1503	
	energy, ft-lb:	2198	1711	1315	1003	
	arc, inches:		+3.0	-1.3	-17.5	
Rem. 150 PSP Core-Lokt	velocity, fps:	2300	1874	1506	1218	1039
	energy, ft-lb:	1762	1169	755	494	359
	arc, inches:		0	-8.6	-32.6	
Rem. 200 SP Core-Lokt	velocity, fps:	2080	1698	1376	1140	1001
	energy, ft-lb:	1921	1280	841	577	445
	arc, inches:		0	-10.7	-40.1	
Win. 200 Power-Point	velocity, fps:	2020	1646	1335	1114	985
	energy, ft-lb:	1812	1203	791	551	431
	arc, inches:		0	-12.1	-43.9	

.356 Winchester

CARTRIDGE BULLET	RANGE, YARDS:	0	100	200	300	400
Win. 200 Power-Point	velocity, fps:	2460	2114	1797	1517	1284
	energy, ft-lb:	2688	1985	1434	1022	732
	arc, inches:		+1.6	-3.8	-20.1	-51.2

.358 Winchester

CARTRIDGE BULLET	RANGE, YARDS:	0	100	200	300	400
Win. 200 Silvertip	velocity, fps:	2490	2171	1876	1610	1379
	energy, ft-lb:	2753	2093	1563	1151	844
	arc, inches:		+1.5	-3.6	-18.6	-47.2

.35 Whelen

CARTRIDGE BULLET	RANGE, YARDS:	0	100	200	300	400
Federal 225 Trophy Bonded	velocity, fps:	2600	2400	2200	2020	1840
	energy, ft-lb:	3375	2865	2520	2030	1690.
	arc, inches:		+2.3	0	-9.4	-27.3
Rem. 200 Pointed Soft Point	velocity, fps:	2675	2378	2100	1842	1606
	energy, ft-lb:	3177	2510	1958	1506	1145
	arc, inches:		+2.3	0	-10.3	-30.8
Rem. 250 Pointed Soft Point	velocity, fps:	2400	2197	2005	1823	1652
	energy, ft-lb:	3197	2680	2230	1844	1515
	arc, inches:		+1.3	-3.2	-16.6	-40.0

.358 Norma Magnum

CARTRIDGE BULLET	RANGE, YARDS:	0	100	200	300	400
A-Square 275 Triad	velocity, fps:	2700	2394	2108	1842	1653
	energy, ft-lb:	4451	3498	2713	2072	1668
	arc, inches:		+2.3	0	-10.1	-29.8
Norma 250 TXP Swift A-Fr.	velocity, fps:	2723	2467	2225	1996	
	energy, ft-lb:	4117	3379	2748	2213	
	arc, inches:		+2.1	0	-9.1	
Norma 250 Woodleigh	velocity, fps:	2799	2442	2112	1810	
	energy, ft-lb:	4350	3312	2478	1819	
	arc, inches:		+2.2	0	-10.0	
Norma 250 Oryx	velocity, fps:	2756	2493	2245	2011	
	energy, ft-lb:	4217	3451	2798	2245	
	arc, inches:		+2.1	0	-9.0	

.358 STA

CARTRIDGE BULLET	RANGE, YARDS:	0	100	200	300	400
A-Square 275 Triad	velocity, fps:	2850	2562	2292	2039	1764
	energy, ft-lb:	4959	4009	3208	2539	1899.
	arc, inches:		+1.9	0	-8.6	-26.1

9.3x57

CARTRIDGE BULLET	RANGE, YARDS:	0	100	200	300	400
Norma 232 Vulkan	velocity, fps:	2329	2031	1757	1512	
	energy, ft-lb:	2795	2126	1591	1178	
	arc, inches:		+3.5	0	-14.9	
Norma 232 Oryx	velocity, fps:	2362	2058	1778	1528	
	energy, ft-lb:	2875	2182	1630	1203	
	arc, inches:		+3.4	0	-14.5	
Norma 285 Oryx	velocity, fps:	2067	1859	1666	1490	
	energy, ft-lb:	2704	2188	1756	1404	
	arc, inches:		+4.3	0	-16.8	
Norma 286 Alaska	velocity, fps:	2067	1857	1662	1484	
	energy, ft-lb:	2714	2190	1754	1399	
	arc, inches:		+4.3	0	-17.0	

9.3x62

CARTRIDGE BULLET	RANGE, YARDS:	0	100	200	300	400
A-Square 286 Triad	velocity, fps:	2360	2089	1844	1623	1369
	energy, ft-lb:	3538	2771	2157	1670	1189
	arc, inches:		+3.0	0	-13.1	-42.2
Norma 232 Vulkan	velocity, fps:	2625	2327	2049	1792	
	energy, ft-lb:	3551	2791	2164	1655	
	arc, inches:		+2.5	0	-10.8	
Norma 232 Oryx	velocity, fps:	2625	2294	1988	1708	
	energy, ft-lb:	3535	2700	2028	1497	
	arc, inches:		+2.5	0	-11.4	
Norma 250 A-Frame	velocity, fps:	2625	2322	2039	1778	
	energy, ft-lb:	3826	2993	2309	1755	
	arc, inches:		+2.5	0	-10.9	
Norma 286 Plastic Point	velocity, fps:	2362	2141	1931	1736	
	energy, ft-lb:	3544	2911	2370	1914	
	arc, inches:		+3.1	0	-12.4	
Norma 286 Alaska	velocity, fps:	2362	2135	1920	1720	
	energy, ft-lb:	3544	2894	2342	1879	
	arc, inches:		+3.1	0	-12.5	

9.3x64

CARTRIDGE BULLET	RANGE, YARDS:	0	100	200	300	400
A-Square 286 Triad	velocity, fps:	2700	2391	2103	1835	1602
	energy, ft-lb:	4629	3630	2808	2139	1631
	arc, inches:		+2.3	0	-10.1	-30.8

9.3x74 R

CARTRIDGE BULLET	RANGE, YARDS:	0	100	200	300	400
A-Square 286 Triad	velocity, fps:	2360	2089	1844	1623	
	energy, ft-lb:	3538	2771	2157	1670	
	arc, inches:		+3.6	0	-14.0	
Hornady 286	velocity, fps	2360	2136	1924	1727	1545
	energy, ft-lb	3536	2896	2351	1893	1516
	arc, inches	-1.5	0	-6.1	-21.7	-49.0
Norma 232 Vulkan	velocity, fps:	2625	2327	2049	1792	
	energy, ft-lb:	3551	2791	2164	1655	
	arc, inches:		+2.5	0	-10.8	
Norma 232 Oryx	velocity, fps:	2526	2191	1883	1605	
	energy, ft-lb:	3274	2463	1819	1322	
	arc, inches:		+2.9	0	-12.8	

Ballistics Tables for Modern Sporting Rifles

9.3X74 R TO .375 REMINGTON ULTRA MAGNUM

CARTRIDGE BULLET	RANGE, YARDS:	0	100	200	300	400
Norma 285 Oryx	velocity, fps:	2362	2114	1881	1667	
	energy, ft-lb:	3532	2829	2241	1758	
	arc, inches:		+3.1	0	-13.0	
Norma 286 Alaska	velocity, fps:	2362	2135	1920	1720	
	energy, ft-lb:	3544	2894	2342	1879	
	arc, inches:		+3.1	0	-12.5	
Norma 286 Plastic Point	velocity, fps:	2362	2135	1920	1720	
	energy, ft-lb:	3544	2894	2342	1879	
	arc, inches:		+3.1	0	-12.5	

.375 Winchester

CARTRIDGE BULLET	RANGE, YARDS:	0	100	200	300	400
Win. 200 Power-Point	velocity, fps:	2200	1841	1526	1268	1089
	energy, ft-lb:	2150	1506	1034	714	
	arc, inches:		0	-9.5	-33.8	

.375 H&H Magnum

CARTRIDGE BULLET	RANGE, YARDS:	0	100	200	300	400
A-Square 300 SP boat-tail	velocity, fps:	2550	2415	2284	2157	2034
	energy, ft-lb:	4331	3884	3474	3098	2755
	arc, inches:		+5.2	+6.0	0	-13.3
A-Square 300 Triad	velocity, fps:	2550	2251	1973	1717	1496
	energy, ft-lb:	4331	3375	2592	1964	1491
	arc, inches:		+2.7	0	-11.7	-35.1
Federal 250 Trophy Bonded	velocity, fps:	2670	2360	2080	1820	1580
	energy, ft-lb:	3955	3100	2400	1830	1380
	arc, inches:		+2.4	0	-10.4	-31.7
Federal 270 Hi-Shok	velocity, fps:	2690	2420	2170	1920	1700
	energy, ft-lb:	4340	3510	2810	2220	1740
	arc, inches:		+2.4	0	-10.9	-33.3
Federal 300 Hi-Shok	velocity, fps:	2530	2270	2020	1790	1580
	energy, ft-lb:	4265	3425	2720	2135	1665
	arc, inches:		+2.6	0	-11.2	-33.3
Federal 300 Nosler Partition	velocity, fps:	2530	2320	2120	1930	1750
	energy, ft-lb:	4265	3585	2995	2475	2040
	arc, inches:		+2.5	0	-10.3	-29.9
Federal 300 Trophy Bonded	velocity, fps:	2530	2280	2040	1810	1610
	energy, ft-lb:	4265	3450	2765	2190	1725
	arc, inches:		+2.6	0	-10.9	-32.8
Federal 300 Tr. Bonded HE	velocity, fps:	2700	2440	2190	1960	1740
	energy, ft-lb:	4855	3960	3195	2550	2020
	arc, inches:		+2.2	0	-9.4	-28.0
Federal 300 Trophy Bonded Sledgehammer Solid	velocity, fps:	2530	2160	1820	1520	1280.
	energy, ft-lb:	4265	3105	2210	1550	1090
	arc, inches, s:		0	-6.0	-22.7	-54.6
Hornady 270 SP HM	velocity, fps:	2870	2620	2385	2162	1957
	energy, ft-lb:	4937	4116	3408	2802	2296
	arc, inches:		+2.2	0	-8.4	-23.9
Hornady 300 FMJ RN HM	velocity, fps:	2705	2376	2072	1804	1560
	energy, ft-lb:	4873	3760	2861	2167	1621
	arc, inches:		+2.7	0	-10.8	-32.1
Norma 300 Soft Point	velocity, fps:	2549	2211	1900	1619	
	energy, ft-lb:	4329	3258	2406	1747	
	arc, inches:		+2.8	0	-12.6	
Norma 300 TXP Swift A-Fr.	velocity, fps:	2559	2296	2049	1818	
	energy, ft-lb:	4363	3513	2798	2203	
	arc, inches:		+2.6	0	-10.9	
Norma 300 Oryx	velocity, fps:	2559	2292	2041	1807	
	energy, ft-lb:	4363	3500	2775	2176	
	arc, inches:		+2.6	0	-11.0	
Norma 300 Barnes Solid	velocity, fps:	2493	2061	1677	1356	
	energy, ft-lb:	4141	2829	1873	1234	
	arc, inches:		+3.4	0	-16.0	
PMC 270 PSP	velocity, fps:					
	energy, ft-lb:					
	arc, inches:					
PMC 270 Barnes X	velocity, fps:	2690	2528	2372	2221	2076
	energy, ft-lb:	4337	3831	3371	2957	2582
	arc, inches:		+2.0	0	-8.2	-23.4
PMC 300 Barnes X	velocity, fps:	2530	2389	2252	2120	1993
	energy, ft-lb:	4263	3801	3378	2994	2644
	arc, inches:		+2.3	0	-9.2	-26.1
Rem. 270 Soft Point	velocity, fps:	2690	2420	2166	1928	1707
	energy, ft-lb:	4337	3510	2812	2228	1747
	arc, inches:		+2.2	0	-9.7	-28.7
Rem. 300 Swift A-Frame	velocity, fps:	2530	2245	1979	1733	1512
	energy, ft-lb:	4262	3357	2608	2001	1523
	arc, inches:		+2.7	0	-11.7	-35.0
Speer 285 Grand Slam	velocity, fps:	2610	2365	2134	1916	
	energy, ft-lb:	4310	3540	2883	2323	
	arc, inches:		+2.4	0	-9.9	
Speer 300 African GS Tungsten Solid	velocity, fps:	2609	2277	1970	1690	
	energy, ft-lb:	4534	3453	2585	1903	
	arc, inches:		+2.6	0	-11.7	-35.6
Win. 270 Fail Safe	velocity, fps:	2670	2447	2234	2033	1842
	energy, ft-lb:	4275	3590	2994	2478	2035
	arc, inches:		+2.2	0	-9.1	-28.7
Win. 300 Fail Safe	velocity, fps:	2530	2336	2151	1974	1806
	energy, ft-lb:	4265	3636	3082	2596	2173
	arc, inches:		+2.4	0	-10.0	-26.9

.375 Dakota

CARTRIDGE BULLET	RANGE, YARDS:	0	100	200	300	400
Dakota 270 Barnes X	velocity, fps:	2800	2617	2441	2272	2109
	energy, ft-lb:	4699	4104	3571	3093	2666
	arc, inches:		+2.3	+1.0	-6.1	-19.9
Dakota 300 Barnes X	velocity, fps:	2600	2316	2051	1804	1579
	energy, ft-lb:	4502	3573	2800	2167	1661
	arc, inches:		+2.4	-0.1	-11.0	-32.7

.375 Ruger

CARTRIDGE BULLET	RANGE, YARDS:	0	100	200	300	400
Hornady 270 SP	velocity, fps	2840	2600	2372	2156	1951
	energy, ft-lbs	4835	4052	3373	2786	2283
	arc, inches	-1.5	+1.8	0	-8.0	-23.6
Hornady 300 Solid	velocity, fps	2660	2344	2050	1780	1536
	energy, ft-lb	4713	3660	2800	2110	1572
	arc, inches	-1.5	+2.4	0	-10.8	-32.6

.375 Weatherby Magnum

CARTRIDGE BULLET	RANGE, YARDS:	0	100	200	300	400
A-Square 300 SP boat-tail	velocity, fps:	2700	2560	2425	2293	2166
	energy, ft-lb:	4856	4366	3916	3503	3125
	arc, inches:		+4.5	+5.2	0	-11.9
A-Square 300 Triad	velocity, fps:	2700	2391	2103	1835	1602
	energy, ft-lb:	4856	3808	2946	2243	1710
	arc, inches:		+2.3	0	-10.1	-30.8
Wby. 300 Nosler Part.	velocity, fps:	2800	2572	2366	2140	1963
	energy, ft-lb:	5224	4408	3696	3076	2541
	arc, inches:		+1.9	0	-8.2	-23.9

.375 JRS

CARTRIDGE BULLET	RANGE, YARDS:	0	100	200	300	400
A-Square 300 SP boat-tail	velocity, fps:	2700	2560	2425	2293	2166.
	energy, ft-lb:	4856	4366	3916	3503	3125
	arc, inches:		+4.5	+5.2	0	-11.9
A-Square 300 Triad	velocity, fps:	2700	2391	2103	1835	1602
	energy, ft-lb:	4856	3808	2946	2243	1710
	arc, inches:		+2.3	0	-10.1	-30.8

.375 Remington Ultra Magnum

CARTRIDGE BULLET	RANGE, YARDS:	0	100	200	300	400
Rem. 270 Soft Point	velocity, fps:	2900	2558	2241	1947	1678
	energy, fps:	5041	3922	3010	2272	1689
	arc, inches:		+1.9	0	-9.2	-27.8

Ballistics Tables for Modern Sporting Rifles

CARTRIDGE BULLET	RANGE, YARDS:	0	100	200	300	400
Rem. 300 Swift A-Frame	velocity, fps:	2760	2505	2263	2035	1822
	energy, fps:	5073	4178	3412	2759	2210
	arc, inches:		+2.0	0	-8.8	-26.1

.375 A-Square

CARTRIDGE BULLET	RANGE, YARDS:	0	100	200	300	400
A-Square 300 SP boat-tail	velocity, fps:	2920	2773	2631	2494	2360
	energy, ft-lb:	5679	5123	4611	4142	3710
	arc, inches:		+3.7	+4.4	0	-9.8
A-Square 300 Triad	velocity, fps:	2920	2596	2294	2012	1762
	energy, ft-lb:	5679	4488	3505	2698	2068
	arc, inches:		+1.8	0	-8.5	-25.5

.376 Steyr

CARTRIDGE BULLET	RANGE, YARDS:	0	100	200	300	400
Hornady 225 SP	velocity, fps:	2600	2331	2078	1842	1625
	energy, ft-lb:	3377	2714	2157	1694	1319
	arc, inches:		+2.5	0	-10.6	-31.4
Hornady 270 SP	velocity, fps:	2600	2372	2156	1951	1759
	energy, ft-lb:	4052	3373	2787	2283	1855
	arc, inches:		+2.3	0	-9.9	-28.9

.378 Weatherby Magnum

CARTRIDGE BULLET	RANGE, YARDS:	0	100	200	300	400
A-Square 300 SP boat-tail	velocity, fps:	2900	2754	2612	2475	2342
	energy, ft-lb:	5602	5051	4546	4081	3655
	arc, inches:		+3.8	+4.4	0	-10.0
A-Square 300 Triad	velocity, fps:	2900	2577	2276	1997	1747
	energy, ft-lb:	5602	4424	3452	2656	2034
	arc, inches:		+1.9	0	-8.7	-25.9
Wby. 270 Pointed Expanding	velocity, fps:	3180	2921	2677	2445	2225
	energy, ft-lb:	6062	5115	4295	3583	2968
	arc, inches:		+1.3	0	-6.1	-18.1
Wby. 270 Barnes X	velocity, fps:	3150	2954	2767	2587	2415
	energy, ft-lb:	5948	5232	4589	4013	3495
	arc, inches:		+1.2	0	-5.8	-16.7
Wby. 300 RN Expanding	velocity, fps:	2925	2558	2220	1908	1627.
	energy, ft-lb:	5699	4360	3283	2424	1764
	arc, inches:		+1.9	0	-9.0	-27.8
Wby. 300 FMJ	velocity, fps:	2925	2591	2280	1991	1725
	energy, ft-lb:	5699	4470	3461	2640	1983
	arc, inches:		+1.8	0	-8.6	-26.1

.38-40 Winchester

CARTRIDGE BULLET	RANGE, YARDS:	0	100	200	300	400
Win. 180 Soft Point	velocity, fps:	1160	999	901	827	
	energy, ft-lb:	538	399	324	273	
	arc, inches:		0	-23.4	-75.2	

.38-55 Winchester

CARTRIDGE BULLET	RANGE, YARDS:	0	100	200	300	400
Black Hills 255 FN Lead	velocity, fps:	1250				
	energy, ft-lb:	925				
	arc, inches:					
Win. 255 Soft Point	velocity, fps:	1320	1190	1091	1018	
	energy, ft-lb:	987	802	674	587	
	arc, inches:		0	-33.9	-110.6	

.41 Magnum

CARTRIDGE BULLET	RANGE, YARDS:	0	100	200	300	400
Win. 240 Platinum Tip	velocity, fps:	1830	1488	1220	1048	
	energy, ft-lb:	1784	1180	792	585	
	arc inches:		0	-15.0	-53.4	

.450/.400 (3")

CARTRIDGE BULLET	RANGE, YARDS:	0	100	200	300	400
A-Square 400 Triad	velocity, fps:	2150	1910	1690	1490	
	energy, ft-lb:	4105	3241	2537	1972	
	arc, inches:		+4.4	0	-16.5	

.450/.400 (3 l/4")

CARTRIDGE BULLET	RANGE, YARDS:	0	100	200	300	400
A-Square 400 Triad	velocity, fps:	2150	1910	1690	1490	
	energy, ft-lb:	4105	3241	2537	1972	
	arc, inches:		+4.4	0	-16.5	

.450/.400 Nitro Express

CARTRIDGE BULLET	RANGE, YARDS:	0	100	200	300	400
Hornady 400 RN	velocity, fps	2050	1815	1595	1402	
	energy, ft-lb	3732	2924	2259	1746	
	arc, inches	-1.5	0	-10.0	-33.4	

.404 Jeffery

CARTRIDGE BULLET	RANGE, YARDS:	0	100	200	300	400
A-Square 400 Triad	velocity, fps:	2150	1901	1674	1468	1299
	energy, ft-lb:	4105	3211	2489	1915	1499
	arc, inches:		+4.1	0	-16.4	-49.1
Hornady 400 DGS, DGX	velocity, fps	2300	2046	1809	1592	
	energy, ft-lbs	4698	3717	2906	2251	
	arc, inches	-1.5	0	-6.9	-24.4	
Norma 450 Woodleigh SP	velocity, fps	2150	2048	1949	1853	1760
	energy, ft-lbs	4620	4191	3795	3430	3096
	arc, inches	-1.5	+.2	0	-2.5	-7.6

.405 Winchester

CARTRIDGE BULLET	RANGE, YARDS:	0	100	200	300	400
Hornady 300 Flatpoint	velocity, fps:	2200	1851	1545	1296	
	energy, ft-lb:	3224	2282	1589	1119	
	arc, inches:		0	-8.7	-31.9	
Hornady 300 SP Interlock	velocity, fps:	2200	1890	1610	1370	
	energy, ft-lb:	3224	2379	1727	1250	
	arc, inches:		0	-8.3	-30.2	

.500/416 Nitro Express

CARTRIDGE BULLET	RANGE, YARDS:	0	100	200	300	400
Norma 450 Woodleigh SP	velocity, fps	2100	1991	1886	1785	1688
	energy, ft-lbs	4408	3963	3556	3185	2849
	arc, inches	-1.5	+.3	0	-2.7	-8.2

.416 Taylor

CARTRIDGE BULLET	RANGE, YARDS:	0	100	200	300	400
A-Square 400 Triad	velocity, fps:	2350	2093	1853	1634	1443
	energy, ft-lb:	4905	3892	3049	2371	1849
	arc, inches:		+3.2	0	-13.6	-39.8

.416 Hoffman

CARTRIDGE BULLET	RANGE, YARDS:	0	100	200	300	400
A-Square 400 Triad	velocity, fps:	2380	2122	1879	1658	1464
	energy, ft-lb:	5031	3998	3136	2440	1903
	arc, inches:		+3.1	0	-13.1	-38.7

.416 Remington Magnum

CARTRIDGE BULLET	RANGE, YARDS:	0	100	200	300	400
A-Square 400 Triad	velocity, fps:	2380	2122	1879	1658	1464
	energy, ft-lb:	5031	3998	3136	2440	1903
	arc, inches:		+3.1	0	-13.2	-38.7
Federal 400 Trophy Bonded Sledgehammer Solid	velocity, fps:	2400	2150	1920	1700	1500
	energy, ft-lb:	5115	4110	3260	2565	2005
	arc, inches:		0	-6.0	-21.6	-49.2
Federal 400 Trophy Bonded	velocity, fps:	2400	2180	1970	1770	1590
	energy, ft-lb:	5115	4215	3440	2785	2245
	arc, inches:		0	-5.8	-20.6	-46.9
Rem. 400 Swift A-Frame	velocity, fps:	2400	2175	1962	1763	1579
	energy, ft-lb:	5115	4201	3419	2760	2214
	arc, inches:		0	-5.9	-20.8	

.416 Rigby

CARTRIDGE BULLET	RANGE, YARDS:	0	100	200	300	400
A-Square 400 Triad	velocity, fps:	2400	2140	1897	1673	1478
	energy, ft-lb:	5115	4069	3194	2487	1940
	arc, inches:		+3.0	0	-12.9	-38.0
Federal 400 Trophy Bonded	velocity, fps:	2370	2150	1940	1750	1570
	energy, ft-lb:	4990	4110	3350	2715	2190
	arc, inches:		0	-6.0	-21.3	-48.1
Federal 400 Trophy Bonded Sledgehammer Solid	velocity, fps:	2370	2120	1890	1660	1460
	energy, ft-lb:	4990	3975	3130	2440	1895
	arc, inches:		0	-6.3	-22.5	-51.5

Ballistics Tables for Modern Sporting Rifles

.416 RIGBY TO .450 MARLIN

CARTRIDGE BULLET	RANGE, YARDS:	0	100	200	300	400
Federal 410 Woodleigh Weldcore	velocity, fps:	2370	2110	1870	1640	1440
	energy, ft-lb:	5115	4050	3165	2455	1895
	arc, inches:		0	-7.4	-24.8	-55.0
Federal 410 Solid	velocity, fps:	2370	2110	2870	1640	1440
	energy, ft-lb:	5115	4050	3165	2455	1895
	arc, inches:		0	-7.4	-24.8	-55.0
Norma 400 TXP Swift A-Fr.	velocity, fps:	2350	2127	1917	1721	
	energy, ft-lb:	4906	4021	3266	2632	
	arc, inches:		+3.1	0	-12.5	
Norma 400 Barnes Solid	velocity, fps:	2297	1930	1604	1330	
	energy, ft-lb:	4687	3310	2284	1571	
	arc, inches:		+3.9	0	-17.7	

.416 Ruger

CARTRIDGE BULLET	RANGE, YARDS:	0	100	200	300	400
Hornady 400 DGS, DGX	velocity, fps	2400	2151	1917	1700	
	energy, ft-lbs	5116	4109	3264	2568	
	arc, inches	-1.5	0	-6.0	-21.6	

.416 Rimmed

CARTRIDGE BULLET	RANGE, YARDS:	0	100	200	300	400
A-Square 400 Triad	velocity, fps:	2400	2140	1897	1673	
	energy, ft-lb:	5115	4069	3194	2487	
	arc, inches:		+3.3	0	-13.2	

.416 Dakota

CARTRIDGE BULLET	RANGE, YARDS:	0	100	200	300	400
Dakota 400 Barnes X	velocity, fps:	2450	2294	2143	1998	1859
	energy, ft-lb:	5330	4671	4077	3544	3068
	arc, inches:		+2.5	-0.2	-10.5	-29.4

.416 Weatherby

CARTRIDGE BULLET	RANGE, YARDS:	0	100	200	300	400
A-Square 400 Triad	velocity, fps:	2600	2328	2073	1834	1624
	energy, ft-lb:	6004	4813	3816	2986	2343
	arc, inches:		+2.5	0	-10.5	-31.6
Wby. 350 Barnes X	velocity, fps:	2850	2673	2503	2340	2182
	energy, ft-lb:	6312	5553	4870	4253	3700
	arc, inches:		+1.7	0	-7.2	-20.9
Wby. 400 Swift A-Fr.	velocity, fps:	2650	2426	2213	2011	1820
	energy, ft-lb:	6237	5227	4350	3592	2941
	arc, inches:		+2.2	0	-9.3	-27.1
Wby. 400 RN Expanding	velocity, fps:	2700	2417	2152	1903	1676
	energy, ft-lb:	6474	5189	4113	3216	2493
	arc, inches:		+2.3	0	-9.7	-29.3
Wby. 400 Monolithic Solid	velocity, fps:	2700	2411	2140	1887	1656
	energy, ft-lb:	6474	5162	4068	3161	2435
	arc, inches:		+2.3	0	-9.8	-29.7

10.57 (.416) Meteor

CARTRIDGE BULLET	RANGE, YARDS:	0	100	200	300	400
Lazzeroni 400 Swift A-Fr.	velocity, fps:	2730	2532	2342	2161	1987
	energy, ft-lb:	6621	5695	4874	4147	3508
	arc, inches:		+1.9	0	-8.3	-24.0

.425 Express

CARTRIDGE BULLET	RANGE, YARDS:	0	100	200	300	400
A-Square 400 Triad	velocity, fps:	2400	2136	1888	1662	1465
	energy, ft-lb:	5115	4052	3167	2454	1906
	arc, inches:		+3.0	0	-13.1	-38.3

.44-40 Winchester

CARTRIDGE BULLET	RANGE, YARDS:	0	100	200	300	400
Rem. 200 Soft Point	velocity, fps:	1190	1006	900	822	756
	energy, ft-lb:	629	449	360	300	254
	arc, inches:		0	-33.1	-108.7	-235.2
Win. 200 Soft Point	velocity, fps:	1190	1006	900	822	756
	energy, ft-lb:	629	449	360	300	254
	arc, inches:		0	-33.3	-109.5	-237.4

.44 Remington Magnum

CARTRIDGE BULLET	RANGE, YARDS:	0	100	200	300	400
Federal 240 Hi-Shok HP	velocity, fps:	1760	1380	1090	950	860
	energy, ft-lb:	1650	1015	640	485	395
	arc, inches:		0	-17.4	-60.7	-136.0
Rem. 210 Semi-Jacketed HP	velocity, fps:	1920	1477	1155	982	880
	energy, ft-lb:	1719	1017	622	450	361
	arc, inches:		0	-14.7	-55.5	-131.3
Rem. 240 Soft Point	velocity, fps:	1760	1380	1114	970	878
	energy, ft-lb:	1650	1015	661	501	411
	arc, inches:		0	-17.0	-61.4	-143.0
Rem. 240 Semi-Jacketed Hollow Point	velocity, fps:	1760	1380	1114	970	878
	energy, ft-lb:	1650	1015	661	501	411
	arc, inches:		0	-17.0	-61.4	-143.0
Rem. 275 JHP Core-Lokt	velocity, fps:	1580	1293	1093	976	896
	energy, ft-lb:	1524	1020	730	582	490
	arc, inches:		0	-19.4	-67.5	-210.8
Win. 210 Silvertip HP	velocity, fps:	1580	1198	993	879	795
	energy, ft-lb:	1164	670	460	361	295
	arc, inches:		0	-22.4	-76.1	-168.0
Win. 240 Hollow Soft Point	velocity, fps:	1760	1362	1094	953	861
	energy, ft-lb:	1650	988	638	484	395
	arc, inches:		0	-18.1	-65.1	-150.3
Win. 250 Platinum Tip	velocity, fps:	1830	1475	1201	1032	931
	energy, ft-lb:	1859	1208	801	591	481
	arc, inches:		0	-15.3	-54.7	-126.6.

.444 Marlin

CARTRIDGE BULLET	RANGE, YARDS:	0	100	200	300	400
Rem. 240 Soft Point	velocity, fps:	2350	1815	1377	1087	941
	energy, ft-lb:	2942	1755	1010	630	472
	arc, inches:		+2.2	-5.4	-31.4	-86.7
Hornady 265 Evolution	velocity, fps:	2325	1971	1652	1380	
	energy, ft-lb:	3180	2285	1606	1120	
	arc, inches:		+3.0	-1.4	-18.6	
Hornady 265 FP LM	velocity, fps:	2335	1913	1551	1266	
	energy, ft-lb:	3208	2153	1415	943	
	arc, inches:		+ 2.0	-4.9	-26.5	

.45-70 Government

CARTRIDGE BULLET	RANGE, YARDS:	0	100	200	300	400
Black Hills 405 FPL	velocity, fps:	1250				
	energy, ft-lb:					
	arc, inches:					
Federal 300 Sierra Pro-Hunt. HP FN	velocity, fps:	1880	1650	1430	1240	1110
	energy, ft-lb:	2355	1815	1355	1015	810
	arc, inches:		0	-11.5	-39.7	-89.1
PMC 350 FNSP	velocity, fps:					
	energy, ft-lb:					
	arc, inches:					
Rem. 300 Jacketed HP	velocity, fps:	1810	1497	1244	1073	969
	energy, ft-lb:	2182	1492	1031	767	625
	arc, inches:		0	-13.8	-50.1	-115.7
Rem. 405 Soft Point	velocity, fps:	1330	1168	1055	977	918
	energy, ft-lb:	1590	1227	1001	858	758
	arc, inches:		0	-24.0	-78.6	-169.4
Win. 300 Jacketed HP	velocity, fps:	1880	1650	1425	1235	1105
	energy, ft-lb:	2355	1815	1355	1015	810
	arc, inches:		0	-12.8	-44.3	-95.5
Win. 300 Partition Gold	velocity, fps:	1880	1558	1292	1103	988
	energy, ft-lb:	2355	1616	1112	811	651
	arc, inches:		0	-12.9	-46.0	-104.9.

.450 Bushmaster

CARTRIDGE BULLET	RANGE, YARDS:	0	100	200	300	400
Hornady 250 SST-ML	velocity, fps	2200	1840	1524	1268	
	energy, ft-lb	2686	1879	1289	893	
	arc, inches	-2.0	+2.5	-3.5	-24.5	

.450 Marlin

CARTRIDGE BULLET	RANGE, YARDS:	0	100	200	300	400
Hornady 325 FTX	velocity, fps	2225	1887	1585	1331	
	energy, ft-lbs	3572	2569	1813	1278	
	arc, inches	-1.5	+3.0	-2.2	-21.3	

CARTRIDGE BULLET	RANGE, YARDS:	0	100	200	300	400
Hornady 350 FP	velocity, fps:	2100	1720	1397	1156	
	energy, ft-lb:	3427	2298	1516	1039	
	arc, inches:		0	-10.4	-38.9	

.450 Nitro Express (3¼")

CARTRIDGE BULLET	RANGE, YARDS:	0	100	200	300	400
A-Square 465 Triad	velocity, fps:	2190	1970	1765	1577	
	energy, ft-lb:	4952	4009	3216	2567	
	arc, inches:		+4.3	0	-15.4	
Hornady 450 DGS, DGX	velocity, fps	2150	1872	1618	1397	
	energy, ft-lbs	4927	3733	2792	2080	
	arc, inches	-1.5	0	-8.5	-30.4	
Hornady 450 DGS, DGX	velocity, fps	2150	1872	1618	1397	
	energy, ft-lbs	4927	3733	2792	2080	
	arc, inches	-1.5	0	-8.5	-30.4	

.450 #2

CARTRIDGE BULLET	RANGE, YARDS:	0	100	200	300	400
A-Square 465 Triad	velocity, fps:	2190	1970	1765	1577	
	energy, ft-lb:	4952	4009	3216	2567	
	arc, inches:		+4.3	0	-15.4	

450 Rigby Rimless

CARTRIDGE BULLET	RANGE, YARDS:	0	50	100	150	200
Norma 550 Woodleigh SP	velocity, fps	2100	1992	1887	1787	1690
	energy, ft-lbs	5387	4847	4352	3900	3491
	arc, inches	-1.5	+.3	0	-2.7	-8.2

.458 Winchester Magnum

CARTRIDGE BULLET	RANGE, YARDS:	0	100	200	300	400
A-Square 465 Triad	velocity, fps:	2220	1999	1791	1601	1433
	energy, ft-lb:	5088	4127	3312	2646	2121
	arc, inches:		+3.6	0	-14.7	-42.5
Federal 350 Soft Point	velocity, fps:	2470	1990	1570	1250	1060
	energy, ft-lb:	4740	3065	1915	1205	870
	arc, inches:		0	-7.5	-29.1	-71.1
Federal 400 Trophy Bonded	velocity, fps:	2380	2170	1960	1770	1590
	energy, ft-lb:	5030	4165	3415	2785	2255
	arc, inches:		0	-5.9	-20.9	-47.1
Federal 500 Solid	velocity, fps:	2090	1870	1670	1480	1320
	energy, ft-lb:	4850	3880	3085	2440	1945
	arc, inches:		0	-8.5	-29.5	-66.2
Federal 500 Trophy Bonded	velocity, fps:	2090	1870	1660	1480	1310
	energy, ft-lb:	4850	3870	3065	2420	1915
	arc, inches:		0	-8.5	-29.7	-66.8
Federal 500 Trophy Bonded Sledgehammer Solid	velocity, fps:	2090	1860	1650	1460	1300
	energy, ft-lb:	4850	3845	3025	2365	1865
	arc, inches:		0	-8.6	-30.0	-67.8
Federal 510 Soft Point	velocity, fps:	2090	1820	1570	1360	1190
	energy, ft-lb:	4945	3730	2790	2080	1605
	arc, inches:		0	-9.1	-32.3	-73.9
Hornady 500 FMJ-RN HM	velocity, fps:	2260	1984	1735	1512	
	energy, ft-lb:	5670	4368	3341	2538	
	arc, inches:		0	-7.4	-26.4	
Norma 500 TXP Swift A-Fr.	velocity, fps:	2116	1903	1705	1524	
	energy, ft-lb:	4972	4023	3228	2578	
	arc, inches:		+4.1	0	-16.1	
Norma 500 Barnes Solid	velocity, fps:	2067	1750	1472	1245	
	energy, ft-lb:	4745	3401	2405	1721	
	arc, inches:		+4.9	0	-21.2	
Rem. 450 Swift A-Frame PSP	velocity, fps:	2150	1901	1671	1465	1289
	energy, ft-lb:	4618	3609	2789	2144	1659

CARTRIDGE BULLET	RANGE, YARDS:	0	100	200	300	400
	arc, inches:		0	-8.2	-28.9	
Speer 500 African GS Tungsten Solid	velocity, fps:	2120	1845	1596	1379	
	energy, ft-lb:	4989	3780	2828	2111	
	arc, inches:		0	-8.8	-31.3	
Speer African Grand Slam	velocity, fps:	2120	1853	1609	1396	
	energy, ft-lb:	4989	3810	2875	2163	
	arc, inches:		0	-8.7	-30.8	
Win. 510 Soft Point	velocity, fps:	2040	1770	1527	1319	1157
	energy, ft-lb:	4712	3547	2640	1970	1516
	arc, inches:		0	-10.3	-35.6	

.458 Lott

CARTRIDGE BULLET	RANGE, YARDS:	0	100	200	300	400
A-Square 465 Triad	velocity, fps:	2380	2150	1932	1730	1551
	energy, ft-lb:	5848	4773	3855	3091	2485
	arc, inches:		+3.0	0	-12.5	-36.4
Hornady 500 RNSP or solid	velocity, fps:	2300	2022	1776	1551	
	energy, ft-lb:	5872	4537	3502	2671	
	arc, inches:		+3.4	0	-14.3	
Hornady 500 InterBond	velocity, fps:	2300	2028	1777	1549	
	energy, ft-lb:	5872	4535	3453	2604	
	arc, inches:		0	-7.0	-25.1	

CARTRIDGE BULLET	RANGE, YARDS:	0	50	100	150	200
Norma 500 Woodleigh SP	velocity, fps	2100	1982	1868	1758	1654
	energy, ft-lbs	4897	4361	3874	3434	3039
	arc, inches	-1.5	+.3	0	-2.8	-8.4

.450 Ackley

CARTRIDGE BULLET	RANGE, YARDS:	0	100	200	300	400
A-Square 465 Triad	velocity, fps:	2400	2169	1950	1747	1567
	energy, ft-lb:	5947	4857	3927	3150	2534
	arc, inches:		+2.9	0	-12.2	-35.8

.460 Short A-Square

CARTRIDGE BULLET	RANGE, YARDS:	0	100	200	300	400
A-Square 500 Triad	velocity, fps:	2420	2198	1987	1789	1613
	energy, ft-lb:	6501	5362	4385	3553	2890
	arc, inches:		+2.9	0	-11.6	-34.2

.450 Dakota

CARTRIDGE BULLET	RANGE, YARDS:	0	100	200	300	400
Dakota 500 Barnes Solid	velocity, fps:	2450	2235	2030	1838	1658
	energy, ft-lb:	6663	5544	4576	3748	3051
	arc, inches:		+2.5	-0.6	-12.0	-33.8

.460 Weatherby Magnum

CARTRIDGE BULLET	RANGE, YARDS:	0	100	200	300	400
A-Square 500 Triad	velocity, fps:	2580	2349	2131	1923	1737
	energy, ft-lb:	7389	6126	5040	4107	3351
	arc, inches:		+2.4	0	-10.0	-29.4
Wby. 450 Barnes X	velocity, fps:	2700	2518	2343	2175	2013
	energy, ft-lb:	7284	6333	5482	4725	4050
	arc, inches:		+2.0	0	-8.4	-24.1
Wby. 500 RN Expanding	velocity, fps:	2600	2301	2022	1764	1533.
	energy, ft-lb:	7504	5877	4539	3456	2608
	arc, inches:		+2.6	0	-11.1	-33.5
Wby. 500 FMJ	velocity, fps:	2600	2309	2037	1784	1557
	energy, ft-lb:	7504	5917	4605	3534	2690
	arc, inches:		+2.5	0	-10.9	-33.0

.500/.465

CARTRIDGE BULLET	RANGE, YARDS:	0	100	200	300	400
A-Square 480 Triad	velocity, fps:	2150	1928	1722	1533	
	energy, ft-lb:	4926	3960	3160	2505	
	arc, inches:		+4.3	0	-16.0	

Ballistics Tables for Modern Sporting Rifles

.470 NITRO EXPRESS TO .700 NITRO EXPRESS

CARTRIDGE BULLET	RANGE, YARDS:	0	100	200	300	400
.470 Nitro Express						
A-Square 500 Triad	velocity, fps:	2150	1912	1693	1494	
	energy, ft-lb:	5132	4058	3182	2478	
	arc, inches:		+4.4	0	-16.5	

CARTRIDGE BULLET	RANGE, YARDS:	0	100	200	300	400
Federal 500 Tr. Bonded	velocity, fps	2150	1890	1660	1450	
	energy, ft-lbs	5130	3975	3045	2320	
	arc, inches	-1.5	0	-9.4	-29.3	
Hornady 500 DGX, DGS	velocity, fps	2150	1885	1643	1429	
	energy, ft-lbs	5132	3946	2998	2267	
	arc, inches	-1.5	0	-8.9	-30.9	

CARTRIDGE BULLET	RANGE, YARDS:	0	50	100	150	200
Norma 500 Woodleigh SP	velocity, fps	2100	2002	1906	1814	1725
	energy, ft-lbs	4897	4449	4035	3654	3304
	arc, inches	-1.5	+.3	0	-2.7	-8.0
.470 Capstick						
A-Square 500 Triad	velocity, fps:	2400	2172	1958	1761	1553
	energy, ft-lb:	6394	5236	4255	3445	2678
	arc, inches:		+2.9	0	-11.9	-36.1
.475 #2						
A-Square 480 Triad	velocity, fps:	2200	1964	1744	1544	
	energy, ft-lb:	5158	4109	3240	2539	
	arc, inches:		+4.1	0	-15.6	
.475 #2 Jeffery						
A-Square 500 Triad	velocity, fps:	2200	1966	1748	1550	
	energy, ft-lb:	5373	4291	3392	2666	
	arc, inches:		+4.1	0	-15.6	
.495 A-Square						
A-Square 570 Triad	velocity, fps:	2350	2117	1896	1693	1513
	energy, ft-lb:	6989	5671	4552	3629	2899
	arc, inches:		+3.1	0	-13.0	-37.8
.500 Nitro Express (3")						
A-Square 570 Triad	velocity, fps:	2150	1928	1722	1533	
	energy, ft-lb:	5850	4703	3752	2975	
	arc, inches:		+4.3	0	-16.1	
Federal, 570 Swift A-Fr.	velocity, fps	2100	1850	1630	1420	
	energy, ft-lbs	5580	4335	3340	2560	
	arc, inches	-.9	0	-9	-31	
Hornady 570 DGX, DGS muzzle	velocity, fps	2150	1881	1635	1419	
	energy, ft-lbs	5850	4477	3384	2547	
	arc, inches	-.9	0	-9.0	-31.1	

CARTRIDGE BULLET	RANGE, YARDS:	0	50	100	150	200
Norma 570 Woodleigh SP	velocity, fps	2100	2000	1903	1809	1719
	energy, ft-lbs	5583	5064	4585	4145	3742
	arc, inches	-1.5	+.3	0	-2.7	-8.0

CARTRIDGE BULLET	RANGE, YARDS:	0	100	200	300	400
.500 Jeffery						
Norma 570 Woodleigh SP	velocity, fps	2200	2097	1997	1901	1807
	energy, ft-lbs	6127	5568	5050	4573	4134
	arc, inches	-1.5	+.2	0	-2.4	-7.1
.500 A-Square						
A-Square 600 Triad	velocity, fps:	2470	2235	2013	1804	1620
	energy, ft-lb:	8127	6654	5397	4336	3495
	arc, inches:		+2.7	0	-11.3	-33.5
.505 Gibbs						
A-Square 525 Triad	velocity, fps:	2300	2063	1840	1637	
	energy, ft-lb:	6166	4962	3948	3122	
	arc, inches:		+3.6	0	-14.2	

CARTRIDGE BULLET	RANGE, YARDS:	0	50	100	150	200
Norma 600 Woodleigh SP	velocity, fps	2100	1998	1899	1803	1711
	energy, ft-lbs	5877	5319	4805	4334	3904
	arc, inches	-1.5	+.3	0	-2.7	-8.1

CARTRIDGE BULLET	RANGE, YARDS:	0	100	200	300	400
.577 Nitro Express						
A-Square 750 Triad	velocity, fps:	2050	1811	1595	1401	
	energy, ft-lb:	6998	5463	4234	3267	
	arc, inches:		+4.9	0	-18.5	
.577 Tyrannosaur						
A-Square 750 Triad	velocity, fps:	2460	2197	1950	1723	1516
	energy, ft-lb:	10077	8039	6335	4941	3825
	arc, inches:		+2.8	0	-12.1	-36.0
.600 Nitro Express						
A-Square 900 Triad	velocity, fps:	1950	1680	1452	1336	
	energy, ft-lb:	7596	5634	4212	3564	
	arc, inches:		+5.6	0	-20.7	
.700 Nitro Express						
A-Square 1000 Monolithic Solid	velocity, fps:	1900	1669	1461	1288	
	energy, ft-lb:	8015	6188	4740	3685	
	arc, inches:		+5.8	0	-22.2	

Ballistics Tables for Modern Sporting Rifles

Data shown here is taken from manufacturers' charts; your chronograph readings may vary. Barrel lengths for pistol data vary, and depend in part on which pistols are typically chambered in a given cartridge. Velocity variations due to barrel length depend on the baseline bullet speed and the load. Velocity for the .30 Carbine, normally a rifle cartridge, was determined in a pistol barrel.

Listings are current as of February the year *Shooter's Bible* appears (not the cover year). Listings are not intended as recommendations. For example, the data for the .25 Auto gives velocity and energy readings to 100 yards. Few handgunners would call the little .25 a 100-yard cartridge.

Abbreviations: Bullets are designated by loading company, weight (in grains) and type, with these abbreviations for shape and construction: BJHP=brass-jacketed hollowpoint; FN=Flat Nose; FMC=Full Metal Case; FMJ=Full Metal Jacket; HP=Hollowpoint; L=Lead; LF=Lead-Free; +P=a more powerful load than traditionally manufactured for that round; RN=Round Nose; SFHP=Starfire (PMC) Hollowpoint; SP=Softpoint; SWC=Semi Wadcutter; TMJ=Total Metal Jacket; WC=Wadcutter; CEPP, SXT and XTP are trademarked designations of Lapua, Winchester and Hornady, respectively.

.25 AUTO TO .32 S&W LONG

.25 Auto

CARTRIDGE BULLET	RANGE, YARDS:	0	25	50	75	100
Federal 50 FMJ	velocity, fps:	760	750	730	720	700
	energy, ft-lb:	65	60	60	55	55
Hornady 35 JHP/XTP	velocity, fps:	900		813		742
	energy, ft-lb:	63		51		43
Magtech 50 FMC	velocity, fps:	760		707		659
	energy, ft-lb:	64		56		48
PMC 50 FMJ	velocity, fps:	754	730	707	685	663
	energy, ft-lb:	62				
Rem. 50 Metal Case	velocity, fps:	760		707		659
	energy, ft-lb:	64		56		48
Speer 35 Gold Dot	velocity, fps:	900		816		747
	energy, ft-lb:	63		52		43
Speer 50 TMJ (and Blazer)	velocity, fps:	760		717		677
	energy, ft-lb:	64		57		51
Win. 45 Expanding Point	velocity, fps:	815		729		655
	energy, ft-lb	66		53		42
Win. 50 FMJ	velocity, fps:	760		707		
	energy, ft-lb	64		56		

.30 Luger

CARTRIDGE BULLET	RANGE, YARDS:	0	25	50	75	100
Win. 93 FMJ	velocity, fps:	1220		1110		1040
	energy, ft-lb	305		255		225

7.62x25 Tokarev

CARTRIDGE BULLET	RANGE, YARDS:	0	25	50	75	100
PMC 93 FMJ	velocity and energy figures not available					

.30 Carbine

CARTRIDGE BULLET	RANGE, YARDS:	0	25	50	75	100
Win. 110 Hollow SP	velocity, fps:	1790		1601		1430
	energy, ft-lb	783		626		500

.32 Auto

CARTRIDGE BULLET	RANGE, YARDS:	0	25	50	75	100
Federal 65 Hydra-Shok JHP	velocity, fps:	950	920	890	860	830
	energy, ft-lb:	130	120	115	105	100
Federal 71 FMJ	velocity, fps:	910	880	860	830	810
	energy, ft-lb:	130	120	115	110	105
Hornady 60 JHP/XTP	velocity, fps:	1000		917		849
	energy, ft-lb:	133		112		96
Hornady 71 FMJ-RN	velocity, fps:	900		845		797
	energy, ft-lb:	128		112		100
Magtech 71 FMC	velocity, fps:	905		855		810
	energy, ft-lb:	129		115		103
Magtech 71 JHP	velocity, fps:	905		855		810
	energy, ft-lb:	129		115		103
PMC 60 JHP	velocity, fps:	980	849	820	791	763
	energy, ft-lb:	117				
PMC 70 SFHP	velocity, fps:	velocity and energy figures not available				
PMC 71 FMJ	velocity, fps:	870	841	814	791	763
	energy, ft-lb:	119				
Rem. 71 Metal Case	velocity, fps:	905		855		810
	energy, ft-lb:	129		115		97
Speer 60 Gold Dot	velocity, fps:	960		868		796
	energy, ft-lb:	123		100		84
Speer 71 TMJ (and Blazer)	velocity, fps:	900		855		810
	energy, ft-lb:	129		115		97
Win. 60 Silvertip HP	velocity, fps:	970		895		835
	energy, ft-lb	125		107		93
Win. 71 FMJ	velocity, fps:	905		855		
	energy, ft-lb	129		115		

.32 S&W

CARTRIDGE BULLET	RANGE, YARDS:	0	25	50	75	100
Rem. 88 LRN	velocity, fps:	680		645		610
	energy, ft-lb:	90		81		73
Win. 85 LRN	velocity, fps:	680		645		610
	energy, ft-lb	90		81		73

.32 S&W Long

CARTRIDGE BULLET	RANGE, YARDS:	0	25	50	75	100
Federal 98 LWC	velocity, fps:	780	700	630	560	500
	energy, ft-lb:	130	105	85	70	55
Federal 98 LRN	velocity, fps:	710	690	670	650	640
	energy, ft-lb:	115	105	100	95	90
Lapua 83 LWC	velocity, fps:	240		189*		149*
	energy, ft-lb:	154		95*		59*
Lapua 98 LWC	velocity, fps:	240		202*		171*
	energy, ft-lb:	183		130*		93*
Magtech 98 LRN	velocity, fps:	705		670		635
	energy, ft-lb:	108		98		88
Magtech 98 LWC	velocity, fps:	682		579		491
	energy, ft-lb:	102		73		52
Norma 98 LWC	velocity, fps:	787	759	732		683
	energy, ft-lb:	136	126	118		102

Ballistics Tables for Modern Sporting Rifles

.32 S&W LONG TO 9MM LUGER

CARTRIDGE BULLET	RANGE, YARDS:	0	25	50	75	100
PMC 98 LRN	velocity, fps:	789	770	751	733	716
	energy, ft-lb:	135				
PMC 100 LWC	velocity, fps:	683	652	623	595	569
	energy, ft-lb:	102				
Rem. 98 LRN	velocity, fps:	705		670		635
	energy, ft-lb:	115		98		88
Win. 98 LRN	velocity, fps:	705		670		635
	energy, ft-lb:	115		98		88

.32 Short Colt

CARTRIDGE BULLET	RANGE, YARDS:	0	25	50	75	100
Win. 80 LRN	velocity, fps:	745		665		590
	energy, ft-lb	100		79		62

.32-20

CARTRIDGE BULLET	RANGE, YARDS:	0	25	50	75	100
Black Hills 115 FPL	velocity, fps:	800				
	energy, ft-lb:					

.32 H&R Mag

CARTRIDGE BULLET	RANGE, YARDS:	0	25	50	75	100
Black Hills 85 JHP	velocity, fps	1100				
	energy, ft-lb	228				
Black Hills 90 FPL	velocity, fps	750				
	energy, ft-lb					
Black Hills 115 FPL	velocity, fps	800				
	energy, ft-lb					
Federal 85 Hi-Shok JHP	velocity, fps:	1100	1050	1020	970	930
	energy, ft-lb:	230	210	195	175	165
Federal 95 LSWC	velocity, fps:	1030	1000	940	930	900
	energy, ft-lb:	225	210	195	185	170

9mm Makarov

CARTRIDGE BULLET	RANGE, YARDS:	0	25	50	75	100
Federal 90 Hi-Shok JHP	velocity, fps:	990	950	910	880	850
	energy, ft-lb:	195	180	165	155	145
Federal 90 FMJ	velocity, fps:	990	960	920	900	870
	energy, ft-lb:	205	190	180	170	160
Hornady 95 JHP/XTP	velocity, fps:	1000		930		874
	energy, ft-lb:	211		182		161
PMC 100 FMJ-TC	velocity, fps:	velocity and energy figures not available				
Speer 95 TMJ Blazer	velocity, fps:	1000		928		872
	energy, ft-lb:	211		182		161

9x21 IMI

CARTRIDGE BULLET	RANGE, YARDS:	0	25	50	75	100
PMC 123 FMJ	velocity, fps:	1150	1093	1046	1007	973
	energy, ft-lb:	364				

9mm Luger

CARTRIDGE BULLET	RANGE, YARDS:	0	25	50	75	100
Black Hills 115 JHP	velocity, fps:	1150				
	energy, ft-lb:	336				
Black Hills 115 FMJ	velocity, fps:	1150				
	energy, ft-lb:	336				
Black Hills 115 JHP +P	velocity, fps:	1300				
	energy, ft-lb:	431				
Black Hills 115 EXP JHP	velocity, fps:	1250				
	energy, ft-lb:	400				
Black Hills 124 JHP +P	velocity, fps:	1250				
	energy, ft-lb:	430				
Black Hills 124 JHP	velocity, fps:	1150				
	energy, ft-lb:	363				
Black Hills 124 FMJ	velocity, fps:	1150				
	energy, ft-lb:	363				
Black Hills 147 JHP subsonic	velocity, fps:	975				
	energy, ft-lb:	309				
Black Hills 147 FMJ subsonic	velocity, fps:	975				
	energy, ft-lb:	309				
Federal 105 EFMJ	velocity, fps:	1225	1160	1105	1060	1025
	energy, ft-lb:	350	315	285	265	245

CARTRIDGE BULLET	RANGE, YARDS:	0	25	50	75	100
Federal 115 Hi-Shok JHP	velocity, fps:	1160	1100	1060	1020	990
	energy, ft-lb:	345	310	285	270	250
Federal 115 FMJ	velocity, fps:	1160	1100	1060	1020	990
	energy, ft-lb:	345	310	285	270	250
Federal 124 FMJ	velocity, fps:	1120	1070	1030	990	960
	energy, ft-lb:	345	315	290	270	255
Federal 124 Hydra-Shok JHP	velocity, fps:	1120	1070	1030	990	960
	energy, ft-lb:	345	315	290	270	255
Federal 124 TMJ TMF Primer	velocity, fps:	1120	1070	1030	990	960
	energy, ft-lb:	345	315	290	270	255
Federal 124 Truncated FMJ Match	velocity, fps:	1120	1070	1030	990	960
	energy, ft-lb:	345	315	290	270	255
Federal 124 Nyclad HP	velocity, fps:	1120	1070	1030	990	960
	energy, ft-lb:	345	315	290	270	255
Federal 124 FMJ +P	velocity, fps:	1120	1070	1030	990	960
	energy, ft-lb:	345	315	290	270	255
Federal 135 Hydra-Shok JHP	velocity, fps:	1050	1030	1010	980	970
	energy, ft-lb:	330	315	300	290	280
Federal 147 Hydra-Shok JHP	velocity, fps:	1000	960	920	890	860
	energy, ft-lb:	325	300	275	260	240
Federal 147 Hi-Shok JHP	velocity, fps:	980	950	930	900	880
	energy, ft-lb:	310	295	285	265	255
Federal 147 FMJ FN	velocity, fps:	960	930	910	890	870
	energy, ft-lb:	295	280	270	260	250
Federal 147 TMJ TMF Primer	velocity, fps:	960	940	910	890	870
	energy, ft-lb:	300	285	270	260	245
Hornady 115 JHP/XTP	velocity, fps:	1155		1047		971
	energy, ft-lb:	341		280		241
Hornady 124 JHP/XTP	velocity, fps:	1110		1030		971
	energy, ft-lb:	339		292		259
Hornady 124 TAP-FPD	velocity, fps:	1100		1028		967
	energy, ft-lb:	339		291		257
Hornady 147 JHP/XTP	velocity, fps:	975		935		899
	energy, ft-lb:	310		285		264
Hornady 147 TAP-FPD	velocity, fps:	975		935		899
	energy, ft-lb:	310		285		264
Lapua 116 FMJ	velocity, fps:	365		319*		290*
	energy, ft-lb:	500		381*		315*
Lapua 120 FMJ CEPP Super	velocity, fps:	360		316*		288*
	energy, ft-lb:	505		390*		324*
Lapua 120 FMJ CEPP Extra	velocity, fps:	360		316*		288*
	energy, ft-lb:	505		390*		324*
Lapua 123 HP Megashock	velocity, fps:	355		311*		284*
	energy, ft-lb:	504		388*		322*
Lapua 123 FMJ	velocity, fps:	320		292*		272*
	energy, ft-lb:	410		342*		295*
Lapua 123 FMJ Combat	velocity, fps:	355		315*		289*
	energy, ft-lb:	504		397*		333*
Magtech 115 JHP +P	velocity, fps:	1246		1137		1056
	energy, ft-lb:	397		330		285
Magtech 115 FMC	velocity, fps:	1135		1027		961
	energy, ft-lb:	330		270		235
Magtech 115 JHP	velocity, fps:	1155		1047		971
	energy, ft-lb:	340		280		240
Magtech 124 FMC	velocity, fps:	1109		1030		971
	energy, ft-lb:	339		292		259
Norma 84 Lead Free Frangible (Geco brand)	velocity, fps:	1411				
	energy, ft-lb:	371				
Norma 124 FMJ (Geco brand)	velocity, fps:	1120				
	energy, fps:	341				
Norma 123 FMJ	velocity, fps:	1099	1032	980		899
	energy, ft-lb:	331	292	263		221

BALLISTICS

Ballistics Tables for Modern Sporting Rifles

CARTRIDGE BULLET	RANGE, YARDS:	0	25	50	75	100
Norma 123 FMJ	velocity, fps:	1280	1170	1086		972
	energy, ft-lb:	449	375	323		259
PMC 75 Non-Toxic Frangible	velocity, fps:	1350	1240	1154	1088	1035
	energy, ft-lb:	303				
PMC 95 SFHP	velocity, fps:	1250	1239	1228	1217	1207
	energy, ft-lb:	330				
PMC 115 FMJ	velocity, fps:	1157	1100	1053	1013	979
	energy, ft-lb:	344				
PMC 115 JHP	velocity, fps:	1167	1098	1044	999	961
	energy, ft-lb:	350				
PMC 124 SFHP	velocity, fps:	1090	1043	1003	969	939
	energy, ft-lb:	327				
PMC 124 FMJ	velocity, fps:	1110	1059	1017	980	949
	energy, ft-lb:	339				
PMC 124 LRN	velocity, fps:	1050	1006	969	937	908
	energy, ft-lb:	304				
PMC 147 FMJ	velocity, fps:	980	965	941	919	900
	enerby, ft-lb:	310				
PMC 147 SFHP	velocity, fps:	velocity and energy figures not available				
Rem. 101 Lead Free Frangible	velocity, fps:	1220		1092		1004
	energy, ft-lb:	334		267		226
Rem. 115 FN Enclosed Base	velocity, fps:	1135		1041		973
	energy, ft-lb:	329		277		242
Rem. 115 Metal Case	velocity, fps:	1135		1041		973
	energy, ft-lb:	329		277		242
Rem. 115 JHP	velocity, fps:	1155		1047		971
	energy, ft-lb:	341		280		241
Rem. 115 JHP +P	velocity, fps:	1250		1113		1019
	energy, ft-lb:	399		316		265
Rem. 124 JHP	velocity, fps:	1120		1028		960
	energy, ft-lb:	346		291		254
Rem. 124 FNEB	velocity, fps:	1100		1030		971
	energy, ft-lb:	339		292		252
Rem. 124 BJHP	velocity, fps:	1125		1031		963
	energy, ft-lb:	349		293		255
Rem. 124 BJHP +P	velocity, fps:	1180		1089		1021
	energy, ft-lb:	384		327		287
Rem. 124 Metal Case	velocity, fps:	1110		1030		971
	energy, ft-lb:	339		292		259
Rem. 147 JHP subsonic	velocity, fps:	990		941		900
	energy, ft-lb:	320		289		264
Rem. 147 BJHP	velocity, fps:	990		941		900
	energy, ft-lb:	320		289		264
Speer 90 Frangible	velocity, fps:	1350		1132		1001
	energy, ft-lb:	364		256		200
Speer 115 JHP Blazer	velocity, fps:	1145		1024		943
	energy, ft-lb:	335		268		227
Speer 115 FMJ Blazer	velocity, fps:	1145		1047		971
	energy, ft-lb:	341		280		241
Speer 115 FMJ	velocity, fps:	1200		1060		970
	energy, ft-lb:	368		287		240
Speer 115 Gold Dot HP	velocity, fps:	1200		1047		971
	energy, ft-lb:	341		280		241
Speer 124 FMJ Blazer	velocity, fps:	1090		989		917
	energy, ft-lb:	327		269		231
Speer 124 FMJ	velocity, fps:	1090		987		913
	energy, ft-lb:	327		268		230
Speer 124 TMJ-CF (and Blazer)	velocity, fps:	1090		989		917
	energy, ft-lb:	327		269		231
Speer 124 Gold Dot HP	velocity, fps:	1150		1030		948
	energy, ft-lb:	367		292		247
Speer 124 Gold Dot HP+P	velocity, ft-lb:	1220		1085		996
	energy, ft-lb:	410		324		273
Speer 147 TMJ Blazer	velocity, fps:	950		912		879
	energy, ft-lb:	295		272		252
Speer 147 TMJ	velocity, fps:	985		943		906
	energy, ft-lb:	317		290		268
Speer 147 TMJ-CF (and Blazer)	velocity, fps:	985		960		924
	energy, ft-lb:	326		300		279
Speer 147 Gold Dot	velocity, fps:	985		960		924
	energy, ft-lb:	326		300		279
Win. 105 Jacketed FP	velocity, fps:	1200		1074		989
	energy, ft-lb:	336		269		228
Win. 115 Silvertip HP	velocity, fps:	1225		1095		1007
	energy, ft-lb:	383		306		259
Win. 115 Jacketed HP	velocity, fps:	1225		1095		
	energy, ft-lb:	383		306		
Win. 115 FMJ	velocity, fps:	1190		1071		
	energy, ft-lb:	362		293		
Win. 115 EB WinClean	velocity, fps:	1190		1088		
	energy, ft-lb:	362		302		
Win. 124 FMJ	velocity, fps:	1140		1050		
	energy, ft-lb:	358		303		
Win. 124 EB WinClean	velocity, fps:	1130		1049		
	energy, ft-lb:	352		303		
Win. 147 FMJ FN	velocity, fps:	990		945		
	energy, ft-lb:	320		292		
Win. 147 SXT	velocity, fps:	990		947		909
	energy, ft-lb:	320		293		270
Win. 147 Silvertip HP	velocity, fps:	1010		962		921
	energy, ft-lb:	333		302		277
Win. 147 JHP	velocity, fps:	990		945		
	energy, ft-lb:	320		291		
Win. 147 EB WinClean	velocity, fps:	990		945		
	energy, ft-lb:	320		291		

9 x 23 Winchester

CARTRIDGE BULLET	RANGE, YARDS:	0	25	50	75	100
Win. 124 Jacketed FP	velocity, fps:	1460		1308		
	energy, ft-lb:	587		471		
Win. 125 Silvertip HP	velocity, fps:	1450		1249		1103
	energy, ft-lb:	583		433		338

.38 S&W

CARTRIDGE BULLET	RANGE, YARDS:	0	25	50	75	100
Rem. 146 LRN	velocity, fps:	685		650		620
	energy, ft-lb:	150		135		125
Win. 145 LRN	velocity, fps:	685		650		620
	energy, ft-lb:	150		135		125

.38 Short Colt

CARTRIDGE BULLET	RANGE, YARDS:	0	25	50	75	100
Rem. 125 LRN	velocity, fps:	730		685		645
	energy, ft-lb:	150		130		115

.38 Long Colt

CARTRIDGE BULLET	RANGE, YARDS:	0	25	50	75	100
Black Hills 158 RNL	velocity, fps:	650				
	energy, ft-lb:					

.380 Auto

CARTRIDGE BULLET	RANGE, YARDS:	0	25	50	75	100
Black Hills 90 JHP	velocity, fps:	1000				
	energy, ft-lb:	200				
Black Hills 95 FMJ	velocity, fps:	950				
	energy, ft-lb:	190				
Federal 90 Hi-Shok JHP	velocity, fps:	1000	940	890	840	800
	energy, ft-lb:	200	175	160	140	130
Federal 90 Hydra-Shok JHP	velocity, fps:	1000	940	890	840	800
	energy, ft-lb:	200	175	160	140	130
Federal 95 FMJ	velocity, fps:	960	910	870	830	790
	energy, ft-lb:	190	175	160	145	130

Ballistics Tables for Modern Sporting Rifles

.380 AUTO TO .38 SPECIAL

CARTRIDGE BULLET	RANGE, YARDS:	0	25	50	75	100
Hornady 90 JHP/XTP	velocity, fps:	1000		902		823
	energy, ft-lb:	200		163		135
Magtech 85 JHP + P	velocity, fps:	1082		999		936
	energy, ft-lb:	221		188		166
Magtech 95 FMC	velocity, fps:	951		861		781
	energy, ft-lb:	190		156		128
Magtech 95 JHP	velocity, fps:	951		861		781
	energy, ft-lb:	190		156		128
PMC 77 NT/FR	velocity, fps:	1200	1095	1012	932	874
	energy, ft-lb:	223				
PMC 90 FMJ	velocity, fps:	910	872	838	807	778
	energy, ft-lb:	165				
PMC 90 JHP	velocity, fps:	917	878	844	812	782
	energy, ft-lb:	168				
PMC 95 SFHP	velocity, fps:	925	884	847	813	783
	energy, ft-lb:	180				
Rem. 88 JHP	velocity, fps:	990		920		868
	energy, ft-lb:	191		165		146
Rem. 95 FNEB	velocity, fps:	955		865		785
	energy, ft-lb:	190		160		130
Rem. 95 Metal Case	velocity, fps:	955		865		785
	energy, ft-lb:	190		160		130
Rem. 102 BJHP	velocity, fps:	940		901		866
	energy, ft-lb:	200		184		170
Speer 88 JHP Blazer	velocity, fps:	950		920		870
	energy, ft-lb:	195		164		148
Speer 90 Gold Dot	velocity, fps:	990		907		842
	energy, ft-lb:	196		164		142
Speer 95 TMJ Blazer	velocity, fps:	945		865		785
	energy, ft-lb:	190		160		130
Speer 95 TMJ	velocity, fps:	950		877		817
	energy, ft-lb:	180		154		133
Win. 85 Silvertip HP	velocity, fps:	1000		921		860
	energy, ft-lb:	189		160		140
Win. 95 SXT	velocity, fps:	955		889		835
	energy, ft-lb:	192		167		147
Win. 95 FMJ	velocity, fps:	955		865		
	energy, ft-lb:	190		160		
Win. 95 EB WinClean	velocity, fps:	955		881		
	energy, ft-lb:	192		164		

.38 Special

CARTRIDGE BULLET	RANGE, YARDS:	0	25	50	75	100
Black Hills 125 JHP +P	velocity, fps:	1050				
	energy, ft-lb:	306				
Black Hills 148 HBWC	velocity, fps:	700				
	energy, ft-lb:					
Black Hills 158 SWC	velocity, fps:	850				
	energy, ft-lb:					
Black Hills 158 CNL	velocity, fps:	800				
	energy, ft-lb:					
Federal 110 Hydra-Shok JHP	velocity, fps:	1000	970	930	910	880
	energy, ft-lb:	245	225	215	200	190
Federal 110 Hi-Shok JHP +P	velocity, fps:	1000	960	930	900	870
	energy, ft-lb:	240	225	210	195	185
Federal 125 Nyclad HP	velocity, fps:	830	780	730	690	650
	energy, ft-lb:	190	170	150	130	115
Federal 125 Hi-Shok JSP +P	velocity, fps:	950	920	900	880	860
	energy, ft-lb:	250	235	225	215	205
Federal 125 Hi-Shok JHP +P	velocity, fps:	950	920	900	880	860
	energy, ft-lb:	250	235	225	215	205
Federal 125 Nyclad HP +P	velocity, fps:	950	920	900	880	860
	energy, ft-lb:	250	235	225	215	205
Federal 129 Hydra-Shok JHP+P	velocity, fps:	950	930	910	890	870
	energy, ft-lb:	255	245	235	225	215
Federal 130 FMJ	velocity, fps:	950	920	890	870	840
	energy, ft-lb:	260	245	230	215	205
Federal 148 LWC Match	velocity, fps:	710	670	630	600	560
	energy, ft-lb:	165	150	130	115	105
Federal 158 LRN	velocity, fps:	760	740	720	710	690
	energy, ft-lb:	200	190	185	175	170
Federal 158 LSWC	velocity, fps:	760	740	720	710	690
	energy, ft-lb:	200	190	185	175	170
Federal 158 Nyclad RN	velocity, fps:	760	740	720	710	690
	energy, ft-lb:	200	190	185	175	170
Federal 158 SWC HP +P	velocity, fps:	890	870	860	840	820
	energy, ft-lb:	280	265	260	245	235
Federal 158 LSWC +P	velocity, fps:	890	870	860	840	820
	energy, ft-lb:	270	265	260	245	235
Federal 158 Nyclad SWC-HP+P	velocity, fps:	890	870	860	840	820
	energy, ft-lb:	270	265	260	245	235
Hornady 125 JHP/XTP	velocity, fps:	900		856		817
	energy, ft-lb:	225		203		185
Hornady 140 JHP/XTP	velocity, fps:	825		790		757
	energy, ft-lb:	212		194		178
Hornady 140 Cowboy	velocity, fps:	800		767		735
	energy, ft-lb:	199		183		168
Hornady 148 HBWC	velocity, fps:	800		697		610
	energy, ft-lb:	210		160		122
Hornady 158 JHP/XPT	velocity, fps:	800		765		731
	energy, ft-lb:	225		205		188
Lapua 123 HP Megashock	velocity, fps:	355		311*		284*
	energy, ft-lb:	504		388*		322*
Lapua 148 LWC	velocity, fps:	230		203*		181*
	energy, ft-lb:	254		199*		157*
Lapua 150 SJFN	velocity, fps:	325		301*		283*
	energy, ft-lb:	512		439*		388*
Lapua 158 FMJLF	velocity, fps:	255		243*		232*
	energy, ft-lb:	332		301*		275*
Lapua 158 LRN	velocity, fps:	255		243*		232*
	energy, ft-lb:	332		301*		275*
Magtech 125 JHP +P	velocity, fps:	1017		971		931
	energy, ft-lb:	287		262		241
Magtech 148 LWC	velocity, fps:	710		634		566
	energy, ft-lb:	166		132		105
Magtech 158 LRN	velocity, fps:	755		728		693
	energy, ft-lb:	200		183		168
Magtech 158 LFN	velocity, fps:	800		776		753
	energy, ft-lb:	225		211		199
Magtech 158 SJHP	velocity, fps:	807		779		753
	energy, ft-lb:	230		213		199
Magtech 158 LSWC	velocity, fps:	755		721		689
	energy, ft-lb:	200		182		167
Magtech 158 FMC-Flat	velocity, fps:	807		779		753
	energy, ft-lb:	230		213		199
PMC 85 Non-Toxic Frangible	velocity, fps:	1275	1181	1109	1052	1006
	energy, ft-lb:	307				
PMC 110 SFHP +P	velocity, fps:	velocity and energy figures not available				
PMC 125 SFHP +P	velocity, fps:	950	918	889	863	838
	energy, ft-lb:	251				
PMC 125 JHP +P	velocity, fps:	974	938	906	878	851
	energy, ft-lb:	266				
PMC 132 FMJ	velocity, fps:	841	820	799	780	761
	energy, ft-lb:	206				
PMC 148 LWC	velocity, fps:	728	694	662	631	602
	energy, ft-lb:	175				
PMC 158 LRN	velocity, fps:	820	801	783	765	749
	energy, ft-lb:	235				

Ballistics Tables for Modern Sporting Rifles

.38 SPECIAL TO .357 MAGNUM

CARTRIDGE BULLET	RANGE, YARDS:	0	25	50	75	100
PMC 158 JSP	velocity, fps:	835	816	797	779	762
	energy, ft-lb:	245				
PMC 158 LFP	velocity, fps:	800		761		725
	energy, ft-lb:	225		203		185
Rem. 101 Lead Free Frangible	velocity, fps:	950		896		850
	energy, ft-lb:	202		180		162
Rem. 110 SJHP	velocity, fps:	950		890		840
	energy, ft-lb:	220		194		172
Rem. 110 SJHP +P	velocity, fps:	995		926		871
	energy, ft-lb:	242		210		185
Rem. 125 SJHP +P	velocity, ft-lb:	945		898		858
	energy, ft-lb:	248		224		204
Rem. 125 BJHP	velocity, fps:	975		929		885
	energy, ft-lb:	264		238		218
Rem. 125 FNEB	velocity, fps:	850		822		796
	energy, ft-lb:	201		188		176
Rem. 125 FNEB +P	velocity, fps:	975		935		899
	energy, ft-lb:	264		242		224
Rem. 130 Metal Case	velocity, fps:	950		913		879
	energy, ft-lb:	261		240		223
Rem. 148 LWC Match	velocity, fps:	710		634		566
	energy, ft-lb:	166		132		105
Rem. 158 LRN	velocity, fps:	755		723		692
	energy, ft-lb:	200		183		168
Rem. 158 SWC +P	velocity, fps:	890		855		823
	energy, ft-lb:	278		257		238
Rem. 158 SWC	velocity, fps:	755		723		692
	energy, ft-lb:	200		183		168
Rem. 158 LHP +P	velocity, fps:	890		855		823
	energy, ft-lb:	278		257		238
Speer 125 JHP +P Blazer	velocity, fps:	945		898		858
	energy, ft-lb:	248		224		204
Speer 125 Gold Dot +P	velocity, fps:	945		898		858
	energy, ft-lb:	248		224		204
Speer 158 TMJ +P (and Blazer)	velocity, fps:	900		852		818
	energy, ft-lb:	278		255		235
Speer 158 LRN Blazer	velocity, fps:	755		723		692
	energy, ft-lb:	200		183		168
Speer 158 Trail Blazer LFN	velocity, fps:	800		761		725
	energy, ft-lb:	225		203		184
Speer 158 TMJ-CF +P	velocity, fps:	900		852		818
(and Blazer)	energy, ft-lb:	278		255		235
Win. 110 Silvertip HP	velocity, fps:	945		894		850
	energy, ft-lb:	218		195		176
Win. 110 Jacketed FP	velocity, fps:	975		906		849
	energy, ft-lb:	232		201		176
Win. 125 Jacketed HP	velocity, fps:	945		898		
	energy, ft-lb:	248		224		
Win. 125 Jacketed HP +P	velocity, fps:	945		898		858
	energy, ft-lb:	248		224		204
Win. 125 Jacketed FP	velocity, fps:	850		804		
	energy, ft-lb:	201		179		
Win. 125 Silvertip HP + P	velocity, fps:	945		898		858
	energy, ft-lb:	248		224		204
Win. 125 JFP WinClean	velocity, fps:	775		742		
	energy, ft-lb:	167		153		
Win. 130 FMJ	velocity, fps:	800		765		
	energy, ft-lb:	185		169		
Win. 130 SXT +P	velocity, fps:	925		887		852
	energy, ft-lb:	247		227		210
Win. 148 LWC Super Match	velocity, fps:	710		634		566
	energy, ft-lb:	166		132		105
Win. 150 Lead	velocity, fps:	845		812		
	energy, ft-lb:	238		219		
Win. 158 Lead	velocity, fps:	800		761		725
	energy, ft-lb:	225		203		185
Win. 158 LRN	velocity, fps:	755		723		693
	energy, ft-lb:	200		183		168
Win. 158 LSWC	velocity, fps:	755		721		689
	energy, ft-lb:	200		182		167
Win. 158 LSWC HP +P	velocity, fps:	890		855		823
	energy, ft-lb:	278		257		238

.38-40

CARTRIDGE BULLET	RANGE, YARDS:	0	25	50	75	100
Black Hills 180 FPL	velocity, fps:	800				
	energy, ft-lb:					

.38 Super

CARTRIDGE BULLET	RANGE, YARDS:	0	25	50	75	100
Federal 130 FMJ +P	velocity, fps:	1200	1140	1100	1050	1020
	energy, ft-lb:	415	380	350	320	300
PMC 115 JHP	velocity, fps:	1116	1052	1001	959	923
	energy, ft-lb:	318				
PMC 130 FMJ	velocity, fps:	1092	1038	994	957	924
	energy, ft-lb:	348				
Rem. 130 Metal Case	velocity, fps:	1215		1099		1017
	energy, ft-lb:	426		348		298
Win. 125 Silvertip HP +P	velocity, fps:	1240		1130		1050
	energy, ft-lb:	427		354		306
Win. 130 FMJ +P	velocity, fps:	1215		1099		
	energy, ft-lb:	426		348		

.357 Sig

CARTRIDGE BULLET	RANGE, YARDS:	0	25	50	75	100
Federal 125 FMJ	velocity, fps:	1350	1270	1190	1130	1080
	energy, ft-lb:	510	445	395	355	325
Federal 125 JHP	velocity, fps:	1350	1270	1190	1130	1080
	energy, ft-lb:	510	445	395	355	325
Federal 150 JHP	velocity, fps:	1130	1080	1030	1000	970
	energy, ft-lb:	420	385	355	330	310
Hornady 124 JHP/XTP	velocity, fps:	1350		1208		1108
	energy, ft-lb:	502		405		338
Hornady 147 JHP/XTP	velocity, fps:	1225		1138		1072
	energy, ft-lb:	490		422		375
PMC 85 Non-Toxic Frangible	velocity, fps:	1480	1356	1245	1158	1092
	energy, ft-lb:	413				
PMC 124 SFHP	velocity, fps:	1350	1263	1190	1132	1083
	energy, ft-lb:	502				
PMC 124 FMJ/FP	velocity, fps:	1350	1242	1158	1093	1040
	energy, ft-lb:	512				
Rem. 104 Lead Free Frangible	velocity, fps:	1400		1223		1094
	energy, ft-lb:	453		345		276
Rem. 125 Metal Case	velocity, fps:	1350		1146		1018
	energy, ft-lb:	506		422		359
Rem. 125 JHP	velocity, fps:	1350		1157		1032
	energy, ft-lb:	506		372		296
Speer 125 TMJ (and Blazer)	velocity, fps:	1350		1177		1057
	energy, ft-lb:	502		381		307
Speer 125 TMJ-CF	velocity, fps:	1350		1177		1057
	energy, ft-lb:	502		381		307
Speer 125 Gold Dot	velocity, fps:	1375		1203		1079
	energy, ft-lb:	525		402		323
Win. 105 JFP	velocity, fps:	1370		1179		1050
	energy, ft-lb	438		324		257
Win. 125 FMJ FN	velocity, fps:	1350		1185		
	energy, ft-lb	506		390		

.357 Magnum

CARTRIDGE BULLET	RANGE, YARDS:	0	25	50	75	100
Black Hills 125 JHP	velocity, fps:	1500				
	energy, ft-lb:	625				
Black Hills 158 CNL	velocity, fps:	800				

BALLISTICS

Ballistics Tables for Modern Sporting Rifles

.357 MAGNUM TO .40 S&W

CARTRIDGE BULLET	RANGE, YARDS:	0	25	50	75	100
	energy, ft-lb:					
Black Hills 158 SWC	velocity, fps:	1050				
	energy, ft-lb:					
Black Hills 158 JHP	velocity, fps:	1250				
	energy, ft-lb:					
Federal 110 Hi-Shok JHP	velocity, fps:	1300	1180	1090	1040	990
	energy, ft-lb:	410	340	290	260	235
Federal 125 Hi-Shok JHP	velocity, fps:	1450	1350	1240	1160	1100
	energy, ft-lb:	580	495	430	370	335
Federal 130 Hydra-Shok JHP	velocity, fps:	1300	1210	1130	1070	1020
	energy, ft-lb:	490	420	370	330	300
Federal 158 Hi-Shok JSP	velocity, fps:	1240	1160	1100	1060	1020
	energy, ft-lb:	535	475	430	395	365
Federal 158 JSP	velocity, fps:	1240	1160	1100	1060	1020
	energy, ft-lb:	535	475	430	395	365
Federal 158 LSWC	velocity, fps:	1240	1160	1100	1060	1020
	energy, ft-lb:	535	475	430	395	365
Federal 158 Hi-Shok JHP	velocity, fps:	1240	1160	1100	1060	1020
	energy, ft-lb:	535	475	430	395	365
Federal 158 Hydra-Shok JHP	velocity, fps:	1240	1160	1100	1060	1020
	energy, ft-lb:	535	475	430	395	365
Federal 180 Hi-Shok JHP	velocity, fps:	1090	1030	980	930	890
	energy, ft-lb:	475	425	385	350	320
Federal 180 Castcore	velocity, fps:	1250	1200	1160	1120	1080
	energy, ft-lb:	625	575	535	495	465
Hornady 125 JHP/XTP	velocity, fps:	1500		1314		1166
	energy, ft-lb:	624		479		377
Hornady 125 JFP/XTP	velocity, fps:	1500		1311		1161
	energy, ft-lb:	624		477		374
Hornady 140 Cowboy	velocity, fps:	800		767		735
	energy, ft-lb:	199		183		168
Hornady 140 JHP/XTP	velocity, fps:	1400		1249		1130
	energy, ft-lb:	609		485		397
Hornady 158 JHP/XTP	velocity, fps:	1250		1150		1073
	energy, ft-lb:	548		464		404
Hornady 158 JFP/XTP	velocity, fps:	1250		1147		1068
	energy, ft-lb:	548		461		400
Lapua 150 FMJ CEPP Super	velocity, fps:	370		527*		303*
	energy, ft-lb:	664		527*		445*
Lapua 150 SJFN	velocity, fps:	385		342*		313*
	energy, ft-lb:	719		569*		476*
Lapua 158 SJHP	velocity, fps:	470		408*		359*
	energy, ft-lb:	1127		850*		657*
Magtech 158 SJSP	velocity, fps:	1235		1104		1015
	energy, ft-lb:	535		428		361
Magtech 158 SJHP	velocity, fps:	1235		1104		1015
	energy, ft-lb:	535		428		361
PMC 85 Non-Toxic Frangible	velocity, fps:	1325	1219	1139	1076	1025
	energy, ft-lb:	331				
PMC 125 JHP	velocity, fps:	1194	1117	1057	1008	967
	energy, ft-lb:	399				
PMC 150 JHP	velocity, fps:	1234	1156	1093	1042	1000
	energy, ft-lb:	512				
PMC 150 SFHP	velocity, fps:	1205	1129	1069	1020	980
	energy, ft-lb:	484				
PMC 158 JSP	velocity, fps:	1194	1122	1063	1016	977
	energy, ft-lb:	504				
PMC 158 LFP	velocity, fps:	800		761		725
	energy, ft-lb:	225		203		185
Rem. 110 SJHP	velocity, fps:	1295		1094		975
	energy, ft-lb:	410		292		232
Rem. 125 SJHP	velocity, fps:	1450		1240		1090
	energy, ft-lb:	583		427		330
Rem. 125 BJHP	velocity, fps:	1220		1095		1009
	energy, ft-lb:	413		333		283
Rem. 125 FNEB	velocity, fps:	1450		1240		1090
	energy, ft-lb:	583		427		330
Rem. 158 SJHP	velocity, fps:	1235		1104		1015
	energy, ft-lb:	535		428		361
Rem. 158 SP	velocity, fps:	1235		1104		1015
	energy, ft-lb:	535		428		361
Rem. 158 SWC	velocity, fps:	1235		1104		1015
	energy, ft-lb:	535		428		361
Rem. 165 JHP Core-Lokt	velocity, fps:	1290		1189		1108
	energy, ft-lb:	610		518		450
Rem. 180 SJHP	velocity, fps:	1145		1053		985
	energy, ft-lb:	542		443		388
Speer 125 Gold Dot	velocity, fps:	1450		1240		1090
	energy, ft-lb:	583		427		330
Speer 158 JHP Blazer	velocity, fps:	1150		1104		1015
	energy, ft-lb:	535		428		361
Speer 158 Gold Dot	velocity, fps:	1235		1104		1015
	energy, ft-lb:	535		428		361
Speer 170 Gold Dot SP	velocity, fps:	1180		1089		1019
	energy, ft-lb:	525		447		392
Win. 110 JFP	velocity, fps:	1275		1105		998
	energy, ft-lb:	397		298		243
Win. 110 JHP	velocity, fps:	1295		1095		
	energy, ft-lb:	410		292		
Win. 125 JFP WinClean	velocity, fps:	1370		1183		
	energy, ft-lb:	521		389		
Win. 145 Silvertip HP	velocity, fps:	1290		1155		1060
	energy, ft-lb:	535		428		361
Win. 158 JHP	velocity, fps:	1235		1104		1015
	energy, ft-lb:	535		428		361
Win. 158 JSP	velocity, fps:	1235		1104		1015
	energy, ft-lb:	535		428		361
Win. 180 Partition Gold	velocity, fps:	1180		1088		1020
	energy, ft-lb:	557		473		416

.40 S&W

CARTRIDGE BULLET	RANGE, YARDS:	0	25	50	75	100
Black Hills 155 JHP	velocity, fps:	1150				
	energy, ft-lb:	450				
Black Hills 165 EXP JHP	velocity, fps:	1150 (2005: 1100)				
	energy, ft-lb:	483				
Black Hills 180 JHP	velocity, fps:	1000				
	energy, ft-lb:	400				
Black Hills 180 JHP	velocity, fps:	1000				
	energy, ft-lb:	400				
Federal 135 Hydra-Shok JHP	velocity, fps:	1190	1050	970	900	850
	energy, ft-lb:	420	330	280	245	215
Federal 155 FMJ Ball	velocity, fps:	1140	1080	1030	990	960
	energy, ft-lb:	445	400	365	335	315
Federal 155 Hi-Shok JHP	velocity, fps:	1140	1080	1030	990	950
	energy, ft-lb:	445	400	365	335	315
Federal 155 Hydra-Shok JHP	velocity, fps:	1140	1080	1030	990	950
	energy, ft-lb:	445	400	365	335	315
Federal 165 EFMJ	velocity, fps:	1190	1060	970	905	850
	energy, ft-lb:	520	410	345	300	265
Federal 165 FMJ	velocity, fps:	1050	1020	990	960	935
	energy, ft-lb:	405	380	355	335	320
Federal 165 FMJ Ball	velocity, fps:	980	950	920	900	880
	energy, ft-lb:	350	330	310	295	280
Federal 165 Hydra-Shok JHP	velocity, fps:	980	950	930	910	890
	energy, ft-lb:	350	330	315	300	290
Federal 180 High Antim. Lead	velocity, fps:	990	960	930	910	890
	energy, ft-lb:	390	365	345	330	315

BALLISTICS

Ballistics Tables for Modern Sporting Rifles

.40 S&W TO .41 REMINGTON MAGNUM

CARTRIDGE BULLET	RANGE, YARDS:	0	25	50	75	100
Federal 180 TMJ TMF Primer	velocity, fps:	990	960	940	910	890
	energy, ft-lb:	390	370	350	330	315
Federal 180 FMJ Ball	velocity, fps:	990	960	940	910	890
	energy, ft-lb:	390	370	350	330	315
Federal 180 Hi-Shok JHP	velocity, fps:	990	960	930	910	890
	energy, ft-lb:	390	365	345	330	315
Federal 180 Hydra-Shok JHP	velocity, fps:	990	960	930	910	890
	energy, ft-lb:	390	365	345	330	315
Hornady 155 JHP/XTP	velocity, fps:	1180		1061		980
	energy, ft-lb:	479		387		331
Hornady 155 TAP-FPD	velocity, fps:	1180		1061		980
	energy, ft-lb:	470		387		331
Hornady 180 JHP/XTP	velocity, fps:	950		903		862
	energy, ft-lb:	361		326		297
Hornady 180 TAP-FPD	velocity, fps:	950		903		862
	energy, ft-lb:	361		326		297
Magtech 155 JHP	velocity, fps:	1025		1118		1052
	energy, ft-lb:	500		430		381
Magtech 180 JHP	velocity, fps:	990		933		886
	energy, ft-lb:	390		348		314
Magtech 180 FMC	velocity, fps:	990		933		886
	energy, ft-lb:	390		348		314
PMC 115 Non-Toxic Frangible	velocity, fps:	1350	1240	1154	1088	1035
	energy, ft-lb:	465				
PMC 155 SFHP	velocity, fps:	1160	1092	1039	994	957
	energy, ft-lb:	463				
PMC 165 JHP	velocity, fps:	1040	1002	970	941	915
	energy, ft-lb:	396				
PMC 165 FMJ	velocity, fps:	1010	977	948	922	899
	energy, ft-lb:	374				
PMC 180 FMJ/FP	velocity, fps:	985	957	931	908	885
	energy, ft-lb:	388				
PMC 180 SFHP	velocity, fps:	985	958	933	910	889
	energy, ft-lb:	388				
Rem. 141 Lead Free Frangible	velocity, fps:	1135		1056		996
	energy, ft-lb:	403		349		311
Rem. 155 JHP	velocity, fps:	1205		1095		1017
	energy, ft-lb:	499		413		356
Rem. 165 BJHP	velocity, fps:	1150		1040		964
	energy, ft-lb:	485		396		340
Rem. 180 JHP	velocity, fps:	1015		960		914
	energy, ft-lb:	412		368		334
Rem. 180 FN Enclosed Base	velocity, fps:	985		936		893
	energy, ft-lb:	388		350		319
Rem. 180 Metal Case	velocity, fps:	985		936		893
	energy, ft-lb:	388		350		319
Rem. 180 BJHP	velocity, fps:	1015		960		914
	energy, ft-lb:	412		368		334
Speer 105 Frangible	velocity, fps:	1380		1128		985
	energy, ft-lb:	444		297		226
Speer 155 TMJ Blazer	velocity, fps:	1175		1047		963
	energy, ft-lb:	475		377		319
Speer 155 TMJ	velocity, fps:	1200		1065		976
	energy, ft-lb:	496		390		328
Speer 155 Gold Dot	velocity, fps:	1200		1063		974
	energy, ft-lb:	496		389		326
Speer 165 TMJ Blazer	velocity, fps:	1100		1006		938
	energy, ft-lb:	443		371		321
Speer 165 TMJ	velocity, fps:	1150		1040		964
	energy, ft-lb:	484		396		340
Speer 165 Gold Dot	velocity, fps:	1150		1043		966
	energy, ft-lb:	485		399		342
Speer 180 HP Blazer	velocity, fps:	985		951		909
	energy, ft-lb:	400		361		330
Speer 180 FMJ Blazer	velocity, fps:	1000		937		886
	energy, ft-lb:	400		351		313
Speer 180 FMJ	velocity, fps:	1000		951		909
	energy, ft-lb:	400		361		330
Speer 180 TMJ-CF (and Blazer)	velocity, fps:	1000		951		909
	energy, ft-lb:	400		361		330
Speer 180 Gold Dot	velocity, fps:	1025		957		902
	energy, ft-lb:	420		366		325
Win. 140 JFP	velocity, fps:	1155		1039		960
	energy, ft-lb:	415		336		286
Win. 155 Silvertip HP	velocity, fps:	1205		1096		1018
	energy, ft-lb	500		414		357
Win. 165 SXT	velocity, fps:	1130		1041		977
	energy, ft-lb:	468		397		349
Win. 165 FMJ FN	velocity, fps:	1060		1001		
	energy, ft-lb:	412		367		
Win. 165 EB WinClean	velocity, fps:	1130		1054		
	energy, ft-lb:	468		407		
Win. 180 JHP	velocity, fps:	1010		954		
	energy, ft-lb:	408		364		
Win. 180 FMJ	velocity, fps:	990		936		
	energy, ft-lb:	390		350		
Win. 180 SXT	velocity, fps:	1010		954		909
	energy, ft-lb:	408		364		330
Win. 180 EB WinClean	velocity, fps:	990		943		
	energy, ft-lb:	392		356		

10 mm Auto

CARTRIDGE BULLET	RANGE, YARDS:	0	25	50	75	100
Federal 155 Hi-Shok JHP	velocity, fps:	1330	1230	1140	1080	1030
	energy, ft-lb:	605	515	450	400	360
Federal 180 Hi-Shok JHP	velocity, fps:	1030	1000	970	950	920
	energy, ft-lb:	425	400	375	355	340
Federal 180 Hydra-Shok JHP	velocity, fps:	1030	1000	970	950	920
	energy, ft-lb:	425	400	375	355	340
Federal 180 High Antim. Lead	velocity, fps:	1030	1000	970	950	920
	energy, ft-lb:	425	400	375	355	340
Federal 180 FMJ	velocity, fps:	1060	1025	990	965	940
	energy, ft-lb:	400	370	350	330	310
Hornady 155 JHP/XTP	velocity, fps:	1265		1119		1020
	energy, ft-lb:	551		431		358
Hornady 180 JHP/XTP	velocity, fps:	1180		1077		1004
	energy, ft-lb:	556		464		403
Hornady 200 JHP/XTP	velocity, fps:	1050		994		948
	energy, ft-lb:	490		439		399
PMC 115 Non-Toxic Frangible	velocity, fps:	1350	1240	1154	1088	1035
	energy, ft-lb:	465				
PMC 170 JHP	velocity, fps:	1200	1117	1052	1000	958
	energy, ft-lb:	543				
PMC 180 SFHP	velocity, fps:	950	926	903	882	862
	energy, ft-lb:	361				
PMC 200 TC-FMJ	velocity, fps:	1050	1008	972	941	912
	energy, ft-lb:	490				
Rem. 180 Metal Case	velocity, fps:	1150		1063		998
	energy, ft-lb:	529		452		398
Speer 200 TMJ Blazer	velocity, fps:	1050		966		952
	energy, ft-lb:	490		440		402
Win. 175 Silvertip HP	velocity, fps:	1290		1141		1037
	energy, ft-lb:	649		506		418

.41 Remington Magnum

CARTRIDGE BULLET	RANGE, YARDS:	0	25	50	75	100
Federal 210 Hi-Shok JHP	velocity, fps:	1300	1210	1130	1070	1030
	energy, ft-lb:	790	680	595	540	495
PMC 210 TCSP	velocity, fps:	1290	1201	1128	1069	1021
	energy, ft-lb:	774				

BALLISTICS

Ballistics Tables for Modern Sporting Rifles

.41 Remington Magnum to .45 Automatic (ACP)

Cartridge Bullet	Range, yards:	0	25	50	75	100
PMC 210 JHP	velocity, fps:	1289	1200	1127	1068	1020
	energy, ft-lb:	774				
Rem. 210 SP	velocity, fps:	1300		1162		1062
	energy, ft-lb:	788		630		526
Win. 175 Silvertip HP	velocity, fps:	1250		1120		1029
	energy, ft-lb:	607		488		412
Win. 240 Platinum Tip	velocity, ft-lb:	1250		1151		1075
	energy, ft-lb:	833		706		616

.44 Colt

Cartridge Bullet	Range, yards:	0	25	50	75	100
Black Hills 230 FPL	velocity, fps:	730				
	energy, ft-lb:					

.44 Russian

Cartridge Bullet	Range, yards:	0	25	50	75	100
Black Hills 210 FPL	velocity, fps:	650				
	energy, ft-lb:					

.44 Special

Cartridge Bullet	Range, yards:	0	25	50	75	100
Black Hills 210 FPL	velocity, fps:	700				
	energy, ft-lb:					
Federal 200 SWC HP	velocity, fps:	900	860	830	800	770
	energy, ft-lb:	360	330	305	285	260
Federal 250 CastCore	velocity, fps:	1250	1200	1150	1110	1080
	energy, ft-lb:	865	795	735	685	645
Hornady 180 JHP/XTP	velocity, fps:	1000		935		882
	energy, ft-lb:	400		350		311
Magtech 240 LFN	velocity, fps:	750		722		696
	energy, ft-lb:	300		278		258
PMC 180 JHP	velocity, fps:	980	938	902	869	839
	energy, ft-lb;	383				
PMC 240 SWC-CP	velocity, fps:	764	744	724	706	687
	energy, ft-lb:	311				
PMC 240 LFP	velocity, fps:	750		719		690
	energy, ft-lb:	300		275		253
Rem. 246 LRN	velocity, fps:	755		725		695
	energy, ft-lb:	310		285		265
Speer 200 HP Blazer	velocity, fps:	875		825		780
	energy, ft-lb:	340		302		270
Speer 200 Trail Blazer LFN	velocity, fps:	750		714		680
	energy, ft-lb:	250		226		205
Speer 200 Gold Dot	velocity, fps:	875		825		780
	energy, ft-lb:	340		302		270
Win. 200 Silvertip HP	velocity, fps:	900		860		822
	energy, ft-lb:	360		328		300
Win. 240 Lead	velocity, fps:	750		719		690
	energy, ft-lb	300		275		253
Win. 246 LRN	velocity, fps:	755		725		695
	energy, ft-lb:	310		285		265

.44 Remington Magnum

Cartridge Bullet	Range, yards:	0	25	50	75	100
Black Hills 240 JHP	velocity, fps:	1260				
	energy, ft-lb:	848				
Black Hills 300 JHP	velocity, fps:	1150				
	energy, ft-lb:	879				
Federal 180 Hi-Shok JHP	velocity, fps:	1610	1480	1370	1270	1180
	energy, ft-lb:	1035	875	750	640	555
Federal 240 Hi-Shok JHP	velocity, fps:	1180	1130	1080	1050	1010
	energy, ft-lb:	740	675	625	580	550
Federal 240 Hydra-Shok JHP	velocity, fps:	1180	1130	1080	1050	1010
	energy, ft-lb:	740	675	625	580	550
Federal 240 JHP	velocity, fps:	1180	1130	1080	1050	1010
	energy, ft-lb:	740	675	625	580	550
Federal 300 CastCore	velocity, fps:	1250	1200	1160	1120	1080
	energy, ft-lb:	1040	960	885	825	775
Hornady 180 JHP/XTP	velocity, fps:	1550		1340		1173
	energy, ft-lb:	960		717		550
Hornady 200 JHP/XTP	velocity, fps:	1500		1284		1128
	energy, ft-lb:	999		732		565
Hornady 240 JHP/XTP	velocity, fps:	1350		1188		1078
	energy, ft-lb:	971		753		619
Hornady 300 JHP/XTP	velocity, fps:	1150		1084		1031
	energy, ft-lb:	881		782		708
Magtech 240 SJSP	velocity, fps:	1180		1081		1010
	energy, ft-lb:	741		632		623
PMC 180 JHP	velocity, fps:	1392	1263	1157	1076	1015
	energy, ft-lb:	772				
PMC 240 JHP	velocity, fps:	1301	1218	1147	1088	1041
	energy, ft-lb:	900				
PMC 240 TC-SP	velocity, fps:	1300	1216	1144	1086	1038
	energy, ft-lb:	900				
PMC 240 SFHP	velocity, fps:	1300	1212	1138	1079	1030
	energy, ft-lb:	900				
PMC 240 LSWC-GCK	velocity, fps:	1225	1143	1077	1025	982
	energy, ft-lb:	806				
Rem. 180 JSP	velocity, fps:	1610		1365		1175
	energy, ft-lb:	1036		745		551
Rem. 210 Gold Dot HP	velocity, fps:	1450		1276		1140
	energy, ft-lb:	980		759		606
Rem. 240 SP	velocity, fps:	1180		1081		1010
	energy, ft-lb:	721		623		543
Rem. 240 SJHP	velocity, fps:	1180		1081		1010
	energy, ft-lb:	721		623		543
Rem. 275 JHP Core-Lokt	velocity, fps:	1235		1142		1070
	energy, ft-lb:	931		797		699
Speer 240 JHP Blazer	velocity, fps:	1200		1092		1015
	energy, ft-lb:	767		636		549
Speer 240 Gold Dot HP	velocity, fps:	1400		1255		1139
	energy, ft-lb:	1044		839		691
Speer 270 Gold Dot SP	velocity, fps:	1250		1142		1060
	energy, ft-lb:	937		781		674
Win. 210 Silvertip HP	velocity, fps:	1250		1106		1010
	energy, ft-lb:	729		570		475
Win. 240 Hollow SP	velocity, fps:	1180		1081		1010
	energy, ft-lb:	741		623		543
Win. 240 JSP	velocity, fps:	1180		1081		
	energy, ft-lb:	741		623		
Win. 250 Partition Gold	velocity, fps:	1230		1132		1057
	energy, ft-lb:	840		711		620
Win. 250 Platinum Tip	velocity, fps:	1250		1148		1070
	energy, ft-lb:	867		732		635

.44-40

Cartridge Bullet	Range, yards:	0	25	50	75	100
Black Hills 200 RNFP	velocity, fps:	800				
	energy, ft-lb:					
Hornady 205 Cowboy	velocity, fps:	725		697		670
	energy, ft-lb:	239		221		204
Magtech 225 LFN	velocity, fps:	725		703		681
	energy, ft-lb:	281		247		232
PMC 225 LFP	velocity, fps:	725		723		695
	energy, ft-lb:	281		261		242
Win. 225 Lead	velocity, fps:	750		723		695
	energy, ft-lb:	281		261		242

.45 Automatic (ACP)

Cartridge Bullet	Range, yards:	0	25	50	75	100
Black Hills 185 JHP	velocity, fps:	1000				
	energy, ft-lb:	411				

Ballistics Tables for Modern Sporting Rifles

.45 AUTOMATIC (ACP) TO .45 GAP

CARTRIDGE BULLET	RANGE, YARDS:	0	25	50	75	100
Black Hills 200 Match SWC	velocity, fps:	875				
	energy, ft-lb:	340				
Black Hills 230 FMJ	velocity, fps:	850				
	energy, ft-lb:	368				
Black Hills 230 JHP	velocity, fps:	850				
	energy, ft-lb:	368				
Black Hills 230 JHP +P	velocity, fps:	950				
	energy, ft-lb:	460				
Federal 165 Hydra-Shok JHP	velocity, fps:	1060	1020	980	950	920
	energy, ft-lb:	410	375	350	330	310
Federal 165 EFMJ	velocity, fps:	1090	1045	1005	975	942
	energy, ft-lb:	435	400	370	345	325
Federal 185 Hi-Shok JHP	velocity, fps:	950	920	900	880	860
	energy, ft-lb:	370	350	335	315	300
Federal 185 FMJ-SWC Match	velocity, fps:	780	730	700	660	620
	energy, ft-lb:	245	220	200	175	160
Federal 200 Exp. FMJ	velocity, fps:	1030	1000	970	940	920
	energy, ft-lb:	470	440	415	395	375
Federal 230 FMJ	velocity, fps:	850	830	810	790	770
	energy, ft-lb:	370	350	335	320	305
Federal 230 FMJ Match	velocity, fps:	855	835	815	795	775
	energy, ft-lb:	375	355	340	325	305
Federal 230 Hi-Shok JHP	velocity, fps:	850	830	810	790	770
	energy, ft-lb:	370	350	335	320	300
Federal 230 Hydra-Shok JHP	velocity, fps:	850	830	810	790	770
	energy, ft-lb:	370	350	335	320	305
Federal 230 FMJ	velocity, fps:	850	830	810	790	770
	energy, ft-lb:	370	350	335	320	305
Federal 230 TMJ TMF Primer	velocity, fps:	850	830	810	790	770
	energy, ft-lb:	370	350	335	315	305
Hornady 185 JHP/XTP	velocity, fps:	950		880		819
	energy, ft-lb:	371		318		276
Hornady 200 JHP/XTP	velocity, fps:	900		855		815
	energy, ft-lb:	358		325		295
Hornady 200 HP/XTP +P	velocity, fps:	1055		982		925
	energy, ft-lb:	494		428		380
Hornady 200 TAP-FPD	velocity, fps:	1055		982		926
	energy, ft-lbs:	494		428		380
Hornady 230 FMJ/RN	velocity, fps:	850		809		771
	energy, ft-lb:	369		334		304
Hornady 230 FMJ/FP	velocity, fps:	850		809		771
	energy, ft-lb:	369		334		304
Hornady 230 HP/XTP +P	velocity, fps:	950		904		865
	energy, ft-lb:	462		418		382
Hornady 230 TAP-FPD	velocity, fps:	950		908		872
	energy, ft-lb:	461		421		388
Magtech 185 JHP +P	velocity, fps:	1148		1066		1055
	energy, ft-lb:	540		467		415
Magtech 200 LSWC	velocity, fps:	950		910		874
	energy, ft-lb:	401		368		339
Magtech 230 FMC	velocity, fps:	837		800		767
	energy, ft-lb:	356		326		300
Magtech 230 FMC-SWC	velocity, fps:	780		720		660
	energy, ft-lb:	310		265		222
PMC 145 Non-Toxic Frangible	velocity, fps:	1100	1045	999	961	928
	energy, ft-lb:	390				
PMC 185 JHP	velocity, fps:	903	870	839	811	785
	energy, ft-lb:	339				
PMC 200 FMJ-SWC	velocity, fps:	850	818	788	761	734
	energy, ft-lb:	321				
PMC 230 SFHP	velocity, fps:	850	830	811	792	775
	energy, ft-lb:	369				
PMC 230 FMJ	velocity, fps:	830	809	789	769	749
	energy, ft-lb:	352				
Rem. 175 Lead Free Frangible	velocity, fps:	1020		923		851
	energy, ft-lb:	404		331		281
Rem. 185 JHP	velocity, fps:	1000		939		889
	energy, ft-lb:	411		362		324
Rem. 185 BJHP	velocity, fps:	1015		951		899
	energy, ft-lb:	423		372		332
Rem. 185 BJHP +P	velocity, fps:	1140		1042		971
	energy, ft-lb:	534		446		388
Rem. 185 MC	velocity, fps:	1015		955		907
	energy, ft-lb:	423		375		338
Rem. 230 FN Enclosed Base	velocity, fps:	835		800		767
	energy, ft-lb:	356		326		300
Rem. 230 Metal Case	velocity, fps:	835		800		767
	energy, ft-lb:	356		326		300
Rem. 230 JHP	velocity, fps:	835		800		767
	energy, ft-lb:	356		326		300
Rem. 230 BJHP	velocity, fps:	875		833		795
	energy, ft-lb:	391		355		323
Speer 140 Frangible	velocity, fps:	1200		1029		928
	energy, ft-lb:	448		329		268
Speer 185 Gold Dot	velocity, fps:	1050		956		886
	energy, ft-lb:	453		375		322
Speer 185 TMJ/FN	velocity, fps:	1000		909		839
	energy, ft-lb:	411		339		289
Speer 200 JHP Blazer	velocity, fps:	975		917		860
	energy, ft-lb:	421		372		328
Speer 200 Gold Dot +P	velocity, fps:	1080		994		930
	energy, ft-lb:	518		439		384
Speer 200 TMJ/FN	velocity, fps:	975		897		834
	energy, ft-lb:	422		357		309
Speer 230 FMJ (and Blazer)	velocity, fps:	845		804		775
	energy, ft-lb:	363		329		304
Speer 230 TMJ-CF (and Blazer)	velocity, fps:	845		804		775
	energy, ft-lb:	363		329		304
Speer 230 Gold Dot	velocity, fps:	890		845		805
	energy, ft-lb:	405		365		331
Win. 170 JFP	velocity, fps:	1050		982		928
	energy, ft-lb:	416		364		325
Win. 185 Silvertip HP	velocity, fps:	1000		938		888
	energy, ft-lb:	411		362		324
Win. 185 FMJ FN	velocity, fps:	910		861		
	energy, ft-lb:	340		304		
Win. 185 EB WinClean	velocity, fps:	910		835		
	energy, ft-lb:	340		286		
Win. 230 JHP	velocity, fps:	880		842		
	energy, ft-lb:	396		363		
Win. 230 FMJ	velocity, fps:	835		800		
	energy, ft-lb:	356		326		
Win. 230 SXT	velocity, fps:	880		846		816
	energy, ft-lb:	396		366		340
Win. 230 JHP subsonic	velocity, fps:	880		842		808
	energy, ft-lb:	396		363		334
Win. 230 EB WinClean	velocity, fps:	835		802		
	energy, ft-lb:	356		329		

.45 GAP

CARTRIDGE BULLET	RANGE, YARDS:	0	25	50	75	100
Federal 185 Hydra-Shok JHP	velocity, fps:	1090	1020	970	920	890
And Federal TMJ	energy, ft-lb:	490	430	385	350	320
Federal 230 Hydra-Shok	velocity, fps:	880	870	850	840	820
And Federal FMJ	energy, ft-lb:	395	380	3760	355	345

Ballistics Tables for Modern Sporting Rifles

.45 GAP TO .500 SMITH & WESSON

CARTRIDGE BULLET	RANGE, YARDS:	0	25	50	75	100
Win. 185 STHP	velocity, fps:	1000		938		887
	energy, ft-lb:	411		361		323
Win. 230 JHP	velocity, fps:	880		842		
	energy, ft-lb:	396		363		
Win. 230 EB WinClean	velocity, fps:	875		840		
	energy, ft-lb:	391		360		
Win. 230 FMJ	velocity, fps:	850		814		
	energy, ft-lb:	369		338		

.45 Winchester Magnum

CARTRIDGE BULLET	RANGE, YARDS:	0	25	50	75	100
Win. 260 Partition Gold	velocity, fps:	1200		1105		1033
	energy, ft-lb:	832		705		616
Win. 260 JHP	velocity, fps:	1200		1099		1026
	energy, ft-lb:	831		698		607

.45 Schofield

CARTRIDGE BULLET	RANGE, YARDS:	0	25	50	75	100
Black Hills 180 FNL	velocity, fps:	730				
	energy, ft-lb:					
Black Hills 230 RNFP	velocity, fps:	730				
	energy, ft-lb:					

.45 Colt

CARTRIDGE BULLET	RANGE, YARDS:	0	25	50	75	100
Black Hills 250 RNFP	velocity, fps:	725				
	energy, ft-lb:					
Federal 225 SWC HP	velocity, fps:	900	880	860	840	820
	energy, ft-lb:	405	385	370	355	340
Hornady 255 Cowboy	velocity, fps:	725		692		660
	energy, ft-lb:	298		271		247
Magtech 250 LFN	velocity, fps:	750		726		702
	energy, ft-lb:	312		293		274
PMC 250 LFP	velocity, fps:	800		767		736
	energy, ft-lb:	355		331		309
PMC 300 +P+	velocity, fps:	1250	1192	1144	1102	1066
	energy, ft-lb:	1041				
Rem. 225 SWC	velocity, fps:	960		890		832
	energy, ft-lb:	460		395		346
Rem. 250 RLN	velocity, fps:	860		820		780
	energy, ft-lb:	410		375		340
Speer 200 FMJ Blazer	velocity, fps:	1000		938		889
	energy, ft-lb:	444		391		351
Speer 230 Trail Blazer LFN	velocity, fps:	750		716		684
	energy, ft-lb:	287		262		239
Speer 250 Gold Dot	velocity, fps:	900		860		823
	energy, ft-lb:	450		410		376
Win. 225 Silvertip HP	velocity, fps:	920		877		839
	energy, ft-lb:	423		384		352
Win. 255 LRN	velocity, fps:	860		820		780
	energy, ft-lb:	420		380		345
Win. 250 Lead	velocity, fps:	750		720		692
	energy, ft-lb:	312		288		266

.454 Casull

CARTRIDGE BULLET	RANGE, YARDS:	0	25	50	75	100
Federal 300 Trophy Bonded	velocity, fps:	1630	1540	1450	1380	1300
	energy, ft-lb:	1760	1570	1405	1260	1130
Federal 360 CastCore	velocity, fps:	1500	1435	1370	1310	1255
	energy, ft-lb:	1800	1640	1500	1310	1260
Hornady 240 XTP-MAG	velocity, fps:	1900		1679		1483
	energy, ft-lb:	1923		1502		1172
Hornady 300 XTP-MAG	velocity, fps:	1650		1478		1328
	energy, ft-lb:	1813		1455		1175
Magtech 260 SJSP	velocity, fps:	1800		1577		1383
	energy, ft-lb:	1871		1437		1104
Rem. 300 Core-Lokt Ultra	velocity, fps:	1625		1472		1335
	energy, ft-lb:	1759		1442		1187
Speer 300 Gold Dot HP	velocity, fps:	1625		1477		1343
	energy, ft-lb:	1758		1452		1201
Win. 250 JHP	velocity, fps:	1300		1151		1047
	energy, ft-lb:	938		735		608
Win. 260 Partition Gold	velocity, fps:	1800		1605		1427
	energy, ft-lb:	1871		1485		1176
Win. 260 Platinum Tip	velocity, fps:	1800		1596		1414
	eneryg, ft-lb:	1870		1470		1154
Win. 300 JFP	velocity, fps:	1625		1451		1308
	energy, ft-lb:	1759		1413		1141

.460 Smith & Wesson

CARTRIDGE BULLET	RANGE, YARDS:	0	25	50	75	100
Hornady 200 SST	velocity, fps:	2250		2003		1772
	energy, ft-lb:	2248		1395		1081
Win. 260 Supreme Part. Gold	velocity, fps	2000		1788		1592
	energy, ft-lb	2309		1845		2012

.475 Linebaugh

CARTRIDGE BULLET	RANGE, YARDS:	0	25	50	75	100
Hornady 400 XTP-MAG	velocity, fps:	1300		1179		1093
	energy, ft-lb:	1501		1235		1060

.480 Ruger

CARTRIDGE BULLET	RANGE, YARDS:	0	25	50	75	100
Hornady 325 XTP-MAG	velocity, fps:	1350		1191		1076
	energy, ft-lb:	1315		1023		835
Hornady 400 XTP-MAG	velocity, fps:	1100		1027		971
	energy, ft-lb:	1075		937		838
Speer 275 Gold Dot HP	velocity, fps:	1450		1284		1152
	energy, ft-lb:	1284		1007		810
Speer 325 SP	velocity, fps:	1350		1224		1124
	energy, ft-lb:	1315		1082		912

.50 Action Express

CARTRIDGE BULLET	RANGE, YARDS:	0	25	50	75	100
Speer 300 Gold Dot HP	velocity, fps:	1550		1361		1207
	energy, ft-lb:	1600		1234		970
Speer 325 UCHP	velocity, fps:	1400		1232		1106
	energy, ft-lb:	1414		1095		883

.500 Smith & Wesson

CARTRIDGE BULLET	RANGE, YARDS:	0	25	50	75	100
Hornady 350 XTP Mag	velocity, fps:	1900		1656		1439
	energy, ft-lb:	2805		2131		1610
Hornady 500 FP-XTP	velocity, fps:	1425		1281		1164
	energy, ft-lb:	2254		1823		1505
Win. 350 Super-X	velocity, fps	1400		1231		1106
	energy, ft-lb	1523		1178		951
Win. 400 Platinum Tip	velocity, fps:	1800		1647		1505
	energy, ft-lb:	2877		2409		2012

Glossary

Annealing: Heating metal to soften it. Brass cartridge cases become hard in the neck after repeated resizing.

Splits and separations result. You can anneal a case to restore its ductility by heating it a cherry red, then quenching it in cold water. With steel, such an operation would *increase* hardness. Brass is different.

Antimony: A metallic element alloyed with lead to increase bullet hardness. In big game bullets, the usual ratio is 97.5 percent lead, 2.5 antimony. A little antimony makes a big difference. Six percent is about the limit. Sierra uses three alloys for rifle bullets, with antimony proportions of 1.5, 3 and 6 percent.

Anvil: A rearward-facing part of the primer or primer pocket against which a striker crushes the soft primer cup, pinching the priming compound. The percussive force and friction ignite the primer, which shoots a jet of flame through the flash-hole(s) behind the anvil.

Ball: Literally, a lead ball used in muzzle-loaders, but also a bullet as in "Ball Cartridge" and a (typically double-base) powder whose hard spherical grains roll and slide like tiny shot pellets.

Ballistics: The science of projectiles in motion, comprising internal, external and terminal ballistics—that is, what happens during the launch of a bullet (internal), the flight characteristics of that bullet (external) and the penetration and upset of a bullet in animals (terminal).

Ballistic coefficient: The ratio of a bullet's sectional density to its coefficient of form, a measure of the bullet's ability to cleave the air. Ballistic coefficient ("C" in formulas) is reflected in a bullet's rate of velocity loss, and in its vertical drop over distance.

Battery cup: A type of primer that comprises anvil and main primer cup inside another cup. Shotshell primers are battery cup primers; modern rifle and pistol primers are not.

Belted case: A cartridge case with a thick ring immediately forward of the extractor groove. The ring or belt serves as a headspacing device and has nothing to do with reinforcing the case. Most belted cartridges are called magnums or belted magnums. But not all magnums are belted.

Berdan primer: A type of primer with no integral anvil. The anvil is part of the primer pocket. Common in European cartridges, Berdan primers were named for Hyram Berdan, an American. Primer flame reaches the powder through double flash-holes, on either side of the anvil. Berdan-primed cases cannot be decapped by the central pin in standard handloading dies. The alternative: a special hook or hydraulic pressure.

Black powder: A propellant comprising potassium nitrate (saltpeter), charcoal and sulfur in specified proportion. Black powder substitutes like Pyrodex can be used in guns designed for black powder, which generates lower pressures than smokeless powder. However, Pyrodex and other substitutes vary in bulk density. To match a charge of black powder, their measure must be taken by volume, not by weight.

Boat-tail: The tapered rear of a bullet designed for long-range shooting (also, "tapered heel"). Standard bullet bases are flat; hence, "flat-base." The ballistic advantage of the more aerodynamic boat-tail bullet is seldom realized at ranges short of 300 yards or so.

Bore: The inside of a rifle or shotgun barrel. Bore diameter is the measure taken from land to land in a rifled bore, or the inside diameter of the tube before rifling ("land diameter," as opposed to "groove diameter," which is greater). "Bore sighting" is a preliminary alignment of the sight with the bore, before zeroing the firearm by shooting at a target from a bench.

Boxer primer: The common type of primer used in centerfire rifle and pistol cartridges in the US Named after a British colonel, this primer has an integral anvil. A central flash-hole makes decapping easy in a die with a central pin.

Brass: Alloy of copper and zinc used to make cartridge cases (also, a collective term to describe cartridge cases, as in "I have lots of .223 brass").

Bullet: A single conical projectile fired from a cartridge case, usually but not necessarily through a rifled bore (not to be confused with "cartridge," which comprises bullet, case, primer and powder).

Caliber: A measure of a bullet, from the Latin term "qua libra" or "what pound." Initially it was applied to weight, but then exclusively to diameter. A .308 bullet is a 308-caliber bullet. Caliber can be expressed in hundredths or thousandths of an inch (.22 or .224). It is part of cartridge nomenclature but cannot by itself describe a cartridge. There are, for example, many cartridges using .308 bullets—and many of them are designated ".300." The .300 represents bore diameter, the .308 groove diameter or bullet diameter. Case dimensions of the various .300 cartridges are not the same, though all can use the same bullets. You can't load .300 Weatherby Magnum cartridges in a .300 Winchester Magnum rifle, and shouldn't fire a .308 in a .30 Gibbs. But the same .308 bullets can be used in any of those cartridges.

Cannelure: Circumferential groove around a bullet to identify it and to mark the proper case mouth location for crimping after seating the bullet in the cartridge case.

Canister powder: Gunpowder ready for retail sales to the public, typically in plastic or cardboard containers or canisters. "Bulk powder" refers to the powders blended to form canister powders in the laboratories and loading rooms of powder manufacturers.

Cartridge: A unit of ammunition, comprising bullet, powder, primer and case. "Cartridge" also applies to shotgun ammunition, but "shell" and "shotshell" are by far the more popular terms.

Case: The hull or shell of a cartridge, the housing that contains the powder and holds the primer and bullet to form a cartridge. "Case head" is the rear portion that fits against the bolt face of a gun and is gripped by the firearm's extractor.

Centerfire: A cartridge whose primer is a removable unit held in a primer pocket at the rear of the case, in the center of the head. Some early cartridge designations included "CF." The ".30 WCF" (Winchester Center Fire) is another name for the .30-30.

Chamber: In a rifle, pistol or shotgun, the rear portion of the bore reamed to precise dimensions to accept a cartridge ready for firing. A chamber is big enough to allow easy insertion of the appropriate cartridge, but small enough to prevent undue case stretch when the cartridge is fired. A "chamber cast" is sometimes taken of relic guns to determine chamber dimensions.

Charge: Amount of powder, usually by weight, specified in a load. Charge also includes the type of powder, as in 90 grains FFg or 56.5

grains H-4350. A compressed charge is one that fills the case to a point above the normal seating depth of the bullet, so that the bullet presses the powder down during seating. Black powder charges are always compressed by the ball or bullet, which must be tightly seated to avoid an air space and a pressure wave that spikes when it hits the immobile projectile.

Chronograph: An instrument for measuring bullet speed. Most chronographs record bullet passage over two points by registering the bullet's shadow with two electric eyes. The distance between the points is known, and when the chronograph comes up with the time interval (hence, "chrono") between crossings, speed can be calculated. For a long time, chronographs were laboratory instruments. Beginning in the 1970s, Dr. Ken Oehler made them available to shooters with portable, inexpensive models—much like Bill Weaver gave riflemen an affordable, functional rifle scope in the 1930s.

Collimator: An optical device used in bore-sighting rifles and pistols. A collimator attaches to the muzzle. Its screen has a grid you use to align your sight with the bore's axis. It's important to shoot at a distance to establish a zero after using a collimator. This instrument merely helps ensure that your first bullets land close to point of aim.

Corrosive primer: A primer whose residue is hygroscopic (attracts moisture), causing rust in the bore. The corrosive agent in many early primers was potassium chlorate. Corrosive priming was discontinued shortly after World War II, when lead styphnate became the primary ingredient in military and commercial small arms primers.

Crimp: An inward bending of the case mouth to bite into the cannelure of a bullet. Crimping increases bullet pull and helps secure heavy bullets with short shanks, such as big-bore pistol bullets. Crimping is also used on dangerous-game ammunition to prevent the bullets in a loaded magazine from backing out under recoil and seizing the magazine. Ammunition for tubular magazines and revolvers likewise warrants a crimp, particularly if recoil is severe. Because there's some bullet deformation, crimped ammo may not give you the best accuracy. A lot of factory ammunition is crimped, however, and can be expected to deliver good hunting accuracy. Bullets without cannelures should not be crimped.

CUP: Copper units of pressure, a measure of breech pressure obtained by measuring a copper pellet of specified starting dimensions after it has been crushed by a piston thrust outward through a hole in the barrel of a test gun. Copper crushers gauge the pressure of high-performance rifle and pistol ammunition. Lead units of pressure are generally used for shotguns and low-pressure pistol loads.

Drift: Lateral movement of a bullet away from the bore-line during flight. Drift is the horizontal equivalent of drop, which results from gravity's pull on the bullet. Unlike gravity, the air movement that causes drift is not always present. And when it is, its speed and direction cannot be assumed. Good "wind-dopers" know that wind action (and drift) may differ at different points along the bullet's path.

Energy: The amount of "work" that can be done by a moving bullet a given distance from launch. Muzzle energy is a common standard, calculated by squaring the velocity of the bullet (fps), multiplying that figure by the bullet's weight (grains) and dividing the product by 450,240.

Erosion: Wearing of the bore caused by the friction and heat of firing. Erosion occurs whether or not you clean the bore and no matter what type of powder, primer or bullet you use. It accelerates as bullet velocity increases. The most severe erosion occurs in the throat, just ahead of the chamber, where temperatures and pressures are highest. Small-bore, high-speed cartridges with slow-burning powders generate the most erosion. Erosion can be kept to a minimum by letting the barrel cool between shots.

Expansion ratio: Interior case volume divided by bore volume. Cartridges with very high expansion ratios are said to be "overbore capacity." That is, they have big powder chambers relative to the bore size. Slow powders and long barrels are necessary to get the most from these rounds.

Extrusion: The result of material flow under pressure. Bullet jackets and cores are formed by extrusion in dies. So is tubular powder, which is then diced into short kernels. An extruded primer, in which the striker dimple has a raised perimeter, can be caused by too much pressure, excess headspace or an oversize striker hole in the bolt face.

fps: Feet per second, a measure of a bullet's speed, like miles per hour for an automobile.

Fireform: Shaping a case to new dimensions by firing it in a chamber of those new dimensions. This is a common practice with non-standard or "wildcat" cartridges but is safe only if the proper headspaces has already been established. A cartridge cannot be safely fired to establish a new headspace dimension!

Firing pin: A rod that strikes the primer of a cartridge when you pull the trigger of a gun. Shapes vary, as do lengths. In early revolvers, a nipple on the hammer nose served the function. The spring-loaded striker in a bolt rifle can be considered a firing pin, though most incorporate a long rear shank of larger diameter.

Flash-hole: The tunnel connecting the primer pocket to the powder chamber of the case through the web.

Boxer-primed cases have one flash-hole; Berdan-primed cases have two. The flash-hole conducts the primer's flame to the powder charge, just as a touch-hole introduced spark in early muzzleloaders.

Foot-pounds: A unit of energy commonly used for bullets, the force required to raise a one-pound weight a foot against the resistance of gravity.

Forcing cone: The beveled forward edge of a chamber that brings chamber diameter down to bore diameter. Most commonly this term applies to shotguns, which have relatively long forcing cones.

Form factor: A multiplier determined by the shape of a bullet and used, with sectional density, to determine its ballistic coefficient (C).

Freebore: An unrifled section of bore immediately in front of the chamber. Freebore can include a parallel section or be cut so as to slope gradually from chamber mouth to full land height. It is this variability that causes some confusion. Freebore is loosely used as a substitute term for throat, the section of bore between chamber mouth and full land diameter. But a steep, short throat is not freebored. Freebore describes long throats, which allow the bullet to start moving without interference, reducing upward slope of the pressure curve. Some rifles, notably Weatherby's, are noted for freebore, which allows more aggressive powder charges than do rifles with shorter throats. Higher velocity results. Also, the freebore lets you seat bullets shallowly, boosting case capacity and, again, velocity. Freebore does not generally improve accuracy.

Full metal jacket: A bullet type designed to maintain its shape during penetration, as opposed to a softpoint or hollowpoint designed to expand and create a large wound channel. Full-jacket (FMJ) bullets are used for some types of competitive shooting, because the jacketed nose is a good airfoil and won't easily deform in handling. The design also applies to "solids" for hunting large African game. The jacket up front protects the lead core from deformation during entry, ensuring minimal resistance to penetration. In their simplest form, full-jacket bullets are inexpensive to produce. Not only are they standard issue in military cartridges; they're a first choice for "plinkers" who use lots of ammo for informal target shooting.

Gilding metal: An alloy of copper and zinc commonly used for bullet jackets. Zinc makes up 5 to 10 percent of this alloy, copper the rest.

Grain: In shooting, a unit of weight, not a description of a particle. That is, 54 grains of powder means that charge weighs 54 grains. It may have hundreds of *kernels* of powder. There are 7,000 grains to a pound, 437.5 to an ounce. Bullets and powder are thus weighed by the same measure.

Grooves: Spiral channels cut or ironed into the bore of a barrel by single cutter, broach button or high-pressure hammers. Grooves and lands (the uncut sections between grooves) comprise rifling, which spins the bullet around its axis, making it stable in flight and more accurate than a bullet from a smooth bore. A bullet's unfired diameter is, ideally, groove diameter. The lands cut into the bullet, grabbing and spinning it as it is shoved forward on firing.

Hangfire: A delayed ignition of the main charge of powder after the striker hits the primer. Hangfires can be caused by a large air spaces in the case, a weak primer, powder that is hard to ignite. They are ruinous to accuracy because the bullet leaves late, when your sights are no longer perfectly aligned. A hangfire that delays more than a fraction of a second is rare, but misfires should be treated as hangfires for safety's sake, the rifle kept pointed downrange for 30 seconds before you open the bolt.

Headspace: The measure between the bolt face and that part of the chamber that acts as a cartridge stop when the round is fully chambered. Headspace on rimmed cases is measured to the front of the rim, on belted cases to the front of the belt. Rimless bottleneck cartridges headspace on a datum line on the case shoulder. A few pistol cartridges like the .45 Automatic headspace on the case mouth. Headspace in any firearm is measured with steel "go" and "no go" gauges, precisely machined to minimum and maximum dimensions. A rifle's bolt should close on a "go" gauge but not on a "no go" gauge. Too much headspace allows the cartridge to move forward when the striker hits the primer. When the expanding gas irons the pliable front of the case tight to the chamber wall, there is nothing to keep the thicker rear of the case (the head) from moving rearward, stretching the brass forward of the case web, sometimes to the point of separation. Released into the chamber through a crack in the case wall, high-pressure gas can damage a rifle and maim the shooter.

Improved: A case design fashioned by "blowing out" a standard cartridge in a chamber of more generous dimensions, typically with less body taper and a sharper shoulder. Result: more powder capacity. Improved cartridges generally take the name of their parent, e.g., the .257 Improved, .280 Improved. Headspace is not changed. If the new chamber does have a different headspace measurement, the factory round cannot safely be fireformed; iIt must first be reshaped to establish proper headspace.

IMR: Improved Military Rifle, a powder designation of E.I. DuPont de Nemours, which replaced the old Military Rifle line of propellants with IMR powders in the 1920s, when four-digit numbers supplanted the two-digit MR designations. In 1986, DuPont sold its powder business to EXPRO, and the IMR Powder Company was established as a testing and marketing arm of that firm. IMR powders are still manufactured for handloaders; only the corporate umbrellas have changed.

Ingalls Tables: Ballistics tables computed by Colonel James Ingalls and first published in 1916. These tables have since served American ammunition makers and ballisticians as the basis for calculating ballistic coefficients and bullet flight characteristics. As with French ballisticians in his day, Ingalls' work followed that of Isaac Newton, Galileo, Benjamin Robins (who developed the ballistic pendulum), the Krupp factory in Germany (which, with other agencies, conducted firing tests to determine ballistic coefficients) and a nineteenth-century Russian named Mayevski (who fashioned a mathematical model of standard drag deceleration of the Krupp bullet). In France, the Gavre Commission had found a flaw in the assumption that drag on a bullet was proportional to some power of the velocity within a range of velocities. At high speed (above 6,000 fps) there was a sharp rise in retardation. The Gavre Commission developed tables to show this—really, the first ballistics tables ever. British ballisticians came up with a better one in 1909, another in 1929. The Ingalls tables were produced using a bullet much like the one-pound, 1 inch-diameter British projectile with its 2-caliber ogive. They are valid to velocities of about 3,600 fps, at which point the British 1909 tables must be used.

Jacket: A metal covering or envelope that protects a bullet's lead core from the heat of friction produced in its travel down the bore. Unjacketed lead bullets were sufficient in early muzzleloaders and black powder cartridge guns that kept velocities under 1,800 fps. Higher bullet speeds stripped lead from the bullets, ruining accuracy and fouling the bore. Bullet jackets are typically copper or gilding metal (copper alloyed with zinc), but steel jackets have been used. Jacket material and thickness can affect breech pressures. With jacket design, they also have a lot to do with how an expanding bullet opens in a game animal.

Keyhole: The perforation made by a bullet entering a target sideways. Keyholing is the mark of a tumbling bullet that is both inaccurate and ballistically inefficient. Tumbling can be caused by insufficient rifling twist, a defective bullet, or bullet contact with a twig or other obstruction.

Lands: The raised sections of rifling with a bore. Lands lie between the grooves and engrave the bullet as it is force down the bore by powder gas. Land diameter is less than groove or bullet diameter, so the lands are really what spin the bullet, making it stable in flight like a well-thrown football. Some caliber designations reflect land diameter, some groove diameter. The .300 Savage and .308 Winchester both use .308 bullets in bores with land diameters of .300.

Leade: Same as throat, that section of the bore between the chamber mouth and full land diameter.

Loading density: In ammunition, the ratio of the volume of the powder charge, expressed in grains weight, to the volume of the case, also in grains weight.

Lock time: In a firearm, the interval between release of the sear by the trigger, and detonation of the primer.

LUP: Lead units of pressure, a measure of breech pressure obtained by measuring a lead pellet of specified starting dimensions after it has been crushed by a piston thrust outward through a hole in the barrel of a test gun. Lead units of pressure are generally used for shotguns and low-pressure pistol loads. Copper crushers measure the pressure of high-performance rifle and pistol ammunition.

Magnum: A cartridge (or, by extension, a firearm) of unusually high performance. A magnum designation may indicate the existence of a standard cartridge of the same bore dimensions but lesser power (the .270 Weatherby Magnum drives a .270 bullet faster than the .270 Winchester because it has a bigger case and more powder). But some magnums, like the .264 Winchester Magnum, have no standard counterpart. Magnum rifle cartridges are generally belted; not so the .357 and .44 Magnum handgun cartridges. The term "magnum" may not by itself identify a cartridge, because there are several commercial .300 magnums, all of different dimensions and ballistic potential.

Maximum ordinate: The point at which a bullet reaches its greatest vertical distance above line of sight, typically just over half the zero distance for ordinary hunting bullets in rifles zeroed at normal ranges. "Max ord" can move farther downrange, relative to midpoint, as zero range is increased. That is because a bullet's arc is parabolic. So the term "midrange trajectory" is really a misnomer for maximum ordinate.

Meplat: The diameter of the flat nose tip of a bullet.

Mercuric primer: An old primer used successfully with black powder arms because the bulky black powder residue absorbed the primer's residue. But with clean-burning smokeless rounds, the mercury fulminate was left to attack the brass cartridge case, weakening it. Non-mercuric primers arrived when potassium chlorate replaced mercury fulminate as primary ingredient. Non-mercuric, non-corrosive primers followed in the 1940s.

Metal fouling: Deposits of bullet jacket left in the rifling.

Minute of angle: A term describing shot dispersion. A circle of 100 yards radius has 360 degrees of roughly 60 inches per degree on its perimeter. Each degree can be divided into 60 minutes of about an inch on the perimeter (totaling 21,600 minutes). A 1-minute group is a series of shots whose greatest dispersion to the centers of the outside holes in the target measures an inch (really, a minute is 1.047 inch) at 100 yards. A 1 inch group is the same size. But a 1 inch group at *200* yards is a *half-minute* group. A one-minute group at 200 yards measures 2 inches; at 300 it measures 3 inches. Bullet divergence from group centers increases with distance, though rate of divergence remains the same (or may even decrease as the rotating bullet "goes to sleep" at long range). A benchrest rifle is expected to shoot groups as small as a quarter minute; a rifle for prairie dogs should shoot well under a minute. A big game rifle, however, needn't be so accurate, because a deer's chest is a big target. Two-minute accuracy will allow you to keep all your shots in the deer's vitals out to 400 yards, a very long shot. Most modern rifles and loads are capable of better accuracy, however, and it's not too much to expect 1-½ inch groups from your hunting rifle.

Mushroom: Shape of a bullet after expansion in game. Softpoint bullets designed for big game are made to mushroom, delivering energy as the bullet slows and plowing a wide wound channel. Frangible bullets for small animals like coyotes and prairie dogs, where penetration is not an issue, are made to disintegrate for a lightning-like kill.

Ogive: The curved portion of a bullet between nose and shank. "Secant ogive" and "tangent ogive" refer to the placement of a compass used to scribe the arc that determines the nose profile. The radius of the curve is typically expressed in calibers. A 2-caliber ogive would be a curve with a radius twice bore diameter.

Overbore: A condition or cartridge characterized by a high expansion ratio; that is, the cartridge case is big in relation to bore diameter. Overbore cartridges have produced the highest bullet velocities, but they don't operate efficiently in short barrels, and they typically require large charges of very slow-burning powder. Because of high throat temperatures and the exit of considerable unburned powder from the case during firing, throat erosion proceeds more rapidly in rifles chambered to overbore cartridges.

Patched ball: A ball or bullet, usually in black-powder muzzle-loading rifles, that has a cloth or paper patch protecting it from powder gas and sealing that gas behind. Patches also reduce fouling.

Point-blank range: Any distance at which you can hit your target without aiming high or low to correct for the trajectory of the bullet. Maximum point-blank range is the farthest distance at which you can hold in the middle and not hit too low. Point blank ranges vary, depending on the load, the target and the acceptable deviation from center. The less deviation you tolerate, the shorter will be your maximum point-blank range. If you don't mind your bullet hitting a couple of inches high or low with a center hold (that's not too much deviation for most big game hunters), you'll extend your point-blank range farther than if you insisted on hitting no more than half an inch high or low. If you're shooting competitively at targets, point-blank range is the range at which your target is fixed, the range at which you've zeroed. On the other hand, point-blank range is often used colloquially to describe very short-range shooting, where sights aren't used at all.

Port pressure: In a gas-operated autoloading firearm, the gas pressure at the port, typically some distance down the barrel.

Powder: Here gunpowder, which includes black powder, semi-smokeless and smokeless powder, as well as black powder substitutes. Powder is a granular fuel (not really a "powder") that burns very fast. It does not detonate from impact as does a primer. Gas formed from burning powder expands to push a bullet or shot charge down the barrel. Powder granules are of various shapes and sizes, depending on their intended use. Coarse, slow-burning powder in large-volume cases move fast bullets. Small cases with big mouths call for powders of faster burn rates. Single-base powders are mainly nitrocellulose, while double-base powders have a significant amount of nitroglycerine. Progressive-burning powders are either shaped or treated to release energy in a controlled way, increasing gas production over time rather than "burning down" from a high initial energy release. Powder charges are measured in grains weight (437.5 grains to the ounce). Black powder substitutes do not all have the same bulk density. They're formulated to be measured in black-powder measures, bulk for bulk. Labels on shotshell boxes show charges in "drams equivalent," a designation held over from when the propellant was black powder. A dram is a unit of weight; 16 drams equal one ounce. When smokeless supplanted black powder at the turn of the century, it was of a type known as "bulk powder" and could be loaded in place of black powder "bulk for bulk" (not by weight). "Dense" smokeless powders came later. They took up less space, so neither bulk nor weight measures transferred. A "3 ¼ dram equivalent" is a smokeless charge that approximates the performance of a 3 ¼-dram black-powder charge. It has nothing to do with the amount of smokeless powder loaded.

Primer: A small metal cup containing a sensitive detonating compound which, when crushed by the blow of a firearm's striker, hammer or firing pin against an internal anvil, throws a spark. The anvil may be part of the primer (Boxer) or part of the primer pocket (Berdan). The spark travels through a flash-hole in the case web to ignite the main charge of powder. You can buy standard and magnum primers (magnums give you a spark of longer duration) and primers for "large rifle," "small rifle," "large pistol," and "small pistol" cases. "Battery cup" primers for shotshells are encased in a larger cup that adds support in the thin shotshell head.

Pyrodex: A black powder substitute developed by Dan Pawlak, who died in a powder fire at his factory in Washington state. Hodgdon powder company bought the rights to manufacture and market Pyrodex.

Rifling: In the bore of a rifle or pistol (and now shotguns designed to shoot slugs), lands and grooves that spin a bullet. Rifling gives any projectile (even a patched ball) greater accuracy and, by keeping bullets nose-first, greater range. Rifling twist is the rate at which a bullet is spun, expressed as the distance it travels while making one complete revolution. A 1-in-14 twist means the bullet turns over one time for every 14 inches of forward travel. The proper rate of twist varies with bullet profile, weight and even speed. In 1879 Briton Sir Alfred George Greenhill came up with a formula that works for most bullets most of the time: The required twist, in calibers, is 150 divided by the length of the bullet in calibers. So if you have a 180-grain .30-caliber bullet 1.35 inches long, you first divide 1.35 by .30 to get the length in calibers (4.5). Then you divide 150 by 4.5 and get a fraction over 33. That's in calibers, so to bring it into inches of linear measure, you multiply it by .30. The final number is very close to 10, a useful rate of spin for most popular 30-caliber hunting cartridges, from the .308 to the .300 Weatherby Magnum.

Rim: In cartridges, the edge of the case head the extractor seizes to pull the case from the chamber. Rimless cases have a rim behind a deep extractor groove, but it's the same diameter as the body of the case and does not protrude beyond as does a rimmed or semi-rimless case. A rimmed case headspaces on the rim and does not need an extractor groove. A rebated rim is one that is smaller in diameter than the case body (e.g., the .284 Winchester). British rimmed cartridges are typically said to be "flanged."

Sabot: A lightweight hull or envelope, typically of groove diameter, that carries a smaller, more ballistically efficient projectile out the barrel, then falls away. A central projectile (commonly a shotgun slug or small-diameter bullet), is spun by the sabot but bears none of the rifling marks. It benefits from the sabot's large-diameter base during launch but is not burdened with excess weight or diameter in flight. The sabot idea was first tested in French artillery.

Seating: The act of inserting a bullet in a case neck. Seating depth is a critical element in getting the most accuracy from a firearm, and can affect pressures as well.

Sectional density: A bullet's weight in pounds divided by the square of its diameter in inches. Sectional density and the bullet's profile or form combine to yield ballistic coefficient, a measure of the bullet's effectiveness in battling drag in flight.

Spitzer: A pointed bullet, derived from a German term that described the first 8mm German military bullets of aerodynamic shape. Spitzers have a more streamlined form and, thus, higher ballistic coefficients than flat-nose or round-nose bullets of the same weight.

Throat: The unrifled section of bore between the case mouth and full land diameter (also known as leade and, not quite correctly, as freebore).

Web: The solid portion of a cartridge case between its base and the powder chamber. The primer pocket is at the rear of the web, and the flash-hole is drilled or punched through the web.

Wildcat: A cartridge that is not loaded commercially. Wildcat cartridges are designed by handloaders who want something different. They're made by reshaping parent cases in special dies so they headspace safely. Firing in the wildcat chamber—as with "improved" cartridges"—completes case-forming.

Zero: In shooting, the range at which the sightline crosses the bullet's path the second time, farthest from the gun. The bullet begins to drop as soon as it leaves the muzzle, but the sightline maintains a slight angle to the bore and meets the descending bullet arc a few yards (typically 25 to 35) from the muzzle. The angle of the sightline brings it into the bullet's arc again as the bullet's rate of drop accelerates with distance. That final crossing is the zero range. Zeroing at 200 yards gives riflemen a useful "point-blank" range for most big game rounds. Bullets then strike between 2 and 3 inches high at mid-range or maximum ordinate. They drop 3 inches low somewhere around 250 yards. Bullets with steeper trajectories must be zeroed at shorter range. Foster-style shotgun slugs might call for a 75-yard zero, as does the .22 Long Rifle cartridge in rifles. Many handguns are zeroed even closer.